PEARSON

ALWAYS LEARNING

Supervision in Canada Today

by Joan L. Condie, Stephen P. Robbins and David De Cenzo

Fourth Edition

ISBN 10: 1-256-91430-4
ISBN 13: 978-1-256-91430-3

BRIEF CONTENTS

CONTENTS

ACKNOWLEDGEMENTS

Many thanks to those who shared their stories with me (including those who wish to remain anonymous), and to those who led me to them:

Aseel Abdulrazzak
Bill Angelopoulos
Carol Appleby
Jay Athia
Jason Aurora
Robin Bender
Nichola Campbell
Wendy Chiu
Garth Dallman
Shelby D'Ambrogio
Adam Derewonko
Kim Derko
Stephanie Dimech
Zoe Dirse
Jamie Dumas
Mostafa Elborno
Jana Fifoot
Kevin Gallant

Sandra Gillis
Ailsa Goncalves
David Goncalves
Debbie Hinz
Diane Hebert
Galya Kabbani
Kathryn Karcz
Haji Khurshid
Katerina Kollaras
Radhika Luthra
Joy Martel
Peter May
RJ McDowell
Ann McInnes
Ron McLester
Jennifer Mills
Chris Mitchell
James Moncarz

Christopher Nicolson
Sue O'Hara
Tim O'Shea
Steve Risavy
Heather Robertson
Sue Ropchan
Bonnie Russell
Michelle Scianitti
Bonnie Shepherd
Anne Terweil
Karen Tourloukis
Pam Van Loenen
Bob Warner
Rob Watson
Ainslie White
Christine Whorwood

And special thanks to Ryan Anderson.

PART ONE

INTRODUCTION

1. THE SUPERVISOR'S JOB AND CHALLENGES FOR THE 21st CENTURY

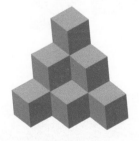

1

THE SUPERVISOR'S JOB AND CHALLENGES FOR THE 21ST CENTURY

Courtesy of Yuri Arcurs/Shutterstock

LEARNING OBJECTIVES

After reading this chapter, you should be able to:

1. Define supervisor.
2. Explain the difference between supervisors, middle managers, and senior management.
3. Explain the pros and cons of being a supervisor.
4. Identify the four functions in the management process.
5. Describe the four essential management competencies.
6. Explain why the supervisor's job will be increasingly important and complex in the future.
7. Describe how the supervisor's role has changed from boss to coach.
8. Explain the impact that shrinking, growing, and changing the organization's structure can have on a supervisor.
9. Define what is meant by workforce diversity.
10. Explain how technology has affected the supervisor's job.
11. Describe the changing legal obligations a supervisor faces.

CHAPTER OUTLINE

Shelby D'Ambrogio started working at AMC Theatres at age 15 in a frontline crew position, moving on to a crew lead position, and then a supervisor. Now at 22 she is an operations manager, running the human resources and administration department at her theatre complex while also completing her education.

As a supervisor, Shelby's job was to coordinate the efforts of the theatre film crew, to optimize guest satisfaction and profitability in a professional and safe work environment. Shelby hired, did training and scheduling, completed employee files, coached employees and disciplined them when needed. As well as ensuring operations were running smoothly, Shelby examined how to improve operations and worked with the general manager to create and implement an action plan; for example, focusing on cleanliness, doing nightly audits, ensuring managers the night before did everything they were supposed to do, ensuring the filing system was up-to-date.

She also dealt with the problems staff had challenges with. "Every night there's a guest angry about something—from stepping on food to noisy kids. I had an incident where one of the staff had difficulty handling a situation. A group was waiting for an 18A movie, were drinking and didn't have tickets; they were asked to step aside and were confrontational. My staff member was frustrated with them and asked me to deal with it. I raised my voice, let them know I needed them to be separated and indicated I was in a position to call the police for assistance if they did not cooperate. I was calm and they listened. The staff all wrote down statements and did an incident report so the home office knows what happened. The same night someone was drinking and cut open their hand. I had to do first aid and get information (e.g. when they ate, if they had any allergies) before the paramedics arrived."

Shelby has had to build credibility very deliberately because of her young age. "Sometimes it's hard to get respect so people will trust and follow your direction and realize you've earned your position. There have been a few occasions with both older staff and with guests where my authority has been challenged because of my age. With older staff, I have done my best to explain the situation, the role I'm in, and say that I wouldn't be in this position if I couldn't handle it. With guests I assure them that I can help them with any issues they have."

Transitioning into a position where she was supervising friends was difficult. ""It was tough at first. The employees thought they could do

what they wanted. They tested me. I told them I don't want to write you up but I will if I have to. People may sometimes think I'm stern, but I have to be so they know I'm serious. It's OK to take it easy on a quiet Monday night, to socialize and get to know the staff on a different level, show I have a sense of humour. I'm on the social committee and the Health and Safety committee. They know I care. I also make small incentives for staff to have some fun, like making a contest where whoever sells the most Rolos will get a $10 gift certificate."

"When it comes to delegating, I'm not one to say "It's your job, just do it. I will say, "Do you mind sweeping the floor for me, please? Hey, that washroom needs stocking, do you mind doing it for me? It seems like a choice but it's not really. This approach gets a better reaction. And I say thanks for a good job. Saying please and thank you is the key to everything."

Shelby is learning a lot from her general manager, whose approach she appreciates. "He is consistent and communicates well with everyone. If a follow-up is not completed by an employee, he asks why and when it will be done. He's friendly and approachable and at the same time holds people accountable, expecting them to do their job."

When asked why she is so effective in her job, Shelby replies, "It's personality. You need a passion for people and patience for everyone's learning style. You need to communicate with everyone on their level effectively. This concern for other's perspective can't be taught."

This book is about supervisors. It assumes that you are reading it because you would like to be a supervisor and are preparing yourself for that event, or you are already a supervisor and are interested in developing your skills. In this book, you will learn about being an effective supervisor from actual supervisors and from the theorists who study them. Shelby's story demonstrates the typical path into a supervisory position, the range of duties, and the challenges of a supervisory role.

SUPERVISORS AND THE MANAGEMENT PROCESS

Let's start by looking at the role that supervisors play in the big picture. This means beginning with examining the concept of organizations since all supervisors work within an organizational setting.

An organization is a systematic grouping of people brought together to accomplish some specific purpose. Such groupings include businesses set up for profit such as Bombardier, nonprofit organizations such as the Victorian Order of Nurses, educational institutions such as New Brunswick Community College, churches, hospitals, and others. All organizations have three characteristics.

First, every organization has a purpose—a distinct reason for being. Second, organizations require people to act in order to turn that purpose into reality. Third, all organizations develop a systematic structure that defines the roles of those people, and that often sets limits on their work behaviours. This could include writing job descriptions to clarify responsibilities, forming work teams, developing rules, regulations and procedures, and giving some people supervisory control over others.

In most traditional organizations, we can depict this structure as a pyramid with four general categories.

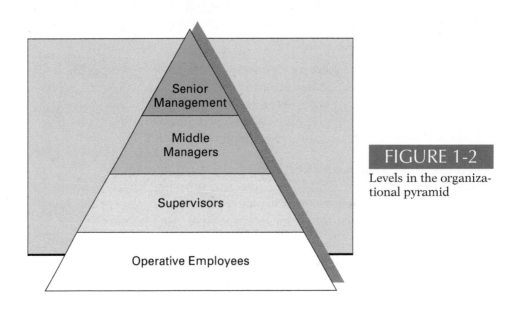

FIGURE 1-2

Levels in the organizational pyramid

Operative employees form the base of the pyramid. These are the front-line workers who actually produce the organization's goods or provide its services. Such employees include the assembly-line worker at Ford, the postal carrier who delivers mail, and the salesperson at a Chapters store. It also includes many professional employees such as engineers, doctors, and computer specialists. What all operative employees have in common is that they do not manage or oversee the work of any other employees.

Moving from the base of the pyramid to the top of the pyramid, we find **senior management**. These people are responsible for establishing the organization's overall objectives and developing the policies and strategies to accomplish these goals. Sample titles are CEO, vice president, museum director, and superintendent of schools.

Down one level, **middle managers** include all managers below the top management level who manage other managers. Titles could include sales director, division manager, area manager, or high school principal.

Middle managers
All employees below the top-management level who manage other managers.

WHO ARE SUPERVISORS?

Returning to the organizational pyramid, the only level not yet described is **supervisors**. Like senior and middle management, supervisors are part of management. However, they are unique in that they oversee operative employees. Supervisors, then, are the only managers who don't manage other managers. This is reflected in the term **first-level managers**. This means that, from the base of the pyramid moving up, supervisors represent the first level in the management hierarchy.

Supervisors
First-level managers who oversee the work of operatives or nonmanagement employees.

What kinds of titles are likely to indicate that someone is a supervisor? Assistant manager, coach, foreman, team leader, shift supervisor or department head are typical. Titles can be misleading, however. As you read about the various Canadian supervisors described and quoted in this book, you'll find one called a director because she directs a major project, but she is still the first-level manager. Another supervisor's title as coordinator may not sound impressive but she supervises staff at four different locations. So titles can be deceiving. What links all supervisors is the responsibility for operative employees.

An interesting aspect of supervisory positions is that many supervisors also engage in operative tasks like their employees. Jamie Dumas supervises a fitness centre for the City of Mississauga but she also leads some fitness classes herself. Garth Dallman not only supervises work on dinosaur installations for Research Casting International, he often pitches in as part of the production team. As supervisor at a Crabby Joe restaurant, Galya Kabbani also bartends and helps out in the dining room when needed.

A second interesting aspect of the supervisor's role is their position as the link between operations and management, the "doing" side of the organization and the planning side. This means that the supervisor is in a position to implement policies and direction set by upper management. Supervisors are also in a position to inform upper management about what is actually happening, where the issues are, what is working and not working. This position in the middle can put the supervisor in a stressful position where each side may expect the supervisor to be their advocate. The supervisor can feel torn loyalties, knowing they are in management and must uphold management decisions, but aware that those decisions may look different at ground level when they are implemented.

FIGURE 1-3

Jamie Dumas supervises a fitness centre but also leads classes herself

WHAT IS MANAGEMENT?

Management
The process of getting things done, effectively and efficiently, through and with other people.

The term **management** refers to the process of getting things done, effectively and efficiently, through and with other people. There are several components in this definition that warrant some discussion. These are the terms *process*, *effectively*, and *efficiently*.

Process
The primary activities supervisors perform.

The term **process** in the definition of management represents the primary activities supervisors perform. In management terms, we call these the *functions of management*. The next section will describe these functions.

Effectiveness
Doing the right task, producing the intended result, attaining the desired goal

Effectiveness means doing the right task, producing the intended result, attaining the desired goal. Supervisors must get things done. But they do not have unlimited resources of time, money and labour. This is where efficiency comes in. **Efficiency** refers to doing the task in the right manner with the least waste of time, effort and resources. The need for efficiency has a profound impact on effectiveness. Because supervisors typically work within constraints, their challenges often involve not "how do I get this done?" but "how do I get this done without going over-budget?" or "how do I get it done when I have to get this other project done at the same time, using the same people and equipment?"

Efficiency
Doing the task in the right manner with the least waste of time, effort and resources.

WHAT DO MANAGERS DO?

Management functions
The four managerial functions of planning, organizing, leading, and controlling.

All managers engage in **management functions**. By that we mean they plan, organize, lead, and control. Since supervisors are part of management, we need to briefly review these four generic functions.

Imagine a boat with eight rowers, each rowing madly but each with a different direction in mind. The result is that they go nowhere and waste a lot of time and energy on the way. All members of a group need a common purpose and a common understanding of the means to get there. This is what **planning** is about. A plan sets out a common direction. In the planning function, managers must define objectives and develop a comprehensive set of plans to integrate and coordinate the activities necessary to achieve those objectives. Managers must also communicate this plan effectively so employees understand and accept it. Acceptance is much more likely if they recognize the "why" behind the plan.

Planning
Defining objectives and the means of attaining them.

Change the rowboat to a large sailboat with several sails, a rudder and a variety of tasks. Not everyone can steer. It must be decided what tasks are to be done, when, and by whom. This refers to the **organizing** function. A manager must divide the work to be done into manageable components and coordinate the activities. Employees must understand what they are responsible for, how their work is grouped, where decisions are to be made, and who reports to whom.

Organizing
Dividing work into manageable components and coordinating results to achieve objectives.

Sailing is fun on a brilliant sunny day with a brisk wind when everything is "shipshape," but what about the days when you are becalmed, or when you must face gale force winds? What about when you have to work with equipment that is in disrepair yet there is no money, time, or opportunity in sight? This is when the third management function of **leading** becomes particularly important. Subordinates need a leader to keep them going when times are tough, to resolve the unexpected difficulties, and to let them know how they are doing. When managers motivate employees, direct employees in their daily activities, communicate effectively, or resolve conflicts among team members, they are leading.

Leading
Directing and coordinating people.

When a boat is "shipshape," it is due to the crew's effort to keep everything in top condition, ready to fulfill its function. This is part of the **controlling** function. To ensure that things are operating as they should, management must monitor activities and measure performance. Actual performance must be compared with the previously set objectives. If there are any significant deviations, it is management's responsibility to get things back on track. This process of measuring, comparing, and correcting is what we mean when we refer to the controlling function. This brings to mind the image of the captain checking position on a compass and ordering an adjustment to the person at the helm. Note that the captain doesn't wait until the ship is far off course before correcting. Measurement and feedback are applied consistently to keep performance on target.

Controlling
Monitoring activities to ensure that objectives are being met as planned, and correcting any significant deviations.

All managers perform the four functions of planning, organizing, leading, and controlling. The specifics of each function and the emphasis on each will vary with the level of management, however. For example, while we find senior managers focusing on long-term, strategic planning such as what business the company should be in, supervisors emphasize short-term, tactical planning such as scheduling unit workloads for the upcoming week. Similarly, top management is concerned with designing the overall organization while supervisors focus on designing the jobs of individuals and groups.

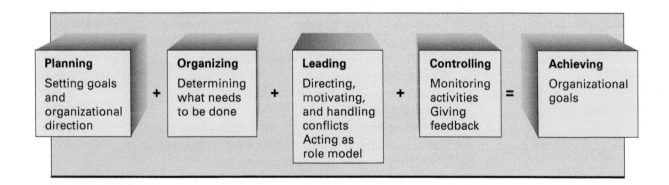

FIGURE 1-4

Management functions

- Motivate employees to change or improve their performance.

- Provide ongoing performance feedback to employees.

- Take action to resolve performance problems in your work group.

- Blend employees' goals with organization's work requirements.

- Identify ways of improving communications among employees.

- Inform employees about procedures and work assignments.

- Keep track of employees' training and special skills as they relate to job assignments to aid their growth and development.

FIGURE 1-5

Key supervisory tasks (based on a survey of more than 650 supervisors). (Based on Allen I. Kraut and others, "The Role of the Manager: What's Really Important in Different Management Jobs," *Academy of Management Executive*, November 1989, p. 287.)

While top managers spend most of their time organizing and planning, supervisors spend much of their time in activities related to the leading function (see Figure 1-4). Figure 1-5 lists the tasks identified by 650 supervisors as very important to performing their job successfully.[1]

THE TRANSITION FROM EMPLOYEE TO SUPERVISOR

"For a year I was one of them. Then, all of a sudden I was in charge. Some didn't buy into it," explains Tammy Abel.

"The micromanagement was a surprise for me when I first became a supervisor. I found a lot of employees turned to management to make decisions that they could make themselves," reported Daniel Quondam.

Diane McArthur's "biggest concern about becoming a supervisor and having direct reports was performance management. What would I do about the employee who isn't performing?"

As you can see from these comments, the move from operative employee to supervisor can involve anxiety and surprises. In this section, we'll look at the primary routes people take to becoming supervisors and the challenges they face in mastering a new identity.

WHERE DO SUPERVISORS COME FROM?

Most supervisors are promoted from within the ranks of their own organization. In the chapter opening, you read about Shelby D'Ambrogio who started in a frontline crew position at AMC Theatres, then became a crew lead, and finally a supervisor.

Employers tend to promote operative employees to first-line management jobs for several reasons. Operative employees know the job, understand the organization and typically know the people they'll be supervising. And the organization knows a lot about the candidate. When management promotes "one of their own," it minimizes risk. Finally, and importantly, promoting from within acts as an employee motivator; it provides an incentive for employees to work hard and excel.

What criteria do management tend to use in deciding whom to promote to supervisor? Employees with good work records and an interest in management tend to be favoured. Ironically, good operative employees don't always make good supervisors. People with strong technical skills don't necessarily have the skills needed to manage others. Those organizations that successfully promote from within tend to select employees with adequate technical skills and then provide them with supervisory training early in their new positions.

Shelby D'Ambrogio became supervisor through internal promotions.

The second source of supervisory personnel is new college or university graduates. But even here, it is unusual for the graduate to move directly into supervision. Typically the graduate must put in some time as an operative employee to learn and appreciate the tasks they will later be supervising.

A third source of supervisors is hiring people from other organizations who have relevant experience. This is more risky than hiring from within as the information the organization has about the candidate is limited and of questionable validity.

MASTERING A NEW IDENTITY

Moving from an operational position to a supervisory position is a much more significant change than further promotions up the ladder of management positions. That first move into management represents a much more significant change in duties, responsibilities and relationships.

Here are the typical experiences and discoveries[2].

The initial view of the manager as "boss" is incorrect. Before accepting a supervisory job, many expect they will walk into a position with power where they will be in control. "I'll be the one calling the shots." However, shortly into the position, they discover they are typically carrying out plans and policies determined by someone else. Rather than "boss", their primary role seems to be one of being a trouble-shooter and juggler. They describe themselves as problem-solvers who make decisions, organize resources and help others.

They are unprepared for the demands and ambiguities they would face. New supervisors tend to be surprised by the unrelenting workload and pace. On a typical day, they have to work on multiple problems simultaneously and are met with constant interruptions.

Technical expertise is no longer the primary determinant of success or failure. Organizations often promote people based on technical expertise so that those skills can support others. So new supervisors are used to excelling by performing specific technical tasks and being individual contributors, not by getting things done through others.

> *"One of the biggest hurdles was transitioning from hands on to hands off. It wasn't that I didn't trust my staff but I was used to a concrete sense of accomplishment. Now the achievements are more abstract, less concrete and I need to look at it in a different way."* (Debbie Hinz, Production Manager, Precision Biologic, Dartmouth)

> *"The hardest part was letting go. People would call and say something is not working and I was tempted to jump in and fix it. I needed to learn to mentor and coach my team in solving issues, to show them the ropes."* (Ainslie White, Manager of Information Systems, Precision Biologic, Dartmouth)

A supervisor's job comes with administrative duties. Routine communication activities to exchange information, or document and follow up on actions, or comply with company policies and procedures are time-consuming and are seen as an imposition.

They aren't prepared for the people challenges of the job. Many new supervisors describe the most challenging part of their position as learning how to manage people. This is particularly difficult for those who have moved into a position where they are supervising former colleagues.

> *"When I was first promoted, the others were the same age and were friends so it was hard to get them to do what I wanted. I convinced them by saying do it now or we'll have to stay late to get it done. If staff didn't do it, I would say "you wouldn't make a friend stay late?" (I would have to do their work). With newer staff I could be more straightforward: this is your task. But I had a tough time delegating. I felt that, if I didn't do it, it wasn't done right. I would always have to check."* (Pam Van Loenen)

FIGURE 1-7

Pam Van Loenen found it a challenge to supervise friends.

"I wasn't prepared. I erred by trying to maintain my friendships with the group while becoming their supervisor. I needed someone to coach me through the social skills; for example, no, I shouldn't go out for drinks with them, plan vacations together, share gossip. People take advantage. I walked into the receiving area and saw a bunch of salespeople doing nothing. I spoke to them diplomatically about going back to work. The response from one was, "Oh, Ryan, you don't need to be like that." And they all ignored my request to return to work. I walked away and did the work myself instead of dealing with the situation." (Ryan Anderson, Chapters)

"It was a difficult transition. I saw who my friends were – they embraced me and encouraged me and helped me along. Others were offended it was not them, because I was newer and younger. (David Goncalves, Mother Parkers)

"Becoming a manager, you have to set the line out. You can't be a buddy, can't buy into the gossip and the rumour mill. You have to stop doing what you used to do, have faith in those who do it, and trust staff to make the right call." (Rob Watson, Fusion Homes)

Almost as difficult as moving into supervision for the first time is the challenge of moving from a supervisory position at one organization to another organization. The people are different and it is likely that the policies, procedures and systems are different as well. The supervisor has to build credibility and establish relationships quickly in order to get things accomplished.

"I came from a specialist position where I dealt with one client to become a manager at an outsourcing company where I had multiple clients and didn't know any of them. I didn't know the internal processes so I had to learn the systems and the terminology. I had to really depend on employees because they had more knowledge than I had, even though I had come from a company where I was the expert." (Sue O'Hara)

DO YOU REALLY WANT TO BE A SUPERVISOR?

The fact that you're learning about supervision indicates that you're interested in understanding how to supervise people. As in any job, though, the person who goes in with open eyes and realistic expectations is more likely to be successful and more likely to last. We'll cover the cons and then the pros of becoming a supervisor.

Supervisory positions are not easy. Many of the items in the previous list of surprises for new supervisors could be seen as "cons" – the paperwork, the workload, the stress. Let's add a few more. One is that supervising may mean longer hours. Rob Mastrotto, team leader for the Inserts Finishing Team at Husky Injection Molding Systems in Bolton, Ontario, supervises about 45 people who work over three shifts. Rob typically arrives at work at 7 a.m. and stays until 6:30 p.m. to be in contact with all three shifts daily. He stays later when needed and sometimes comes in on weekends as well.

One of the reasons that Tina Payton came to Robinson-Blackmore printing company in St. John's, Newfoundland was the hours at her previous workplace, a daily newspaper. As a supervisor there she was on call seven days a week, 24 hours a day. She had to be accessible at all times, which meant that she couldn't even go far away on weekends. And, for printing a newspaper, the most critical hours are 11 p.m. to 4 a.m.—so this was when she was most likely to get the "We need you" emergency calls. Although both of these examples are at the extreme end, most supervisors do put in much more time than they are paid for.

These long hours are just one element of another issue for supervisors: stress. The increased responsibilities, accompanied by a limited amount of control, can be draining. Alex Lawrence has worked for years in a profit-focused corporate environment where expectations are high. Annually she has to rate all staff, including noting the bottom 10%, who may be let go as a result. As times got tougher and budgets tighter, she had to accomplish more with less and ultimately had to terminate people whose jobs were repositioned outside North America.

Downsizing always causes stresses for supervisors as it means releasing good employees and drastically increasing the workload for the remaining employees, who are understandably anxious about their own future. "It was really difficult to supervise through the recession. Because of the poor economy, there were layoffs but no less work so the remaining people were overworked. Whereas in the past three people covered three roles, now two covered three roles while still getting the same money. So morale was affected. There was no pay increase and there were fewer incentives even though the work demands were higher. Staff did what they had to in order to keep their jobs. In the past staff would do more than they were asked, but not anymore." (Haji Khurshid, workshop manager for a large used car centre)

Your pay as a supervisor also needs to be considered. As discussed above, it is unlikely that you will receive any overtime pay for all those extra hours. As a result, it is possible that operatives working fewer hours than you do may actually earn more because of overtime pay or commissions.

Another consideration focuses not on a negative but on a necessary shift in perspective. Your success as a supervisor will now typically come through other people's success. As an operative employee you were accustomed to tangible and immediate indication that you had performed your job well. As a supervisor, however, the feedback takes longer and is less closely tied to your own personal skills and efforts. This can be frustrating for some supervisors, leading them to keep their

FIGURE 1-10

Haji Khurshid found it especially tough to supervise in the recession.

Becoming a supervisor is a challenging opportunity. Some individuals look forward to "taking the helm" of a crew of workers, while others are put into this situation with little advance notice—or training. As you consider going into a supervisory position—or making yourself a more effective supervisor than you are today—think about the following two areas.

1. List five reasons why you want to be a supervisor.

   _____

   _____

   _____

   _____

   _____

2. Identify five potential problems or difficulties that you may encounter when you become a supervisor.

   _____

   _____

   _____

   _____

   _____

hand in more than they should on the operative side. This can overload you and cause resentment among the operative employees.

Despite the concerns expressed above, people still choose to move into management and then choose to stay in management. Why? Some of the positives include challenging yourself, learning new skills, getting the opportunity to work with a different group of people, making more money (yes, sometimes that happens), and having the opportunity to influence how things are done. "I enjoy working with the people, getting to know them, and I enjoy the challenge of making good quality product and getting it out the door by deadline", says Paula Aylward, a shift manager at a Cavendish Farms French fries plant in P.E.I. Diane McArthur of ServiceOntario says, "the most rewarding thing is to see someone who works for you succeed and move to the next level and know you had a little part in it."

Ron McLester, the Special Advisor to the Vice-President Student Services, Aboriginal Education & Student Services, Mohawk College explains "What do I like about being in management? It's way more macro-oriented. I am a macro-level thinker. I like pulling a team together who are all subject matter experts and then letting each find their own sweet spot."

Moving into management is a great opportunity for those who want to make a difference, who will enjoy acquiring a new skill set, and who will accept the challenges the position brings as part of the package.

COMPETENCIES OF SUPERVISORS

What does it take to be an effective manager? Are the competencies or skills needed the same, regardless of a manager's level in the organization? These questions will be answered in this section.

Management competencies
General categories of skills necessary to perform a managerial job.

Forty years ago, Robert Katz identified three essential **management competencies**: technical, interpersonal, and conceptual.[3] They are as relevant today as when Katz originally described them. And they have been joined by a fourth general category of management skills: political competence.

TECHNICAL COMPETENCE

Senior management is composed of generalists who don't need to be intimately familiar with the mechanics of the operative employee's job. Instead, senior management activities—such as strategic planning, developing the organization's overall structure and culture, maintaining relationships with major customers, investors, and so on—are generic in nature. The technical demands on senior managers tend to be related to knowledge of the industry and a general understanding of the organization's processes and products. But this is not true for managers at other levels.

Technical competence
The ability to apply specialized knowledge or expertise.

Unlike top management, most other managers manage within areas of specialized knowledge: for example, *sales* manager, *call centre project* manager, *ATM production* manager, *student placement* coordinator, *finishing line* supervisor. These managers need **technical competence**—the ability to apply specialized knowledge or expertise. It's difficult, if not impossible, to effectively manage people with specialized skills if you lack understanding of their jobs. You will have little credibility with them and will be unable to fulfill the "troubleshooting" role so commonly expected of supervisors.

INTERPERSONAL COMPETENCE

A supervisor's job is working with and through other people. So **interpersonal competence** is critical—the ability to work with, understand, and motivate other people, both individually and in groups. Supervisors must listen well, speak well, and understand the needs of others. They need to give bad news and negative feedback, resolve conflicts, and confront unacceptable behaviour. They need to tune in to the varying motivations of people and act accordingly, yet still be viewed as fair.

This is a tall order and I suspect you have encountered a manager or two in your time who, although technically competent, failed in a leadership role because of inadequate interpersonal skills. "**Emotional intelligence**" is a concept now popularly used to describe a set of skills that correlate highly with effectiveness at work and in other realms. Goleman describes it as consisting of five basic emotional and social skills:[4]

- Self-awareness (a realistic assessment of one's abilities and shortcomings; use of awareness of one's feelings to guide actions appropriately)
- Self-regulation (conscientiousness, emotional control, the ability to delay gratification, self-discipline)
- Motivation (use of one's values and needs to take initiative; intent on improvement despite setbacks)
- Empathy (the ability to "tune in" to others' feelings and perspectives, to create rapport with diverse people)
- Social skills (smooth interaction with others, accurate reading of social situations and networks, and use of these skills to influence others, handle conflict, and promote cooperation)

The skills described above would certainly enhance any supervisor's ability to work with and through others. And they are skills, like technical competence, that can be consciously developed once one is aware of the need to develop them. One of the effective uses of 360-degree feedback, where a selection of employees who work with a supervisor all contribute their appraisals of his or her performance, is getting subordinates to anonymously give feedback to their supervisor on his or her skills. The feedback often most appreciated by supervisors, and often surprising to them, is the feedback on elements of their interpersonal competence.

CONCEPTUAL COMPETENCE

Managers must have the ability to analyze and diagnose complex situations. This is **conceptual competence**. Strong conceptual abilities allow a manager to see the "big picture" of the organization and its interrelated parts, and the bigger picture including the industry, community, and

Interpersonal competence
The ability to work with, understand, and motivate other people, both individually and in groups.

Emotional intelligence
A set of skills including self-awareness, self-regulation, motivation, empathy and social skills that correlate highly with effectiveness at work.

Conceptual competence
The mental ability to analyze and diagnose complex situations.

economy. On a more day-to-day level, these conceptual abilities allow a manager to anticipate events, plan more thoroughly, understand the priorities when faced with overwhelming demands, and make better decisions.

Stacy Goodale of Imperial Oil in Toronto notes, "I have to be a good analyst. To get things done, I not only have to articulate my ideas well, I have to know my audience and the context, know what is in my control, and know what is important. When should I be aggressive and push for my ideas in interfacing with senior management? What are they interested in?"

POLITICAL COMPETENCE

Political competence
A supervisor's ability to enhance his or her power, build a power base, and establish the "right" connections in the organization.

Supervisors also need to possess **political competence**. This refers to the supervisor's ability to enhance his or her power, build a power base, and establish the "right" connections in the organization. Politics is something supervisors engage in when they attempt to influence the advantages and disadvantages in a situation.[5] It is beyond normal work duties and their job description.

Jason Aurora, a human resources (HR) manager, showed his political astuteness the first day he started at the Canadian headquarters of a multinational company. When he went to the cafeteria, he realized it was like high school with everyone sitting in their cliques (admin staff together, executives together, engineers...). Jason decided not to follow the pattern. Instead he deliberately sat down at different tables, introduced himself and started chatting. Soon everyone knew him. This was perfect for his role in HR because he was now perceived as approachable and welcoming. It was also a great source of information as the others would forget he was there and his role so he would hear about issues and concerns informally before they made it through the official routes to him in the HR office.

COMPETENCIES AND MANAGERIAL LEVEL

While managers need to possess all three competencies, the importance that each competency plays in the manager's job varies with the manager's level in the organization. Here are some general rules:

1. Technical competence declines in importance as managers rise in the organization.
2. Conceptual competencies increase in importance as managerial responsibility rises.
3. Interpersonal competencies are a constant to success, regardless of level in the organization.
4. Political competence grows in importance as managers rise in the organization.

Technical abilities have the greatest relevance for first-level managers. This is true for two reasons. First, many perform technical work as well as managerial work. In contrast to other levels of management, the distinction between individual contributor and first-line manager is often blurred. Second, supervisors spend more time on training and developing their employees than do other managers. This requires them to have a greater technical knowledge of their employees' jobs than that needed by middle- and senior-level managers.

The importance of conceptual competence increases as managers move up in the organization because of the type of problems and decisions that managers make at different levels. Generally speaking, the higher a manager rises in an organization, the more the problems he or she faces tend to be complex, ambiguous, and ill defined. This requires custom-made solutions. In contrast, first-level managers generally have more straightforward, familiar, and easily defined problems that lend themselves to more routine decision making. Ill-structured problems and custom-made solutions make greater conceptual demands on managers than do structured problems and routine decision making.

There is overwhelming evidence that interpersonal abilities are critical at all levels of management. This shouldn't come as a shock, because we know that managers get things done through other people. But supervisors are particularly in need of interpersonal competencies because they spend so much of their time in leading-function activities. For instance, Rod Guild, senior foreman at Highland Valley Copper Mine in British Columbia, emphasizes the importance of interpersonal skills: "Listen to your people as they have experience and ideas that you don't. Also, the simple act of listening to their input often ensures they become more interested and involved in the job. For example, we were building a road and needed good quality rock for it. Talking it over with the cat operator, who had run the cat longer than I had been alive, I suggested hauling rock in from an ore shovel with good material. His suggestion was to cut the rock from a bank immediately beside him. This saved 25 percent of the time to do the job and didn't interrupt ore flow to the crushers."

FIGURE 1-11

Rod Guild, senior foreman at a B.C. copper mine, emphasizes the importance of interpersonal skills in his position. Courtesy of Brad Aie

Finally, the higher one climbs in the organization's hierarchy, the more critical political competence becomes. Because resource allocation decisions are made at higher levels in an organization, middle and top managers are "fighting" for their piece of the organizational pie. Their need to develop alliances, support one project over another, or influence certain situations, involves higher-level political skills. But don't interpret this as implying that politics are less important for supervisors. Because so much of the supervisor's job is not well defined, he or she needs strong political skills to get the unit's work completed, and to survive.

FROM CONCEPTS TO SKILLS

Supervision does come more easily to some than others. It helps if you've worked for a good manager so you have a role model to emulate. Or if you've grown up with parents, relatives or friends who were managers, you may have gained insights into the job and the skills needed. If your parents helped you set realistic goals, provided positive feedback, encouraged independence, communicated openly, and fostered the development of a strong self-concept in you, you have learned skills that will help you function as a manager. However, anyone can improve his or her supervisory abilities.

This book will help you to be an effective supervisor by focusing on both conceptual knowledge and practical skills. In each chapter there will be a section called "From Concepts to Skills" that focuses on a specific skill, inviting readers to assess themselves on the skill, consider the basics, and then apply the skill in an activity (see the list below in Figure 1-12). In the next chapter, for example, we'll discuss the importance of planning to a supervisor's success and show how setting goals is a key part of planning. Then we'll present specific techniques for helping employees set goals and provide you with an opportunity to practice and develop your goal-setting skills.

Skill
The ability to demonstrate a system and sequence of behaviour that is functionally related to attainment of a performance goal.

What exactly is a skill? **A skill** is the ability to demonstrate a system and sequence of behaviour that is functionally related to attaining a performance goal.[6] No single action constitutes a skill. For example, the ability to write clear communications is a skill. People who have this skill know the particular sequence of actions to be taken to propose a project or summarize a report. They can separate primary from secondary ideas. They can organize their thoughts in a logical manner. They can simplify convoluted ideas. But none of these actions is by itself a skill. A skill is a system of behaviour that can be applied in a wide range of situations.

WHAT ELSE DO I NEED TO KNOW ABOUT SUPERVISING?

If by now you're somewhat amazed at what a supervisor has to do and the skills he or she must have to succeed in an organization, there are nonetheless several other elements that you should consider. Specifically, what are the personal issues that you should address?

One of the first things you'll need to do is to recognize that as a supervisor, you are part of management. This means that you support the organization and the wishes of management above you. Although you might disagree with those wishes, you must, as a supervisor, be loyal to the organization. You must also develop a means of gaining respect from your employees, as well as from your peers and boss. In order to be effective as a supervisor, you'll need to develop their trust and build credibility with them. One means of doing this is to continually keep your skills and

Chapter	From Concepts to Skills topic
2	Goal Setting
3	Budgeting
4	Creative Problem-Solving
5	Delegating
6	Interviewing for Hiring
7	Conducting Appraisal Interviews
8	Coaching
9	Designing Motivating Jobs
10	Networking
11	Active Listening
12	Negotiation
13	Stress Reduction
14	Disciplining
15	Handling Grievances

FIGURE 1-12

competencies up to date. You must continue your "education," not only because it helps you, but also because it sets an example for your employees. It communicates that learning matters.

Supervisors in various fields understand this need for continuing education. "Every time I turn around there's an upgrade. There's always new software coming out as well as new equipment. It's a constant challenge to keep up with it all and you have to take the initiative to keep up. We are currently reviewing new equipment to keep us on the leading edge of technology. We will be attending a huge graphic trade show in Chicago soon to research this equipment as well as checking out what else is new in the industry," says Tina Payton, prepress supervisor at Robinson-Blackmore, a printing company in St. John's. On the other hand, when Tricia Mah moved into her position as director of support services at an intermediate care residential home in Vancouver, she was in charge of food services, laundry, and housekeeping, knowing a great deal about food services but very little about the other areas. Since no courses were available to teach her the necessary information, she contacted colleagues in management at acute-care facilities and asked one friend to spend a day helping her to "learn the ropes." She also took a correspondence course in housekeeping methodology.

You'll also have to understand what legitimate power you have been given by the organization because you direct the activities of others. This legitimate power is your authority to act and to expect others to follow your directions. Yet, be aware that ruling with an iron fist may not work.

You'll need to know when to assert your authority and how to get things done without resorting to "because I told you so." Supervisors play a key role in affecting turnover - people tend to leave managers, not organizations. To get things done in the organization, you need to develop interpersonal skills that help you influence others. This is particularly true when dealing with organizational members whom you don't supervise.

Finally, you'll need to recognize that organizational members differ from one another—not only in their talents, but also as individuals. You'll need to be sensitive to their needs, tolerate and even celebrate their differences, and be empathetic to them as individuals. Success, in part, will begin with understanding the meaning of flexibility.

SUPERVISORY CHALLENGES FOR THE 21ST CENTURY

The world of management has changed drastically because of the increasing use of computer technology, massive downsizings and restructurings to meet intense competition, new legislation and the diversity of today's workforce. In the remainder of the chapter, we will review some of the most significant forces now affecting supervisors.

CHANGING EXPECTATIONS OF SUPERVISORS

Forty years ago, if you asked a group of top executives what they thought a supervisor's or foreman's job was, you'd get a fairly standard answer. They'd describe a man (which it was likely to be back then) who made and enforced decisions, told employees what to do, closely watched over those employees to make sure they did as they were told, disciplined them when they broke the rules, and fired those who didn't "shape up." Supervisors were the bosses on the "operating floor" and their job was to keep the employees in line and get the work done.

If you asked senior executives that same question today, you'd find a few who still hold to the supervisor-as-boss perspective. But you'd be far more likely to hear executives describe today's supervisor with terms such as "trainer," "adviser," "mentor," "facilitator," or "coach." In this section, we will look at how top management, the public, and even operative employees have developed changing expectations of supervisory managers.

ROLE AMBIGUITY

The supervisor's job—unique in that it bridges both the management and operative ranks—has long had an ambiguous role. For example, each of the following offers a different perspective of the supervisor's role:[7]

Key person.   Supervisors serve as the critical communication link in the organization's chain of authority. They are like the hub of a wheel around which all operating activities revolve.

Person in the middle.   Because they are "neither fish nor fowl," supervisors must interact and reconcile the opposing forces and competing expectations from higher management and workers. If unresolved, this ambiguous status can create frustration and stress for supervisors.

Just another worker.   To some, particularly among upper-level managers, supervisors are often viewed as "just another worker" rather than as management. This is reinforced when their decision-making authority is limited, when they're excluded from participating in upper-level decisions, and when they perform operating tasks alongside the people they supervise.

Behavioural specialist.   Consistent with the belief that one of the most important abilities needed by supervisors is strong interpersonal skills, we can view them as behavioural specialists. To succeed in their jobs, supervisors must be able to understand the varied needs of their staff; and be able to listen, motivate, and lead.

While each of these four role descriptions has some truth to it, each also offers a slanted view of the supervisor's job. Our point is that different people hold different perceptions of this job, which can create ambiguity and conflicts for today's supervisor.

INCREASED IMPORTANCE

Despite differing perceptions of the supervisor's role, the job has always been important and complex. It will likely become even more so in the future for at least three reasons.[8]

First, organizations are implementing significant change programs to cut costs and increase productivity. Examples include quality improvement, new technology, the use of teams, group bonus plans, and stress-reduction programs. These programs tend to focus on the work activities of operative employees. Supervisors are, therefore, important because they are the ones typically responsible for implementing these change efforts on the operating floor.

Second, many organizations have imposed extensive cutbacks in their numbers of employees. Middle management and support-staff personnel have been particularly thinned out. Because there are fewer middle managers, supervisors tend to have more people reporting to them: a span of control of 50 employees per supervisor is not uncommon today yet was unheard of not long ago. Many of the tasks previously performed by support personnel are now moving to supervisors; for example, scheduling and quality control.

Finally, employee training is increasing in importance as organizations seek to improve productivity. New employees, many of whom lack literacy or numeracy skills, and some immigrants with limited English, require basic training in reading and writing. Current employees typically need occasional but ongoing training to keep their skills up-to-date. Supervisors carry the primary burden of identifying skill deficiencies, and sometimes also design and deliver the training.

SOMETHING TO THINK ABOUT
• AND TO PROMOTE CLASS DISCUSSION •

IT'S TOUGHER TO BE A MANAGER NOW

Barbara Moses[9] believes it is becoming "tougher to be a manager" and reports the following typical complaints by managers:

Needy employees: acting like children, seeking approval for minor tasks

- "It's like I spend most of my time being mommy – wiping noses, kissing boo-boos and getting everyone to play nice."

Sense of entitlement: unreasonable expectations

- "I have three employees who are now lobbying for a promotion or exceptional performance rating. One made a retirement party, another stayed an hour late, and the third helped someone with their technology problem."

Lack of boundaries: overstepping appropriate worker-boss talk

- Would you believe there are some "who feel a need to tell me about their sex life?"

Need for direction: need for hand-holding, coaching through simple tasks

- "One manager was consulted on what colour the icing should be on a birthday cake for a team member. Another was asked by a senior professional, for the third time, to review a 20-page proposal. The changes: a few minor grammatical revisions."

Bureaucracy: filling out forms to get anything done

- "One middle manager said she spent a whole day trying to determine which form to fill out to request an ergonomic chair for an employee; the next day, she ate up four hours completing forms for someone going on maternity leave."

Leaders don't walk the talk: top brass not living up to the organizational values

- For example, "executives who proclaimed to care about work/life balance – and then scheduled meetings at, say, 6 pm, with full knowledge of staffers' childcare responsibilities."

Action before thinking: being expected to provide immediate responses to complicated problems

- "Produce, produce, produce. This is not a fast food restaurant."

Time and resources squeeze: feeling maxed out

- "Many feel they have neither the time nor the resources to feel they have successfully accomplished even one small thing."

FIGURE 1-13

Management isn't easy
Courtesy of bullet74/Shutterstock

FROM BOSS TO COACH

Marlene Roy is supervisor of the Labour Market Information Unit of HRDC in Winnipeg, but she is also formally referred to as the team leader. Rob Mastrotto supervises over 40 people at Husky Injection Molding Systems but his official title is Inserts Finishing Team Leader.

These titles are significant. The focus for supervisors now in most companies is not on being a boss but rather on "coaching" or leading a team. The analogy with a sports team can be expanded even further. Today's supervisor is expected to identify and develop skills, as well as support and motivate individuals. The supervisor ensures that each employee learns to play his or her part, but also facilitates employees' movement towards a cohesive, synergistic whole. Supervisors are also expected to make tough decisions when things are going badly.

Note that the skills of a coach include the technical, conceptual, and political skills noted earlier. But a major emphasis for a coach must be on his or her interpersonal skills. People obey a boss because they have to "or else." People go along with a coach because they consider it to be in their best interest, they respect the coach, and they want to contribute to the team.

CHANGING THE SIZE OR THE STRUCTURE OF THE ORGANIZATION

DOWNSIZING

Downsizing
A reduction in the workforce and reshaping of operations to create "lean and mean" organizations. The goals of organizational downsizing are greater efficiency and reduced costs.

Many Canadian organizations have attempted to become "lean and mean" by reducing their workforce, or **downsizing**. The goal in each case was to create greater efficiency and cut costs. Many activities were outsourced and there has been increased use of contract workers to give the organization greater flexibility.

Downsizing can have various effects on supervisors. Employees who are laid off and those left behind, feeling insecure and overloaded with work, may become angry. Despite not being the one to make the downsizing decision, the supervisor may take the brunt of employees' resentment. The supervisor may also have had the excruciating responsibility of helping to decide which employees were to be let go. Many supervisors feel that the worst thing they have ever had to do in their position was to lay off an excellent performer and loyal employee simply because that person had less seniority than others.

An important challenge for supervisors is to motivate the remaining staff, who may feel resentful, less committed, stressed, and disloyal. Downsizing may also cause increased competition among the employees, trying to outdo each other to protect their position. They may be less likely to help each other. In such a situation the idea of a team seems ridiculous.

Along with the loss of staff through downsizing, it is unlikely that the demand on the department's productivity will become any less. Work systems and procedures may need to be altered drastically, and this will likely be the supervisor's responsibility. Workloads for all, including the supervisor, will be heavier. Productivity and/or quality may suffer, and the supervisor must answer for this.

GROWTH

To be a supervisor in an organization that is healthy and growing may seem ideal; however, such a situation brings its own problems. Production demands are high. New employees must be recruited, hired, given the appropriate orientation and training, and integrated into the workflow. But, due to production demands, they may be thrown on the floor without adequate preparation and then cause quality problems. The supervisor must train employees, deal with the quality problems, push production, and interview new staff while his or her own workload is incredibly high. It's a challenging and stimulating endeavour but it can also be extremely draining for the individuals involved.

RESTRUCTURING

Organizations may change their organizational structure for a variety of reasons, for example, in an attempt to streamline activities, make them more responsive to customer demands, or save money. For example, an organization may move from a traditional functional structure to one that is more responsive to customers. In a traditional structure, employees are grouped by function—marketing people are grouped together, production staff are grouped, finance people are grouped, and so on. This can focus employee attention and loyalty on their unit rather than on the organization and the customer. As a result, many companies have now moved to a customer base structure where a department may consist of a selection of people from all those functions who are grouped to meet the needs of one particular customer to whom they are assigned. The supervisory role in these two structures is very different—moving from one of technical specialist and troubleshooter to coordinator.

MANAGING TECHNOLOGY

Few jobs today are unaffected by technology. As he drives around the large mine site in his truck, Rod Guild of Highland Valley Copper in British Columbia uses a digital handheld voice recorder and a handheld computer notebook to note his observations. He regularly consults these notes when he is in a position to act on his observations. He has no office. As assistant manager at a large clothing store Katerina Kollaras had to communicate with her staff through headsets. "The headsets were mostly used for the staff to communicate amongst one another in each zone of the store in regards to clothing, assistance that they may have needed, and to communicate sales goals. I would coach them when necessary. For example, "I just watched a customer walk by and you didn't greet them." It almost felt like we were spying on them. All staff hear what is said on the headset so you have to be really careful what you say and how you say it. It means that coaching one person on the headset sets an example for all but there's no privacy and it's not as personal as I would like." As a supervisor at AMC theatres, Shelby D'Ambrogio's decisions are based on information provided by technology. "We have software that indicates the number of guests, number of transactions, dollar spent per person, auditorium levels. I need to decide whether auditoriums need swapping due to demand and if I need to cut staff hours because guest attendance is down."

Undoubtedly, technology has had a positive effect on internal operations within organizations. How, specifically, has it changed the supervisor's job? To answer that question we need only to look at the way the typical office is set up. Organizations today have become integrated communications centres. By linking computers, telephones, fax machines, copiers, printers, and the like, supervisors can get more complete information

FIGURE 1-14
Katerina Kollaras uses a headset to communicate with staff in a large clothing store.

more quickly than ever before. With that information, they can better formulate plans, make faster decisions, more clearly define the jobs that workers need to perform, and monitor work activities on an "as-they-happen" basis. In essence, technology today has enhanced supervisors' ability to more effectively and efficiently perform their jobs!

Technology is also changing where a supervisor's work is performed. Historically in organizations, the supervisor's work site was located close to the operations site. As a result, employees were in close proximity to their bosses. A supervisor could observe how the work was being done, as well as easily communicate with employees face-to-face. Through technological advancements, supervisors are now able to supervise employees in remote locations (see Something to Think About, below). Face-to-face interaction has decreased dramatically. Work, for many, occurs where their computers are. Telecommuting capabilities—linkage of a remote worker's computer and modem with coworkers and management at an office—have made it possible for employees to be located anywhere in the global village. Communicating effectively with individuals in remote locations, and ensuring that their performance objectives are being met, are some of the supervisor's new challenges.

Communication technology also makes huge demands on supervisors. They can be reached anytime anywhere through technology and data can be easily shared, leading to an expectation that they will be able to provide instant answers. In CASE 1.A, Diane Hebert expresses the frustrations that many supervisors feel over this.

SOMETHING TO THINK ABOUT
• A N D   T O   P R O M O T E   C L A S S   D I S C U S S I O N •

THE OFF-SITE EMPLOYEE

If you were to go back some 150 years in Canadian history, you'd find that it was not uncommon for most workers to be performing their jobs at home. Most goods were not mass-produced. Individuals produced a finished product and then took it to market to sell. Then along came the Industrial Revolution, which changed how work was done. Now we may be coming full circle—once again working at home. It is estimated that off-site employees comprise about one-quarter of the Canadian workforce today, and that number is expected to rise. Most of these workers are in such professions as sales, medicine, law, accounting, and a wide range of service occupations.[10]

What benefits do you see for organizations that have work done off site? What benefits do you believe exist for employees who work at home? What are the potential problems a supervisor may face in supervising off-site workers?

The primary implications for supervisors of advances in computer technology relate to training, overcoming resistance to change, and dealing with a vastly greater amount of communication than previously. Many supervisors deal with literally dozens of e-mail and voice-mail messages daily.

Managing Workforce Diversity

Canada's workforce reflects its society and, particularly in urban areas, that workforce is multicultural. As well as increasing in cultural diversification, the Canadian workforce is composed of a greater percentage of women than it used to be, is better educated, and also comes with an almost endless variety of "family" systems to return home to. See Figure 1-17 for a summary of how the Canadian workforce has changed.

The implications of **workforce diversity** for management are widespread. Employees don't set aside their cultural values and lifestyle preferences when they come to work. As a result, management must be accommodating and flexible enough to meet the needs of valued workers. For example, this may mean more flexible work schedules to allow those responsible for children, the elderly, or others needing special care to work, or benefit programs may need to be redesigned to reflect employees' varied needs.

Workforce diversity The increasing heterogeneity of organizations with the inclusion of different groups.

On a day-to-day level, supervisors must set an example of tolerating and embracing differences. A supervisor must be careful not to use inappropriate words or use humour that may be offensive. Inappropriate words or actions by subordinates indicating discrimination or lack of respect must be confronted. A supervisor may need to give extra support to an employee having difficulties outside of work that are affecting his or her performance at work. A supervisor may also need to strive to build a relationship with an employee whose culture includes extreme deference to authority. That person may be extremely reluctant to ask for help or make suggestions.

In addition to the diversity brought about by such factors as lifestyle, gender, nationality, and race, supervisors must be aware of the age differences they'll encounter. Today, there are four general age groups in the work place: the Traditionalists (born before 1946), the Baby Boomers (born 1946-1964), Gen X (1964-1980) and Gen Y or Millenials (born after 1980). The different age clusters do tend to have different values and different expectations and the supervisor has to deal with all of them. Debbie Hinz, production manager at Precision Biologic in Dartmouth, explains: "There is a difference in the new generation. I need to make adjustments and try not to judge. I try to understand their perspective but I also have to take the business perspective. Twenty year olds are much more likely to use their cell phones during work to call or text and they are more likely to question work/life balance issues. But they are also much more comfortable with computers and automation. On the other hand, the fifty year olds have lower comfort with computers but they are less likely to question the need for working overtime."

In general terms, the age groups differ in their comfort level with technology and with change, and prefer different means of communication. But no assumptions can be made about individuals according to their age. The potential damage from age differences may be more due to stereotyped perceptions of other ages rather than the actual characteristics. See Figure 1-15 for the results of a Conference Board of Canada study on the self-perceptions of different age groups and their perceptions of other generations. Regardless of age, all employees would like flexibility, fairness and respect. If a supervsior provides these and also addresses individual needs, there is the basis for strong working relationships.

Unfortunately, supervisors themselves may need to deal with others in the organization who discriminate against them. For example, Paula Aylward of Cavendish Farms says, "I need to have more [guts] than anything. If I don't, the fight is twice as hard." Paula is a shift manager of a production plant, one of only eight women in management. When she first moved into management, some of the men she supervised would question her decisions, uncomfortable with a woman directing them. Even in dealing with upper management, Paula believes that her gender has affected how she is treated.

	Self-Perception	Perception of Other Generations
Baby Boomers	*Boomers say that they:* "have more respect for the boss" "tend to take the job more seriously" "like a social atmosphere" "will give the extra effort when needed" "are looking for stability" "are more likely to be content in their jobs" "tend to stick with organizations and try to change them from within" "can be set in their ways" "are the ones most willing to learn" "take more time to learn technology, but learn it on a more in-depth basis"	*Boomers say that Gen Xers:* "are willing to learn, to work in teams, easily adapt to technology" "are not committed to the company"; "are loners"; "lack patience" "try hard to get ahead, and if they don't, quickly move on" "have no loyalty. They want to get ahead at any cost" "have difficulty reporting to an authority figure" *Boomers say that Gen Yers:* "are more adaptable to change and learn new technology more easily" "are only there for a paycheque. They have no loyalty to the employer or to the other employees with whom they work." "seek shortcuts and don't like to assume responsibilities" "do not like to follow rules." "do too much communication digitally"

	Gen Xers say that they:	Gen Xers say that Boomers:
Gen X (1965–1980)	"are trying to find a balance between work and family life" "are more willing to question authority" "have always lived in the shadow of the Baby Boomers" "are frustrated at being caught in the middle of two generations" "want to move up in an organization but can't because there are a lot of old people biding their time until retirement" "can lean either way toward Baby Boomer tendencies or Gen Y tendencies, depending on previous life and work experiences"	"seem to be more dedicated to the employer" "are more experienced and 'know how to get things done'" "lack computer skills" and "like things done 'the old way'" "know their job, but have a hard time 'stepping out of the bubble'" "have difficulty giving up control" "are dependable, but like to stick with the same routine" *Gen Xers say that Gen Yers:* "are capable and technology obsessed" "tend to be more self-absorbed; more interested in protecting their own interests even at the expense of an organization" "often miss details, concerned more with getting done now, not right" "are lazy, expecting salaries will be handed to them with no effort" "think they know everything, but actually know very little"
	Gen Yers say that they:	Gen Yers about Boomers:
Gen Y (after 1980)	"love using technology" "are more open to suggestions than the 'older generations'" "strive to have a life that will make them happy. This causes conflict when it comes to personal days or vacation" "tend to do things their own way, and do not always follow the rules" "are results-oriented. This can cause problems, as one group strictly wants to follow processes while the other wants to get stuff done"	"are less accepting of technology" "don't tend to take suggestions from young people" "want to follow procedure, even if there is a better or faster way" "are not comfortable thinking 'outside the box.' They'd rather stick to tried and tested procedures." "live to work rather than work to live" *Gen Yers about Xers:* "are comfortable with technology, [and] can handle some change" "are well-motivated, but not as much as the older generation" "are annoying and aggressive" "are more likely to share information with Gen Y" "make the company run, but often don't get as much credit or pay as the Boomers"

FIGURE 1-15 *(CONTINUED)*

Supervision in *Action*

The Cultural Variables

To date, the framework most valuable in helping managers better understand differences between national cultures is one developed by Geert Hofstede.[12] He surveyed over 116 000 IBM employees in 40 countries, and found that supervisors and employees vary in four dimensions of national culture:

1. individualism versus collectivism
2. power distance
3. uncertainty avoidance
4. quantity versus quality of life[13]

Individualism refers to a loosely knit social framework in which people are expected to look after their own interests and those of their immediate family. This is made possible because of the large amount of freedom that such a society allows individuals. Its opposite is *collectivism*, which is characterized by a tight social framework. People expect others in groups to which they belong (such as a family or an organization) to look after them and protect them when they are in trouble. In exchange for this, they feel they owe absolute allegiance to the group.

Power distance is a measure of the extent to which a society accepts the fact that power in institutions and organizations is distributed unequally. A high power-distance society accepts wide differences in power within organizations. Employees show a great deal of respect for those in authority. Titles, rank, and status carry a lot of weight. In contrast, a low power-distance society plays down inequalities as much as possible. Supervisors still have authority, but employees are not fearful or in awe of the boss.

A society that is high in *uncertainty avoidance* is characterized by an increased level of anxiety among its people, which manifests itself in greater nervousness, stress, and aggressiveness. Because people feel threatened by uncertainty and ambiguity in these societies, mechanisms are created to provide security and reduce risk. Their organizations are likely to have more formal rules, there will be less tolerance for deviant ideas and behaviours, and members will strive to believe in absolute truths. Not surprisingly, in organizations in countries with high uncertainty avoidance, employees demonstrate relatively low job mobility, and lifetime employment is widely practised.

Quantity versus quality of life, like individualism and collectivism, represents a dichotomy. Some cultures emphasize the quantity of life, and value things such as assertiveness and the acquisition of money and material goods. Other cultures emphasize the quality of life, placing importance on relationships and showing sensitivity and concern for the welfare of others.

Where do Canadian supervisors fit within this framework? Which cultures would be likely to involve the biggest adjustment problems for Canadian supervisors? To answer these questions, we must identify those countries that are most and least like Canada on the four dimensions.[14] Canada is strongly individualistic, but low on power distance. This same pattern is exhibited by Great Britain, Australia, the United States, the Netherlands, and New Zealand. Those least similar to Canada on these dimensions are Venezuela, Colombia, Pakistan, Singapore, and the Philippines.

Canada scored low on uncertainty avoidance and high on quantity of life. This same pattern was shown by Ireland, Great Britain, the United States, New Zealand, Australia, India, and South Africa. Those least similar to Canada on these dimensions are Chile and Portugal.

The study supports what many suspected—that the Canadian supervisor who transfers to London, New York, Melbourne, or a similar "Anglo" city has the fewest adjustments to make. The study further identifies the countries in which "culture shock" is likely to be the greatest, suggesting a need to radically modify the Canadian supervisory style.

USE OF CONTRACT WORKERS

At Mother Parkers Tea and Coffee where David Goncalves is a production supervisor, he has eight full-time people on his team but can also have up to 24 agency employees working with them at any one time, depending on projects. For example, if there is a special request from a customer for special packaging, there may be no capability for automation so hand packing is necessary and a lot more hands are needed.

Organizations are now much more likely than previously to hire temporary help through the use of contract workers. This allows them to get the job done by people with exactly the skills needed without incurring the additional costs of extensive training, benefits, and employment insurance. Organizations can then terminate their relationship with contract workers when the demand for them no longer exists. How does this affect the super-

FIGURE 1-16

David Goncalvez often uses contract workers so the expanded team can deal with more demanding projects.

FIGURE 1-17

The diversification
of the Canadian
workforce

Characteristic	1950s	Today
Gender	Predominantly male	Male and Female
Race	Caucasian	Caucasian, Asian-Canadian, African-Canadian
Ethnic Origin	European descent	European descent, Asian, Middle Eastern, African
Age	20 to 65	16 to 80+ (with a higher average age)
Family Status	Single or married with children	Single, married with children, married with no children, cohabitating, dependent elders, dual-career couple, commuter relationship
Sexual Orientation	Heterosexual	Heterosexual, gay, lesbian, bisexual
Physical Abilities	Physically able	Physically able and physically challenged
Education Level	High school	About half with post-secondary education.

visor who likely supervises a mixed staff of full-time and contract workers? When work is done by a series of contract workers rather than full-time workers, supervisors must do more hiring and training. The team's structure is upset somewhat every time personnel change. The contract worker may know the job but cause difficulties because he or she doesn't understand the culture, the "way things are done here" and the supervisor ends up working with the employee to overcome that, and working to put out the fires created.

Stacy Goodale has had several contract workers on her project and explains, "It can be a challenge building their credibility to others in the organization so they can get their job done. And sometimes I feel like a football blocker because a contract worker is criticized for putting his nose in where it doesn't belong. I need to deflect the comments so it doesn't become an issue—for the contract worker, the team, or the project."

INCREASING LEGAL OBLIGATIONS

Supervisors have always had to be concerned about compliance with collective agreements in a unionized workplace and compliance with company policies and procedures in any organization. There is also an awareness of provincial employment standards that govern things like required vacation, and minimum wage but most supervisors assume someone from head office (like HR) will ensure those considerations are taken care of. Supervisors rarely thought of themselves as being in a position where the law is applied. This is changing, principally because of legislation related to health and safety and to workplace harassment or bullying.

Canadian provincial legislation has long made workplace safety a joint responsibility of workers, supervisors and employers. But the recent amendment to the Criminal Code by the federal government's Bill C-45 makes it possible for employers and their representatives (e.g. supervisors) to be convicted for safety violations. Also known as the Westray Bill, its genesis lay in the 1992 Westray mining disaster where 26 miners were killed. Safety concerns at the mine had been raised but the company made few changes; as a result the company was considered to blame for those deaths by most people. Yet the legislation current at the time did not lead to a successful conviction of the company or its managers. A Royal Commission made recommendations that eventually led to the 2004 creation of Bill C-45, adding Section 217.1 to the Criminal Code which reads:

> "217.1 Every one who undertakes, or has the authority, to direct how another person does work or performs a task is under legal duty to take reasonable steps to prevent bodily harm to that person, or any other person, arising from that work or task."

The first conviction under the amendment was against Transpavé, a Quebec manufacturer of concrete blocks. In 2005, 23-year-old employee Steve L'Ecuyer was crushed to death by a concrete press as he was trying to manually free stones that were blocking the machine. A safety barrier meant to prevent the machine from operating when someone was underneath it had been disabled because it was causing production slowdowns. Mr. L'Ecuyer had not been trained properly to recognize the dangers and members of management were aware of the dangerous situation but did nothing to correct it. Transpavé pled guilty on December 7, 2007, to the criminal negligence charge and was ordered to pay a fine of $110,000. In 2010, Pasquale Scrocca, a landscape contractor, was found guilty of criminal negligence causing the death of an employee. Aniello Boccanfuso was killed when a backhoe driven by Scrocca failed to brake and pinned him against a wall. The backhoe, purchased in 1976, had not been inspected by a certified mechanic in at least five years. Inspection after the incident found that the machine had a braking capacity of less than 30 per cent, and 14 additional major issues including nonfunctioning horn, brake lights, parking brake and brake pressure gauge. Found guilty of criminal negligence causing death, Scrocca was sentenced to two years less a day, to be served in the community with conditions.

The other area in which supervisors are seeing new responsibilities is to maintain a workplace free of workplace harassment or bullying. Legislation in Quebec, Ontario, Manitoba, Saskatchewan and BC now provides this protection to workers. Employers are required to ensure that workplaces are free of harassment (such as intimidation, bullying and humiliation) by developing and implementing policies and practices to prevent harassment and address it if it occurs. When Quebec was the first North American to introduce this legislation, there was concern that it would open the floodgates to complaints from employees about any workplace incident. That has not happened. Over 95% of workplace harassment complaints are settled either at the investigation stage or through early mediation, and few end up in a formal hearing[15]. However, some supervisors are apprehensive about engaging in performance management or discipline activities because of the potential for employees interpreting it as harassment.

Perhaps the biggest challenge for supervisors is handling change. The challenges noted above all combine together and do not have a distinct finish line. All supervisors must deal with never-ending change, both planned and unplanned. Trish Mah, who works at an intermediate care home in Vancouver, saw the home suddenly expand from 90 beds to over 150. "All the systems had to change. And change is hard for everyone." Daniel Quondam explains that there is such demand for his product, components for cellular phones, that customers keep changing their orders, yet still expect them to be ready as soon as possible. As a result, it is extremely difficult to forecast sales and plan production accurately. Daniel becomes mired in trying to meet planned production, plus squeezing in the extra demands.

In the midst of all this change, supervisors need to use those emotional intelligence skills to keep themselves calm and motivated, and work with others to accept the changes and then implement them. It's a challenge, but never boring, and supervisors will be kept alert and developing. More specifics on managing change will be discussed in Chapter 13.

SUMMARY

This summary is organized by the Learning Objectives.

1. A supervisor is a first-level manager who oversees the work of operative or nonmanagement employees.
2. While supervisors, middle managers, and senior management are all part of the managerial ranks, they differ by their level in the organization. Supervisors are first-level managers—they manage operative employees. Middle management includes managers who manage managers. Senior management is composed of the highest-level managers—responsible for establishing the organization's overall objectives and developing the policies to achieve those objectives.
3. Being a supervisor offers challenge, the development of new skills, stimulating and ever-changing demands, and, often, more money and recognition to match the increased responsibility. However, supervisory responsibilities may be accompanied by greater stress, longer hours (and no overtime pay), the loss of immediate and tangible results from one's work, and paperwork demands.
4. The four functions of planning, organizing, leading, and controlling comprise the management process.
5. The four essential management competencies are technical, interpersonal, conceptual, and political competencies.
6. The supervisor's job will be increasingly important and complex in the future because of programs that focus on the work activities of operating employees, middle-management cutbacks (which have increased supervisory responsibilities), and the increased focus on training employees, which will be substantially implemented at the supervisory level.
7. Supervisors are now expected to coach a team of employees, treating them with respect and motivating them to reach their potential. They are no longer expected to "tell" employees what to do, but rather to explain what is needed and facilitate their achievement.
8. A shrinking staff sees the supervisor dealing with surviving employees who are frightened of their own security and may be overwhelmed with work demands. A growing company forces the supervisor to deal with high production demands while hiring and training new workers. Restructuring the organization can change the number of subordinates, the type of subordinates, and the demands on a supervisor.

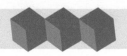

9. Workforce diversity seeks to increase the heterogeneity of organizations with the inclusion of different groups. This includes, but is not limited to, women, members of racial minority groups, immigrants, and people with disabilities.

10. Technology has changed the equipment with which workers produce the company's product and service and introduced computers to many aspects of work. Supervisors use computers in their daily work (for example, creating reports or communicating via e-mail) and need to work with increased skill demands placed on workers by the newer technologies. Communication technologies have increased access and demands.

11. Supervisors have increasing obligations for ensuring safety in the workplace due to the Bill C-45 amendment to the Criminal Code. In several provinces they now have obligations to maintain a workplace that is free of harassment (or bullying) due to new legislation.

KEY TERMS AND CONCEPTS

Baby boomers	Management functions
Bill C-45	Management process
Collectivism	Middle managers
Conceptual competence	Operative employees
Controlling	Organizing
Downsizing	Planning
Effectiveness	Political competence
Efficiency	Power distance
Emotional intelligence	Process
First-level managers	Senior management
Gen X	Skill
Gen Y	Supervisors
Individualism	Traditionalists
Interpersonal competence	Technical competence
Leading	Uncertainty avoidance
Management	Workforce diversity
Management competencies	

REVIEWING YOUR KNOWLEDGE

1. What differentiates supervisory positions from all other levels of management?
2. Is the owner-manager of a small store, with three employees, an operative, supervisor, or senior manager? Explain.
3. What specific tasks are common to all managers?
4. Contrast time spent on management functions by supervisors versus time spent by senior management.
5. "The best rank-and-file employees should be promoted to supervisors." Do you agree or disagree with this statement? Explain.
6. Why is conceptual competence more important for senior managers than for first-level supervisors?
7. How can a supervisor be both a "key person" and "just another worker"?
8. What challenges does workforce diversity create for first-level managers?
9. Do you believe that changes in technology will be perceived as a stressful demand by the younger generation of supervisors?
10. What, if anything, can organizations do to help managers and employees alike learn to thrive on constant change?

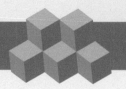

CASE 1.A

Technology— Boon or Nightmare?

Diane Hebert, with experience as a human resources manager in government, mining and lumber industries, has strong feelings on the impact of technology.

"I am burned out because of technology. I'm 57, I've always worked hard, I can pack a lot in and be effective. I remember when I would get a phone call and needed to wait for something by fax or mail and I would have time to consider how to deal with it. I always had time to plan and organize. Now there are constant demands with expectations of instant answers or information. They have 24/7 access to me. I have learned, rather than giving answers, to say "What do you think?" so they know I expect them to have done some work on their own. But many managers get caught up in feeling the need to provide an immediate answer and there is an expectation that they have to respond to an email immediately with the sender not knowing that you may have received 150 emails that day.

Just last week I had a demand for a budget report in three days. It is complex information that cannot be assembled with the snap of a finger and I still had a full workload to deal with. Technology makes it too easy to demand from others.

Technology has not done me any favours. A lot of managers have little time to plan strategically and be creative because of these demands.

I also find that a lot of contact that used to be done in person is now being done by text or email so there is less human contact. Now emails are more common than meeting in person and everyone is overworked. Technology allows more work from everyone. I'm very cognizant of it in my staff. I watch their workloads. One has a tendency to do a lot at home. I do not allow her to bring work home, saying she needs more work/life balance. She still does it occasionally but not as often as before. I don't want her to burn out at 35." Just because everyone has access to me 24/7 does not mean that I will allow them to have access to my staff 24/7.

It sounds like I hate technology and the opposite is the case. My biggest issue is the access to me that it has given people. If two or three people above me do not have work/life balance and work 18 hours a day, they are generating work for those below and believe me, when they want something, they don't want to hear any excuse as to why you can't provide it. I'm one of those managers that absolutely refuse to allow that kind of stress to flow down which puts me in a very small minority. Unfortunately, it adds to my workload."

RESPONDING TO THIS CASE

1. Describe the competencies Diane is exhibiting in this case.
2. Discuss the apparent conflict between effectiveness and efficiency in this case.
3. Describe what Diane is dealing with in terms of the various perspectives on the supervisor's role in the "Role Ambiguity" section.
4. How does this case illustrate the "cons" of being a supervisor?

FIGURE 1-18

Diane Hebert finds increasing and unreasonable demands made on her and her staff due to communication technology.

CASE 1.B

A Short-lived Career as a Dairy Manager[1]

Justin was dairy manager at a grocery store for one year. Quitting the position to return to school, he was glad to be rid of it. It was a lot of responsibility and very stressful.

Justin had not expected it to be so challenging. Before he was promoted at 19, he had worked in the industry for five years, with experience in most grocery departments. Now he was responsible for a 30-foot dairy department, in charge of all the orders, dealing with sales reps, cleaning, organizing, and allocating duties to the part-time employee whose work hours rarely overlapped with Justin's.

When he applied for the position, there were five duties listed on the posting. When he started the job, he soon realized there were about 50 duties. The job as presented to him was very general; for example, complete dairy orders. But there were actually three different types of orders to be done on different days at different times requiring different things. It was much more complex than he expected. He was trained for one week by the store owner, who was very busy and couldn't devote the time needed. Justin was only given the order book for milk as a tool, just a simple chart of what was ordered previously. There were no planning tools. There were no goals set. Justin had no idea if he was doing a great job or a poor job because there was no feedback. He did not know whether to focus on sales or shrinkage (damaged or expired products). There were no explanations from the store manager, no praise and no thanks. But, as he was never disciplined and there were no complaints, he figured he was doing okay.

The manager said Justin would get a bonus at the end of the year "if things looked good". What success would look like was never defined. In the end Justin was told he would not get the bonus because of a health and safety audit. The auditor failed the temperature log (taking the temperature around the store twice a day) because some times were missed. Justin had been tasked with that job and admitted he had missed an occasional measure. But he had been allocated the task without being told what the ramifications were or without clarity on who would record the measures when he was absent.

Glad in the end to walk away from the job, Justin still recognizes that he learned a lot: a lot about running the various aspects of the grocery business; and a lot about what can go wrong when someone is put into a position without preparation or support.

RESPONDING TO THIS CASE

1. Using concepts from the chapter, outline why you believe Justin's transition from employee to supervisor was not successful and what could have been done both by Justin and by his employer to avoid these issues.
2. Describe the apparent competencies of Justin's manager given what you observe in this case.
3. There is no discussion of awareness or application of legislation in this case. However, given what you have read, what would you expect in terms of the employer's compliance with legislation and why? What are the implications for the organization?

---

[1] Based on a true story, with name changed.

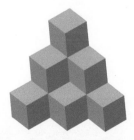

2 SUPERVISORY PLANNING AND TIME MANAGEMENT

Courtesy of Dmitriy Shironosov/Shutterstock

LEARNING OBJECTIVES

After reading this chapter, you should be able to:

1. Explain what planning is and what gets planned.
2. Describe how planning differs with management level yet also links those levels.
3. Contrast policies and rules.
4. Explain why managers create single-use plans.
5. Describe the Gantt chart.
6. Describe the characteristics of effective goals.
7. Contrast response time and discretionary time.
8. List the five steps to better time management.

CHAPTER OUTLINE

PERFORMING EFFECTIVELY

WHAT IS PLANNING?

WHAT GETS PLANNED?

PLANNING AND MANAGERIAL LEVEL
  Planning Breadth
  Planning Time Frame
  Linking Managerial Levels
  Something to Think About

KEY PLANNING GUIDES
  Standing Plans
  Single-Use Plans

SETTING GOALS
  Characteristics of Effective Goals
  Management by Objectives

TIME MANAGEMENT
  Time as a Scarce Resource
  Focusing on Discretionary Time
  Five Steps to Better Time Management
  Something to Think About
  Some Additional Points to Ponder

FROM CONCEPTS TO SKILLS: GOAL SETTING
  Assessing Yourself: Are You a Good Goal Setter?
  Skill Basics
  Applying Your Skills

UNDERSTANDING THE BASICS
  Summary
  Key Terms and Concepts
  Reviewing Your Knowledge

PERFORMING YOUR JOB
  Case 2.A: Is This the Beginning of the End?
  Case 2.B: No Time and Getting Blamed!

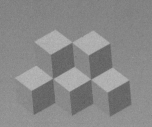

Garth Dallman is project manager and assistant production manager at Research Casting International (RCI), one of the world's largest providers of museum technical services. This includes specimen preparation, restoration, casting, molding, and mounting, exhibit fabrication and exhibit moving. RCI has been commissioned to provide hundreds of cast dinosaur, mammal and reptile skeletons to museums around the world.

Located in Trenton, Ontario, RCI operates out of a large state of the art facility that can accommodate dinosaur, mammal and reptile fossil restoration, casting and mounting commissions and other museum exhibit projects of any size and complexity. The company maintains a staff of experienced craftsmen and artists who are dedicated to the restoration and preservation of the world's rarest paleontological specimens and artifacts. Sample projects include restoring and remounting the famous Brachiosaurus exhibit on display in the grand atrium of Berlin's Museum für Naturkunde; molding, casting and mounting a bronze Tyrannosaurus Rex (6500 pound skeleton) for the Museum of the Rockies in Montana; and collecting and mounting a variety of Canadian whale skeletons for the Royal Ontario Museum.

Many specimens the RCI team works with are rare and very special. "Palaeontologists and curators are often nervous about moving specimens. Because of our experience, our job is to put their minds at ease. We plan as well as we can, knowing we might not have all the answers at the start, because every project is different."

Software programs help with both planning and controlling RCI projects, with the two processes closely tied. "We have a web-based program that helps us take a project from quote through completion. In many administrative environments there are often spreadsheets and database bits or data islands that have important information but are not integrated with one another. With this program the databases and spreadsheets are all integrated. A quote to a client is essentially the end product of an important planning process for what has to be done and what resources will be needed. When we

FIGURE 2-1

Garth Dallman of Research Casting International works with his team to plan dinosaur exhibits

provide a quote to a client, the price and estimates are based on tracking of past similar projects. To initially gather this information to more accurately quote projects, we had all staff fill out timesheets that indicate the time it takes to perform a particular task within a project. The allocation of effort to particular projects is then clear. This time and material allotment allows us to more accurately price similar projects in the future. In the case of skeleton mounting it is extremely valuable because a mounted skeleton is a known quantity compared to some of the other unique exhibit projects that come our way where we have no frame of reference for how long it might take. At the outset of a mount or project we gather and document details from the client. We send a client information form asking about the size of door openings, height restrictions et cetera. This will allow us to determine if there are any potential problems that will increase time or complicate the project. The web based program allows us to enter potential material costs and other unique details of the project to determine an accurate quote.

One of the most valuable resources the web based program creates is a pipeline of potential projects that assist in future planning of the company. Some of the quotes will become projects and others will never go ahead but at any time we can call up the pipeline to determine potential revenue, material usage and staff that may be needed. Quotes that are rolled to project are tracked for work being done and also integrated with our invoicing so that we know when to invoice, how much and when payment has been made.

The project is broken down into tasks and rough time estimates. Staff know how much time has been assigned to a project and when it is due. Staff track their hours daily on a work sheet and then enter them into the computer weekly because they work on several projects simultaneously. With staff entering their hours regularly it is possible to track a project week to week to ensure a project is on schedule and budget."

WHAT IS PLANNING?

Garth Dallman's description of planning at RCI illustrates Chapter 1's definition of planning. **Planning** refers to the process of defining objectives and the means of attaining them. A plan sets out a common direction for all involved and integrates and coordinates the activities necessary for successful achievement of the desired outcome. The RCI example demonstrates the importance of planning to the company's business and its integration with controlling and leading. It shows the use of both recurring plans for standard projects and single use plans for unique projects. Many managers engage in informal planning that is spontaneous and undocumented. In this chapter, when we use the term 'planning', we'll be implying the formal variety (see Something to Think About).

Planning
Defining objectives and the means of attaining them.

WHAT GETS PLANNED?

The complex planning involved in creating RCI's dinosaur exhibits also demonstrates the various aspects of planning:

Activities:	What specifically needs to be done?
Time and Timing:	What is the deadline?
	What are the milestones or checkpoints?
	What is the sequencing of the various steps in the process and how do we integrate them effectively?
Resources:	What skills are needed?
	Who has these skills?
	Are these people available given other work commitments?
	Is any training needed?
	What budget is required to support the work?
Information:	Do we have the technology and systems to handle the information flow and track the work effectively?
	Do we need to set up any new approaches to work with this particular project?
	Do we need information from external people (like the paleontologists)? How will we ensure we get it and do so in a timely way?
Assets:	What machinery, equipment, space and materials will be required?
	Are they available or can they be made available when needed?
	Does the space or equipment need to be shared with other projects and how might we accomplish this effectively?

PLANNING AND MANAGERIAL LEVEL

All managers plan but the type of planning they do tends to vary with their level in the organization.

PLANNING BREADTH

Strategic planning
Plans focus on the entire organization, establishing goals and positioning the organization's products or services.

A common way to distinguish types of planning is to separate strategic planning from tactical or operational planning. **Strategic planning** focuses on the entire organization, establishing goals and positioning the organization's products or services. In a for-profit organization, this would mean positioning against the competition, determining what would distinguish this organization from the others. In a not-for-profit organization, this would mean determining a focus—the organization cannot be all things to all people and must target its efforts. Strategic planning's big picture focus is done at the senior level of the company. At RCI, for instance, it would be part of senior management's strategic plan for the company to go beyond Canadian or North American projects and seek international projects. Once a strategic plan is in place, an organization needs tactical planning to convert the strategy into action. A person or department needs to plan just how those international projects will be won. **Tactical planning** refers to specific plans on how to achieve the overall goals. In Garth's case, a higher level in the company strategically plans which projects to bid on and it is up to Garth, once a project is won, to determine how to manage that project, creating a museum exhibit that will meet the client's needs. He puts the strategic plans into operation, which is why tactical plans are often called operational plans.

Tactical planning
Specific plans on how to achieve the overall goals.

PLANNING TIME FRAME

Planning often occurs in three time frames—short term, intermediate term, and long term.

Short-term plans are less than one year in length. **Long-term plans** cover a period of five years or more. Plans of one to five years are **intermediate-term plans**. A supervisor's planning horizon tends to emphasize the short term: preparing plans for the next month, week or day. Garth Dallman's project plans fall under short term planning with their emphasis on months and weeks.

Short-term plans
Plans that are less than one year in length.

Long-term plans
Plans covering more than five years.

Intermediate-term plans
Plans that cover from one to five years.

LINKING MANAGERIAL LEVELS

It's important to keep in mind that effective planning is integrated and coordinated throughout the organization. Long-term strategic planning sets the direction for all other planning. That is, once senior management has defined the organization's overall strategy and goals and the general plan for getting there, then, in descending order, the other levels of the organization develop plans.

Figure 2-2 illustrates this linking of plans from the top to the bottom of an organization. The president, vice president, and other senior executives define the organization's overall strategy. Then upper-middle managers, such as regional sales directors, formulate their plans. And so on down to first-level managers. Ideally, these plans will be coordinated through joint participation. In the case of Figure 2-2, for instance, the Vancouver territory manager would participate with other territory managers by providing information and ideas to the B.C. district manager as she formulates plans for her entire district. If planning is properly linked, then the successful achievement of all the territory managers' goals

Formalized planning became very popular in the 1960s, and, for the most part, it's still popular today. It makes sense to establish some direction. But recently, critics have begun to challenge some of the basic assumptions underlying planning.

Canadian management expert Henry Mintzberg believes that plans may create rigidity.[1] Formal planning efforts can lock organizational members into specific goals to be achieved within specific timetables. When these objectives are set, assumptions may be made that the "outside world" won't change during the period that the objectives cover. This may be a faulty assumption. Nevertheless, rather than remaining flexible—and possibly scrapping the plan—some supervisors may continue to fulfill the actions required to achieve the originally set objectives.

Other experts believe that formal plans can't replace intuition and creativity.[2] Formal planning efforts typically follow a specific methodology—making it a routine event. That can spell disaster for an organization. For instance the rapid rise of Apple Computer Inc between the late 1970s and the late 1980s was attributed, in part, to the creativity and anti-corporate attitudes of its cofounder, Steve Jobs. However, as the company grew, Jobs felt a need for more formalized management—a style he was personally uncomfortable with. He hired a CEO who ultimately ousted Jobs from his own company. With Jobs' departure came increased organizational formality—the very thing Jobs despised so much because it hampered creativity. Soon the company had lost much of its creativity and was struggling to survive. When Jobs was brought back on board, he successfully revived Apple's fortunes with his informal and more intuitive approach.[3]

Finally, there's a perception that while formal planning may reinforce success, it may also lead to failure.[4] We have been taught that success breeds success. That's been a North American "tradition." After all, if it's not broken, don't fix it—right? Well, maybe not! Success may, in fact, breed failure in the changing world of work. It's tough to change or discard successful plans—leaving the comfort of what works for the anxiety of the unknown. Formal plans may provide a false sense of security, generating more confidence than is warranted. Consequently, supervisors often won't deliberately face that unknown until forced to do so by changes in the environment. Unfortunately, by then it may be too late!

So, given these facts, should we still plan formally? Is it worth it? What do you think?

Why is it that, as a company grows in size, it is much more likely to engage in formal planning?

should result in the B.C. district manager achieving her goals. If all the district managers meet their goals, this should lead to the successful attainment of the regional sales manager's goals, and so on up each level in the organization.

In Garth's case, because RCI is a small company, there are no middle managers to bridge the long-term strategic to the short-term operational side. Garth often works directly with the company president to ensure integration of plans.

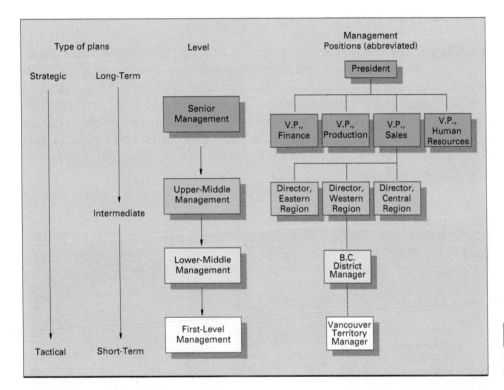

FIGURE 2-2

Planning and managerial levels

KEY PLANNING GUIDES

Once an organization's strategy and overall goals are in place, management will design additional plans to help guide decision makers. Some of these plans will be **standing plans**. Once designed, they can be used repeatedly by managers faced with recurring activities. Others will be **single-use plans**, which are detailed courses of action used once or only occasionally to deal with situations that don't occur repeatedly.

In this section we'll review the popular types of each plan.

Standing plans
Plans used over and over again for recurring activities.

Single-use plans
Detailed courses of action used once or only occasionally.

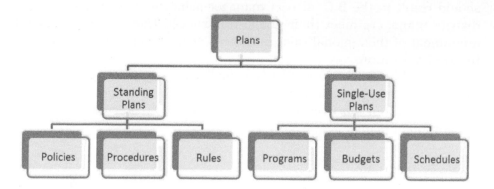

FIGURE 2-3

Types of Plans

STANDING PLANS

Standing plans allow managers to save time by handling similar situations in a predetermined and consistent manner. For example, mounting the skeleton of a standard dinosaur type is a common project for Garth's team at RCI. Because they have done it so many times, they have developed an efficient and effective plan for accomplishing future mountings with careful attention to time, resources and costs. In this section, we'll review the three major types of standing plans: policies, procedures, and rules.

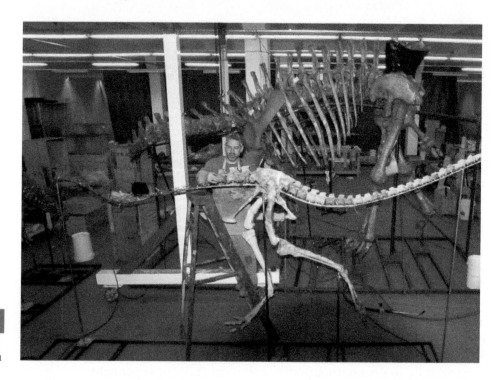

FIGURE 2-4

Garth Dallman works on a dinosaur skeleton

POLICIES

"We promote from within wherever possible." "Do whatever it takes to satisfy the customer." "Our employees should be paid competitive wages." These three statements are examples of **policies**. That is, they're broad guidelines for managerial action. Typically established by senior management, they define the limits within which managers must stay as they make decisions.

Policies
Broad guidelines for managerial action.

Supervisors rarely make policies. Rather, they interpret and apply them. Within the parameters that policies set, supervisors must use their judgment. For instance, the organization's policy specifying "sustainability is a foundation for all organizational activities" does not tell a supervisor exactly how sustainability concerns are to affect his planning on equipment or materials use. Does this mean only recycled material should be used? How can energy requirements for a project be reduced while still accomplishing the tasks in a timely way? The supervisor has to make judgments in converting the policy into action. The tricky part is that, while aware that sustainability must be included as a decision parameter, the supervisor will also have to consider all the other parameters of importance to senior management (like profitability).

PROCEDURES

A **procedure** is a series of steps for responding to a recurring problem or situation. And a procedure can be a good friend to a supervisor who must deal with a problem employee. For example, Paula Aylward, a shift manager at Cavendish Farms' New Annan French-fries plant, explains, "You never fire anyone; they do it themselves. If I follow the steps in a disciplinary procedure for someone who, for example, is late consistently, I give them the appropriate verbal and written warnings. They know the consequences if they repeat the offence. They can't argue when they are fired. The union has never contested a firing I've been involved in."

Procedure
A series of steps for responding to a recurring problem or situation.

Where procedures exist, managers only have to identify the specific situation or problem. Once the problem is clear, so is the procedure to handle it. Other examples of procedures include hiring, completing purchasing requisitions with the right information and signatures, and handling overtime payment.

Procedures are more specific than policies. But, as with policies, procedures provide consistency. By defining the steps to be taken and the order in which they should be carried out, procedures provide a standardized way of responding to situations. As a result, the supervisor using these procedures appears fair and actions are carried out in a timely, cost-effective way.

Supervisors follow procedures set by higher levels of management and also create their own procedures for staff to follow. As conditions change and new situations surface that tend to be recurring, supervisors develop standardized procedures for handling them. For example, Rita

Cupitt, the Manager of Human Resources at Eagle's Flight in Guelph, Ontario, developed a hiring manual for team leaders outlining their "preflight checklist" of all the steps to follow. This was done because, without a clear and consistent hiring process and the requirement to get specific approvals from Finance and the CEO, crucial steps were being overlooked and the organization's recruiting goals were not being met. At RCI, Garth Dallman describes a standard procedure for planning a project and creating a quote, starting with gathering specific information from the client and using past experience on similar projects to estimate material costs and usage, labour required, and time.

RULES

A **rule** is an explicit statement that tells an employee about specific behaviour that is either required (e.g., all staff must wear safety boots in this area) or prohibited (e.g., no smoking). Similar to policies and procedures, rules ensure consistency. For example, if the rule says that no jewellery may be worn in the machine shop, the supervisor should ensure that all employees are aware of this rule and comply with it.

The main issue that arises with respect to rules is inconsistent enforcement. Nothing makes it more difficult for a supervisor to enforce a rule (e.g., employees are only allowed 15-minute breaks) than his or her subordinates knowing that their colleagues in another area are allowed to break the rule without consequence. In recent years, one of the most common areas of inconsistency concerns "smoke breaks." If some supervisors allow smokers to take extra breaks (beyond the normal breaks allowed to everyone else), this leads to the nonsmokers feeling cheated and the other supervisors being challenged on their attempts to enforce the strict adherence to break times. What can a supervisor do? This is an issue that should be addressed at a supervisors' meeting or through their common manager. The only way a rule can be enforced is if it is enforced by a united front.

SINGLE-USE PLANS

In contrast to the previous discussions of standing plans, single-use plans are designed for a specific activity or time period. The most popular types of these plans are programs, budgets, and schedules.

PROGRAMS

When an organization must plan to deal with a new situation, a **program** is created. A program is a single-use set of plans for a specific major undertaking.

Garth Dallman gives an RCI example. "A major challenge we faced was molding a rock face of the earliest life forms known to have existed 550 million years ago at Mistaken Point in Newfoundland. It was a collaborative project with a variety of other institutions. This project posed logistical challenges due to its location in a protected environment prohibiting vehicles near the site. We had to helicopter in supplies, make the large scale mold of a rock face, and then remove everything and clean up. It went smoothly because of careful planning. We came in with good solutions to transport in large amounts of working materials, there was close collaboration with all parties involved, and the staff was dedicated to making it happen."

Sue (manager at a systems outsourcing and consulting firm) discusses the difference between a program (for a new project) and standing plans (for established projects): "For established activities like handling a current client with known system needs, it's a matter of ensuring the continuation of strong service. Little planning is needed; it's more a matter of checking to ensure all continues to run smoothly by allocating the right people, ensuring appropriate operational practices are in place and standards are clear. If I've set out standards and they're following them, I shouldn't have to be involved in the nitty-gritty. For new projects, planning is critical, starting with establishing the outcomes desired. I work with the client to analyze their business requirements. I then provide a draft solution to the client (so I don't move forward on the wrong path). Then I work backwards from the desired outcomes to assess what activities will lead to those outcomes, and how those activities can be broken down into a series of tasks with specific items, deadlines, and people assigned. Review points and approvals are also built into the project task list."

All managers develop **programs**. A major program—such as building a new manufacturing plant or merging two companies and consolidating their headquarters' staff—will tend to be designed and overseen by senior management, can extend over several years, and may even require its own set of policies and procedures. But supervisors frequently must create programs for their departments. Examples include the creation of a comprehensive ad campaign for a new client by an account manager of an advertising firm, and the development of a unique training program by the regional sales supervisor to help her people learn the intricacies of the company's new computerized inventory system. Note the common thread through all these examples: These are nonrecurring undertakings that require a set of integrated plans to accomplish their objectives.

Program
A single-use set of plans for a specific major undertaking.

BUDGETS

Budgets are numerical plans. They typically express anticipated results in dollar terms for a specific time period. For example, a department may budget $8000 this year for travel. But budgets can also be calculated in nondollar terms, such as employee hours, capacity utilization, or units of production. And budgets can cover daily, weekly, monthly, quarterly, semi-annual, or annual periods.

Budgets are certainly important planning guides as they give direction. However, they also serve other functions. One such function is

Budgets
Numerical plans.

coordination, forcing the person creating the budget to seek pertinent information from the other parts of the business that influence it, and to focus on the goals of the unit and the organization.

Budgets also enforce communication. Through the allocation of funds, budgets clearly identify the important activities to others. They also place the creator in the position of justifying the specific details of the budget, thereby communicating the underlying plans and priorities to others.

Third, budgets act as a control device. They typically set out standards for comparison with actual performance (e.g., Were expenses beyond what was set out? Were hours within reason of the budgeted number? Are we on target for material costs?). Budgeting is discussed in more detail in the From Concepts to Skills section at the end of the next chapter on Designing and Implementing Controls.

A fourth function of budgets is performance evaluation. Whether a unit performed within budget is often an important aspect of a supervisor or manager's performance evaluation, addressing both their ability as planners and as doers.

Ainslie White's experience in budgeting (as the manager of information systems at Precision Biologic in Nova Scotia) demonstrates budgeting's value as a planning guide, as a tool to promote coordination and communication and as a control device. "I start with a wish list. I talk to

Department Expense Budget
Calendar Year 2013

ITEM	QUARTER			
	1ST	2ND	3RD	4TH
Salaries/Fixed	$70 800	$70 800	$70 800	$70 800
Salaries/Variable	9 000	15 000	9 000	30 000
Overtime/Bonuses				36 000
Office Supplies	2 400	2 400	2 400	2 400
Photocopying	3 000	3 000	3 000	3 000
Telephone	7 500	7 500	7 500	7 500
Mail	2 400	2 400	2 400	2 400
Travel	7 500	3 000	3 000	3 000
Employee Development	1 800	1 800	1 800	1 800
Total Quarterly Expenses	$104 400	$105 900	$99 900	$156 900

FIGURE 2-6

An example of a budget that could be used as a planning guide

the team leads in the company about what they would like for the next year. I get them to prioritize their list, telling me the top five, and keep paring it down. Once we have collected this information the IT team meets to consider costs and implementation, what can be accomplished. We get very detailed. The controller loves our budget because we give a detailed layout of what will be spent each month, some listed as goals, others as routine maintenance. We always put aside backup money for the unexpected, like a printer dying. We meet with the accounting team to review the IT decisions. We have to have an overall picture, what's the biggest payoff for the business. We get as much information from people as we can, decide what we can and cannot do, and people understand our decisions when we show them the priorities. The budgeting is closely aligned with workload planning activities. For example, if we are replacing 10 desktop computers over the next 5 months, we know that each team member will be involved with 2 or 3 installs per month."

Many supervisors become involved in budgets. For instance, supervisors typically prepare their department's expense budget and submit it to the manager at the next higher level for review and approval (see Figure 2-6). Once approved by higher management, these budgets set specific standards for supervisors and their unit staff to achieve. Budgeting is discussed further in the From Concepts to Skills section in Chapter 3.

SCHEDULES

If you were to observe a group of supervisors or department managers for a few days, you'd see them regularly detailing what activities have to be done, the order they are to be done in, who is to do each, and when they are to be completed. These managers are **scheduling**.

Scheduling
Determining what activities have to be done, the order they are to be done in, who is to do each, and when they are to be completed.

Scheduling can involve daily, weekly or monthly activities, regular activities and unexpected ones, all the while attempting to balance organizational needs with employee preferences. Jamie Dumas, fitness centre supervisor fitness centre with the City of Mississauga, describes her challenge: "For me, scheduling is based on demographics, understanding what the clientele needs; then looking at space availability and instructor availability."

Scheduling would be easier if the supervisor had control of all the factors influencing departmental work. Given this is not the case, the supervisor is in a delicate position of planning what needs to be done, knowing there will be disruptions that could throw the schedule off. As IT manager at Precision Biologic, Ainslie White has to schedule the installation and replacement of equipment and maintenance of the system, all the while keeping in mind the need to be available for the unexpected. Just-in-time delivery is common in many organizations and can be a major pain for scheduling, as explained by David Goncalves, production supervisor a Mother Parkers Tea and Coffee: "Just-in-time delivery means that they can be ready to pack, but then if some material is late, it has a domino effect. Coffee only has so many hours before it becomes stale, so we have to start shuffling schedules and may even lose a block. I could be stressed but it's counterproductive. Accept it, this is what has happened, what are we going to do about it?"

Two popular scheduling techniques that can help you prioritize activities and complete work on time are the Gantt chart and the PERT chart. In the rest of this section, we'll describe each.

Gantt chart
A bar graph, with time on the horizontal axis and activities to be scheduled on the vertical axis, that shows planned and actual activities.

The **Gantt chart** was developed early in this century by an industrial engineer named Henry Gantt. The idea was inherently simple but has proved extremely helpful in scheduling work activities. The Gantt chart is essentially a bar graph with time on the horizontal axis and activities to be scheduled on the vertical axis. The bars show output, both planned

Task	Week 1	Week 2	Week 3	Week 4	Week 5	Week 6	Week 7	Week 8
Review and edit job description	■							
Use to create job posting		■						
Determine where to advertise		■						
Select hiring committee		■						
Schedule committee and room			■					
Advertise			■					
Finalize interview questions				■				
Applicant screening					■			
Interviews						■		
Reference checks								
Job offer								
Closure with other candidates								

■ Task completed   ▧ Task remaining

FIGURE 2-7

Hiring process in a Gantt chart.

and actual, over a period of time. The Gantt chart visually shows when tasks are supposed to be done and compares that to the actual progress on each. As we stated, it is a simple but important device that allows managers to detail easily what has yet to be done to complete a job or project and to assess whether it is ahead, behind, or on schedule.

Figure 2-7 depicts a simplified Gantt chart that was developed for hiring. Time is expressed in weeks across the top of the chart. The major activities are listed down the left side. The planning comes in deciding what activities must be done to accomplish the hiring, the order in which they need to be done, and the time that should be allocated to each activity. Where a box sits within a time frame reflects its planned sequence. The shading represents actual progress. The chart becomes a control device when the manager looks for deviations from the plan.

Gantt charts are helpful as long as the activities being scheduled are few in number and independent of each other. But what if a supervisor has to plan a large project such as a departmental reorganization, the launching of a cost-reduction campaign, or the installation of a major piece of new equipment that requires the coordination of inputs from a number of different sources? Such projects often require the coordination of hundreds of activities, some of which must be done simultaneously and some of which cannot begin until earlier activities have been completed. If you're constructing a building, for example, you obviously can't start erecting walls until the foundation is laid. How, then, can you schedule such a complex project? You could use a Program Evaluation and Review Technique (PERT) chart.

The PERT chart was originally developed in the late 1950s for coordinating the more than 3000 contractors and agencies working on the Polaris submarine weapon system.[5] This project was incredibly complicated, with hundreds of thousands of activities that had to be coordinated. PERT is reported to have cut two years off the completion date for the Polaris project. A PERT chart can be a valuable tool in the hands of a supervisor.

A **PERT chart** is a diagram that depicts the sequence of activities needed to complete a project and the time or costs associated with each activity. With a PERT chart, a supervisor must think through what must be done, determine which events depend on one another, and identify potential trouble spots. A PERT chart makes it easy to compare what effect alternative actions will have on scheduling and costs. Thus PERT allows supervisors to monitor a project's progress, identify possible bottlenecks, and shift resources as necessary to keep the project on schedule.

To understand how to construct a PERT chart, you need to know three terms: *events*, *activities*, and *critical path*. Let's define these terms, outline the steps in the PERT process, and then work through an example.

Events are end points that represent the completion of major activities. **Activities** represent the time or resources required to progress from one event to another. The **critical path** is the longest or most time-consuming sequence of events and activities in a PERT chart.

PERT chart
A technique for scheduling complex projects.

Developing a **PERT** chart requires the supervisor to identify all key activities needed to complete a project, rank them in order of dependence, and estimate each activity's completion time. This can be translated into five specific steps:

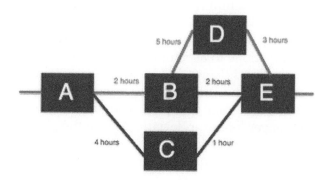

FIGURE 2-8

Simplified PERT chart

1. Identify every significant activity that must be achieved for a project to be completed. The accomplishment of each activity results in a set of events or outcomes.

2. Ascertain the order in which these events must be completed.

3. Diagram the flow of activities from start to finish, identifying each activity and its relationship to all other activities. Use circles to indicate events and arrows to represent activities. This results in the diagram that we call the **PERT** chart.

4. Compute a time estimate for completing each activity.

5. Finally, using a **PERT** chart that contains time estimates for each activity, the supervisor can determine a schedule for the start and finish dates of each activity and for the entire project. Any delays that occur along the critical path require the most attention because they delay the entire project. That is, the critical path has no slack in it; therefore any delay along that path immediately translates into a delay in the final deadline for the completed project.

SETTING GOALS

"If you don't give people targets, they don't know what to strive for. If you do, they will care more, they will flag problems, and the goal will become a personal goal, not a company goal," explains Daniel Quondam, highlighting the importance of giving employees specific targets to accomplish.

Daniel's description of the motivational importance of goals or objectives differs from the traditional use of goals for control purposes. Historically, goals were imposed by senior management who then told the next level of management what they had to accomplish, who then told the next layer, and so on, down to operative employees. This one-way process assumed that senior management knew best because only senior managers could accurately see the "big picture." The current use of goal setting is much more likely to be participative, allowing the employees who must achieve the goals to help determine the goals themselves. This makes it much more likely that the goals will be realistic and that the employees will "buy in" to the goals.

Colleen Murray, director of marketing and sales for Parks and Recreation at the City of Brampton, agrees with Daniel Quondam's emphasis on goals. Colleen supervises 17 marketing coordinators who provide marketing for the many recreational programs and facilities offered by the City. When she meets with them for their mid-year and end-of-year performance reviews, employees know they are expected to bring specific information on their goals for discussion at that meeting. What training will they be undertaking? What is their business plan? What is their marketing plan? Specifically, how do they plan to achieve their participation numbers? (The City's main objective is to achieve 50 percent participation in leisure activities through direct programming such as swim lessons at the aquatic centres and indirect programming such as minor sports leagues.) And, finally, what is their financial goal for their area? Colleen has had great feedback on her new approach. After the first mid-year review, every coordinator had achieved at least 50 percent of his or her year's objectives and they all said it was simple because, for the first time, expectations were clear. Interestingly, it was the coordinators who actually created the clear expectations, although Colleen had insisted that they do so.

Colleen uses this emphasis on goals not just for long-term planning but also for short-term planning. For example, at the start of each departmental meeting, she will identify the focus of the meeting. "What are we trying to achieve? What specific objectives do we have for this meeting?" In fact, an agenda forms the objectives for many meetings. And, for those who have attended a meeting without an agenda, you'll appreciate the direction and focus provided by an agenda.

CHARACTERISTICS OF EFFECTIVE GOALS

The characteristics of effective goals are often summarized under the acronym **SMART**. Good goals are:

Specific—they can be described in terms of exact behaviours or outcomes

Measurable—because they are specific, they can be quantified; this way there will be much less dispute than if the results are subjectively evaluated

Accepted—participation in setting the goals will greatly increase their acceptability to subordinates but, as long as they are viewed as reasonable and the logic supporting them is valid, employees may be willing to go along with goals set for them by others

Reasonable—part of this is that the circumstances surrounding the achievement of the goal are under the control of the employee; if reaching the goal depends partly on coworkers and their cooperation, it is not fair to make one person responsible for its success

Time-bound—there should be a deadline; as you probably know from personal experience, if there is no deadline, there is not much motivation to complete a goal

Being **SMART** is what makes goals effective. But what are they then effective at doing? Goals certainly offer clarity and direction, thereby fulfilling a planning role. The request to set specific goals forces someone to think carefully through what they want to happen and how they can achieve it. Goals can also increase motivation, involvement, and commitment, which may result from participation in setting the goals. Such commitment can also result from the feedback that is naturally generated when specific measurable goals are set and a procedure is set up to monitor progress. Another benefit from goals is their occasional use to create fair, objective criteria for performance appraisal and for allocating rewards. Finally, the use of goal setting as a process involving both supervisor and subordinate can improve the relationship between the two levels of employees. Unlike the many circumstances where a supervisor seems to have little real understanding of a subordinate's position and little concern for the frustrations in it, when a supervisor must work with a subordinate on jointly setting goals, the supervisor must understand the employee's position. The supervisor must also commit him- or herself to supporting the employee in those goals because the supervisor agrees that they are reasonable. The resulting communication and sharing of information likely brings the two parties to a closer and common understanding of each other's expectations.

Figure 2-9 illustrates the issues with non-**SMART** goals and how specific examples can be converted into more effective **SMART** goals.

Management by objectives (MBO)
A system in which subordinates jointly determine specific performance objectives with their superiors, progress toward objectives is periodically reviewed, and rewards are allocated on the basis of this progress.

MANAGEMENT BY OBJECTIVES

Some organizations formalize the goal-setting process into a regular activity undertaken by all in the organization, and integrated so that all goals work together. This is referred to as **management by objectives** (MBO). In MBO, objectives cascade down through the organization, set at first at the top. But this does not mean the objectives are imposed. Rather, each supervisor or manager works with each employee to create a set of objectives for that particular employee. While doing this, the man-

Non-SMART Goal	Issue	Making it into a SMART Goal
1. Improve your customer service.	What is to be changed and how will it be measured? No deadline. How can an employee accept it and see it as reasonable if it is vague?	Return all customer contacts within 24 hours.
2. Lower costs.	How? By when?	By next Friday, come up with a specific plan to reduce 10% from the budget for the next quarter.
3. Organize the department.	How? By when? How will it be measured?	By the end of the year, all staff will have created a manual of activities, FAQs and contacts for their specific function for use by others who are new or filling in.

FIGURE 2-9

Converting Goals to SMART Goals

ager will, of course, be keeping in mind the objectives he or she has committed to in his or her own position. So the employees' objectives must ultimately help the manager achieve his or her objectives. This is exactly the point of MBO—coordinating everyone's activities to work towards the corporate good.

A form of MBO is used at Fusion Homes in Guelph, Ontario. Rob Watson, Vice President of Construction explains: "Annually, all managers at Fusion choose objectives for their team members in terms of business and personal development, prepared in the SMART format. The number of objectives varies based on what is needed to move the company forward from either a business or personal development perspective, and these are split into smaller attainable stages. They fit into the company's larger vision and the president's own goals."

MBO has seen substantial success but not all attempts to use it have been successful. Some employees find the paperwork too overwhelming. Others find that upper managers exempt themselves from the process, which destroys the mandate of the program and allows others to take it less seriously. Also, goals cannot be applied to certain jobs. Applying goals to a repetitive job where the work is controlled by the machine or the customer rather than the employee means that goal setting doesn't work. Furthermore, not all work has easily measured outcomes or behaviours. For example, how do you measure how effective someone is as a teacher in inspiring a love for the material or an interest in the area? How do you measure the quality of a consultant's handling of a project if it has never been done before, there are no comparisons, and it was difficult to forecast what a "good" outcome would look like as compared to a "bad" one?

TIME MANAGEMENT

"I'm always on the go, dealing with machines, people, quality, safety. I rarely have a moment to myself. I'm usually juggling 10 balls at a time." (Paula Aylward, shift manager, Cavendish Farms, P.E.I.).

"I work from 8:30 to 5:30 but I'm on call 24 hours a day. When I come in in the morning, I do a walkabout to take care of concerns, and gravitate to areas where I'm needed. I just have to go with the flow." (Trish Mah, director of support services, Royal Arch Home, Vancouver)

"I work from 7 a.m. to about 6:30 p.m. and I occasionally come in on weekends. It's definitely not a 9 to 5 job. I'm never out of something to do." (Catalino Misenas, sales manager, Russell Food Equipment, Vancouver)

"The biggest challenge for me is creating the time to lead people, to let people know I'm there for them. I can get very caught up in the administrative work. And it can be difficult to make the time to coach people, even though my typical work day starts at 7 and ends at 6." (Susan Pander, manager of human resources, SaskTel, Regina)

The most effective supervisors have learned to manage their time. Like Catalino and Susan, many put in long hours. Others put in a more normal workday but it is a day crammed with pressures to do an incredible amount. In this section, we'll discuss how **time management** is actually a personal form of scheduling. Supervisors who use their time effectively know what they want to accomplish and when.

Time management
A personal form of scheduling; maximizing the allocation of the use of time.

TIME AS A SCARCE RESOURCE

Time is a unique resource in that, if it's wasted, it can never be replaced. While people talk about saving time, the fact is that time can never actually be saved. It can't be stockpiled for use in some future period. If wasted, it can't be retrieved. When a minute is gone, it's gone forever.

The positive side of this resource is that all supervisors have it in equal abundance. While money, personnel, and other resources are distributed unequally in organizations, thus putting some supervisors at a disadvantage, every supervisor is allotted 24 hours every day and seven days every week. Some just use their allotments better than others.

Response time
Responding to requests, demands, and problems initiated by others.

Discretionary time
The portion of a supervisor's time that is under his or her control.

DISCRETIONARY TIME AND PRIORITIES

Supervisors can't control all their time. They are routinely interrupted and have to respond to unexpected crises. It's necessary, therefore, to differentiate between **response time** and **discretionary time**.

Most of a supervisor's time is spent responding to requests, demands, and problems initiated by others. We call this response time and treat it as uncontrollable. The portion that is under a supervisor's control is called discretionary time. Most of the suggestions offered to improve time management apply to its discretionary component. Why? Because only this part is manageable.

How well do you use your time? How much of it is typically response time and how much is discretionary? You can determine this by keeping a log of your activities for a period of time and then evaluating the data. It is advisable to break the log into 15-minute intervals and track your activities over at least one and preferably two weeks. Then take a look at how you spent your time, what you accomplished and whether you spent your time wisely.

The major issue with the use of discretionary time is not whether you get things done but whether you get the right things done. There are always more demands than time. The critical skill for a supervisor is recognizing priorities and organizing time spent on activities according to urgency and importance. What will the impact be if something is not done immediately? Will anyone else be affected? Is this activity strategically critical and therefore a high priority?

Ryan Anderson explains: "I use a digital calendar tool. I can separate items based on urgency, create reminders for myself, and create "to do" lists. I organize items in the daily calendar by colour because I'm a visual person so it's helpful—the colours capture my attention. The calendar is synched with my computer and my Smartphone so I can always get access no matter where I am. But, you know, all the digital time management tools won't work if you are not personally disciplined enough to use it. It's easy to get distracted. In most situations, time management is a matter of your own maturity, realizing priorities, and having the self-discipline to not let yourself get sidetracked."

FIGURE 2-10

Ryan Anderson relies on a digital calendar but recognizes he needs self-discipline to use it well

FIVE STEPS TO BETTER TIME MANAGEMENT

The essence of time management is to use your time effectively. This requires that you know the objectives you want to accomplish, the activities that will lead to their accomplishment, and the importance and urgency of each activity. We've translated this into a five-step process.

1. **Make a list of your objectives.** What do you want to accomplish? You're familiar with this from having created "to do" lists.
2. **Rank the objectives according to their importance.** You are setting priorities because time is limited and you should get the important things done first.
3. **List the activities necessary to achieve your objectives.** To really know where your time is going, you need to consider *all* the things you must do in order to accomplish an objective. Sometimes we overload ourselves because we commit to too much, having underestimated the time that activities will take. Remember how

Below are listed many of the typical factors that supervisors cite as time wasters. Check all those that apply to you in both Column A and Column B.

Column A

____ Interruptions

____ Attending meetings

____ Drop-in visitors

____ Telephone calls

____ Red tape

____ Unclear expectations

____ Lack of clear goals

____ Lack of help

____ Unrealistic time estimates

____ Too many bosses

____ Lack of motivation

Column B

____ Procrastinations

____ Too much work to do

____ Complete easy tasks first

____ Messy desk

____ Unnecessary email

____ Can't say no

____ Failure to listen

____ Waiting for others

____ Lack of self-discipline

____ Visual distractions

____ Misplaced items

After you've checked those that apply, study your time wasters. Do they have anything in common?

Irrespective of what you checked, did you see any relationship between the items in the two columns? If you observed closely, you probably found that Column A includes those things that waste your time but are not in your direct control. In Column B are time wasters we bring on ourselves. However, time management isn't that simple. Contrary to what most of us want to believe, every item in each column is within our control. Many of those things in Column A that we shrug off as impossible to deal with can in fact be addressed. That's the purpose of good time management.

How will you address your time wasters? How will you face these issues? What will you do to correct your time management "problems"?

meetings get postponed, information is not always available when it should be, and computers go down so that work is delayed.

4. **Assign priorities to the various activities required to reach each objective.** Assign priorities to the various activities required to reach each objective. This imposes a second set of priorities. Here, you need to emphasize both importance and urgency. Decide what you *must* do, what you *should* do, what you will do *when you can*, and what you can *delegate to others*.

5. **Schedule your activities according to the priorities you've set.** At the beginning of each day or last thing before you leave work for the day, list the five or so most important things you want to do for the day. Then set priorities on these.

SOME ADDITIONAL POINTS TO PONDER

FOLLOW THE 20-80 PRINCIPLE

The Pareto principle says that you achieve 80% of your results from just 20% of your efforts. The trick is to focus your efforts on the important 20% and not get caught up in an activity trap that confuses action with accomplishment. Some supervisors achieve this by blocking the first chunk of their day to work on high priority items.

PLAN TO PLAN

Whether you spend the last half hour of each day planning for the next day, or allocate time on Friday looking ahead to the next week, it's worth looking ahead to see what is coming up, anticipate potential disruptions or changes and prepare materials needed. It is also valuable to make time every few months to look at the bigger picture and whether you are on-track to accomplishing the major goals. If you do not book time to plan, it may never be available. The lack of planning time will later mean scrambling, stress and disappointment.

SCHEDULE REGULAR TIME WITH YOUR TEAM MEMBERS

Block regular time off as office hours when staff know they can reach you. Set up regular meetings with individuals and/or with the team. By connecting regularly with staff you will catch issues when they are small and avoid later, more disruptive, surprises.

ENSURE IT'S YOUR RESPONSIBILITY

Does the task belong to the supervisor or someone else on the team? Sometimes supervisors take on work that really belongs to their staff. It may be tempting to step in and do operational work—it gives immediate results. But it takes time that could be spent on other tasks and may offend the staff who feel that the supervisor does not trust them.

DELEGATE WHERE POSSIBLE

Which of your tasks could you give away? Treat it as a developmental opportunity for the staff member. Supervisors may hesitate to do this because of the time involved in explaining and monitoring, but it is building skills in the employee that will later save the supervisor time. Train your employee to think for themselves—don't answer every question that comes to you. Put it back on them, e.g. what would you do if I wasn't here? They often rise to the challenge.

ORGANIZE

Organize your desk, your office, your computer files and your email so that you have quick and easy access to information and don't waste time looking for things.

KNOW YOUR PRODUCTIVITY CYCLE

Each of us has a daily cycle. Some of us are morning people, while others are late-afternoon or evening people. Supervisors who know their cycle and schedule their work accordingly can significantly increase their effectiveness. They handle their most demanding problems during the high part of their cycle, when they are most alert and productive. They relegate their routine and undemanding tasks to their low periods.

REMEMBER PARKINSON'S LAW

Parkinson's Law says that work expands to fill the time available. The implication for time management is that you can schedule too much time for a task. If you give yourself an excess amount of time to perform an activity, you're likely to pace yourself so that you use up the entire time allotted. On the other hand, don't block your calendar with back-to-back activities. Buffer time is needed, to deal with the unexpected and to catch your breath.

GROUP LESS IMPORTANT ACTIVITIES TOGETHER

Set aside a regular time period each day to make phone calls, do follow-ups, and perform other kinds of busywork. Ideally, this should be during your low cycle. This avoids duplication, waste, and redundancy; it also prevents trivia from intruding on high-priority tasks.

MINIMIZE DISRUPTIONS

When possible, try to minimize disruptions by setting aside a part of the day when you are most productive as a block of discretionary time. Then, try to insulate yourself. During this time—which may only be 20 or 30 minutes—limit access to your work area and avoid interruptions. Refuse phone calls or visits during this period. You can set aside other blocks of time each day to be accessible, and to initiate or return all your calls.

KNOW YOUR POLYCHRONICITY

People differ in terms of their preference for doing one thing at a time rather than doing two or more things simultaneously. People range from being highly monochronic (focusing entirely on doing one thing at a time) to highly **polychronic** (having no difficulty writing a report, talking on the phone, eating a snack, and watching a television program simultaneously). In terms of time management, highly polychronic types are more flexible in their schedules. They're less likely to be precise in scheduling completion times for tasks; have little trouble in grouping certain tasks together to be performed during the same time period; and are more likely to add, delete, and alter their priorities as the day proceeds. Maybe most interestingly, the highly polychronic person is much better at responding to unscheduled events. An unplanned phone call, for instance, typically has little effect on the highly polychronic type's work schedule, while it is a distinct distraction and likely to interrupt the monochronic's scheduled activities.

Polychronicity
The degree to which a person prefers doing two or more things simultaneously.

LEARN TO SAY NO

Some supervisors become overloaded because they accept everything they are asked to do. Sometimes it's appropriate to say no. For example, if your manager asks you to undertake a big task that will make it difficult to complete what you're already committed to doing, don't just work a lot of unpaid overtime to complete both tasks. Instead, ask your manager which task has the higher priority because you can't accomplish both in the time allowed. Put the decision back on your manager. If subordinates ask you what to do in a particular situation, it may not be best to simply give the answer. If you ask them instead what they think they should do or could do, you are helping them problem-solve in a way that may get them solving the problem on their own next time instead of coming back to you.

GOAL SETTING

Now we turn to skill development and application. In this section, we introduce a skill in three parts.

1. You complete a self-assessment "Check Yourself" exercise relating to a specific supervisory skill.

2. We present some basic skill information.

3. We present a skill application on which you can practise.

For this chapter, the skill is goal setting. Each of the remaining chapters of this book will conclude with a section entitled From Concepts to Skills, which will introduce a supervisory skill using the same three-part approach.

ASSESSING YOURSELF: ARE YOU A GOOD GOAL SETTER?

For each of the following questions, check the answer that best describes your relationship with direct reports. Remember to respond as you have behaved or would behave, not as you think you should behave. If you have no supervisory experience, answer the questions assuming you are a supervisor.

THE PEOPLE WHO WORK FOR ME HAVE:

	Usually	Sometimes	Seldom
1. Specific and clear goals.	❑	❑	❑
2. Goals for all key areas relating to their job performance.	❑	❑	❑
3. Challenging but reasonable goals (neither too hard nor too easy).	❑	❑	❑
4. The opportunity to participate in setting their goals.	❑	❑	❑
5. A say in deciding how to implement their goals	❑	❑	❑
6. Deadlines for accomplishing their goals.	❑	❑	❑
7. Sufficient skills and training to achieve their goals.	❑	❑	❑
8. Sufficient resources (i.e., time, money, equipment) to achieve their goals.	❑	❑	❑

9. Feedback on how well they are progressing toward their goals. ❏ ❏ ❏

10. Rewards (e.g., pay, promotions) allocated to them according to how well they reach their goals. ❏ ❏ ❏

SCORING KEY AND INTERPRETATION

For all questions, give yourself 3 points for "Usually," 2 points for "Sometimes," and 1 point for "Seldom."

Total up your points. Scores of 26 or higher demonstrate a strong use or understanding of goal-setting techniques. A score of 21 to 25 indicates you can improve your goal-setting skills. Scores of 20 or less suggest that you have significant room for improvement.

SKILL BASICS

Let's begin by summarizing the five basic rules that should guide you in defining and setting goals.

1. **Make your goals specific.** Goals are only meaningful when they're specific enough to be verified and measured.

2. **Make your goals challenging.** Goals should be set so as to require employees to stretch in order to reach them. If they're too easy, they offer no challenge. If set unrealistically high, they create frustration and are likely to be abandoned.

3. **Impose specific time limits for accomplishment of the goals.** Open-ended goals are likely to be neglected because no sense of urgency is associated with them.

4. **Goals should be jointly determined by the supervisor and the employee.** Participation increases an employee's goal-aspiration level. Additionally, jointly set goals are often more readily accepted, and accepted goals are more likely to be achieved.

5. **Provide feedback on performance.** Feedback lets people know if their level of effort is sufficient or needs to be increased. It can also induce them to raise their goal level after attaining a previous goal and can inform them of ways in which they can improve their performance.

Effective goal-setting skills can be condensed to eight specific behaviours. When you follow all eight you will have mastered the skill of goal setting.

1. **Identify an employee's key job tasks.** Goal setting begins by defining what it is that you want your employees to accomplish. The best source for this information is each employee's job description, if one is available. It details what task an employee is expected to perform, how these tasks are to be done, what outcomes the employee is responsible for achieving, and the like.

2. **Establish specific and challenging goals for each task.** This is self-explanatory. Consider making the goals public. When a person's goals are made public—announced in a group or posted for others to see—the individual seems to be more highly committed to them.

3. **Specify deadlines for each goal.** Goals should include a specific time limit for accomplishment.

4. **Allow the subordinate to actively participate.** Employees are less likely to question or resist a process in which they actively participate than one that is imposed upon them from above.

5. **Prioritize goals.** When someone is given more than one goal, it is important to rank the goals in order of importance. The purpose of this step is to encourage the employee to take action and expend effort on each goal in proportion to its importance.

6. **Rate goals for difficulty and importance.** Goal setting should not encourage people to choose easy goals in order to ensure success. So goal setting should take into account the difficulty of the goals selected and whether individuals are emphasizing the right goals. When these ratings are combined with the actual level of goal achievement, you will have a more comprehensive assessment of overall goal performance. This procedure gives credit to individuals for attempting difficult goals even if they don't fully achieve them.

7. **Build in feedback mechanisms to assess goal progress.** Ideally, feedback on goal progress should be self-generated rather than provided externally. When an employee is able to monitor his or her own progress, the feedback is less threatening and less likely to be perceived as part of a management control system.

8. **Make rewards contingent on goal attainment.** Offering money, promotions, recognition, time off, or similar rewards to employees

contingent on goal achievement is a powerful means to increase goal commitment. When the going gets tough on the road toward meeting a goal, people are prone to ask themselves, "What's in it for me?" Linking rewards to the achievement of goals helps employees to answer this question.

APPLYING YOUR SKILLS

PART A

For each of the following goals, identify what is wrong with it and rewrite it to be more effective.

Increase your sales by 10 percent.

Improve your relationship with your coworkers.

Manage your time better.

Tidy up your work area.

Put together a comprehensive report on how to cut costs by 25 percent in this department.

Eliminate the stress in your life.

Improve production output by 50 percent without incurring greater costs or sacrificing quality.

Get a major newspaper to publish an article on the success of our change efforts.

Improve quality.

Get those two people who are thinking of quitting to stay.

PART B—SETTING GOALS TOGETHER

This is a role-play exercise. Break into groups of three or four students. One student in each group will assume the role of Kelly and one will assume the role of Brad. The other students will serve as observers and evaluators.

Kelly has finally hired someone to take on part of her workload. The 80-hour weeks she has been putting in running her new specialty store for runners were beginning to take the thrill out of entrepreneurship. She will continue to do all the buying but will spend less time on the shop floor. Brad, her new employee, will work full-time selling the shoes. Kelly wants to reduce her hours overall and to spend more time getting back into running herself, connecting with running clubs in the area, and writing a blog about running.

Kelly wants to start off well with Brad. She knows he is experienced in sales and has athletic interests since he was a hockey player who has just started running. But since so much of the business's future will depend on how well Brad handles himself, she has decided that they should work together to create a set of goals for him. Kelly has set up a meeting to begin this goal-setting process.

The object of the exercise is to end up with a set of goals for Brad. They might address issues such as training goals (e.g. customer service expectations, using the sales and inventory system, becoming familiar with major brands and their features), performance goals (e.g. sales, sales floor display) and development goals (e.g. becoming familiar with runners, running issues, running products). Both Brad and Kelly are expected to come to the meeting with some suggestions as to appropriate goals and reasonable timelines for achieving them.

This exercise should take no more than 20 minutes. When completed, the observers from each group should discuss with the role players how their goal-setting session went. Focus specifically on the skill behaviours presented in this section and any problems that surfaced.

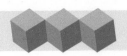

SUMMARY

This summary is organized by the Learning Objectives.

1. Planning is the process of defining objectives and the means of attaining them. This means planning typically focuses on activities, time, resources, information and assets.
2. Whereas senior management focuses on strategic long-term planning, supervisors focus on short-term operational plans. The intermediate-term planning of middle managers helps convert strategic plans to tactical ones. Plans at each level help to accoumplish those for the level above.
3. Policies and rules are both standing plans. Policies are broad and leave room for managerial discretion, while rules are explicit statements that allow no discretion.
4. Managers create single-use plans to cover specific activities or time periods. They provide detailed courses of action to handle new, unique or nonrecurring activities.
5. The Gantt chart is a simple scheduling device. It is a bar graph with time on the horizontal axis and activities on the vertical axis. It shows planned and actual activities, and allows managers to easily identify the status of a job or project.
6. Effective goals are SMART. That is, they are specific, measurable, accepted by the person who must implement them, reasonable, and time-bound with a specific deadline.
7. Response time is uncontrollable and encompasses the time one spends responding to actions initiated by others. Discretionary time is controllable and within the discretion of the individual.
8. A five-step process to better time management includes making a list of your objectives, ranking the objectives according to their importance, listing the activities necessary to achieve the objectives, assigning priorities to the various activities required to reach each objective, and scheduling your activities according to their importance and urgency.

KEY TERMS AND CONCEPTS

Activities
Budgets
Critical path
Discretionary time
Events
Gantt chart
Intermediate-term plans
Long-term plans
Management by objectives
Pareto principle
PERT chart
Planning
Policies

Polychronicity Procedures
Procedures
Programs
Response time
Rules
Scheduling
Short-term plans
Single-use
SMART goals
Standing plans
Strategic Planning
Tactical planning
Time Management

REVIEWING YOUR KNOWLEDGE

1. Contrast the planning senior managers do with that done by first-level managers.
2. Explain how budgets are both a planning and a control device.
3. How might you use a Gantt chart to schedule a group term paper for a college class?
4. What are the implications of the critical path for PERT analysis?
5. Contrast MBO with traditional objective setting.
6. Why is goal setting effective in some jobs and ineffective in others?
7. What specific things can you do, that you're not currently doing, to make you better at managing your time?
8. Why are highly polychronic people likely to be more flexible in their schedules?

CASE 2.A

Is This the Beginning of the End?*

Deanna watches Peter pass by the office window. He doesn't look happy these days. There are rumours that he is looking for another position. Such a move would be disastrous for the company. As production manager, Peter is the person who keeps everything together at this place. And Peter is so good he should have no problems finding another job. But if Peter goes, several other managers will also probably go. Everyone is fed up. If Peter goes, maybe Deanna will also leave.

Deanna is the human resources manager at a food processing company in southeast Ontario. It began about 15 years ago as a small operation but has grown amazingly in the last few years, expanding its product line and becoming the main supplier to two very large companies. But the growing pains are becoming debilitating. The owner/president of the company has turned most of the company management over to a handpicked successor, the vice president, while the owner concentrates on sales. But he still sticks his nose in every once in a while and dictates what should happen. The vice president doesn't dare refuse him. Both the owner and the vice president know the older staff intimately and give them special treatment. It has frustrated Deanna that she has worked hard with management to create a set of policies, rules, and guidelines for staff yet they are constantly undermined. The supervisors really wanted clear policies and rules so they knew what they could and couldn't do and had some firm guidance in confronting problem behaviour. But the rules and procedures have not had the desired impact because the senior employees who don't like a rule just go to the owner or vice president who then give them permission to ignore the rule.

Deanna arrived two years ago to create a human resources function in the company of 250 people that had no such function. She set about creating job descriptions so everyone knew their responsibilities, and lines of authority were clear. That project remains unfinished since the assistant assigned to work with Deanna was pulled to work on other matters closer to production. Deanna still shares three support people with Production but knows that her demands are lower priority and can be shoved aside at a moment's notice. Most of Deanna's time is spent on recruiting. The company has a very high turnover rate. The jobs are not exciting, the pay is not particularly high, there are few benefits (e.g., they are not paid any sick days), and the employees without seniority must work the afternoon or evening shift since only the long-term employees get to work the more desirable day shift. Deanna shudders at the thought of staffing the new plant that is planned for construction next year out of province.

Peter is the production manager and a friend of Deanna's. He began as an operative employee and worked his way up, proving himself in each position to be competent and able. But he finds his job very difficult. Like Deanna, he has no budget to work with. The company has always simply spent money as needed and tried to keep costs as low as possible. He is now expected to keep up production while half the machines are being moved into a newly expanded plant space. That was supposed to happen during the summer downtime but then they discovered at the last minute that the new end of the plant had not been supplied with sufficient electrical power to handle the machines so it needed to be rewired. And now the move is happening in the fall, their busiest time of the year. Peter also has to deal with catastrophes like the recent debacle with a major customer because it made a huge error on a shipment. This did not happen because production failed but because there was a miscommunication to production and a critical adjustment to the machine settings was not implemented, thereby allowing a whole lot of useless product to be churned out. It was only when the customer received a batch of food that did not meet their specifications that the mistake was realized.

Peter has not decided definitely to leave the company but he is feeling more and more like that each day. The company has great potential and he feels almost like he would be abandoning family members, but the working situation has become too stressful and he feels he can't make a difference. Deanna and other managers know that Peter is the one link pin holding things together. This is why Deanna feels that, if Peter goes, she'll also need to leave.

RESPONDING TO THIS CASE

1. Explain all the ways in which this company appears to be ignoring planning advice. Then attempt to explain why the company does not follow typical planning guidelines and how it has managed to be successful despite this.
2. Explain the impact that the lack of planning has had on employees, on management, and on the success of the company as a whole.
3. Explain how this case demonstrates the link between planning and time management.

* This case is based on a real situation. The names and certain details have been changed to disguise the identity of the individuals and organization.

CASE 2.B

No Time and Getting Blamed!

Amanda puts in long hours at her job as a college department head. She typically starts work around 8 doing emails at home over breakfast, delaying her commute until the worst of the traffic is over. She is in meetings much of the day so often stays until 7 or 8 in the evening to get things done. With about 30 full-time faculty and 50 part-time faculty teaching in the diploma and degree programs in her portfolio, Amanda is responsible for hiring, for assigning teaching loads (who is to teach what the next term), and doing regular classroom visits to give feedback to probationary faculty. Amanda also deals with issues of student dishonesty, with student complaints and with student grade appeals.

A number of frustrations challenge Amanda. She feels so caught up in the day-to-day demands that she knows she is not planning for the future. And when she tries, through initiatives to develop new academic programs, she gets resistance from the faculty whose help she needs. They want time on their assigned workload contract to recognize new development efforts but she is reluctant to do this because she needs them assigned to classes in order to meet the teaching targets dictated by college management. As a result, Amanda ends up taking on much of the development work herself, trying to squeeze it into her busy schedule (and then she gets resistance from some faculty who disagree with what she has produced). Other department heads somehow manage to get their faculty to do this work with less hassle. She feels the other department heads must have much easier faculty to work with. There are a number of things that her faculty members refuse to do or delay doing; for example, completing annual reviews of their courses and programs, getting students to do feedback surveys, completing college training around new processes or policies. Amanda ends up taking on some of this herself or making apologies to management over why things were not done in a timely way.

Other people are frustrated with Amanda. Faculty feel she is often not available when they need to speak with her about things that arise; she has no set office hours when they know she'll be free. Other people around the college find she does not respond in a timely way to email or voicemail and they often have to resend information because she can't find it. Amanda seems to react as if requests from other parts of the college (like the registrar's office, finance office or co-op office) for information or discussion are impositions that she has no time for and are low priority. As a result those offices sometimes have to go to her supervisor, the dean, to get things done. This angers Amanda further. The dean knows that Amanda is well-intentioned and hard-working but believes Amanda could be much more efficient in her use of time and able to accomplish more with less stress. She has seen it in other department heads and she accomplished it herself when in that position.

RESPONDING TO THE CASE

1. Amanda believes her problems can be blamed to a great extent on her having a tough group of employees to work with. Do you believe it is possible that the 20 other department heads all have employees who are different from Amanda's and much more "cooperative"? What is the danger in Amanda believing this?
2. What tactical planning is Amanda involved in? What suggests she is involved in potential strategic planning as well?
3. What standing plans does it seem Amanda works with?
4. How might goal-setting assist Amanda?
5. Explain how Amanda seems to be violating the principles of effective time management.
6. Describe what steps you would recommend to Amanda to improve her time management.

3

DESIGNING AND IMPLEMENTING CONTROLS

Courtesy of Hybrid Images/cultura/Corbis Images

LEARNING OBJECTIVES

After reading this chapter, you should be able to:

1. Compare and give examples of preventive, concurrent and corrective controls.
2. Explain the importance of performance measurements.
3. Explain how a supervisor can reduce costs.
4. Describe the need for due diligence in supervisors.
5. Describe what a supervisor can do to control employee behaviour.
6. List the characteristics of an effective control system.
7. Explain potential negative outcomes that controls can create.
8. Distinguish incremental budgeting from zero-base budgeting.

CHAPTER OUTLINE

PERFORMING EFFECTIVELY

TYPES OF CONTROL
Preventive Control
Something to Think About
Concurrent Control
Corrective Control
Measuring Performance
Some Measurement Tools

FOCUS OF CONTROL
Costs
Inventories
Quality
Safety
Building a Supervisory Skill: Job Safety Analysis
Employee Performance
Something to Think About

CHARACTERISTICS OF EFFECTIVE CONTROLS

POTENTIAL NEGATIVE OUTCOMES OF CONTROLS
Employee Resistance
Assessing Yourself: How Willing Are You to Encourage Self-Control?
Misdirection of Effort
Ethics and Control Devices

FROM CONCEPTS TO SKILLS: BUDGETING
Assessing Yourself: What Do You Know about Budgeting?
Skill Basics
Applying Your Skills

UNDERSTANDING THE BASICS
Summary
Key Terms and Concepts
Reviewing Your Knowledge

PERFORMING YOUR JOB
Case 3A: Pam Van Loenen
Case 3B: Katerina Kollaras

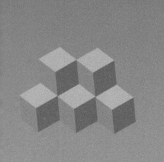

PERFORMING EFFECTIVELY

Debbie Hinz is the production manager at Precision Biologic in Dartmouth, Nova Scotia. The company manufactures medical products (e.g., plasmas, reagents, diagnostic kits) and Debbie manages the lab where all finished products are made, supervising three people on the production side (who bottle the products, package and store them in freezers) and three manufacturing technologists who make the controls and calibrators for coagulation labs. Quality is critical. To achieve this quality there are many processes, procedures, and documents that ensure everyone is carrying out what they need to do.

"All employees have role dimensions which describe their responsibilities. We have training plans and a training database which serve to describe and document what training each role requires and who has completed various areas of training and when. We have SOP's (Standard Operating Procedures), Work Instructions and forms which specifically describe what is required for a process (equipment, materials, chemicals, etc.) and how to carry out the process. Also, from our new ERP system, we generate Work Orders which contain the bills of materials which define everything needed for a particular product and when it's scheduled to be made.

Throughout all of these processes are various in-process checks and there is also final finished goods Quality Control testing at the end. Quality Assurance approves the final release of all finished goods." Debbie herself provides part of the control process in the lab by keeping an eye on things. With all the systems, rules, training and instructions in place, there is still room for human error or for the unexpected. For example, "I had a situation with a young person hired as a maternity replacement who was often texting at work. I find that, for many young people, texting is like breathing and they don't understand why it is not acceptable at work. She was shocked that it was an issue. When I spoke with her I explained why it was inappropriate. One, we have lab areas in the building with strict biosafety rules so texting is a safety issue—people remove their gloves to handle the phone and then do not wash their hands so they are contaminating. Two, if you are texting, your focus is not on your work and this opens the door to mistakes—in her case there had been instances of errors. There are specific processes we follow in the production lab and there is no room for interruption of these processes."

FIGURE 3-1

Debbie Hinz, second from the right, with the production team and the dispensing, labeling, and capping machine affectionately known as Stella

The greatest plans still depend on execution to realize their potential. And how does a supervisor know if the plan is being achieved? The supervisor won't know, unless he or she has developed controls.

As described in Chapter 1, controlling is the management function concerned with monitoring activities to ensure that activities are being accomplished as planned, and with correcting any significant deviations. In this chapter, we will show you how effective supervisors perform the controlling function. Specifically, we'll detail the controlling process, discuss the timing of controls, identify the major areas where supervisors concentrate their control activities, describe the characteristics of effective controls, and discuss some of the potentially undesirable side effects of controls that supervisors need to guard against.

Controlling
Monitoring activities to ensure that objectives are being met as planned, and correcting any significant deviations.

TYPES OF CONTROL

PREVENTIVE CONTROLS

Preventive controls anticipate and prevent undesirable outcomes. They set up clear expectations about what is acceptable and what is not. Because of their existence, deviations are less likely to happen. Debbie Hinz described a number of preventive controls in place in her lab at Precision Biologic: role dimensions, training plans, standard operating procedures, work instructions and forms which specifically describe what is required for a process and how to carry out the process, work orders which contain the bills of materials.

Examples of preventive controls:

Policies (e.g. discrimination and harassment policy)

Rules (e.g. rules on expenses to be reimbursed for business travel and meals)

Procedures (e.g. opening and closing procedures; lockdown procedures; reporting injuries)

Budgets (specifying what expenses are to be expected and seen as reasonable)

Non-compete clauses in hiring contract (e.g. guaranteeing that, for a period of one year after leaving the company, the employee will not conduct any business with any of its clients)

Code of Conduct (e.g. IBM's Business Conduct Guidelines outline topics such as conflicts of interest, intellectual property, dealing with organizations outside of IBM, the use of IBM assets and premises, speaking publicly and social media[1])

Job descriptions (a written description of what a jobholder does, how and why)

Training (preparing people with skills before they need them on the job)

Preventive maintenance practices (e.g. standard practice to overhaul machinery on regular schedule, even if no problems apparent)

Job Safety Analysis (identifying potential hazards and determining how to avoid them)

Legislation (e.g. employment standards, and health and safety)

Preventive controls are typically created by authorities (e.g. legislation by the government; polices and rules by senior management or their staff experts). Supervisors may have a hand in some of the preventive controls (e.g. information they give to prospective hires, how they orient and train new employees). The supervisor's role is more typically one of communicating the controls, ensuring employees know what the rules and policies are, and then enforcing them. Of course, supervisors must comply with the preventive controls pertinent to their own behaviour. For example, procedures regarding carrying out and documenting employee performance appraisals and disciplining have been crafted to avoid problems (like a charge of harassment) while effectively managing performance.

In order to communicate, enforce and comply themselves with the preventive controls, it is essential that supervisors are aware of them. Federal and provincial governments have enacted legislation to prevent problems in the workplace and it is important that supervisors are aware of these imposed controls. See *Something to Think About* for information on relevant legislation.

SOMETHING TO THINK ABOUT
• LEGISLATIVE CONTROLS AFFECTING SUPERVISORS •

EMPLOYMENT STANDARDS
Employers must abide by legislated rules about employment standards such as minimum vacation and minimum wage. In many companies, these issues are dealt with by the human resources department. However, in small companies without such a department it is incumbent on management to be aware of workplace employment standards and apply them. The standards vary by jurisdiction. Below is a sample.

Jurisdiction	Minimum Wage	Hours of Work & Overtime	Paid Public Holiday	Vacation	Emergency Leave/Sick Leave	Termination of Employment
Alberta	$9.40/hour	max. 12 hours/day, 6 days/week, overtime when 8 hour/day and/ or 44 hrs/week exceeded	9 days	2 weeks/year 3 wks/yr after 5 yrs	Nil	1 week after 3 months 2 wks after 2 yrs 4 wks after 4 yrs 5 wks after 6 yrs 6 wks after 8 yrs 8 wks after 10 yrs
Newfound-land and Labrador	$10.00/hour	overtime after 40 hours/week 24 consecutive hours off each week 3 hours call-in	6 days	2 weeks/year 3 weeks/year after 15 years	3 days bereavement (1 day paid) 7 day sick leave	1 week after 3 months 2 wks after 2 yrs 3 wks after 5 yrs 4 wks after 10 yrs 6 wks after 15 yrs
Nunavut	$11.00/hour	8 hours/day, 40 hours/week, overtime when this is exceeded; up to 10 hours/day, 60 hours/week with a permit 4 hours call-in	9 days	2 weeks/year 3 weeks/year after 5 years	Nil	2 weeaks after 90 days additional week per year after 3 years to a maximum of 8 weeks
Federal	rate of provincial minimum where work is per-formed	max. 48 hours /week, overtime when 8 hours/day and/or 40 hours/week exceeded	9 days	2 weeks/year 3 weeks/year after 6 years	3 days bereavement (paid) 12 weeks sick leave	2 weeks after 3 months and two days wages per year employed

FIGURE 3-2 Select Workplace Standards: Alberta, Newfoundland, Nunavut and Federal (August 2012)[1] Canadian flag courtesy of jannoon028/Shutterstock, Nunavut flag courtesy of Luftikus/Shutterstock, Newfoundland flag courtesy of Atlaspix/Shutterstock, Alberta flag courtesy of Atlaspix/Shutterstock

ANTI-BULLYING LEGISLATION

Quebec, Ontario, Manitoba, B.C. and Saskatchewan have all enacted leg-islation to protect workers from harassment or bullying. Employers and supervisors in those jurisdictions now have a duty to protect workers from hazards not only to physical health but also to mental health. For example, Saskatchewan's Occupational Health and Safety Act declares that:

> "Every employer shall ensure, insofar as is reasonably practical, that the employer's workers are not exposed to harassment with respect to any matter or circumstance arising out of the worker's employment."

---

[1] See particular legislation for up-to-date information. Exceptions and special circumstances apply to the standard information provided.

The legislation defines harassment as:

> "any inappropriate conduct, comment , display, action, or gesture by a person; that either adversely affects the worker's psychological or physical well-being and that the person knows or ought reasonably know to know would cause a worker to be humiliated or intimidated..."

What is the role of the supervisor? Supervisors must enforce relevant organizational policies, monitor staff behaviours, investigate all complaints, and deal with inappropriate behaviours promptly.

CONCURRENT CONTROLS

Concurrent controls are enacted while an activity is in progress. Debbie Hinz at Precision Biologic referred to in-process checks that can detect issues before activities are completed. She also provides concurrent control by watching and giving feedback and guidance to employees.

Examples of concurrent controls

Observation

Gauges (e.g. that measure temperature, pressure)

Error identification built into a system (e.g. software that questions potential spelling errors)

Much of a supervisor's day-to-day activities involve concurrent control. It occurs whenever a supervisor directly oversees employee work and corrects problems as they occur.

CORRECTIVE CONTROLS

Corrective controls provide feedback after an activity is finished in order to prevent future deviations. At Precision Biologic, Debbie Hinz referred to the quality control testing of final finished goods and the fact that Quality Assurance approves the final release of all finished goods.

Examples of corrective controls:

Inspection of finished goods

Mid-year budget reports (noting how close the activity matches what was planned)

Annual employee performance appraisals

Financial audits

Annual inventory taking

The obvious shortcoming of corrective control is that, by the time there is awareness of a problem, it's too late to do anything about it. The damage has occurred. For example, if a supervisor learns in August that 120% of the annual budget for office expenses is spent, there's nothing she can do to correct the overexpenditure.

Looking at the examples of preventive, concurrent corrective controls, you will note that the list for preventive controls is longest. This is appropriate—the clearer expectations are upfront, the less need for concurrent and corrective controls. It is efficient to put greater energy into ensuring success than correcting errors.

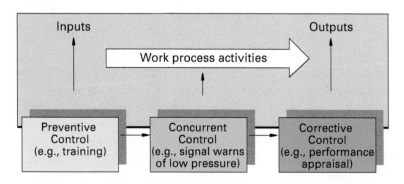

FIGURE 3-3

Three types of controls

MEASURING PERFORMANCE

Note that both concurrent and corrective controls mean that we must have information regarding the adequacy of performance. We need to measure it and be able to compare it to standards or expectations and determine if there are deviations needing correction.

What we measure is critical. This is because measurement is highly visible and sends a strong message about what is important to the organization. Employees will focus on the activities and behaviours that are measured rather than those that are not measured. This sounds obvious and appropriate but can lead to unintended results. For example, if a company focuses solely on sales and does not pay attention to customer service, what happens? Staff want to focus only on sales opportunities. They do not want to handle returns, they ignore the customer with a small sale when there is the potential for a bigger sale, and they avoid duties like stocking, maintenance and taking inventory. Customer service and other aspects of the job end up suffering because only one aspect of performance is measured and, often, the only one rewarded.

Supervisors will have some common performance measures, like absenteeism, turnover, activity costs and employee satisfaction. Beyond this, the specific types of measures will vary depending on the job and the goals of the department. Some will show up in statistical reports or charts whereas others will be obvious from personal observation. It's important that supervisors have tools that make it easy for them to track the information they need. Diane Hebert says: "It's not enough to say "We need to look at absenteeism issues." You need to develop a system, a way of tracking absenteeism and dealing with it. For example, create a three-month probation tool so managers know what to look for and how to evaluate it. You can't leave it up to managers to simply 'know'."

SOME MEASUREMENT TOOLS

Any discussion of how you measure would be incomplete without a discussion of the basic techniques used to control variability. In this section, we'll describe the more popular statistical process control techniques.

Cause-effect diagrams
Diagrams used to depict the causes of a problem and to group them according to common categories such as machinery, methods, personnel, finances, or management.

Cause and Effect Diagrams. **Cause-effect diagrams** (also sometimes called fish-bone or Ishikawa diagrams) are used to depict the causes of a certain problem and to group the causes according to common categories such as machinery, materials, methods, personnel, finances, or management.

As shown in Figure 3-4, these diagrams look somewhat like a fish skeleton, with the problem—the effect—as the "head." On the "bones," growing out of the "spine," are the possible causes of production problems. They're listed in order of possible occurrence. Cause-effect diagrams provide guidance for analyzing the influence that alternative courses of action will have on a given problem.

Business Process Maps
Visual representations of the sequence of events for a particular process that clarify how things are being done, so that efficiencies can be identified and the process improved.

Business Process Maps (or Flow Charts). **Flow charts** (or process mapping) are visual representations of the sequence of events for a particular process. They clarify exactly how things are done so that inefficiencies can be identified and the process improved. Figure 3-5 provides an illustration, showing the steps in a car repair process at a dealership, and the people involved.

Lenny Jackson, a manager at CBC Halifax television, has been involved in several work-flow assessments. In one, he and a Vancouver manager interviewed 65 people involved in program production at a major production centre. They examined the production work-flow process from program approval through to the completion of production. The resultant flow chart showing the people connections so jammed with processes that it had to be constructed with an overlay so that others could understand the issues. The duplication spelled out what appeared to be a less-than-efficient process. This chart provided the basis for a focused redesign of the process, streamlining it to reduce redundancy and make the process more efficient and effective.

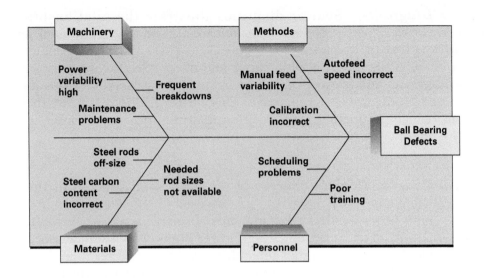

FIGURE 3-4

Example of a fish-bone diagram.

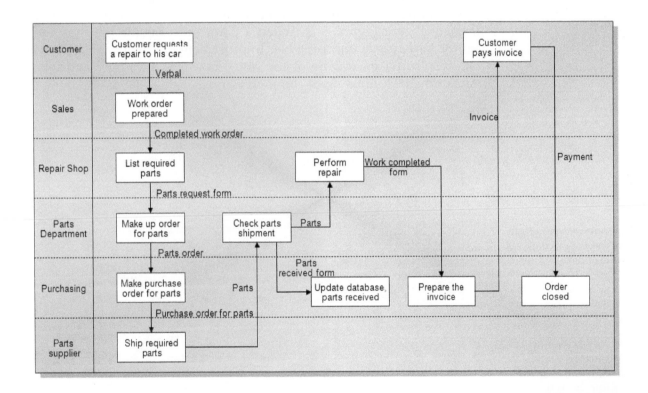

FIGURE 3-5

A business process map illustrating a car repair process.

Scatter Diagrams. **Scatter diagrams** illustrate the relationship between two variables such as height and weight, or the hardness of a ball bearing and its diameter (see Figure 3-6). These diagrams visually depict correlations and possible cause-and-effect. So, for instance, a scatter diagram could reveal that the percentage of rejects increases as the size of production runs increase. This, in turn, might suggest the need to reduce production runs or re-evaluate the process in order to improve quality.

Control Charts. **Control charts** are the most sophisticated of the statistical techniques we'll describe. They are used to reflect variation in a system. Control charts reflect measurements of sample products averaged with statistically determined upper and lower limits. For instance, Coca Cola samples its one-litre bottles after they are filled to determine their exact quantity. These data are then plotted on a control chart, which tells management when the filling equipment needs adjustment. As long as the process variables fall within the acceptable range, the system is said to be "in control" (see Figure 3-7). When a point falls outside the limits set, then the variation is unacceptable. Improvements in quality should, over time, result in a narrowing of the range between the upper and lower limits through elimination of common causes.

FIGURE 3-6

Example of a scatter diagram. (Reprinted with permission of the publisher. From *Putting Total Quality Management to Work*, p. 170, copyright © 1993 by Marshall Sashkin and Kenneth J. Kiser, Berrett-Koehler Publishers, Inc., San Francisco, CA. All rights reserved.)

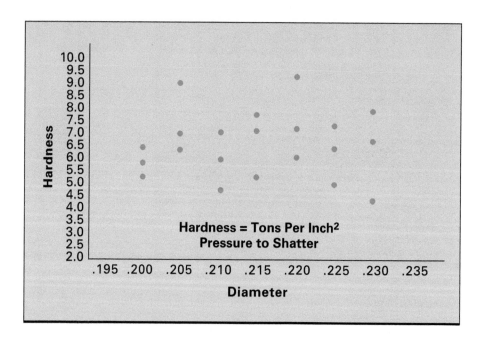

Hardness = Tons Per Inch² Pressure to Shatter

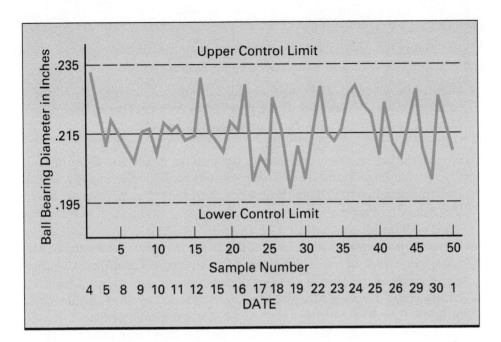

FIGURE 3-7

Example of a control chart. (Reprinted with permission of the publisher. From *Putting Total Quality Management to Work*, p. 176, copyright © 1993 by Marshall Sashkin and Kenneth J. Kiser, Berrett-Koehler Publishers, Inc., San Francisco, CA. All rights reserved.)

FOCUS OF CONTROL

What do supervisors control? Most of their control efforts are directed at one of five areas (see Figure 3-8):

- costs
- inventories
- quality
- safety
- employee performance

COSTS

Supervisors are regularly under pressure to keep their costs in line. Let's look at those cost categories and present a general program for cost reduction.

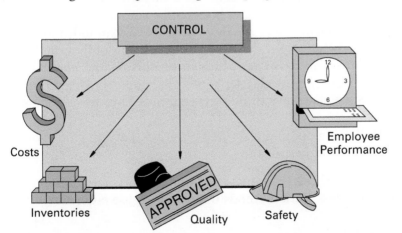

FIGURE 3-8

Focus of control

MAJOR COST CATEGORIES

The following list presents the major cost categories that a supervisor will come in contact with and which need to be monitored.

- **Direct labour costs.** Expenditures for labour that are directly applied in the creation or delivery of the product or service. Examples: Machine operators in a factory or teachers in a school.
- **Indirect labour costs.** Expenditures for labour that are not directly applied in the creation or delivery of the product or service. Examples: Cost accountants, human resource recruiters, public relations specialists.
- **Raw material costs.** Expenditures for materials that go directly into the creation of a product or service. Examples: Sheet steel at a Mazda plant or hamburger buns at a McDonald's.
- **Supportive supplies costs.** Expenditures for necessary items that do not become part of the finished product or service. Examples: Cleaning compounds at the Mazda plant or photocopying costs at Sun Life.
- **Utility costs.** Expenditures for electricity, gas, water, and similar utilities. Example: Monthly electric bill for a regional office.
- **Maintenance costs.** Material and labour expenditures incurred to repair and maintain equipment and facilities. Examples: Repair parts for equipment or jet-engine maintenance technicians at Air Canada.
- **Waste costs.** Expenditures for products, parts, or services that cannot be reused. Examples: Unsold French fries at McDonald's.

Typically, supervisors will have a budget for each major cost category. Then, by monitoring expenditures, costs can be kept within their budget plans. (See the skill module on budgeting at the end of this chapter.)

COST-REDUCTION PROGRAMS

When costs are too high, managers will implement a cost reduction program. In a difficult economy, Canadian corporations often focus on how to reduce costs and improve their competitive position in relation to their global competitors. Much of this cost-cutting has a direct effect on supervisors. For instance, direct labour costs have been cut by automating jobs and redesigning work around teams that are more productive than individuals; and indirect labour costs have been slashed by laying off tens of thousands of support personnel in research, finance, human resources, and clerical functions. Budgets for training, travel, telephone calls, photocopying, computer software, office supplies, and similar expenditures have undergone significant cuts.

The following outlines a six-step program that can guide you in reducing costs in your department.[2]

1. **Improve methods.** Eliminate any unnecessary activities and introduce new work methods that can increase efficiency.

2. **Level the work flow.** Peaks and valleys in a work flow imply inefficiencies. By levelling the work flow, you can manage with fewer employees and reduce overtime.
3. **Minimize waste.** Burning lights in unused areas, misuse of office supplies, underemployed workers, underutilization of equipment, and wasteful use of raw materials add considerably to a supervisor's departmental costs.
4. **Install modern equipment.** Budget for new equipment to replace obsolete and worn-out machinery, computers, and the like.
5. **Invest in employee training.** People, like machines, can become obsolete in that their skills become dated.
6. **Make cuts selectively.** Avoid across-the-board cuts. Some people and groups contribute significantly more than others. Make cuts where they will generate the greatest efficiencies.

INVENTORIES

Supervisors are routinely responsible for ensuring that adequate inventories of materials and supplies are available for activities under their jurisdiction. For a shift supervisor at Burger King, that would include paper products, buns, burger patties, French fries, condiments, cooking utensils, cleaning supplies, and even proper change for the cash register. For a nursing supervisor at a hospital, it might mean supplies such as pharmaceuticals, gloves, hypodermic needles, and bed linen.

The challenge in monitoring inventory costs is balancing the costs of maintaining inventories against the cost of running out of inventory. If excessive inventory is carried, money is needlessly tied up and unnecessary storage costs are incurred. Excessive inventory also adds to insurance premiums and taxes. And, of course, there are potential obsolescence costs—unused inventory may remain unused because products change. If inventories drop too low, operations can be disrupted and sales lost. A stock-out of paper can bring a publisher's printing to a halt. And if a Tim Horton's supervisor fails to monitor the inventory of milk, there may be some very disgruntled coffee customers.

The **just-in-time (JIT) inventory** system is a popular inventory system that attempts to balance the trade-offs between costs of having too much or too little inventory. In this system, inventory items arrive from suppliers as they are needed in the production process rather than being stored in stock. Despite its apparently ideal setup, JIT is not used by all organizations as it requires a great deal of planning. Backup plans to cover the inevitable occasion when parts are not delivered on time must be created. What if the received inventory does not meet quality requirements and must be returned? A strong relationship with suppliers, including excellent and complete communication of quality, quantity, and delivery needs, is required.

When JIT works as designed, it results in a number of positive benefits for a manufacturer: reduced inventories, reduced setup time, better

Just-in-Time (JIT) Inventory System A system in which inventory items arrive when they are needed in the production process instead of being stored in stock.

work flow, shorter manufacturing time, less space consumption, and even higher quality. Of course, suppliers who can be depended on to deliver quality materials on time must be found. Because there are no inventories, there is no slack in the system to absorb defective materials or delays in shipments.

Materials requirement planning (MRP) is another inventory control tool used in some organizations. This system uses a bill of materials, which is essentially a recipe for the product specifying what is needed and in what order. The bill of materials is used to instruct the computer program that controls inventory and schedules production. MRP is similar to JIT in that it tries to ensure that the right raw materials and parts arrive at the right time in the right place.

Gantt and PERT charts, described in the last chapter as planning tools, also provide scheduling control in the production process.

QUALITY

With the possible exception of controlling costs, achieving high quality has become a primary focus of today's organizations. Many North American products were criticized as being shoddy in quality compared to their Japanese and German counterparts. On the other hand, companies such as Bombardier have thrived by focusing on quality products or services. With this emphasis has come increased demand on supervisors to engage in quality control.

Quality control refers to monitoring quality (weight, strength, consistency, colour, taste, reliability, and so on) to ensure that it meets pre-established standards. It is needed at multiple points in a process. It begins with the receipt of inputs. Are the raw materials satisfactory? Do new employees have the proper skills and abilities? It continues with work in process and in all steps up to the completion of the final product or service. Assessments at intermediate stages of the transformation process are typically part of quality control. Early detection of a defective part or process can save the cost of further work on the item.

A comprehensive quality control program would encompass preventive, concurrent, and corrective controls. For example, controls would inspect incoming raw materials, monitor operations while they are in progress, and include final inspection and rejection of unsatisfactory outputs. Of course, this same comprehensive program could be applied to services. For instance, a claims supervisor for Dominion Insurance could hire and train her people to ensure that they fully understand their jobs, monitor their daily work flow to ensure it is done properly and on time, review completed claims for accuracy and thoroughness, and follow up with customers to determine their degree of satisfaction with the way their claims were handled.

Quality has taken on a meaning larger than quality control in the expanded perspective of **Six Sigma** and **total quality management (TQM)**

Six Sigma
A structured quality approach that seeks to improve the quality of outputs by identifying and removing the causes of defects and minimizing variability in processes.

Total quality management
(TQM) A philosophy of management that is driven by the attainment of customer satisfaction through the continuous improvement of all organizational processes.

programs. Six Sigma is a comprehensive approach that seeks to improve the quality of outputs by identifying and removing the causes of defects and minimizing variability in processes. A six sigma process is one in which 99.99966% of manufactured products are expected to be free of defects. Originated by Motorola, it uses a set of quality management methods, and creates a special infrastructure of people within the organization ("Black Belts", "Green Belts", etc.) who are experts in these methods. Each Six Sigma project follows a specific sequence of steps and has quantified financial targets. A supervisor within a Six Sigma organization will use some of the tools already mentioned (e.g. fishbone diagram, control charts, scatter diagrams) as well as many other statistical and analytical tools. One analytical method is Root Cause Analysis or The 5 Whys, because it refers to exploring the potential causes underlying an issue by persistently asking "Why?." When a problem presents itself, and you ask "Why did this happen?," don't stop at the answer to this first question. Keep asking "Why?" until you reach the root cause.

TQM is based on the ideas of W. Edwards Deming, an American whose ideas found an interested audience in postwar Japan (see Figure 3-9) before they were accepted in North America. Among his ideas was the use of statistics to analyze variability in production processes. A well-managed organization, according to Deming, was one in which statistical control reduced variability and resulted in uniform quality and predictable quantity of output. TQM's management philosophy sees customers as

1. **Focus on the customer.** The customer includes not only outsiders who buy the organization's products or services, but also internal customers (such as shipping or accounts payable personnel) who interact with and serve others in the organization.

2. **Continuous improvement.** TQM is a commitment to never being satisfied. "Very good" is not enough. Quality can always be improved.

3. **Improvement of the quality of everything the organization does.** TQM uses a very broad definition of quality. It relates not only to the final product, but also to the way the organization handles deliveries, how rapidly it responds to complaints, how politely the phones are answered, and the like.

4. **Accurate measurement.** TQM uses statistical techniques to measure every critical variable in the organization's operations. These are compared against standards or benchmarks to identify problems, trace them to their roots, and eliminate their causes.

5. **Involvement of employees.** TQM involves the people on the line in the improvement process. Teams are widely used in TQM programs for finding and solving problems.

FIGURE 3-9

The foundations of TQM

everyone who interacts with the organization's product or service, internally or externally, thereby including employees and suppliers as well as clients who purchase the organization's output. The objective is to create an organization committed to continuous improvement. There is never enough quality. Quality improvement is an ongoing, never-ending process.

If a supervisor works in an organization focused on TQM, that supervisor must be familiar with statistical control processes but also comfortable working closely with subordinates on quality. TQM is based on the participation of the people closest to the work. Employees are respected for their ideas on continuous improvement and a supervisor is expected to support and seek their input.

ISO registration is another quality initiative used by many companies that influences work procedures and, therefore, the supervisor's job. It is often part of a company's TQM strategy.

The International Standards Organization developed the ISO 9000 series of standards. To be certified as meeting these standards, thereby proving that certain quality assurance procedures and documentation are in place, a company must be audited both when it applies for registration and then on a regular, ongoing basis. Elements of the ISO guidelines refer to management responsibility, control of customer-supplied product, document and data control, design control, process control, inspection and testing, handling, packaging, storage, preservation and delivery, training and control of quality records, among others.

Tina Payton, prepress supervisor at Robinson-Blackmore printing company in St. John's, Newfoundland, says that her company's ISO registration significantly affected her job. "There are very strict policies and procedures to follow. It reduces errors so it is beneficial. The downside is that it takes a lot of time, for example, on preventative maintenance on equipment. And there's more paperwork, for example, signing off that a disk coming in from a client is not damaged, doing weekly calibrations on equipment, and recording the results. The controls created are time-consuming but important, improving productivity in the long run. One aspect that has improved is that not as much time is wasted tracking down information needed to carry out a job. Sales representatives would not fill out all the areas of the job docket, which would cause unnecessary downtime trying to collect information needed. With these policies in place, these problems have decreased significantly."

SAFETY

Paula Aylward at Cavendish farms of P.E.I knows that, of all her priorities, safety is at the top. At Suncor's oil production facility in Fort McMurray, Larry Bowzeylo agrees: "You must make the work as safe as possible. You can't replace people." Safety is a concern to any supervisor but particularly to those in production facilities where the equipment or chemicals used could have dangerous consequences. In a manufacturing facility, the supervisor will always be on the lookout for potential sources of accidents: loose tiles or grease, signs of stress on scaffolding or ladders, anything clogging aisles and walkways, employees not following safety rules.

OCCUPATIONAL HEALTH AND SAFETY LEGISLATION

Protecting worker safety is not just an ethical obligation and the best thing for business. It is also a legal obligation. All jurisdictions (federal and provincial) impose an "internal responsibility" system recognizing that workers, supervisors and employers are all responsible for maintaining a safe workplace. They share a common goal of preventing work-related injury or illness and are all in a position to identify and prevent circumstances leading to injury or illness in the workplace. The legislation identifies rules for this joint accountability in the form of duties, rights and responsibilities. As a result, employers and supervisors have been fined for not taking steps to protect workers adequately.

The game changer has been the 2004 amendment to the Criminal Code through the passing of Bill-C45, the "Westray Bill". Now employers and their representatives (read: supervisors and other managers) can be held criminally responsible for safety violations. The amendment added Section 217.1 to the Criminal Code which reads:

> "217.1 Every one who undertakes, or has the authority, to direct how another person does work or performs a task is under legal duty to take reasonable steps to prevent bodily harm to that person, or any other person, arising from that work or task."

Test your awareness of health and safety legislative principles in the following. True or False?

1.	T	F	Supervisors must take all reasonable care to protect the well-being of employees or co-workers.
2.	T	F	Supervisors can be disciplined for refusing to direct workers to perform tasks they have reasonable cause to believe are dangerous.
3.	T	F	Employers and supervisors must immediately investigate unsafe acts and conditions reported by workers, and make sure each unsafe act or condition is remedied without delay.
4.	T	F	A supervisor cannot be held liable for a workplace accident unless he or she holds the official title of supervisor.

Answers:
1. True.
2. False. Supervisors have the right to refuse to direct workers to perform work they consider unsafe. Just as workers have the right to refuse to perform any work they consider unsafe.
3. True.

4. False. In most jurisdictions, a supervisor need not have the title "supervisor" to be held liable. What is critical is that they were in charge of a workplace or had authority over a worker. In Ontario there have been several key cases relying on this definition that ruled that a person without a supervisory title still carried out the functions that made him/her a supervisor. For example,[3] one was a "crew lead" and another was a "working foreman."

If there is an accident on the job, a supervisors will not be held liable if it can be shown that the supervisor showed **due diligence**. This means that the supervisor took all reasonable care to prevent the incident.

Due Diligence
Taking all reasonable care to prevent the occurrence of an incident or event.

EVIDENCE OF SUPERVISORY DUE DILIGENCE

The following are elements demonstrating due diligence:

- Verify appropriate training and education
- Ensure qualified operators use equipment
- Identify and correct hazards (see *Building a Skill*: Job Safety Analysis)
- Correct unsafe acts and conditions
- Take part in investigations
- Report accidents
- Enforce rules
- Encourage workers to report hazards
- Document (e.g. inspections, training records, discipline, equipment logs, safety meetings)

Even if a supervisor undertakes these actions, certain workers are at more risk of injury. These are new or young workers (see *Something to Think About*). It's important to pay special attention to these workers, explaining the job and hazards in detail to them, explaining what safety precautions must be taken and why, and ensuring their understanding and compliance.

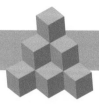

Building a Supervisory Skill

JOB SAFETY ANALYSIS[4]

ABOUT THE SKILL

Job safety analysis (JSA) is a process of identifying potential hazards on a job and recommending the safest way to do the job. So it is a preventive control. It is done through a process of either watching a worker actually perform the job and/or experienced workers and supervisors completing the analysis together based on their joint expertise.

Steps in Job Safety Analysis:

- Select the job or the task to be analyzed
- Break it down into a series of steps
- Identify potential hazards
- Determine preventive measures to overcome hazards

Figure 3-10 illustrates an example of a job safety analysis worksheet where hazards related to specific steps were identified and then appropriate preventive measures were recorded.

Job Safety Analysis Worksheet		
Job:		
Analysis by:	Reviewed By:	Approved by:
Date:	Date:	Date:
Sequence of Steps	**Potential Accidents or Hazards**	**Preventive Measures**
Park Vehicle	a) Vehicle too close to passing trafic b) Vehicle on uneven, soft ground c) Vehicle may roll	a) Drive to area well clear of traffic. Turn on emergency flashers. b) Choose a firm, level parking area. c) Apply the parking brake; leave transmission in PARK; place blocks in front and back of the wheel diagonally opposite to the flat.
Remove spare and tool kit	a) Strain fromlifting spare	a) Turn spare into upright position in the wheel well. Using your legs and standing as close as possible, lift spare out of truck and roll to flat tire.
Pry off hub cap and loosen lug bolts	a) Hub cap may pop off and hit you. b) Lug wrench may slip.	a) Pry off hub cap using steady pressure. b) Use proper wrench; apply steady pressure slowly.
And so on...	a) ...	a) ...

FIGURE 3-10

Sample Job Safety AnalysisWorksheet

PREFERRED WAYS OF DETERMINING PREVENTIVE MEASURES

The final stage in a JSA is to eliminate or control the hazard.

1. Eliminate the Hazard.

   • For example, choose a different process, substitute with a less hazardous substance, or change equipment

2. Contain the hazard

   • For example, use enclosures, machine guards or worker booths

3. Revise work procedures

   • For example, modify hazardous steps, add additional steps (like locking out energy sources)

4. Reduce the exposure

   • For example, use personal protective equipment, reduce the frequency of contact (e.g. modify equipment so less maintenance necessary)

What happens once a job safety analysis is complete? Now the information must be communicated to those who are, or will be, performing the job. For example, the recommendations will affect training plans, standard operating procedures, and work instructions. The supervisor will ensure they are enforced.

SAFETY - THE SPECIAL CASE OF YOUNG WORKERS

Nick Perry, 19, had his back broken at a lumberyard when a forklift load shifted and fell on him. Sean Kells, 19, was killed when a highly flammable chemical he was handling ignited and exploded. Jennifer Fourchalk, 19, lost three fingers when her hand was caught in a pizzeria dough machine.[5]

FACT: Young men are more likely to be injured on the job than any other group of workers.

FACT: Most young worker injuries occur within a worker's first six months on the job.

Why are young workers more likely to be injured? The following could be contributing factors:[6]

- They believe nothing bad could happen.
- They have little experience with the equipment to know what could go wrong.
- They are reluctant to ask questions for fear of looking stupid.
- They accept physically demanding or dangerous tasks as part of the job.
- They may choose not to wear safety equipment because they feel it's not "cool."

Why do you think the rates for young workers are so much higher than for other workers? What should supervisors do to prevent this?

FIGURE 3-11

Sean Kells, killed at 19 in a workplace accident

EMPLOYEE PERFORMANCE

Supervisors accomplish things through other people. They need and depend on subordinates to achieve their unit goals. It is, therefore, important for them to get their employees to perform in ways they consider desirable. But how do supervisors ensure that employees are performing as they are supposed to? How do you, for example, minimize employee lateness, absenteeism, and accidents? How do you control the quantity and quality of employee effort? Obvious means include direct supervision and performance appraisals.

Researchers examined the job expectations of bank tellers working for the same large multinational bank in the United States, Australia, Japan, and Hong Kong, and compared these with the expectations of their supervisors. It was discovered that, in all countries, supervisors had broader definitions of the teller job role than did their subordinates. It appears that, within the teller role, supervisors include any actions that could reasonably be taken by the subordinate to improve efficiency and effectiveness. The subordinate is less likely to have such a wide-open perception of the job, instead focusing on specific expected duties.[7]

1. What could be the consequences of these differing perceptions?

_____

_____

_____

_____

_____

2. How could these differences in perception be reduced?

_____

_____

_____

_____

_____

An employee typically behaves with the best intentions in mind. So, if there is a problem with performance, it can often be traced to the employee not understanding fully what expectations the supervisor had in mind, for example, concerning quality, or documentation or safety procedures. It is essential that the supervisor ensure that each employee is informed about the organization's expectations toward that employee. As you'll see in Something to Think About, a supervisor's perception of what a subordinate's job role includes often differs from the subordinate's perception—and it does so in the same way in several countries.

On a day-to-day basis, supervisors oversee employees' work and correct problems as they occur. The supervisor who notices an employee taking an unnecessary risk when operating his or her machine can point out the correct way to perform the task and tell the employee to do it the correct way in the future.

Supervisors assess the work of their employees in a more formal way by means of systematic performance appraisals. An employee's recent performance is evaluated. If performance is positive, the employee's behaviour can be reinforced with a reward such as a pay increase. If performance is below standard, the supervisor will seek to correct it or, depending on the nature of the deviation, discipline the employee.

As Figure 3-13 demonstrates, supervisors have at their disposal a considerably larger menu of behavioural control devices. In actual practice, supervisors use almost all of the options described in the figure to increase the likelihood that employees will perform as desired.

CHARACTERISTICS OF EFFECTIVE CONTROLS

Effective control systems tend to have certain qualities in common (these qualities are summarized in Figure 3-14). The importance of these characteristics varies with the situation, but the following can provide guidance to supervisors in designing their unit's control system.

TIMELINESS

Controls should alert the supervisor to a problem as soon as possible. The best information has little value if it is dated. Therefore, an effective control system must provide timely information.

ECONOMY

A control system must be economically reasonable to operate. Any system of control has to justify the benefits that it gives in relation to the costs it

FIGURE 3-12

Giving performance appraisals is a significant part of a supervisor's controls function.
Courtesy of J.R. Bale/Alamy

- **Selection.** Identify and hire people whose values, attitudes, and personality fit with what the supervisor desires.
- **Goals.** When employees accept specific goals, the goals then direct and limit behaviour.
- **Job design.** The way jobs are designed determines, to a large degree, the tasks that a person does, the work pace, the people he or she interacts with, and similar behaviours.
- **Orientation.** New-employee orientation defines what behaviours are acceptable and what aren't.
- **Direct supervision.** The physical presence of supervisors acts to shape employee behaviour and allows for rapid detection of undersirable behaviour.
- **Training.** Formal training programs teach employees desired work practices.
- **Regulations.** Formal rules, policies, job descriptions, and other regulations define acceptable practices and constrain undesirable behaviour.
- **Performance appraisals.** Employees will behave so as to look good on the criteria by which they will be appraised.
- **Rewards.** Pay raises, recognition, desired job assignments, and similar rewards act as reinforcers to encourage desired behaviours and to extinguish undesirable ones.

FIGURE 3-13

Behavioural control devices

1. **Timeliness** ensures quick response.

2. **Economy** ensures that the benefits of control exceed the cost.

3. **Flexibility** provides the ability to adjust to change.

4. **Understandability** increases the likelihood that controls will be used.

5. **Reasonable criteria** ensure that controls will not act as demotivators.

6. **Critical placement** recognizes that controls can't be imposed on everything and, therefore, need to be located where there is the greatest potential for harm.

7. **Emphasis on the exception** lessens the chance that a manager will be overwhelmed with information on variations from standard.

FIGURE 3-14

Characteristics of effective controls

incurs. To minimize costs, supervisors should try to impose the least amount of control necessary to produce the desired results. The widespread use of computers is due to a large extent to their ability to provide timely and accurate information in a highly efficient manner.

FLEXIBILITY

Effective controls must be flexible enough to adjust to adverse change or to take advantage of new opportunities. In today's dynamic and rapidly changing world, supervisors should design control systems that can adjust to the changing nature of departmental objectives, work assignments, and job tasks.

UNDERSTANDABILITY

Controls that cannot be understood by those who must use them are of little value. It is sometimes necessary, therefore, to substitute less complex controls for sophisticated devices. A control system that is difficult to understand can cause unnecessary mistakes, frustrates employees, and is eventually ignored.

REASONABLE CRITERIA

Consistent with our discussion of goals in the previous chapter, control standards must be reasonable and attainable. If they are too high or unreasonable, they no longer motivate. Since most employees don't want to risk being labelled as incompetent for telling their bosses that they ask too much, employees may resort to unethical or illegal shortcuts. Controls should, therefore, enforce standards that are reasonable; they should challenge and stretch people to reach higher performance levels without being demotivating or encouraging deception.

CRITICAL PLACEMENT

Supervisors can't control everything that occurs within their department. Even if they could, the benefits couldn't justify the costs. As a result, they should place controls on those factors that are critical to their unit's performance goals. Controls should cover the critical activities, operations, and events within their unit. That is, they should focus on where variations from standard are most likely to occur or where a variation would do the greatest harm. In a department where labour costs are $20 000 a month and postage costs are $50 a month, a 5 per cent overrun in the former is more critical than a 20 per cent overrun in the latter. Hence, we should establish controls for labour and a critical dollar allocation, whereas postage expenses would not appear to be critical.

EMPHASIS ON THE EXCEPTION

Since supervisors can't control all activities, they should place their strategic control devices where they can call attention only to the exceptions. **A control by exception** system ensures that a manager is not overwhelmed by information on variations from standard. For instance, the accounts receivable supervisor at a Sears store instructs her people to only inform her when an account is 15 days past due. The fact that 90 per cent of the store's customers pay their bills on time or no more than two weeks late means she can devote her attention to the 10 per cent exceptions.

Control by exception
Strategic control devices should call attention only to exceptions from standard.

POTENTIAL NEGATIVE OUTCOMES OF CONTROLS

Controls can create their own problems. The introduction of controls comes with potential negatives that you will need to guard against. These include employee resistance, misdirection of employee effort, and ethical dilemmas for supervisors concerning control devices. Let's take a brief look at each.

EMPLOYEE RESISTANCE

Many people don't like to be told what to do or to know that they're being "checked up on." When work performance is deficient, few people enjoy being criticized or corrected. The result is that employees often resist controls. They view their supervisor, daily production reports, performance appraisals, and similar control devices as evidence that their employer doesn't trust them.

Reality tells us that controls are a way of organizational life because management has a responsibility to ensure that activities are going as planned. So what can you, as a supervisor, do to lessen this resistance?

First, wherever possible, encourage employee self-control (see Assessing Yourself). Once employees know their goals, give them the benefit of the doubt and leave them alone. Let them monitor and correct their own performance. Supplement this with regular communication so they can let you know what problems they've encountered and how they've solved them. The assumption with self-control is that employees are responsible, trustworthy, and capable of personally correcting any significant deviation from their goals. Only if this assumption proves incorrect do you need to introduce more formalized external control mechanisms.

When external controls are needed, here are a few suggestions to minimize employee resistance.

- Have employees participate in setting the standards. This lessens the likelihood that they'll view them as unrealistic or too demanding.

- Explain to employees how they will be evaluated. Surprisingly, the problem is often not the controls themselves creating resistance but the lack of understanding of how information will be gathered and how it will be used.
- Provide employees with regular feedback. Ambiguity causes stress and resistance, so it makes sense to let people know how they're doing.
- Finally, treat controls as a device for helping employees improve rather than for punishing them. Most people want the satisfaction that comes from doing their work better and want to avoid the pain and embarrassment that comes with discipline.

Assessing Yourself

HOW WILLING ARE YOU TO ENCOURAGE SELF-CONTROL?

For each of the following eighteen statements, rate each on a scale of 1 to 5, where 5 = strongly agree, 4 = agree somewhat, 3 = neither agree nor disagree, 2 = disagree somewhat, and 1 = strongly disagree.

	Strongly Agree			Strongly Disagree	
1. I'd let others do more, but it appears the jobs never seem to get done the way I want them to be done.	5	4	3	2	1
2. I don't feel I have the time to explain to others what to do.	5	4	3	2	1
3. I carefully check on others' work without letting them know I'm doing it, so I can correct their mistakes if necessary, before they cause too many problems.	5	4	3	2	1
4. I let others control the whole job—giving them the opportunity to complete it without any of my involvement. Then I review the result.	5	4	3	2	1
5. When I have given clear instructions and the task isn't done right, I get upset.	5	4	3	2	1
6. I feel that others may lack the commitment I have. Any task I ask them to do won't get done as well as I'd do it.	5	4	3	2	1
7. I'd let others control things more, but I feel I can do the job better than the person I might have given the job to.	5	4	3	2	1

8. I'd let others control more, but if the individual I give this responsibility to does an incompetent job, I'll be severely criticized. 5 4 3 2 1

9. If I were to give up control, my job wouldn't be nearly as much fun. 5 4 3 2 1

10. When I give up control, I often find that the outcome is such that I end up doing the task over again myself. 5 4 3 2 1

11. I have not really found that giving up control saves any time. 5 4 3 2 1

12. I tell others exactly how something should be accomplished. 5 4 3 2 1

13. I can't give up control as much as I'd like to because others lack the necessary experience. 5 4 3 2 1

14. I feel that when I give up control, I lose control. 5 4 3 2 1

15. I would give up control more, but I'm pretty much a perfectionist. 5 4 3 2 1

16. I work longer hours than I should. 5 4 3 2 1

17. I can give others the routine tasks, but I feel I must do nonroutine tasks myself. 5 4 3 2 1

18. My own boss expects me to keep very close to all details of my job. 5 4 3 2 1

SCORING

Total your score by adding the circled numbers for the eighteen statements.

WHAT THE INSTRUMENT MEANS

How much control you're willing to give up or share is directly related to how willing you are to assign this "authority" to others. Depending on your total score, the following interpretations can be made:

> 72–90 points = ineffective assignment of self-control
> 54–71 points = assigning self-control habits needs substantial improvement
> 36–53 points = assigning self-control habits are positive, but some improvement needed
> 18–35 points = superior assignment of self-control

Source: Reprinted by permission of the publisher from *Management Review*, May 1982 ©1982, American Management Association, New York. All rights reserved.

MISDIRECTION OF EFFORT

Three managers at a General Motors plant installed a secret control box in a supervisor's office to override the control panel that governed the speed of the assembly line.[8] The device allowed the managers to speed up the assembly line—a serious violation of GM's contract with the United Auto Workers. When caught, the managers explained that, while they knew what they had done was wrong, the pressure from higher-ups to meet unrealistic production goals was so great that they felt the secret control panel was the only way they could meet their targets. As described by one manager, senior GM executives would say (regarding the high production goals), "I don't care how you do it—just do it."

Have you ever been frustrated by the "service" you receive when trying to get some information, fill out a form, or solve a problem?

Some employees can be so fixated on ensuring that every rule is followed that they lose sight of the fact that their job is to serve the public, not hassle them! This tendency illustrates another potential problem with controls: People may misdirect their efforts in order to look good on the control criteria.

Because any control system has imperfections, problems occur when individuals or organizational units attempt to look good exclusively in terms of the control devices while in actuality, the result is dysfunctional in terms of the organization's goals. More often than not, this situation is

FIGURE 3-15

Customers sometimes suspect that government workers are evaluated based on following rules rather than customer service. Courtesy of Ryan Remiorz/AP Images.

CHAPTER 3   DESIGNING AND IMPLEMENTING CONTROLS

109

caused by incomplete measures of performance. If the control system evaluates only the quantity of output, people will ignore quality. Similarly, if the system measures activities rather than results, people will spend their time attempting to look good on the activity measures.

What can you, as a supervisor, do to minimize this problem? Two things. First, make sure that control standards are reasonable. Very importantly, this should not merely be your perception. The employees must believe the standards are fair and within their capability. Second, you should select and evaluate criteria that are directly related to achievement of employee job goals. If the licensing supervisor in the motor vehicle office evaluates her people on how well they follow rules rather than on how effectively they serve the needs of clients, then her employees will not give much attention to satisfying clients. Finding the right criteria will often mean using a multiple set of standards. For instance, the goal of "serving clients" might require the licensing supervisor to evaluate her clerks on criteria such as "greets all clients with a smile and friendly greeting," "answers all client questions without seeking outside assistance," and "solves the client's problems in one visit." In addition, the supervisor might set up a client comment box in her licensing department where individual employees could be praised or criticized on their service, and then use this feedback as one measure of how well employees were doing their jobs.

ETHICS AND CONTROL DEVICES

Just because a supervisor *can* monitor the most minute details of an employee's work day doesn't mean he or she *should*. This has become a particularly sensitive issue in recent years as sophisticated communication systems and computer software make it possible for a supervisor's control capability to potentially interfere with an employee's right to privacy.

Supervisors at General Electric's Answering Centre record and review employees' handling of customer telephone inquiries. At Vantreight's huge flower farm in Saanichton, British Columbia, supervisors use handheld computers to track each picker's output. The technology now exists for "big brother" to directly and indirectly monitor employees. But is it ethical?

We have no absolute answer. It can be argued that this type of computer performance monitoring helps people do their jobs better. It enables supervisors to review employee performance and provide feedback that can improve the quality of the employees' work. But employees certainly should be aware that this monitoring is going on. Even then, studies have shown that stress-related complaints increase when employees know that somebody may be listening in on their phone calls.[9] This suggests that great care needs to be taken by supervisors as advanced technology expands their control capability.

BUDGETING

ASSESSING YOURSELF: WHAT DO YOU KNOW ABOUT BUDGETING?

For each of the following statements, record your response by circling the corresponding number.

WHEN DESIGNING AND CONTROLLING A BUDGET, I WOULD:

		Strongly Agree	Agree	Neutral	Disagree	Strongly Disagree
1.	Begin the budget process by focusing on the goals of the organization and my department.	5	4	3	2	1
2.	Delegate responsibility for developing my budget to a team of employees.	1	2	3	4	5
3.	Use last period's budget as a guide for developing this period's budget, especially in times of significant departmental change.	1	2	3	4	5
4.	Use the budget process as a way to convey to upper management new programs and responsibilities that my department might pursue.	5	4	3	2	1
5.	Focus on controlling costs because expense budgets are the most frequently used supervisory budgets.	5	4	3	2	1
6.	Try to underspend my current budget because that typically results in a larger budget in the next budget period.	1	2	3	4	5

SCORING KEY AND INTERPRETATION

Add up your score. The higher your total, the better your understanding of budgeting. Individuals with scores below 20, in particular, should find the following coverage of budgeting valuable.

Skill Basics

An organization needs to forecast its financial needs in order to be able to meet them adequately at the right time. A budget is essentially a forecast of financial needs. It then operates also as a control tool to keep expenses in check with the forecast and to avoid shortfalls and unexpected debt.

A company will typically prepare a long-term capital budget to forecast expenses that will occur over a long time, for example, predicting when equipment will need to be replaced or hardware and software upgraded or a new plant built. A supervisor will have some input into this capital budget in that the supervisor has information to contribute to that forecast (such as incidence of breakdown, leading to forecasts of equipment replacement).

But the supervisor is much more likely to get involved with short-term operational budgets, forecasting financial needs over the next year, breaking that down typically into quarters. Because the supervisor is so close to where the work is accomplished, he or she is best qualified to make the most accurate judgement of what expenses will be incurred in the near future. Given that the creation of this short-term expense budget is a common expectation for supervisors, we'll use the expense budget as the focus for our discussion.

INCREMENTAL vs. ZERO-BASE BUDGETS

Incremental budget
A budget that develops out of the previous budget.

The traditional budget is incremental in nature. It develops out of the previous budget. In the **incremental budget**, each period's budget begins by using the last period as a reference point. Then adjustments are made to individual items within the budget. The major problems with the incremental approach are that it tends to hide inefficiencies and waste, encourages continual increases, and hinders change. Inefficiencies tend to grow because, in the typical incremental budget, nothing ever gets cut. Each budget begins with the funds allocated for the last period—to which are added a percentage for inflation and requests for new or expanded activities. So, unfortunately, this approach to budgeting often provides money for activities long after the need is gone. And because incrementalism builds on the past, this type of budget also tends to constrain bold or radical changes.

Zero-base budget
A budget that makes no reference to previous appropriations; all items must be justified.

An option that deals directly with the incremental budget's limitations is the **zero-base budget** (ZBB). With the ZBB, the entire budget begins from scratch and each budget item must be justified. No reference is made to previous appropriations. The major advantage to the ZBB is that all programs, projects, and activities taking place within every department in the organization are reassessed in terms of benefits and costs. You previously read about Ainslie White's experience budgeting as the IT manager at Precision Biologic. His approach exemplifies a zero-based approach, starting from scratch. "I start with a wish list. I talk to the team leads in the company about what they would like for the next year. I get them to prioritize their list, telling me the top five, and keep paring it down. Once we have collected this information the IT team meets to consider costs and implementation, what can be accomplished." The primary drawbacks of ZBB include increased paperwork and preparation time, the tendency for managers to exaggerate the benefits of activities they want funded, and the negative effect on intermediate and long-term planning. On this last point, when departmental budgets have to be completely justified every year, the potential for dramatic ups and downs in funding can create chaos for managers and make intermediate and long-term planning almost impossible.

While most organizations rely on incremental budgeting, the zero-base approach continues to have its advocates. We suggest that when organizations are developing new strategies, making major shifts in the products and services they offer, undertaking a significant reorganization, or introducing similar organization-wide change programs, managers should at least temporarily utilize zero-base budgeting. This approach will lessen the likelihood that outdated or less important activities will continue to receive their prior level of funding.

TOP-DOWN vs. BOTTOM-UP BUDGETING

Another decision that must be made about budgeting is where the budget will initially be prepared. **Top-down budgeting** originates at the upper levels of the organization. Budgets are initiated, controlled, and directed by senior management. This approach assumes senior management is best able to allocate resources among alternative uses within the organization. These budgets are then given to middle-level and lower-level managers, who are responsible for carrying them out. This method has the advantage of simplifying the budgeting process and focusing attention on the organization's overall strategy and goals. However, the top-down approach has some huge disadvantages. It assumes that top management has comprehensive data on all activities within the organization. This assumption is rarely valid, especially in relatively large organizations. Since operating personnel and lower-level managers have no input, the top-down approach also does nothing to build support for and commitment to budgets.

Top-down budgeting
Budgets that are initiated, controlled, and directed by top management.

Bottom-up budgeting
Budget requests are prepared by those who implement them and then sent to higher levels of management for approval.

Most organizations today have moved to **bottom-up budgeting**, where the initial budget requests are prepared by those who must implement them. These requests are then sent up for approval to higher levels of management where modifications may be suggested. When differences occur, they are negotiated. The process is followed upward until an organization-wide budget is developed. This is the case for Ainslie, who drafts the budget based on requests for IT activity in the next year, and then gets it approved through upper management (the controller). The bottom-up approach to budgeting essentially has the opposite advantages and disadvantages to those of budgets initiated from the top. Because supervisors and other lower-level managers are more knowledgeable about their needs than are managers at the top, they are less likely to overlook important funding requirements. And very importantly, lower-level managers are also much more likely to enthusiastically accept and try to meet budgets they had a hand in shaping.

THE BUDGETING PROCESS

You're a new supervisor who has been asked to submit your first budget. What do you do? The following steps will provide you with some guidance:

1. **Review the organization's overall strategy and goals.** Understanding your organization's strategy and goals will help you focus on where the overall organization is going and your department's role in that plan.

2. **Determine your department's goals and the means to attain them.** What activities will allow you to reach your departmental goals and help the organization achieve its overall goals? What resources will you require to achieve these goals? Think in terms of factors such as staffing requirements, workloads, and the materials and equipment you'll need. This is also your opportunity to formulate new programs and propose new responsibilities for your department.

3. **Gather cost information.** You'll need accurate cost estimates of those resources you identified in step 2. Old budgets may be of some help. But you'll also want to talk with your immediate manager, other superiors, colleagues in similar positions, key subordinates, and use other contacts you have developed both inside and outside your organization.

4. **Share your goals and cost estimates with superiors.** Your immediate manager will need to approve your budget, so his or her support is necessary. Discuss your goals, cost estimates, and other

ideas with your immediate manager and key superiors before you include them in your budget. This will ensure that they align with upper management's vision of your department's role and will build consensus for your proposed submission.

5. **Draw up your proposed budget.** Once your goals and costs are in place, constructing the actual budget is fairly simple. But be sure to show the linkage between your budget items and your departmental goals. You need to justify your requests. And be prepared to explain and sell your budget to your immediate manager and upper management. Remember that there will almost certainly be other managers competing for some of the same resources that you want.

6. **Be prepared to negotiate.** It's unlikely that your budget will be approved exactly as you submitted it. Be prepared to negotiate changes that upper management suggests and to revise your original budget. Recognize the politics in the budget process and negotiate from the perspective of building credits for future budgets. If certain projects aren't approved this time, use this point in the budget process to get some assurance that they will be reconsidered next time.

7. **Monitor your budget.** Once approved and implemented, you'll be judged on how well you carry out your budget. Manage by exception. Set variance targets that include both percentages and dollars. For instance, you could set a decision rule that says you'll investigate all monthly variances of 15 per cent or larger where the actual dollar variance is $200 or more.

8. **Keep superiors informed of your progress.** Keep your immediate manager and other relevant parties advised on how you're doing in terms of meeting your budget. This is likely to help protect you if you exceed your budget for reasons beyond your control. Also, don't expect to be rewarded for underspending your budget. In incremental budgets, underspending will only mean you'll be allocated fewer funds in the next budget period!

The prospect of budgeting frightens some supervisors and many potential supervisors. They are uncomfortable with the idea, anticipating it will be beyond their skills. David Goncalves, a production supervisor at Mother Parkers Tea and Coffee has gone from fear to active, engaged involvement. "I never used to be involved with bills, budgeting, the financials. Now the plant manager is getting me involved in budgets, showing me as we go along, how we're hitting or

FIGURE 3-16

David Goncalves used to be afraid of handling a budget. Now actively involved in budgeting, he finds it a valuable tool.

missing budgets. I was scared at first—how am I going to handle this? I was honest, asking people to talk to me as if I've never seen these numbers before or heard these terms—I'm a simple person. The financial manager went through the numbers with me. It looked like a scary picture but she broke it down for me so I could understand. It became interesting—I started thinking, what can I change in the routine to hit these numbers? If I can't, maybe those numbers aren't accurate. Budgets are sometimes like a wish list, and not really true. I had never seen the gas and hydro bills until the last few months. That understanding is now helping me pull the pieces together. We've started putting together next year's budget and I can see, here's our utilities and our labour costs; I can see what may have to change. It helps make decisions if we can track these costs. Because I'm juggling so much, I'm now passing on some of my duties to my team, including the basics of budgeting. They are understanding what it means to be on target, ahead of target, and why it is important."

APPLYING YOUR SKILLS

You wish to attend a three-day training course in Halifax. To get approval, you need to submit a cost estimate to your supervisor. This estimate will also serve as your budget for the trip.

1. Describe how you would approach this cost estimate. For example, what information will you need and where will you get it? Remember to apply the appropriate steps of the budgeting process.

2. Create a proposed budget using cost estimates for all items. Then look at your completed budget and decide which items are negotiable and why.

3. Now take the role of the *manager* who will be receiving the above request.

    a) Assuming you approve the trip, would you prefer to cover the costs of the trip in advance or reimburse afterwards? Explain why. What are the implications for control?

    b) You want to encourage employee development, yet at the same time keep costs down. What kinds of expenses on the submitted budget might you decide to declare as personal expenses that the company will not cover? Which expenses should the company accept and why?

    c) What "controls" might your company apply to ensure that all such travel and training expenses are both legitimate and within reason?

UNDERSTANDING THE BASICS

SUMMARY

This summary is organized by the Learning Objectives.

1. Preventive control is implemented before an activity begins (e.g. rules, procedures). It anticipates and prevents undesirable outcomes. Concurrent control takes place while an activity is in progress (e.g. supervisory observation, temperature gauge). Corrective control is implemented after an activity is finished and facilitates the prevention of future deviations (e.g. performance appraisal, finished goods inspection).
2. Measurement of performance is necessary to determine whether correction is necessary. It also focuses attention on what is considered important.
3. Supervisors can reduce costs in their departments by improving work methods, levelling the work flow, reducing waste, installing more modern equipment, investing in employee training, and making selective cuts that will generate the greatest efficiencies.
4. Supervisors must take all reasonable care to prevent the occurence of a health and safety incident. This includes actions like education, training, hazard identification and correction, and enforcing rules.
5. To control employee behaviour, supervisors can select employees who will fit well in the department, provide specific goals, control the design of jobs, use new-employee orientation to convey acceptable behaviour, engage in direct supervision, provide formal training, impose formal regulations, use performance appraisals, and reward desirable behaviour.
6. An effective control system should be timely, economical, flexible, and understandable; have reasonable standards and strategically placed controls; and emphasize the exception.
7. Some potential negative outcomes from controls include employee resistance, employees directing their efforts to the wrong activities, and ethical dilemmas created by advances in control technology.
8. An incremental budget develops out of the previous budget whereas a zero-base makes no reference to the previous budget and all items must be justified.

KEY TERMS AND CONCEPTS

Bottom-up budgeting
Business process maps
Cause-effect diagrams
Concurrent controls

Control by exception
Control charts
Corrective control
Due diligence

Employment standards

Harassment

Incremental budget

Job safety analysis

Just-in-time inventory system

Materials requirement planning

Preventive controls

Range of variation

Scatter diagrams

Six Sigma

Top-down budgeting

Total quality management

Zero-base budget

REVIEWING YOUR KNOWLEDGE

1. Which type of control is preferable—preventive, concurrent, or corrective? Why? What type do you think is most widely used in practice?
2. What is the challenge of monitoring inventory costs?
3. In terms of characteristics of an effective control system, where do you think most control systems fail? Why?
4. Why should a supervisor control "by exception"?
5. How can a supervisor lessen employee resistance to controls?
6. How can a supervisor minimize the problem of people trying to look good on control criteria?
7. Contrast incremental and zero-base budgets. Which is best for facilitating change? Why?
8. Why do most organizations use bottom-up budgeting?

CASE 3.A

Pam Van Loenen

"As a supervisor in a fast food franchise, I would often open the store but more commonly was responsible for closing, which included daily inventory counts, counting the tills, and filling out an envelope to compare debits/cash sales to the register to ensure a balance, cleaning the store and locking up. Usually I had two cashiers and one cook working under me. As supervisor I was supposed to be in the centre of the kitchen packaging orders, telling the cook what to do, and dealing with customer complaints. I also had to keep my eye on the speed of service times, keeping it to less than one minute in the drive-through, and know what was in the warmers. But, if we were really busy, I may also need to clean the lobby, do the dishes, sweep and mop, and help take down a machine. We can't simply say we'll do things later because we need to keep labour costs down. Staff hours are budgeted based on predicted sales, which may not match what actually happens. For example, Wednesdays are usually dead and you can assume it will be quiet so you can get a lot of cleaning done. But then a bus pulls in and we go crazy. The customer always comes first.

The main reason I think I was effective was because I was organized. I know my paperwork, and am comfortable with numbers. Each day I needed to examine the inventory control sheet showing what was sold yesterday, then figure out overs and shorts to ensure no theft. Then I would do production planning for the same day the next year, using every year to reference. On Sundays I did a count of the entire inventory in the store, doing a larger control sheet than the daily one, considering sales, coupons etc. Every quarter we also counted paper products (cups, bags, cartons) to ensure we were keeping costs down. Math skills are important. We had a manager in training who was weak in math and had to use a calculator for everything, which slowed things down. It's simple math but it is needed (for example, handling multiples like 5 buckets of 15 items equals 75). I ordered a couple of times a week, completing paperwork for this. Technically there are procedures to follow for ordering with procedures based on last year's sales, but sometimes you need to go on your gut because there are unusual circumstances. There are rules and procedures that are supposed to standardize everything we do in the store but I can't say we actually always followed all of them. For example, we're supposed to wear protective equipment when cleaning ovens but no one does because then you can't clean the over properly so we just get burns and don't report them.

There are certain standards set by the company the franchise is connected with but then there are things that vary with the local store. Management turnover is high (we had four managers in my six years there) which meant the rules changed and the staff had to adapt each time. It can be particularly hard for the supervisor in between the manager and the staff. A lazy manager sets an example that the cashiers follow and then the supervisor has to work a lot harder. The store can disintegrate if there is a poor manager. That's why I ended up taking on so much of the paperwork – she would leave it for me knowing I would do it and do it well."

FIGURE 3-17

Pam Van Loenen

1. Identify the preventive, concurrent and corrective controls in this case.
2. Which of the control areas (costs, inventories, quality, safety, and employee performance) are the main focus of control and why? Generate examples of organizations whose control emphasis would be different and explain why.
3. Pam reports that the staff do not follow the rule about wearing protective equipment when cleaning the ovens. Why is this rule (a preventive control) not effective? What are the potential consequences? What should be done to better control this behaviour?
4. Pam reports that a poor manager can have a major impact on performance in the store. Explain why by using control concepts.

CASE 3.B

Katerina Kollaras

Katerina Kollaras, 24, describes her experience as assistant manager at a clothing store.

"I would zone staff within the store, give them their sales quotas at the start of the shift, then do hourly sales reads throughout the day, coaching each one on what their read was and how they could improve. If people did well in their first hour, they became either motivated and tried harder, or they would begin to slow down and take it easy. I had to learn how each person would take the information. If an employee's sales are slow, I would suggest ways to improve sales, e.g. I notice customers weren't in your area and went straight to the sales area. Perhaps you could connect with them as soon as they enter the store and before they get to the sales area."

Katerina worked in two store locations, first in a smaller community, then in a city with more traffic, loud music, a much larger space and 20 to 25 employees, requiring a different approach. "We used headsets to communicate with staff and would coach them when necessary. For example, "I just watched a customer walk by and you didn't greet them." It almost felt like we were spying on them. All staff hear what is said on the headset so you have to be really careful what you say and how you say it. It means that coaching one person on the headset sets an example for all but there's no privacy and it's not as personal as I would like."

Staff would also share information about customers on the headset. One day an employee complained about a customer and warned the other staff through the headset that the customer was rude, not responding at all when the salesperson had approached her and tried to speak with her. Katerina decided to approach the customer. When there was no response, Katerina touched her lightly on the arm. She turned with interest toward Katerina and asked for pen and paper to communicate because she was hearing impaired. "I ended up spending a lot of time with her, selling her a number of items. It taught me to be patient with people and not to jump to conclusions."

Katerina's duties also included opening and closing procedures, selling on the floor herself, answering emails, dealing with cash, ensuring coverage if an employee was ill, doing weekly/monthly/quarterly reports on sales, monitoring sales compared to other stores, and coming up with plans for improvements. "It was a challenge keeping up with everything. I had to set goals for the store and organize myself. I needed an overall strategy to complete everything I had to do plus monitor staff." Daily sales quotas are sent out by the head office at the beginning of each week, then broken down and assigned to staff by Katerina depending on the number of hours each employee works. "From the weekly and monthly reports sent out by head office each store could see how the entire district was

FIGURE 3-18

Katerina Kollaras.

doing and if the store was on track to meeting their daily, weekly, and monthly sales quotas, as well as being able to see where each store stood within the district. Management also had sales quotas, which were usually higher than the other employees and on top of meeting our sales goals we also had to complete our other daily duties."

RESPONDING TO THIS CASE

1. What are the ethical implications of the communication headsets?
2. What resistance might you expect to the controls Katerina describes and why?

4

PROBLEM SOLVING AND DECISION MAKING

Courtesy of StockLite/Shutterstock

LEARNING OBJECTIVES

After reading this chapter, you should be able to:

1. Distinguish programmed from nonprogrammed decisions.
2. List the eight steps in the decision-making process.
3. Describe expected value analysis.
4. Explain the value of decision trees.
5. Contrast data with information.
6. Describe the four types of decision styles.
7. Explain three different ethical viewpoints.
8. Compare and contrast group and individual decision making.
9. List three techniques for improving group decision making.

CHAPTER OUTLINE

PERFORMING EFFECTIVELY
  Programmed and
    Nonprogramed Decisions

THE DECISION-MAKING PROCESS
  Identify the Problem
  Define the Objective and
    Criteria
  Collect Relevant Information
  Develop Alternatives
  Evaluate Each Alternative
  Select the Best Alternative
  Implement the Decision
  Follow Up and Evaluate

EMOTIONS IN DECISION MAKING

DECISION TOOLS
  Expected Value Analysis
  Decision Trees
  Marginal Analysis
  Risk Analysis
  Gap Analysis and the Five Why's
  Matrix Assessments
  Cause-and-Effect Diagrams
  Management Information
    Systems

DECISION-MAKING STYLES
  *Assessing Yourself: What's Your
    Decision-Making Style?*

ETHICS IN DECISION MAKING
  *Dealing with a Difficult Issue:
    Hiring a Friend*
  Common Rationalizations
  Three Different Views on Ethics
  Some Ethical Decision Guides
  Fairness in Decision Making
  *Building a Supervisory Skill:
    Guidelines for Acting
    Ethically and
    Compassionately*

GROUP DECISION MAKING
  Advantages and Disadvantages
  A Guide to When to Use Group
    Decision Making

Types of Group Decision
  Making
*Building a Supervisory Skill:
  Conducting a Group
  Meeting*
Techniques for Improving
  Group Decision Making
*Something to Think About:
  New Ways of Meeting*
*Something to Think About: A
  Changing Work World
  will Affect Decision
  Making*

FROM CONCEPTS TO SKILLS:
CREATIVE PROBLEM SOLVING
  Assessing Yourself: How
    Creative Are You?
  Skill Basics
  Applying Your Skills

UNDERSTANDING THE BASICS
  Summary
  Key Terms and Concepts
  Reviewing Your Knowledge

PERFORMING YOUR JOB
  Case 4.A: Wendy Chiu
  Case 4.B: How Can You
    Make the Decision?

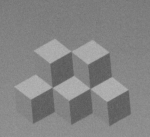

In Chapter 3 we were introduced to Debbie Hinz, the production manager at Precision Biologic, a Nova Scotia company that manufactures medical products. She manages the lab where all finished products are made, supervising three people on the production side and three manufacturing technologists.

"Last year we had two major challenges that happened at the same time. We had a new ERP (Enterprise Resource Planning) system installed across the company and we automated production in our area. Because we create products in tiny amounts (.5 ml, 1, 1.5) the automation system was custom built for us so there were growing pains. We had challenges learning the automated system and some hairballs with the process itself. The manufacturing technologists were helping support the production crew and there was lots of turmoil. It was tough to keep production moving and everyone happy while we were dealing with these changes. And people react differently to the stresses. We dealt with it as a team, but this took some planning. When the turmoil was happening, people were becoming unhappy, so I started to have meetings to deal with it. We started by discussing the attributes of a strong team. Everyone had to contribute to this and we built a picture of a team that was flexible, trusted each other and had fun. Then we set this aside and tackled what we felt was the current state of the production group. We always strive for honesty at Precision Biologic and we needed to be honest about the current state. It took a few meetings and a lot of honesty until we got a clear picture of the current state. Then we asked where do we want to go from here? What are the parts of the current picture that are worth keeping and what do we want to change? Out of these discussions, we created a final document that became our team pact. We all agreed to it. We know that when things get rough and there are stresses, people can drift away from the strong team. So we agreed that when a team member is straying, someone on the team would call it out in a nice way to remind them it's not how we agreed to react. We all agreed on being called out if we were the guilty party.

We have referred to this team document many times. Last week in a meeting, we discussed slightly altering a process. Someone who had previously supported it now did not and could not provide any good reasons. Put to a team decision, three of the four said okay but one person crossed her arms and shrugged. I held up an imaginary paper, saying nothing. She said, "I know, I'm just nervous to do it." I had to do something because she wanted to be quiet but our agreement is that no one is allowed to opt out of the team. Either you're on board or not; it's not okay to say nothing. We tried the process and it seems to work very well. Having a document all agree to is important. Beforehand, someone would snap or make a judgement and all would go quiet. No one would say anything. Now we have those courageous conversations to get over the hump.

Looking back over all the changes last year, one of the biggest things was being there to listen while it was all happening, especially when they were struggling so no one felt alone. We had planned for automation but we still had to deal with a lot. We worked to fix what we could but some things couldn't change. My listening to the team's issues was important so they felt supported.

FIGURE 4-1

Debbie Hinz (third from right) and the production team at Precision Biologic.

Debbie Hinz knew decisions needed to be made regarding how to bring a stressful situation under control. These were not routine, straightforward decisions—these changes were new to her as well as her team. And she required her team to accept the decisions in order for them to move forward. In accomplishing this, Debbie illustrated many of the concepts in this chapter—she applied the steps of the decision-making process, she showed a particular decision making style, and she chose a particular decision making approach, overcoming obstacles in the process. We will return to Debbie's example as we work through the chapter.

The power and the responsibility to make decisions is one of the key elements distinguishing a supervisor's job from operative employees. Decision making is where supervisors make things happen and it is the source of much of their stress. In this chapter we will discuss the types of decisions made by supervisors, the decision making process, decision making tools, styles, and ethics, and when and how group decision making can be effective.

PROGRAMMED AND NONPROGRAMMED DECISIONS

Programmed decision
A simple, routine matter for which the supervisor has an established decision rule.

Nonprogrammed decision
A complex and nonroutine decision requiring a creative solution.

Supervisors make a wide range of decisions, ranging from simple, routine matters for which the supervisor has an established decision rule (**programmed decisions**) to complex and nonroutine decisions requiring creative solutions (**nonprogrammed decisions**). Ordering additional inventory when the current stock gets below a certain level is an example of a programmed decision. As a supervisor at AMC Theatres, Shelby D'Ambrogio sometimes had to decide whether auditoriums need swapping due to demand and if she needed to cut staff hours because guest attendance was down. There was no guesswork involved. She had software indicating the number of guests, number of transactions, dollar spent per person, and auditorium levels. She also had company guidelines that indicated what steps to take and when. Those guidelines also give her decision rules around things like handling drunk guests and dealing with customer complaints.

Nonprogrammed decisions involve situations where there are no decision rules. The situation is new, complex and demanding. Debbie Hinz's situation, requiring her to determine how to facilitate the team's adaptation to two new systems at once, is an example of a nonprogrammed decision. Other nonprogrammed decisions could include dealing with a request for the team to be involved in an entirely new kind of project—could they do it and, if so, what would be the best use of skills and time? Or dealing with a sudden timetable change that throws all the normal activities out of whack. Supervisory positions tend to focus much more on dealing with programmed decisions. As one moves up the management hierarchy, there is more responsibility for nonprogrammed decisions. This is because strategy is, by its nature, nonroutine and complex.

Fortunate are the supervisors whose own managers prepare them to make decisions by involving them in their own challenges. Christopher Nicolson, the president of Tourism Sun Peaks, is grooming someone to take his place in the future. "I actively involve the person in discussions. And I use adversity intentionally. When an issue is occurring, I bring them in to see what is going on, what I have to deal with in my position, but also to think through the troubleshooting with me. I think highly of their opinion." David Goncalves at Mother Parkers Tea and Coffee has had experience on both sides of this opportunity. "My plant manager gets me to come up with ideas, gets me involved in decisions. He tells me it's better to make a decision than not. If it's the wrong decision, you learn from it. If you scrape your knee, you pick yourself up and try something else. He supports me in risk-taking. But he also encourages me to think through the situation before I make a decision. I use the same techniques with my team members. When we hit a tough situation, I ask them for options. We have a 5 minute powwow to consider what we're going to do. I might say, "I see x as a possibility, what else?" We discuss, they scatter and get it done. I joke with them that I should take more vacations because they can handle everything."

THE DECISION-MAKING PROCESS

Decisions with no established rules to simplify them require a process. Here is an eight-step, rational way of looking at decisions (see Figure 4-2)

1. Identify the problem.
2. Define the objective and decision criteria.
3. Collect relevant information.
4. Develop alternatives.
5. Evaluate each alternative.
6. Select the best alternative.
7. Implement the decision.
8. Follow up and evaluate.

IDENTIFY THE PROBLEM

The decision-making process begins with the existence of a **problem**, or an opportunity. Debbie Hinz recognized that there were challenges arising with the installation of the new ERP system as well as the new automation process. She felt things needed to be done to smooth and support the processes. This required decision-making: what needed to be done and how?

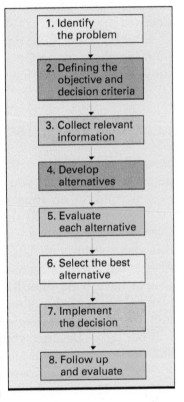

FIGURE 4-2

The decision-making process

Problem
A discrepancy between an existing and a desired state of affairs.

In the real world, problems don't come with neon signs identifying them as such. Many of the problems supervisors will confront aren't as obvious as Debbie's need. One of the most difficult tasks at this stage, then, is separating symptoms from problems. Is a five per cent decline in sales a problem? Or are declining sales merely a symptom of another problem, such as product obsolescence or an inadequate advertising budget?

DEFINE THE OBJECTIVE AND THE CRITERIA

Before you start looking for solutions to the identified issue, it is important to clarify what it is that you want and how you will be able to judge the alternatives. Ultimately, Debbie Hinz knew that efficient and effective production under the two new systems was the ideal. So she could investigate aspects of the situation in terms of what was interfering with that smooth production. She also specified that another objective was for her team to be happy under the new systems.

COLLECT RELEVANT INFORMATION

Now you need to gather the relevant facts and information. Why has the problem occurred now? How is it affecting productivity in my department? What organizational policies, if any, are relevant for dealing with this problem? What time limitations exist for solving it? What costs are involved?

Debbie Hinz investigated the issues regarding learning and implementing the new systems by speaking to those mired in the middle of those challenges—her team.

DEVELOP ALTERNATIVES

Now all possible alternatives need to be identified. It is at this step in the decision process that you demonstrate your creativity. What alternatives exist beyond the obvious or those that may have been used previously?

Keep in mind that this step requires only that you *identify* alternatives. So no alternative—no matter how unusual—should be discarded at this stage. If an alternative isn't viable, you'll find out at the next stage. Also avoid the tendency to stop searching for alternatives after only a couple have been identified. If you see only two or three choices, you probably haven't thought hard enough. Remember that, generally speaking, the more alternatives you can generate, the better your final solution will be. Why? Because your final choice can only be as good as the best alternative you've generated.

Debbie's team discussed a number of alternatives left unspecified in the case. These might have included additional training, coaching, a buddy system, or changing duties assigned to individuals.

EVALUATE EACH ALTERNATIVE

Now all the strengths and weaknesses of each alternative need to be evaluated. For example, what will each cost? How long will each take to implement? What's the most favourable outcome I could expect from each? Most unfavourable outcome?

In this step in particular, it's important to guard against biases. Undoubtedly some alternatives will look more attractive when initially identified. Others, at first glance, may seem unrealistic or exceedingly risky. As a result, you may have a tendency to prematurely favour some outcomes over others and then bias your analysis accordingly. Try to put your initial prejudices on hold and evaluate each alternative as objectively as you can. Of course, no one is perfectly rational. But you can improve the final outcome if you acknowledge your biases and overtly attempt to control them.

As a result of their discussions, the Precision Biologic team created a team pact that outlined expectations for the members.

SELECT THE BEST ALTERNATIVE

After analyzing the pros and cons for each alternative, it is time to select the best alternative. Of course, what's "best" will reflect any limitations or biases that you bring to the decision process. It depends on things such as the comprehensiveness and accuracy of the information gathered in step 2, your ingenuity in developing alternatives in step 3, the degree of risk that you're willing to take, and the quality of your analysis in step 4.

IMPLEMENT THE DECISION

Even if you've made the proper choice, the decision may still fail if it is not implemented properly. This means you need to convey the decision to those affected and get their commitment to it. You'll specifically want to assign responsibilities, allocate necessary resources, and clarify any deadlines.

In Debbie's case, the implementation of the team pact was not entirely smooth, with resistance from one member. But a gentle reminder of her commitment to the pact brought her back on board.

FOLLOW UP AND EVALUATE

The last phase in the decision process is to follow up and evaluate the outcomes of the decision. Did the choice accomplish the desired result? Did it correct the problem that was originally identified in step 1?

Debbie's team has used the team pact repeatedly, finding it a useful tool to address the change process. Production has settled down under the new systems and the team are happy both with the new circumstances and with how they achieved the adaptation together. The objectives have been reached.

If the follow-up and evaluation indicate that the sought-after results weren't achieved, you'll want to review the decision process to see where you went wrong. In that case, you essentially have a brand-new problem and you should go through the decision process again with a new perspective.

EMOTIONS IN DECISION MAKING

The rational decision making process described above is ideal but not typical. We err at step 1 by identifying something as a problem to be solved when actually it is only a symptom of a deeper problem. We don't clarify what exactly we need before we go gathering information and generating alternatives. We leap to choose a solution without thoroughly examining it. We do these things because we are not as consistently rational as we may like to think we are. But we also do it because we are impatient and perhaps anxious about moving forward. We get excited about a potential idea and want to implement it immediately. Let's examine how emotions are a part of decisions, in both positive and negative ways.

Emotions are often seen as contaminants: rational decisions are good, emotional ones are bad. However, decisions stripped of emotional considerations are flawed. It is emotional observations that often trigger our awareness that a problem exists; for example, noticing a customer is displeased, or team morale is poor, or a disappointed reaction from an executive. Knowing the importance of emotions ensures that emotional reactions are considered when decision criteria and objectives are articulated—we want something people will accept. Emotional awareness helps us evaluate alternative solutions by anticipating people's reactions. And tuning into emotions is important in the follow up stage to a decision implementation to see how things are actually rolling out. So awareness and consideration of emotions are important parts of decision making.

On the other hand, emotions can lead us to make the wrong decisions because we emphasize the emotional aspect over other equally important aspects. For example, Diane Hebert says, "Many managers haven't clued in to the importance of tying hiring decisions to skills as opposed to liking or knowing the person." Ryan Anderson concurs: "I see a "similarity" error happening frequently, where managers hire based on being comfortable with the person, connecting with them. 'Oh, you like dogs? So do I. You must be the right person for the job.' It causes a lot of grief because decisions are not based on logic." Under highly emotional conditions, people do not look at the whole picture or the various alternatives; they tend to zero in on whatever is causing them to react so strongly. So, when supervisors must make decisions, they need to do so in a calm and relatively unemotional frame of mind. If they are not feeling calm, it's a good idea to defer the decision until they can achieve that perspective (see CASE 4.A Wendy Chiu).

Ultimately, in making decisions, supervisors need to accomplish a balancing act—considering and valuing both their own emotions and those of others but not letting those emotions override other critical considerations. This issue comes up later in the book as we discuss conflict management (Chapter 12) and emotional intelligence in leadership (Chapter 10).

DECISION TOOLS

A number of tools and techniques have been developed over the years to help supervisors improve their decision-making capabilities. In this section, we'll present several of them.

EXPECTED VALUE ANALYSIS

Fred Cassidy, the co-owner and manager of Larry's Sports in Hamilton, Ontario, is looking at several brands of hockey skates. Given his space and budget limitations, he can only purchase one of these brands to add to his department. Which one should he choose?

Expected value analysis could help with this decision. It permits decision makers to place a monetary value on the various consequences likely to result from the selection of a particular course of action. The procedure is simple. You calculate the expected value of a particular alternative by weighting its possible outcomes by the probability (0 to 1.0, with 1.0 representing absolute certainty) of achieving the alternative, then summing up the totals derived from the weighting process.

Let's say Fred is looking at three lines of skates: Bauer, CCM, and Graf. He's constructed the payoff table in Figure 4-3 to summarize his analysis. Based on his past experience and personal judgement, he's calculated the potential yearly profit from each alternative and the probabil-

Expected value analysis
Calculating the expected value of a particular alternative. This is achieved by weighting its possible outcomes according to the probability of achieving the alternative, then summing up the totals derived from the weighting process.

Alternative	Possible Outcome	Probability	Expected Value
Bauer	$ 12 000	0.2	$ 2 400
	10 000	0.6	6 000
	6 000	0.2	1 200
			$ 9 600
CCM	$ 10 000	0.4	$ 4 000
	6 000	0.5	3 000
	2 000	0.1	200
			$ 7 200
Graf	$ 9 000	0.2	$ 1 800
	6 000	0.6	3 600
	4 000	0.2	800
			$ 6 200

FIGURE 4-3

Payoff table for hockey skate decision

ity of achieving that profit. The expected value of each alternative ranged from $6200 to $9600. Based on this analysis, the supervisor could anticipate the highest expected value that could be reached by purchasing the Bauer line of skates.

DECISION TREES

Decision trees
A diagrammatic technique for analyzing decisions by assigning probabilities to various outcomes and calculating payoffs for each outcome.

Decision trees are a useful way to analyze hiring, marketing, investment, equipment purchases, pricing, and similar decisions that involve a progression of decisions. They're called decision trees because, when diagrammed, they resemble a tree and its branches. Typical decision trees encompass expected value analysis by assigning probabilities to each possible outcome and calculating payoffs for each decision path.

Figure 4-4 illustrates a decision facing Mike Rosen, the eastern region site-selection manager for a large bookstore chain. Mike supervises a small group of specialists who analyze potential locations and make store-site recommendations to the eastern region's manager. The lease on the company's store in Moncton, New Brunswick, is expiring and the landlord has decided not to renew it. So Mike and his group must make a relocation recommendation to the regional manager.

Mike's group has identified an excellent site in a nearby shopping mall. The mall owner has offered him two comparable locations: one with 4000 square metres (the same as he has now) and the other a larger 6000-square-metre space. Mike has an initial decision to make about whether to recommend renting the larger or smaller location. If he chooses the larger space and the economy is strong, he estimates the store will make $320 000 profit. However, if the economy is poor, the high operating costs of the larger store will mean only $50 000 in profit will be made. With the smaller store, he estimates the profit at $240 000 with a good economy and $130 000 with a poor one.

As you can see from Figure 4-4, the expected value for the larger store is $239 000 [(.70 × 320 000) + (.30 × 50 000)]. The expected value for the smaller store is $207 000 [(.70 × 240 000) + (.30 × 130 000)]. Given these results, Mike is planning to recommend the rental of the larger store space.

But what if Mike wants to consider the implications of initially renting the smaller space and then possibly expanding if the economy picks up? He can extend the decision tree to include this second decision point. He has calculated three options: no expansion, adding 1000 square metres, and adding 2000 square metres. Following the approach used for Decision Point 1, he could calculate the profit potential by extending the branches on the tree and calculating expected values for the various options.

MARGINAL ANALYSIS

Marginal analysis
Analyzing decisions in terms of their incremental costs

The concept of marginal, or incremental, analysis helps decision makers to optimize returns or minimize costs. **Marginal analysis** deals with the

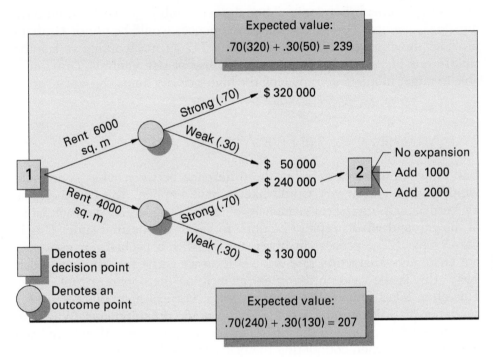

Expected value:

.70(320) + .30(50) = 239

$ 320 000

Strong (.70)

Rent 6000
sq. m

Weak (.30)

$ 50 000

$ 240 000

No expansion

2 Add 1000

Add 2000

Rent 4000
sq. m

Strong (.70)

1

Weak (.30)

$ 130 000

Denotes a
decision point

Denotes an
outcome point

Expected value:

.70(240) + .30(130) = 207

FIGURE 4-4

Decine tree and
expected values for
renting a large or
small retail space

additional cost in a particular decision, rather than the average cost. For example, the operations supervisor for a large commercial dry cleaner wonders whether she should take on a new customer. She should consider not the total revenue and the total cost that would result after the order was taken, but rather what additional revenue would be generated by this particular order and what additional costs incurred. If the incremental revenues exceed the incremental costs, total profits would be increased by accepting the order.

RISK ANALYSIS

Another way of approaching a decision situation uses **risk analysis** as opposed to expected value analysis. Either the decision tree or expected value analysis formats described above could be used, replacing value with risk. Graham Van Brunt, the director of Plant Operations and Maintenance at Churchill Falls Labrador Corporation's hydro power plant, knows that his 25-year-old equipment will soon need replacing. But he cannot afford the huge expense of replacing everything at once. The old way of doing maintenance was essentially accomplished by following manufacturer's recommended procedures for refurbishment, repair and/or replacement. But this starts to get very expensive as a plant ages (it could, for example, recommend simultaneous replacement of similar parts). Instead, Graham and his team assess the risk involved in not replacing a

Risk analysis
Analyzing decisions in terms of their relative risk.

piece of equipment. For some old equipment, failure to work would have dire consequences. For others, the consequences would be minor. Graham provides the analogy of landing gear on a 747 jet not working versus the sink in one of its many washrooms. Because of risk analysis, Graham is able to target money into replacing the high-priority items.

GAP ANALYSIS AND THE FIVE WHYS

Gap analysis
Gap analysis involves defining the difference between what is actually happening and what you would like to have happening.

Gap analysis involves defining the difference between what is actually happening and what you would like to have happen. You can then use backward-chaining logical sequences of actions to identify the root cause of the gap and what needs to be done to get to the desired state. This is the "5 whys." The process involves starting with a problem or gap (e.g., our customer satisfaction rate is lower than we wish) and asking yourself "why" this is the case until you can determine the apparent root cause. This often takes four or five or more whys. For example, one reason for customer dissatisfaction relates to errors made on shipments. Why? We have many new people in the customer service centre and they have been making errors when completing the order forms. Why? They have a very short training period and the procedural manual is outdated. Why? We are so short-staffed that we need new employees on the floor immediately and no one has time to update the manual. Why? Turnover is high. Why? The job is very stressful and doesn't pay well. Why? The company does not think the skills needed are worth much and basically sets employees up for failure by not training them well and not giving them the tools to do the job well (such as an up-to-date manual). Why? The company seems to believe that anyone can do a customer service job, and that it is low skill and low priority.

At the end of this analysis, you get some immediate ideas for correcting the problem. One of the interesting aspects of this technique is that, as you do the gap analysis and "whys" for different issues in the organization, you often find that certain themes or basic root causes emerge. The problems often arise out of very few basic concerns (such as a company treating its customer service people as low-priority, low-skill employees). This tool was noted in Chapter 3 as a Six Sigma quality tool.

MATRIX ASSESSMENTS

Matrix assessment
Sets up a comparison between alternatives based on weighted criteria.

When there are a number of alternative actions being considered and you, or you and your team, want to assess them in a clearly logical way, you may choose to use a **matrix assessment**. There are many types of matrices, but basically you want to judge the alternatives on the impor-

Hiring Criterion	Weighting of Criterion (1 low to 10 high)	Candidate 1 Sam	Candidate 2 Lorenzo	Candidate 3 Satwinder	Candidate 4 Reg	Candidate 5 Petra
Knowledge of SAP software (1 low to 10 high)	7	Score 1 X7 =7	Score 8 X7 =56	Score 10 X7 =49	Score 4 X7 =28	Score 6 X7 =42
Experience (two or more years) in related business (1 low to 10 high)	9	Score 3 X9 =27	Score 9 X9 =81	Score 10 X9 =90	Score 6 X9 =54	Score 7 X9 =63
"Fit" with team (1 low to 10 high)	10	Score 9 X10 =90	Score 6 X10 =60	Score 6 X10 =60	Score 3 X10 =30	Score 10 X10 =100
Degree None = 1 Bach=5 Masters = 10	3	Score 10 X3 =30	Score 5 X3 =15	Score 1 X3 =3	Score 5 X3 =15	Score 5 X3 =15
Willingness to travel and work unusual hours (1 low to 10 high)	10	Score 10 X10 =100	Score 9 X10 =90	Score 10 X10 =100	Score 7 X10 =70	Score 8 X10 =80
Total		254	302	302	197	310
Summary		4	2 (tied)	2 (tied)	5	1

FIGURE 4-5

Hiring decision matrix — the decision makers have determined the pertinent criteria and their weighting beforehand, then rate the candidates on each criterion, and combine the scores in the matrix to see who has the top score; that person should be the one recommended for the hire.

tant criteria and conclude with a priority ranking of those alternatives. You can set up whatever comparisons you want.

Two examples are provided. Figure 4-5 looks at how to choose among candidates for a position, having decided on what the hiring criteria should be and weighted them according to importance. Note that, as in most hiring situations, there are some strong candidates and others who are not as strong. The criteria end up being important in separating the top one from the two close behind.

The other matrix, Figure 4-6, looks at a ranking of continuous improvement initiatives, using predetermined criteria choosing, this time, not to weight the criteria to reflect their importance. Note that, although the structure provided by the matrix promotes a focus on the most important factors, it does not eliminate subjectivity. The actual scores of the choices on the criteria are still subjective judgements by the decision maker(s).

	Alternative Continuous Improvement Ideas			
	Train supervisors on supervisory skills	Top management holds monthly town hall meeting with employees	Redesign order form	Post weekly production results
Criterion				
Ease of doing (1 difficult to 10 easy)	5	8	7	9
Cost of doing (1 expensive to 10 inexpensie)	2	9	9	10
Assists in meeting department quality goal (1 low to 10 high)	5	1	2	3
Assists in achieving customer service goal (1 low to 10 high)	3	1	6	1
Improves team work (1 low to 10 high)	6	2	1	3
Total	21	21	25	26
Summary	3 (tied)	3 (tied)	2	1

FIGURE 4-6

Decision-making matrix to select continuous improvement initiatives (once ideas are generated, they are assessed regarding their relative ease and cost as well as their contributing to departmental goals).

CAUSE-AND-EFFECT DIAGRAMS (FISHBONE DIAGRAMS)

Cause-and-effect diagrams
Used to speculate on potential effects of taking an action, grouping the effects according to common categories.

In Chapter 3 on controlling, you read about using a **cause-and-effect diagram** to assist you in looking at the myriad of potential causes of a problem. This diagram (see Figure 4-7) can be used in a different way to determine what the effects of an action *will* be by reversing the setup of the fishbone—having the head to the left and the bones or arrows leading to the right and recording possible consequences of a planned action. By laying out these ideas, encouraging participants to look at many different subsets of consequences, it is more likely that the action's impact will be thoroughly explored.

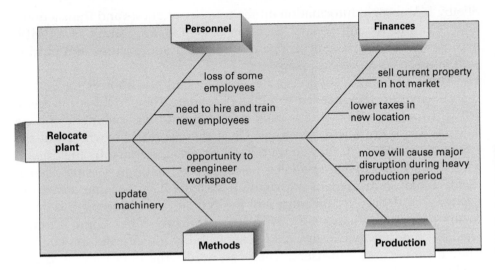

Sample cause-and-effect diagram. Start with proposed decision, then generate potential consequences to consider.

MANAGEMENT INFORMATION SYSTEMS

How can supervisors improve their ability to collect the information needed for assessing problems and for accurately evaluating alternatives? The answer is to learn to effectively use their organization's management information system.

A **management information system (MIS)** is a mechanism to provide managers with needed and accurate information on a regular and timely basis. It can be manual or computer-based, although recently almost all discussion of MIS focuses on computer-supported applications.

The term "system" in MIS implies order, arrangement, and purpose. Further, an MIS focuses specifically on providing management with information, not merely data. These two points are important and require elaboration.

A library provides a good analogy. Although it can contain millions of volumes, a library doesn't do users much good if they can't quickly find what they want. That's why libraries spend a lot of time cataloguing their collections and ensuring that volumes are returned to their proper locations. Organizations today are like well-stocked libraries. There is no scarcity of data. The limitation is in the ability to process it so that the right information is available to the right person when he or she needs it. An MIS has data organized in some meaningful way so you can access the information in a reasonable amount of time. Data are raw, unanalyzed facts such as names, numbers, or quantities. As data, these facts are relatively useless to managers. When data are analyzed and processed, they become information. An MIS collects data and turns them into relevant information for managers to use. The AMC Theatre software that gives

Management information system (MIS)
A mechanism to provide managers with needed and accurate information on a regular and timely basis.

Shelby D'Ambrogio information on the number of guests and transactions, auditorium levels and dollars spent per person is an example of an MIS, and allows her to make decisions on swapping auditoriums and cutting staff hours.

Thirty years ago, supervisors essentially had two choices for getting the information they needed to make decisions. They could get it themselves through crude methods such as looking in files, making telephone calls, asking questions in meetings. Or, if they worked anywhere but the smallest organization, they could rely on reports generated by the organization's data processing specialist or centralized data processing department. Today, management information systems have become decentralized; that is, decisions and control of the systems have been pushed down to the users (see Figure 4-8). With decentralization has come a major change—supervisors can now take responsibility for information control. They have become end-users. They can access the data they need and analyze that data on their personal computers. As a result, today's supervisors need to be knowledgeable about their information needs and accept responsibility for their systems' operations.

The good news is that sophisticated management information systems dramatically improve the quantity and quality of information available to supervisors, as well as the speed with which it can be obtained. Gone are the long delays between the appearance of a serious discrepancy and a supervisor's ability to find out about it. On-line, real-time systems allow supervisors to identify problems almost as they occur. Database management programs allow supervisors to look things up or get to the facts without either going to other people or digging through piles of paper. This reduces a supervisor's dependence on others for data and makes fact gathering far more efficient. Today's supervisor can identify alternatives quickly, evaluate those alternatives by using a spreadsheet program, pose a series of what-if questions, and finally select the best alternative on the basis of answers to those questions.

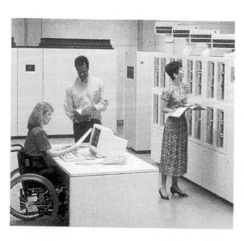

FIGURE 4-8

Thirty years ago, large mainframe computers drove an organization's MIS. Today, supervisors are end-users.
Courtesy of PhotoDisc, Inc.

DECISION-MAKING STYLES

Each of you brings your own unique personality and experiences to the decisions you make. For instance, if you're someone who is basically conservative and uncomfortable with uncertainty, you're likely to value decision alternatives differently from someone else who enjoys uncertainty and risk taking. These facts have led to research that has sought to identify individual decision styles.[1] To make the following discussion more personal, take 10 minutes to complete the Assessing Yourself questionnaire.

The basic foundation for a decision-style model is the recognition that people differ along two dimensions. The first is their way of thinking. Some people are logical and rational, and process information serially. In contrast, some people are intuitive and creative, and perceive things as a whole. The other dimension addresses a person's tolerance for ambiguity. Some people have a high need to structure information in ways that minimize ambiguity, while others are able to process many thoughts at the same time. When these two dimensions are diagrammed, they form four styles of decision making (see Figure 4-9). These are directive, analytic, conceptual, and behavioural.

DIRECTIVE STYLE

People using the directive style have low tolerance for ambiguity and seek rationality. They are efficient and logical. But their efficiency concerns result in their making decisions with minimal information and after assessing few alternatives. Directive types make decisions fast and they focus on the short run.

ANALYTIC STYLE

The analytic type has a much greater tolerance for ambiguity than does a directive manager. This leads to the desire for more information and consideration of more alternatives than is true for directives. Analytic managers

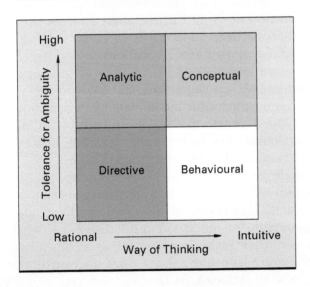

FIGURE 4-9

Decision-style model

would be best characterized as careful decision makers with the ability to adapt or cope with new situations.

CONCEPTUAL STYLE

Individuals with a conceptual style tend to be very broad in their outlook and consider many alternatives. Their focus is long range and they are very good at finding creative solutions to problems.

BEHAVIOURAL STYLE

The final category—the behavioural style—characterizes decision makers who work well with others. They're concerned with the achievement of subordinates. They're receptive to suggestions from others and rely heavily on meetings for communicating. This type of supervisor tries to avoid conflict and seeks acceptance.

SUMMARY

Although these four categories are distinct, most supervisors have characteristics that fall into more than one. So it's probably best to think in terms of a manager's dominant style and his or her backup styles. While some supervisors rely almost exclusively on their dominant style, more flexible supervisors can make shifts depending on the situation. Referring to the Assessing Yourself results, the box with the highest score reflects your dominant style. The closer a person is to a score of 75 in each category, the greater flexibility he or she shows.

Business students, supervisors, and senior executives tend to score highest in the analytic style. That's not surprising, given the emphasis that formal education, particularly business education, gives to developing rational decision-making skills. For instance, courses in accounting, statistics, and finance all stress analytical thinking.

Focusing on decision styles can be useful in helping you understand how two intelligent people, with access to the same information, can differ in the ways they approach decisions and in the final choices they make. It can also explain conflicts between supervisors and their subordinates. For example, the directive supervisor expects work to be performed rapidly and gets frustrated by the slowness and deliberate actions of a conceptual or analytic subordinate. At the same time, the analytic supervisor might criticize a decisive subordinate for incomplete work or acting too hastily. And the analytic supervisor will have great difficulty with his or her behavioural counterpart because of lack of understanding of why feelings rather than logic have been used as the basis for a decision.

The fact is, there is no single decision style ideal for all situations. All are valuable, and a combination of approaches to a decision situation is likely to yield a strong approach. This is one of the reasons why group decision making can be so powerful. "As much as I'm interested in giving my sense of direction, I also want their ideas. I approach it as a collaborative thing. Far more answers come from me asking what do you think rather than being top-down." (Garth Dallman, RCI)

WHAT'S YOUR DECISION-MAKING STYLE?

INSTRUCTIONS

1. Use the following numbers to answer each question:
   8: when the question is *most* like you.
   4: when the question is *moderately* like you.
   2: when the question is *slightly* like you.
   1: when the question is *least* like you.

2. Each of the numbers must be inserted in the box following the answers to each question.

3. *Do not* repeat any number on a given line.

4. For example, the numbers you might use to answer a given question could look as follows: 8 2 1 4

5. Notice that each number has been used only once in the answers for a given question.

6. In answering the questions, think of how you *normally* act in your work situation.

7. Use the first thing that comes to your mind when answering the question.

8. There is no time limit in answering the questions and there are no right or wrong answers.

9. Your responses reflect how you feel about the questions and what you prefer to do, not what you think might be the *right* thing to do.

Score the following questions based on the instructions given. Your score reflects how you see yourself, not what you believe is correct or desirable, as related to your work situation. It covers typical decisions that you make in your work environment.

		I		II		III		IV	
1.	My prime objective is to:	Have a position with status	☐	Be the best in my field	☐	Achieve recognition for my work	☐	Feel secure in my job	☐
2.	I enjoy jobs that:	Are technical & well defined	☐	Have a considerable variety	☐	Allow independent action	☐	Involve people	☐
3.	I expect people working for me to be:	Productive and fast	☐	Highly capable	☐	Committed and responsive	☐	Receptive to suggestions	☐

	I		II		III		IV	
4. In my job, I look for:	Practical results	☐	The best solutions	☐	New approaches or ideas	☐	Good working environment	☐
5. I communicate best with others:	In a direct one-to-one basis	☐	In writing	☐	By having a group discussion	☐	In a formal meeting	☐
6. In my planning I emphasize:	Current problems	☐	Meeting objectives	☐	Future goals	☐	Developing people's careers	☐
7. When faced with solving a problem, I:	Rely on proven approaches	☐	Apply careful analysis	☐	Look for creative approaches	☐	Rely on my feelings	☐
8. When using information I prefer:	Specific facts	☐	Accurate and complete data	☐	Broad coverage of many options	☐	Limited data which is easily understood	☐
9. When I am not sure about what to do, I:	Rely on intuition	☐	Search for facts	☐	Look for a possible compromise	☐	Wait before making a decision	☐
10. Whenever possible I avoid:	Long debates	☐	Incomplete work	☐	Using numbers or formulas	☐	Conflict with others	☐
11. I am especially good at:	Remembering dates & facts	☐	Solving difficult problems	☐	Seeing many possibilities	☐	Interacting with others	☐
12. When time is important, I:	Decide and act quickly	☐	Follow plans and priorities	☐	Refuse to be pressured	☐	Seek guidance or support	☐
13. In social settings I generally:	Speak with others	☐	Think about what is being said	☐	Observe what is going on	☐	Listen to the conversation	☐
14. I am good at remembering:	People's names	☐	Places we met	☐	People's faces	☐	People's personalities	☐
15. The work I do provides me:	The power to influence others	☐	Challenging assignments	☐	Achieving my personal goals	☐	Acceptance by the group	☐
16. I work well with those who are:	Energetic and ambitious	☐	Self-confident	☐	Open-minded	☐	Polite and trusting	☐
17. When under stress, I:	Become anxious	☐	Concentrate on the problem	☐	Become frustrated	☐	Am forgetful	☐
18. Others consider me:	Aggressive	☐	Disciplined	☐	Imaginative	☐	Supportive	☐
19. My decisions typically are:	Realistic and direct	☐	Systematic or abstract	☐	Broad & flexible	☐	Sensitive to the needs of others	☐
20. I dislike:	Losing control	☐	Boring work	☐	Following rules	☐	Being rejected	☐

SCORING THE DECISION-STYLE INVENTORY

1. Add the points in each of the four columns—I, II, III, IV.
2. The sum of the four columns should be 300 points. If your sum does not equal 300 points, check your addition and your answers.
3. Place your scores in the appropriate box—I, II, III, IV.

Analytic II	Conceptual III
Directive I	Behavioural IV

Source: A. J. Rowe, R. Mason, and K. Dickel, *Strategic Management and Business Policy.* Reading, MA: Addison-Wesley, 1982, p. 217. Reproduced by permission of Alan J. Rowe.

ETHICS IN DECISION MAKING

Decision making is a prime instance of an occasion when supervisors have to confront ethical concerns (see Dealing with a Difficult Issue). For instance, one alternative may generate a considerably higher financial return than the others but might be ethically questionable because it compromises employee safety.

Given an alternative that will make the supervisor look high profile but be relatively ineffective in the long run and another alternative that is much more promising for the company but low key for the supervisor, will the supervisor make the "right" choice? A supervisor may feel torn about dealing with an employee's poor performance—dealing with it in a proper coaching way that will take a lot of time or transferring the employee to a another part of the company where he will make someone else look bad.

Dealing with a Difficult Issue

HIRING A FRIEND

In making hiring decisions, supervisors often face difficult issues. Take the following situation:

Your company is advertising for a new employee to work in your department. The person in this position will be important because the work directly affects the quality and quantity of your performance. One of your friends needs a job and you think he is qualified for the position. But you feel you *could* find better qualified and more experienced candidates if you keep looking.

What would you do? What might influence your decision? Would you tell your friend? How do you handle this sensitive situation?

COMMON RATIONALIZATIONS

Through the ages, people have developed some common rationalizations to justify questionable conduct.[2] These rationalizations provide some insights into why supervisors might make poor ethical choices.

"It's not really *illegal or immoral."* Where is the line between being smart and being shady? Between an ingenious decision and an immoral one? Because this line is often ambiguous, people can rationalize that what they've done is not really wrong. If you put enough people in an ill-defined situation, some will conclude that whatever hasn't specifically been labelled as wrong must be acceptable, especially if there are rich rewards for attaining certain goals and the organization's appraisal system doesn't look too carefully at how those goals are achieved. The practice of profiting on a stock tip through insider information seems often to fall in this category.

"It's in my (or the organization's) best interest." The belief that unethical conduct is in a person's or an organization's best interests nearly always results from a narrow view of what those interests are. For instance, supervisors can come to believe that it's acceptable to bribe officials if the bribe results in the organization's getting a contract, or to falsify financial records if this improves their unit's performance record.

"No one will find out." This rationalization accepts the wrongdoing but assumes that it will never be uncovered. It is often stimulated by inadequate controls, strong pressures to perform, the appraisal of performance results while ignoring the means by which they're achieved, the allocation of big salary increases and promotions to those who achieve these results, and the absence of punishment for those who get caught.

"Since it helps the organization, the organization will condone it and protect me." This response represents loyalty gone berserk. Managers come to believe that not only do the organization's interests override the

laws and values of society, but also that the organization expects its employees to exhibit unqualified loyalty. Such managers believe that, even if he or she is caught, the organization will support and reward him or her for showing loyalty. Managers who use this rationalization to justify unethical practices place the organization's good name in jeopardy.

THREE DIFFERENT VIEWS ON ETHICS

In this section we will present three different ethical positions. They can help us to see how individuals can make different decisions by using different ethical criteria (see Figure 4-10).

THE UTILITARIAN VIEW

The first position is the **utilitarian view of ethics**, in which decisions are made solely on the basis of their outcomes or consequences. The goal of utilitarianism is to provide the greatest good for the greatest number. This view tends to dominate business decision making because it's consistent with the goals of efficiency, productivity, and high profits. By maximizing profits, for instance, a manager can argue that he or she is securing the greatest good for the greatest number.

Utilitarian view of ethics
Decisions are based solely on the basis of their outcomes; the goal is to provide the greatest good for the greatest number.

THE RIGHTS VIEW

Another ethical perspective is the **rights view of ethics**. This calls upon individuals to make decisions consistent with fundamental liberties and privileges as set forth in documents such as the Charter of Rights and Freedoms. The rights view of ethics is concerned with respecting and protecting the basic rights of individuals; for example, the right to privacy, free speech, and due process. This position would protect employees who report unethical or illegal practices by their organization to the press or government agencies on the grounds of their right to free speech.

Rights view of ethics
Decisions emphasize respecting and protecting the basic rights of individuals.

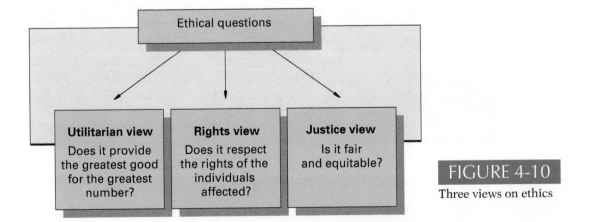

FIGURE 4-10

Three views on ethics

THE JUSTICE VIEW

Justice view of ethics
Decisions seek fair and
impartial distribution
of benefits and costs.

The final perspective is the **justice view of ethics.** This requires individuals to impose and enforce rules fairly and impartially so there is an equitable distribution of benefits and costs. Union members typically favour this view. It justifies paying people the same wage for a given job, regardless of performance differences, and it uses seniority as the criterion in making layoff decisions (see Figure 4-11).

DISCUSSION OF THE THREE VIEWS

The same decision can be judged very differently in terms of its ethics, depending on which of the three views is the basis of the judgement. For example, you may catch an employee going through the papers on another employee's desk after hours. Your reaction may be that it is an invasion of privacy, and therefore unethical (rights view). The employee may justify the action based on either of the other two views. For example, "Hey, she has locks on her desk and her filing cabinet. It's an open office area and she knows to lock anything away that is sensitive" (justice view). Or, "Look, here's the information I've been looking for. It's been holding me up and now I can get my report done, which is good for the whole department, right?" (utilitarian view).

FIGURE 4-11

The justice view suggests the junior employee gets laid off in tough times, even if a stronger performer than a senior employee, in a unionized organization.

Each of these three perspectives has advantages and liabilities. The utilitarian view promotes efficiency and productivity, but it can result in the rights of some individuals—particularly those with minority representation in the organization—being ignored. The rights perspective protects individuals from injury and is consistent with freedom and privacy, but it can create an overly legalistic work environment that hinders productivity and efficiency. The justice perspective protects the interests of the underrepresented and less powerful, but it can encourage a sense of entitlement that reduces risk taking, innovation, and productivity.

Even though each of these perspectives has its individual strengths and weaknesses, as we noted, managers in business tend to focus on utilitarianism. But times are changing and so too must supervisors and other managers. New trends toward individual rights and social justice mean that supervisors need ethical standards based on nonutilitarian criteria. This is a solid challenge to today's supervisor because making decisions using criteria such as individual rights and social justice involves far more ambiguities than using utilitarian criteria such as effects on efficiency and profits.

SOME ETHICAL DECISION GUIDES

There is no simple credo that we can provide to ensure that you won't err in your ethical judgements. What we can offer are some questions that you can—and should—ask yourself when making important decisions, or decisions with obvious ethical implications.[3]

1. How did this problem occur in the first place?
2. Would you define the problem differently if you stood on the other side of the fence?
3. To whom and to what do you give your loyalty as a person and as a member of your organization?
4. What is your intention in making this decision?
5. What is the potential for your intentions to be misunderstood by others in the organization?
6. How does your intention compare with the probable result?
7. Whom could your decision injure?
8. Can you discuss the problem with the affected parties before you make the decision?
9. Are you confident that your position will be as valid over a long period of time as it seems now?
10. Could you disclose your decision to your boss or your immediate family?
11. How would you feel if your decision was described, in detail, on the front page of your local newspaper?

FAIRNESS IN DECISION MAKING

The ethics of a decision could be judged partly on whether it is seen as fair. The perceived fairness of a decision is critical, regardless of the type of decision being made. If others perceive a decision as just and reasonable, they are much more likely to accept it and implement it, and less likely to resist. "It's important to be fair in this role. Especially sensitive areas include vacations, pay increases, workload, ensuring people get their say. Don't show any favouritism or preferential treatment. For example, in the allocation of tasks, divide it up, so the team shares between the crappy less visible jobs." (Ainslie White, Precision Biologic)

There are various kinds of fairness or justice: **distributive justice** (fairness in who gets what), **procedural justice** (fairness in how things are done) and **interactional justice** (fairness in how people are treated). All are important. If your manager gives your colleague a larger bonus than you and you feel it was well deserved based on performance (distributive justice), you may still react in a negative way to the decision because in announcing the bonuses, the manager belittled your work (low interactional justice). Or, if it became clear that the manager based the decision on favouritism and not on performance, you may still be angry about the decision even though you recognize the colleague did have a stronger performance than you.

How can a supervisor enhance the perceived fairness of decisions?

- Explain how decisions are made so the underlying rationale and process are clear.
- Be consistent in the way similar decisions are made.
- Involve those affected by a decision wherever possible, leading to greater information about the situation and acceptance of the ultimate decision.

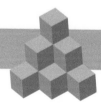

Building a Supervisory Skill

GUIDELINES FOR ACTING ETHICALLY AND COMPASSIONATELY

ABOUT THE SKILL

Ethical dilemmas Situations requiring one to define right and wrong conduct.

Making decisions can be difficult for supervisors when there seems to be an **ethical dilemma**. Yes, you must follow the law and you are supposed to follow the organization's rules and regulations. But do you want to discipline someone for leaving a little early from their shift when you know it's because they are going for cancer treatments? Should you recognize someone for an excellent report when you know they asked someone else to do most of the work even though you can't prove it?

As a supervisor you will face a lot of "grey" areas where you don't like what is happening but it isn't clear what you should do, if anything. For example, Marlene Roy at Winnipeg's Labour Market Information Unit of Human Resources Development Canada speaks of private consultants coming in to get specialized information from her office free of charge. What really irks her and her staff is that they know some of the consultants then go back to their clients and charge a lot of money for that information. Meanwhile, the client could have got the information for free if they had known. Her office therefore doesn't like dealing with those particular consultants. But do they have a choice, as a government information service?

Rob Mastrotto of Husky Injection Molding Systems says, "As bad as my day may be, it's sad to see how much personal misery some people have to endure outside of the workplace yet come into work in a high-pressure environment." If Rob knows these personal circumstances, can he allow this knowledge to affect the way he treats one employee compared to another?

Here are some guidelines for choosing what to do.

1. **Know your organization's policy on ethics.** Company policies on ethics, if they exist, describe what the organization perceives as ethical behaviour and what it expects you to do. This policy will help you clarify what is permissible for you to do—the managerial discretion you have. It will become your code of ethics to follow.

2. **Understand the ethics policy.** Just having the policy in your hand does not guarantee that it will achieve what it is intended to do. You need to fully understand it. Ethical behaviour is rarely a "cut and dried" process. With the help of the policy as a guiding light, you will have a basis from which to resolve ethical questions in the organization. Even if a policy doesn't exist, there are several steps you can take when confronted with a difficult situation.

3. **Think before you act.** Ask yourself, why are you doing what you're about to do? What led up to the problem? What is your true intention in taking some action? Is it for a valid reason, or are there ulterior motives behind it—such as demonstrating organizational loyalty? Will your action injure someone? Would you define the problem differently if you stood on the other side of the fence? Can you discuss the problem with the affected parties before you make the decision? Can you disclose to your manager or your family what you're going to do? Remember, it's your behaviour that will be seen in your actions. You need to make sure that you are not doing something that will jeopardize your role as a manager, your organization, or your reputation.

4. **Ask yourself "what if" questions.** When you think ahead about why you're doing something, you should also be asking yourself "what if" questions. For example, the following questions may help you shape your actions: What if you make the wrong decision—what will happen to you? To your job? What if your actions were described, in detail, on your local TV news or in the newspaper? Would it bother or embarrass you or those around you? What if you get caught doing something unethical? Are you prepared to deal with the consequences?

5. **Seek opinions from others.** If it is something major that you must do, and you're uncertain about it, ask for advice from other managers. Maybe they've been in a similar situation and can give you the benefit of their experiences. If not, maybe they can just listen and act as a sounding board for you.

6. **Do what you truly believe is right.** You have a conscience and you are responsible for your behaviour. Whatever you do, if you truly believe it is the right action to take, then what others say (or what the proverbial "Monday morning quarterbacks" say) is immaterial. You need to be true to your own ethical standards. Ask yourself: Can you live with what you've done?

GROUP DECISION MAKING

Decisions in organizations are increasingly being made by groups rather than by individuals. There seem to be at least two primary reasons for this. First is the desire to develop more and better alternatives. The adage "two heads are better than one" translates into groups being able to generate a greater number, and potentially a more creative set, of decision alternatives. We have already discussed that different decision making styles complement each other and yield better decisions. "As much as I'm interested in giving my sense of direction, I also want their ideas. I approach it as a collaborative thing. Far more answers come from me asking what do you think rather than being top-down." (Garth Dallman, RCI). Second, organizations are relying less on the historical idea that departments and other organizational units should be separate and independent decision units. To get the best ideas and to improve their implementation, organizations are increasingly turning over their decision making to teams that cut across traditional departmental lines. This choice requires group decision-making techniques (see Figure 4-12).

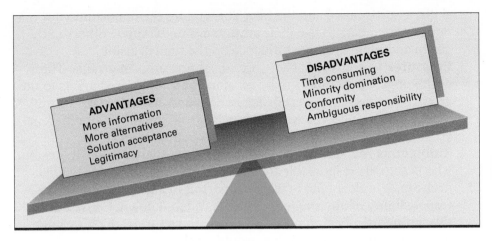

FIGURE 4-12

The advantages and disadvantages of group decision-making

Advantages and Disadvantages

Individual and group decisions each have their own set of strengths. Neither is ideal for all situations. Let's begin by reviewing the advantages that group decisions have over an individual decision maker.

1. **Provides more complete information.** A group will bring a diversity of experience and perspective to the decision process that an individual, acting alone, cannot.
2. **Generates more alternatives.** Because groups have a greater quantity and diversity of information, they can identify more alternatives than can an individual.
3. **Increases acceptance of a solution.** Many decisions fail after the final choice has been made because people do not accept the solution. If the people who will be affected by a certain solution and who will help implement it get to participate in the decision making itself, they will be more likely to accept the decision and to encourage others to accept it.
4. **Increases legitimacy.** The group decision-making process is consistent with democratic ideals and therefore may be perceived as more legitimate than decisions made by a single person.

If groups are so good, how did the phrase "A camel is a racehorse put together by a committee" become so popular? The answer, of course, is that group decisions are not without their drawbacks. The major disadvantages of group decision making are as follows

1. **Time consuming.** It takes time to assemble a group. Additionally, the interaction that takes place once the group is in place is frequently inefficient. The result is that groups almost always take more time to reach a solution than an individual making the decision alone.
2. **Minority domination.** Members of a group are never perfectly equal. They may differ in terms of rank in the organization, experience, knowledge about the problem, influence with other members, verbal

skills, assertiveness, and the like. This creates the opportunity for one or more members to use their advantages to dominate others in the group and impose undue influence on the final decision.

3. **Pressures to conform.** There are social pressures in groups. The desire of group members to be accepted and considered assets to the group can quash any overt disagreement and encourage conformity among viewpoints. The withholding by group members of different views in order to appear in agreement is called **groupthink.**

4. **Ambiguous responsibility.** Group members share responsibility, but who is actually responsible for the final outcome? In an individual decision, it is clear who is responsible, but in a group decision the responsibility of any single member is watered down. Conscious of this, group members may not give their full effort or think through the issue as thoroughly as they would on their own.

Groupthink
Group members withhold different views in order to appear to be in agreement.

A GUIDE TO WHEN TO USE GROUP DECISION MAKING

When are groups better than individuals and vice versa? That depends on what you mean by better. Let's look at four criteria frequently associated with "better" decisions: accuracy, speed, creativity, and acceptance.

Group decisions tend to be more accurate. The evidence indicates that, on the average, groups make more accurate decisions than individuals. This doesn't mean, of course, that all groups outperform every individual. Rather, group decisions have been found to be more effective than those that would have been reached by the average individual in the group. However, groups are seldom as good as the best individual.

If *better* is defined in terms of decision speed, individuals are superior. Group decision processes are characterized by give and take, a process that is often time-consuming.

Decision quality can also be assessed in terms of the degree to which a solution demonstrates creativity. If creativity is important, groups tend to do better than individuals. This requires, however, minimizing the forces that foster groupthink—pressure to repress doubts about the group's shared views or the validity of favoured arguments, excessive desire by the group to give an appearance of consensus, and the assumption that silence or abstention by members is a "yes" vote.

As noted previously, because group decisions have input from more people, they are likely to result in solutions that will have a higher degree of acceptance.

TYPES OF GROUP DECISION MAKING

The process used by a group to make a decision will influence the effectiveness of the decision. There is no single best process, though. The way the group should make its decision depends on the needs of the group as well as on the situation and on how much time is available.

The most commonly used method is **majority vote**. It offers the appeal of a democratic process and is as quick as it takes to get 51 percent of the members to agree. It can leave a powerful minority very dissatisfied, however. This can harm the implementation of the decision. Majority vote is fine if the decision is not a critical one and not worth spending a lot of time on. For instance, Larry Bowzeylo at Suncor in Fort McMurray believes in involving his people in decisions that affect them. They needed new Control Room chairs and he brought them three to try and recommend. From the 25 guys, he got three different recommendations out but one chair got 90% acceptance so they went with that one.

Deciding by **consensus** is highly desirable. If there is sufficient time, it provides the best decisions and the most commitment to the decision. And, in practice, reaching a consensus does not mean everyone agrees absolutely but that all members are willing to support the decision, knowing that everyone has been heard and the issues have been thoroughly addressed. This decision-making method is not often used, however. Not only does it take time but it takes effort and skill, particularly on the part of the chair, to keep the discussion progressing in a constructive way. Each morning Rod Guild, the senior shift supervisor at Highland Valley Copper mine in B.C., tours the two mine pits in a crew cab with engineers and the mine superintendent. The engineers have already created a mine plan for the day but the final decision is a joint decision of the five or six people in the truck. Rod's field experience is as respected as the engineers' theoretical knowledge. The final plan for mining is agreed upon by all of them by the end of the morning tour. Debbie Hinz's decision situation in the introductory chapter case illustrated Debbie using a consensus style. The team pact solution required the commitment of all.

Sometimes a group uses its power to turn the decision-making authority over to someone else. The group may choose someone deemed an **expert** to make the decision. That choice itself could be made via consensus or majority vote. A second form of decision referral is the use of minority vote. In its legitimate form, this involves assigning a decision to a committee made up of a few members of the larger group. Its illegitimate form occurs when a subgroup railroads a decision through, quickly forcing a decision before real debate can occur. In either expert decision or minority vote, the advantages include putting the decision in the hands of potentially more qualified people and at the same time freeing up time for the remainder of the group.

A final method of group decision making is **authority after discussion**. In this, the supervisor holds a full discussion with the whole group to hear their ideas and issues. Then the supervisor makes the final decision, which may or may not reflect the wishes of the group. In practice, this method is often similar to consensus because a group trend becomes apparent and the supervisor simply applies official approval. However, the supervisor may choose not to follow the group if the group's goals are not in the best interests of the organization.

Majority vote
Agreement to a decision by at least 51 percent of a group's members.

Consensus
Agreement to support a decision by all members of a group.

Decision by expert
Decision delegated to a person with special skill or knowledge in a particular field.

Decision by minority vote
Decision-making power held by a subgroup of a larger group.

Decision by authority after discussion
Decision-making by a group leader after weighing group members' opinions.

The choice of a specific approach will depend on what is needed by the situation but also on comfort level for the supervisor. Ron McLester, the Special Advisor to the Vice-President Student Services, Aboriginal Education & Student Services at Mohawk College in Hamilton, explains that he has tried different approaches and settled into one that is working for him. "In our language (Iroquois), "chief" means "he speaks for the people". I believe in a consensus style of management and that's what I strive for. Sometimes in meetings, the team will override my views. That's OK. When I started in management, I was too much into consensus and they pushed back, saying they needed someone to make decisions. So I flipped and became much more directive but that didn't work either. I think I now have found a middle ground where we work hard to decide together but I can and do make decisions that are needed at a management level."

Basically, it is a good idea to involve people in group decision making whenever there is time and the decision is pertinent to them. Group decision making as seen in Figure 4-13 can make the group more cohesive, can be an important forum for learning and sharing, and can improve motivation.

Whichever decision technique is used, it is likely that the context will often be a meeting conducted by you. And running a good meeting is a challenge, as you've probably discovered by attending meetings that were a waste of time. See "Building a Supervisory Skill: Conducting a Group Meeting" for guidance running meetings.

FIGURE 4-13

Meetings are a widely used, excellent vehicle for implementing decisions.
Courtesy of Dmitriy Shironosov/Shutterstock

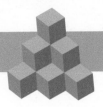

Building a Supervisory Skill

CONDUCTING A GROUP MEETING

ABOUT THE SKILL

Many supervisors report that they spend many hours a week in meetings. Many of these are called and run by others.

When it's your responsibility to conduct a meeting, do you know what to do? Experts say one-third of the time spent in meetings is a waste. What can you do to cut out that waste and make your meetings both efficient and effective? We'll provide you with the answers in this section.

STEPS IN PRACTISING THE SKILL

The following summarizes the key actions you should take as a leader to increase the likelihood that the meetings you conduct are run efficiently and effectively.

1. **Prepare a meeting agenda.** An agenda defines what you hope to accomplish at the meeting. It should state the meeting's purpose. Is the purpose only to exchange information or is it to make decisions? Will all relevant parties in the organization be included or merely their representatives? And if decisions are to be made, how are they to be arrived at? Will consensus be sought? If decisions are to be made by voting, what constitutes approval: a simple majority, a two-thirds majority? These issues should be clarified ahead of time. The agenda should also identify who will be in attendance; what, if any, preparation is required of each participant; a detailed list of items to be covered; the specific time and location of the meeting; and a specific finishing time.

2. **Distribute the agenda in advance.** If you want specific people to attend your meeting, and particularly if participants need to do some homework beforehand, get your agenda out well in advance of the meeting. What's an adequate lead time? That depends on such factors as the amount of preparation necessary, the importance of the meeting, and whether the meeting will be recurring or is being called once to deal with an issue that has arisen and will be repeated only under similar circumstances.

3. **Consult with participants before the meeting.** An unprepared participant can't contribute to his or her full potential. It is your responsibility to ensure that members are prepared. What data will they need ahead of time? Do they have that data? If not, what can you do to help them get it?

4. **Prepare your "stage."** Check the meeting location beforehand to ensure it is suited to the purpose and everything you need is there and in working order (e.g., projector, room not too hot or cold, extension cord). Consider whether you want to alter the seating arrangement, where it would be best for you and others to sit, and whether any refreshments should be available.

5. **Establish specific time parameters.** Meetings should begin on time and have a specific time for completion. It is your responsibility to specify these time parameters and to hold to them.

6. **Maintain focused discussion.** As chairperson, it is your responsibility to give direction to the discussion; to keep it focused on the issues; and to minimize interruptions, disruptions, and irrelevant comments. If participants begin to stray from the issue under consideration, intercede quickly to redirect the discussion. Similarly, one or a few members cannot be allowed to monopolize the discussion or to dominate others. Appropriate preventive action can range from a subtle stare, a raised eyebrow, or other nonverbal communication, on up to an authoritative command such as ruling someone "out of order" or withdrawing someone's right to continue speaking.

7. **Encourage and support participation by all members.** Participants were not selected randomly. Each is there for a purpose. To maximize the effectiveness of problem-oriented meetings, each participant must be encouraged to contribute. Quiet or reserved personalities must be drawn out so their ideas can be heard.

8. **Maintain a balanced style.** You need to exert the appropriate level of control. The style of leadership can range from authoritative domination to laissez-faire. The effective group leader pushes when necessary and is passive when need be.

9. **Encourage the clash of ideas.** You need to encourage different points of view, critical thinking, and constructive disagreement. Your goals should be to stimulate participants' creativity and to counter the group members' desire to reach an early consensus.

10. **Discourage the clash of personalities.** An effective meeting is characterized by the critical assessment of ideas, not attacks on people. When running a meeting, you must quickly intercede to stop personal attacks or other forms of verbal insult.

11. **Exhibit effective listening skills.** If your group meeting is to achieve its objectives, you need to listen actively rather than passively. Do whatever is necessary to get the full intended meaning from a speaker's comments. Effective listening reduces misunderstandings, improves the focus of discussion, and encourages the critical assessment of ideas.

Even if other group members don't exhibit good listening skills, you can keep the discussion focused on the issues and facilitate critical thinking if you listen well.

12. **Bring proper closure.** Close a meeting by summarizing the group's accomplishments; clarifying what actions, if any, need to follow the meeting; and allocating follow-up assignments. If any decisions have been made, you also need to determine who will be responsible for communicating and implementing them. Formal minutes recording actions and commitments can be distributed.

SUGGESTIONS FOR OVERCOMING OBSTACLES AT A MEETING

The Talker. If the person's points are on topic, tactfully interrupt, summarize the person's point, and ask for others to comment on it. If the person is discussing an issue off-topic, interrupt, make a positive comment on what the person was discussing, for example, "I wish we had time to discuss that right now but we have to...", and steer the discussion back to the proper focus.

Chit-Chat on the Sidelines. If the private conversation continues for more than a short time and seems to be distracting others, call one of the people by name, asking for their contribution on the point being discussed, or confront him or her tactfully on whether there is something you have missed that they wish to bring to your attention. Or, you may think it most suitable to make a joke about their conversation, for example, "Hey, you two, we know you haven't seen each other in two weeks since your offices were moved but we'd like to get in on the reunion, too."

The Silent Meeting Member. Ask that person specifically for their input, remembering to word it as an open question rather than closed so they cannot respond with a one-word answer. You may refer to something you know the person has done or said pertinent to the topic and draw him or her into the discussion in that way.

The Critic. If someone makes non-productive comments, you may discourage further comments by simply ignoring them. If that doesn't work, ask the person for a positive suggestion or specific proof for their criticism. For example, "You say that won't work. We've discussed specific situations where it has worked in the past. I'd like to hear about specific negative instances so I can understand your pessimism." Or, "Yes, you're right, that would cost a lot the way we have been picturing it. Do you see a way to achieve the same objective without it costing so much?"

TECHNIQUES FOR IMPROVING GROUP DECISION MAKING

When group members physically confront and interact with one another, they create the potential for groupthink. They can censor themselves and pressure other group members into agreement. There are three techniques that you might want to consider as ways to stimulate creativity in group decision making.

BRAINSTORMING

Brainstorming
An idea-generation process that specifically encourages any and all alternatives while withholding any criticism of those alternatives.

Brainstorming is a relatively simple technique for overcoming pressures for conformity that can retard the development of creative alternatives. It achieves this by using an idea-generating process that actively encourages any and all alternatives while withholding any criticism of those alternatives.

In a typical brainstorming session, group members sit around a table. The group leader states the problem in a clear manner so it is understood by all participants. Members then "freewheel" as many alternatives as they can in a given time. No criticism is allowed, and all the alternatives are recorded for later discussion and analysis.

Brainstorming, however, is merely a process for generating ideas, not for choosing among them. The next techniques go further by offering ways to arrive at a preferred solution.

NOMINAL GROUP TECHNIQUE

Nominal group technique
A group decision technique where all members are present but operate independently.

The nominal group restricts discussion during the decision-making process, hence the term **nominal group technique**. Group members are all physically present, as in a traditional committee meeting, but the members are required to operate independently. Specifically, the following steps take place:

1. Members meet as a group; however, before any discussion takes place, each member independently writes down his or her ideas on the problem.
2. This silent period is followed by each member presenting one idea to the group. Each member takes his or her turn, going around the table, presenting one idea at a time until all ideas have been presented and recorded (typically on a flip chart or chalkboard). No discussion takes place until all ideas have been recorded.
3. The group now discusses the ideas for clarity and evaluates them.
4. Each group member silently and independently assigns a rank to the ideas. The final decision is determined by choosing the idea with the highest aggregate ranking (i.e., majority vote).

Because the rankings are confidential, members are less likely to experience groupthink or the pressure to conform.

DELPHI TECHNIQUE

A more complex and time-consuming alternative is the **Delphi technique**, which is similar to the nominal group technique except that it doesn't require the physical presence of group members. This is because the Delphi technique never allows the group members to meet face to face. The following steps characterize the Delphi technique:

1. The problem is identified, and members are asked to provide potential solutions through a series of carefully designed questionnaires.
2. Each member anonymously and independently completes the first questionnaire.
3. Results of the first questionnaire are compiled at a central location, transcribed, and reproduced.
4. Each member receives a copy of the results.
5. After reviewing the results, members are again asked for their solutions. The results typically trigger new solutions or cause changes in the original position.
6. Steps 4 and 5 are repeated as often as necessary until consensus is reached.

In this technique there is a gradual evolution of ideas with the benefit of individual contributions and group feedback. However, it misses the energy and speed of meetings that allow synchronous discussions (See Something to Think About).

Delphi technique
A group decision technique where members independently and anonymously contribute to a group "discussion" through systematic compilation of their thoughts.

SOMETHING TO THINK ABOUT
• A N D   T O   P R O M O T E   C L A S S   D I S C U S S I O N •

NEW WAYS OF MEETING

Increasing numbers of people are "meeting" at a distance. They may use conference calls to do this or a tool like Skype that allows visual contact as well as voice. A third option is to use a digital tool like Collaborate that allows voice and visual contact but also allows the sharing of documentation so people can work collaboratively on the same information.

What are the advantages? It saves travel time and costs and supports sustainability efforts. Meetings tend to start on time and have much less socializing. It is harder to have personal chats off to the side of the meeting.

What are the potential disadvantages? It is more difficult to develop relationships with people through these means if they are not complemented by opportunities to meet face to face. Technical problems can be a diversion and can prevent participation. Some are still uncomfortable with using technology to meet and prefer to be in the same room seeing people face to face.

Have you had experience with any of these types of meetings at work or on school projects? What did you think? Do the same recommendations about how to run an efficient meeting apply to these types?

FIGURE 4-14

Courtesy of Dan Krauss/Stringer/Getty Images

PART 2   PLANNING AND CONTROL

160

A CHANGING WORK WORLD WILL AFFECT DECISION MAKING

The Conference Board of Canada's study—Navigating Through the Storm: Leaders and the World of Work in 2020[4]—predicted major changes that leaders need to understand now:

- Boomers won't leave. Generations will mix.
- Visible minorities will be on the verge of becoming the majority in urban workplaces.
- We will all be linked to work, through technology, whether we want to be or not.
- The office will be where we say it is.
- Social media will be the community halls of the future, where work can be done collaboratively.
- Real companies will have virtual locations.
- Management will be pushed down and out as organizations decentralize.
- Contingent workers (including contractors, part-time, casual and seasonal workers) and volunteers will become unconditionally important.
- Teamwork will be a learned skill, not just a nice attitude.

What will be the effect of these changes on decision making in organizations?

CREATIVE PROBLEM SOLVING

ASSESSING YOURSELF: HOW CREATIVE ARE YOU?

How creative are you? The following test helps determine if you have the personality traits, attitudes, values, motivations, and interests that comprise creativity. It is based on several years' study of attributes possessed by men and women in a variety of fields and occupations who think and act creatively.

INSTRUCTIONS

For each statement, write in the appropriate letter:

>   A = Agree
>   B = Undecided or Don't Know
>   C = Disagree

Be as frank as possible. Try not to second-guess how a creative person might respond.

____ 1. I always work with a great deal of certainty that I am following the correct procedure for solving a particular problem.

____ 2. It would be a waste of time for me to ask questions if I had no hope of obtaining answers.

____ 3. I concentrate harder on whatever interests me than do most people.

____ 4. I feel that a logical step-by-step method is best for solving problems.

____ 5. In groups I occasionally voice opinions that seem to turn some people off.

____ 6. I spend a great deal of time thinking about what others think of me.

____ 7. It is more important for me to do what I believe to be right than to try to win the approval of others.

____ 8. People who seem uncertain about things lose my respect.

___ 9. More than other people, I need to have things interesting and exciting.

___ 10. I know how to keep my inner impulses in check.

___ 11. I am able to stick with difficult problems over extended periods of time.

___ 12. On occasion I get overly enthusiastic.

___ 13. I often get my best ideas when doing nothing in particular.

___ 14. I rely on intuitive hunches and the feeling of "rightness" or "wrongness" when moving toward the solution of a problem.

___ 15. When problem solving, I work faster when analyzing the problem and slower when synthesizing the information I have gathered.

___ 16. I sometimes get a kick out of breaking the rules and doing things I am not supposed to do.

___ 17. I like hobbies that involve collecting things.

___ 18. Daydreaming has provided the impetus for many of my more important projects.

___ 19. I like people who are objective and rational.

___ 20. If I had to choose from two occupations other than the one I now have, I would rather be a physician than an explorer.

___ 21. I can get along more easily with people if they belong to about the same social and business class as myself.

___ 22. I have a high degree of aesthetic sensitivity.

___ 23. I am driven to achieve high status and power in life.

___ 24. I like people who are most sure of their conclusions.

___ 25. Inspiration has nothing to do with the successful solution of problems.

___ 26. When I am in an argument, my greatest pleasure would be for the person who disagrees with me to become a friend, even at the price of sacrificing my point of view.

___ 27. I am much more interested in coming up with new ideas than in trying to sell them to others.

___ 28. I would enjoy spending an entire day alone, just "chewing the mental cud."

___ 29. I tend to avoid situations in which I might feel inferior.

___ 30. In evaluating information, the source is more important to me than the content.

___ 31. I resent things being uncertain and unpredictable.

___ 32. I like people who follow the rule, "business before pleasure."

___ 33. Self-respect is much more important than the respect of others.

___ 34. I feel that people who strive for perfection are unwise.

___ 35. I prefer to work with others in a team effort rather than solo.

___ 36. I like work in which I must influence others.

___ 37. Many problems that I encounter in life cannot be resolved in terms of right or wrong solutions.

___ 38. It is important for me to have a place for everything and everything in its place.

___ 39. Writers who use strange and unusual words merely want to show off.

Below is a list of terms that describe people. Choose ten words that best characterize you.

❏ energetic	❏ alert
❏ persuasive	❏ curious
❏ observant	❏ organized
❏ fashionable	❏ unemotional
❏ self-confident	❏ clear-thinking
❏ persevering	❏ understanding
❏ original	❏ dynamic
❏ cautious	❏ self-demanding
❏ habit-bound	❏ polished
❏ resourceful	❏ courageous
❏ egotistical	❏ efficient
❏ independent	❏ helpful
❏ stern	❏ perceptive
❏ predictable	❏ quick
❏ formal	❏ good-natured
❏ informal	❏ thorough

❑ dedicated   ❑ impulsive

❑ forward-looking   ❑ determined

❑ factual   ❑ realistic

❑ open-minded   ❑ modest

❑ tactful   ❑ involved

❑ inhibited   ❑ absent-minded

❑ enthusiastic   ❑ flexible

❑ innovative   ❑ sociable

❑ poised   ❑ well liked

❑ acquisitive   ❑ restless

❑ practical   ❑ retiring

Source: Eugene Raudsepp, President, Princeton Creative Research, Inc. Reprinted by permission from *How Creative Are You?* (1981). First published by Perigee Books.

SCORING DIRECTIONS

To compute your score, circle and add up the values assigned to each item. The values are as follows:

	A Agree	B Undecided or Don't Know	C Disagree		A Agree	B Undecided or Don't Know	C Disagree
1.	0	1	2	21.	0	1	2
2.	0	1	2	22.	3	0	-1
3.	4	1	0	23.	0	1	2
4.	-2	0	3	24.	-1	0	2
5.	2	1	0	25.	0	1	3
6.	-1	0	3	26.	-1	0	2
7.	3	0	-1	27.	2	1	0
8.	0	1	2	28.	2	0	-1
9.	3	0	-1	29.	0	1	2
10.	1	0	3	30.	-2	0	3
11.	4	1	0	31.	0	1	2
12.	3	0	-1	32.	0	1	2
13.	2	1	0	33.	3	0	-1
14.	4	0	-2	34.	-1	0	2
15.	-1	0	2	35.	0	1	2
16.	2	1	0	36.	1	2	3
17.	0	1	2	37.	2	1	0
18.	3	0	-1	38.	0	1	2
19.	0	1	2	39.	-1	0	2
20.	0	1	2				

40. The following have values of 2:

energetic	dynamic	perceptive	dedicated
resourceful	flexible	innovative	courageous
original	observant	self-demanding	curious
enthusiastic	independent	persevering	involved

The following have values of 1:

self-confident	determined	informal	forward-looking
thorough	restless	alert	open-minded

The rest have values of 0.

TOTAL SCORE

95–116	Exceptionally creative		20–39	Average
65–94	Very creative		10–19	Below average
40–64	Above average		Below 10	Noncreative

SKILL BASICS

There's good news on the creativity front! Most of us have creative potential, but we get into psychological ruts. In this skill module, we want to show you how you can unleash your creative problem-solving talent.

CHARACTERISTICS OF THE EXCEPTIONALLY CREATIVE PERSON

Let's begin with the obvious. People differ in their inherent creativity. Einstein, Picasso, and Mozart were individuals of exceptional creativity. What personality characteristics do the exceptionally creative share? Generally they are independent, risk-taking, persistent, and highly motivated. They're also nonconformists who can be hard to get along with. Additionally, highly creative individuals prefer complex and unstructured tasks. Disorder doesn't make them anxious.

How widespread is exceptional creativity? Not very! A study of lifetime creativity of 461 men and women found that fewer than one per cent were exceptionally creative.[5] But 10 percent were highly creative and about 60 percent were somewhat creative. As you'll see, even if you didn't score in the exceptionally creative category on the self-assessment exercise, there are ways to improve your potential.

THE ORGANIZATION MATTERS

Your creative potential is also influenced by characteristics of the organization in which you work. For instance, rigidly structured organizations that inhibit communication between departments tend to limit creativity.

Every organization has a culture. This organizational culture represents a shared perception of the organization's values. It's sort of an organizational equivalent of an individual's personality. That is, just as some people are open, or aggressive, or controlling, so too are organizations. The difference is that in organizational culture, all members of the organization tend to share a common understanding about the organization, how things are done in it, and the way members are supposed to behave. Certain organizational cultures can restrict creativity. Specifically, these are cultures that punish risk-taking and failure, and reward excessive loyalty and conformity. Creative cultures promote interaction and experimentation.

STIMULATING YOUR CREATIVITY

Creativity is the ability to combine ideas in a unique way to make unusual associations between them. Each of us has the ability to be creative, yet some use their creativity more than others. Although creative people are sometimes referred to as "artsy," and their precise characteristics are difficult to describe, there are certain steps you can take in becoming more creative.[6]

1. **Think of yourself as creative.** Although it's a simple suggestion, research shows that if you think you can't be creative, you won't be. Just as the little train in the children's fable says, "I think I can," if we believe in ourselves, we can become more creative.

2. **Pay attention to your intuition.** Everyone has a subconscious mind that works well. Sometimes answers come when we least expect them. For example, when you are about to go to sleep, your relaxed mind sometimes comes up with solutions to problems you face. You need to listen to this intuition. In fact, many creative people keep a note pad near their bed and write down those "great" ideas when they come to them. That way, they are not forgotten.

3. **Move away from your comfort zone.** Every individual has a comfort zone in which certainty exists. But creativity and the known often don't mix. To be creative, we need to move away from the status quo, and focus on something new.

4. **Engage in activities that put you outside your comfort zone.** Not only must we think differently, we need to do things differently. By engaging in activities that are different to us, we challenge ourselves. For example, learning to play a musical instrument or learning a foreign language may open the mind up and allows it to be challenged.

5. **Seek a change of scenery.** As humans, we are creatures of habit. Creative people force themselves out of their habits by changing their scenery. Going into a quiet and serene area where you can be alone with your thoughts is a good way to enhance creativity.

6. **Find several right answers.** Just as we set boundaries in rationality, we often seek solutions that are only good enough. Being creative means continuing to look for other solutions, even when you think you have solved the problem. A better, more creative solution just might be found.

7. **Play your own devil's advocate.** Challenging yourself to defend your solutions helps you develop confidence in your creative efforts. Second guessing may also help you find more correct answers.

8. **Believe in finding a workable solution.** Like believing in yourself, you also need to believe in your ideas. If you don't think you can find a solution, one won't be found. Having a positive mental attitude, however, may become a self-fulfilling prophecy.

9. **Brainstorm with others.** Creativity is not an isolated activity. By bouncing ideas off others, a synergistic effect occurs.

10. **Turn creative ideas into action.** Coming up with ideas is only half of the process. Once the ideas are generated, they must be implemented. Great ideas that remain in someone's mind, or on papers that no one reads, do little to expand one's creative abilities.

APPLYING YOUR SKILLS

Form groups of four or five. You are a committee of employees at the student centre on campus. The centre has several fast-food franchises and a pub. The centre is doing well but analysis of the statistics reveals that much of that success is due to strong liquor and beer sales in the pub. This concerns the committee because the student mix on campus is changing. There are now many more mature students, who don't spend nearly as much on liquor and beer as the younger students. In fact, the mature students are much less likely to spend time in the student centre.

You have 30 minutes for your committee to develop a list of ideas for how the student centre can attract more of the older students, both to "hang out" and mix with the other students, and to spend their money there. Be prepared to discuss a) your top three recommendations, and b) what your committee believes to be its most creative option.

SUMMARY

This summary is organized by the Learning Objectives.

1. A programmed decision is a simple, routine matter for which there is an established decision rule. A nonprogrammed decision is a complex, nonroutine decision requiring a creative solution.

2. The eight steps in the decision-making process are: 1. identify the problem; 2. define the objective and decision criteria. 3. collect relevant information; 4. develop alternatives; 5. evaluate each alternative; 6. select the best alternative; 7. implement the decision; 8. follow up and evaluate.

3. Expected value analysis calculates the expected value of a particular alternative by weighting its possible outcomes by the probability of achieving the alternative, then summing up the totals derived from the weighting process.

4. Decision trees are a device for analyzing decisions that involve a progression of decisions. They help decision makers visualize key decision points and outcomes.

5. Data are raw, unanalyzed facts. Data become information when they are analyzed and processed. It is information that is most relevant for making informed decisions.

6. There are four types of decision styles. The directive type is efficient and logical. The analytic type is careful, with the ability to adapt or cope with new situations. The conceptual type considers many alternatives and is good at coming up with creative solutions. The behavioural type emphasizes suggestions from others and conflict avoidance.

7. The utilitarian view of ethics makes decisions based on the greatest good for the greatest number. The rights view of ethics makes decisions consistent with fundamental liberties and privileges. The justice view of ethics seeks fairness and impartiality.

8. Group decisions are based on more complete information, more alternatives, increased acceptance of a solution, and increased legitimacy. Individual decisions take less time, have clear accountability and are not subject to pressures to conform.

9. Techniques for improving group decision making include brainstorming, nominal group technique and Delphi technique.

UNDERSTANDING THE BASICS

KEY TERMS AND CONCEPTS

Brainstorming
Cause-and-effect diagram
Consensus
Creativity
Decision by authority
    after discussion
Decision by expert
Decision by minority vote
Decision trees
Delphi technique
Distributive justice
Ethical dilemma
Expected value analysis
Gap analysis
Groupthink

Interactional justice
Justice view of ethics
Majority vote
Management information system
Marginal analysis
Matrix assessment
Nominal group technique
Nonprogrammed decision
Problem
Procedural justice
Programmed decision
Risk analysis
Rights view of ethics
Utilitarian view of ethics

REVIEWING YOUR KNOWLEDGE

1. In which step of the decision-making process do you think creativity would be most helpful? In which step would quantitative analysis tools be most helpful?
2. Discuss the emotional element to decision making.
3. Calculate your estimated grade average this term using expected value analysis.
4. What is meant by the expression "supervisors are increasingly becoming end-users in MIS"?
5. How might certain decision styles fit better with specific jobs? Give examples.
6. What rationalizations do people use to justify questionable conduct?
7. Which view of ethics dominates in business firms? Why?
8. When should managers use groups for decision making? When should they use individuals?
9. Contrast the nominal group technique and Delphi technique.

CASE 4.A

Wendy Chiu

Wendy Chiu is the President and Managing Director of Katalogic Inc., Human Resource Systems Outsourcing and Consulting Specialists. As the president of a small company she is involved in both strategic decisions and operational, day-to-day decisions like working with clients on special projects.

"One of the toughest parts of being in management is finding a balance between relationship/emotional decisions and logical business decisions. When I like someone I want to hire them even if I know they don't have the skills I need—I want to give them a chance. I sometimes have a hard time delivering bad news. Because I get emotionally attached to people it can take me a long time to make some decisions. I sometimes delay if I know the right decision is not what they want to hear. I know bad decisions are made on emotion (like hiring the wrong person). On the other hand, when I have tried to toughen up I have sometimes overcompensated and been seen as cold. This issue transcends across how I manage employees to how I deal with customers. There's a lot to be gained from having good relationships with customers, but then there is the temptation to give away too much. Yet customers may not respond well when charged for something they weren't expecting because you have developed a friendly relationship.

I have learned over the years that I need to take time and talk myself through these conflicting situations. I do not make any sudden decisions when I am feeling torn between the business side and the people side. For example, I laid off someone a year ago due to their insufficient skills. The person approached me recently looking to be rehired and I was tempted because I like the person. I needed a few weeks time to talk out the situation with others who were involved and to remind myself about the business decision I made and to stick to it."

RESPONDING TO THIS CASE

1. Explain what aspects of the eight-step decision making process Wendy is forcing herself to consider when she takes the time to talk herself through these conflicting situations.
2. Suggest how Wendy could benefit from using one of the decision tools in making the decision regarding the laid off worker.
3. Based on what you have read in the case and on the fact that Wendy is the president of a successful company, what decision style or styles would you say are likely typical of her? Why?
4. Wendy refers to talking through the hiring situation with others who are involved in order to help to make the decision. Considering the advantages and disadvantages of group decision making, is this appropriate? Why or why not?
5. What does this case suggest to you about the emotional aspects of decisions—both the value and the cautions?

FIGURE 4-15
Wendy Chiu

CASE 4.B

How Can You Make the Decision?

You have just moved to Mississauga from Fredericton for your spouse to accept a new position. In response to a Workopolis ad, you applied for a position running a storefront business centre that supplies photocopying, printing, and other services for local businesses. It is a very busy place, staffed by four people. The owner has been managing the business until hiring you to take over. He has decided to concentrate on two other businesses he is running. Although you have never run a business exactly like this one, you have been an office manager as well as a retail manager in a computer store, and you are familiar with all the services offered in this business. You are very familiar with typical business software and your supervisory skills are strong.

You decide to spend your first week learning as much as possible about the state of this business and figuring out what is needed. At the end of this time, your list of observations includes the following:

The scheduling of staff did not cover the peak customer times adequately.

Two of the four staff seem to know their customers very well, having strong and friendly relationships; one seems to be knowledgeable but is much quieter, not chatting with either customers or other staff; the fourth staff person seems to find anything to do that involves working on her own and avoiding both staff and customers; there appears to be tension between that person and the two sociable staff members.

The good customer relationships seem to be in spite of an apparent problem in getting work orders done on time; staff appear to make unrealistic promises.

Equipment seems to be needing replacement, judging by the amount of downtime and the recent repair costs you have found in examining the books.

You find the organization of inventory inappropriate; it is difficult to find some things, items that relate are not shelved together, some stock is split into two storage areas, making it difficult to ascertain inventory levels.

The staff members turn to you for approval for many of their actions; this puzzles you as they obviously have more experience in this environment and many of the approvals seem a silly waste of time; you guess that the owner demanded to check everything and they expect you to do the same.

You know a lot needs to be done in the store.

RESPONDING TO THIS CASE

1. What decisions need to be made?
2. What decision-making methods and/ or tools from the chapter would be appropriate?
3. What decision-making methods or tools from the chapter would not be appropriate?
4. As a new manager, what do you want to achieve in the next few months in addition to getting the store into better shape? How do these aims influence your choice of how to approach decision making?

PART THREE

ORGANIZING, STAFFING, AND EMPLOYEE DEVELOPMENT

5. ORGANIZING AN EFFECTIVE DEPARTMENT

6. ACQUIRING THE RIGHT PEOPLE

7. DEVELOPING YOUR EMPLOYEES

8. PERFORMANCE MANAGEMENT AND APPRAISAL

5

ORGANIZING AN EFFECTIVE DEPARTMENT

Courtesy of Dmitriy Shironosov/Shutterstock

LEARNING OBJECTIVES

After reading this chapter, you should be able to:

1. Define organizing.
2. Describe why division of labour can increase economic efficiency.
3. Explain how the span of control affects an organization's structure.
4. Contrast line and staff authority.
5. Explain why organizations are increasingly becoming decentralized.
6. Describe functional departmentalization.
7. Identify the strengths and weaknesses of the matrix.
8. Explain the value of job descriptions.
9. Identify the four-step process of delegation.

CHAPTER OUTLINE

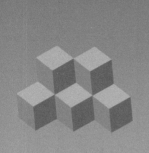

Susan Miller is the vice president of Enbridge Technology, an international engineering consulting firm. The firm is headquartered in Edmonton with Enbridge Pipelines, but has staff working all over the world. There are 14 full-time employees in the organization but up to 50 contract people can also be working at any given time. Shortly after Susan's move to Enbridge Technology, she reported to her boss that it looked like it was imploding, in that parts of the company were working against each other. Despite the fact that all employees were supposed to be working together for the success of the company, Susan found that they were actually divided into three silos (training, advising, and engineering) that communicated poorly and failed to cooperate. Susan believed that this internal competition was hurting the company and she undertook a reorganization to create a team. As a result, there was turnover. Most people moved to Enbridge's operating divisions, and some were laid off. The new "green" team started with a team focus. All individual performance indicators were removed from performance appraisals. Instead, the focus became corporate goals and team achievement.

As you can see, the way in which people are grouped has an impact on the organization. It creates loyalties, lines of communication and cooperation, and barriers, too. Often, the supervisor has no choice as to the grouping or structure. The supervisor of a unit must work within the opportunities and restrictions created by that structure. The structure itself can influence the unit's activity and effectiveness, as Susan observed at Enbridge Technology. A supervisor can, however, sometimes affect the organization of his or her subordinates through, for example, an influence on job descriptions, or through exerting effort to turn the work group into a team.

When we examine the impact of structure, many questions arise. How many people can one person supervise effectively? When does the supervisor have authority to make a decision? What tasks can a supervisor delegate? These are all dependent on the organization of the company. This chapter examines the basics of organization within a company and within a department, and looks at ways in which organizational structures are changing.

In the 1920s and 1930s, as organizations got bigger and more formal, supervisors felt a need to provide more coordination of activities and tighter control over operations. Early business researchers argued that formal bureaucracies would best serve the company—and that was true many years ago. These bureaucratic structures flourished. By the 1980s, the world began to change drastically. The global marketplace, rapid technological advancements, diversity in the workforce, and socioeconomic conditions made these formal bureaucracies inefficient for many businesses. As a result, many organizations have restructured to be more customer- and market-oriented, and to increase productivity.

It is critical today for an organization to have the right structure. Although setting up the organization's structure is typically done by senior management in an organization (or the owner in a small business), it is important for all organizational members to understand how these structures work. Why? Because you'll understand your job better if you know why you're "arranged" as you are. For example, how many people can you effectively supervise? When do you have authority to make a decision and when is it merely advice that you're providing? What tasks can you delegate to others? Will you supervise employees who produce a specific product? Will your department exist to serve a particular customer, a geographic region, or some combination of these? You'll see how to find the answers to questions like these in this chapter. We'll look at the traditional components that go into developing an organization's structure, discuss the various ways that employees may be grouped, and look at how organizational structures change over time.

WHAT IS ORGANIZING?

Organizing is arranging and grouping jobs, allocating resources, and assigning work in a department so that activities can be accomplished as planned. The senior management team in an organization typically establishes the overall organization structure. They'll determine, for instance, how many layers there will be in the organizational chart (e.g., number of management levels). They will also decide the extent to

Organizing
Arranging and grouping jobs, allocating resources, and assigning work in a department so that activities can be accomplished as planned.

which lower-level managers will have to follow formal rules and procedures in carrying out their jobs. In large corporations, it's not unusual for there to be five to eight levels from top to bottom; hundreds of departments; and dozens of manuals (for example, purchasing, human resources, accounting, engineering, maintenance, sales) that define procedures, rules, and policies within departments. Once the overall structure is in place, individual supervisors will need to organize their departments. In this chapter, we'll show you how to do that.

Keep in mind that our discussion here is with the formal arrangement of jobs and groups of jobs. These are defined by management. In addition, individuals and groups will develop informal alliances that are neither formally structured nor organizationally determined. Almost all employees in all organizations develop these informal arrangements to meet their needs for social contact. We'll discuss informal groups later in the book.

BASIC ORGANIZING CONCEPTS

The early writers on management developed a number of basic organizing principles that today's supervisors often use as they organize their departments.

DIVISION OF LABOUR

Division of labour
The breakdown of jobs into narrow tasks.

Division of labour (also known as work specialization) means that an entire job is broken down into a number of steps, each step being completed by a different individual. In essence, individuals specialize in doing part of an activity rather than the entire activity. Assembly-line production, in which each worker does the same standardized task over and over again, is an example of division of labour.

Until very recently, designers of organizations have felt that greater economic gains are achieved by breaking jobs down into smaller steps. In most organizations, some tasks require highly developed skills; others can be performed by the untrained. If all workers were engaged in each step of, say, an organization's manufacturing process, all would require the skills necessary to perform the most demanding and the least demanding jobs. The result would be that, except when performing the most highly skilled or highly sophisticated tasks, employees would be working below their skill level. Since skilled workers are paid more than unskilled workers and their wages tend to reflect their highest level of skill, it is not economical to pay highly skilled workers to do easy tasks. It also takes more time and money to train skills. If someone must only do a repetitive task, it is faster to train them and easier to replace them.

Today, supervisors understand that while division of labour provides economic efficiencies, it is not an unending source of increased productivity. There is a point at which the human costs of division of labour—boredom, fatigue, stress, low productivity, poor quality, increased absenteeism, repetitive strain injury, and high turnover—exceed the economic advantages. Contemporary supervisors utilize the division-of-labour concept in designing jobs but also recognize that, in an expanding number of situations, productivity, quality, and employee motivation can be increased by giving employees a variety of activities to perform, allowing employees to do a whole and complete piece of work, and joining employees together in teams.

SPAN OF CONTROL

It's not very efficient for a supervisor to direct only one or two subordinates. Conversely, it's pretty obvious that even the best of supervisors

FIGURE 5-3

The advantages of division of labour are evident on an assembly line, such as the one at this plant. Each worker performs a narrow and standardized operation. This requires a limited range of skills and allows for increased efficiency. Courtesy of Mark Antman/The Image Works

Span of control
The number of subor-
dinates a supervisor
can direct efficiently
and effectively.

would be overwhelmed if he or she had to directly oversee several hundred people. This, then, begs the **span of control** question: How many subordinates can a supervisor effectively direct?

There is, unfortunately, no universal answer. For most supervisors, the optimum number is probably somewhere between five and thirty. Where, within that range, the exact span should be depends on a number of factors.

- How experienced and competent is the supervisor? The greater his or her abilities, the larger the number of subordinates that can be handled.
- What level of training and experience do subordinates have? The higher their abilities, the fewer demands they'll make on their supervisor and the more subordinates that supervisor can directly oversee.
- How complex are the subordinates' activities? The more difficult the employees' jobs, the narrower the span of control.
- How many different types of jobs are under the supervisor's direction? The more varied the jobs, the narrower the span.
- How extensive are the department's formal rules and regulations? Supervisors can direct more people when employees can find solutions to their problems in organizational manuals rather than having to go to their immediate manager.

An important trend currently taking place in organizations is for spans of control to be almost universally expanded (see Figure 5-4). It is a way for management to reduce costs. By doubling the span size, the number of supervisors you need is cut in half. Of course, this move to wider spans couldn't be effectively carried out without modifications in work assignments and improvements in skill levels. So, in order to make wider spans work, organizations are spending more on supervisory and employee training, as well as redesigning jobs around teams so individuals can help each other solve problems without needing to go to their manager.

Something else important is taking place in organizations that involves a supervisor's span of control. This is the increased use of telecommuting. **Telecommuting** allows employees to do their work at home on a computer that is linked to their office (see Figure 5-5). The big advantage of telecommuting is that it gives employees more flexibility. It frees them from the constraints of commuting and fixed hours, and increases opportunities for meeting family responsibilities. For supervisors, telecommuting means managing people they rarely see. Where it is used, supervisors usually have a fairly wide span of control. This is because telecommuters tend to be skilled professionals and clerical employees—computer programmers, marketing specialists, financial analysts, and administrative support personnel—who make minimal demands on their supervisors.

Telecommuting
The linking by com-
puter and modem of
workers at home with
coworkers and man-
agement at an office.

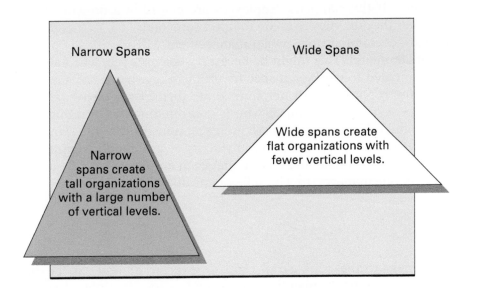

FIGURE 5-4

Contrasting spans of control

Narrow Spans

Wide Spans

Narrow spans create tall organizations with a large number of vertical levels.

Wide spans create flat organizations with fewer vertical levels.

FIGURE 5-5

The increased use of telecommuting means supervisors may be managing more people, and people they seldom see
Courtesy of image-egami/Shutterstock

UNITY OF COMMAND

The **unity of command** principle states that a subordinate should have one and only one superior to whom he or she is directly responsible. No person should report to two or more managers. Otherwise, a subordinate might have to cope with conflicting demands or priorities from several people at once. If this happens, employees are placed in a no-win situation. Whatever they do, they're going to upset someone.

There are occasional times when management will specifically break the unity of command. This might be necessary, for instance, when a project team is created to work on a specific problem or when a sales representative must report to both her immediate district supervisor and a marketing specialist at head office who is coordinating the introduction of a new product. Nevertheless, these are exceptions to the rule. For the most part, when allocating tasks to individuals or grouping assignments in your department, you should ensure that each employee has one manager, and only one manager, to whom he or she directly reports.

LINE, STAFF AND FUNCTIONAL AUTHORITY

Authority refers to the managerial right to give orders and expect the orders to be obeyed. Each supervisory position has specific rights that are acquired from the position's rank or title. Authority, therefore, relates to one's position within an organization and ignores the personal characteristics of the individual supervisor. Employees obey individuals in authority not because they like or respect them but because of the rights inherent in their position.

There are three different types of authority relations: line, staff, and functional (see Figure 5-6). The most straightforward and easiest to understand is **line authority**. This is the authority that gives the supervisor the right to direct the work of his or her employees and make certain decisions without consulting others.

Staff authority supports line authority by advising, servicing, and assisting, but it is typically limited. For instance, the assistant to the department head has staff authority. She acts as an extension of the department head and can give advice and suggestions, but they needn't be obeyed. However, the assistant may be given the authority to act for the department head. In such cases, she gives directives under the line authority of her boss. For instance, she might issue a memo and sign it "Sue Wilson for R.L. Dalton." In this instance, Wilson is only acting as an extension of Dalton. Staff authority allows Dalton to get more things done by having an assistant who can act on his behalf.

A third type of authority, **functional authority**, represents rights over individuals outside one's own direct areas of responsibility. For example, it is not unusual for a supervisor in a manufacturing plant to find that his immediate boss has line authority over him but that someone in corporate headquarters has functional authority over some of his activities and decisions. The supervisor in charge of a plant purchasing department is responsible to that plant's manager and the corporate director of purchasing at the company's head office.

Why, you might wonder, would the organization create positions of functional authority? After all, it breaks the unity of command principle

Unity of command
The principle that a subordinate should have one and only one superior to whom he or she is directly responsible.

Authority
The managerial right to give orders and expect the orders to be obeyed.

Line authority
The authority that entitles a supervisor to direct the work of his or her employees, and to make certain decisions without consulting others.

Staff authority
A limited authority that supports line authority by advising, servicing, and assisting.

Functional authority
Rights over individuals outside one's own direct areas of responsibility.

FIGURE 5-6

Organization chart depicting line, staff, and functional authority relationships

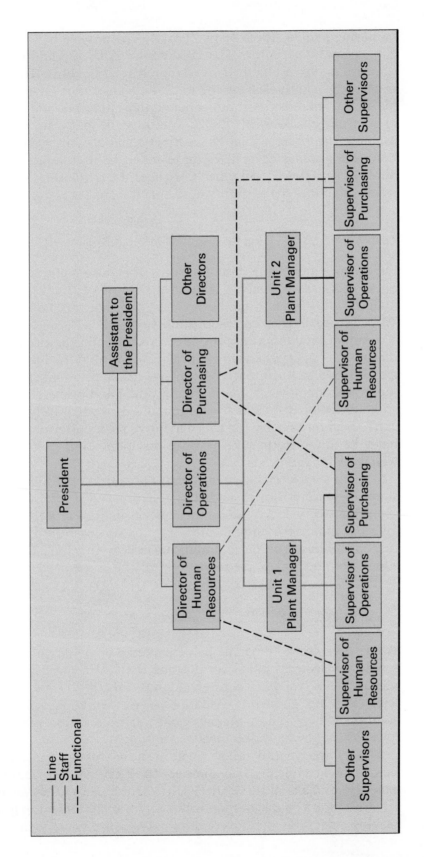

Line
Staff
Functional

President

Assistant to the President

Director of Human Resources

Director of Operations

Director of Purchasing

Other Directors

Unit 1 Plant Manager

Supervisor of Human Resources

Supervisor of Operations

Supervisor of Purchasing

Other Supervisors

Unit 2 Plant Manager

Supervisor of Human Resources

Supervisor of Operations

Supervisor of Purchasing

Other Supervisors

by having people report to two bosses. The answer is that it can create efficiencies by permitting specialization of skills and improved coordination. Its major problem is overlapping relationships. This is typically resolved by clearly designating to an individual the activities over which his or her line boss has authority and those that fall under the direction of someone else with functional authority. To follow up our purchasing example, the director might have functional authority to specify corporation-wide purchasing policies on forms to be used and common procedures to be followed. All other aspects of the purchasing supervisor's job would fall under the authority of the plant manager.

EQUATING AUTHORITY AND RESPONSIBILITY

Supervisory jobs come with authority. They also come with obligations. Supervisors are obliged to achieve their unit's goals, keep costs within budget, follow organizational policies, and motivate their subordinates. We call these obligations **responsibility**.

Responsibility
An obligation to perform assigned activities.

Authority without responsibility creates opportunities for abuse. For instance, a supervisor who isn't held responsible for his or her actions may become inclined to make excessive demands on an employee, resulting in that employee being injured on the job. Conversely, responsibility without authority creates frustration and the feeling of powerlessness. If you're held responsible for your territory's sales performance, you should have the authority to hire, reward, discipline, and fire the salespeople who work for you.

When senior management creates organizational units such as divisions, regions, territories, and departments—and allocates managers with specific goals to achieve and other responsibilities to fulfill—it must also give the managers enough authority to successfully carry out those responsibilities. The more ambitious and far-reaching the goals that a supervisor undertakes, the more authority he or she needs to be given.

CENTRALIZED VS. DECENTRALIZED AUTHORITY

Where does decision making lie? The design of any organization requires senior management to answer this question. If the answer is "with senior management," you have **centralized authority**. With centralization, problems "flow up" to senior executives, who then choose the appropriate solution. Where senior management pushes decision making down to lower levels, you have **decentralized authority**.

Centralized authority
Decision making is done by senior management.

Decentralized authority
Senior management pushes decision making down to lower levels of organization.

Years ago, centralization ruled in most organizations. Why? Senior management typically had the necessary critical information and the expertise to make most key decisions. Additionally, time was not a problem. If it took a couple of months for senior management to get around to making a decision, there were minimal negative consequences. That's no longer true. As jobs have become more complex, it's become nearly impossible for senior managers to keep current and knowledgeable on everything going on in their organization. Moreover, the dynamics of competition make it increasingly necessary for organizations to make decisions fast. Because speedy decision making and centralization don't usually go together, senior management has in recent years been forced to decentralize decision making.

Today, more than any time in recent years, supervisors and employees are being actively included in the decision-making process. As organizations have cut costs and streamlined their organizational design to respond better to custom er needs, they have pushed decision-making authority down to the lowest levels in the organization and empowered employees. In this way, those people most familiar with a problem are able to quickly size it up and solve it. We'll present specific delegation skills later in this chapter, which will show you how to effectively push decision-making authority downward. Note that decentralization also is sometimes chosen because of its link to acceptance of change and perceived fairness. As we will see in a later chapter, employees who are involved in the decision making of a change are much more likely to accept the change and less likely to resist it. Also, involving employees in decision making can motivate them (see Chapter 9) and lead them to believe the decisions made are fair.

GROUPING EMPLOYEES

Early business experts argued that activities in the organization should be specialized and grouped into departments. Work specialization creates specialists who need coordination. This coordination is facilitated by putting specialists together in departments under the direction of a supervisor. Creation of these departments is typically based on the work functions being performed, the product or service being offered, the target customer or client, the geographic territory being covered, or the process being used to turn inputs into outputs. This process of grouping jobs is called **departmentalization**. No single method of departmentalization was advocated by the early experts. The method or methods used should reflect the grouping that would best contribute to the attainment of the organization's objectives and the goals of individual units.

Specialization is found throughout organizations. For instance, when a company appoints vice presidents for marketing, finance, production, and research, it is dividing up organizational activities by specialization. While major decisions—such as what departments an organization will have and how they will interrelate—are typically made by senior management, supervisors still make organizing decisions. These decisions are confined to activities within their own areas of responsibility. As a result,

Departmentalization Grouping jobs according to work functions, product or service, target customer or client, geographic territory, or the process used to turn inputs into outputs.

supervisors need to understand various options for organizing their departments and for grouping activities. These are, incidentally, the same options available to senior managers when they make decisions about the organization's overall structure. Thus, as a supervisor, you can departmentalize on the basis of work function, product or service, geographic territory, target customer or client, or the process being used to turn inputs into outputs.

FUNCTION

Functional departmentalization Grouping activities by functions performed.

One of the most popular ways to group activities is by functions performed—**functional departmentalization**. When you see a company that separates engineering, accounting, manufacturing, human resources, and purchasing specialists into common departments, you have an example of departmentalizing by function (see Figure 5-7). Similarly, hospitals use this approach when they create departments devoted to research, patient care, accounting, and so forth.

Why is the functional department so popular? Because it most directly takes advantage of occupational specialization. By placing together jobs that are performed by people with the same kinds of training and experience, it is easier for people within the department to communicate with each other. It also makes it easier for the supervisor to coordinate activities, because he or she will be overseeing activities that have a somewhat common component.

One downside of functional specialization is that it can encourage greater loyalty to one's functional area, such as marketing, than to the organization as a whole, and can create competition between different functional areas. Companies want all of their employees on the same side, not vying with each other.

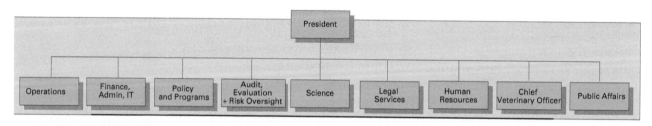

FIGURE 5-7

Functional Departmentalization at the Canadian Food Inspection Agency

PRODUCT/SERVICE

Another way to departmentalize is by product or service provided. This means that each major product area in the organization is under the authority of a manager who is a specialist in, and responsible for, everything to do with his or her product line or service.

In contrast to functional departments, **product or service departmentalization** creates relatively independent units. Any problem or issue that surfaces related to a product will fall under the responsibilities of that product's manager. Thus a major advantage of organizing around products is that it places ultimate responsibility for everything concerning a specific product with one manager, thus eliminating the potential for "passing the buck." It also coordinates and focuces energy on achieving product results.

A segment of the Procter and Gamble organizational chart demonstrates a product-based departmentalization. See Figure 5-8a. Rogers Communications organizational chart illustrates a service-based departmentalization (see Figure 5-8b). It also coordinates and focuses energy on achieving product results.

> **Product or service departmentalization**
> Grouping activities by product line or service.

GEOGRAPHY

Another way to departmentalize is on the basis of geography or territory—**geographic departmentalization**. For instance, the Canadian Forestry

> **Geographic departmentalization**
> Grouping activities on the basis of territory.

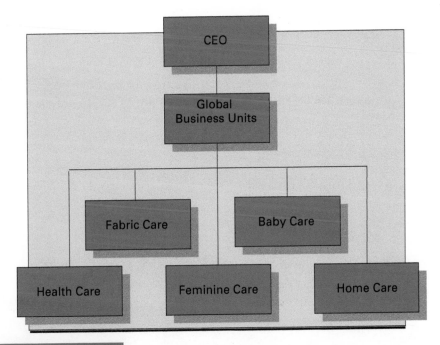

FIGURE 5-8a

Product departmentalization at Procter and Gamble

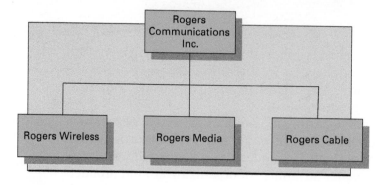

FIGURE 5-8b

Service departmentalization at the Procter and Gamble

Service has five regional centres reporting to an assistant deputy minister (see Figure 5-9).

What's the advantage to this form of departmentalization? It puts decision-making authority close to where the work is being done. If activities are physically dispersed and different locations face different types of problems, management will want to ensure that the people who make the decisions understand those differences. For instance, Denison Hydraulics has Western Canada, Central Canada, and Quebec sales and distribution centres. The Ontario Provincial Police have major operational units to cover northeastern Ontario, northwestern, central, western, and eastern Ontario.

Customer departmentalization Grouping activities on the basis of common customers.

CUSTOMER

The fastest-growing form of departmentalizing is by customer. Why? Because companies are learning that success requires staying close to the

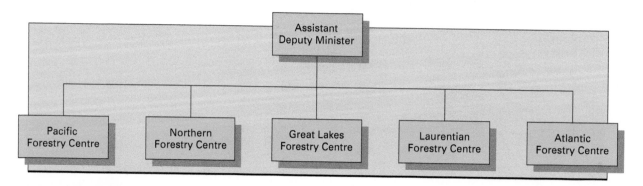

FIGURE 5-9

Geographic departmentalization at the Canadian Forestry Service

customer. Organizations that lose touch with the changing needs of their diverse customer base aren't likely to be around for too long. The primary force that has driven the growth of many current companies has been careful listening to and response to the needs of their customers.

Where an organization has a diverse set of customers that can be grouped around common interests, concerns, or needs, then a customer form of departmentalization makes sense. For instance, most provincial governments organize departments to service different customers. Alberta Provincial Court has specialized court divisions for small claims, traffic, youth, family and criminal issues. British Columbia's Northern Health Authority has special divisions for Aboriginal health, mental health and addictions, public health, and home and community care. Private sector companies also value structuring to focus on different customer types. Wolseley is a national distributor of plumbing, hydronic, HVAC/R and PVF products and solutions and it organizes based on the customers it is dealing with (e.g. professional contractors, retailers, industrial users; see Figure 5-10).

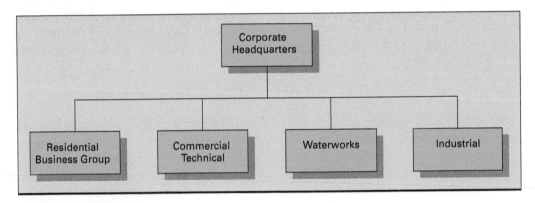

FIGURE 5-10

Customer departmentalization at Wolseley Canada

PROCESS

The final pure form of departmentalization is by process. Figure 5-11 depicts the various production departments at Hamilton Works, U.S. Steel Canada.[1] Iron ore, coke and fluxes are cooked at high temperatures in huge blast furnaces to create molten iron; the molten iron is converted to steel at even higher temperatures and then poured into castings. The castings are sent to the hot strip mill for hotrolling where slabs are rolled into scaly coils of steel. Next, the pickling process cleans the scale. Then the coils go to cold rolling where they are rolled again but to a much more accurate tolerance since the surface is clean. After cold rolling the steel is annealed to remove the stress in the metal from the cold rolling operation. The metal then goes to a galvanizing line to be coated against rust. Since each process requires

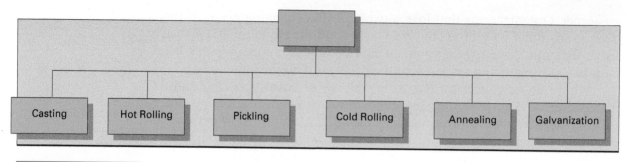

FIGURE 5-11

Process departmentalization in steel production

Process
departmentalization
Grouping activities on
the basis of product or
customer flow.

different skills and specialized equipment, this method offers a basis for the categorizing of activities.

Process departmentalization can be used for processing customers as well as products. If you have ever arrived at a major airport after an international flight, you probably went through several departments between leaving the plane and heading for home. Immigration verifies your eligibility to enter Canada, you pick up your luggage at the arrivals carousel, and the customs department verifies your purchases for import.

BLENDING FUNCTION AND PRODUCT: THE MATRIX

The functional department offers the advantages of specialization but can create internal competion. The product department has a greater focus on results but suffers from duplication of activities and resources (e.g. sales, human resources, finance repeated in each product area). Does any form combine the advantages of functional specialization with the focus and accountability that product departmentalization provides? The answer is yes, and it's called the **matrix**.

Matrix
A structural design
that assigns specialists
from functional
departments to work
on one or more pro-
jects that are led by
a project manager.

The matrix structure creates a dual chain of command. It explicitly breaks the principle of unity of command. Functional departmentaliza-tion is used to gain the economies of specialization. But overlaying the functional departments is a set of supervisors who are responsible for specific *products*, *projects*, or *programs* within the organization. (We'll use the terms products, projects, and programs interchangeably, since matrix structures can use any of the three).

Figure 5-12 illustrates the matrix structure of an aerospace firm. Notice that along the top of the figure are the familiar functions of engineering, accounting, human resources, and so forth. Along the verti-cal dimension, however, have been added the various projects that the aerospace firm is currently working on. Each project is directed by a supervisor who staffs his or her project with people from the functional departments. The addition of the vertical dimension to the traditional

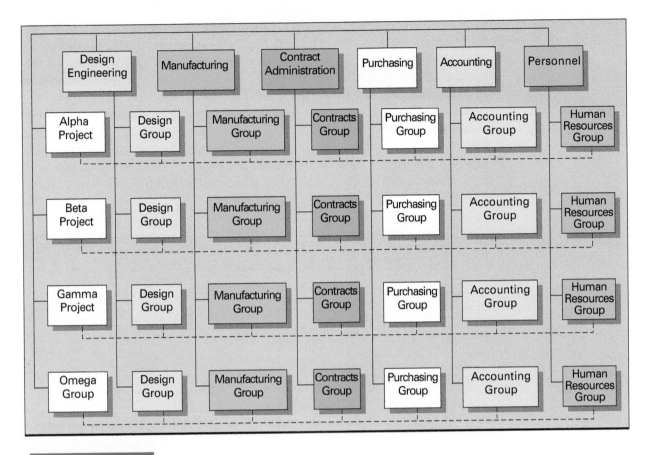

FIGURE 5-12

A matrix structure in an aerospace firm

functional departments in effect weaves together elements of functional and product departmentalization—hence the term *matrix*.

How does the matrix work? Employees in the matrix report to two managers—their functional departmental supervisor and their product or project supervisor (see Dealing with a Difficult Issue). The project supervisors have authority over the functional members who are part of that supervisor's project team. For instance, the purchasing specialists who work on the Gamma project are responsible to both the supervisor of purchasing and the Gamma project supervisor. Authority is shared between the two supervisors. Typically, this is done by giving the project supervisor authority over project employees relative to the project's goals, while decisions such as promotions, salary recommendations, and annual reviews remain the functional supervisor's responsibility. To work effectively, project and functional supervisors must communicate regularly and coordinate the demands upon their common employees.

The matrix creates a structure that possesses the strengths of both functional and product departmentalization, while avoiding the weaknesses of both. That is, the strength of the functional form lies in putting like specialists together, minimizing the numbers, and allowing for the pooling and sharing of specialized resources across products. Its primary drawback is the difficulty in coordinating the tasks of the specialists so that their activities are completed on time and within budget. The product form, on the other hand, has exactly the opposite benefits and disadvantages. It facilitates the coordination among specialists to achieve on-time completion and meet budget targets, and furthermore provides clear responsibility for all activities related to a product or project. But no one is responsible for the long-run technical development of the specialists, and this results in duplication of costs.

Dealing with a Difficult Issue

DO MATRIX STRUCTURES CREATE CONFUSED EMPLOYEES?

Workers in matrix structures face a difficult issue that never arose in traditional organizational structures. That is, they have at least two bosses. They are responsible to their functional supervisor, who has the responsibility to evaluate their performance and make salary increase determinations. Concurrently, these employees are responsible to their project leader for specific project tasks.

In this situation, whose authority takes precedence? Do employees give their functional supervisor's requests priority because, after all, it is this individual who handles the administrative and personnel-related paperwork? Or is it the project leader—who is more involved with the employees on a day-to-day basis—who gets the "top-billing"? Failure to complete the required tasks on the project could result in being removed from the project team—a decision that may place an employee's job in jeopardy. Are both supervisors given equal priority? Should employees simply accept that they have to serve "two masters"? What do you think?

WHY IS THERE MOVEMENT TO SIMPLER EMPLOYEE GROUPINGS?

Many of the departmentalizations mentioned above are highly complex and formalized, and decisions are made in a centralized fashion—resulting in rigid, often massive, multilevelled structures. Although they were designed to promote efficiency, they do not easily adjust to the dynamic world around them. As a result, more emphasis today has been given to organizations that focus on simplicity. As discussed in Chapter 1, changing organizational structures is one of the challenges facing many supervisors today. Let's look at what we mean by a simple structure.

If "bureaucracy" is the term that best describes most large organizations, "simple structure" is the one that best characterizes most small ones. A **simple structure** is defined more by what it is not than by what it is. It is not an elaborate structure.[2] If you see an organization that appears to have almost no structure, it is probably of the simple variety. By that we mean that it is low in complexity, has little formalization, and has its authority centralized in a single person. The simple structure is a "flat" organization; it usually has only two or three levels, employees who perform a variety of tasks, and one individual who makes most of the decisions.

The simple structure is most widely practised in small businesses in which the manager and the owner are one and the same. This is illustrated in Figure 5-13—an organization chart for a men's clothing retail store. Jack Singleton owns and manages this store. Although Jack employs five full-time salespeople, a cashier, and part-time weekend help, he "runs the show."

Simple structure
A non-elaborate structure low in complexity, with little formalization, and with authority centralized in a single person; a "flat" organization with only two or three levels.

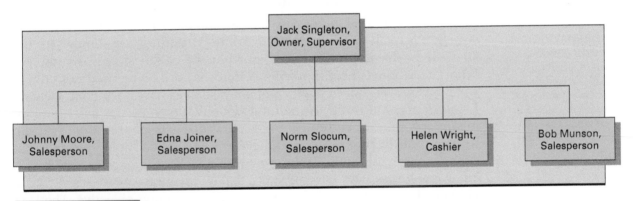

FIGURE 5-13
Jack Singleton's structure

The strengths of the simple structure should be obvious. Communications are efficient, accountability is clear, and it has flexibility to respond to the changing environment. One major weakness is the challenge of dealing with growth. It can become increasingly inadequate as an organization grows, because the low degree of formalization and high degree of centralization result in information overloads at the top. As size increases, decision making can become slower and eventually come to a standstill as the single person in charge tries to continue making all the decisions. This often proves to be the undoing of many small businesses. The simple structure's other weakness is that it is risky: everything depends on one person. One heart attack, or a fatal auto accident on the way to work, can literally destroy the organization—for the only one who held the critical information is now gone. However, these weaknesses were not necessarily the fault of the simple structure. Rather, those in charge just couldn't give up the control that they had so enjoyed.

ARE THERE SIMPLE STRUCTURES FOR LARGER ORGANIZATIONS?

If yesterday's organizations had one feature in common, it was the rigid boundaries that separated employees from other members of the organization. Employees were often segregated by the jobs they did and rarely interacted with others in different parts of the business. A select few "ran the show." That setup may no longer provide the best advantage in organizations. Some of those boundaries are being broken down, giving employees more interaction with others whom they count on for getting jobs done. In business today, we call this arrangement the horizontal structure.

THE HORIZONTAL STRUCTURE

Horizontal structures Very flat structures used in small businesses as well in as giant companies in which job-related activities cut across all parts of the organization.

Before we begin this discussion, let's set the record straight. A horizontal structure is really nothing new. **Horizontal structures** are simply very flat structures—basically the same as what we called simple structures. What's new about them, however, is that they are being used not only in small businesses, but in giant companies such as AT&T, Du Pont, General Electric, and Motorola. Horizontal organizations, as the term implies, means job-related activities cut across all parts of the organization. Rather than having employees perform specialized jobs and work in departments with people who do similar tasks, they are grouped with other employees who have different skills—forming a work team. These individuals come together to work toward a common objective. They are given the authority to make the necessary decisions to do the work, and are held accountable for measurable outcomes.[3] Their jobs encompass the entire work to be completed, from beginning to end—rather than focusing on individualized job tasks.[4] In a horizontal structure, control shifts from those in management to supervisors and workers.

Working in a horizontal organization brings about other changes for supervisors. For instance, supervisors reward employees for mastering multiple skills, rather than just a few specialized skills. The more jobs employees can do, the more valuable they are. Additionally, rather than being evaluated on the work one individual does, the rewards are based on how the team performs. In a horizontal organization, the supervisor's evaluations are no longer the only ones. Instead, employees are likely to be evaluated by anyone who has knowledge of their work. This could include a selection of subordinates, coworkers, and customers, as well as the supervisor. Known as 360-degree evaluation or multisource evaluation, it is being increasingly used in organizations, both for developmental information and evaluative feedback. Horizontal structures may also provide incentive for collaborative performance through their bonus structure. For example, bonuses may be decided based 50% on organizational performance, 30% on team performance and 20% on individual performance, emphasizing the importance of working together.

BLENDED DEPARTMENTALIZATION

Because the organizing structure needs to meet the needs of the organization, many companies actually mix different types of departmentalization. Take a look at Figure 5-14. As departments that serve all parts of the company, Finance and Human Resources are organized as functional departments operating out of headquarters. Then there is product specialization for the manufacturing of different products. The sales department is organized on a geographic basis to meet the needs of the regional customers.

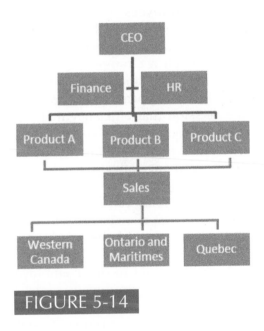

FIGURE 5-14

STRUCTURAL PARALLELS WITHIN A DEPARTMENT

As a supervisor, you may have leeway in how to organize your department along lines parallel to the concepts we have just discussed. For example, assume you supervise a shop that sells and services bicycles. If you chose a functional structure, within the shop you would have people allocated specifically to sales or office administration or repair. This takes advantages of specific strengths – few people would be effective at all these activities. If you chose a product structure you would have the staff become specialists in certain brands and types of bicycles, both selling and repairing "their" types of bikes. You might consider a customer specialization as an angle so that one salesperson is the bridge with the local bike clubs and racers. Chances are you will end up selecting a blended model that starts with a functional structure but overlays customer and product considerations in order to suit the needs and strategy of the shop and the skills of your staff.

FITTING EMPLOYEE GROUPING TO THE SITUATION

Although the movement toward simple structures brings with it many strengths and may provide an exciting work atmosphere, keep one thing in mind. Simple structures must be used only where appropriate. The question then arises: When does each of the different groupings work best? For example, in industries where efficiency of mass production is warranted, grouping employees by the jobs they perform may better serve the organization. The answer will depend on the environment in which you work.

Organizations group employees in a given way for a particular reason. They don't implement structures haphazardly for the fun of it. It's too expensive, and very difficult, to make these changes. When an organization does make such a change, you should learn from it. Recognize what the structure is telling you as a supervisor. If grouping employees by the job performed appears to be the norm, then your organization has made the decision that efficiency matters most. Therefore, to be successful in this element of your supervisory job, you need to focus on being efficient and continue refining your current skills. That may mean emphasizing work specialization for your employees—and yourself, too. In such an arrangement, you'll also be given clues on how best to make some of your decisions. You'll want to give greater weight to the alternatives that are most cost effective or provide greater output for a given input. Play to the strength of the employee grouping—that's usually what you'll be rewarded for.

Similar guidelines can be found in other employee groupings. For example, grouping by the product produced means that the "bigger" picture is most important. That is, achieving organizational goals is a "must," and the company is willing to use resources to do it.

ORGANIZING YOUR EMPLOYEES' JOBS

Once your departmental structure is in place, you need to organize the specific jobs of each of your employees. How do you do that? By identifying the tasks to be done, combining them into jobs, and then formalizing the process by creating job descriptions. The critical issue for organizing your employees is deciding and communicating exactly what their jobs entail. Who will do what, when and how? How will they coordinate? What authority and responsibility will they have? Once you have decided what the different positions in the department will be, the details of those positions need to be pinned down. Every job needs a clear job description.

CREATING JOB DESCRIPTIONS

A **job description** is a written statement of what a jobholder does, how the job is done, and why it is done. It typically portrays job duties, working conditions, and operating responsibilities. Figure 5-16 illustrates a job description for a secretary. Note each of its elements. It lists the job title, to whom the position reports, and the department to which the position is assigned. There is a brief description of the job followed by a more specific list of duties, all of which are phrased using action verbs. This list must be comprehensive and accurate. Qualifications are also listed. There are omissions from this particular job description, however, that could lead to potential problems for a supervisor. It does not say who created the description or when. Without this, the supervisor does not know whether the description is up-to-date and accurate.

Why do supervisors need to write job descriptions for each job in their department? For two reasons. First, the job description provides the supervisor with a formal document describing what the employee is supposed to be doing. It acts as a standard against which the supervisor can determine how well the employee is performing. This, in turn, can be used to make performance appraisal, feedback, wage adjustment, and training decisions. Second, the job description helps employees learn their job duties and clarifies the results that management expects them to achieve.

Diane Hebert, experienced as an HR manager in mining, lumber and government organizations, concurs with the importance of job descriptions. "At a recent employer, they had no job descriptions despite being a large company. As the new HR manager, I brought job descriptions in. At first they referred to them as "Diane's little job descriptions" but now they're addicted to them. They use them for recruitment, performance development and evaluations, for planning. Now they're used as they're meant to be, incorporated into everything, but it took a long time to convince them. Why were they resistant? They hung on to the myth that if you write down what employees are supposed to do, they will refuse to do anything else. They're not unionized but they're still suspicious. They thought they would get refusals, but I have yet to see this happen in any workplace."

How does a job description get created? There are sources through the government; for example, the National Occupation Classification (NOC) provides profile information based on extensive research. But using someone else's description of a job may mean a mismatch with what is needed in your organization.

The best source of an accurate job description is a thorough job analysis.

FIGURE 5-15

Diane Hebert introduced job descriptions into a company that first resisted them, and now appreciates their value.

Job Title: Secretary
Department: Marketing
Main functions: The secretary supports the work of the Marketing Director by handling calls, visitors, mail and email, and the Director's calendar, by creating and maintaining effective office systems to manage the flow and archiving of information, and by completing documentation. The secretary will work under general supervision, dealing with both planned and ad hoc tasks and changing priorities, showing independent judgement.
Reports to: Marketing Director
Duties: • Answers telephone and relays messages • Greets visitors, enquires the nature of their business and directs them to the appropriate person • Schedules and confirms appointments for the Director; handles the director's calendar • Opens and distributes general departmental mail and other material and coordinates the flow of information within the department • Opens and administers regular and electronic mail for the Director and follows up, when required, to ensure proper action is taken on all incoming mail • Determines and establishes office administration procedures • Coordinates and manages office services, such as equipment and supplies • Arranges travel schedule of director • Uses word processing and spreadsheet skills to complete documentation • Performs any other duties related to the position of secretary as directed by the Marketing Director
Working Conditions: • Monday to Friday, 8:30 to 5:30, with one hour paid lunch; occasional paid overtime required • Frequent exposure to noise and interruptions with a regular flow of people around the office • Changing priorities assigned on frequent basis
Employment Requirements: • Post-secondary program in office administration completed • At least five years related experience • Advanced skills in WORD and EXCEL • Excellent spoken and written English • Courteous manners; punctual, meticulous and reliable

FIGURE 5-16

A job description for a
secretary

JOB ANALYSIS

A **job analysis** is the process of collecting information to define a job in terms of its component tasks or duties and the knowledge or skills required to perform them. An effective job analysis ensures accurate information that can be used to assist in making important decisions like what skills should be sought in hiring and what the person should be paid. Not only does it support fairness and good business practice, but it also provides important information in the case of a legal challenge.

How is a job analysis done? Given your own past work experience, you will realize that a supervisor often does not realize the entire scope and challenge of a job, or may be biased in their assessment. Job analysis involves a structured approach to gathering information that will paint an accurate picture. This typically means involving job incumbents (those in the position at the moment) through structured interviews or questionnaires, and may also mean direct observation of their performance. Sometimes other experts contribute, like those formerly in the position or supervising the department.

Information is collected on what tasks are involved, how much time is spent on each task and how frequently they occur, what resources are needed, what physical and cognitive demands are made on the incumbent, what hazards exist in the job, and how the person interacts with other people. It also examines the education, experience, and skills needed.

Here are some of the questions asked on a job analysis questionnaire:

- Describe a key issue or problem frequently encountered on the job that you would generally handle on your own. How is it identified? Explain the analysis used to determine a solution(s) for the situation and/or problem. What resources are there to assist you?
- Does your work require you to develop new work methods, procedures or manuals?
- During the course of a working day, what period of time are you required to: sit at a desk or machine; walk; stand at a counter or machine; stoop/crouch/kneel; climb up or down stairs?
- Indicate the types of tools, equipment, machines, etc that you are required to use or operate in carrying out your job duties
- Which statement best describes the likely consequences of an error in doing your work (e.g. "An error would have little or no direct consequence to others. I could correct it myself." to "Others could suffer permanent physical/psychological impairment. Addressing errors could involve major expenditure of time or resource. Could cause severe damage to reputation of company.")
- From the list provided, identify the usual contacts you are required to make in your job. Describe the nature or purpose of the contact.
- From the list provided of disagreeable work conditions, select those that are applicable, indicating frequency and giving an example.

Job Analysis
The process of collecting information to define a job in terms of its component tasks or duties and the knowledge or skills required to perform them.

- List the duties you regularly perform each day; each week; each month; once a year or occasionally.
- Do you require a license, formal or professional designation or diploma/certificate for your job?
- Indicate the education level you consider is required to do your job.

Job analysis is not an easy or quick task, as you can surmise from the questions above. A job analysis questionnaire can often run to 20 or 30 pages. This is why they are only done periodically to ensure up-to-date information on which business decisions are made.

USES FOR JOB ANALYSIS

Job specification
The minimum acceptable qualifications an employee must possess to perform a given job successfully.

Job evaluation
An assessment of the worth of a job.

A job analysis provides information that can be used to create job descriptions, job specifications and job evaluations. The job description has already been described as a written description of what an employee does, how and why. A **job specification** outlines in detail the minimum acceptable qualifications an employee must possess to perform a given job successfully (this information is sometimes added to the job description). Information from both the job description and the job specifications will be used to create a job posting when a new hire is needed and the organizations goes looking for suitable candidates. A **job evaluation** is an assessment of the worth of a job, used to establish the compensation rate. One of the reasons why standard job analysis questionnaires are used across all positions in an organization is so that different jobs can be fairly compared on common components (like risk, degree of responsibility, education required) when making assessments of value.

THE INCREASING USE OF TEAMS

Team
Members are committed to a common purpose, have a set of specific performance goals, and hold themselves mutually accountable for the team's results.

Teams are increasingly becoming the prime vehicle around which work is being designed. Why? Because teams typically outperform individuals when the tasks being done require multiple skills, judgement, and experience. As organizations restructure themselves to compete more effectively and efficiently, they are turning to teams as a way to better utilize employees' talents. Organizations are finding that teams are more flexible and responsive to changing events than are departments or other forms of permanent groupings. They can be quickly assembled, deployed, refocused, and disbanded.

Teams fall into one of three categories, depending on their objectives. Some organizations use teams to provide advice. For instance, they create temporary task forces to recommend ways to cut costs, improve quality, or select a site for a new plant. Some organizations use teams to manage. They introduce management teams at various levels in the organization to run things. However, supervisors are most likely to be involved with teams that are created to make or do things. They include production teams, design teams, and office teams that handle administrative work.

Companies such as Pratt and Whitney Canada, Honeywell, Motorola, and Imperial Oil have made work teams the centrepiece in creating new work units. For instance, the Imperial Oil refinery in Dartmouth, Nova Scotia, previously threatened with closure, is now surviving thanks to its organizational redesign based on teams.

In organizations reorganizing work around teams, supervisors are learning to effectively coordinate team activity. In many cases, management's emphasis has been on creating self-managed teams. As we'll see, this is redefining the supervisor's managerial role.

TURNING GROUPS INTO TEAMS

Groups and teams are not necessarily the same thing. Many formal work groups are merely individuals who sporadically interact, but who have no collective commitment that requires joint effort. That is, the group's total performance is merely the sum of the individual group members' performance.

What differentiates a team is that members are committed to a common purpose, have a set of specific performance goals, and hold themselves mutually accountable for the team's results. Teams, in other words, are something greater than the sum of their parts. Figure 5-17 illustrates how a work group evolves into a real team. The primary force that moves a work group toward a real high-performing team is its emphasis on performance.

A working group is a group of individuals who interact primarily to share information and to make decisions, in order to help each other perform within a given area of responsibility. Members of such a group

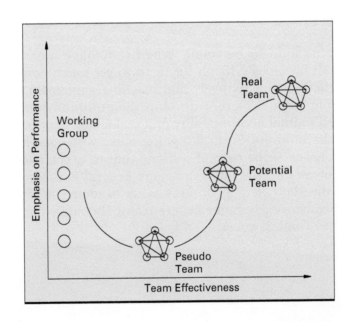

FIGURE 5-17

Comparing groups
and teams

have no need or opportunity to engage in collective work that requires joint effort, so their performance is merely the sum of each group member's individual contribution. There is no positive synergy to create an overall level of performance that is greater than the sum of the inputs.

A *pseudoteam* is the product of negative synergy. The performance or output of the whole is less than the potential of the individual parts, because of factors such as poor communication, antagonistic conflicts, and avoidance of responsibilities. Even though members may call themselves a team, they're not. Because it doesn't focus on collective performance and because members have no interest in shaping a common purpose, a pseudoteam actually underperforms a working group.

"Going in the right direction but not there yet" is the best way to describe a *potential team*. It recognizes the need for, and is really trying hard to achieve, higher performance, but some roadblocks are in the way. Its purpose and goals may need greater clarity or the team may need better coordination. The result is that it has not yet established a sense of collective accountability.

The ultimate goal is to become a real team. This is a unit with a set of common characteristics that lead to consistently high performance.

BUILDING REAL TEAMS

Studies of effective teams have found that they contain a small number of people with complementary skills who are equally committed to a common purpose, goals, and working approach for which they hold themselves mutually accountable.[5] This section describes the six characteristics of real teams.

SMALL SIZE

The best teams tend to be small. When they have more than about 10 members, it becomes difficult for them to get much done. They have trouble interacting constructively and reaching agreement. Large numbers of people usually cannot develop the common purpose, goals, approach, and mutual accountability of a real team. They tend merely to go through the motions. So in designing effective teams, keep them to 10 people or fewer. If the natural working unit is larger, and you want a team effort, break the group into subteams. Federal Express, for instance, has divided the 1000 clerical workers at its headquarters into teams of five to ten members each. Some believe teams should be composed of an odd number to avoid tie votes.

COMPLEMENTARY SKILLS

To perform effectively, a team requires three types of skills. First, it needs people with *technical expertise*. Second, it needs people with the *problem-solving and decision-making skills* to identify problems, generate alternatives, evaluate those alternatives, and make competent choices. Finally, teams need people with good *interpersonal skills* (listening, feedback, conflict resolution).

No team can achieve its performance potential without developing all three types of skills. The right mix is crucial. Too much of one at the expense of others will result in lower team performance.

Teams don't need to have all the complementary skills at the beginning. Where team members value personal growth and development, one or more members often take responsibility to learn the skills in which the group is deficient, as long as the skill potential exists. Additionally, personal compatibility among members is not critical to the team's success if the technical, decision-making, and interpersonal skills are in place.

COMMON PURPOSE

Does the team have a meaningful purpose that all members aspire to? This purpose is a vision. It's broader than any specific goals. High-performing teams have a common and meaningful purpose that provides direction, momentum, and commitment for members.

For example, the development team at Apple Computer that designed the Macintosh was almost religiously committed to creating a user-friendly machine that would revolutionize the way people used computers.

Members of successful teams put a tremendous amount of time and effort into discussing, shaping, and agreeing upon a purpose that belongs to them collectively and individually. This common purpose, when accepted by the team, becomes the equivalent of what celestial navigation is to a ship captain—it provides direction and guidance under any and all conditions.

SPECIFIC GOALS

Successful teams translate their common purpose into specific, measurable, and realistic performance goals. Just as goals lead individuals to higher performance (see Chapter 2), they also energize teams. Specific goals facilitate clear communication and help teams maintain their focus on getting results. Examples of specific team goals might be responding to all customers within 24 hours, cutting production-cycle time by 30 per cent over the next six months, or maintaining equipment at a level of zero downtime every month.

COMMON APPROACH, SHARED "MENTAL MODELS"

Goals are the ends a team strives to attain. Defining and agreeing upon a common approach assures that the team is unified on the *means* for achieving those ends.

Recent research suggests that sharing "mental models" greatly enhances a team's effectiveness.[6] This means that the more alike team members are in terms of their understanding, the more quickly they can cooperate to cope with difficult and changing conditions. To adapt effectively, team members need to be able to predict what their coworkers will do and what they will need to do it. Common understanding will greatly enhance this adaptability. This means common understanding of the technology and equipment—functioning, limitations, likely problems; the job itself—procedures, likely scenarios, task strategies; team interaction—who is responsible for what, how communication and information flow; and the team members—individual strengths and weaknesses, attitudes, and preferences. To achieve this, there needs to be frequent interaction and communication, and an underlying sense of trust that encourages sharing.

MUTUAL ACCOUNTABILITY

The final characteristic of high-performing teams is accountability at both the individual and group level.

Successful teams make members individually and jointly accountable for the team's purpose, goals, and approach. Members understand what they are individually responsible for and what they are jointly responsible for.

Social loafing
The tendency of group members to do less than they are capable of individually when their individual contribution is not measured.

Studies have shown that when teams focus only on group-level performance targets, and ignore individual contributions and responsibilities, team members often engage in **social loafing**.[7] They reduce their efforts because their individual contributions can't be identified. In effect, they become "free riders" and coast on the group's effort. The result is that the team's overall performance suffers. This reaffirms the importance of measuring both individual contributions to the team as well as the team's overall performance. And successful teams have members who collectively feel responsible for their team's performance (see Figure 5-18).

OVERCOMING THE OBSTACLES

Critical obstacles that can prevent a team from becoming high performers include a weak sense of direction, infighting, shirking of responsibilities, lack of trust, critical skill gaps, and lack of external support.

There are a number of things supervisors can do to overcome the obstacles mentioned and help teams to reach their full potential.

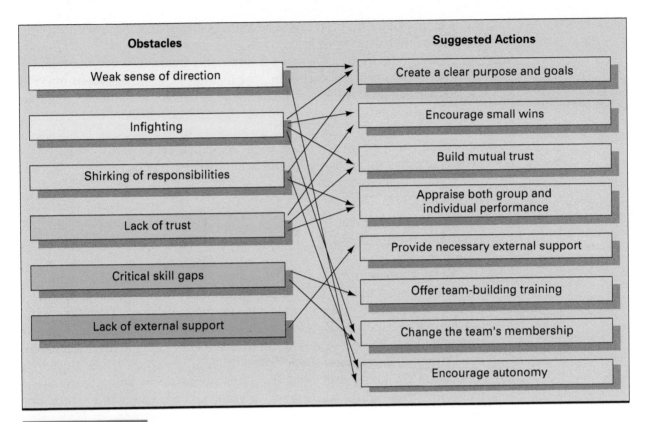

FIGURE 5-18
Creating effective teams

CREATE A CLEAR PURPOSE AND GOALS

High-performance teams have both a clear understanding of their goals and a belief that the goals embody a worthwhile or important result. Moreover, the importance of these goals encourages individuals to sublimate personal concerns to the team goals. In effective teams, members are committed to the team's goals, know what they are expected to accomplish, and understand how they will work together to achieve these goals.

As a supervisor, your job is to ensure that teams under your leadership have a clear purpose and goals. Whether you participate in setting them or delegate this task to the team itself, it's your responsibility to make sure that it is accomplished. Make the goals "front-of-mind" by posting them, mentioning them at meetings, giving frequent feedback regarding their accomplishment, and questioning decisions and proposals in terms of those goals.

ENCOURAGE TEAMS TO GO FOR SMALL WINS

The building of real teams takes time. Team members have to learn to think and work as a team. New teams can't be expected to hit home runs, right at the beginning, every time they come to bat. So encourage the team to begin by trying to hit singles.

Help the team identify and set attainable goals. The eventual goal of cutting overall costs by 30 percent, for instance, can be dissected into five or ten smaller and more easily attainable goals. As the smaller goals are attained, the team's success is reinforced. Cohesiveness is increased and morale improves. Confidence builds. Success breeds success, but it's a lot easier for young teams to reach their goals if they start with small wins. When they do win, recognize it and celebrate.

BUILD MUTUAL TRUST

Trust is fragile. It takes a long time to build and can be easily destroyed. However, there are things a supervisor can do to create a climate of mutual trust.[8]

Keep team members informed by explaining upper-management decisions and policies and by providing accurate feedback. Create a climate of openness where employees are free to discuss problems without fear of retaliation. Be candid about your own problems and limitations. Make sure you're available and approachable when employees need support. Be respectful and listen to team members' ideas. Develop a reputation for being fair, objective, and impartial in your treatment of team members. Show consistency in your actions, and avoid erratic and unpredictable behaviour. Finally, be dependable and honest. Make sure you follow through on all explicit and implied promises.

Interestingly, the way trust appears to work within a work group is that high trust translates into group effort, whereas low trust translates into individual effort.[9] Lack of trust, therefore, does not destroy performance, but it does redirect the effort to behaviour which the individual can control. As a result, performance that depends on coordination and cooperation is much more likely to suffer.

APPRAISE BOTH GROUP AND INDIVIDUAL PERFORMANCE

Team members should all share in the glory when their team succeeds, and they should share in the blame when it fails. So a large measure of each member's performance appraisal should be based on the overall team's performance. But members need to know that they can't ride on the backs of others. Therefore, each member's individual contribution should also be identified and made a part of his or her overall performance appraisal.

PROVIDE THE NECESSARY EXTERNAL SUPPORT

You're the link between the teams and upper management. As such, it's your responsibility to make sure that teams have the necessary organizational resources to accomplish their goals. That means you should be prepared to make the case to your boss and other key decision makers in the organization for tools, equipment, training, personnel, physical space, or other resources the teams may require.

OFFER TEAM-BUILDING TRAINING

Teams, especially in their early stages of formation, will need training to build their skills. Typically, these skills include problem solving, communication, negotiation, conflict resolution, and group process. If you can't personally provide this kind of skill training for your team members, look to specialists in your organization who can, or secure the funds to bring in outside facilitators who specialize in this kind of training.

CHANGE THE TEAM'S MEMBERSHIP

When teams get bogged down in their own inertia or internal fighting, allow them to rotate members. You might want to manage this change by considering how certain personalities will mesh, and reforming teams in ways that will better combine skills. If lack of leadership is the problem, use your knowledge of the people involved to create teams in which there will be a high probability that a leader will emerge.

ENCOURAGE AUTONOMY

The supervisor can refuse to make decisions or solve problems until the team has attempted to deal with it. Paul, a production manager with over 90 people organized into self-directed teams reporting to him, supports this concept wholeheartedly. When an individual comes to him about an issue, he will first ask, "What have you done about it?" Once the individual has tried to work within the team to solve a problem, Paul is then willing to come in as a conciliator or adjudicator. The attempt must be made first within the team, however. For example, there was some grumbling over perceived unfairness when two pregnant employees were given light duties. Paul refused to step in. Subsequently, the whole team discussed the issue and resolved it. As a result, their problem-solving skills had grown and they felt they had accomplished something as a team.

A study of over 100 construction and road crews in the northeastern United States[10] investigated the effect of performance barriers on the work crews' effectiveness, which crews were more successful in overcoming those barriers, and why. To no one's surprise, performance constraints, such as machine breakdowns, had a negative impact on performance. However, some groups were more likely than others to take action to prevent these problems or minimize their impact. What was distinctive about those groups that were much more effective in their problem management strategies? They were more likely to be self-managing—already given the responsibility for making decisions for the team. They also had strong teamwork processes in that they were confident in approaching their tasks, their experience had led them to a common understanding of what might go wrong and what to do about it, and there was excellent communication and coordination among the team members. Their managers were also distinctive in that they tended to encourage self-management and autonomy. For example, forepeople encouraged their crews to plan activities, set performance goals, encourage each other, and monitor their performance and work processes. County managers linked with these crews provided the crews some discretion in decision making, recognized crews regularly, and provided resource support.

What do you see as the potential difficulties in giving work crews more power? Could the above scenario be possible in a unionized environment? What are the challenges for a supervisor of a self-managed team? What in the road crews' task and environment might help them pull together as a team? Are these conditions present in most jobs?

EMPOWERING OTHERS
THROUGH DELEGATION

Contemporary supervisors need to learn to empower others. Empowerment means increasing your employees' involvement in their work through making decisions and taking responsibility for work outcomes. Two ways to empower people are to delegate authority to them and to redesign their jobs. In this section, we'll address delegation. In Chapter 9, we'll show you how to empower people through job design.

ASSESSING YOURSELF: ARE YOU WILLING TO DELEGATE?

Think of times when you have been in charge of a group - this could be a full-time or part-time work situation, a student work group, or similar experience. Complete the following questionnaire by recording how you feel about each statement according to this scale. Remember to be honest in your answers.[11]

5 = Strongly disagree

4 = Disagree

3 = Neutral

2 = Agree

1 = Strongly agree

When in charge of a group I find:

___ 1. Most of the time other people are too inexperienced to do things, so I prefer to do them myself.

___ 2. It often takes more time to explain things to others than to just do them myself.

___ 3. Mistakes made by others are costly, so I don't assign much work to them.

___ 4. Some things simply should not be delegated to others.

___ 5. I often get quicker action by doing a job myself.

___ 6. Many people are good only at very specific tasks, and thus can't be assigned additional responsibilities.

___ 7. Many people are too busy to take on additional work.

___ 8. Most people just aren't ready to handle additional responsibility.

___ 9. In my position, I should be entitled to make my own decisions.

SCORING KEY AND INTERPRETATION

This questionnaire gives you an idea of your willingness to empower others through delegation. Add up your score on the nine items. Possible total scores range from 9 to 45. The higher your score, the more willing you appear to be to delegate to others. A score of 36 or higher indicates a strong willingness to allow others to assume workplace responsibilities and exercise self-control in their work. Scores in the 25-35 range imply serious reluctance to give up authority and control. Consider what past experiences may lie behind this score and whether you feel this level of willingness to delegate is suitable for your future as a supervisor.

SKILL BASICS

There is no question that effective supervisors need to be able to delegate. But supervisors tell us that it's hard for them. Why? They're typically afraid to give up control. Tammy Abel of the Winnipeg Student Employment Centre says, "One of the hardest things to do is delegate. I'm new in my position and I like to know exactly what is happening. It is hard to let go and let someone else do something even when I know I should because I don't have time or because it would be a great opportunity to develop staff." Tammy is learning, however. This year she was approached by a Quebec HRDC office asking whether her centre would compete in a national résumé contest. At first Tammy declined, due to her workload, but then realized she did not have to do it herself and delegated it to one of her staff. Another situation arose in which one of her senior staff members approached her about an idea. There was a new morning variety show on local television called The Big Breakfast. The show suggested that the employment centre participate in a regular slot on the show advertising their services and the job opportunities currently available for students. Previously, Tammy had been in charge of media relations and had enjoyed her experiences. She was also aware of the need to be careful in presenting the right image. However, she knew she needed to take a backseat role in this situation. Tammy delegated the entire project to the senior staff member, coaching him, but letting him do all the preparation and the actual "on air" episodes for 10 weeks during the summer. He loved doing it and did a good job.

In this section, we will show that delegation increases a supervisor's effectiveness and that, when done properly, still provides supervisory control.

WHAT IS DELEGATION?

Delegation is frequently depicted as a four-step process: 1. allocation of duties; 2. delegation of authority; 3. assignment of responsibility; and 4. creation of accountability.

1. **Allocation of duties.** Duties are the tasks and activities that a manager desires to have someone else do. Before you can delegate authority, you must allocate to a subordinate the duties over which the authority extends. You must explain to the person exactly what you wish him or her to do.

2. **Delegation of authority.** The essence of the delegation process is empowering the subordinate to act for you. It is passing to the subordinate the formal rights to act on your behalf. Ask yourself: Did I give my subordinate enough authority to get the materials, the equipment, and the support from others necessary to get the job done?

3. **Assignment of responsibility.** When authority is delegated, you must assign responsibility. That is, when you give someone "rights," you must also assign to that person a corresponding "obligation" to perform. This means clarifying not only the duties but also the standards and the deadlines.

4. **Creation of accountability.** To complete the delegation process, you must create **accountability**; that is, you must hold your subordinate answerable for properly carrying out his or her duties. So while responsibility means a subordinate is obliged to carry out assigned duties, accountability means the subordinate must perform the assignment in a satisfactory manner. Subordinates are responsible for the completion of tasks assigned to them, and are accountable to you for the satisfactory performance of that work. If you establish follow-up checkpoints, they will keep their accountability in mind.

Delegation
A four-step process of allocating duties, delegating authority, assigning responsibility, and creating accountability.

Accountability
Holding a person to performing an assignment in a satisfactory manner.

DELEGATION IS NOT ABDICATION

If you dump tasks on a subordinate without clarifying exactly what is to be done, the range of the subordinate's freedom, the expected level of performance, when the tasks are to be completed, and similar concerns, you are abdicating responsibility and inviting trouble. But don't fall into the trap of assuming that, in order to avoid the appearance of abdicating, you should minimize delegation. Unfortunately, this is the approach taken by many new and inexperienced supervisors. Lacking confidence in their subordinates, or fearful that they will be criticized for their subordinates' mistakes, they try to do everything themselves.

It may very well be true that you're capable of doing the tasks you delegate to your subordinates better, faster, or with fewer mistakes. The catch is that your time and energy are scarce resources. It's not possible for you to do everything yourself. So you need to learn to delegate if you're going to be effective in your job. This suggests two important points. First, you should expect and accept some mistakes by your subordinates. It's part of delegation. Mistakes are often good learning experiences for your subordinates, as long as their costs are not excessive. Second, to ensure that the costs of mistakes don't exceed the value of the learning, you need to put adequate controls in place. As we'll show, delegation without proper feedback controls that let you know when there are serious problems is abdication.

DELEGATION SKILLS

A number of actions differentiate the effective from the ineffective delegator. The following summarizes those actions.

1. **Clarify the assignment.** Begin by determining what is to be delegated and to whom. You need to identify the person best capable of doing the task, then determine if he or she has the time and motivation to do the job.

   Assuming you have a willing and able subordinate, it is your responsibility to provide clear information on what is being delegated, the results you expect, and any time or performance expectations you hold. Bill Angelopoulos, assistant manager at a clothing store, explains: "My approach is to explain what needs to be done and why and the time expectation. If they need more time, they are to come back and speak with me. It's important to give a specific task and time frame around it so they have a deadline and can't just slack off. They know I'll come back to check progress and see if they need help—which sometimes happens because these tasks are beyond being on the sales floor helping clientele, which is their prime task."

Unless there is an overriding need to adhere to specific methods, you should delegate only the end results. That is, get agreement on what is to be done and the end results expected, but let the subordinate decide on the means. By focusing on goals and allowing the employee the freedom to use his or her own judgement as to how those goals are to be achieved, you increase trust between you and the employee, improve the employee's motivation, and enhance accountability for the results. Diane McArthur at ServiceOntario works with subordinates who need to produce important reports. Even though she is an excellent writer herself, she cannot do all the reports, so they must be delegated. Diane thinks carefully, however, about the feedback she gives her subordinates after reports, keeping her focus on the position being expressed in the paper—was the right concept described, capturing the full breadth of the pertinent information? Diane tries not to make editorial comments about the writing itself because everyone expresses him- or herself differently and she needs to give her subordinates that freedom.

2. **Specify the subordinate's range of discretion.** Every act of delegation comes with constraints. You're delegating authority to act, but not unlimited authority. What you're delegating is authority to act on certain issues and, on those issues, within certain guidelines. You need to specify all guidelines so subordinates know, in no uncertain terms, the range of their discretion. When this has been successfully communicated, both you and the subordinate will have the same idea of the limits to the latter's authority and how far he or she can go without checking further with you.

How much authority do you give a subordinate? In other words, how tightly do you draw the guidelines? The best answer is that you should allocate enough authority to allow the subordinate to successfully complete the task. Your level of confidence in the employee's ability should help establish appropriate guidelines.

3. **Allow the subordinate to participate.** If you allow employees to participate in determining what is delegated, how much authority is needed to get the job done, and the standards by which they'll be judged, you increase employee motivation, satisfaction, and accountability for performance.

Be aware, however, that participation can present its own set of potential problems. For example, some subordinates are personally motivated to expand their authority beyond what they need and beyond what they are capable of handling. Allowing such people too much participation in deciding the tasks they should take on and the level of authority they must have can undermine the effectiveness of the delegation process.

4. **Inform others that delegation has occurred.** Delegation should not take place in a vacuum. The supervisor, the employee, and anyone else who may be affected by the delegation act all need to be informed. This includes people outside the organization as well as inside. If you fail to follow through on this step, your subordinate's authority will probably be called into question. Failure to inform others makes conflicts likely and decreases the chances that your subordinate will be able to accomplish the delegated task efficiently.

5. **Establish feedback controls.** There is always the possibility that a subordinate will misuse the discretion that he or she has been delegated. The establishment of controls to monitor the subordinate's progress increases the likelihood that important problems will be identified early and that the task will be completed on time and to the desired specifications.

   Ideally, controls should be determined at the time of the initial assignment. Agree on a specific time for completion of the task, and then set progress dates when the subordinate will report back on how well he or she is doing and any major problems that have surfaced. This can be supplemented with periodic spot checks to ensure that authority guidelines are not being abused, organization policies are being followed, and proper procedures are being met. But too much of a good thing can be harmful. If the controls are too constraining, the subordinate will be deprived of the opportunity to build self-confidence. A well-designed control system permits your subordinate to make small mistakes, but quickly alerts you when big mistakes are imminent.

6. **When problems surface, insist on recommendations from the subordinate.** Many supervisors fall into the trap of letting subordinates reverse the delegation process: the subordinate runs into a problem and then comes back to the supervisor for advice or a solution. Avoid being sucked into reverse delegation by insisting from the beginning that when subordinates want to discuss a problem with you, they come prepared with a recommendation. When you delegate downward, the subordinate's job includes making necessary decisions. Don't allow the subordinate to push decisions back upward to you.

Applying Your Skills

This is a role-playing exercise. Break into groups of four to six students. One student in each group will assume the role of Chris Hall and one the role of Dale Morgan. The other students will serve as observers and evaluators.

Students playing the roles of Chris and Dale should read the Situation and his or her respective role *only*. Observers should read the Situation and *both* roles, and record observations on their Observer's Sheet.

SITUATION

CHRIS HALL is Director of Research and Development for a small pharmaceutical manufacturer. Chris has six direct subordinates: Sue Traynor (Chris's secretary), **DALE MORGAN** (the laboratory supervisor), Todd Connor (quality standards supervisor), Linda Peters (patent coordination supervisor), Ruben Gomez (market coordination supervisor), and Marjorie England (senior project supervisor). Dale is the most senior of the five supervisors, and is generally acknowledged as the chief candidate to replace Chris when Chris is promoted.

CHRIS HALL'S ROLE

You have received your annual instructions from the CEO to develop next year's budget for your area. The task is relatively routine but takes quite a bit of time. In the past, you've always done the annual budget yourself. But this year, because your workload is exceptionally heavy, you've decided to try something different. You're going to assign budget preparation to one of your supervisors. The obvious choice is Dale Morgan. Dale has been with the company longest, is highly dependable, and, as your probable successor, is most likely to gain from the experience. The budget is due on your boss's desk in eight weeks. Last year it took you about 30 to 35 hours to complete. However, you had done a budget many times before. For a novice, it might take double that amount of time.

The budget process is generally straightforward. You start with last year's budget and modify it to reflect inflation and changes in departmental objectives. All the data that Dale will need are in your files or can be obtained from your other supervisors.

You have decided to walk over to Dale's office and inform him or her of your decision.

DALE MORGAN'S ROLE

You like Chris Hall. You think Chris is a first-rate manager and you've learned a lot from him or her. You also consider yourself Chris's heir apparent. To better prepare yourself to take Chris's job, you'd like to take on more of Chris's responsibilities.

Running the lab is a demanding job. You regularly come in around 7:00 a.m. and it's unusual for you to leave before 7:00 p.m. Four of the last five weekends, you've even come in on Saturday mornings to get your work done. But, within reasonable limits, you'd try to find the time to take on some of Chris's responsibilities.

As you sit behind your desk reviewing a lab report, Chris walks into your office.

SKILL APPLICATION—OBSERVER'S SHEET

INSTRUCTIONS

This exercise should take no more than 10 to 15 minutes. When completed, representatives from each group should discuss with the entire class how their delegation exercise went. Focus specifically on the skill behaviours presented in the previous section and any problems that surfaced.

	1 Poor	2	3 Good	4	5 Excellent
1. Chris was clear in defining the assignment—expected results, deadlines	☐	☐	☐	☐	☐
2. Chris specified the range of discretion—guidelines and authority	☐	☐	☐	☐	☐
3. Chris allowed Dale to participate in the delegation process	☐	☐	☐	☐	☐
4. Chris discussed informing others of Dale's involvement	☐	☐	☐	☐	☐
5. Chris established feedback controls—times, sessions	☐	☐	☐	☐	☐

SUMMARY

This summary is organized by the Learning Objectives.

1. Organizing is arranging jobs and groups of jobs in a department so that activities can be accomplished as planned.
2. Division of labour increases economic efficiency by allocating the most difficult and complex tasks to those employees with the highest skill level and paying other people less to do the less difficult and less skilled tasks. It is easier to train and replace staff who are specialized.
3. The narrower the span of control, the more management levels are necessary to directly oversee activities. Wider spans create fewer managerial levels and flatter organization structures.
4. Line authority refers to the right to direct the work of subordinates. Supervisors with staff authority, on the other hand, advise, and assist line supervisors in accomplishing their job. So only line authority allows individuals to make decisions independently and without consulting others.
5. Organizations are becoming increasingly decentralized in order to meet competitive challenges through knowledgeable and rapid decision making.
6. Functional departmentalization means that group activities are organized around functions performed—for example, accounting, engineering, manufacturing, personnel, and purchasing.
7. The strength of the matrix is that it provides the economies of functional specialization with the accountability of product departmentalization. Its major weakness is that, because the principle of unity of command is broken, it is difficult to coordinate tasks of people who have more than one manager.
8. Job descriptions provide supervisors with a formal document describing what the employee is supposed to be doing, help employees understand their job duties, and clarify the results that management expects.
9. Delegation consists of 1. allocation of duties, 2. delegation of authority, 3. assignment, and 4. creation of accountability.

KEY TERMS AND CONCEPTS

Accountability
Authority
Blended departmentalization
Centralized authority
Customer departmentalization
Decentralized authority
Delegation
Departmentalization
Division of labour
Empowerment
Functional authority
Functional departmentalization
Geographic departmentalization
Horizontal structures
Job analysis
Job description

Job evaluation
Job specifications
Line authority
Matrix
Organizing
Process departmentalization
Product or service departmenta-
  lization
Responsibility
Simple structure
Social loafing
Span of control
Staff authority
Team
Telecommuting
Unity of command

REVIEWING YOUR KNOWLEDGE

1. What are the limitations, if any, to division of labour?
2. How might wider spans of control lead to cost reductions for an organization?
3. What is functional authority? When is it useful to an organization?
4. What happens when authority and responsibility are out of balance?
5. What are the advantages of a) product, b) geographic, c) customer, and d) process departmentalization?
6. Why would an organization use a matrix structure?
7. Differentiate the following: job analysis, job description, job evaluation, job specifications.
8. Describe the four-step delegation process.
9. Is delegation synonymous with abdication? Discuss.

CASE 5.A

Trickle Down Restructuring

Alex Lawrence[1] has spent many years managing the North American client satisfaction unit of a multinational company that provides business systems, software and services. Her team is composed of client satisfaction advisors, working with various internal client groups to interpret the results of client satisfaction surveys and strategize how to address any issues uncovered. Her team advises company staff who consult with, sell to or service the actual customers.

When the company restructures, as it has done several times, Alex's group is immediately affected. The structure when Alex first started clustered organizational units based on client groups (e.g. financial services, industrial, communications, distribution) so each of her team members would be assigned to work with a group of internal stakeholders who work with a particular industry. For example, two advisors worked with staff selling to financial services clients across North America.

Then the company reorganized to units based on region (e.g. Canada, north-eastern U.S., western U.S.). Alex's team members were each allocated a new set of internal stakeholders. An advisor who had previously worked with company units focused on one industry now worked with company units who dealt with all clients in a region (e.g. Canada), regardless of their industry.

What did the change mean to Alex's staff? "It meant entirely new relationships had to be created, trust built. The client issues don't change hugely, regardless of industry or region, but my staff now needed to establish their credibility with new internal people so that their advising would be effective."

The most recent reorganization has focused on assessment of client account profitability. Clients have been divided into A clients (that are growing more than 15% a year), B clients (that are large and stable, like banks) and C clients (everyone else). The company strategy is to focus on the clients offering more potential profitability. The effect on Alex's team has been to really focus on supporting strong relationships with A and B clients. Little support is now offered for those dealing with C clients. There has been pushback from internal stakeholders who want the same support they are used to, and Alex has had to explain that those resources have been removed. When the issue is escalated above Alex, the answer is the same—there has been a decision to focus resources strategically on certain parts of the business, and this means removing supports people were used to. Not all clients are considered equal.

Why does the company make these changes? "The company reinvents itself every few years, examining the markets and economy and reflecting on whether the company structure supports what is needed. It has worked; after decades in business, we continue to be successful, never resting on our laurels."

The switch from one structure to a second to a third described above is a simplified summary. As Alex explains, in fact, all the structures are in place at any time; it's the primary structure that changes. "So when we changed to a regional structure, there were still industry specialists in the company who kept an eye on what was happening in their industry across all regions. I may have had only one manager who did my appraisal but several others had some say in it—I had to satisfy not only the regional bosses but also the industry specialists that my team were doing their best to deal with client satisfaction issues."

---

[1] Names and details have been changed to protect the identity of "Alex".

RESPONDING TO THIS CASE

1. Outline the progression of structural changes using concepts from the chapter.
2. Explain what the changes in organizational structure likely mean to Alex in working with her staff. Do you see any need for job analysis when the structure changes? Are job descriptions, specifications or evaluation likely to change?
3. Alex describes her performance appraisal being shaped by several managers even though she formally only reports to one. What structural concept does this illustrate?
4. In their work with client groups on how to improve client satisfaction scores, do Alex's staff members have line, staff or functional authority? Why?
5. Alex describes her staff as "team members". Are they really a team? Why or why not?

CASE 5.B

The Social Chainsaw

Ace[1] is a skilled professional who has worked in a number of small and successful companies. He tells the story of his short experience at one organization memorable for the owner. In Ace's words, that owner is a 'social chainsaw'. We'll refer to him as 'Buzz'.

Buzz is the owner of a company that manufactures and distributes a technological device. It is a simple and flat structure, with all employees reporting to Buzz. He hires well, building a small staff of young, smart people. But he micromanages them. "Buzz wouldn't show up at the office for days at a time but would still insist that everything had to go through him. He would task people but they had to get his approval on next steps and he did not make time to see staff."

Buzz is reluctant to spend money. The office manager had to spend her own money on stamps because Buzz wouldn't authorize payment for them. "UPS shut down our account because he didn't pay their bill; it was our lifeline." Ace felt

the employees were used as creditors because Buzz took months to reimburse employees who had funded business flights and hotels themselves. He would question expense reports (do you have to drink that many coffees?) and delay payment further. Dealing with hundreds of pieces of inventory coming from many places, the staff wanted an inventory system. No, Buzz said they could simply use a spreadsheet. Ace felt Buzz wanted the analysis without providing the tool.

Part of what bothered Ace the most was the promise of autonomy and the reneging on that promise. "I saw him hire a bright, energetic guy to spearhead business development. He asked him to come help grow the business, do partnership and marketing. This guy did great marketing plans but then Buzz deleted his email. He wanted him to do 20 cold calls a day, wanted to use him as a grunt; couldn't stomach anyone else having a leadership role."

How was Buzz a social chainsaw? "He was rude and harsh. He would sit in his office and yell, "Do this". I remember one day he told me "I've forgotten more about this than you will ever know", almost sneering at me. He hired an excellent office manager who was organized and polite. He treated her like garbage, giving her a long list of tasks, expecting her to work 12 hours a day for $30,000. And she would have to beg him to sign cheques. He negotiated quarterly bonuses with us, we would earn them, and then he would "forget" to pay them." Turnover was high.

Sharing information was, unsurprisingly, not a strong point for Buzz. "There were four areas to the company and they felt like four silos. We had no idea what each other did. He wouldn't let others see the books so we had no idea what was coming in or going out."

"It was a cancerous environment. Buzz was very smart but he was socially retarded. Brains will only take you so far. It's all about relationships. He hired good guys who were so beaten down they didn't care; people who wanted to grow, learn, build and invest in themselves. Buzz only wanted soldiers to shoot on command."

---

[1] Ace is a pseudonym chosen by the narrator of this case who did not wish to be identified.

Responding to This Case

1. Describe the way Buzz has chosen to organize his company in terms of the following concepts: centralized versus decentralized authority, unity of command, line/staff/functional authority, span of control.

2. Explain what the results of Buzz's organizational choices are.

3. Describe how Buzz's organization illustrates the potential problems with a simple structure.

4. Buzz has no job descriptions; he delivers verbal explanations only to staff. What do you see as the problem with this approach?

5. Buzz obviously does not know how to delegate effectively. Assuming you had to make a pitch to convince Buzz of the value of delegating, summarize what the advantages would be and how he should approach delegating.

6. Even if Buzz wanted to create teams in his organization, he would not be successful. Explain why.

6

ACQUIRING THE RIGHT PEOPLE

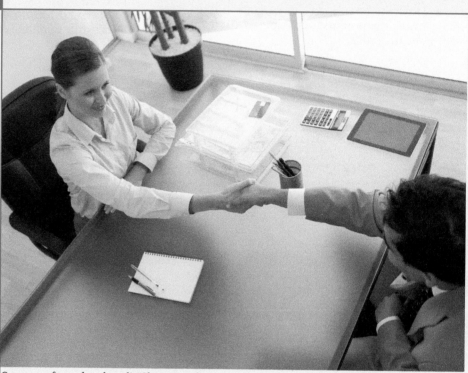

Courtesy of wavebreakmedia/Shutterstock

LEARNING OBJECTIVES

After reading this chapter, you should be able to:

1. Identify key laws and regulations affecting human resource practices.
2. Define the three steps in human resource planning.
3. Explain the purpose of the job specification.
4. List the primary sources for job candidates.
5. Discuss the different problems created by accept errors and reject errors.
6. Identify the strengths and weaknesses of the best-known selection devices.
7. Explain how to conduct an effective hiring interview, including the use of behaviour-based questions.

CHAPTER OUTLINE

PERFORMING EFFECTIVELY

SUPERVISORS AND THE HUMAN RESOURCES DEPARTMENT

UNDERSTANDING EQUAL EMPLOYMENT OPPORTUNITY
Laws and Regulations
Human Rights Legislation
Your Role in Employment Equity
EEO Goes Beyond Hiring
Employment Standards

DETERMINING STAFFING NEEDS
Current Assessment
Future Assessment
Developing a Future Program

FROM JOB DESCRIPTIONS TO JOB SPECIFICATIONS
Something to Think About

RECRUITING CANDIDATES
Internal Search
Advertisements
Employee Referrals
Employment Agencies
Schools, Colleges, and Universities
Professional Organizations
Casual or Unsolicited Applicants
Unemployment Agencies and Centres
Other Sources

EMPLOYEE SELECTION
Foundations of Selection
Selection Devices
Something to Think About
Building a Supervisory Skill

NEW-EMPLOYEE ORIENTATION
Supervision in Action: The Realistic Job Preview

FROM CONCEPTS TO SKILLS: INTERVIEWING
Assessing Yourself: Do You Have Good Interviewing Skills?
Skill Basics
Applying Your Skills

UNDERSTANDING THE BASICS
Summary
Key Terms and Concepts
Reviewing Your Knowledge
Answers to the Pop Quizzes

PERFORMING YOUR JOB
Case 6.A Hiring Horror Stories
Case 6.B Was Anyone Unethical Here?

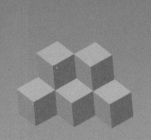

FIGURE 6-1

Ainslie White of
Precision Biologic in
Nova Scotia.

FIGURE 6-2

Christopher Nicolson of
Tourism Sun Peaks in
British Columbia.

Ainslie White is the manager of information systems at Precision Biologic in Dartmouth, Nova Scotia. He takes hiring decisions seriously.

"I put a lot of stock into hiring people, ensuring the right fit. It's not just skills. I put emphasis on fit and problem-solving. I want someone who can interact with others well. There are a lot of smart, skilled computer people but you also need social skills to work in a business. In hiring at Precision Biologic, we might do 4 or 5 interviews, spending a lot of time. It's part of our culture. Someone joked we almost do three months of probation in the screening process. We throw out scenarios for them to say how they'd deal with it, we chat, we check technical knowledge. There are no quick decisions on hiring in my area. I have to ensure they click with me and the team. When we went from 2 to 3 people, the other person was involved in the hiring with me. I wanted her sense of whether she could work with the person. It has paid off; the IT team is great. It saves a lot of headaches in the long run.

The job is not set in stone when we are looking for someone. I like considering the role in my head as we consider possible candidates to see what skills the person can bring and what skills could be developed. In a sense, we fit the job to them."

In a totally different industry, Christopher Nicolson, the president of Tourism Sun Peaks (a ski resort) has a similar approach. "Our hiring is a pretty informal process. I do work with the resume for skills but a lot depends on the interaction with me and the rest of the team. I introduce them to the team so I can get feedback from others. I like the team feedback for gut feel and soft skills. They meet everyone and get the Tourism Sun Peaks 101 orientation so they know what they would be getting into. I give a lot of situational analogies to see what they come up with because initiative and empowerment are important to me. Sometimes I'll ask them to actually demonstrate something. For example a public relations media person has to be out there, so I ask them to go and get interviews in the street."

Christopher and Ainslie both put a lot of effort into hiring the right people, with "right" referring to fit with the team and the organization as well as having the needed skills and knowledge. Hiring is a time-consuming process, as are the orientation and training to support a new hire fitting in. But not taking the time to do it well means performance management issues and possibly termination down the road, as well as the morale issues that come when a team member is let go. It's critical to put time in upfront to clarify what kind of employee is needed, then hire someone suitable, and support their integration into the role and the organization.

In this chapter we'll address a number of issues around recruitment and selection. Let's start, however, by considering the typical role of the human resources department in staffing decisions.

SUPERVISORS AND THE HUMAN RESOURCES DEPARTMENT

Some readers may be thinking, "Sure, human resources decisions such as recruitment and selection are important, but aren't they made by specialists in the human resources department? These aren't decisions that supervisors get involved in:"

It's true that many organizations have human resources (HR) departments. But the people in these departments rarely make specific staffing decisions. Rather, as staff specialists, they help supervisors by writing and placing employment ads, screening applicants, and providing legal advice on various issues. They may also assist with the recruitment strategy and with creating appropriate interview questions, and by training on effective interview techniques. At the request of managers, HR can join in the interviews. However, HR is primarily a support that rests behind the scenes. The final decision, typically, is the supervisor's. Moreover, many small organizations don't have human resources departments. In such cases, supervisors typically have sole responsibility for hiring.

Every supervisor will be involved in staffing decisions. So, regardless of the size of your organization or the presence of a human resources department staffed with specialists, there will be certain activities you need to understand. These include, at a minimum, human resources planning, how to conduct employment interviews, and techniques for new-employee orientation. Also, very importantly, every supervisor must have a fundamental understanding of the current laws and regulations governing equal employment opportunity (EEO).

UNDERSTANDING EQUAL EMPLOYMENT OPPORTUNITY

Ron had worked in the lumber business for more than 20 years, but he'd never held a management position before. About five months ago he was hired as a supervisor in the finishing department at a small lumber mill. When he recently had an opening in his department, he interviewed four candidates sent to him by the firm's human resources department. During an interview with one of the applicants, a woman who was not made a job offer, he asked her a number of questions. Two of them were "Are you married?" and "Do you have any children at home?" He didn't, however, ask those questions of the male candidates he interviewed. Ron learned today, from his boss, that this applicant has filed a discrimination suit against him and the company. When Ron's boss asked if it was true that he had asked the woman about her marital status and whether she had children, Ron responded, "Sure. I was concerned she might miss work because of family responsibilities." Ron's boss was shocked. "Let me tell you something, Ron. Regardless of your intentions, you've just gotten yourself and this company into a heck of a mess!"

Ron broke the law by asking questions of women job candidates that he didn't ask of men, questions that in fact may not even have been job-relevant. In so doing, he made himself and his employer potentially liable for damages.

Bona fide Occupational Requirements
Skills or qualifications essential for performance in the role.

Hiring must be based on **bona fide occupational requirements** (BFOR), that is, the skills or qualifications used in a hiring decision must be essential for performance in the role. All candidates should be screened on those BFORs and no additional screening questions should be used for some and not others. The example of Ron illustrates the importance of every supervisor understanding the law and its effect on human resource practices. In large companies, there will be policies, procedures and training to support effective hiring and reduce the risk of discrimination. There will also be efforts to ensure that hiring practices and recruitment strategies reach as wide an audience as possible and do not target specific groups or omit certain groups. For supervisors in small firms, hiring assistance may be provided through consultants or an outsourced HR function, or the supervisor may simply have to turn to upper management for guidance. As we briefly review equal employment opportunity, remember that engaging in discrimination not only exposes you and your organization to potential liability, but also deprives you of hiring the applicant who is most qualified.

LAWS AND REGULATIONS

In Canada, human rights legislation guarantees each person's right to equal opportunity for employment. Depending on your place of employment, your rights to equal treatment at work are protected by either the Federal Human Rights Act or one of the provincial acts. Although the acts vary in the categories they specify for protection, their basic intent is to prevent discrimination on the basis of race, colour, gender, religion, marital status, age, or handicap (see Figure 6-3). Additionally, each jurisdiction can specify additional "protected groups." The fundamental intent of all the acts is to protect equal opportunity.

HUMAN RIGHTS LEGISLATION

Human rights legislation protects job applicants from possible discriminating practices by prohibiting various questions. The following guidelines from the B.C. Ministry of Attorney General, similar to those offered in other provinces, indicate which questions are allowed and not allowed to ask when recruiting.

Age (18+)
Questions employers may ask:
- "Have you reached BC's legal working age?"
- After hiring, an applicant's age may be asked for benefit and insurance plans.

Questions to avoid:
- Asking about age in general, or about birth certificates.

Race, Creed, Colour, Ancestry, Place of Origin
Questions employers may ask:
- "Are you legally entitled to work in Canada?"
  All those legally entitled to work in Canada must be given equal employment opportunity unless there is a legal restriction stating otherwise.

Questions to avoid:
- Asking about birthplace or nationality, including nationality of relatives or spouse.

Criminal or Summary Conviction
Questions employers may ask:
- Inquiries about criminal or summary convictions are discouraged unless directly related to job duties.
- If bonding is required, ask applicants if they are eligible to be bonded.

Questions to avoid:
- Asking for statements of criminal and/or arrest record, unless job involves working with children.

Education

Questions employers may ask:

- Any educational requirements should be related to job duties.

Mental or Physical Disability

Questions employers may ask:

- Applicants may be asked job-related questions concerning ability to do the essential components of the job.
- An applicant's disability is relevant to the job only if it prevents that person from effectively carrying out the essential components of the job.

Questions to avoid

- Asking for a general statement of disabilities, limitations, or health problems.

Political Belief

Questions to avoid

- Asking for statements of political beliefs and philosophy (except where it is a legitimate requirement, as it may be for employment by a political party).

Religious Belief

Questions employers may ask:

- Applicants may be asked job-related questions such as whether they are available for the required work time.
- Employers must be responsible in accommodating the religious needs of employees.

Questions to avoid:

- Asking for statements concerning religious affiliation, religious beliefs, and church membership.

Sex, Sexual Orientation, Marital/Family Status

Questions employers may ask:

- If job mobility is required, ask the applicants if they are willing to travel or be transferred.
- Information regarding spouse, children and/or dependants required for benefit and pension plans can be obtained after hiring.

Questions to avoid:

- Asking about an applicant's sex or sexual orientation.
- Asking for information regarding pregnancy, childcare arrangements, or child-bearing plans.
- Asking whether the applicant is single, married, divorced, engaged, separated, widowed or living common-law.

YOUR ROLE IN EMPLOYMENT EQUITY

Some employers will institute employment equity programs, with specific goals, to increase the number of women, Aboriginal persons, disabled and minorities in their organization. As a supervisor, you may be asked to actively pursue such candidates and make a good-faith effort to get them into the applicant pool.

Does this mean you must hire an unqualified applicant in order to meet employment equity goals? No! As we'll discuss shortly, before you begin looking to fill a position in your department, you need to know the skills, knowledge, and ability requirements of the job. If candidates meet these criteria, they are qualified. But the law doesn't require you to hire unqualified employees. So you should extend your search for female, disabled, Aboriginal, and minority applicants far and wide—for example, possibly placing ads in papers that are specifically targetted at multicultural groups or sending a notice of your job opening to the local disabled training centre—but you are not forced to hire any individual under this process. The objective of employment equity is to eliminate discrimination, not ensure the hiring of individuals from certain groups.

EEO Goes beyond Hiring

Equal employment opportunity goes beyond recruitment and selection of employees. It also addresses issues such as training, promotion, and eliminating discriminatorily abusive work environments.

TRAINING OPPORTUNITIES

Are you making sure *all* of your employees have equal access to training?

Do your employees need special training to learn to understand and work more effectively with individuals who are different from them? As the workforce becomes more culturally diverse, you will want to ensure that women, racial and ethnic minorities, gay employees, and members of any other group who may be perceived as "different" are not treated prejudicially by others. This may require your employees to participate in awareness and sensitivity workshops to help them better understand and work with people who are unlike themselves.

ELIMINATING SEXUAL HARASSMENT

Few workplace topics have received more attention in recent years than that of sexual harassment.

Sexual harassment generally encompasses sexually suggestive remarks, unwanted touching and sexual advances, requests for sexual favours, and other verbal and physical conduct of a sexual nature. It is considered illegal; it is a violation of the human rights legislation.

Courts have widened the test for sexual harassment to whether a comment or behaviour in a work environment "would reasonably be perceived, and is perceived, as hostile or abusive." In so doing, employees need not show they have been psychologically damaged to prove sexual harassment in the workplace, merely that they are working in a hostile or abusive environment. Sexual harassment is assessed based on how it was

Sexual harassment Sexually suggestive remarks, unwanted touching and sexual advances, requests for sexual favours, and other verbal and physical conduct of a sexual nature.

perceived by the victim. It is not how a joke or advance was "meant" to be taken, but how it was taken.

From a supervisor's standpoint, sexual harassment is a concern because it intimidates employees, interferes with job performance, and exposes the organization to liability. With changing legislation in several provinces, there is also more legal pressure to deal with harassment. Bill 168 in Ontario (amending the Occupational Health and Safety Act) now holds business owners, managers, and supervisors personally and criminally responsible for workplace harassment and violence. To ensure that you do not have a hostile or abusive environment, you must establish a clear and strong position against workplace harassment. If higher management doesn't have a workplace harassment policy, then you need to establish one for your department. The policy should be reinforced by discussion sessions in which employees are reminded of the rule and carefully instructed that even the slightest sexual overture to another employee will not be tolerated. In some companies, employees have been specifically advised that they can be fired for making repeated unwelcome sexual advances, using sexually degrading words to describe someone, or displaying sexually offensive pictures or objects at work.

EMPLOYMENT STANDARDS

While we examine legal implications affecting the way supervisors hire employees and deal with them, it is appropriate to also look at the employment standards with which employers must comply. All jurisdictions have minimum standards that all employers must abide by. These vary somewhat with jurisdiction and were discussed in chapter 3. Figure 3-2 illustrated sample standards for employees working under federal jurisdiction or under provincial jurisdiction in Alberta, Newfoundland and Labrador, and Nunavut.

DETERMINING STAFFING NEEDS

Human resource planning
Ensuring that a department has the right personnel, who are capable of completing those tasks that help the department reach its objectives.

You've organized your department. You've identified the tasks that need to be done and grouped them into jobs. Now you must ensure that you'll have the right number and kinds of people to achieve your department's goals. We call this **human resource planning** and it can be condensed into three steps:

1. assessing current human resources
2. assessing future human resource needs
3. developing a program to meet future human resource needs

Current Assessment

Begin your assessment by reviewing your current human resource status. Your goal is to create a departmental human resource inventory.

To build this inventory, your employees will complete forms for the human resources department. Increasingly, these files can be accessed by computer. This departmental inventory will typically include a list of your employees' names, education, training, prior employment, languages spoken, capabilities, and specialized skills. When completed, this inventory allows you to assess what talents and skills are available within your department. It lets you know what your individual employees can do. Make sure the files are updated periodically so the information is current.

Future Assessment

Future human resource needs are determined by the organization's overall objectives and your departmental goals.

The organization's demand for human resources is directly related to the demand for the organization's products or services. From its estimate of total revenue, top management can attempt to establish the number and mix of human resources needed to reach these revenues. In some cases, the situation may be reversed. Revenues may be determined by human resources if the particular skills are in scarce supply, and are not available in the labour market.

Based on forecasts provided by upper management, you can calculate their implications for your department's operations. What will be the increase or decrease in workload? What new or changing skills will be called for?

Developing a Future Program

After you've assessed both current capabilities and future needs, you'll be able to estimate shortages—both in number and kind—and to highlight areas in which your department will be overstaffed. Additionally, of course, your departmental projections will need to be combined with forecasts made by other supervisors in your organization and coordinated with the human resources department. This is important because it ensures that you can identify individuals with skills and capabilities that cut across departmental lines.

Where shortages are identified, hiring and training plans can be generated. Where overstaffing is forecast, the solution may be movement of people within the company, early retirements, encouraging unpaid sabbaticals, or terminations. Of course, this future planning must also be ready to accommodate the unexpected departure of employees through resignation, illness or death.

FROM JOB DESCRIPTIONS TO JOB SPECIFICATIONS

Job specification
The minimum acceptable qualifications an employee must possess to perform a given job successfully.

You'll remember from the previous chapter that once your departmental structure is in place, you then create job descriptions. These job descriptions tell employees what they're supposed to do. Also mentioned in the last chapter is the **job specification**, which similarly arises from the job analysis and is often included as part of the job description.

The job specification states the minimum acceptable qualifications an employee must possess to perform a given job successfully. It identifies the knowledge, skills, and abilities needed to do the job effectively. In large organizations, job specifications are written by specialists in the human resources department. In smaller organizations, you may develop these yourself. An example of a job specification for an animal technician in a university research lab is shown in Figure 6-4.

ANIMAL TECHNICIAN I

NATURE OF WORK

This is technical work in the care of laboratory research animals. Work involves caring for laboratory animals in accordance with specific directions received from a superior and includes the preparation of special foods, administering medicines, and breeding, weaning and sexing of some species of animals.

REQUIREMENTS OF WORK

- Experience in feeding and caring for laboratory animals; graduation from high school supplemented by courses in animal husbandry; OR graduation from high school supplemented by the successful completion of the University training program; or any equivalent combination of experience and training which provides the following knowledge, abilities and skills:
- Knowledge of the techniques involved in handling, breeding, observing and caring for a variety of laboratory animals.
- Knowledge of common symptoms of illness or abnormality in laboratory animals.
- Ability to perform tasks in the care and feeding of animals.
- Ability to perform custodial tasks related to sanitation and cleanliness of cages and premises.
- Ability to read, understand and interpret written and oral instructions.
- Ability to establish and maintain effective working relationships with subordinates, officials, faculty, and other employees.
- Skill in handling and caring for laboratory animals.
- Possession of a valid Province of Newfoundland and Labrador driver's license.

Source: Memorial University Human Resources, http://www.mun.ca/humanres/jobspecs/pdf/3241.pdf
Reprinted from *www.mun.ca*, January 5, 2004, Memorial University of Newfoundland.

FIGURE 6-4

Sample job specification

Competency research has generated another way of developing a job specification. By researching what distinguishes the top performers in a position from the average performers, one can generate a picture of competencies or skills that go beyond simply being able to do the job. This can take a lot of work, for example, through interviewing the top and mediocre performers or their managers and coworkers, but if there is a huge difference in performance between the two groups, as in sales, the resulting information is worth the effort.[2]

Why is the job specification important? It's the standard against which job applicants will be compared. It keeps your attention focused on the specific necessary and preferred qualifications for an individual to do a job effectively, and it assists you in determining whether candidates are qualified. The criteria to use as a basis for hiring may even include personality characteristics, which adds more complexity to the situation (see "Something to Think About").

Once you've identified a vacancy in your department and have a job specification for that position, you can begin the search for the right candidate to fill that vacancy.

RECRUITING CANDIDATES

If you have a departmental vacancy, where do you look to find potential candidates to fill it? In this section, we'll review the primary sources for job candidates.

INTERNAL SEARCH

Most organizations give preference to current employees for new openings. Employees like this practice because it gives them an advantage over outsiders in applying for lateral transfers and promotions, improving morale and retention. Managers prefer internal candidates because they are more likely to be able to get detailed and accurate information on how the candidate did on prior jobs within the organization. While outside references are often vague and noncommittal, other managers within your organization can typically provide you with the full history of an internal employee's performance record. In addition, internal candidates are already familiar with the organization. They should therefore take less time to adjust to a new job.

When looking for people to staff her brand new library branch, Anne Murphy of the Frank McKechnie library in Mississauga presented a workshop at the library system's staff conference, encouraging people to apply for transfer to the new branch.

Predicting group performance is tricky. We've all seen groups that have not performed exceptionally well despite having exceptional talent. And we've seen groups with mediocre talent pull together and beat the odds. Obviously group potential is more than simply adding up the skill levels of individual members.

One study that supports this points to personality as an influential factor. Neuman and Wright examined the work performance of 316 full-time human resource (HR) representatives who work in teams of four at local stores across the United States in a large whole-sale department store organization.[3] When they were hired, all 316 employees completed commercial tests of personality, cognitive ability, and job-related skills. The scores were *not* used in the hiring decisions. Three years later, each representative's work performance was evaluated by their peers on six dimensions. Each four-person team's performance was measured on the same six dimensions by three department supervisors who work in the same store as the HR team. The supervisors were not aware of the original scores, which prevented bias in their evaluations. Two more measures were taken: work completed—meaning the number of days for one year that team tasks were completed within schedule; and work accuracy—the percentage of forms processed by the team without error in the year.

The results showed that scores on two personality traits predicted peer ratings of individual performance beyond measures of job-specific skills and general cognitive ability. The same two personality measures predicted supervisor ratings of team performance and objective measures of work team accuracy and work completed. These two important personality variables are agreeableness and conscientiousness. Individuals high on these characteristics were more likely to be evaluated as strong performers by their peers, and teams high on these characteristics were more likely to have their work completed accurately and on time, and to be seen as effective teams by supervisors.

Agreeableness refers to the extent to which someone tends to trust others; be straightforward, altruistic, cooperative in conflict situations, and modest; and be able to express sympathy and empathy. Conscientiousness describes a combination of thinking carefully before acting, working hard to achieve goals, following up on commitments, adhering to ethical and moral obligations, and maintaining self-discipline.

How would these personality characteristics influence the team so that its performance is enhanced? Would it be fair to test applicants on these personality traits and use their scores to screen their suitability for a position? Consider how conscientiousness and agreeableness could be explored using behaviour-based questions, described later in this chapter, when hiring someone to work as part of a team.

There are several drawbacks to relying on an internal search. First, it provides a limited set of candidates. You wouldn't want to hire a second-rate employee merely because he or she was there, when excellent candidates are available outside the organization. Second, excessive reliance on internal search tends to perpetuate "inbreeding." Internal candidates are less likely to bring new ideas and fresh perspectives to the job. Third, if past hiring decisions were discriminatory, internal hiring will continue to fail the "equal opportunity" test.

Nevertheless, many companies stand by their "hire from within" policy, giving first crack at job opportunities before the search is opened up.

Advertisements

Effective hiring depends on qualified candidates learning of the job opportunity and applying. Ads for job openings have traditionally been posted in newspapers and at the actual location (e.g. a sign outside a plant reads: "Now Hiring – Experienced Machinists"). Increasingly, companies are depending on the internet to post job openings. Whether paying to post on Workopolis and Monster or using free services like Indeed.ca or eluta.ca, employers find the internet a powerful way to reach a wide audience of potential candidates quickly and effectively. This is sometimes supplemented by the use of social media like Facebook, LinkedIn and Twitter to inform people about the company and invite them to investigate employment opportunities.

Advertisements are an excellent means of informing a wide audience of a vacancy. Also, by careful selection of the medium for the ad, you can target specific minority groups or individuals with similar interests. The major drawback of advertisements is that, unless ads are very carefully worded, they tend to attract many unqualified candidates. Cost must also be considered.

Employee Referrals

One of the best sources of individuals who will perform effectively on the job is a recommendation from a current employee.[4] The reasons are fairly obvious. Employees will rarely recommend someone unless they believe that the referral will perform adequately. Such a recommendation reflects on the recommender and, when someone's reputation is at stake, we can expect the recommendation to be based on relatively strong beliefs. Employee referrals may also have acquired more accurate information about their potential jobs. The recommender often gives the applicant more realistic information about the job than could be conveyed through employment agencies or advertisements. This information reduces unrealistic expectations. As a result of these pre-selection factors, employee referrals tend to be more acceptable applicants, to have a greater probability of accepting an offer if one is made, and, once employed, to have a higher job-survival rate. Some organizations encourage employee referrals by giving "finder's fees" (for example, $500) to employees who recommend someone who is later hired. To avoid employees making a referral only to capitalize on the finder's fee, companies typically do not pay the fee until the new employee has successfully completed a probationary period.

There are, of course, some potentially negative features of employee referrals. For one thing, recommenders may confuse friendship with job-performance competence. Individuals often like to have their friends join them at their place of employment for social and even economic reasons. For example, they may be able to share rides to and from work. As a result, a current employee may recommend a friend for a position without giving unbiased consideration to the friend's job-related competence.

Employee referrals may also lead to nepotism; that is, hiring individuals who are related to persons already employed by the organization. The hiring of relatives is particularly widespread in family-owned organizations. While such actions do not necessarily meet the objective of hiring the most qualified applicant, interest in the organization and loyalty to it may be long-term advantages.

Finally, employee referrals may not help the organization in actively seeking minority and women candidates. Employees often refer someone who shares something with them—religion, demographics, race, etc. Accordingly, an organization that wants to increase the presence of protected groups must guard against over-reliance on employee referrals from members of nonprotected groups.

Employment Agencies

Employment agencies can be divided into three categories: full-service agencies, temporary help services, and executive search firms. Since the last type has little relevance to supervisors—they specialize in placing middle-level and top-level executives—we'll focus on the other two.

The typical full-service agency charges for its services. Their fees can be paid by the employer, the applicant, or on a shared basis. These agencies provide a complete line of services. They advertise the position, screen applicants against the criteria specified by the employer, and usually provide a guarantee covering six months or a year as protection to the employer, in case the applicant does not perform satisfactorily.

An increasingly popular type of employment agency is the one that specializes in temporary employees. Organizations such as Kelly and Manpower can be excellent sources of employees to fill part-time or short-term staffing needs (see Figure 6-5). As employers look for ways to increase their staffing flexibility and at the same time keep benefit costs down, the use of contingent workers hired through temporary help services is seen as a highly attractive alternative.

FIGURE 6-5

Manpower, the world's largest temporary help firm, tests applicants in order to match their skills to employer needs.
Courtesy of Marcio Jose Sanchez/AP Images

SCHOOLS, COLLEGES, AND UNIVERSITIES

Educational institutions at all levels offer opportunities for recruiting recent graduates. Most educational institutions operate placement services where prospective employers can review credentials and interview graduates; and many offer internship and co-op programs where you can find students who are looking for opportunities to practise on the job what they're learning. Whether the educational qualification required for the job is a high school diploma, specific vocational training, or a university background with a bachelor's, master's, or doctoral degree, educational institutions are an excellent source of potential employees for entry-level positions in organizations.

High schools or vocational-technical schools can provide blue-collar applicants; business or secretarial schools can provide white-collar staff; and colleges and universities can provide technical and professional personnel. Institutions can be targeted according to their specializations.

While educational institutions are usually viewed as sources of young, inexperienced entrants to the workforce, it is not uncommon to find individuals with considerable work experience using an educational institution's placement service. They may be workers who have recently returned to school to upgrade their skills, or alumni using their former school's placement centre.

Professional Organizations

Many professional organizations, including labour unions, operate placement services for the benefit of their members and employers. The professional organizations include such varied occupations as accountants, industrial engineers, training specialists, and seafarers.

These organizations publish rosters of job vacancies and distribute these lists to members. It is also common practice to provide placement facilities at regional and national meetings where those looking for employment and companies looking for employees can find each other. The advantage of using professional organizations is that this is "your crowd" and word of mouth within your own professional designation can create a referral.

Casual or Unsolicited Applicants

"Walk-ins," whether they reach an employer by letter, telephone, or in person, can be a major source of applicants. Although the qualification level of unsolicited applicants can depend on economic conditions, the organization's image, and the job seeker's perception of the types of jobs that might be available, this source does provide an excellent supply of stockpiled applicants. Even if there are no particular openings when the applicant makes contact with the organization, the application can be kept on file for later needs. Ryan Anderson refers to this as his virtual bench. He likes to have a selection of potential candidates on his radar and uses social media to keep in contact with these individuals.

Applications from individuals who are already employed can be referred to many months later and can provide applicants who 1. are interested in considering other employment opportunities and 2. regard the organization as a possible employer.

Unsolicited applications made by unemployed individuals, however, generally have a short life. Those individuals who have adequate skills will usually find employment with some other organization that does have an opening. But in tough economic times, excellent prospects are often unable to locate the type of job they desire and may stay actively looking in the job market for some time.

Unemployment Agencies and Centres

Provincial unemployment agencies are another source of available workers. These agencies will provide the service of posting vacancies, matching applicants, and prescreening for job openings. Increasingly, computerized files are simplifying the process of matching available workers to the skills required in available jobs.

OTHER SOURCES

Organizations that are focused on hiring particular types of applicants can use non-traditional sources such as the Canadian Paraplegic Association, that partners with employers with qualified candidates who are disabled; or the Toronto Region Immigrant Employment Council (TRIEC) that helps pair employers with qualified immigrants. Even unions can play a role. For example, the Power Workers' Union prefers the hiring of full-time employees but knows that sometimes organizations face peak demands or special projects that require the use of casual or contractor personnel. So the Power Workers' Hiring Hall works with employers to ensure a supply of qualified, dependable members to fill casual positions.

When you want to reach out and expand the diversity among applicants, sources might include local religious organizations, minority-oriented media, schools in low-income neighbourhoods, multicultural organizations, and agencies dealing with ex-prisoners.

EMPLOYEE SELECTION

You've developed a pool of applicants. Now you need some method for screening the applicants and for identifying the most appropriate candidate. That screening method is the selection process.

FOUNDATIONS OF SELECTION

Selection is a prediction exercise. It seeks to predict which applicants will be successful if hired. "Successful" in this case means performing well on the criteria the organization uses to evaluate employees. In filling a sales position, for example, the selection process should be able to predict which applicants will generate a high volume of sales for the company.

PREDICTION

Consider, for a moment, that any selection decision can result in four possible outcomes. As shown in Figure 6-6, two of these outcomes would indicate correct decisions, but two would indicate errors.

A decision is correct when the applicant was predicted to be successful and later proved to be successful on the job, or when the applicant was predicted to be unsuccessful and would perform accordingly if hired.

In the first case, we have successfully accepted; in the second case, we have successfully rejected. Thus the purpose of selection activities is to develop the outcomes shown as "correct decision" in Figure 6-6.

In selection, a supervisor is open to two different mistakes: reject errors and accept errors.

Reject errors occur when a supervisor eliminates a candidate who would have performed well on the job. The cost of reject errors might be additional recruitment and selection expenses. More significant, and potentially harmful, are the possible claims of discrimination.

Accept errors occur when a supervisor selects a candidate who is unable to perform the job successfully. Here, the costs of a poor decision include extra training, productivity losses, possible severance costs, and ultimately additional recruitment and selection costs. The major thrust of any selection activity is therefore to reduce the probability of making reject errors or accept errors, while increasing the probability of making correct decisions.

VALIDITY

Any selection device that a supervisor uses—such as application forms, tests, and interviews—must demonstrate **validity**. That is, there must be a proven relationship between the selection device and some relevant criterion. For example, the law prohibits management from using a test score as a selection device unless there is clear evidence that individuals with high scores on this test outperform, on the job, individuals with low test scores.

The burden is on management to show that any selection device it uses to differentiate applicants is related to job performance. For instance, while management can give applicants an intelligence test and use the results to help make selection decisions, it must be prepared to demonstrate, if challenged, that this intelligence test is a valid measure; that is,

Reject errors
Rejecting candidates who would later perform successfully on the job.

Accept errors
Accepting those candidates who subsequently perform poorly on the job.

Validity
The proven relationship that exists between a selection device and some relevant criterion.

	Selection Decision	
Later Job Performance	**Accept**	**Reject**
Successful	Correct decision	Reject error
Unsuccessful	Accept error	Correct decision

FIGURE 6-6

Selection decision outcomes

that scores on the test are positively related to later job performance.

RELIABILITY

In addition to being valid, a selection device must demonstrate reliability. **Reliability** indicates whether the device measures the same thing consistently. For example, if a test is reliable, any single individual's score should remain fairly stable over time, assuming that the characteristics it is measuring are also stable.

Reliability
The ability of a selection device to measure the same thing consistently.

The importance of reliability should be evident. No selection device can be effective if it is low in reliability. That is equivalent to weighing yourself everyday on an erratic scale. If the scale is unreliable—randomly fluctuating, say, five to ten kilograms every time you step on it—the results will not mean much. The same applies to selection devices. To be effective predictors, they must possess an acceptable level of consistency.

SELECTION DEVICES

Supervisors can use a number of selection devices to reduce accept and reject errors. The best-known devices include an analysis of the prospect's completed application form, written and performance-simulation tests, interviews, background investigations, and in some cases a physical examination. Let's take a look at each of these devices, noting their respective strengths and weaknesses.

THE APPLICATION FORM

Almost all organizations require candidates to fill out an application (see Figure 6-7). The form might ask a prospect to give his or her name, address, and telephone number. At the other extreme, it might be a comprehensive personal history profile, detailing the applicant's activities, skills, and accomplishments. Are these forms valid?

Hard and relevant biographical data that can be verified—for example, rank in graduating class—have been shown to be valid measures of performance for some jobs.[5] Additionally, when application-form items have been appropriately weighted to reflect job relatedness—that is, points are allocated to variables such as education and experience—the device has proven a valid predictor for such varied groups as sales clerks, engineers, factory workers, clerical employees, and technicians. But typically, only a couple of items on the application prove to be valid predictors, and then only for a specific job. Supervisors are encouraged to use weighted applications for selection purposes, but it is critical that application items be validated for each job and that the items be continually reviewed and updated to reflect changes in weights over time.

Application forms require management review and approval. Subtle discrimination can be built into the form and must be avoided. For example, if there is no reason to know what year a person graduated from high

Job Application

Date: _____

Name: _____
        Last   First   Middle Init.

Address: _____
            Street   City/Town   Prov.   Postal Code

Phone: (_____) _____

Email: _____

Employment History: Last 3 Jobs

1. Employer: _____
   Address: _____
   Phone: (_____) _____
   Position: _____

2. Employer: _____
   Address: _____
   Phone: (_____) _____
   Position: _____

3. Employer: _____
   Address: _____
   Phone: (_____) _____
   Position: _____

Education: Post-Secondary

1. School: _____   Degree earned _____
   Address: _____

2. School: _____   Degree earned _____
   Address: _____

Education: Secondary

Additional information: _____

_____

_____

_____

FIGURE 6-7

Sample application form

school, why ask that question other than as a way of learning their approximate age?

WRITTEN TESTS

Typical written tests include tests of intelligence, aptitude, ability, and interest. Historically, these written tests were popular selection devices, but there has been a marked decline in their use over the past quarter-century. Why? The reason is that these tests have frequently been characterized as discriminatory, and many organizations have been unable to demonstrate that they're job related. In other words, their validity is low.

Tests in intellectual ability, spatial and mechanical ability, perceptual accuracy, and motor ability have shown to be moderately valid predictors for many semiskilled and unskilled operative jobs in industrial organizations.[6] However, remember the burden is on management to demonstrate that any test used is job-related. Since many of these tests examine characteristics that are considerably removed from the actual performance of the job itself, getting high validity scores has often been difficult across a wide spectrum of jobs. The result has been a decreased use of traditional written tests and increased interest in performance simulation tests.

PERFORMANCE SIMULATION TESTS

What better way to find out whether an applicant can do a job successfully than by having him or her do it? The logic of this question has resulted in increased usage of performance simulation tests. Undoubtedly, the enthusiasm for these tests lies in the fact that they are based on actual job behaviours rather than on surrogates. The best-known performance simulation test is called **work sampling** and is designed for routine jobs.

Work sampling involves presenting applicants with a miniature replica of a job and letting them perform a task or set of tasks that are central to the job. Applicants demonstrate that they possess the necessary talents by actually doing the tasks. By carefully devising work samples, supervisors can determine the knowledge, skills, and abilities needed for each job. Each work-sample element is then matched with a corresponding job-performance element. For instance, for a job that involves computations on a calculator, a work sample would require applicants to make similar computations.

Marjane explains her use of a simulation: "I was hiring a researcher who had to do quantitative and qualitative research for the organization. I could gain a lot from the resume and interview but I wanted to get them actually handling some data and interpreting it. So I gave each of them half an hour to answer some questions about a data set recently handled by the current person in the job. Even though it was short, it was very revealing. Their ability to find relevant information, interpret data and then explain it in plain language was immediately clear to all of the committee members."

Work sampling
A selection device in which job applicants are presented with a miniature replica of a job and are asked to perform tasks central to that job.

The results from work-sample experiments have generally been impressive.[7] They have almost always yielded validity scores that are superior to those of written aptitude, personality, or intelligence tests.

INTERVIEWS

The interview, along with the application form, is an almost universal selection device. Not many of us have ever been hired for a job without one or more interviews. Unfortunately, interviews are typically poorly conducted and result in distorted findings.[8] This doesn't mean that interviews can't provide valid and reliable selection information, but rather that untrained interviewers tend to make common mistakes. For example, interviewers often hold a stereotype of what represents a "good" applicant; they often tend to favour applicants who share the interviewer's own attitudes; the order in which applicants are interviewed often influences evaluations, as does the order in which information is elicited; negative information is given unduly high weight; and interviewers forget much of the interview's content within minutes of its conclusion. See "Something to Think About" regarding the questions often used in interviews.

Structured behaviour-based questions are stronger predictors, allowing us to predict future behaviour based on descriptions of past behaviour (See Building a Supervisory Skill—Behaviour-Based Interviewing).

BACKGROUND INVESTIGATIONS

Background investigations are of two types: verification of application data and reference checks. The first type has proven to be a valuable source of selection information, whereas the latter is essentially worthless. Let's briefly review each.

Verifying the "facts" given on an application form pays dividends. The reason is that a significant percentage of job applicants—studies indicate upwards of 15 percent—exaggerate or misrepresent dates of employment, job titles, past salaries, or reasons for leaving a prior position.[9] Confirmation of hard data on the application with prior employers is therefore a worthwhile endeavour.

The reference check is used by many organizations but is extremely difficult to justify. Whether they are work-related or personal, references provide little valid information for the selection decision. Employers are frequently reluctant to give candid evaluations of a former employee's job performance for fear of legal repercussions. In fact, one survey found that only 55 percent of human resource executives would "always" provide accurate references to a prospective employer. Seven percent said they would never give an accurate reference![10] Personal references should also be given little weight. Who among us doesn't have three or four friends who will speak in glowing terms about our integrity, work habits, positive attitudes, knowledge, and skills? There just isn't enough variation among personal references for them to provide supervisors with any meaningful selection information.

PHYSICAL EXAMINATIONS

For jobs that require certain physical requirements—for example, police officers, airline pilots, train engineers—the physical examination has some validity. In most cases, nowadays, the physical examination is done for insurance purposes only. Management wants to eliminate insurance claims for injuries or illnesses contracted prior to being hired.

Great care must be taken to ensure that physical requirements are job-related and do not discriminate. Some physical requirements may exclude persons with disabilities, when, in fact, such requirements do not affect job performance. Similarly, the use of height and weight requirements may discriminate against female and some ethnic minority applicants.

SOMETHING TO THINK ABOUT
•AND TO PROMOTE CLASS DISCUSSION•

What do you think are good interview questions? List three of them below.

_____

_____

_____

Share your questions and then discuss how you could "fake out" the interviewer on these questions, by giving impressive answers that may have nothing to do with your actual suitability for the job.

What are your comments on the following questions?

> Do you have any experience in this area?

> What do you see yourself doing five years from now?

> What are your strengths and weaknesses?

Interviews are widely used and, additionally, tend to be given considerable weight in the final selection decision. As a result, supervisors need to perfect their interviewing skills. In From Concepts to Skills at the end of this chapter, we'll present some guidelines to help you conduct effective employment interviews. More immediately, the "Building a Supervisory Skill" section describes a specific interviewing approach called behaviour-based interviewing, which has been highly successful.

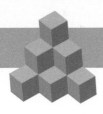

Building a Supervisory Skill

BEHAVIOUR-BASED INTERVIEWING

ABOUT THE SKILL

The best predictor of future behaviour is past behaviour. This is why we are so interested in résumés as a job-selection device. Do we get the whole story from résumés, however?

An increasingly popular form of interviewing that focuses on effectively eliciting specific information about past behaviour is called behaviour-based interviewing, also known as behaviour description interviewing or behavioural event interviewing. It asks candidates to tell a series of true "stories" about themselves, detailing accounts of specific events from their past. It has much higher predictive power than traditional interviews.[11]

STEPS IN PRACTISING THE SKILL

Determine what you are looking for in the candidate. As described earlier, use job descriptions and job specifications to develop a picture of the ideal candidate.

Develop a series of questions based on those desired skills. These will be asked of all job candidates. Each question seeks detailed information on past behaviour. For example, if you were hiring for a retail clerk, you may ask: "Tell me about the last time you handled a slow time in your job." "People are not always easy to deal with. Think about a time you had a challenging customer to deal with. What happened?" "We're a busy workplace. Tell me about a specific time when your workload was very fast-paced and may have seemed overwhelming. Describe it. How did you handle it?" Focus most of the questions on the key aspects of the job or the duties performed most often.

Prepare the candidate by describing this approach before launching into the questions. Candidates may never have been faced with this type of question before and may find it difficult. Before asking the questions, explain what you will be doing. For example, you may say, "I'm going to be asking you to describe in detail some experiences you've been through in your past work. This way I'll get a much clearer picture of your experience. When I ask a question like this, feel free to take time to think about your answer. You may not have had to describe your work in this way before."

Give the person time to think after asking a behaviour-based question. Don't rush the person or feel you need to fill the silence. If they answer that they cannot think of an appropriate situation, consider changing the question slightly or giving some sample situations to describe events that might fit this question.

After the person's initial answer to a behaviour-based question, follow up with probes. For instance, you may ask who was involved, what were you thinking at the time, what did you learn from this, what happened as a result, and what specifically did you say. Persist until you get a clear and complete picture of each event and the candidate's role in it. You may spend five or ten minutes discussing one event. This is considered superior to hypothetical questions, such as "What would you do if..." because people can make up anything for a hypothetical question. You may be thinking that applicants also do that for past events. However, evidence suggests that this is unlikely to happen. By probing a situation fully, you will get a sense of how genuine it is.

Take notes throughout. Recording the answers allows you to refer to them later when making decisions. It also allows you to follow up when doing a reference check to confirm whether a specific event described by the candidate actually happened.

TRY IT YOURSELF

Create a behaviour-based question to get the candidate to describe a past experience related to each of the following:

- Customer interaction skills
- Integrity
- Implementing an unpopular management decision

What would you be looking for in the answers?

NEW-EMPLOYEE ORIENTATION

Once a job candidate has been selected, he or she needs to be introduced to the job and the organization. This introduction is called **orientation** or on-boarding.

Have you ever had the experience of being "dumped" into a position the first day on the job without any preparation, explanation, or introductions? Many people have and know that it does not set them up to be successful or happy in their job. All employees should receive an orientation. The major objectives of orientation are to reduce the initial anxiety all

Orientation
The introduction of a new employee into his or her job and the organization.

Sample Manager's On-boarding Checklist for New Employees

Action:

- ❑ Distribute an email communication or distribute a message via the company newsletter to make staffing announcement prior to or close to the new employee's arrival

- ❑ Personally welcome the new employee – always ensure you are there for their first day at the designated time and location

- ❑ Review the orientation plan for the first day and the week. Include an explanation of the employee's role and roles of the team members in the department (review org. chart)

- ❑ Personally introduce employee to staff in the department

- ❑ Assign a 'buddy" to provide information needed for a successful introduction. Include things such as:
    - ❑ Company history, Mission & Vision statements, Strategic Plan
    - ❑ Newsletters, brochures, marketing materials
    - ❑ Should also include:
    - • Payroll procedures
    - • Normal work hours, break policies
    - • Performance standards: expected outcomes, success metrics, probationary period
    - • Dress code
    - • Confidentiality
    - • Health and Safety including emergency procedures, i.e. Lockdown and Fire Alarms

- ❑ Show the employee their new work area, review all components of phone, internet, calendar and email setup

- ❑ Give tours as required, including: restrooms, staff lounge & cafeteria, other food services, emergency exits, conference rooms, etc.

- ❑ Demonstrate where resources are and how they can access useful information such as staff directories, etc.

- ❑ Review office organization, discuss faxing, mailing, where to find files, supplies, etc.

- ❑ Review Policies

- ❑ Explain safety policy, reporting of all accidents and injuries (when, to whom, and how), first aid facilities, emergency medical attention

- ❑ Describe process and who to notify if sick or on vacation leave

- ❑ Discuss overtime needs and how assignments are given (if applicable)

- ❑ Obtain parking pass and permit from Security

- ❑ Order business cards and name tag (if required)

- ❑ Arrange for lunch with the new employee or assign a 'buddy" to have lunch with him/her

- ❑ Meet with new employee at the end of the day to find out how the day went and answer any questions; review the importance of the position and its accountability within the organization

FIGURE 6-8

Sample orientation or "on-boarding" plan

new employees feel as they begin a new job; to familiarize new employees with the job, the work unit, and the organization as a whole; and to facilitate the outsider-insider transition. Job orientation expands on the information the employee received during the recruitment and selection stages. The new employee's specific duties and responsibilities are clarified, as is the way his or her performance will be evaluated. This is also the time to rectify any unrealistic expectations new employees might hold about the job (see Supervision in Action). Work-unit orientation familiarizes the employee with the goals of the work unit, clarifies how his or her job contributes to the unit's goals, and includes introduction to coworkers. Organization orientation informs the new employee about the organization's objectives, history, philosophy, procedures, and rules. This should include relevant human resource policies and benefits such as work hours, pay procedures, overtime requirements, and fringe benefits. A tour of the organization's physical facilities is often part of the organization orientation. Figure 6-8 illustrates what an orientation program can include to meet its goals.

Many organizations have formal orientation programs. Such a program might include a tour of the offices or plant, a video describing the history of the organization, and a short discussion with a representative from the human resources department, who describes the organization's benefit programs. Eagle's Flight of Guelph, Ontario, puts all new employees through an extensive orientation including having all employees go through the programs that Eagle's Flight sells (experiential training programs for the business community). This way, everyone working for the company in any position is intimately familiar with what Eagle's Flight represents, what it sells and what they, as employees, can be proud of. The formal orientation is also augmented by the written expectation that all supervisors will ensure that all appropriate supports are in place for the new employee when the employee arrives. For example, when requesting a specific hire, supervisors must also complete a form requesting new or changing services, such as a desk, new office equipment, a phone, and an IT user account with specific software access.

Other organizations utilize an informal orientation program in which, for instance, the supervisor assigns the new employee to a senior member of the work unit, who introduces the new employee to immediate coworkers and shows him or her the locations of the rest rooms, cafeteria, coffee machine, and the like.

Supervisors will want to make the integration of the new employee into the organization and department as smooth and as free of anxiety as possible. Successful orientation results in an outsider-insider transition that makes the new member feel comfortable and fairly well adjusted, lowers the likelihood of poor work performance, and reduces the probability of a surprise resignation by the new employee only a week or two into the job.

Supervision in *Action*

The Realistic Job Preview

Supervisors who treat the recruiting and hiring of employees as if the applicants must be sold on the job and exposed only to an organization's positive characteristics set themselves up to have a dissatisfied workforce that is prone to high turnover.[12]

Every job applicant acquires, during the hiring process, a set of expectations about the company and about the job for which he or she is being interviewed. When the information an applicant receives is inflated, a number of things happen that have potentially negative effects on the company. First, mismatched applicants who would probably become dissatisfied with the job and quit soon would be less likely to withdraw from the search process. Second, the absence of accurate information builds unrealistic expectations. Consequently the new employees are likely to become quickly dissatisfied—again leading to premature resignations. Third, new hires are prone to become disillusioned and less committed to the organization when they face the "harsh" realities of the job. In many cases, these individuals feel that they were duped or misled during the hiring process and, therefore, may become problem employees.

To increase job satisfaction among employees and reduce turnover, supervisors should provide a **realistic job preview (RJP)**. An RJP includes both positive and negative information about the job and the company. For example, in addition to the positive comments typically expressed in the interview, the candidate would be told of the downside of joining the company. He or she might be told that there are limited opportunities to talk to coworkers during work hours, that promotional advancement is slim, or that work hours fluctuate so erratically that employees may be required to work during typically off hours (nights and weekends). Applicants who have been given a more realistic job preview hold lower and more realistic job expectations for the jobs they'll be performing and are better able to cope with the job and its frustrating elements. The result is fewer unexpected resignations by new employees.

For supervisors, realistic job previews offer a major insight into the selection process. That is, retaining good people is as important as hiring them in the first place. Presenting only the positive aspects of a job to an applicant may initially entice him or her to join the organization, but it may be an affiliation that both parties quickly regret.

"You need to lay out all the expectations right at the beginning when they are hired so there are no surprises. They must know all aspects of the job, including the not-so-popular parts" says Haji Khurshid, former workshop manager for a large used car centre where he supervised mechanics and apprentices. "A lot of people come in with preconceived notions on what they are to be doing. And for many young people they don't think they should be doing menial tasks like cleaning up. But it's a safety-related environment so any hazardous potential like a spill, it's the apprentice's job to deal with. They need to know that before they step in to the job."

FIGURE 6-9

Haji Khurshid emphasizes the importance of explaining even the negative aspects of a job to candidates. There should be no surprises.

INTERVIEWING

ASSESSING YOURSELF: DO YOU HAVE GOOD INTERVIEWING SKILLS?

Are the following questions true (T) or false (F)? Circle what you believe is the right answer.

1. On an application form, it's illegal to ask an applicant what foreign languages he or she can read, write, or speak fluently. T F
2. It's illegal to ask an applicant about his or her past work experience. T F
3. It's illegal to ask the full names of an applicant's dependants. T F
4. It is better for the interviewer to examine the candidate's resume after the interview rather than before, so that the interviewer is open and lacks preconceived ideas about the candidate. T F
5. It's a good idea to tape record or takes notes during an interview. T F
6. A good interviewer takes control of an interview and does most of the talking. T F
7. An interviewer should avoid asking questions that can be answered with a simple yes or no. T F
8. Early in the interview, you should provide the applicant with as much detail about the job being interviewed for as possible. T F

SCORING INSTRUCTIONS

Questions 3, 5, and 7 are true. Questions 1, 2, 4, 6, and 8 are false. If you got seven or eight correct, you already have some understanding of how to conduct an effective selection interview.

SKILL BASICS

In conducting an employment interview, you're trying to get answers to three questions:

1. Can the applicant do the job?

2. Is the applicant motivated to do the job?

3. Will the applicant fit into your work group and organization?

Everything you do regarding the interview—from preparation to closure—should help you to answer these three questions.

Interviewing is difficult because it is, in effect, an art. Developing the art of the interview is learning what to do and how to do it. Then it's a matter of practice to ensure your interviewing skills don't become stale from lack of use.

STEPS IN PRACTISING THE SKILL

This list summarizes the key actions in preparing for and conducting an interview.

1. **Review job description and job specification.** Reviewing pertinent information about the job provides valuable information about what you'll assess the candidate on. Furthermore, relevant job requirements help to eliminate interview bias.

2. **Prepare a structured set of questions to ask all applicants for the job.** By having a set of prepared questions, you ensure that the information you wish to elicit is attainable. Furthermore, by asking similar questions, you are able to better compare all candidates' answers to a common base. It is preferable to use behaviour-based questions.

3. **Prior to meeting a candidate, review his or her application form and résumé.** This helps you create a complete picture of the candidate in terms of what is represented on the résumé/application and what the job requires. You will also begin to identify areas to explore in the interview. Areas not clearly defined on the résumé/application that are essential for your job should become a focal point in your discussion with the candidate.

4. **Open the interview by putting the applicant at ease and providing a brief preview of the topics to be discussed.** Interviews are stressful for job candidates. By opening with small talk (e.g., the weather or the traffic) you give the candidate time to adjust to the interview setting. By providing a preview of topics to come, you are giving the candidate an "agenda." This helps the candidate to begin framing what he or she will say in response to your questions.

5. **Ask your questions and listen carefully to the applicant's answers.** Select follow-up questions that naturally flow from the answers given. Focus on the responses as they relate to information

you need to ensure that the candidate meets your job requirements. Any uncertainty you may have requires a follow-up question to further probe for the information.

6. **Take excellent notes of applicant responses and allow lots of time at the end of the interview for answering questions.** Good notes allow you to recall and compare candidates later in conversation with others involved in the hiring. Those notes may also be used later to justify hiring decisions in court if there is a legal challenge. Especially for promising candidates, the open time at the end to answer questions allows you to sell the position and provide a realistic job preview.

7. **Close the interview by telling the applicant what's going to happen next.** Applicants are anxious about the status of your hiring decision. Be upfront with the candidate regarding others who will be interviewed and the remaining steps in the hiring process. If you plan to make a decision in two weeks or so, let the candidate know. Additionally, tell the applicant how you will respond to him or her about your decision.

APPLYING YOUR SKILLS

1. Break into groups of three.

2. Spend up to 10 minutes writing up to five challenging job-interview questions that you think would be relevant in the hiring of new college graduates for a sales-management training program at Procter & Gamble. Each hiree will spend 18 to 24 months as a sales representative calling on retail grocers. After this training period, successful candidates can be expected to be promoted to the position of district sales supervisor.

3. Exchange your five questions with another group.

4. Each group should allocate one of the following roles to their three members: interviewer, applicant, and observer. The person playing the applicant should rough out a brief résumé of his or her background and experience, then give it to the interviewer.

5. Role-play a job interview. The interviewer should include, but not be limited to, the questions provided by the other group.

6. When completed, the observer should evaluate the interviewer's behaviours in terms of the skills presented in this section.

SUMMARY

This summary is organized by the Learning Objectives.

1. All employees in Canada are protected by either federal or provincial human rights legislation. Depending on the jurisdiction, different acts specify "protected groups" with the intention of guaranteeing equal employment opportunity. All employess are also protected by minimum employment standards with which employers must comply.

2. The three steps in human resource planning are assessing current human resources, assessing future human-resource needs, and developing a program to meet future human-resource needs.

3. The job specification, which states the minimum acceptable qualifications that an applicant needs for a job, guides supervisors in recruitment and selection by establishing the standard against which job applicants can be compared.

4. The primary sources for job candidates are an internal search; advertisements; employee referrals; employment agencies; schools, colleges, and universities; professional organizations; casual or unsolicited applicants; and nontraditional sources such as disabled and women's organizations.

5. Accept errors increase the costs to employers in the following areas: training, lost productivity, possible severance, and the recruiting and selection costs to find a replacement. Reject errors increase the number of candidates that must be screened. Additionally, they can subject the organization to charges of discrimination if members from protected groups are systematically rejected from jobs for which they are actually qualified.

6. Hard and relevant data on an application form have been shown to provide valid information, but care must be taken not to ask for information that isn't job-relevant. Some written tests demonstrate moderate validity, but they place a burden on management to support job-relatedness. Work samplings are expensive but tend to yield high validity scores. Interviews are widely used and people have confidence in them, but they are typically poorly conducted and result in distorted findings. Verification of facts on an application form is a worthwhile endeavour but reference checks provide little valid information. Physical exams as selection tools are relevant for only a small portion of jobs and care must be taken not to discriminate on the basis of physical requirements.

7. An effective interview uses structured questions focused on the major aspects of the job. The applicant is put at ease throughout and is encouraged to share specific past experiences relevant to the job through targeted behaviour-based questions (e.g. tell me about a time when you...). The same questions are asked of all candidates. Answers are documented, candidate questions are answered and next steps are explained.

KEY TERMS AND CONCEPTS

Accept errors

Behaviour-based interviewing

Bona fide occupational
    requirements

Human resource planning

Job specification

Orientation

Realistic job preview

Reject errors

Reliability

Sexual harassment

Validity

Work sampling

REVIEWING YOUR KNOWLEDGE

1. Why do supervisors need to know the basics of employee recruitment and selection?
2. Explain the importance of hiring based on bona fide occupational requirements.
3. Why has the internet become a major vehicle for job advertisements?
4. Why are employee referrals called "one of the best sources" for job applicants?
5. Explain the importance of validity in a selection device.
6. Explain the importance of reliability in a selection device.
7. Why are work samples more likely to be valid than written tests as selection devices?
8. Why should a supervisor spend time orienting a new employee?

CASE 6.A

Hiring Horror Stories

Ryan Anderson worked in operations management before changing careers to a human resources position where he has worked as a consultant and as a corporate human resources manager. This means he has many experiences working with managers and supervisors on hiring. Ryan offers some warnings about questionable hiring practices based on these experiences.

"Management at one company I worked with insisted on using a particular screening test for electricians. It made my job to recruit electricians almost impossible because the test was unreliable and invalid. People would get 90% one time and 50% another time when retested (which was a fail since 60% was needed to pass). I proved the problems by giving the test to electricians already working for the company who were accepted as highly skilled. Many of them actually failed the test. But management still wanted to use the test because they had used it so long and were creatures of habit. It's critical that screening tools measure the skills you need.

I see a "similarity" error happening frequently, where managers hire based on being comfortable with the person, connecting with them. "Oh, you like dogs? So do I. You must be the right person for the job." It causes a lot of grief because decisions are not based on logic. It's hard to get managers away from this thinking because they are comfortable with it. It's like high school – jocks hang out with jocks, nerds with nerds. But a work team needs a variety of skills. Fit in a company and a work team is important but so are the skills needed to get the job done. Managers need to be aware and avoid this error.

Managers can also get it into their head that there is a magic "fix" to hiring the right person. For example, I had a company president

tell me he had been hearing about something called "locus of control" and he wanted me to "action it" in all the hiring. He wanted me to hire only people with an internal locus of control from now on. Period. (People with an internal locus of control believe they can control events that affect them, whereas external locus of control people do not believe in their own control, instead believing that external forces like other people, fate or chance have a substantial hand in their future). He had read a magazine article that convinced him that internal locus of control people would be much better employees because they would take more initiative because of their beliefs, and would adjust their behaviour to achieve what they wanted. I debated with him the wisdom of hiring only "internals" but he was the boss and he insisted. However, I asked for the opportunity to test people within the company who were willing so that I could have some baseline data for comparison. He agreed so I communicated to employees why I was looking for the data (to establish whether locus of control seemed to correlate with current employee positions) but made sure they knew it was only for this purpose and no one should be fearful that they were testing for their own jobs.

I had to source an appropriate test. I had the vendors' data on validity and reliability of their locus of control tools but I also arranged for the executives to take the tests to see how they felt about the results. They debated the options and we chose one.

Once we had chosen a test, I set about checking its validity with current employees. For ones willing to take the test, I graphed the results by position and job class (sales, technicians, administration, executives...). The president could look at results. He was shocked as the article he had read only said it was the best thing and provided no data. I knew I could not be successful in a war of words with him so I had to show him.

The results were interesting: sales people were high in internal locus of control but the level of locus of control was not correlated with productivity and did not predict success. I think perhaps that reflects the fact that, even if they believe they can control their success by adjusting their approach, it does not guarantee they can successfully do so.

We discovered that some of the lowest scores were among admin support (e.g., executive assistants) who were seen as amazingly effective employees (walk on water) who made things happen and problem-solved constantly (organized travel for all, organized deliveries and lunches). It's not surprising that they scored low because things screw up in their jobs all the time (e.g., a plane is delayed) so their scoring as not feeling in control actually reflects their job conditions.

In the end, we decided to use the locus of control test as one tool in the hiring process. For example, if we get a sales person with an internal locus of control, it will be interesting because they recognize the need to tailor their behaviour but now we need to test to see if they will actually do so; it's not the only selection tool.

FIGURE 6-10

RESPONDING TO THIS CASE

1. Describe the problems with using the electrician screening test, using concepts from the chapter.
2. Explain what the locus of control testing experience teaches us about selection processes.
3. Discuss the ethics of using hiring tools that are not suitable.
4. The company president told Ryan to use a specific approach to hiring even though Ryan knew it was not suitable. Discuss whether you think Ryan handled this situation appropriately or not and why. Discuss the challenges of being a supervisor who is a subject matter expert but being told by a senior manager (who is not a subject matter expert) what you must do.
5. Ryan strongly believes there is no magic "fix" to hiring the right person. What does this mean?

CASE 6.B

Was Anyone Unethical Here?

Danielle is angry. The HR person who had been working with Danielle on hiring for a key position just phoned to say that the successful candidate, Roman, was declining the job offer, the one he had already signed off in February. Now it is the end of April and Roman was supposed to start in a couple of weeks. Danielle had spent a long time on the job search to find the right person for such a crucial position. It had been difficult to find someone with the right combination of skills and there were few people with related experience. Roman was clearly the best job candidate. Danielle's organization had offered Roman an excellent salary and benefits package, the top of the range for the position. Despite desperately needing someone in the position immediately, Danielle had agreed to allow him to work out the end of his current contract and have a vacation break before starting the new position in May. She did not believe it ethical for him to break his contract to make the move. She knew his current employer was also in great need of his services. Being professionally involved with them in an industry association, there was a respect and awareness of the challenges each was facing. When contacted for references, Roman's current employer was glowing in their praise for him and said they would gladly keep him if there was a full-time position available. Danielle felt lucky and relieved that Roman was joining her department and had been planning the orientation and the distribution of projects among staff. They already had organized an employee number, a laptop and an office for him. Now Danielle felt betrayed, both by Roman and by his current employer. It turns out Roman has now been offered a full-time position by them and has chosen to stay. Danielle has major projects lined up with no one to do them. A new search process will take months. Danielle is about to go to the industry association annual event where she is likely to see Roman and his manager, and she feels like spitting in their faces.

Greg hired Roman on contract a year ago, taking somewhat of a risk because Roman had no direct experience in the position. But Greg saw great potential in him and worked hard to train him and support him. Roman had made the most of the opportunity and blossomed into an exceptional employee. As the contract neared an end, Greg felt sick that he was going to lose such a strong employee. Even though the work was definitely there in his department, the company refused to convert the contract into a full-time position. Greg knew Roman was looking for the salary, benefits and security of full-time work and was not surprised when Roman told him he was interviewing for a position at Danielle's company. Greg knew Danielle and her company through a professional association and believed that Roman would enjoy working there and would be a good fit. So, when the HR person from Danielle's company phoned for a reference, he gladly gave him strong support. When Roman accepted their job offer, they were good about letting him work out the end of his contract with Greg's organization rather than requiring he start immediately. But everything then changed. An executive working with Roman on a project learned about Roman leaving and immediately made the resources available to create a full-time position for him. Greg offered Roman the job and he accepted.

Roman was surprised by how much he enjoyed the new and unusual role he stepped into on contract at Greg's company a year ago. Loving the work and knowing that the contract was coming to an end in the spring, he was pleasantly surprised to come across a posting for a full-time position at another company. Getting a job offer at the end of it was wonderful so he had signed off the offer happily and was looking forward to the next step in her career. Mind you, it was going to mean a much longer commute, and establishing relationships with a whole new group of people, but he had confidence all would go well. He had really enjoyed working with Greg in his organization and was relieved that he was allowed to work out the end of the contract, rather than leaving them in the lurch. Then Greg surprised him shortly before he was to leave by offering him a full-time position after all. Roman couldn't refuse. They had matched the salary and benefits offer and it meant he could continue with the work and people he so enjoyed. Plus the commute was no longer an issue. He felt momentarily guilty at reneging on his commitment to Danielle's company. But it was his life after all.

RESPONDING TO THIS CASE

1. Should Danielle be angry?
2. Does Roman's action reveal something about his character that is important? When Danielle told others at her company what he had done, they said, "Good riddance, we wouldn't have wanted someone like that anyway." Are they right?
3. What could Danielle have done in the lag between the acceptance of the job offer and Roman's start date to make it more likely he would not have turned his back on the commitment?
4. Are there any ethics involved here?
5. Danielle is in the position of needing to fill a position for which there will be few qualified candidates. She does not have an unlimited budget to lure someone into the position. What would you recommend she do in the hiring process to attract a strong candidate?

7

DEVELOPING YOUR EMPLOYEES

Courtesy of Goodluz/Shutterstock

LEARNING OBJECTIVES

After reading this chapter, you should be able to:

1. Define training.
2. Identify signs that suggest employee training may be necessary.
3. Describe the role of reinforcement in learning.
4. Explain the learning curve.
5. Describe four on-the-job training methods.
6. Describe four off-the-job training methods.
7. List three skill deficiency categories.
8. Explain the importance of evaluating training effectiveness.
9. Explain diversity training.
10. Explain how asking questions can be a powerful part of the coaching process.

CHAPTER OUTLINE

PERFORMING EFFECTIVELY

EMPLOYEE TRAINING: WHAT IS IT AND WHY IS IT IMPORTANT?

NEEDS ASSESSMENT

ALLOCATING TRAINING RESPONSIBILITIES

DESIGNING THE PROPER TRAINING PROGRAM: UNDERSTANDING HOW PEOPLE LEARN
   Learning Guidelines
   Designing Training Programs

TRAINING METHODS
   On-the-Job Training
   Building a Supervisory Skill: *Asking Logical Consequence Questions*
   Off-the-Job Training

MATCHING TRAINING PROGRAMS TO OBJECTIVES

EVALUATING TRAINING EFFECTIVENESS

HOW IS EMPLOYEE DEVELOPMENT DIFFERENT FROM EMPLOYEE TRAINING?

CURRENT ISSUES IN TRAINING AND DEVELOPMENT
   Diversity Training
   The Shift to Customer Orientation

FROM CONCEPTS TO SKILLS: COACHING
   Assessing Yourself: What is Effective Coaching?
   Skill Basics
   Applying Your Skills

UNDERSTANDING THE BASICS
   Summary
   Key Terms and Concepts
   Reviewing Your Knowledge

PERFORMING YOUR JOB
   Case 7.A: Invisible Coaching
   Case 7.B: Training on the Run

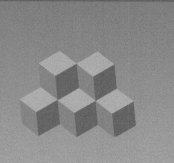

Russell Food Equipment sells over 8000 items to restaurants throughout BC and Catalino Misenas, the Sales Manager, must ensure that the company's sales representatives are familiar with all of them. This means that a major part of Catalino's job is training. New outside sales reps take up to 18 months to become thoroughly knowledgeable and, even at that, the training does not stop. Every second week, Catalino holds a sales meeting with all inside and outside sales reps. Several new products are presented in each one, sometimes by a manufacturer's rep, often by Catalino. "The more senses you use, the more the information will stick. I show them the item, for example a glass or some china, pass it around so they can handle it, they hear about its features and benefits, they read a handout. There is a question and answer time. At the next meeting, I may ask them to draw a sketch of an item from the previous week so I know they can describe it to a client. Sometimes I ask them to recap the highlights so I know they absorbed the information.

"Bringing in new items to show clients helps keep the reps motivated. And I can never train too much. I have to keep reminding them that salespeople can get in reaction mode and forget that their primary purpose is to sell and not take orders."

As for the salespeople at Russell Food Equipment, training today is a major focus for new employees but also an ongoing focus to keep employees up-to-date.

EMPLOYEE TRAINING: WHAT IS IT AND WHY IS IT IMPORTANT?

As we'll show in this chapter, employee training and development is more important today than ever. It's relevant to big companies and small ones, and for businesses and nonprofit organizations alike. Additionally, organizations are increasingly looking to supervisors to identify employee training needs, recommend programs, and even conduct training sessions.

Employee **training** refers to a learning experience that results in a relatively permanent change in an individual that improves his or her ability to perform on the job. It can involve changing skills, knowledge, attitudes, or behaviour. It includes obvious development of technical skills such as operating sophisticated equipment or using new software

Training
Learning experience that results in a relatively permanent change in an individual that improves his or her ability to perform on the job.

programs. But it also includes learning other, more subtle behaviours, such as developing teamwork skills.

In today's fast-changing world, victory increasingly goes to the company whose entire workforce can solve problems and make good decisions. That means investing in training. As companies seek continuous process improvements, employees must be trained to use control charts and other statistical tools. And as technology rapidly transforms the workplace, employees must upgrade or alter their skills to allow new technologies to realize their full potential in increasing productivity.

Training is becoming an integral part of most jobs. The goals of high productivity and avoidance of obsolescence require that employees be in a constant state of learning and adapting. In this chapter, we want to present the fundamental aspects of training and the supervisor's role in these efforts.

NEEDS ASSESSMENT

As a supervisor, how do you tell whether an employee could benefit from training? Begin by assuming that *every* new employee needs orientation training. Joining a new organization and settling into a new job is typically an uncomfortable experience. There are new people to meet and new policies to learn—the "right way" to do a job in one company is not necessarily the "right way" in another company or even in a different department at the same company. Provide initial orientation training to new members in order to reduce their anxiety and to allow them to become comfortable in their new surroundings.

Beyond orientation training, look for signals that suggest employee training may be necessary. What are some of these signals?

1. The introduction of new equipment or processes that may affect an employee's job
2. An increase in the number of errors
3. An increase in the number of questions that employees ask you or their colleagues
4. An increase in complaints by customers or coworkers
5. A rise in the number of accidents
6. A drop in individual or group productivity

If you see any of these signs, you cannot automatically assume the solution is increased training. As noted in the next chapter, training is not the only response to performance problems. If the problem is lack of motivation, a poorly designed job, or external conditions, training is not likely to offer much help. For example, training is not likely to be the answer if a performance deficiency is caused by low salaries, inadequate benefits, a poorly designed work layout, or the trauma of layoffs associated with corporate downsizing.

Once you have been alerted to the need for training, you must determine what specific type of training is needed. An employee might be able to tell you him- or herself. You can use a survey to determine explicit needs or use a focus group. You can simply watch and draw your own conclusions.

When you have determined that training is necessary, specify training goals. What explicit changes or results do you expect the training to achieve? These goals should be clear to both you and the employee. For example, the new service assistant at a Copy Centre is expected to be able to 1. use all photocopying equipment, 2. enlarge and shrink copies, 3. send and receive domestic and international faxes, 4. operate the passport photo machine, 5. operate and answer technical questions about the computer rentals, 6. answer all technical questions regarding photo processing and differences in paper quality, and 7. operate the cash register and make change. These goals then guide the design of the training program and can be used after the program is complete to assess its effectiveness.

ALLOCATING TRAINING RESPONSIBILITIES

Like Catalino, as supervisor you are responsible for ensuring that all those who report to you are adequately trained. Since you'll eventually be judged on the performance of the people who work for you, it is in your best interest to do so.

This doesn't mean, however, that you must necessarily conduct all the training yourself. Exactly what role you play in training your employees will generally depend on the size of your organization, your training budget, and your own training skills. The larger your organization, the more likely it is that there will be a separate training department or training specialists in the human resources group. They can provide valuable support resources and may perform some centralized training functions. Additionally, the size of your departmental training budget will have a large bearing on your role. The more generous the budget, the more you can look to specialists outside your department for assistance. Finally, supervisors vary in their abilities to conduct effective training sessions. The higher your skills, the more of the actual training you can do yourself.

In addition to yourself, there are three other training resources you should consider (see Figure 7-1). As previously noted, where available, you should consult with your firm's *in-house training specialists*. They can help you identify training needs, design specific programs for your employees, provide advice on teaching methods, and assist you in assessing the effectiveness of your training efforts. In most large organizations, these in-house specialists will also conduct centralized training on general

- *You* can provide training for people in your department
- *In-house training specialists* are often available in large organizations
- *Outside trainers* can be hired to provide specialized expertise
- *Your employees* often are capable of training their peers

FIGURE 7-1

Where to look for training resources

issues affecting all employees. For instance, specialists may provide organization-wide training on issues such as company history and policies, employee benefits, basic business economics, math and literacy skills, time management, and interpersonal skills. Job-specific training is then typically left to the responsibility of departmental supervisors.

In small organizations or in cases where very specialized expertise is required, supervisors will rely on *outside trainers*. Outsiders, for instance, may be the best source for teaching your people about the implications of new legislation or for improving their communication skills.

Last, but not least, don't forget the potential of your employees to train their peers. You may want to delegate some training activities to skilled and experienced employees. If you do so, remember that just because employees can do their own job well, it is no assurance that they can teach others. Just as the best athletes don't always make the best coaches, the best workers don't always make the best trainers. The experienced employee must not only know the job, but also know how to train others. So if you use employees as trainers, make sure that they have been properly prepared for these added responsibilities. You may wish to enhance their skills by having them participate in "train-the-trainer" learning.

DESIGNING THE PROPER TRAINING PROGRAM: UNDERSTANDING HOW PEOPLE LEARN

You're developing a training program for your department. You want the program to be effective. That is, you want to create a learning experience that results in changing employees so it improves their ability to perform their jobs. Toward this end, you should understand how people learn. An understanding of learning principles can help you to structure effective training experiences.

LEARNING GUIDELINES

The following suggestions highlight what we know about how people learn.[1]

LEARNING IS ENHANCED WHEN THE LEARNER IS MOTIVATED

Merely exposing an employee to a learning experience is no guarantee that learning will take place. The employee must be motivated to learn. They need to know not only what they learning but why. And the "why" should be meaningful to them. How will it help them in their job, what difference will it make to the results, and how does it tie into their goals? Will it affect promotion opportunities or increased protection from lay-offs? Discuss with the employee the benefits of the training.

CLEAR EXPECTATIONS FOCUS EFFORT

Training is more successful if both trainer and learner know exactly what is expected to be achieved. If the training objectives are articulated upfront, time and effort are not wasted. As with any goal, a training objective should be an observable, measurable performance and any conditions of the performance should also be clarified. Here are some examples of training objectives:

- Given two hours of instruction, the new employee will be able to orally describe all floor hazards present in a selected area of the plant floor of 4,000 square feet. Each description will include the name of the hazard along with a specific reason why it is a hazard.
- By the end of a one hour training session, the participant will be able to orally state the code numbers of at least 10 of the colours found in our indoor latex paint chart. When stating each number you will need to be able to identify the correct colour on the chart.
- By the end of a one-day training session, the personnel trainee will be able to calculate the correct vacation allowance for any employee using an Excel time sheet in 15 minutes or less.

LEARNING REQUIRES FEEDBACK

Feedback on results is necessary so learners can correct mistakes. Only by getting information about how they're doing can they compare results against goals and correct any deviations. Feedback is best when it is immediate rather than delayed: the sooner a learner has some knowledge of how well he or she is performing, the easier it is to correct deficiencies.

REINFORCEMENT INCREASES THE LIKELIHOOD THAT A LEARNED BEHAVIOUR WILL BE REPEATED

Behaviours that are rewarded tend to be repeated and sustained. For instance, if employees are verbally praised when they have properly performed a task, they are likely to continue doing the task this way and be motivated to strive toward performing better work. Frequent reinforcement is powerful when learning. On the other hand, punishment tends to only temporarily suppress behaviour. Moreover, punishment merely tells someone what they're doing wrong; it doesn't convey the right way to do something.

PRACTICE INCREASES A LEARNER'S PERFORMANCE

When learners actually practise what they have read or seen, they gain confidence and are less likely to make errors or forget what they have learned. Active involvement through practice should therefore be made part of any learning experience.

There are basically two ways an employee can practise a job. One is to practise the whole job at once. The other is to break the job into parts and practise each part independently. Which way is best? It depends on the type of job being done. It appears that if the job is narrowly defined and relatively simple—for example, stocking shelves in a grocery store—practice should cover the whole job. If the job is complicated—for example, tracking space satellites—it is better to practise the parts of the job independently.

LEARNING BEGINS RAPIDLY, THEN LEVELS OFF

Learning rates can be expressed as a curve that usually begins gradually and is followed by a steep rise, then increases at a decreasing rate until a plateau is reached. Learning is very fast near the beginning, but then levels off as opportunities for improvement are reduced.

The **learning curve** concept can be illustrated by observing individuals in training to run a kilometre. At first, their time improves rapidly as they get into shape. Then, as their conditioning develops, their improve-

Learning curve Learning begins gradually, followed by a steep rise, then increases at a decreasing rate until a plateau is reached.

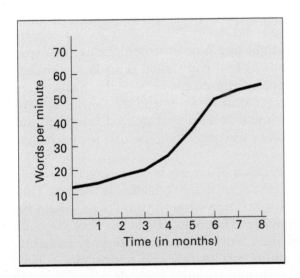

FIGURE 7-2

Learning curve for keyboarding

ment reaches a plateau. Obviously, knocking one minute off a seven-minute kilometre is a lot easier than knocking one minute off a five-minute kilometre. If you have ever learned word processing, you may have had an experience that somewhat follows the pattern shown in Figure 7-2.

Notice the shape of the curve in Figure 7-2. During the first three months, the rate of increase is slow as the subject learns the technique and becomes familiar with the keyboard. During the next three months, learning accelerates as the subject works on developing speed. After six months, learning slows as progress evolves into refinement of technique.

LEARNING MUST BE TRANSFERABLE TO THE JOB

It doesn't make much sense to perfect a skill in the classroom and then find that you can't successfully transfer it to the job. Therefore training should be designed for transferability.

This means that the learning environment should simulate the work situation as closely as possible. In cases where learning is done on the job —such as when a senior employee spends a week with a new worker, showing the new employee specifically what to do and watching as he or she perfects the skill—the transferability requirement is not a relevant issue. Neither is it much of a problem where the off-site simulation is incredibly realistic—as is the case with today's sophisticated flight simulators used to train pilots. Transferability becomes a problem when the learning environment is considerably unlike that of the actual work situation. If a medical surgeon's training was made up completely of reading books and attending lectures on anatomy and physiology, you'd rightly question whether the surgeon could transfer that knowledge to actually operating on a real patient. This explains why surgical training includes a large segment of actual practice and several years of internship—it ensures transferability of surgical skills.

DESIGNING TRAINING PROGRAMS

The previous section provides insight into how to structure training experiences for your employees. It tells us that you should provide motivation by tying the learning experience to the employee's goals. Employees should have the opportunity to perfect their skills and to transfer off-site learning to the job itself. They should receive feedback on how well the training is progressing, as well as praise and other rewards for each step of the process.

It also emphasizes the importance of having a clear target in mind. Designing a training program is best done using "backwards" design. This means starting off at the end with defining what the employee should be able to do at the end of the training. Then you determine how you will assess their achievement and then work backwards to what learning approaches will support their ability to illustrate that performance. This leads us to a consideration of the various training methods.

TRAINING METHODS

Training employees in an economy of constant change has challenged supervisors to react faster and more creatively in preparing employees to perform other jobs. Supervisors are looking for newer, faster, and more effective ways to keep their staff trained to meet the challenges of an increasingly customer-driven market. In this section we'll briefly review various on-the-job and off-the-job training methods and then show that the choice of training methods should reflect the type of problem that needs fixing.

ON-THE-JOB TRAINING

Most training takes place on the job. This is because it's easy to do and gives the impression of being low in cost. **On-the-job training** places employees in actual work situations and makes them appear to be immediately productive. It is learning by doing. For jobs that either are difficult to simulate or can be learned quickly by watching and doing, on-the-job training makes sense.

On-the-job training Training that places employees in actual work situations.

One of the drawbacks of on-the-job training can be low productivity while employees develop their skills and other employees assist them. Another drawback can be the errors made by the trainees while they learn. However, when the damage the trainees can do is minimal, where training facilities and personnel are limited or costly, and where it is desirable for the employees to learn the job under normal working conditions, the benefits of on-the-job training frequently offset its drawbacks. Galya Kabbani, a restaurant supervisor, says: "The best training is shadowing. We have people shadowing for two weeks, 3 shifts a week, getting a training salary and no tips. Then we test them on the menu and on the 12 steps of service."

SIMULATION TRAINING

At the Allan Waters Family Simulation Centre[2] at St. Michael's Hospital in Toronto, health professionals practise skills and learn new ones with no risk to live patients by using computers and life-like mannequins. In the state-of-the-art operating room, trainees are put through real-life medical scenarios or crises to learn how to respond quickly and as a team. In the skills lab they learn and practice the newest surgical and diagnostic procedures. It is the amazing mannequins that make much of this possible through simulating patients. For example, these mannequins can breathe and speak, have pulses and audible heart and breath sounds and respond to medications, CPR and defibrillation. An advanced wireless model has eyes that react to light, can bleed, perspire, cry and seize. A mannequin newborn baby can move all limbs, turn cyanotic, have

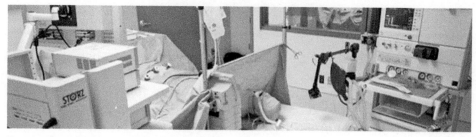

FIGURE 7-3

Simulator technology at St. Micheal's Hospital in Toronto

Source: http://www.stmichaelshospital.com/education/simulation/simulation.php

seizures, and has an umbilical cord for line insertion with fluid feedback. Since the simulation centre is set up for tele-simulation, trainees can practice treating patients at a distance over a secure network. Procedures can be broadcast to anywhere in the world. As with the use of flight simulators for pilot training, the safe rehearsal space offered by medical simulators save lives and money. "Surgeons who have simulation training perform faster, are more accurate and make fewer errors."[3]

Simulation training is an accurate reflection of real world work situations and builds skills that are highly transferable to the working environment. Other examples would include the mock emergency situations that police and other emergency personnel practice handling.

APPRENTICESHIPS

Apprenticeship
A program covering a period of time—typically one to five years—when an individual is considered to be training to learn a skill.

People seeking to enter skilled trades—to become, for example, plumbers, electricians, or ironworkers—are often required to undergo **apprenticeships** before they are accepted to expert status. Typically, this apprenticeship period lasts from one to five years. For instance, a bricklayer's apprenticeship is three years, machinists and printers spend four years, and a patternmaker's apprenticeship requires five years.

Apprenticeship programs put the trainee under the guidance of a master worker (see Figure 7-4). The argument for apprenticeships is that the required job knowledge and skills are so complex as to rule out anything less than a period of time where the trainee understudies a skilled master.

One disadvantage of apprenticeships is that they are designed solely around the skills of a specific trade; they are not tailored to the needs of a specific organization. So when hired, apprentices may have to be retrained to an organization's specific job requirements. The other disadvantage is that apprenticeships are at odds with the current trend toward cross-training and teamwork. Today's employees need versatility. They need to be able to move quickly between a number of jobs as situations change. Apprenticeships grew out of a time when one learned a specific skilled trade and then practised it for a lifetime. Today's jobs often require a broader range of skills that must be continually updated.

FIGURE 7-4

Apprentices learn on the job but also in the classroom. Most training is done by skilled masters. Courtesy of Lisa F. Young/ Shutterstock

COACHING

One of the most significant changes in the supervisor's job over the past few years has been the increased importance placed on coaching employees. **Coaching** is a day-to-day, hands-on process of helping employees recognize opportunities to improve their work performance. A coach analyzes the employee's performance; provides insight as to how that performance can be improved; and offers the leadership, motivation, and supportive climate to help the employee achieve that improvement. Rob Watson, of Fusion Homes, says: "If they make poor decisions, I don't come down hard on them. I ask why they did what they did so I can learn the thinking and the situation. I suggest alternatives so there is no next time. I coach on why something is a mistake and how to prevent it in future." Ainslie White, IT manager at Precision Biologic, also prefers coaching to telling: ""I sit down and listen and then I like to play devil's advocate to spur their thoughts. I don't want to provide the answer. They often generate better answers. I tell them to keep "x" in mind, but want them to come up with potential solutions on their own."

Like training, coaching is a big part of Catalino Misenas's job as sales manager at Russell Food Equipment in British Columbia. "New reps have to give me daily sales reports. I ask them what they did when they went to a particular restaurant. What was the purpose of their visit? What questions did they ask? I ask them questions to get them thinking. What did

Coaching
Day-to-day, hands-on process of helping employees recognize opportunities to improve their work performance.

the kitchen look like? The floor? The rack? Were the dishes sorted? I need the rep to be thinking about what the restaurant could use that they might not realize."

Catalino's description of his coaching illustrates a highlight of effective coaching—the coach asks lots of questions. This may seem odd since the coach is the "expert." However, the questions are important in leading the employee to "think" along the lines of the expert and solve problems later on his or her own. Building a Supervisory Skill describes the coaching skill of using questions to probe logical consequences. And From Concepts to Skills at the end of the chapter looks at developing coaching skills more fully.

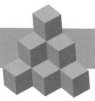

Building a Supervisory Skill

ASKING LOGICAL CONSEQUENCE QUESTIONS AS PART OF COACHING

ABOUT THE SKILL

Asking logical consequence questions refers to asking employees questions to probe the results of specific actions. The purpose is to help employees become more aware of the impact of their actions or of potential actions and to therefore choose their actions more carefully.

For example, an employee says to you, "I don't think I'll have that report done until Monday. It's only going to be a couple of days late." You know there would be grave repercussions to this delay and are tempted to say something sarcastic to that effect. Instead, you respond, "How do you think Peter will feel about that since his work is dependent on your results?" or "How will Sandy be able to make her presentation on Monday to the client without the report with her or without being able to read it and prepare?"

STEPS IN PRACTISING THIS SKILL

Look for an opportunity to ask logical consequence questions. This could be when you and the employee are discussing an error already made, or the employee is discussing what he or she plans to do, or there are a variety of options for the employee to choose from in taking action and you want the employee to think carefully through the choices and their impact. Refrain from asking the question "why," as in "Why did you do it that way?" Although it is a question and it probes their thinking, it tends to put people on the defensive.

Instead of "why," focus on specific consequences through "What happened?" or "What do you think will happen...?". Explore the impact of an action on the customer, coworkers who are linked to the task, equipment, the work environment, the organization, or anything else pertinent to the professional handling of a situation. "How might they react if you chose that option?" "What risk might be involved if you did that?" "What benefits do you see in opting for that solution?"

Ask for alternative actions. For example, "How else could you have done this?" or "What other options do you see in tackling this potential issue?" and pursue the logical consequences of those actions as well.

You may need to actually give pertinent information if it is apparent that an employee is unaware of an important consequence. For example, he or she may not be aware that "fixing" a machine a certain way may get it working in the short term but damages it in the long run. Or the employee may not be aware that if an ad is not placed in your publication for a customer by a certain date, it will be useless, you will not be able to run that ad, and you may lose that customer's future business.

TRY IT YOURSELF

Consider the circumstances in which an employee may say each of the following to you, their supervisor, and create a question in response to the employee that would get him or her thinking about the impact of their action.

"Thanks for the phone message. I'm not going to phone him back, though. He is so difficult to deal with and if I just leave him alone for a while, maybe he'll cool off."

"I don't know whether to handle it myself or give it to the new hire to do since he hasn't done this kind of thing yet."

MENTORING

Most work groups foster a buddy system where new employees are taken under the wing of more experienced employees to ease their transition into the workplace. This is an informal approach to mentoring. **Mentoring** is a formal or informal process for more experienced workers to share their knowledge and guide less experienced workers. In formal mentoring programs, senior employees are assigned junior protégés to whom they lend the benefit of their experience. The focus is typically on helping the employee achieve organizational goals but can also offer support for personal career goals.

Mentoring
A formal or informal process for more experienced workers to share their knowledge and guide less experienced workers.

Not every experienced or high-performing employee makes an effective mentor. Successful mentors are good teachers. They can present ideas clearly, listen well, and empathize with the problems of their protégés. In some cases, supervisors will become formal mentors to one or more of the people who work for them. However, this is not typically a good idea. It can create morale problems among other employees who perceive that protégés are getting favoured treatment. The best mentors for operative employees are other operative employees in their department or work group.

Reverse mentoring describes an initiative taken by some to have less experienced employees mentor more experienced employees. Ernst and Young's[4] Just Ask program matches Generation X and Y and LGBT (lesbian, gay, bisexual and transgender) individuals with more senior staff, who spend time together building bridges and addressing differences. RBC's Diversity Dialogues[5] program matches mid-level females and visible minorities with those in more senior positions but expects the mentorship to work both ways over a 12-month commitment. They believe the less senior have much to teach the more senior.

Reverse Mentoring
Less experienced employees mentor more experienced employees.

JOB ROTATION

Job rotation is an excellent way to broaden employees' perspectives and turn specialists into generalists. It allows employees to increase their experience and absorb new skills.

Job rotation
Moving employees horizontally to broaden their skills, knowledge, or abilities; turning specialists into generalists.

Job rotation can take one of two forms: planned or situational. *Planned rotation* describes a formal program of sequential moves. For instance, an accountant at Xerox may spend six months working in the tax area, then six months in cost analysis, then six months on auditing activities, and so forth. Japanese companies have relied extensively on job rotation to build a labour force of generalists who can perform a wide range of company functions on a variety of teams and have a network of contacts throughout the organization. *Situational rotation* is more informal—employees are moved to different jobs when their current one is no longer challenging, or in order to meet the needs of work scheduling. Many supervisors use the summer months, when employees typically take vacations, as an opportunity to broaden their staff's skills by situationally rotating people into and out of different jobs to cover for those on vacation.

While job rotation fits well with today's increased need for employee flexibility and cross-training, it comes with some serious drawbacks. Initial productivity often suffers when an employee moves into a new job. And an extensive job-rotation program can result in a vast number of employees situated in positions where their job knowledge is very limited. The organization must therefore be equipped to deal with the day-to-day problems that result when inexperienced personnel perform new tasks. That usually means supervisors must be readily available to help with problems.

OFF-THE-JOB TRAINING

Chrysler contracted training for 3000 employees in communications, group motivation and stress management through Sheridan College, a community college in southwestern Ontario. Training sessions were held outside of scheduled production shifts, beginning at 6:00 in the morning or 7:00 in the evening. This training partnership allowed Chrysler to use the expertise of college professors who designed and tailored the **off-the-job training** program directly to the company's needs.

Off-the-job training
Training that takes place outside the direct work area.

VESTIBULE TRAINING

In **vestibule training**, employees learn their jobs on the equipment they will be using, but the training is conducted away from the actual work floor. Many large retail chains train cashiers on their computer cash registers—which are complex because they control inventory and perform other functions in addition to ringing up orders—in specially created vestibule labs that simulate the actual checkout-counter environment. While expensive, vestibule training allows employees to get a feel for doing tasks without real-world interferences such as noise, distractions, and time pressures. Additionally, it minimizes the problem of transferring learning to the job, because vestibule training uses the same equipment the trainee will use on the job.

Vestibule training
Employees learn their jobs on the equipment they will be using, but away from the actual work floor.

SEMINARS, CONFERENCES, AND LONGER-TERM EDUCATION

Giving employees the opportunity to participate in seminars and conferences is an effective way of conveying specific information such as corporate policies, job procedures, business economic data, and industry trends. The presentations tend to rely on a mixed bag of techniques, for example, lectures, videos, demonstrations, case studies, role-plays, and group exercises. They are widely used when orienting large groups of new employees. Organizations also rely on seminars and conferences as ways of keeping professional employees up to date in their fields. Professional development budgets typically plan for some employees to attend professional conferences or workshops. It is common for organizations to reimburse employees for membership dues through their professional organizations and to support accreditations in order to encourage knowledge currency.

Many companies support employees seeking further education through universities and community colleges, some to the extent of helping pay tuition fees or providing educational leave. For example, Statistics Canada provides for educational leave for its employees when appropriate conditions are met.

OUTSIDE READING

It's so basic that it's often overlooked: providing reading material for employees to review in their nonworking hours. Supervisors, for example, can request and purchase subscriptions to job-relevant periodicals and have them mailed to employees' homes. Or, more typically, books, journals, and magazines are provided in rest areas, lunch rooms, and other places where employees may informally gather.

INDUSTRIAL SECTOR TRAINING

In a unique partnership between management and union, a certificate program was developed to cooperatively address training needs within the independent automotive parts manufacturing industry in Canada. The partners, the Automotive Parts Manufacturers' Association (management) and the Canadian Auto Workers Union, must both approve the content and instruction methods. The ultimate aim is to deliver effective long-term training in an integrated curriculum that focuses on communication, industry, and technology. The program relies heavily on the use of peer trainers—production workers recruited from industry. The trainers work at gaining mutual respect for the agendas of management, labour, employers, and workers with an orientation towards the auto parts manufacturing sector. The certificate informational brochure states:

> Management representatives see the value of this process in increased willingness and ability of their employees to participate in changes occurring at their workplace. Labour representatives see its value in increased empowerment of their members to play a leading role in making and implementing decisions about workplace change. Both agree, however, that the title of the program—"Opening Doors"—expresses its essential purpose.[6]

WEB-BASED LEARNING

E-learning
Employees use network technology to gain access to training materials, to "experts," and to other learners.

Also known as on-line learning or **e-learning**, web-based learning uses network technology to give employees access to training materials, to "experts," and to interaction with other learners.

Web-based learning can offer cost-effective training that ensures consistent and quick delivery of information to a large number of people. Rogers employees have access to My E-Learning, an online learning program that offers on-demand courses at no cost, allowing participants to select from a wide range of courses and complete them at their convenience, at their own pace and from any internet location. The courses are designed to align with Rogers Core Competencies: innovation, communication, accountability, customer focus and team work.[7] Many employers roll out specific online modules to ensure employees learn about company initiatives or policies, or new regulations. For example, because of the new Accessibility for Ontarians with Disabilities Act, all employees at the Ontario College of Art and Design have to take the one-hour AODA

Customer Service training provided online.[8] At the University of Western Ontario, all employees must take four required training programs online: a health and safety orientation, workplace hazardous materials information system (WHMIS), preventing harassment and violence, and accessibility.[9]

MATCHING TRAINING PROGRAMS TO OBJECTIVES

Supervisors shouldn't select training methods arbitrarily. Each method has certain strengths and weaknesses. A good deal of the success of any training or development program can be attributed to properly selecting a method that fits your objective.

Most skill deficiencies fall into one of three categories: technical, decision-making, or interpersonal. *Technical deficiencies* address the ability to use the tools, equipment, processes, and techniques needed to perform a job. *Decision-making deficiencies* encompass the abilities to identify problems, develop alternatives, analyze and evaluate alternatives, and arrive at effective solutions. *Interpersonal deficiencies* are concerned with abilities to work and communicate with others. In addition, learning in each of these categories may be from a cognitive or experiential perspective. **Cognitive learning** relies on mental processes. When you learn by reading, watching, or thinking, you're engaged in cognitive learning. When training focuses on actually practising, experiencing, or doing something, then you're engaged in **experiential learning**. As we noted earlier in the chapter, surgical training relies both on cognitive concepts and experiential practice.

On-the-job training methods are either experiential or a combination of cognitive and experiential learning. These are the preferred methods for learning technical skills and for practising interpersonal skills. Vestibule training, while off-the-job, requires learning by doing. It is an excellent means of dealing with technical deficiencies. Web-based learning can be either cognitive or experiential. For example, when you read about computers, it's cognitive. When you practise what you've learned, it's experiential. Seminars and conferences can likewise be designed along either perspective. Lecturing, for instance, relies on cognitive processes for learning. Role-plays, on the other hand, incorporate learning by doing. Outside reading is an example of a purely cognitive learning activity.

When you want to merely know about something, cognitive learning methods are most effective. If you want to understand what a business plan is, or the pros and cons of putting your department on flexible work hours, or the proper steps to take in disciplining an employee, cognitive learning methods work well. However, if you want to actually write a business plan, or learn to implement flexible work hours, or practise disciplining, you should focus on experiential techniques.

Cognitive learning
Learning that occurs via mental processes such as reading, watching, and thinking.

Experiential learning
Learning that relies on practising, experiencing, or doing something.

FIGURE 7-5

Categories of skill deficiencies

Before you choose a training method, ask yourself what it is you want your trainee to learn (see Figure 7-5). What specifically is the skill deficiency? Then design a training program that will most effectively facilitate the learning of that skill.

EVALUATING TRAINING EFFECTIVENESS

It's relatively easy to offer a new training program. But training must be cost-effective. You won't know if it's cost-effective unless you evaluate the training that's taking place. You must be able to show that the benefits gained from the training outweigh the costs of providing the learning experience. The only way to do this is to analyze the outcomes training may have generated.

Is there a way in which training programs are typically evaluated? Frequently, the following scenario takes place. Several individuals—usually representatives from the training department and a group of workers—are asked to critique a recently completed training program. If the comments are generally positive, the program receives a favourable evaluation. Based on that evaluation, the program continues, until something occurs that causes it to be changed or eliminated.

The accuracy of these reactions, however, is questionable. The participants' opinions are often heavily influenced by factors that have little to do with actual training effectiveness—factors such as difficulty, entertainment value, or the personality of the instructor. Obviously, that's not the type of evaluation we're referring to. Rather, you must be certain that employee performance improves. Accordingly, training programs must be evaluated on some performance-based measures. This can be achieved by evaluating how well employees perform their jobs after they have received training, or the differences found between pre- and post-training performance.

HOW IS EMPLOYEE DEVELOPMENT DIFFERENT FROM EMPLOYEE TRAINING?

In many organizations, the terms *training* and *development* are used synonymously. In many respects, that may be correct. But employee development is different. Whereas employee training focuses its attention on the skills needed to do one's current job, **employee development** is more future-oriented. That is, it deals with preparing employees for future positions that require higher-level skills, knowledge, or abilities—like the analytical, human, conceptual, political, and specialized skills needed by all supervisors, which we introduced in Chapter 1. Although the methods of delivering employee development programs are similar to training methods, they focus more heavily on employees' personal growth.

It is important to consider one critical component of employee development in today's organizations. All employees, no matter what their level, can be developed. Historically, development was reserved for supervisory personnel, and those aspiring to be such. Although there's no question that development still must include preparing these individuals, the processes of downsizing and empowering have shown us that non-supervisory personnel need such skills as planning, organizing, leading, and controlling, too. For instance, the use of work teams, workers' greater opportunity to participate in decision making, and the greater emphasis on customer service and quality have all led to development being "pushed" down in the organization. Like training, development efforts must also be evaluated to ensure that the organization is getting its money's worth.

> **Employee development**
> Preparation of employees for future positions that require higher-level skills, knowledge, or abilities.

CURRENT ISSUES IN TRAINING AND DEVELOPMENT

Informal discussions with practising supervisors reveal that, in addition to basic job skills, two other issues are high on their list of training needs. One is *diversity training*. Work groups are increasingly made up of individuals of mixed gender and diverse ethnic backgrounds. Employees need training to help them learn to accept people who are different from themselves and to become aware of the advantages diversity can bring to a work group. The other issue is *customer service training*.

> **Diversity training**
> Training aimed at creating greater awareness of the issues that arise in a staff of varied background and characteristics, encouraging acceptance and appreciation of that variety, and helping employees learn how to accommodate and work with people of diverse backgrounds.

DIVERSITY TRAINING

While some organizations rely on outside consultants to provide **diversity training**, others are doing it in-house with their own employees (see

FIGURE 7-6

This informal, small
group training session
focuses on increasing
diversity awareness
among participants
Courtesy of
Larry Williams/Corbis

Figure 7-6). The Royal Bank of Canada created a website, called Destination Diversity, with educational and training modules that managers can download for sessions with their staff to help manage different elements of diversity, such as cultural diversity, disability issues, or dealing with diverse clients.[10] Imperial Oil offers diversity education programs designed to help managers enhance their understanding of diversity, Imperial's expectations, and ideas for addressing diversity. Over 1,000 leaders have already participated.[11] Bombardier Aerospace's leaders receive training in inclusive recruitment strategies to develop a better understanding of cultural biases and perceptions.[12] Diversity training is mandatory for all TD employees who serve customers. Among other things, employees learn about how best to address the needs of customers with disabilities.[13]

THE SHIFT TO CUSTOMER ORIENTATION

The example described above, of TD providing training to its employees so they can better understand and work with disabled customers, links the focus on diversity training with a second major focus—customer service. As the Canadian economic base becomes more focused on sales and service, supervisors will be challenged to instil a different orientation to customer satisfaction in employees who are accustomed to process-driven jobs. A company that continues to have a world-wide reputation for customer service is Four Seasons Hotels. Strong training and hiring practices along with empowering management have contributed to this. All new employees attend a seven-part introductory training program over a period of 90 days to learn the corporate culture and expectations for exceptional customer service. Then, at select properties, new employees receive a complimentary stay following the successful completion of their probationary period so they can appreciate the Four Seasons experience through the eyes of a guest.[14] Looking for guidance from organizations known for exceptional customer service, some Canadian companies have approached a notable organization entirely out of their industry. Walt Disney Co., having perfected the art of customer service in its theme parks, now offers customer training services through its' consulting arm, the Disney institute. Tim Horton's has sent senior staff to Florida and held a symposium for its franchisees there, with content from the Disney Institute. Ottawa-based developer Minto Group Inc. worked with Disney for two years, leading to a customer-service program called "beInspired."[15].

COACHING

ASSESSING YOURSELF: WHAT IS EFFECTIVE COACHING?

For each of the following statements, answer either True (T) or False (F).

AN EFFECTIVE COACH SHOULD:

1.	Tell employees the right way to do a job.	T	F
2.	Suspend judgment and evaluation.	T	T
3.	Be a role model.	T	F
4.	Provide long-term career planning.	T	F
5.	Use a collaborative style.	T	F
6.	Never use threats.	T	F
7.	Respect an employee's individuality.	T	F
8.	Focus on getting each employee's performance up to a minimum standard.	T	F
9.	Dismiss mistakes.	T	F
10.	Delegate responsibility for coaching outcomes to the employee.	T	F

SCORING KEY

Give yourself one point for each correct answer: 1. F; 2. T; 3. T; 4. F; 5. T; 6. T; 7. T; 8. F; 9. F; and 10. F. Scores of eight or above indicate you have quite a bit of valid knowledge about coaching.

SKILL BASICS

Effective supervisors have learned how to coach their employees. That is, through coaching you help your employees to improve their performance.

Is coaching synonymous with counselling? Both deal with day-to-day issues rather than the long term. But they're different. Coaching deals with ability issues. As a coach, you provide instruction, guidance, advice, and encouragement to help employees improve their job performance.

Counselling, by contrast, deals with personal problems. When employee attitudes or personality are the problem, you need to provide counselling.

Another important dimension of coaching is that it requires you to suspend judgement and evaluation. Supervisors, in the normal routine of carrying out their jobs, regularly express judgements about performance in relation to previously established goals. As a coach, you focus on accepting employees the way they are and helping them to make continual improvement toward the goal of developing to their full potential.

There are three general skills that supervisors should exhibit if they are to help their employees generate breakthroughs in performance.[16] The following reviews these general skills and the specific behaviours associated with each.

1. **Ability to analyze ways of improving an employee's performance and capabilities.**
   a. Observe your employee's behaviour on a day-to-day basis.
   b. Ask questions of the employee: Tell me about how you handled this situation. What other approach could you have used?
   c. Show genuine interest in the person as an individual, not merely as an employee. Respect his or her individuality. The insight you have into the employee's uniqueness is more important than any technical expertise you can provide about improving job performance.
   d. Listen to the employee. You can't understand the world from an employee's perspective unless you listen.

2. **Ability to create a supportive climate.** It's the coach's responsibility to reduce barriers to development and facilitate a climate that encourages performance improvement.
   a. Create a climate that contributes to a free and open exchange of ideas.
   b. Offer help and assistance. Give guidance and advice when asked
   c. Encourage your employees. Be positive and upbeat. Don't use threats.
   d. Focus on mistakes as learning opportunities. Change implies risk and employees must not feel that mistakes will be punished. When failure occurs, ask: "What did we learn that can help us in the future?" "What would you do differently next time?"
   e. Reduce obstacles. What factors do you control that, if changed, would help the employee to improve his or her job performance?
   f. Express to the employee the value of his or her contribution to the department's goals.
   g. Take personal responsibility for the outcome, but don't rob employees of their full responsibility. Validate the employees'

efforts when they succeed, and point to what was missing when they fail. Never blame the employees for poor results.

3. **Ability to influence employees to change their behaviour.** The ultimate test of coaching effectiveness is whether an employee's performance improves. But this is not a static concept. We are concerned with ongoing growth and development.

a. Encourage continual improvement. Recognize and reward small improvements and treat coaching as helping employees to continually work toward improvement. There are no absolute upper limits to an employee's job performance.

b. Use a collaborative style. Employees will be more responsive to accepting change if they participate in identifying and choosing among improvement ideas.

c. Break difficult tasks down into simpler ones. By breaking down more complex jobs into a series of tasks of increasing difficulty, discouraged employees are more likely to experience success. Achieving success on simpler tasks encourages them to take on more difficult ones.

d. Model the qualities you expect from your employees. If you want openness, dedication, commitment, and responsibility from your employees, you must demonstrate these qualities yourself. Your employees will look to you as a role model, so make sure your deeds match your words.

e. Encourage reflection on their decisions and the consequences of those decisions. Every action is based on a choice. Use questions to get them thinking about their thinking: what other options are or were available? What are the pros and cons of the options? What would they like to achieve and what actions would most likely lead to those results? If you influence their thinking, they will choose to change their behaviour, which is your ultimate goal.

APPLYING YOUR SKILLS

Read the following scenario. Depending on the instructions given, be prepared to either write a three- or four-page report or discuss in class how you would handle Todd Corsetti based on the coaching skills in this chapter.

SITUATION

You work for a large mortgage brokering company that has 30 offices located in western Canada. You're the supervisor of the Edmonton office and have seven mortgage brokers, an assistant, and a secretary reporting to you. Your business entails helping home buyers find mortgages and acting as a link between lenders and borrowers in getting loans approved and processed.

Todd Corsetti is one of your brokers. He has been in the office for two and a half years. Before that, he sold commercial real estate. You've been in your Edmonton job for 14 months, prior to which you supervised a smaller office for the same company.

You have not been pleased with Todd's job performance, so you decided to review his personnel file. His first six-month review stated: "Todd is enthusiastic. He is a bit disorganized but willing to learn. Seems to have good potential." After a year, his previous supervisor had written, "Todd seems to be losing interest. Seems frequently disorganized. Often rude to clients. Did not mention these problems to him. Hope he'll improve. His long-term potential now much more in question."

You have not spent much time with Todd. Your offices are far apart. But probably the real reason is that he's not a person who's easy to talk to and you have little in common. When you took this job, you decided that you'd wait some time before tackling any problems to make sure you had a good grasp of the people and the situation.

But Todd's problems have become too visible to ignore. He is consistently missing his quarterly sales projections. Based on mortgages processed, he is your lowest performer. In addition, his reports are constantly late. After reviewing last month's performance reports, you made an appointment yesterday to meet him today at 9:00 a.m. But he wasn't in his office when you arrived for that appointment. You waited 15 minutes and gave up. Your secretary tells you that Todd regularly comes in late for work in the morning and takes extra long coffee breaks. Last week, Valerie Oletta, who has the office next to Todd's, complained to you that Todd's behaviour was demoralizing her and some of the other brokers.

You don't want to fire Todd. It wouldn't be easy to find a replacement. Moreover, he has a lot of contacts with new-home builders, which brings in a number of borrowers to your office. In fact, maybe 60 per cent of the business generated by your entire office comes from builders who have personal ties to Todd. If Todd were to leave your company and go to a competitor, he'd probably be able to convince the builders to take their business somewhere else.

DISCUSSION

Using the three general skills in coaching employees, detail a plan of action that you, as Todd's supervisor, might follow in a coaching meeting with Todd.

SUMMARY

This summary is organized by the Learning Objectives.

1. Training is defined as a learning experience that results in a relatively permanent change in an individual that improves his or her ability to perform on the job.

2. Signs that suggest employee training may be necessary include the entry of a new employee, the introduction of new equipment or processes, an increase in the number of employee errors, an increase in the number of questions employees ask, an increase in complaints by customers or coworkers, a rise in the number of accidents, or a drop in individual or group productivity.

3. The use of reinforcement encourages the repetition of a behaviour. When a new behaviour is exhibited, it can be sustained by use of reinforcement.

4. The learning curve describes the speed with which learning occurs over time. Learning is very fast near the beginning, which means the curve is steep. Then learning levels off as opportunities for improvement lessen.

5. Four on-the-job training methods are apprenticeship, coaching, mentoring, and job rotation.

6. Four off-the-job training methods are vestibule training, seminars and conferences, programmed instruction, and outside reading.

7. Three skill deficiency categories are technical, decision-making, and interpersonal.

8. Evaluating training effectiveness is an important tool to ensure that training dollars are spent on programs that positively influence employee job performance. Rigorous evaluation can help determine if training makes any difference and whether the improvement justifies the cost.

9. Diversity training is aimed at creating greater awareness of the issues that arise in a staff of varied background and characteristics, encouraging acceptance and appreciation of that variety, and helping employees learn how to accommodate and work with people of diverse backgrounds.

10. Through questioning an employee about what they have done or plan to do, alternative actions, and the impact of the various actions, a coach can encourage the employee to think through and carefully choose future actions based on their results.

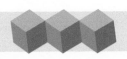

KEY TERMS AND CONCEPTS

Apprenticeship
Coaching
Cognitive learning
Diversity training
E-learning
Employee development
Experiential learning
Job rotation

Learning curve
Mentoring
Off-the-job training
On-the-job training
Reverse mentoring
Training
Vestibule training

REVIEWING YOUR KNOWLEDGE

1. Why is training important?
2. When might training not be the solution to ineffective job performance?
3. What is the supervisor's responsibility regarding training?
4. How can you use learning principles to make training more effective?
5. Discuss this statement in terms of designing a training program: "I hear and I forget. I see and I remember. I do and I understand."
6. What are the advantages of on-the-job training? Off-the-job training?
7. What's the best approach for evaluating training? Why?
8. Is it possible to teach people to get along better with each other? Explain.

CASE 7.A

Invisible Coaching[1]

Bruno describes an employee situation he has been dealing with.

"A challenge I have at the moment is dealing with the bad habits of an employee that he brought with him from another employer. They aren't effective here and they create staff stress and affect product quality. But, on the other hand Colin isn't easily replaceable. He can put out high volume with okay quality but we are a highly skilled team and a company with higher standards.

I had the same problem with him a couple of years ago and spent two weeks working with him on it intensively. But I handled it wrong – I told him how to fix his decisions and it worked for a while but then he slid back. What I really needed to do was to learn how Colin was thinking and seeing the situation and work with him so he would see it differently.

Now I'm approaching it more effectively. Over the last few months, I kept an eye on the daily work list he created for his staff meetings. I reviewed it to see what was being done and the thinking behind it. I noticed a lot of stuff being incomplete. I would approach him, bringing an example, asking "Why this? What's going on? What do you think could happen if you tried this option?" I thought I got his buy-in. I was trying to subtly give him solutions because I couldn't be direct, but I had to ensure the business model didn't suffer (I was worried about customer service ratings). Colin dug himself a hole in one particular situation and then came to me with a solution I had actually suggested. He asked me what to do and this opened the door to a deeper conversation about the current problem and the overall bigger problem. He came up with a game plan and I ensured it was manageable by discussing how it could be broken down into steps, and how we would have measures of whether it was successful or not. Now he has to implement it and I believe it will work. I knew it wouldn't have been effective if I had come down hard on him. He needed to come to me needing my help and being cooperative, and ultimately coming up with a solution that was in line with what the company needed."

RESPONDING TO THIS CASE

1. Explain the signals that Bruno used as a "needs assessment" indicating the employee needed training.
2. How well did Bruno apply the "learning guidelines"?
3. Does Bruno's coaching focus on cognitive learning, experiential learning, or both?
4. Examine Bruno's coaching in light of the three general skills and specific behaviours associated with effective coaching.
5. Given what you have read about Bruno's coaching, which of the skill deficiencies (technical, decision-making, interpersonal) do you believe he is focusing on and why?

CASE 7.B

Training on the Run

Janis, a finance supervisor at a large manufacturing company, believes that keeping up on your skills is tough, whether you're a regular employee or a supervisor. This is especially true in technical areas. Her organization is implementing several new leading-edge software systems that affect her area. This is complicated by the fact that her VP is always suggesting other changes. As soon as he hears the buzz about some new trend, it's "Let's do it." Janis and her

---

[1] Names and details changed to protect anonymity.

staff are expected to become instant experts and implement this "flavour of the month." This is stressful because Janis must jump in and implement as she's learning about something.

When Janis was hired as supervisor, the finance department had been previously decimated by downsizing and early retirements. She was expected to rebuild the team, plus deal with all these software changes. In recruiting and hiring, Janis found it difficult to find candidates with the appropriate software proficiency, so she chose people with the potential to learn. They knew the finance side well and were comfortable in other programs. She knew that, with the right training and support, they would rise to the challenge. But there was no way she could send each one away for a month to learn the new software. And she couldn't expect them to be immediate experts. So, instead, she spaced out the courses for the individuals. First, they would become involved in a process, such as payroll, and then they would attend a course relating software to that function. This improved their learning experience. Janis calls it "just-in-time learning" and claims it works well.

The employees are focused and motivated in the course and describe the experience of a "light bulb" flashing in their head when they make a crucial link in the training.

RESPONDING TO THIS CASE

1. Janis's VP appears to have an interesting view on training needs analysis. Comment.
2. What is wrong with the VP's approach to introducing change and the required training that goes with it?
3. What training method does Janis appear to be using for the software training and why? What other methods might be appropriate for this training? What would be the advantages and disadvantages of each?
4. How might Janis evaluate the effectiveness of the software training?

8

PERFORMANCE MANAGEMENT AND APPRAISAL

Courtesy of auremar/Shutterstock

LEARNING OBJECTIVES

After reading this chapter, you should be able to:

1. Define performance management and explain its four componenets.
2. Contrast the purposes of the performance appraisal.
3. Describe key legal concerns in performance appraisals.
4. Identify the three most popular sets of criteria that supervisors appraise.
5. Contrast absolute and relative standards.
6. Describe the graphic rating scale.
7. Explain behaviourally anchored rating scales.
8. List human errors that can distort performance appraisal ratings.
9. Explain how appraisal errors can be minimized.

CHAPTER OUTLINE

FIGURE 8-1

Despite good intentions, Chrissy Whorwood was unsuccessful as a manager. She was set up for failure by the poor performance management of the employer.

Chrissy Whorwood was made assistant manager at a shoe store when she was 19, supervising 8 people. She had only wanted a sales position, but was made assistant manager due to her experience as a counter manager (with one part-time person under her) for a cosmetics line at The Bay. She was surprised at this and it was not what she wanted, but a full-time job was welcome so she took it.

"One of the staff had wanted the job and several had worked there for years. I had no background in the company or in shoe sales and I had no idea what I was doing, yet I was expected to supervise. I worried I wouldn't get along with them and I worried that I wouldn't be able to do my job.

There was no training, no shadowing, no introductions. On my first shift I sat in the back reading a lot of papers given to me by the district manager. I felt awkward sitting at the back with people coming and going and they didn't know who I was. So I introduced myself and I discovered that the district manager had not informed the staff of my hiring and had not told the employee who wanted the promotion that she did not get it. I told the staff that I'm not going to tell you what to do because you have more experience than I do; there's no need for hard feelings; I didn't even apply for this job. It was very awkward because I needed the staff to train me."

It turned out that the store manager had wanted the store employee promoted and was against the district manager hiring Chrissy. So, when Chrissy started, the store manager disappeared, leaving Chrissy on her own. Chrissy also learned that when she was hired, the store was in the middle of preparing to fire a staff member due to theft. She had no idea and had treated the employee like a friend, not knowing she was supposed to be watching this person. "I was given a low performance appraisal and told it was a problem that I had befriended the staff. When I tried to get the district manager to help me, his response was, "Do you think my job is easy?" After three months I was transferred to another smaller store and my pay was cut. And then I was fired."

"What do I take away from this experience? Never work someplace that is disorganized. Now I know to put my foot down and walk away if I don't want a position. I should have called the district manager more and talked to the person above him – is this supposed to be how I'm trained, how I'm to learn? You can't do a performance appraisal on someone who was never taught. People shouldn't be put in a position where they don't know what is expected and are told not to be friends with those they need to help them learn the job."

Chrissy's unfortunate experience illustrates how an employee can fail despite good intentions because of the company's poor performance management. Beginning with the hiring process and continuing through the lack of training, support and feedback, Chrissy didn't have a chance. The performance appraisal was unfair and inaccurate. In this chapter we'll examine the performance management needed in every company for every position and then focus on one aspect of performance management: the formal performance appraisal.

PERFORMANCE MANAGEMENT

The job of a supervisor is essentially to ensure that operational employees effectively perform the job they were hired to do. The prime focus of a manager's job, then, is on **performance management**. Performance management describes the steps taken to ensure employee performance aligns with the organization's goals. It means ensuring that employees know what to do and why, are capable of achieving the performance, and work in conditions supportive of successful performance. The components of performance management cut across the chapters of this book.

Performance management
Steps taken to ensure employee performance aligns with the organization's goals.

COMPONENTS OF PERFORMANCE MANAGEMENT

1. Set out individual performance expectations.

Employees must know what they are expected to do in their position, including tasks, responsibilities, timelines and standards. Christopher Nicolson of Tourism Sun Peaks says: "Employees want to know what they're accountable for as much as you want them to be doing those things."

Many elements of an employee's experience contribute to understanding expectations. In the hiring process, they saw a job posting and went through a screening that further informed them about the job. Hopefully they were given a realistic job preview. Once hired, they were given a job description, and the orientation and training they received added more information about performance expectations. On a day-to-day basis employees are given work assignments and instructions. Throughout this process, it is critical to explain not just what they are to do, but why. Understanding the reasons helps motivate them and links their role to the department and the organization. Haji Khurshid explains: "You need to explain not just what has to be done but why. And treat them with respect. Supervisors I have worked with wouldn't explain even though it won't take two minutes. They just tell. For example, you need to explain that if it's not done there could be an injury."

Of course, performance expectations are only fair if the employee is capable of meeting those expectations. So the supervisor must ensure that requisite skills are there (through hiring and/or training), that resources of time and equipment are there, and that the expectations are reasonable given competing demands, and the need for coordination with others. When it comes to setting specific performance standard expectations, fairness is more likely if the employee is involved in setting the standards. Through a joint discussion of departmental needs and how the employee can meet those needs, a common understanding will mean full acceptance by the employee and full support by the supervisor.

2. Coach and give ongoing feedback

"I believe people should get frequent feedback, both when they are doing great things and when their performance is not what is expected. How else can we grow and change?" Research supports Debbie Hinz's belief. Timely and specific information about performance is a powerful motivator and allows employees to improve. Feedback is an essential element to learning, as you saw in the last chapter, and performance management is all about employees learning to meet expectations. Coaching was discussed in Chapter 7. How to effectively give feedback is discussed in more detail in Chapter 11.

3. Formally appraise performance

Most companies have annual reviews and some add mid-year or quarterly reviews to discuss an employee's overall performance. This review is often linked to organizational outcomes like bonuses. Nothing in the appraisal should come as a surprise to the employee because they have been getting ongoing feedback from their supervisor. The majority of this chapter will focus on formal performance appraisals.

4. Align consequences with performance

As was discussed in the previous chapter, reinforcement increases the chance that a learned behaviour will be repeated. The supervisor has control over potential reinforcements for performance, like praise, new opportunities, formal recognition (e.g. awards) and bonuses. That is why it is essential that the supervisor responds differently to effective and ineffective performance. Christopher Nicolson of Tourism Sun Peaks: "You cannot reward mediocrity. If you do, valued members take notice. People question why they are working so hard if someone is allowed to get away with poor work." The use of consequences for motivational purposes is further discussed in the next chapter.

Setting clear expectations and giving feedback have been discussed in Chapters 2 (planning) and 3 (controls), and will be further discussed in Chapter 11 (communication). The impact of consequences will be discussed in Chapter 9 (motivation). So we will now concentrate on the remaining component: formal appraisal.

FIGURE 8-2

Components of performance management

THE PURPOSE OF THE PERFORMANCE APPRAISAL

The performance appraisal is a way to ensure employees get feedback (since not all managers are diligent about doing it on an ongoing basis). It is also a key determinant in pay adjustments and promotion decisions. And it is a forum for employee and supervisor to discuss the future.

The **performance appraisal** is both an evaluation tool and a development tool. It reviews *past* performance—emphasizing positive accomplishments as well as deficiencies. In addition, supervisors use the performance appraisal as a means of helping employees improve *future* performance. If deficiencies are found, the supervisor can help employees draft a detailed plan to correct the situation. With emphasis on the future as well as the past, employees are less likely to respond defensively to performance feedback, and the appraisal process is more likely to motivate employees to correct their performance deficiencies. Finally, the performance appraisal functions as an important legal document. Taking action against an employee for poor performance can create a problem if the problem is not well documented, and the performance evaluation serves a vital purpose in providing the documentation necessary for any personnel action that is taken.

Performance appraisal
An evaluation and development tool. Reviewing past performance to identify accomplishments and deficiencies and creating detailed plans to improve future performance.

WHEN SHOULD APPRAISALS BE MADE?

The performance appraisal is both a formal and an informal activity. *Formal performance reviews* should be conducted at least once a year. Twice a year is better. Just as students don't like to have their entire course grade hanging on the results of one final exam, neither do employees appreciate having their careers depend on an annual review. Two formal reviews a year means less "performance" will be appraised at each review, and lessens the tension employees often associate with the formal review.

The *informal performance appraisal* refers to the day-to-day assessment a supervisor makes of an employee's performance, and the ongoing feedback the supervisor gives to the employee. The effective supervisor continually provides informal information to employees—commenting on the positive aspects of their work and pointing out any problems that surface. So while formal reviews may occur only once or twice a year, informal reviews should be taking place all the time. Moreover, when the informal feedback has been open and honest, the formal reviews will be less threatening to the employee and won't present any surprises. It is a good idea for supervisors to document the informal feedback sessions to provide a representation of activities throughout the year when it comes time to do the annual appraisal.

THE SUPERVISOR'S ROLE IN PERFORMANCE APPRAISAL

The supervisor and the employee are the two key players in any appraisal. The supervisor is typically in a position to observe the employee's performance closely, recognizing what is going well and what is not. And the supervisor is also in a position to do something about that performance, whether it is recommending a bonus or arranging for additional training. Yet, despite their key role in appraisals and the importance of those appraisals to the employee's future, many supervisors avoid doing them and leave it to the last minute. Rob Watson of Fusion Homes describes this: "I used to hate getting performance appraisals in my previous job because they were done once a year and prepared the night before, reflecting only recent events so they were a waste of time." Why the procrastination? Appraisals can be seen as time-consuming but also as stressful. Supervisors may feel they don't need to appraise the strong employees and they don't want to appraise the weak ones, because there may be conflict over critical assessments. Those who avoid doing the annual appraisals are also likely those who avoid giving feedback on an ongoing basis, especially the negative kind.

Now Rob is in a position to ensure appraisals are done and done well (as vice president of construction at Fusion Homes). "Our reviews are regular, twice a year—mid-year and final; and the appraisals are living documents. I jot down information as things occur during the year. I find it's hard to get the managers under me to update their records regularly (I suggest at least weekly). I remind them. For example before June reviews, at a bi-monthly general managers meeting in April, I will remind them that the reviews are only two months away and they need to start pulling all their notes together, so it doesn't come across to the employee that they just threw the review together in the past week." The thoughtfulness put into an appraisal that is a "living document" will be appreciated by the employees. And the performance discussions that accompany the appraisal will be much more valuable to both the company and the employee.

FIGURE 8-3

Rob Watson, Fusion Homes, ensures appraisals are done and done well

WILL YOU BE THE SOLE APPRAISER?

Historically, the supervisor was the only performance evaluator of his or her employees. In fact, about 95 per cent of all employee performance appraisals are conducted by supervisors.[1] But supervisors aren't always the sole source of pertinent performance information about employees. Employees themselves often have valuable insights to provide. So, too, do their peers. Hence, in recent years, some organizations have added self-evaluations and peer evaluations to those made by the supervisor.

Self-evaluations get high marks from employees themselves, tend to lessen employees' defensiveness about the appraisal process, and make excellent vehicles for stimulating job performance discussions between employees and their supervisors. Self-assessment should be treated as enhancing the supervisor's evaluation rather than replacing it. The use of self-evaluations, however, is fully consistent with the view of performance appraisal as a developmental rather than a purely evaluative tool.

For some elements of an employee's job, peers are better at judging performance than is the employee's supervisor. In some jobs, for instance, supervisors don't regularly observe their employee's work because their span of control is quite large or because of physical separation. If work is done in teams, the team members are often better at evaluating each other than any supervisor because they have a more comprehensive view of each member's job performance. In such instances, supplementing supervisory appraisals with peer evaluations can increase the accuracy of the appraisal process.

What Forms or Documentation Does the Organization Provide?

Most organizations require supervisors to use a standardized form to guide them in doing their performance appraisals. In some cases, top management or the human resources department will provide an abbreviated form and allow you considerable freedom in identifying and assessing job performance factors. At the other extreme, some organizations provide detailed forms and instructions that all supervisors and managers must follow.

Our point is that supervisors rarely have complete discretion in evaluating the people who report to them. So begin by reviewing any standard forms that your organization uses for appraisals. Familiarize yourself with the information you'll be expected to provide and make sure all the people reporting to you—especially new employees—understand how and on what criteria they will be evaluated.

LEGAL ISSUES IN PERFORMANCE APPRAISALS

A great many lawsuits have arisen because supervisors said or did something that their employees believed adversely affected them. For instance, a supervisor told an employee that he had downgraded the employee's evaluation because he had taken time off work for religious holidays; another employee argued that her supervisor's appraisals were arbitrary and based on subjective judgements; and a third employee was awarded damages because his supervisor failed to follow the company's performance appraisal policies and procedures.

Maybe the two most important legal facts you need to keep in mind concerning performance appraisals are:

1. Performance appraisal policies and procedures, as set forth in organizational handbooks, are being increasingly construed by the courts as binding unilateral contracts; and
2. You must do everything possible to avoid prejudice and discrimination.

Does your company have a published handbook that describes its performance appraisal procedures? If so, the courts in most provinces consider it a binding contract. The organization can be held accountable if those procedures are not followed or are followed improperly. If the handbook states, for instance, that appraisals must be performed annually or that supervisors will counsel employees to correct deficiencies, then you are obliged to fulfill these commitments. On the other hand, the courts have generally supported giving supervisors a wide range of discretion when their organizations have no published performance appraisal policies, as long as fairness and equity are not compromised. So, if your organization has a published handbook that covers its policies on performance appraisal, make sure you fully understand its contents.

The second point above reminds us that human rights laws require that all human resource practices be bias-free—including employee performance appraisals. The appraisal criteria, methods, and documentation must be designed to ensure that they are job-related. They must not create an unfair impact on any protected group. For instance, appraisal judgements must be neutral regarding an employee's race, colour, religion, age, sex, or national origin. An increasing number of organizations are providing supervisory training in the mechanics of performance appraisal specifically to minimize the likelihood that discrimination might occur in the appraisal process.

Another issue that supervisors need to be aware of is the potential charge of defamation of character. Under the law, "qualified privilege" allows you as a supervisor to point out performance problems. In law, it is your duty to honestly, without malicious intent, inform employees of unsatisfactory performance. Your duty may also be extended to other company supervisors who are considering promotions or transfers of employees who are not fulfilling their job requirements.

WHAT DO WE APPRAISE?

As noted in Chapter 3, the criteria that supervisors choose to appraise when evaluating employee performance will have a major influence on what employees do. Consider what happened in an employment agency that served workers seeking employment and employers seeking workers. Employment interviewers were appraised by the number of interviews they conducted. Consistent with the idea that the evaluation criteria influence behaviour, the interviewers tended to focus on the number of interviews they conducted rather than the placement of clients in jobs. Packing in the interviews is not the same as actually placing clients, and only the latter makes money for the organization.

The preceding example demonstrates the importance of criteria in performance appraisal. This, of course, begs the question: What should supervisors appraise? The three most popular sets of criteria are individual task outcomes, behaviours, and traits.

INDIVIDUAL TASK OUTCOMES

If the ends count, rather than the means, then supervisors should evaluate an employee's task outcomes. If task outcomes were used, a carpet cleaner might be judged on the number of square metres he was able to clean per day. A salesperson could be assessed on overall sales volume in her territory, dollar increase in sales, and number of new accounts established. Many organizations now use goals set for specific deadline-driven achievements as the outcomes of most interest.

BEHAVIOURS

Evaluating employees on behaviour requires the opportunity to observe employees or devise a system for reporting to you on specific behaviour criteria. Using the previous examples, behaviours of a carpet cleaner that could be used for performance appraisal purposes might include promptness in reporting to work sites or thoroughness in cleaning equipment at the end of the work day. Pertinent behaviours for the salesperson could be average number of contact calls made per day or sick days used per year.

Some organizations evaluate a set of behaviours expected in employees in a certain group (like management or operational employees) and call these competencies. Figure 8.4 shows an excerpt from one organization's performance appraisal form for managers. It focuses on the competencies of impact and influence, and team effectiveness.

In many cases, it is difficult to identify specific outcomes that can be directly attributable to an employee's actions. This is particularly true of people in staff positions and individuals whose work assignments are intrinsically part of a group effort. In the latter case, the group's performance may be readily evaluated, but the contribution of each group member may be difficult or impossible to identify clearly. In such instances, it is not unusual to appraise the employee's behaviour rather than outcomes.

TRAITS

When you rate people on the degree to which they are dependable, confident, aggressive, loyal, cooperative, and the like, you are judging traits. Experts seem to agree that traits are inferior to both task outcomes and behaviours as appraisal criteria.[3] The reason is that traits refer to potential *predictors* of performance, not performance itself. So the link between traits and job performance is often weak. Additionally, traits typically have a strong subjective component. What, for instance, does *aggressive* mean? Is the meaning "pushy," "dominating," or "assertive"? Your evaluation of someone on this trait is largely determined by what the term means to you. Despite the drawbacks of traits, they are still widely used in organizations for appraising employee performance.

Competencies	Descriptors	Rating		
		Met	Did Not Meet	N/A
Impact and influence Persuading, convincing or influencing	Uses direct persuasion in a discussion or presentation. Appeals to reason, uses data or concrete examples, visual aids, demonstrations etc.			
	Tailors discussion to appeal to the interest or perspectives of others.			
	Anticipates the impact of an action or other detail.			
	Takes more than one action to influence, with each action adapted to the specific audience e.g. uses experts or third parties to influence.			
Team Effectiveness Working cooperatively and productively with others to achieve results. Demonstrates an ability to get people to work effectively together for a common purpose.	Contributes positively by openly sharing information while remaining flexible and adaptive to others points of view, new approaches and ideas.			
	Balances self and team interests to meet collective goals and has the ability to give and receive constructive feedback. Solicits ideas and opinions to help form specific decisions or plans.			
	Recognizes conflicts arise within the team and acts to bring these out into the open. Assists in mediating between team members to resolve conflicts.			
	Establishes and communicates methods and processes designed to get the most out of meetings and group efforts by: facilitating the identification of goals, identifying and breaking down barriers to effective team process, and evaluating the effectiveness of team processes.			

FIGURE 8-4

Selected Competency Components from One Organization's Performance Appraisal

GATHERING PERFORMANCE DATA

Once performance standards have been set, expectations communicated, and appraisal criteria defined, you need to gather performance data. This is an activity every supervisor can and should do.

The best approach is to gather performance data on a continuous basis. Don't wait until a week or so before the appraisal interview. You should keep an ongoing journal for each of your employees, in which you record actual incidents (behaviours and/or outcomes) that affect his or her job success or failure. Such documentation reduces the potential for errors caused by relying on your memory of recent events, and provides supportive evidence to substantiate your eventual ratings. Remember that the more opportunities you have to observe your employee's behaviour firsthand, the more accurate your performance appraisals are likely to be.

PERFORMANCE APPRAISAL METHODS

Once you have your data, you can begin your actual performance appraisals, using the forms provided by the organization (see Figure 8-5). The object is to replace the "global impression" that each of us creates about someone else's overall performance with a systematic procedure for assessing performance. This systematic procedure increases the accuracy and consistency of results.

There are three different approaches for performing appraisals. Employees can be appraised against 1. absolute standards, 2. relative standards, or 3. objectives. No single approach is always best; each has its strengths and weaknesses. However, keep in mind that your choice may be affected by the human resource policies and procedures in your organization.

ABSOLUTE STANDARDS

The use of absolute standards means that employees are not compared against any other person. Rather, employees are evaluated within the context of the behaviour expected of them. Included in this approach are the following methods: the written essay, critical incidents, the checklist, graphic rating scales, and behaviourally anchored rating scales.

FIGURE 8-5

Documenting the appraisal takes time and thoughtfulness.
Courtesy of Robert Daly/ Alamy

WRITTEN ESSAYS

Probably the simplest method of appraisal is to write a narrative describing an employee's strengths, weaknesses, past performance, potential, and suggestions for improvement. The **written essay** requires no complex forms or extensive training to complete. But the results often reflect the ability of the writer to express him- or herself well, the writer's opinion of what is notable, and a totally subjective assessment of those notable events. Comparing an employee's appraisal from one year to the next may be difficult, as will be comparing one employee to another.

Written essay
A performance appraisal technique in which an evaluator writes out a description of an employee's strengths, weaknesses, past performance, and potential, and then makes suggestions for improvement.

CRITICAL INCIDENTS

Critical incidents focus attention on those employee behaviours that are crucial in ensuring that a job is executed effectively. The supervisor writes down examples that describe what the employee did that was especially effective or ineffective. The key here is that only specific behaviours, not vaguely defined personality traits, are cited. A list of critical incidents provides a rich set of examples from which the employee can be shown those behaviours that are desirable and those that call for improvement.

Critical incidents
A performance appraisal technique in which an evaluator lists key behaviours that separate effective from ineffective job performance.

CHECKLISTS

With a **checklist**, a supervisor uses a list of behavioural descriptions and checks off those behaviours that apply to the employee. As Figure 8-6 illustrates, you merely go down the list and check off yes or no to each question.

A major drawback to checklists is the cost. Where an organization has a number of job categories, checklist items must be developed for each category.

Checklist
A performance appraisal technique in which an evaluator uses a list of behavioural descriptions and checks off those behaviours that apply to the employee.

GRAPHIC RATING SCALES

One of the oldest and most popular methods of appraisal is the **graphic rating scale**. An example of some graphic rating scale items is shown in Figure 8-7.

Graphic rating scales can be used to assess factors such as quantity and quality of work, job knowledge, cooperation, loyalty, dependability, attendance, honesty, integrity, attitudes, and initiative. However, this method is most valid when subjective traits such as loyalty or integrity are avoided, unless they can be defined in specific behavioural terms.

With the graphic rating scale, you go down the list of factors and note that point along the scale or continuum that best describes the employee. There are typically 3 to 10 points on the continuum. In the design of the graphic scales, the challenge is to ensure that both the factors evaluated and the scale points are clearly understood by the supervisor doing the rating.

Why are graphic rating scales so popular? Though they don't provide the depth of information that essays or critical incidents do, they are less time-consuming to develop and administer; they allow for easy numerical tallying

Graphic rating scale
A performance appraisal technique in which an evaluator rates a set of performance factors on an incremental scale.

and comparison and, in contrast to the checklist, there is greater standardization of items, so that comparison with other employees in diverse job categories is possible.

However, if you put yourself in the shoes of the employee, how useful are a series of ratings on vague categories in terms of feedback? Do you know what to change in future? Can that standard set of scales dig into the details of your job? Another issue with graphic rating scales is how easy it is for a supervisor to complete them without putting much thought into it, and the tendency to either rate everyone around the middle or near the top. These central tendency and leniency errors are discussed later in the chapter. With the five rating levels offered in Figure 8-7, it makes it especially easy to rate people in the middle so many prefer an even number of levels with no actual "middle" to fall back on.

BEHAVIOURALLY ANCHORED RATING SCALES

Behaviourally anchored rating scales (BARS)
A performance appraisal technique in which an evaluator rates employees on specific job behaviours derived from performance dimensions.

Behaviourally anchored rating scales (BARS) have received more attention in recent years. These scales combine major elements from the critical incident and graphic rating scale approaches: Supervisors rate their employees based on items along a continuum, but the points are examples of actual behaviour on the given job rather than general descriptions or traits.

Behaviourally anchored rating scales specify definite, observable, and measurable job behaviours. Examples of job-related behaviours and per-

	Yes	No
1. Are supervisor's orders usually followed?	_____	_____
2. Does the individual approach customers promptly?	_____	_____
3. Does the individual suggest additional merchandise to customers?	_____	_____
4. Does the individual keep busy when not servicing a customer?	_____	_____
5. Does the individual lose his or her temper in public?	_____	_____
6. Does the individual volunteer to help other employees?	_____	_____

FIGURE 8-6

Sample of items from a checklist

Performance Factor	Performance Rating				
Quality of work is the accuracy, skill, and completeness of work.	**1** Consistently unsatisfactory	**2** Occasionally unsatisfactory	**3** Consistently satisfactory	**4** Sometimes superior	**5** Consistently superior
Quantity of work is the volume of work done in a normal workday.	**1** Consistently unsatisfactory	**2** Occasionally unsatisfactory	**3** Consistently satisfactory	**4** Sometimes superior	**5** Consistently superior
Job knowledge is information pertinent to the job that an individual should have for satisfactory job performance.	**1** Poorly informed about work duties	**2** Occasionally unsatisfactory	**3** Can answer most questions about the job	**4** Understands all phases of the job	**5** Has complete mastery of all phases of the job
Dependability is following directions and company policies without supervision.	**1** Requires constant supervision	**2** Requires occasional follow-up	**3** Usually can be counted on	**4** Requires very little supervision	**5** Requires absolute minimum of supervision

FIGURE 8-7

Example of graphic rating scale items

formance dimensions are found by obtaining specific illustrations of effective and ineffective behaviour for each performance dimension. These behavioural examples are then translated into a set of performance dimensions, each dimension having varying levels of performance. The results of this process are behavioural descriptions, such as *anticipates, plans, executes, solves immediate problems, carries out orders,* and *handles emergency situations.* Figure 8-8 provides an example of a BARS.

Studies conducted on the use of BARS indicate that this method of appraisal tends to reduce rating errors. But its biggest advantage may stem from the dimensions BARS generates rather than from any particular superiority of behaviour anchors over trait anchors. The process of developing the behavioural scales is valuable in and of itself for clarifying to both the employee and supervisor which behaviours reflect good performance and which bad.

However, BARS is not without its drawbacks. It, too, suffers from the distortions inherent in most rating methods. BARS is also costly and time-consuming to develop and to maintain.[4]

FIGURE 8-8

Sample BARS for an employee relations specialist (*Source:* Reprinted from *Business Horizons,* August 1976. Copyright 1976 by the Foundation for the School of Business at Indiana University.)

Performance dimension scale development under BARS for the dimension "Ability to Absorb and Interpret Policies for an Employee Relations Specialist."

This employee relations specialist

9   could be expected to serve as an information source concerning new and changed policies for others in the organization

could be expected to be aware quickly of program changes and explain these to employees   8

7   could be expected to reconcile conflicting policies and procedures correctly to meet HRM goals

could be expected to recognize the need for additional information to gain a better understanding of policy changes   6

5   could be expected to complete various HRM forms correctly after receiving instruction on them

could be expected to require some help and practice in mastering new policies and procedures   4

3   could be expected to know that there is always a problem, but go down many blind alleys before realizing they are wrong

could be expected to incorrectly interpret guidelines, creating problems for line managers   2

1   could be expected to be unable to learn new procedures even after repeated explanations

RELATIVE STANDARDS

In the second category of performance appraisals—relative standards –employees' performance is evaluated by comparing it against other employees' performance. We'll discuss two relative methods: group order ranking and individual ranking.

GROUP ORDER RANKING

Group order ranking A performance appraisal approach that groups employees into ordered classifications.

Group order ranking requires supervisors to place their employees into particular classifications, such as "top 20%" or "bottom 10%." So if you have 20 employees and you're using the group-order ranking method, only four of your people can be in the top fifth, and, of course, two also must be relegated to the bottom 10% (see Figure 8-9).

The advantage of this group ordering method is that it prevents supervisors from inflating their evaluations so everyone looks good, or homogenizing the evaluations so everyone is rated near the average—outcomes that are not unusual with the graphic rating scale. The predominant disadvantages surface when the number of employees being compared is small. At the extreme, if you are assessing only four employees, all of whom may actually be excellent, you are forced to rank them into top quarter, middle, and bottom quarter! Of course, as the sample size increases, the validity of relative scores as an accurate measure also increases.

Another disadvantage, which plagues all relative measures, is the zero-sum consideration. This means that any change must add up to zero. For example, if there are 12 employees in your department performing at different levels of effectiveness, then by definition three are in the top quarter (sometimes called *quartile*), three in the second quarter, and so forth. The sixth-best employee, for instance, would be in the second quarter. But if two of the workers in the third or fourth quarters were to leave the department and not be replaced, then the sixth-best employee would drop into the third quarter. Because comparisons are relative, an employee who is mediocre may score high only because he or she is the "best of the worst"; in contrast, an excellent performer who is matched against tough competition may be evaluated poorly, when in absolute terms his or her performance is outstanding.

INDIVIDUAL RANKING

The **individual ranking** method requires supervisors to list all their employees in order from the highest to lowest performer. In this method, only one can be "best." This method also assumes that differences

Individual ranking
A performance appraisal approach that ranks employees in order from highest to lowest.

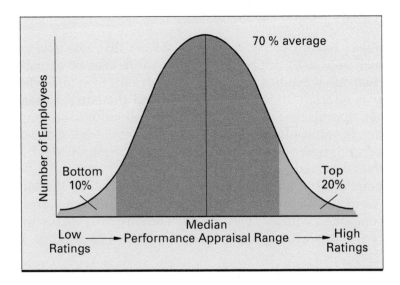

FIGURE 8-9

Group order ranking distribution

between people are uniform. That is, in appraising 30 employees, it is assumed that the difference between the first and second employee is the same as that between the twenty-first and twenty-second. This method allows for no ties—this can be an advantage because it forces supervisors to confront differences in performance levels. But its major drawback is that, in those situations where differences are small or nonexistent, this method magnifies and overemphasizes differences.

OBJECTIVES

Increasingly, organizations are focusing on the achievement of specific goals or objectives as part of the appraisal process. These are unique measurable outcomes jointly established by the employee and supervisor and intended to be accomplished in a specific time period. Figure 8-10 illustrates an excerpt from a performance appraisal form that required the employee to come up with three key performance goals each year. Note that it is broken down into the steps that must be accomplished in order to ultimately reach the goal. Resources needed and potential barriers are discussed and documented. Each goal is also linked to organizational goals or strategies, reminding the employee of the bigger picture.

HURDLES IN THE WAY OF EFFECTIVE APPRAISALS

While you and your employer may seek to make the performance appraisal process free from personal biases, prejudices, and idiosyncrasies, a number of potential problems can creep into the process. As a supervisor, you can try to avoid distorted performance appraisals by recognizing the following errors.

LENIENCY AND HARSHNESS ERRORS

Leniency error
The tendency to appraise a set of employees too high.

Harshness error
The tendency to appraise a set of employees too low

Every appraiser has his or her own value system that acts as a standard against which appraisals are made. Relative to the true or actual performance an individual exhibits, some appraisers mark high and others low. The former is referred to as **leniency error**, and the latter as **harshness error**. When appraisers are lenient in their evaluations, an employee's performance is rated higher than it actually should be. Conversely, a harshness error underrates performance, giving the individual a lower appraisal than deserved.

If all employees in an organization were appraised by the same person, there would be no problem. Although there would be an error factor, it would be applied equally to everyone. The difficulty arises when we have different raters with different leniency errors. For example, assume

Key Performance Goals
September 11, 20XX – September 10, 20XX

Key Performance Goal #3 of 3:	Agreed Outcomes including completion date:	Check Completed	Overall Rating		
			U	S	E
Prepare draft sustainability policy	• _Research current sustainability best practices (Dec.)_ • _Create and distribute sustainability questionnaire to internal stakeholders (Jan.); analyze results and share with advisory group, along with best practices info (Mar.)_ • _Present draft policy to advisory group and edit accordingly (June)_ • _Present edited draft policy to stakeholder focus groups for feedback (July)_ • _Present final draft policy to executive committee (Sept.)_				

Link to Organization's Enablers:	Resources Required:
☐ _Develop People_ ✕ _Build & Deploy Resources Strategically_ ✕ _Responsive Planning & Implementation_	Time Access to research databases on sustainability Admin support assistance to create best practices paper, questionnaire, draft policy documents Assistance of Institutional Research to analyze data **Barriers to Achieving Outcomes:** _Workload (projects X and Y also demanding)_ _Competing priorities for stakeholders so they don't provide timely feedback_

Employee: _____   Manager: _____
Date Completed: _____

FIGURE 8-10

Excerpt from Performance Appraisal that focuses on Achievement of Goals

that Jones and Smith are performing the same job for different supervisors, but they have absolutely identical job performance. If Jones's supervisor tends to err toward leniency, while Smith's supervisor errs toward harshness, we might be confronted with two dramatically different performance appraisals. Smith may end up feeling angry and cheated because the same performance level has resulted in dramatically different bonuses or promotion opportunities.

HALO ERROR

The **halo error** is a tendency to rate an individual high or low on *all* factors as a result of the impression of a high or low rating on *one* specific factor. For example, if an employee tends to be dependable, you might become biased

Halo error
A tendency to rate an individual high or low on all factors due to the impression of a high or low rating on some specific factor.

toward that individual and rate him or her high on many desirable traits. The halo effect is more likely to arise if a supervisor has limited exposure to the employee. For instance, if the supervisor only sees the employee in meetings, and the employee is a very confident and imaginative contributor, the supervisor may assume, incorrectly, that everything else the employee does is just as impressive. Conversely, if the employee is shy and a reluctant meeting participant, the supervisor may assume, again incorrectly, that the employee fades into the background in all aspects of work.

The halo effect confronts the people who design teaching appraisal forms for college students to fill out in order to evaluate the effectiveness of their instructors. Students tend to rate a faculty member as outstanding on all criteria when they are particularly appreciative of a few things he or she does in the classroom. Similarly, a few bad habits—showing up late for lectures, being slow in returning papers, or assigning an extremely demanding reading assignment—might result in students evaluating the instructor negatively across the board.

SIMILARITY ERROR

When appraisers rate other people giving special consideration to those qualities they perceive in themselves, they are making a **similarity error.** For example, the supervisor who perceives himself as aggressive may evaluate others by looking for aggressiveness. Those who demonstrate this characteristic tend to benefit, while others are penalized.

Similarity errors hurt an organization if the rated quality does not further the organization's success.

RECENCY ERROR

Most of us can remember more vividly what happened yesterday than what happened six months ago. This creates the potential for the **recency error** to surface in performance appraisals.

The recency error results in evaluators recalling, and then giving greater importance to, employee job behaviours that have occurred near the end of the performance-measuring period. So if supervisors have to complete an appraisal form on each of their employees every June 1, those accomplishments and mistakes that took place in May tend to be remembered while those behaviours exhibited the previous November tend to be forgotten. Given the reality that we all have good days and bad days—even good and bad months—and that they don't occur at the same time for all employees, a semiannual or annual review may be significantly biased by employee behaviours just prior to their supervisor's review. Employees are aware of this, as indicated by the "best behaviour" they show as appraisal time nears.

CENTRAL TENDENCY ERROR

It's possible that, regardless of who the appraiser evaluates and what characteristics are used, the pattern of evaluation will remain the same. It is also possible that a supervisor's ability to appraise objectively and accurately will be impeded by a failure to use the extremes of the appraising scale. This reluctance to assign extreme ratings, in either direction, is the **central tendency error.**

Raters who are prone to the central tendency error avoid the "excellent" category as well as the "unacceptable" category, and assign all ratings around the "average" or midpoint range. By failing to use the extreme ratings, the pattern of evaluation becomes the same for all employees. For example, if a supervisor rates all subordinates as 3, on a 1 to 5 scale, then no differentiation among the subordinates exists. And by suppressing differences, employees' work performances appear considerably more homogeneous than they really are.

INFLATIONARY PRESSURES

Inflationary Pressures
Tendency to minimize performance differences and be lenient as well so all appraisals are inflated.

A clerical employee at a large insurance company was disappointed by the small salary increase she received following her recent performance review. After all, her supervisor had given her an 86 overall rating. And she knew that the company's appraisal system defined "outstanding performance" as 90 and above, "good" as 80 to 89, "average" as 70 to 79, and "inadequate performance" as anything below 70. This employee was really bewildered when she heard from some friends at work that her pay increase was below the company average. You can imagine her surprise when, after meeting with the assistant director for human resources, she learned that the "average" rating of clerical personnel in the company was 92!

This example illustrates a potential problem in appraisals—inflationary pressures. This problem arises when supervisors both minimize differences among their subordinates *and* push all evaluations into the upper range of the rating scale.

Inflationary pressures have always existed, but they have become more of a problem. As equality has grown in importance, and fear of retribution from disgruntled employees who fail to achieve excellent appraisals has increased, there has been a tendency for evaluators to be less rigorous and to reduce the negative repercussions from the appraisal process by generally inflating or upgrading evaluations.

FUNDAMENTAL ATTRIBUTION ERROR

Fundamental attribution error
The tendency to make attributions to internal causes when focusing on someone else's behaviour.

A potential error underlying all judgements of behaviour is jumping to conclusions about the causes underlying performance. When we assess causation we are making an attribution. And there is a **fundamental attribution error** we all tend to fall victim to, the tendency to make attributions to internal causes when focusing on someone else's behaviour. Whether a performance is strong or weak we will tend to attribute the performance to the person (e.g. skills, effort) rather than to circumstances. For example, when a new staff member has an unusually high sales record the supervisor tends to credit the employee for the success, judging it to be a result of ability and persistence. In fact, the success could be due to a shifting of sales boundaries so a client previously in someone else's region now belongs to this salesperson's region. On the other hand, a new employee with a poor sales record could be blamed for the failure, with the supervisor seeing it as due to laziness. It could be that the employee worked diligently in extremely difficult circumstances and the failure was due to issues with delays in the production and delivery areas that caused him to lose the sales.

How do you avoid attribution errors? To avoid jumping to conclusions, you probe for information that could offer other explanations for the performance. Was the failure due to poor training or lack of support from other areas or equipment problems? Was the workload reasonable? How have

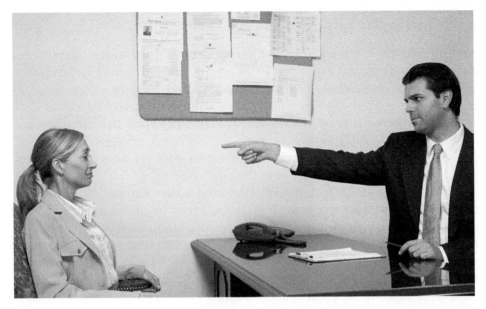

others in similar situations performed? How has this person performed in other circumstances and over time? One of the best sources of explanation is the employee him or herself. Simple questions like "Tell me about why you think this particular event went so well" or "Tell me what you think went wrong and what could have helped you handle it" can yield important information for the supervisor to understand what actually happened.

OVERCOMING THE HURDLES

Just because there are potential hurdles to effective appraisals, supervisors shouldn't give up on the process. There are several things you can do to help overcome these hurdles.

CLARIFY EXPECTATIONS

Make no assumptions that an employee knows exactly what you expect. Discuss your expectations with each subordinate. Colleen Murray, sales and marketing manager for the parks and recreation department at the City of Brampton, believes strongly in communicating expectations so there are no surprises. Colleen jointly sets objectives with her staff and she makes it very clear what they will be measured on through a face-to-face meeting long before the performance appraisal.

According to Susan Pander, HR manager at SaskTel, all managers are expected to work with all employees to ensure that they understand the corporate vision and direction, and where their division is going. Then managers are expected to work with them to set individual objectives within their job description so employees can contribute to the division and the corporation.

CONTINUALLY DOCUMENT EMPLOYEE PERFORMANCE

Keep a file for each of your employees and continually enter notes describing specific instances of accomplishments and behaviours. Include dates and details. When the time comes for you to conduct formal employee appraisals, you'll have a comprehensive history of each employee's performance record during the appraisal period. This will minimize the recency error, increase the accuracy of your ratings, and provide you with specific documentation to support your assessments. You will be much more credible to the employee.

Rod Guild, senior foreman at Highland Valley Copper in BC, uses a digital handheld voice-recorder to make notes as he drives around the site and later records them in a small computer notebook. Rob Mastrotto, at Husky Injection Molding Systems in Bolton, Ontario, carries his black notebook with him constantly. "I write down what happens as I go along. I document all verbal warnings I give. I'm trying to concentrate on also recording more of the good things I observe."

USE BEHAVIOURALLY BASED MEASURES

As we've noted previously, behaviourally based measures are superior to those developed around traits. Many traits often considered to be related to good performance may, in fact, have little or no performance relationship. Traits such as loyalty, initiative, courage, and reliability are intuitively appealing as desirable characteristics in employees. But the relevant question is: Are employees who are evaluated as high on these traits higher performers than those who rate low? We can't answer that question. We know that there are employees who rate high on these characteristics and are poor performers. And we can find others who are excellent performers but don't score well on traits such as these. Our conclusion is that traits such as loyalty and initiative may be prized by organizations, but there is no evidence to support the view that certain traits will be adequate substitutes for performance in a large cross-section of jobs. Additionally, as we noted previously, traits suffer from weak agreement among multiple raters. What you consider "loyalty," I may not.

Behaviourally based measures can deal with both of these objections. Because they deal with specific examples of performance—both good and bad—you avoid the problem of using inappropriate substitutes. Moreover, because you're evaluating specific behaviours, you increase the likelihood that two or more evaluators will see the same thing. You might consider a given employee as "friendly" while I rate her "standoffish." But when asked to rate her in terms of specific behaviours, we might both agree that she "frequently says 'good morning' to customers," "rarely gives advice or assistance to coworkers," and "almost always avoids idle chatter with coworkers."

Perceptions of fairness in the way an organization does things can have a big impact on employee morale, and the performance appraisal is particularly important in this regard. The more accurate and transparent the appraisal is, the more it will be accepted. It will also build trust that the supervisor and company are supportive and fair with employees and are making appropriate decisions.[5]

COMBINE ABSOLUTE AND RELATIVE STANDARDS

A major drawback to absolute standards is that they tend to be biased by inflationary pressures—evaluators lean toward packing their subjects into the high part of the rankings. On the other hand, relative standards suffer when there is little actual variability among the subjects.

The obvious solution is to consider using appraisal methods that combine absolute and relative standards. For example, you might want to use the graphic rating scale and the individual ranking method. It's much more meaningful to compare two employees' performance records when you know that Supervisor A gave Bob Carter an overall rating of 86, which ranked fourth in a department of 17; while Supervisor B gave Tina Blackstone the same overall rating—an 86—but ranked her twelfth in a department of 14. It's possible that Supervisor B has higher-performing employees than Supervisor A. But Supervisor B's ratings may also suffer from inflationary pressures. By providing both absolute and relative assessments, it is easier to more accurately compare employees across departments.

USE MULTIPLE RATERS

As the number of evaluators increases, the probability of attaining more accurate information increases. If rater error tends to follow a normal curve, an increase in the number of appraisers will tend to find the majority congregating about the middle. You see this approach being used in athletic competitions in such sports as diving, gymnastics, and figure skating (see Figure 8-12). A set of evaluators judges a performance, the highest and lowest scores are dropped, and the final performance appraisal is made up from the cumulative scores of those remaining. The logic of multiple raters applies to organizations as well, hence the increasing popularity of an approach known as **360-degree feedback**. This describes the use of multiple sources of evaluation of an employee's performance in order to increase accuracy (e.g. supervisor, employee, team colleagues, other supervisors with whom employee does project work, customers).

FIGURE 8-12

Figure skating performances are judged by multiple raters in order to increase accuracy

360-degree feedback
The use of multiple sources of evaluation of an employee's performance in order to increase accuracy

Rate Selectively

As an employee's direct supervisor, you are not always in a position to comprehensively appraise all the key aspects of that employee's job. You should only rate in those areas where you have significant job knowledge and have been able to observe, first-hand, the employee's job performance. If you appraise only those dimensions that you are in a good position to rate, you make the performance appraisal a more valid process.

If there are important parts of an employee's job in which you aren't able to make accurate judgements, you should supplement your appraisal with self-appraisals, peer evaluations, or even customer appraisals, if that's more appropriate. For instance, a number of sales supervisors use customer input as part of their evaluation of sales representatives. And in cases where supervisors must be away from their work areas frequently, thus limiting their opportunities to observe their employees' job behaviour, the use of peer reviews can improve the validity of the appraisal process.

One study demonstrated that peer ratings were more strongly influenced by interpersonal facilitation skills whereas supervisory ratings were more influenced by technical/administrative task performance, probably due to differing opportunities to observe. Therefore, the inclusion of both types of appraisals towards an overall performance rating probably creates a fuller and more accurate appraisal.[6]

Participate in Appraisal Training

Good appraisers aren't necessarily born. If your appraisal skills are deficient, you should participate in performance-appraisal training because there is evidence that training can make you a more accurate rater.

Common problems such as leniency and halo errors have been minimized or eliminated in workshops where supervisors practise observing and rating behaviours. These workshops typically run from one to three days, but allocating many hours to training may not always be necessary. For instance, one case has been cited where both halo and leniency errors were decreased immediately after exposing evaluators to explanatory training sessions lasting only five minutes.[7] But the effects of training appear to diminish over time, which suggests the need for regular refresher sessions.

PricewaterhouseCoopers uses an interesting training exercise to impress upon managers the impact of performance appraisals. They are asked to sit opposite another manager and form a first impression of that person. Then they are told that they will be reporting that first impression to the person in a few minutes. When the time has expired, they are relieved to find out that, in fact, they won't be asked to share their impressions after all, or receive an appraisal from someone else. However, they have had the experience of knowing how fearfully most people approach being appraised, and the uncomfortable feelings they get when they are asked to appraise someone else.[8] Even when performance appraisals are improved to be more behaviour-based, there are still mental barriers to overcome.

WHAT ABOUT TEAM PERFORMANCE APPRAISALS?

Performance appraisal concepts have been almost exclusively developed with the individual employee as the focus point. This reflects the historic belief that individuals are the core building block around which organizations are built. But as we've noted a number of times in this book, more and more organizations are restructuring themselves around teams: self-managed teams, cross-functional teams, task forces, and the like (see Supervision in Action)

In team-based departments, job performance is a function of each individual's contribution to the team, and of his or her ability to be a good team player. Both these performance dimensions are often better assessed by the team's members than by the team's supervisor. We suggest, therefore, that supervisors include peer evaluations from team members in the performance appraisals of those whose jobs are inherently designed around teamwork. This enhances the autonomy of the team, reinforces the importance of cooperation, and increases the validity of the appraisal process. Additionally, supervisors should consider the benefits of downplaying individual contributions by substituting group performance measures. Where teams have clear responsibilities for achieving specific objectives, it makes more sense to appraise the team's overall performance than to focus on its individual members.

One of the issues that comes up with peer appraisals in a team is the willingness to be totally honest. Particularly if important consequences are attached to the ratings, such as bonuses or reprimands, team members may be reluctant to "tattle" on peers who are likely friends as well. Anne Murphy, branch manager at Frank McKechnie library in Mississauga, encourages honesty in several ways. She chooses five or six people to appraise an individual. Each person must sign his or her name to the appraisal, encouraging accountability, but the feedback is passed on anonymously to the individual being appraised. The peer appraisals are not done annually because they are so time-consuming and the staff is large. People want to make it meaningful and tend to "agonize over the wording." So Anne performs appraisals for new employees, if someone requests it, or when she needs the backing of other staff members to note that improvement is needed. Other than that, she will arrange appraisals for individuals about every two years.

Performance Appraisals in Contemporary Organizations

The foundation of the performance appraisal process is the concept that performance standards are clearly identified.[9] This fundamental fact implies that for workers to perform effectively, they must know and understand what is expected of them. This concept, however, applies only where clear job descriptions and specifications exist, and where variations to the job are minimal. In other words, conventional performance appraisals were designed to fit the needs of the traditional organization. But what happens when the organization is far from traditional? Let's consider some possibilities.

First, setting goals for an employee could become a thing of the past. Your workers may go from project to project, with the demands and requirements of their work rapidly changing. No formalized performance appraisal system may be able to capture the complexities of the jobs being done. Second, employees will likely have several bosses, not just you. Who, then, will have the responsibility for the performance appraisal? It is more likely to be the team members themselves—setting their own goals and evaluating each other's performance. One can even speculate that this will take the format of an ongoing informal process, rather than some formal "ritual" held every 12 months. All in all, while we surmise a drastic change in the performance appraisal process, it should not be interpreted that you will become less concerned with evaluating employee performance. On the contrary, individual performance will still matter most. The major difference is that employee performance information is likely to be collected from a number of sources—from anyone who's familiar with the employee's work.

NOW WHAT? RESPONDING TO PERFORMANCE PROBLEMS

You've completed your employees' performance appraisals. What if you've identified a significant performance deficiency? What are your options?

You can provide personal coaching, attempt to increase employee motivation, provide skill training, reassess the employees, or try to eliminate external performance barriers. Your choice depends on the reason why performance is lacking.[10]

If you realize the performance problem is ability-related, your emphasis becomes one of encouraging training and development efforts. However, when the performance problem is not ability-related, you need to engage the employee in discussion about the issue.[11]

WHAT DO YOU NEED TO KNOW ABOUT DISCUSSING PERFORMANCE ISSUES?

Some fundamental steps should be followed when discussing an issue with an employee (see Figure 8-13).

LISTEN TO WHAT THE EMPLOYEE HAS TO SAY

You can't effectively counsel others unless you listen to what they have to say.[12] Your actions should be tailored to the needs, demands, and personality of your employee. These factors can't be accurately assessed without active listening. Rob Watson: "If they make poor decisions, I don't come down hard on them. I ask why they did what they did so I can learn the thinking and the situation."

When you sit down with your employee, demonstrate your willingness and desire to be helpful. Then, listen to what he or she has to say. Also, listen to what is not being said. How is the employee framing the problem? Who does the employee think is to blame? Are his or her emotions driving out rational thinking? Don't make judgements too quickly.

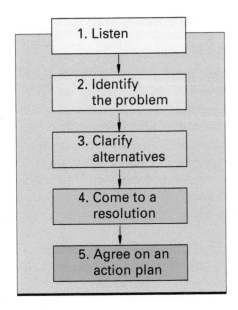

FIGURE 8-13

Dealing with a performance issue.

Try to grasp the employee's perception of the situation without agreeing or disagreeing with that perception. At this point, it's not as important to determine whether the employee is right or wrong as it is to try to fully understand the problem from his or her point of view.

IDENTIFY THE PROBLEM

After you've listened to your employee's initial assessment of the situation, begin the search to identify the problem and its causes. What does the employee think is the problem? Who or what is the cause? How is this problem affecting the employee? What, if any, responsibility is your employee taking for the problem? This discussion helps avoid attribution errors.

CLARIFY ALTERNATIVES, BUT DON'T GIVE ADVICE ON PERSONAL ISSUES

Problems come with options. In most cases a number of alternative actions can correct the problem. These actions need to be explored and clarified. At this step, a participative approach can be particularly valuable because you may see and know things that escape the employee. As a result, the merging of both your insights and those of the employee can result in a larger number of quality options.

Once alternatives are identified, they need to be evaluated. What are the strengths and weaknesses of each? Again, two heads are better than one. Your goal should be to have the employee weigh the pluses and minuses of each course of action.

Avoid giving advice. Identify the options and give information, but don't tell the person what he or she *should* do. Why? If the advice works, the employee may become dependent on you for future advice and less likely to solve problems independently. If the advice does not work, you may be blamed and will lose credibility. The employee may then be reluctant to discuss concerns in the future. Whether advice is good or bad, the simple act of giving advice, especially on a personal matter, can offend some people, making them defiant.

Let's look at an example. An employee's productivity has been suffering and she has been chronically late recently. In discussing this issue with her, you discover that she is dealing with a very sick parent. You can describe possible options such as taking vacation time, going to half-time temporarily, taking a leave of absence, accessing help through community resources, or utilizing the company's Employee Assistance Program. Feel free to discuss the pros and cons of the various options—she'll probably appreciate the support and another perspective on the situation—but don't recommend a particular course of action. She is responsible for her own actions.

Christopher Nicolson: "If I'm unhappy with someone's performance, they are usually also unhappy with their performance. And there are usually things going on. Recognition can help turn things around. I need to

FIGURE 8-14

Christopher Nicolson of Tourism Sun Peaks

set standards, so we both know if something is not acceptable, and work constructively with them: 'You've got a great skill set, so let's use your skills to move forward.'"

COME TO A RESOLUTION

What's the best option for the employee? Remember, the best option for one employee is not necessarily the best option for another. The solution should reflect the unique characteristics of the employee. And ideally, both you and the employee will agree on the solution. You want to be sure the employee buys into the final choice, whether that final choice was made by you, the employee, or jointly. A terrific solution that's not accepted by the employee is unlikely to result in any meaningful change in the problem. Obviously, here we're discussing a work issue rather than an employee's personal issue. For example, an employee is not performing well in a new role. Your discussion with him reveals that he does not enjoy this role because of its isolation from other people and he would prefer to work in a more social setting. Together you can discuss his options, such as altering the current job so it is less isolated, remaining with the job and improving performance until another opening comes up, returning to the old job, or transferring to another position. However, business circumstances may restrict the choices so you may inform him that there is no option but to stay until another opening arises and, therefore, his performance must improve, despite his feelings. If he understood the restrictions, was clear on expectations and consequences, and felt you were being fair, he would likely accept your explanation.

AGREE ON AN ACTION PLAN

Finally, the employee needs to develop a concrete plan of action for implementing the solution. What, specifically, is the employee going to do? When will he or she do it? What resources, if any, will be needed?

It's usually a good idea to end with the employee summarizing what has taken place and the specific actions he or she plans on taking. You should establish a follow-up point at some specific date in the future for reassessing the employee's progress. If a formal meeting isn't needed, request a short memo from the employee updating you on his or her progress. This can be effective as a reminder to the employee that progress is expected, and as a control device for you to assess the employee's progress.

As part of the summarizing of next steps, it also has to be clear what will happen if a performance issue is not resolved. Discussing a performance issue to seek resolution is not disciplining an employee. But if the issue persists, it may become a discipline issue and the employee needs to know that.

Is Your Action Ethical?

What business do you have delving into an employee's personal life? That's a valid question, and it requires us to look at the ethics involved.

Employees bring a multitude of problems and frustrations from their personal lives to their jobs. They have difficulty finding quality day care for infants. A teenage child is expelled from high school. They have fights with their spouses. A family member suffers a nervous breakdown. They get behind in their bills and they're harassed by creditors. A close friend is seriously hurt in an automobile accident. A parent is diagnosed with Alzheimer's disease.

It may seem wise to keep your nose out of your employees' personal lives, but that is often unreasonable. Why? Because there is no clear demarcation that separates personal and work lives. Consider the following scenario involving one of your employees, Denise. Denise's son was arrested last night for drug possession. She spent most of the night with police and lawyers. Today, at work, she is tired and psychologically distant. She has trouble concentrating. Her mind is not on her job. It's naive to believe that employees can somehow leave their personal baggage at the door when they come to work each morning. Colleen Murray is acutely aware of the impact of the aging population and the "sandwich" generation. She has an employee whose mother is dealing with cancer, another whose son has a brain tumour, and one who took time off to help her 80-year-old father through surgery and recovery.

Employees have a right to privacy. However, when personal problems interfere with work performance, you should not consider it beyond your jurisdiction to inquire about the problem, offer yourself as an open ear, and genuinely seek to help with the problem. If your offer is rejected, don't push. If the employee understands how his or her personal problem is affecting work performance, and you make clear what the consequences will be if the work performance doesn't improve, you've reached the ethical limit of your involvement. If the employee is protective of the privacy of his or her personal life, your rights as a supervisor don't extend to helping solve his or her personal problems. However, you do have the right and the obligation to make sure employees understand that if personal problems interfere with their work, they need to solve those personal problems—and you're there to help, if asked.

CONDUCTING THE APPRAISAL REVIEW INTERVIEW

ASSESSING YOURSELF: CONDUCTING THE APPRAISAL INTERVIEW

For each of the following questions, check the answer that best describes your relationship with subordinates. Remember to respond as you have behaved or would behave, not as you think you should behave. If you have no supervisory experience, answer the questions assuming you are a supervisor.

WHEN CONDUCTING AN EMPLOYEE'S PERFORMANCE APPRAISAL REVIEW, I:

	Usually	Sometimes	Seldom
1. Try to put the employee at ease.	❏	❏	❏
2. Make sure I fully understand the employee's job duties and responsibilities.	❏	❏	❏
3. Encourage the employee to engage in self-evaluation.	❏	❏	❏
4. Do most of the talking.	❏	❏	❏
5. Avoid criticism.	❏	❏	❏
6. Focus discussion on the employee's behaviour rather than on his or her personal characteristics.	❏	❏	❏
7. Use specific examples to support my judgments.	❏	❏	❏
8. Try to get the appraisal over with as quickly as possible.	❏	❏	❏

For questions 1, 2, 3, 6, and 7, give yourself 3 points for "Usually," 2 points for "Sometimes," and 1 point for "Seldom." For questions 4, 5, and 8, give yourself 3 points for "Seldom," 2 points for "Sometimes," and 1 point for "Usually."

Add up your points. A score of 21 or higher indicates excellent performance appraisal skills. Scores in the 16–20 range imply some deficiencies in this skill. Scores below 16 denote that you have considerable room for improvement.

SKILL BASICS

There are three basic approaches to conducting the performance review: 1. tell and sell, 2. tell and listen, and 3. problem solve.[13] With *tell and sell*, the supervisor acts as a judge. That is, the supervisor tells the employee how well he or she is doing and then persuades the employee to change in the way the supervisor desires. The *tell and listen* approach is similar, except that the supervisor conveys assessments of the strengths and weaknesses in the employee's performance and then lets the employee respond to these statements. The supervisor tries to understand the employee's feelings by being a good listener and by displaying empathy. The *problem-solving* approach takes a very different tack. In this approach, the supervisor acts as a partner and works jointly with the subordinate to develop the employee's performance. It requires the supervisor to practise both joint goal setting and effective listening.

Most contemporary discussions of the performance review advocate the problem-solving approach. We acknowledge our debt to this approach in developing many of the following guidelines

1. **Schedule the formal appraisal review in advance and be prepared.** Many supervisors treat the entire performance appraisal as a last-minute obligation that they dread. They put neither time nor thought into it.

   If a performance review is to be effective, planning must precede it. Review the employee's job description. Go over your rating sheet. Have you carefully considered the employee's strengths as well as weaknesses? Can you substantiate, with specific examples, all points of praise and criticism? Given your past experiences with the employee, what problems, if any, do you anticipate cropping up in the review? How do you plan to react to these problems? What is the main message you want to convey?

   Once you have worked out these kinds of issues, you should schedule a specific time and place for the review and give the employee ample advance notice. Also give the employee a blank template of the appraisal form so they know what will be discussed, or give them the last appraisal done to remind them of the commitments made in that appraisal. If you expect the employee to do a self-assessment, give lots of time ahead of the meeting to do this, and plan time within the meeting to discuss it. When the meeting itself comes about, you should do whatever is necessary—close your office door, have your phone calls held, and the like—to ensure there are no outside interruptions once the review begins.

2. **Put the employee at ease.** Regardless of your personal feelings about performance reviews—and many supervisors feel uncomfortable judging others, or fear that being honest will create resentment among their employees—you are responsible for creating a supportive climate for the employee. The performance review can be a traumatic experience for the best of employees. People don't like to hear their work criticized. On the other hand, many employees have little confidence that the organization's performance-appraisal system will accurately assess their contribution. Add the fact that people tend to overrate themselves (approximately 60 percent place their own performance in the top 10 percent[14]) and you have the ingredients for tension and confrontation. Recognize that the employee is probably anxious, so be supportive and understanding.

3. **Be sure that the employee understands the purpose of the appraisal review.** What's the purpose of the review? Is it to be used for personnel decisions or to promote the employee's growth and development? The former purpose warrants focusing on the past, while the latter points to the future. In the problem-solving approach, the review is seen as an opportunity to provide recognition for those things the employee is doing well and to discuss any job-related problems that the employee may be experiencing. Regardless of the purpose, however, you should clarify at the start any uncertainty the employee may have about what will transpire during the review and the resulting consequences.

4. **Minimize threats.** You will want to create a helpful and constructive climate. The review should not be an inquisition. Try to maximize encouragement and support, while minimizing threats.

5. **Obtain employee participation.** Effective performance reviews are characterized by high employee participation. Let the employee do the majority of the talking. The evidence indicates the more the employee talks, the more satisfied he or she will be with the appraisal.[15]

6. **Have the employee engage in self-evaluation.** Consistent with high participation, encourage the employee to evaluate his or her own performance. If the climate is supportive, the employee may well openly acknowledge performance problems thus eliminating your need to raise them. Further, the employee may offer viable solutions to these problems. By encouraging self-evaluation and

being a good listener, you become a partner who is helping the employee perform better, rather than a "boss" who is looking for negatives to criticize. The employee might be the best person to identify a training plan or program that will improve his or her own performance.

Starting the review by asking the person for his or her perspective on how things have gone is often an effective beginning. Most employees appreciate this opportunity and, if you prove to be an effective listener, are very open with their comments. This means that the employee is often the first to address the topic of performance problems or particular performance challenges. This takes the supervisor off the hook for mentioning such issues and may even put you in the position of being the one to focus on the employee's positives. Often employees are too hard on themselves.

7. **Criticize performance but not the person.** If you need to criticize, direct the criticism at specific job-related behaviours that negatively affect the employee's performance. Never criticize the employee. It's the person's performance that is unsatisfactory, not the person.

8. **Soften the tone when criticizing, but not the message.** Many of us find it difficult to criticize others. If you believe criticism is necessary, don't water down the message, don't dance around the issue, and certainly don't avoid discussing a problem in the hope that it'll just go away. State your criticism thoughtfully and show concern for the employee's feelings, but don't soften the message. Criticism is criticism, even if it's constructive. When you try to sell it as something else, you're liable to create ambiguity and misunderstanding.

9. **Don't exaggerate**. Many of us tend to make extreme statements in order to make our point. Don't stretch the facts. If an employee has been late for four out of five recent meetings, don't say, "You're always late for meetings." Whenever possible, avoid absolutes such as "always" or "never." Such terms encourage defensiveness and undermine your credibility. An employee only has to introduce one exception to your "always" or "never" statement to destroy the entire statement's validity. Instead, list the four occasions on which the employee was late for the meeting.

Another example of exaggeration that is likely to cause repercussions is a statement like "You've got a bad attitude." This comment attacks the person, and generalizes to all circumstances. Rather than noting a "bad attitude," be more specific in your feedback. For example, you might say, "There have been three customer complaints about you in the last six months. All focused on apparent unwillingness to help, and resentment about taking you away from another task."

10. **Use specific examples to support your ratings.** Document your employee's performance ratings with specific examples. This adds credibility to your ratings and helps employees to better understand what you mean by "good" and "bad" performance. If you use critical instances to record specific actions in each employee's file, it will be easier to support your rating.

11. **Give positive as well as negative feedback.** No matter how poorly an employee is performing, he or she will have exhibited some strengths worthy of recognition. State what was done well and why it deserves recognition. What you want to avoid is turning the performance review into a totally negative feedback session. Interestingly, research indicates that those areas of job performance that are most criticized are least likely to show an improvement.[16] Of course, you want to avoid the other extreme, too, of unjustified blanket praise. If blanket praise is given, the employee is reinforced for mediocre as well as excellent behaviour.

    Some people believe in making a "feedback sandwich" by starting and finishing with positive observations and including the constructive criticism in the middle. However you combine them, it is important that employees don't dismiss the positive statement by waiting for the "But..." that leads to a negative. People are far more sensitive to the negative than the positive and will recall one criticism much more than five compliments.

12. **Have the employee sum up the appraisal review.** As the review nears its conclusion, encourage the employee to summarize the discussion that has taken place. This gives your subordinate an opportunity to put the entire review into perspective. It will also tell you whether you have succeeded in clearly communicating your evaluation. How do you do this? For example, you may say, "I want to make sure I've been clear and that we've covered everything. So I'd appreciate your recapping what you believe we've discussed."

13. **Detail a future plan of action.** Where there are serious performance deficiencies, the final part of the review should be devoted to helping the employee draft a detailed, step-by-step plan to correct the situation. Your role should be supportive: "What can I do to provide assistance?" Do you need to make yourself more available to answer questions? Do you need to give the employee more freedom or responsibility? Would securing funds to send the employee to professional meetings, workshops, or training programs help? The object is to demonstrate your support for the employee by asking him or her where you can provide assistance and then committing to provide that assistance. In effect, you fulfill your partnership role by helping employees clear the obstacles on the road toward their goals. Remember, outstanding employees also need to know future plans for their own advancement.

Ryan Anderson: "If there is any requirement of the job in which the employee is not meeting expectations, there should be a clear and documented improvement plan. And at the end of any appraisal meeting, there should be discussion about follow-up meetings and commitments (e.g. for intermediate targets) and all documentation should be completed and signed."

FIGURE 8-15

Ryan Anderson notes the importance of creating clear plans of action and following up on them.

APPLYING YOUR SKILLS

PART A—WHAT'S WRONG WITH THIS PERFORMANCE APPRAISAL?

Read the following script and "appraise the appraisal". Better yet, ask two class members to act out the roles. Use the following observer's sheet to assess Sarah. At the end, discuss what was not done well. How should it have been done?

Characters: Sarah, the supervisor, and Mike, the subordinate

> *(Mike knocks on Sarah's door)*

> Mike: "Hi, Sarah, I'm here for the appraisal meeting."

> Sarah: "Oh, dear, was that today?"

> Mike: "Well, that's what you e-mailed me."

> Sarah *(waving him to a seat, pulling open a drawer and removing a file):* "Well, I guess you're right then. Have a seat. So, tell me how you think I should rate you."

> Mike: "Well, that's kind of hard. What are you rating me on?"

Sarah: "Everything that's important in your job, of course. So tell me what's important and then how you've done." *(phone rings)* "Hold on a minute. I'd better take this."

(Sarah takes the call and mumbles quietly for two or three minutes. Mike looks increasingly uncomfortable. Sarah hangs up the phone and starts to speak again:) "Mike, how long is it since we've looked at that project of yours anyway? It must have been a couple of weeks, eh?"

Mike: "Actually, it's been two months."

Sarah: "Boy, time flies in this business. Well, let's start by looking at your punctuality. You know, I can recall several instances recently where you were late. Not good."

Mike: "When was that? I don't remember anyone saying anything to me about lateness."

Sarah: "Look, I don't memorize everything around here so I can't give you the exact dates. But punctuality is important. Let's move on to the next item—unit productivity. I have written here that the goal was an increase of five percent. Have you reached that?"

Mike: "Uh, I think so."

Sarah: "Great. Now, what else should we look at... Oh, I remember, I'm going to have to put a note in your file about not contributing to that meeting on future project management in the division. You should have been there."

Mike: "I wasn't even invited to that meeting."

Sarah: "Mike, you've got to show some initiative." *(phone rings again, Sarah answers it briefly and says, "OK, I'll be there right away", then hangs up and turns to Mike)* "Look, Mike, something's come up and I'm going to have to leave. Don't worry, you're a great employee and I see no real issues. You'll get a good appraisal. I'll chat to you soon."

(Sarah stands and reaches out to shake Mike's hand)

Mike *(looking unhappy)*:

"Okay. See you."

As the role-play proceeds, record Sarah's skill in the performance appraisal.

	1 not used	2	3	4 used very well
1. Put employee at ease	❏	❏	❏	❏
2. Clearly set out the purpose of the interview	❏	❏	❏	❏
3. Obtain employee participation	❏	❏	❏	❏
4. Ask for self-evaluation	❏	❏	❏	❏
5. Criticize performance, not the person	❏	❏	❏	❏
6. Soften the tone, not the message, when criticizing	❏	❏	❏	❏
7. Don't exaggerate	❏	❏	❏	❏
8. Use specific examples	❏	❏	❏	❏
9. Give positive feedback	❏	❏	❏	❏
10. Detail a future plan	❏	❏	❏	❏

SUMMARY

This summary is organized by the Learning Objectives.

1. Performance management describes the steps taken to ensure employee performance aligns with the organization's goals. The four components include: setting out individual performance expectations, giving ongoing feedback, formally appraising performance, and aligning consequences with performance.

2. Performance appraisal is both an evaluation/development tool and a legal document. It reviews past performance to identify accomplishments and deficiencies; it offers a detailed plan to improve future performance through training and development. It also becomes a legal document that can be used to justify or support personnel actions.

3. To minimize legal problems, supervisors should ensure that they carefully follow all performance appraisal policies and procedures set forth in the organization's handbooks (if any), and make every effort to avoid prejudice and discrimination.

4. The three most popular sets of criteria used by supervisors in appraisals are individual task outcomes, behaviours, and traits. The first two are almost always preferable to the third.

5. Absolute standards compare the employee's performance against specific traits or behaviours rather than against other people. In contrast, relative standards compare employees against other employees.

6. The graphic rating scale lists a set of factors—traits or behaviours—that are related to job performance. The rater then uses a 3- to-10-point scale to rate the employee on each of these factors.

7. Behaviourally anchored rating scales have received increased interest because they focus on job-related behaviours specific to a given job. This tends to reduce rating error and increase the validity of findings.

8. Common human errors that can distort appraisals include leniency, halo, similarity, recency, central tendency, inflationary pressures and the fundamental attribution error.

9. Appraisal errors can be minimized by clarifying expectations, maintaining continuous documentation of performance, using behaviourally based measures and multiple raters, combining absolute and relative standards, rating selectively and participating in appraisal training.

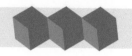

UNDERSTANDING THE BASICS

KEY TERMS AND CONCEPTS

Absolute standards
360-degree feedback
Behaviourally anchored
   rating scales (**BARS**)
Central tendency error
Checklist
Critical incidents
Fundamental attribution error
Graphic rating scale
Group order ranking

Halo error
Harshness error
Individual ranking
Leniency error
Performance appraisal
Performance management
Recency error
Relative standards
Similarity error
Written essay

REVIEWING YOUR KNOWLEDGE

1. Why is performance management a prime focus of a supervisor's job?
2. Why do many supervisors dislike and even avoid giving employees performance feedback?
3. Contrast the advantages of supervisor-conducted appraisals, self-evaluations, and peer appraisals.
4. What is the relationship between goal setting and performance appraisal?
5. If appraising behaviours is superior to appraising traits, why do you think so many organizations evaluate their employees on criteria such as effort, loyalty, and dependability?
6. Do formal performance appraisals replace informal feedback sessions? Discuss.
7. Compare written essay appraisals with **BARS**.
8. Would human errors in the appraisal process be eliminated in small organizations where one person does all the appraisals?

CASE 8.A

Relative Performance Ratings—A Challenge for Supervisors

Employee performance can be assessed against performance standards or against the performance of others. Some companies prefer the latter because they believe it is too easy for managers to be lenient and not make tough decisions about performance. Here are the stories of three managers working under such a system.

Alex:

"At my organization I have to rate my employees as high, medium or low and these ratings are related to salaries and bonuses. I have to distribute the scores; they can't all be high. I have to look at my team and identify laggards and standouts, and then communicate this with them. When there was lots of money, all 20 could be seen as top performers but not now. Sales is different because they have quotas, and if all get 200% of their quota they can all be rated as top performers. My staff are paid against work goals, but also compared to others and the market (each year the company looks at competitors and positions to see if certain professions are being paid more or are flat). My company used to pay top dollar for all employees but now only pays top dollar for top performers. If someone is struggling with their goals, it is up to me to provide coaching and support and education where needed but I can't change the goals. They are set from above and describe what is required to deliver the expected results to the corporation. It's hard to deal with someone who has been rated at medium and now is low; someone always has to be at bottom, and every year the bar is set higher so not everyone can keep up with the increasing expectations."

Radko:

"My organization has adopted a performance ranking system which supports the "refreshing" of a certain percentage of the staff annually. Each supervisor must rank all their employees into a bell curve that divides an employee group into the 20% that are above expectations, the 70% that meet expectations and the 10% that are operating below expectations. Those in the bottom 10% are put on a performance improvement plan. The assessments are made quarterly and if a person continues to be in the bottom 10%, they will eventually be let go. This performance evaluation system can be a challenge for supervisors, particularly if they have done their hiring, training and coaching well and believe all employees meet expectations. They are still forced to designate some in the bottom 10% and then have to work with other managers to see whose employees are really the weakest and should be let go, because in the end, 10% of employees are let go each year. So it can become political. One of the good aspects of the ranking system is the expectation that there is a focus on the top 20%. Once those people are identified, their supervisors are accountable for supporting their coaching and development for a continuing career at the company."

Andy:

"We use a distribution curve for performance so most are to be scored in the middle and very few at the top. Plus we must designate some as poor performers. I find this difficult when my staff are actually all strong. It tends to mean that the people who are new in their positions get the low ratings—this is because they are not as strong as those with experience. But they may have tremendous potential. Nevertheless they may not get the chance to demonstrate that potential, if they're let go because of their rating. And it's discouraging for them to get such critical judgements when they really are trying hard and achieving what is expected of someone just learning."

1. Explain why an organization may prefer to use relative standards as opposed to absolute standards. Alex, Radko and Andy all happen to work for large, multi-national organizations. Why might this kind of organization be interested in using relative rankings?
2. Discuss what problems or errors a relative ranking system seems to avoid. What errors still may exist? What new "problems" are created by using a relative system, as noted by Alex, Radko and Andy?
3. Discuss the challenges of using relative ratings to provide feedback for future improvement to employees.
4. How would you feel about being appraised as an employee under this approach? About being a supervisor expected to rank your employees?

CASE 8.B

Who is Managing the Performance?

Here is a performance management story from a supervisor who prefers to remain anonymous to protect the people involved.

"When I came in as manager, I had a lot of resistance from one particular staff member. He had been the only person in the department for years, working hard in isolation to represent his portfolio and make sure things happened the way they should. So he had developed quite a militant style and had not been under close supervision from anyone. As the department grew, a management position emerged. I was brought in, younger and with a very different style. I have a collaborative approach but I also have clear expectations and needed the staff to work to accountabilities. He did not like this. I dealt with this employee mainly through communication—I increased team meetings and strategic meetings, instituted operational plans and performance plans. I ensured that expectations were absolutely clear so he could not say he did not know. Accountabilities were clear to all. The situation was complicated by the fact that my manager, the vice president, was also new and he was hearing two very different sides to the story. He didn't know whether to trust the long-time employee or me, his new manager. I had no real support from him in dealing with the situation until he immersed himself in it and realized what was going on. He did back me up but he chose to deal with the situation quite differently than I wanted to. Because we have different locations, he decided to give this employee much more autonomy to work from the other locations rather than the central office where I was. I wanted to deal much more directly with his behaviour and ensure he was meeting expectations, which is something I really couldn't do from afar. Ironically, even though the vice president increased his autonomy, the employee reacted in a negative way, like he typically does to anything coming from management, saying "Now I'm isolated and I don't feel part of the team." Things have become more manageable with this employee in the eighteen months since I started but not really resolved. So now the vice president has decided to give the guy a paid sabbatical for a while. I think he's hoping that the employee will choose not to come back. From my point of view, at least it allows me to build the team further without his disruptive influence. By the time he comes back, things may be so different, he may not want to return."

1. Discuss how the supervisor was attempting to apply the components of performance management. Contrast this with the vice president's apparent approach to performance management. Comment on which you believe is likely to be more effective and why.
2. There is no mention of doing a formal performance appraisal in this situation. If the supervisor had to perform a

performance appraisal on the resistant employee, what would be the challenges of documenting an accurate appraisal assessment and doing an effective performance appraisal interview?

3. Assume the supervisor is coming up to his own performance appraisal with his boss, the vice president. Explain why we have reason to believe this appraisal may be controversial.

PART FOUR

STIMULATING INDIVIDUAL AND GROUP PERFORMANCE

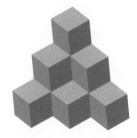

9 MOTIVATING YOUR EMPLOYEES

Courtesy of Gary Laufman Photography

LEARNING OBJECTIVES

After reading this chapter, you should be able to:

1. Define *motivation*.
2. Identify and define five personality characteristics relevant to understanding the behaviour of employees at work.
3. Explain the elements and the focus of the three early theories of motivation.
4. Identify the characteristics that stimulate the achievement drive in high achievers.
5. Explain how reinforcement is related to motivation.
6. Describe the role that equity can play in motivation.
7. Identify the three relationships in expectancy theory that determine an individual's level of effort.
8. List those actions a supervisor can take to maximize employee motivation.
9. Contrast the challenges in motivating low-pay service workers versus professional employees.

CHAPTER OUTLINE

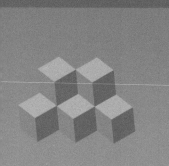

Darren didn't think twice about leaving the contract HR job when offered a way out. He had been working at a large database software company for six months, replacing someone on maternity leave, when he got an offer for a full-time job at an engineering firm. He was slightly hesitant about giving the two weeks' notice to the software company, knowing that they would be short staffed, and he would be hard to replace. However, the reaction of his manager to the news quickly reminded him why he had gone looking for another position. She angrily demanded to know why he was leaving. He told her it was a chance to get full-time work but it was also a matter of fit; that it just didn't feel like he was the kind of person they wanted as part of their team.

Darren wanted to be much more explicit about how he felt but did not want to ruin the remainder of his employment by telling her that she had treated him and the other contract employee badly from the start. There had been no orientation and no training. Darren had had to introduce himself to his client groups within the company, interview them to learn their needs and organize his work from scratch. The manager had failed to clarify expectations or coach him, had never given any praise, and clearly excluded him from the core "team" of five full-time employees.

The final two weeks of his employment saw a continuation of this behaviour. Darren worked hard to stay professional while being ignored by his boss, who did not return his calls or emails. He had offered to organize a handover of his client group to colleagues. She did not respond. He attended the weekly team meeting where the manager brought coffees for each one of the full-time employees, handing it to each one in person, and pointedly failed to give one to Darren or the other contract employee (who had not resigned and would be continuing her employment). At the lunch break, the manager and full-time employees announced they were going out for lunch and would meet Darren and the other contract employee again afterwards.

Darren understands that the full-time team had been a tight knit and consistent group for years before events caused two of them to go on leave, leading to the hiring of two contract workers, including himself. And he has worked other places where there is a mix of full-time and contract or part-time workers—the blend can be a challenge. But he has never worked anyplace else with such an exclusionary culture and is glad to be out of it. His colleague told him that things became even worse after he left. His choice to leave was seen as some kind of betrayal that painted all contract workers in an evil light. She was soon gone herself.

Darren is a reminder that people tend to leave supervisors, not jobs. He was skilled enough to handle the contract job but he was demotivated by the circumstances in which he worked. Recognizing his value to the group too late, the manager did not want him to leave. Seeing it as a desertion, she was blind to the role she played in his decision to leave. In this chapter, we examine what influences employee motivation and what supervisors can do to support and enhance motivation.

WHAT IS MOTIVATION?

Motivation is the energizing force creating a willingness to act. Every supervisor wants a motivated employee. But no supervisor can actually make anyone be motivated. Motivation is an internal psychological state conditioned by the action's ability to satisfy some need for the individual. A **need**, in our terminology, means a physiological or psychological deficiency that makes certain outcomes seem attractive. So the chapter will focus on how we can understand those needs and offer opportunities and conditions that both meet the needs of the employee (thereby motivating them) and meet the needs of the organization (leading to strong performance).

Motivation
The energizing force creating a willingness to act.

Need
A physiological or psychological deficiency that makes certain outcomes seem attractive.

WHY MOTIVATION MATTERS

Motivation influences the direction, intensity and persistence of effort. You want qualified candidates motivated to apply for your job opening, not someone else's — you want to influence the direction of their effort. Similarly, you want an employee to choose to focus on their work rather than texting their friend and you want them to focus on the high priority items rather than the easy ones. In terms of effort, you want employees to put effort into attaining both quality and quantity of performance. You want effort put into problem-solving challenges and generating innovative ideas. Persistence is also an important outcome of motivation. You want someone to keep going, despite challenges. You do not want them to slack off at work and you do not want qualified, hardworking people like Darren to quit.

Motivation is as important to performance as is skill level. Those with high skill but no motivation choose not to direct their attention to a task, put little effort into it and give up as soon as they can. Organizations therefore need to focus on hiring and building skill levels but also on creating motivating conditions. This will contribute to stronger performance, lower absenteeism and lower turnover.

UNDERSTANDING INDIVIDUAL DIFFERENCES

An error that new supervisors commonly make is to assume that other people are like them and motivated by the same things. If they're ambitious, they think others are also ambitious. If they place a high value on spending evenings and weekends with their family, they assume that others feel the same way. Big mistake! People are different because their needs vary. What's important to me is not necessarily important to you.

Not everybody, for instance, is driven by the desire for money. Yet a lot of supervisors believe a bonus or the opportunity for a pay increase should make every employee want to work harder. If you're going to be successful in motivating people, you have to begin by accepting and trying to understand individual differences. And you have to be willing to treat different people differently.

To make our point, let's look at personality. Most of us know people who are loud and aggressive. We know others who are quiet and passive. A number of personality characteristics have been singled out as having relevance to understanding the behaviour and motivation of employees at work. These include locus of control, Machiavellianism, self-esteem, self-monitoring, and risk propensity.

Some people believe that they are masters of their own fate. Other people see themselves as pawns of fate, believing that what happens to them in their lives is due to luck or chance. **Locus of control** in the first case is internal; these people believe they control their destiny. Because of this, they thrive on autonomy and flexibility in their job and will respond enthusiastically to an enriched job design (see From Concepts to Skills at the end of the chapter). Those who see their life controlled by outsiders have an external locus of control. Studies tell us that employees who rate high in externality are less satisfied with their jobs, more alienated from the work setting, and less involved in their jobs than are internals. For instance, employees with an external locus of control may be less enthusiastic about their jobs because they believe that they have little personal influence on the outcome of their performance appraisals. If they receive a poor appraisal, they're apt to blame it on their supervisor's prejudice, their coworkers, or other events outside their control. As a supervisor, you may need to adjust your style according to locus of control, backing off and giving more freedom to the internal locus of control person and creating much more structure for the person with an external locus of control.

The characteristic of **Machiavellianism** (Mach) is named after Niccolo Machiavelli, who wrote in the sixteenth century on how to gain and manipulate power. An individual exhibiting strong Machiavellian tendencies is manipulative and believes ends can justify means. Some might even see these people as ruthless. High Machs tend to be motivated on jobs where there are few rules to confine them, jobs that require bargaining (such as labour negotiator), or where there are substantial rewards for winning (as in commissioned sales). But they can get frustrated in jobs where there are specific rules that must be followed or where rewards are based more on using the proper means rather than on the achievement of outcomes.

People differ in the degree to which they like or dislike themselves. This trait is called **self-esteem**. Studies confirm that people high in self-esteem (SE) believe that they possess more of the ability they need in order to succeed at work. But the most significant finding on self-esteem is that low-SEs are more susceptible to external influence than are high-SEs. Low-SEs are dependent on receiving positive evaluations from others. As a result, they are more likely to seek approval from others and more prone to conform to the beliefs and behaviours of those they respect than are high-SEs. An employee with low self-esteem will greatly appreciate supportive conditions from his or her supervisor and will likely respond well to praise and recognition. The employee with high self-esteem will also appreciate recognition but will likely expect much more challenge from the job, and an opportunity to participate in decisions.

Some individuals are very adaptable and can easily adjust their behaviour to changing situations. Others are rigid and inflexible. The personality trait that captures this difference is called **self-monitoring**. Individuals high in self-monitoring show considerable adaptability in adjusting their behaviour to external situational factors. They are highly sensitive to external cues and can behave differently in different situations. High self-monitors are capable of presenting striking contradictions between their public personas and their private selves. Low self-monitors can't disguise themselves this way. They tend to display their true feelings and beliefs in every situation. The evidence tells us that high self-monitors tend to pay closer attention to the behaviour of others and are more capable of conforming than are low self-monitors. Additionally, because high self-monitors are flexible, they adjust better than low self-monitors to job situations that require individuals to play multiple roles in their work groups.

Self-monitoring
A personality trait that measures an individual's ability to adjust his or her behaviour to external, situational factors.

People differ in their willingness to take chances. Individuals with a high **risk propensity** make more rapid decisions and use less information in making their choices than low risk-propensity individuals. Not surprisingly, high-risk seekers tend to prefer, and are more satisfied in, jobs such as stockbroker or firefighter on an oil platform.

Risk propensity
The degree to which people are willing to take chances.

HOW CAN AN UNDERSTANDING OF PERSONALITY HELP YOU BE A MORE EFFECTIVE SUPERVISOR?

The major value of understanding personality differences probably lies in selection. You are likely to have higher performing and more satisfied employees if there is a strong person-role fit. In addition, there may be other benefits. By recognizing that people approach problem solving, decision making, and job interactions differently, you can better understand why, for instance, an employee is uncomfortable making quick decisions or insists on gathering as much information as possible before addressing a problem. You can also anticipate that individuals with an external locus of control may be less satisfied with their jobs than "internals," and also that they may be less willing to accept responsibility for their actions.

Understanding personality differences can also help delegate more appropriately; adjust supervisory style, for example, being more or less structuring depending on the employee's locus of control; and understand which rewards may be particularly appreciated by an employee.

EARLY APPROACHES TO MOTIVATION

Once we accept individual differences, we begin to understand why there is no single motivator that applies to all employees. Because people are complex, any attempt to explain their motivations will also tend to be complex. We see this in the number of approaches that have been taken in developing theories of employee motivation. In the following pages, we'll review the most popular of these approaches.

FOCUS ON NEEDS

The most elementary approach to motivation was developed by Abraham Maslow.[1] He identified a set of basic needs which, he argued, were common to all individuals; and he said individuals should be evaluated in terms of the degree to which these needs are fulfilled. According to Maslow's **hierarchy of needs theory**, a satisfied need no longer creates tension and therefore doesn't motivate. The key to motivation then, according to Maslow, is to determine where an individual is located on the needs hierarchy and focus motivation efforts at the point where needs become essentially unfulfilled.

> **Hierarchy of needs theory**
> There is a hierarchy of five needs—physiological, safety, social, esteem, and self-actualization. As each need is sequentially satisfied, the next need becomes dominant.

Maslow proposed that within every human being there exists a hierarchy of five needs. These needs are:

1. **Physiological**—includes hunger, thirst, shelter, sex, and other bodily needs.
2. **Safety**—includes security and protection from physical and emotional harm.
3. **Social**—includes affection, a sense of belonging, acceptance, and friendship.

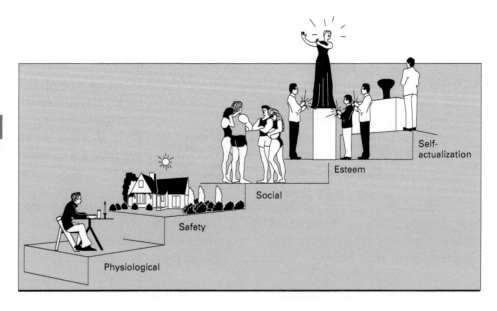

FIGURE 9-1

Maslow's Hierarchy of Needs. (*Source:* By permission of the Modular Project of Organizational Behavior and Instructional Communications Centre. McGill University, Montreal, Canada.)

4. **Esteem**—includes internal factors such as self-respect, autonomy, and achievement; and external factors such as status, recognition, and attention.
5. **Self-actualization**—the drive to become what one is capable of becoming; includes growth, achieving one's potential, and self-fulfillment.

As each of these needs becomes substantially satisfied, the next need becomes dominant. In terms of Figure 9-1, the individual moves up the hierarchy. From the standpoint of motivation, the theory would say that although no need is ever fully gratified, a substantially satisfied need no longer motivates.

Research indicates Maslow's theory is not useful in predicting the motivations of individuals, so it is not an effective guide for supervisors. But the theory was instrumental in emphasizing the importance of the upper level needs. Canadian workers typically have their basic lower level needs met, meaning employers should be focusing on meeting social, self-esteem and self-actualization needs.

FOCUS ON THE NATURE OF PEOPLE

Some supervisors believe their employees are hard working, committed, and responsible. Other supervisors view their employees as essentially lazy, irresponsible, and lacking ambition. This observation led Douglas McGregor to propose his **Theory X–Theory Y** view of human nature and motivation.[2]

McGregor argued that a supervisor's view of the nature of human beings is based on assumptions, and that supervisors tend to mould their behaviour toward subordinates according to these assumptions rather than how their employees actually behave.

Under Theory X, the four assumptions held by supervisors are:

1. Employees inherently dislike work and, whenever possible, will attempt to avoid it.
2. Since employees dislike work, they must be coerced, controlled, or threatened with punishment to achieve desired goals.
3. Employees will shirk responsibility and seek formal direction whenever possible.
4. Most workers place security above all other factors associated with work, and will display little ambition.

In contrast to these negative views toward the nature of human beings, McGregor listed four other assumptions that he called Theory Y:

1. Employees can view work as being as natural as rest or play.
2. Employees will exercise self-direction and self-control if they are committed to the objectives.
3. The average person can learn to accept, even seek, responsibility.

Theory X–Theory Y Two diametrically opposed views of human nature. Theory X assumes people are essentially lazy, irresponsible, and lacking ambition; Theory Y assumes people are hard working, committed, and responsible.

4. The ability to make good decisions is widely dispersed throughout the population, and not necessarily the sole province of those in management.

What are the motivational implications of Theory X–Theory Y? McGregor argued that Theory Y assumptions were more valid than those of Theory X. As a result, he proposed ideas such as participation in decision making, responsible and challenging jobs, and good group relations as approaches that would maximize an employee's job motivation.

In fact, neither Theory X nor Theory Y accurately describes all people. But research does suggest that many people do respond positively to the motivating conditions suggested by McGregor. And other research suggests that a supervisor's Theory X or Theory Y attitude can become a self-fulfilling prophecy: those treated with trust and respect will often live up to the high expectations, and those treated as if they are lazy, untrustworthy employees may show little effort because of their resentment.

FOCUS ON SATISFACTION AND DISSATISFACTION

"First, describe situations in which you felt exceptionally good about your job. Second, describe situations in which you felt exceptionally bad about your job." Beginning in the late 1950s, Frederick Herzberg asked these two questions of a number of workers. He then tabulated and categorized their responses. What he found was that the replies people gave when they felt good about their jobs were significantly different from the replies given when they felt bad. Certain characteristics tend to be consistently related to job satisfaction (when they felt "good"), and others to job dissatisfaction (when they felt "bad"). Intrinsic factors such as achievement, recognition, the work itself, responsibility, and advancement seemed to be related to job satisfaction. When those questioned felt good about their work, they tended to attribute these characteristics to themselves. On the other hand, when they were dissatisfied, they tended to cite external factors, such as company policy and administration, supervision, interpersonal relations, and working conditions.

Motivation-hygiene theory
Intrinsic factors are related to job satisfaction, while extrinsic factors are associated with dissatisfaction.

Herzberg took these results and formulated what he called **motivation-hygiene theory**[3]. He said the responses suggest that the opposite of satisfaction is not dissatisfaction, as was traditionally believed. Removing dissatisfying characteristics from a job does not necessarily make the job satisfying. Herzberg proposed that his findings indicate the existence of a dual continuum: the opposite of "Satisfaction" is "No Satisfaction," and the opposite of "Dissatisfaction" is "No Dissatisfaction" (see Figure 9-2).

According to Herzberg, the factors leading to job satisfaction are separate and distinct from those that lead to job dissatisfaction. Therefore, supervisors who seek to eliminate factors that can create job dissatisfaction may bring about peace, but not necessarily motivation. They will be placating their employees rather than motivating them. As a result, such characteristics as company policy and administration, supervision, interpersonal relations, working conditions, and salary have been characterized by Herzberg as hygiene factors. When they're adequate, people will not be dissatisfied; however, neither will they be satisfied. If we want to motivate people on their jobs, Herzberg suggests emphasizing achievement, recognition, the work itself, responsibility, and growth. These motivating factors are the characteristics that people find intrinsically rewarding.

The motivation-hygiene theory is important because it was the primary initiating force encouraging managers, beginning in the 1960s, to redesign jobs in order to make them more intrinsically interesting and challenging for employees.

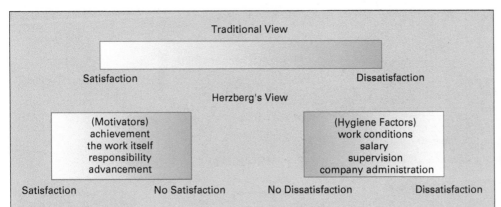

FIGURE 9-2

Contrasting views of satisfaction–dissatisfaction

CONTEMPORARY THEORIES OF MOTIVATION

While the previous theories are well known, they unfortunately have not held up well under close examination. However, all is not lost. Some contemporary theories have one thing in common: each has a reasonable degree of valid supporting documentation. The following theories represent the current "state-of-the-art" explanations of employee motivation.

FOCUS ON LEARNED NEEDS

David McClelland's research suggested that there are three learned needs that people emphasize at different levels, depending on their upbringing.[4] These are the need for achievement, need for power, and need for affiliation. All three affect people's reactions to work situations.

People with a high **need for achievement** are a supervisor's dream because they choose to work hard for the sense of personal achievement. They have a desire to do things better or more efficiently than it has been done before. They are self-motivated, requiring little of a supervisor's

Need for achievement
The need to do things better or more efficiently

time. But the supervisor does have the potential to affect the high achiever's motivation. High achievers seek situations where they can attain personal responsibility for finding solutions and problems, where they can receive rapid and unambiguous feedback on their performance to see whether they are improving or not, and where they can set moderately challenging goals (see Figure 9.3). They are not gamblers. Supervisors can support the motivation of high achievers by giving them work that is challenging but not high-risk, giving them autonomy and responsibility in their role and ensuring they get feedback. Despite high achievers typically performing well, that does not guarantee they will make effective project leaders or managers. This is because they enjoy personal achievement and may not get the same satisfaction out of leading others toward accomplishments.

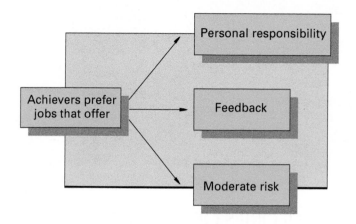

FIGURE 9-3

Matching achievers and jobs

Need for power
The need to exert influence

People with a **high need for power** enjoy exerting influence. This does not mean they are power hungry. Many managers and supervisors have a high need for power and it is the motivation that keeps them going in situations that many others would see as inequitable. Supervisors working long hours in highly stressful situations for outcomes similar to their staff keep doing it because they are meeting a need important to them, getting the chance make a difference. If you have an employee who you believe has a high need for power, consider what opportunities there may be for this person to get involved in decision making, to join committees, and to meet people in the organization that have power.

Need for affiliation
The need for social interaction and strong relationships with others

Those with a high **need for affiliation** thrive in a social atmosphere because they have a need for social interaction and strong relationships with others. This does not mean they will not work hard at their job. But they will tend to work harder if it is part of a cooperative group project rather than if they are isolated. Relationships are important to these people and can greatly affect their decisions. For example, they may turn down an opportunity for a promotion if it means moving into a supervisory position over colleagues they consider friends, or if it means moving to an entirely new position and leaving their friends behind.

As with the personality differences discussed earlier, supervisors have to respect these individual differences in needs. There are no right or wrong motivations. People are the way they are.

FOCUS ON REINFORCEMENT

In Chapter 7, in our discussion of learning principles, we said that reinforcement increases the likelihood that a learned behaviour will be repeated. The concept of reinforcement also has application as an approach to motivation.

Reinforcement theory states that people will exert higher levels of effort in tasks that are reinforced. A reinforcer is any consequence that, when immediately following a response, increases the probability that the behaviour will be repeated. This would include piece-rate pay plans where workers are paid a fixed sum for each unit of production completed, sales commissions, prizes given to employees for achieving perfect attendance, and compliments to employees when they do something nice for a customer.

Reinforcement theory
People will exert higher levels of effort in tasks that are reinforced.

The current popularity of pay-for-performance programs in organizations is clearly a direct response to the logic of reinforcement theory. Instead of compensating people on the basis of, for example, seniority, paying workers for performance outcomes increases their effort because the higher their performance, the larger their compensation. But in its pure form, reinforcement theory totally ignores the inner state of an individual and concentrates solely on what happens to a person when he or she takes some action. It's hard to believe that feelings, attitudes, expectations, and similar cognitive variables have no impact on behaviour, but that's what reinforcement theory proposes. Our conclusion is that you should recognize that reinforcement undoubtedly has an important influence on motivation but it is not the only influence.

FOCUS ON EQUITY

Equity refers to perceived fairness. Consider the following situation and how your perception of the fairness involved may affect your motivation.

Your company just hired someone new to work in your department, doing the same job as you are doing. That person is about the same age as you, with almost identical educational qualifications and experience. The company is paying you $6000 a month (which you consider very competitive). How would you feel if you found out that the company is paying the new person—whose credentials are not one bit better than yours—$7000 a month? You'd probably be upset and angry. You'd probably think it wasn't fair. You're now likely to think you're underpaid. And you might direct your anger into actions such as reducing your work effort, taking longer coffee breaks, or taking extra days off by calling in "sick."

Your reactions illustrate the role that equity plays in motivation. People make comparisons of their job inputs and outcomes relative to others, and inequities have a strong bearing on the degree of effort that employees exert.[5]

Equity theory
Employees perceive what they get from a job situation (outcomes) in relation to what they put into it (inputs), then compare their input-outcome ratio with the input-outcome ratio of others; and then respond so as to eliminate any inequities.

Equity theory (see Figure 9-4) states that employees perceive what they can get from a job situation (outcomes) in relation to what they put into it (inputs), and then compare their input/outcome ratio with the input/outcome ratio of others. If they perceive their ratio to be equal to the relevant others with whom they compare themselves, a state of equity is said to exist.

Equity does not mean being treated the same. You may be fine seeing a colleague paid substantially more if you see that is balanced by the colleague having better credentials, taking on more of the responsibility and spending more hours at work.

On the other hand, if you perceive the ratios as unequal, you perceive inequity and may be motivated to do something about it. If the inequity favours you (for example, you believe you really get more than you deserve compared to others), you may be motivated to work harder. But research suggests we tend to rationalize that situation rather than work harder. What is clear from research is that inequitable situations where we feel under rewarded can be very damaging[6] to motivation, causing people to reduce effort, produce lower quality work, sabotage the system, skip work days or even resign.

All of this points to the importance of a supervisor keeping perceived equity in mind. Are employees truly aware of how hard their colleagues work and how much they contribute? Is there some way of this information being better understood so that rewards are perceived in the right context? Are outcomes actually linked to performance differences so those who perform better have preferable outcomes to those with weaker performance? Can the supervisor use rewards more effectively to recognize strong performance? Do people understand how decisions about outcomes are made?

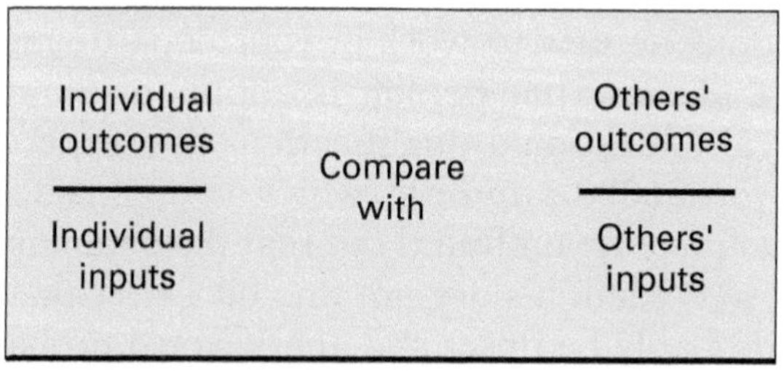

Individual outcomes	Compare with	Others' outcomes
Individual inputs		Others' inputs

FIGURE 9-4

Equity theory

Underlying equity theory's ideas are two concepts of justice: distributive justice and procedural justice.[7] **Distributive justice** refers to the fairness involved in who gets what. **Procedural justice** refers to the fairness in the process by which outcomes are decided. This brings us back to the importance of fairness in organizational procedures like performance appraisals. Employees will not be motivated by outcomes if they feel they did not get their fair share or if they feel the process for deciding outcomes was invalid or biased. It is important that, in all interactions, supervisors are sensitive to possible perceptions of inequity and address them where possible. Explaining what lies behind decisions, correcting misinformation about processes and decisions and being open to questions about decisions can help build trust.

Distributive justice
Fairness involved in who gets what.

Procedural justice
Fairness in process by which outcomes are decided.

FOCUS ON GOALS

Goal setting was introduced as a planning tool in Chapter 2. However, it is also a powerful motivational tool. Edwin Locke's research suggests that the simple fact of having a specific goal, with no reward attached to its accomplishment, is highly motivating. In field experiments, employees who were given specific performance targets consistently outperformed others who were simply told to do their best. This is not surprising in that we enjoy having a sense of direction and purpose in our actions. Having a measurable goal also sets you up for feedback and recognition as well as giving you a better idea of exactly what "exceptional" performance is.

Goal setting
Setting specific and measurable performance targets is motivating.

FOCUS ON JOB DESIGN

The design of a job creates opportunities for motivation. Hackman and Oldham's Job Characteristics Model was the first to focus on analyzing the characteristics of jobs themselves and people's reactions to them[8]. Their research led to the creation of tools for diagnosing jobs and advice for redesigning jobs with a low motivating potential to make them more effective. Details on how to apply their concepts are described in From Concepts to Skills: Designing Motivating Jobs at the end of the chapter. For now, let's focus on a major result of job design research: the importance of the meaningfulness an employee perceives in the role.

People are highly motivated to do work that they find meaningful. What makes it meaningful? A variety of factors contribute, including evidence that the task is significant and affects others, the knowledge that one is accomplishing an entire task rather than just a piece and using a variety of skills to do it, and the knowledge that one was personally responsible for achieving the results.[9] It is also enhanced by feedback that indicates progress and by opportunities to be in contact with those who benefit from their work.[10] You can be very proud of accomplishing a task that may seem unimpressive on the surface if you know it has truly made a difference to someone or if it was a real stretch for you to accomplish and represents significant growth.

FOCUS ON EXPECTANCIES

Expectancy theory
The strength of a tendency to act depends on the strength of an expectation that the act will be followed by a given outcome and on the attractiveness of that outcome to the individual.

The final perspective we'll present is an integrative approach to motivation. It focuses on expectations. Specifically, **expectancy theory** argues that individuals analyze three relationships: effort-performance, performance-rewards, and rewards-personal goals. Their level of effort depends on the strengths of their expectations that these relationships can be achieved.[11] According to expectancy theory, an employee will be motivated to exert a high level of effort when he or she believes that effort will lead to a good performance; that a good performance will lead to organizational rewards like a bonus, a salary increase, or a promotion; and that the rewards will satisfy the employee's personal goals. The theory is illustrated in Figure 9-5.

Expectancy theory has proven to provide a powerful explanation of employee motivation. It helps explain why many workers aren't motivated on their jobs and merely do the minimum necessary to get by. This can be made clearer if we look at the theory's three relationships in a little more detail. We'll present them as questions that, if supervisors want to maximize employee motivation, need to be answered affirmatively by those employees.

1. **If I give maximum effort, will I achieve an excellent performance?** The answer may be no, because the employee has not been fully trained or there are insufficient resources and time to do the job well or there are obstacles preventing excellent performance.

2. **If I achieve an excellent performance, will it be recognized by my supervisor**, for example, in my performance evaluation? For many employees, the answer is no. Why? The supervisor may only give negative feedback on a day-to-day basis. Or the company's performance appraisal system may be poorly designed—assessing traits, for example, rather than behaviours—making it difficult or impossible for the employee to achieve a strong evaluation. Still another possibility is that the employee, rightly or wrongly, perceives that her supervisor doesn't like her. As a result, she expects to get a poor appraisal regardless of her level of performance. These examples suggest that one possible source of low employee motivation is the employee's belief that no matter how hard she works, the likelihood of getting a good performance appraisal is low.

3. **If my performance is noticed and I get a good performance appraisal, will it lead to organizational rewards?** Many employees

see the performance-reward relationship in their job as weak. The reason is that organizations reward many things besides just performance. For example, when pay is allocated to employees based on factors such as seniority, being cooperative, or "kissing up" to the boss, employees are likely to see the performance-reward relationship as being weak and demotivating.

4. **If I'm rewarded, is the reward one that I find personally attractive?** The employee works hard in hope of getting a promotion, but gets a pay raise instead. Or the employee wants a more interesting and challenging job, but receives only a few words of praise. Unfortunately, many supervisors are limited in the rewards they can distribute. This makes it difficult to tailor rewards to individual employees. Still other supervisors incorrectly assume that all employees want the same thing, thus overlooking the motivational effects of differentiating rewards. In either case, employee motivation is submaximized.

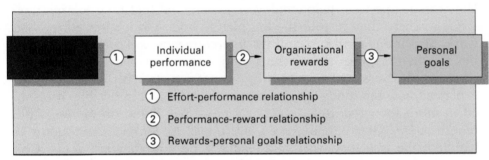

① Effort-performance relationship
② Performance-reward relationship
③ Rewards-personal goals relationship

FIGURE 9-5

Expectancy theory

APPLYING MOTIVATION CONCEPTS

We've presented a number of approaches to motivation in this chapter. If you're a supervisor, concerned with motivating your employees, how do you apply the various concepts introduced? While there is no simple, all-encompassing set of guidelines, the following suggestions provide valuable insight.

BE CLEAR IN COMMUNICATING WHAT IS EXPECTED

Recall two specific assignments you have received from teachers in the past. One was absolutely clear—as you read it, you knew exactly what you must do, what standard would achieve an "A," when it was due, what format was expected, how long it should be, and what resources were available and where. The other assignment was not clear—as you read it, you felt your heart sinking because you were confused as to what the instructor wished you to do and you didn't know where to start. These two situations are sometimes replicated in work circumstances. The outcome is predictable—when you are absolutely clear on expectations, the reaction is to jump right in and get going on it. When you are confused as to what you are supposed to do, the result is hesitation, procrastination, and anxiety.

When you are in the position of communicating expectations to employees, remember the school assignment analogy and ensure that you communicate clearly every aspect of your assignment. Describe it in various ways. Ask the employee to recap your points or demonstrate to you so you know your instructions were clear. Encourage questions, recognizing that many people are reluctant to ask questions and risk appearing ignorant.

HELP EMPLOYEES FIND MEANINGFULNESS IN THEIR JOBS

FIGURE 9-6

Rob Watson: "I want all employees to feel part of something bigger and something successful."

Rob Watson of Fusion Homes exemplifies this when he says: "I want all employees to feel part of something bigger and something successful." How can a supervisor help employees understand that their job matters? Explain where they fit into the big picture and who is affected by their work. Map it out so they see all the interconnections. Provide opportunities for them to meet those who benefit from their work. For example, when fundraisers had one 15-minute interaction with a student who explained how the funds they raised made an impact in her life, it resulted in more than five times the average weekly donation money a full month later.[12] Give employees an entire task to complete, autonomy to handle it the way they wish, and feedback on how they are doing. Give them work that uses a variety of skills and stretches them. Pass on good news about performance connected to the department and note their role in that success.

RECOGNIZE INDIVIDUAL DIFFERENCES

If there is one thing we've learned over the years, it's that employees are not homogeneous. People have different needs. While you may be driven by the need for recognition, I may be far more concerned with satisfying my desire for security. And we identified earlier in the chapter that a number of employees have a high need for achievement. Your job as a supervisor includes learning to recognize the dominant needs of each of your employees. Susan Mocsan notes, "The key is everyone is motivated by different things so you need to know what they need and how often. For example, more work and challenge, or a pat on the back and a thank-you. And you need to find creative ways to motivate when there are things you can't do, for example, if someone is at the top of their salary range yet want more money, I could send them to Los Angeles to a conference. You have to get to know your staff personally so you understand when they are having down times and know not to push them then. Some like you joking around with them but not on a bad day. You have to read them."

MATCH PEOPLE TO JOBS

There is abundant evidence to support the idea that motivational benefits accrue from carefully matching people to jobs. Some people prefer routine work with repetitive tasks, while others need constant new challenges to keep them interested. Many people enjoy being part of a team, while others do their best work when they're isolated from other people and able to do their jobs independently. Since jobs differ in terms of autonomy, the variety of tasks to be done, the range of skills they demand, and the like, you should try to match employees to jobs that best fit with their capabilities and personal preferences. Matching with capabilities is important in that success in performance leads to a sense of achievement and pride. This then motivates employees to work even harder.

FIGURE 9-7

Jamie Dumas believes a strong job-person match leads to passion

Jamie Dumas, supervisor at a City of Mississauga fitness centre, believes that matching the person to the job leads to passion. "Having passion for a job makes a big difference; it means they're always thinking about it, trying to develop means and methods for implementing the programs. Community jobs, trying to help make things better in the community — the attitude shows; when staff talk the talk and walk the walk, you know they'll get things done and go places."

SET CHALLENGING GOALS

We talked in Chapter 2 about the importance of goals. In that discussion, we showed how challenging goals can be a source of motivation. When people accept and are committed to a set of specific and difficult goals, they will work hard to achieve them. Locke's research, described earlier in the chapter, clearly indicates the power of goals in influencing employee behaviour. Based on that earlier evidence, we suggest that you sit down with each of your employees and jointly set tangible, verifiable, and measurable goals for a specific time period; and then create a mechanism by which these employees will receive ongoing feedback on their progress toward achieving these goals. If done properly, this goal-setting process should act to motivate employees.

EMPOWER EMPLOYEES

"Listen to your people as they have experience and ideas that you don't. Also, the simple act of listening to their input often ensures they become more interested and involved in the job. For example, we were building a road and needed good quality rock for it. Talking it over with the cat operator, who had run cat longer than I had been alive, I suggested hauling rock in from an ore shovel with good material. His suggestion was to cut the rock from a bank immediately beside it. This saved 25 percent of the time to do the job and didn't interrupt the ore flow to the crushers," says Rod Guild, senior foreman at the Highland Valley Copper mine in BC.

From his experience as assistant manager at a clothing store, Bill Angelopoulos also believes in involving employees in decisions: "I get employee opinions on what should be ordered or not. Each store has some leeway in what they order so that they can adapt to local customer tastes. Employees know what customers are asking for that we don't have, and how customers are reacting to what they see. Ordering becomes a team effort so they feel their experience and opinions count. When they see products come in, they know we listened to them and their word was trusted."

Participation is empowering. It allows people to take ownership of decisions. Examples of decisions in which employees might participate include setting work goals, choosing their own benefit packages, and selecting preferred work schedules and assignments. Participation, of course, should be the option of the employee. No one should feel compelled to participate in decision making. While participation is associated with increasing employee commitment and motivation, consistent with our earlier discussion of individual differences, some people may prefer to waive their rights to participate in decisions that affect them. Those preferences should be heeded. If you ask for participation, make sure the involvement is real and not just a token request. Otherwise you may create cynicism and a resistance to getting involved in the future.

TRUST EMPLOYEES

Employees hate being micromanaged, feeling every move is being watched. They do want support, knowing assistance will be there when needed, but they want to feel trusted to be able to handle their job. This means being given a chance to handle challenges without the supervsior taking over. Wendy Chiu, President of Katalogic, describes what she has observed: "Even if a supervisor is aware of a tendency to jump in and fix things themselves and consciously backs off personal involvement, that changes under stress. I've seen them jump right in. This robs their staff members of opportunities and they feel like their supervisor doesn't trust them. Employees want to learn and want challenges. Seeing the supervisor take over, they may think, "Doesn't he think I can do it? Am I not worth spending time on?"

FIGURE 9-8

Wendy Chiu believes that stepping in to fix something can send a message to employees that you don't trust them

Trust shows in day-to-day things like tracking time, as Ainslie White of Precision Biologic describes: "Occasionally we are required to do evening or weekend work. If that happens, I tell them to come in late the next day or trade off for when they have an appointment or they're getting their mortgage done. If we got into clocking hours then I'd go crazy. I don't want to count the number of hours so as to ensure that they only take off that much. People communicate and trust. They don't want to be monitored and they appreciate flexibility, especially when I know they will be reading at home and come across something relevant to work and will pursue it on their own time." A report from the 2010 Great Place to Work Rankings notes that 90 percent of employees in those organizations that made the top list believe that management trusts them without looking over the shoulder and 92 percent say they are given a lot of responsibility.[13]

FIGURE 9-9

Ainslie White trusts his staff to handle their work time responsibly

INDIVIDUALIZE REWARDS

Since employees have differing needs, what acts as a reinforcer for one may not work for another. You should use your knowledge of individual differences to customize the rewards over which you have control. Some of the more obvious rewards that supervisors allocate include pay, job assignments, work hours, and the opportunity to participate in goal setting and decision making (see Dealing with a Difficult Issue). The difficulty here may be in ensuring that rewards that are different are still perceived to be equal.

GIVE RECOGNITION

Again, some words from Rod Guild about motivating employees: "Follow up on the work they've done. Often it seems supervisors just give instructions and think that is all that is required. Checking on the job part way through shows you are interested and allows mistakes to be corrected before it is too late. Following up at the end of the job allows you to give positive reinforcement. For example, when I first started looking after the equipment operators, one operator—not the most ambitious in the world —took it upon himself to build a rock road over a soft mud dump. At the end of the shift when I climbed up on his cat, he looked apprehensive, wondering what I was doing. When I thanked him for doing such a good job, especially without being asked, he visibly relaxed and was very enthusiastic. From then on he showed far more initiative and interest. I really believe that if the supervisor doesn't show an interest he has no right to expect the worker to show one."

In many jobs, it is difficult to measure degrees of success or failure because there's no bottom-line figure or hard data directly related to performance. People working in such jobs may have difficulty feeling a sense of achievement or progress, so the supervisor, who is one of the few people aware of their efforts, is an important source of recognition.

Ainslie White, IT Manager at Precision Biologic: "A lot of IT jobs are not visible so I jump in and say 'Thanks to so-and-so for working all weekend to get "X" done'." David Goncalves, production supervisor at Mother Parkers Tea and Coffee: "Just like we tend to give the most attention to the child who has been bad, the same thing happens at work. It's the easiest mistake to make, forgetting about the people who put in every day, are never late and never need to be reminded about anything. You need to ensure they get the attention they deserve. For example, a verbal acknowledgement — 'Thanks, you guys really pulled it through.' I get vendors giving me golf tees or hats. I never bring them home. I give them to staff. And if there isn't enough for everyone, then I raffle it off. I've gone to the boss and asked for gift cards, to hand out to the guys as a surprise; even a $25 gift card goes a long way. Sometimes when my boss knows I've been putting in really long hours, he'll tell me to take my wife, Ailsa, out to dinner, and bring him the bill." Wendy Chiu at Katalogic: "People are more productive when they feel they've done a good job. Money is great

FIGURE 9-10

David Goncalvez warns that we tend to overlook the quiet, steady employees who work hard, are never late, and never need to be reminded.

but what's really important to people is, 'Did you know I just put in 60 hours and did something I've never done before.' Managers need to be aware of what employees are doing so they can comment when an employee gets through something stressful or challenging. Two minute verbal energizers can work wonders."

LINK REWARDS TO PERFORMANCE

In both reinforcement theory and expectancy theory, motivation is maximized when supervisors make rewards contingent on performance. To reward factors other than performance will only act to reinforce and encourage those other factors. Key rewards such as pay increases and promotions should be allocated for the attainment of the employee's specific goals. To maximize the impact of the reward contingencies, supervisors should look for ways to increase the visibility of rewards. Publicizing performance bonuses and allocating annual salary increases in a lump sum (rather than spreading them out over the entire year) are examples of actions that will make rewards more visible and potentially more motivating.

Unfortunately, sometimes supervisors unwittingly reward poor performance or low motivation and must deal with the consequences (see Dealing with a Difficult Issue).

BE FAIR

Rewards or outcomes should be perceived by employees as equalling the inputs they give. At a simplistic level, this should mean that experience, abilities, effort, and other obvious inputs should explain differences in pay, responsibility, and other obvious outcomes. The problem, however, is complicated by the fact that there are dozens of inputs and outcomes, and that employee groups place different degrees of importance on them. This suggests that one person's equity is another's inequity, so an ideal reward system should probably weight inputs differently in order to arrive at the proper rewards for each job. In many cases, communication of rewards can reduce perceived inequities in employees' minds. As a supervisor, it can help to announce who is being rewarded and why.

HAVE FUN

David Goncalves: "We work hard and we have fun. We have a lot of lunches, potlucks, we celebrate birthdays – the birthday person is expected to bring a box of donuts to share." What fun looks like at each workplace will differ. But a supervisor can do a lot to support a friendly work atmosphere that values each team member and has a sense of humour about the things that go wrong.

REWARDING THE WRONG BEHAVIOUR

"The squeaky wheel gets the oil." The squeaky wheel at work may not be the best performer, but because this person is much more vocal in his or her demands or complaints, the supervisor gives more attention and help to this person. Meanwhile, the other staff member who simply goes about his or her job competently with no complaint is ignored. How will this person react if he or she sees the supervisor giving a lot of attention to the poorer performer and trying to please the person? At the same time, the supervisor may be making the situation worse by giving the competent worker much more work, or the harder tasks, or the more unpleasant ones. This is because the supervisor knows the job will get done well and in time, and the employee will probably not complain. It appears, though, that the good worker is being punished by being given more work whereas the slow or poor worker is allowed to slack off.

Have you seen this happen? What were the consequences? How do you think the supervisor *should* handle a worker who is very loud in his or her demands? How can a supervisor ensure that the quiet, competent worker is not ignored?

DON'T IGNORE MONEY!

Our last suggestion may seem incredibly obvious. But it's easy to get so caught up in setting goals or providing opportunities for participation that you can forget that money is a major reason why most people work. So the allocation of performance-based wage increases, piece-work bonuses, and other pay incentives are important in influencing employee motivation. Maybe the best case for not overlooking money as a motivator is a review of 80 studies evaluating motivational methods and their impacts on employee productivity.[14] Goal setting alone produced, on average, a 16 per cent increase in productivity; efforts to redesign jobs in order to make them more interesting and challenging yielded 8 to 16 per cent increases; employee participation in decision making produced a median increase of less than 1 per cent; while monetary incentives led to an average increase of 30 per cent.

CHALLENGES FOR MOTIVATING TODAY'S EMPLOYEES

Today's supervisors have challenges in motivating their employees that their counterparts of 30 or 40 years ago didn't have. This is most evident when we look at some of the fastest growing employee subgroups.

MOTIVATING A DIVERSIFIED WORKFORCE

Don Connelly (not his real name) supervises four workers in a government office located in Toronto that deals with the public all the time. One employee is Colombian, another Chinese, one is African-Canadian, and the fourth is Jamaican. Two are male and two are female. Their skills in written and spoken English vary widely as does their motivation to improve these skills. They have different ideas about punctuality and what constitutes a full day's work. Don feels vulnerable as a white male in this supervisory situation. To him, it seems he is constantly being monitored for any inkling of racism or sexism in his actions or words. The supervisory job alone is tough enough to handle without this extra complication. Like many managers, he says it's impossible to please everyone no matter how hard he tries.

Diversity has become the norm in organizations. You are likely to supervise departments that include women and men, ethnic minorities, immigrants, people with physical disabilities, seniors, and others from diverse groups. This diversity presents a number of motivation challenges. For instance, diverse group members often have different needs and expectations. If you're going to maximize motivation, you must be able to understand and respond to this diversity.

The key word to guide you should be flexibility. Be ready to design work schedules, benefits, physical work settings, and the like to reflect your employees' varied needs. This might include offering childcare, flexible work hours, and job sharing for employees with family responsibilities. You might offer flexible leave policies for immigrants who want to return occasionally to their homelands. Or consider allowing employees who are attending school to be able to vary their work schedules from semester to semester.

MOTIVATING LOW-PAY SERVICE WORKERS

You're supervising counter workers at McDonald's, clerks at Walmart, orderlies in a hospital, or a building maintenance crew. These examples represent some of the fastest-growing job categories. Such jobs represent a challenge: how do you motivate people in low-paying jobs that offer limited opportunities for advancement? In contrast to low-skill, blue-collar manufacturing jobs that paid well in the 1960s, today's low-skill ser-

How to Demotivate

What can supervisors do to demotivate their staff? Motivation is an emotional issue rather than a rational one. Anything a supervisor can do to make an employee feel good while working is likely to contribute to motivation. Anything the supervisor does that makes the employee feel bad is likely to demotivate them.

What can you add to the list below?

An employee may feel **over-whelmed** if...	<ul><li>The supervisor hands off a large volume of work with no indication of priorities</li><li>The supervisor gives the employee work to do which the employee has never done before and there is no support or training offered</li></ul>
An employee may feel **mistrusted** if...	<ul><li>The supervisor withholds information</li><li>The supervisor continues to check everything once competence is established</li></ul>
An employee may feel **devalued or shamed** if...	<ul><li>The supervisor is dismissive of the employee's ideas or is sarcastic</li><li>The supervisor questions whether the employee actually did a piece of work by him/herself</li></ul>
An employee may feel **insecure** if...	<ul><li>The supervisor micromanages</li><li>The supervisor does not clearly define tasks and timelines</li></ul>
An employee may feel **angry** if...	<ul><li>The supervisor takes credit for work done by the employee</li><li>The supervisor is unfair/inconsistent in dealing with employee issues</li></ul>
An employee may feel **unappreciat-ed** if...	<ul><li>The supervisor offers only criticism and no praise</li><li>The supervisor praises a trivial accomplishment and ignores a major one</li></ul>
An employee may feel **resentful** if...	<ul><li>The supervisor shows favouritism to colleagues</li><li>The supervisor fails to deal with a colleague's poor performance</li></ul>

vice jobs are paying minimum wage—barely enough to satisfy basic needs and far from allowing the worker to move into the middle class.

So what can you do? Pay might be increased a bit, but significantly higher basic wages can't be passed on to consumers. The public isn't ready yet for the $10 Big Mac. So what you're left with are options such as offering job flexibility and variety, providing recognition, and capitalizing on the role of social support. Give employees flexibility in choosing their work hours. Increase variety by allowing them to change tasks and rotate among jobs. And build group cohesiveness, support, and commitment by encouraging employees to be part of a winning team.

MOTIVATING PROFESSIONALS

How do you motivate the professional librarian, civil engineer, registered nurse, or lawyer? How do you get the most effort from the C.A. at Price Waterhouse, the software programmer at RIM, or the Calgary Flames hockey player earning $1 million a year?

Professional employees provide a unique challenge in terms of motivation. Money, in an absolute sense, does not tend to be high on their needs list. They tend to be sensitive to the design of their jobs. And they're more likely to attach their identity to their profession than to the organization that employs them.

FIGURE 9-12

Colin Kirby spent the summer supervising fifteen students painting campus buildings. What motivated them? Colin made their duties clear, pitched in and helped, used humour and challenges; plus they got a bonus for finishing the job.

When asked about motivation issues, Heather Cook (manager of Halton Region Children's Assessment and Treatment Centres) said of the psychologists and social workers, "We deal more with the other end of the continuum. People tend to take on too much; they push themselves because it's hard to say no to urgent, difficult cases."

Since professionals tend to be relatively well paid, money is more likely to be an issue of equity than of absolute amount. Many professionals are equity sensitive; they are likely to compare their salary, job assignments, benefit packages, office furnishings, and the like with those of their colleagues and associates. A $5000 bonus tends to carry significantly more weight to a $25 000-a-year retail worker than to a $150 000-a-year professional.

Professionals tend to place a high value on job factors such as autonomy, personal growth, recognition, and challenging work. Their motivation is closely tied to the degree to which their job satisfies these needs. Much of the discussion that follows on designing motivating jobs is particularly relevant to professionals.

Finally, one characteristic that typically differentiates professional employees from others is that professionals put their allegiance to their field of expertise ahead of their allegiance to the organization. A corporate lawyer who works for MacMillan Bloedel will tend to see his or her identity as being more closely tied to the legal profession than to MacMillan Bloedel. This presents a challenge to supervisors, because the rewards offered outside the organization often take precedence over those from within. For example, recognition by professional peers through articles in newsletters, awards, appointment to important committees, or election to a high-ranking office within the professional organization can be powerful motivators to the professional employee. Unfortunately, the typical supervisor has little influence over these outside sources of rewards.

SHOULD EMPLOYEES BE PAID FOR PERFORMANCE OR FOR TIME ON THE JOB?

What's in it for me? That's a question every person consciously or subconsciously asks before engaging in any form of behaviour. Our knowledge of motivation tells us that people do what they do to satisfy some need. Before they do anything, therefore, they look for a payoff or reward. Although there may be many different rewards offered by organizations, most of us are concerned with earning an amount of money that allows us to satisfy our needs and wants. Because pay, as one type of reward, is an important variable in motivation, we need to look at how we can use pay to motivate high levels of employee performance. This principle explains the intent and logic behind pay-for-performance programs.

Pay-for-performance programs
Compensation plans that pay employees on the basis of some performance measure.

Pay-for-performance programs are compensation plans that pay employees on the basis of some performance measure.[15] Piece-rate plans, sales commissions, gainsharing, wage incentive plans, profit sharing, and lump sum bonuses are examples of pay-for-performance programs.[16] What differentiates these forms of pay from more traditional compensation plans is that instead of paying an employee for time on the job, pay is adjusted to reflect some measures of performance. These performance measures might include such things as individual productivity, team or work group productivity, departmental productivity, or the overall organization's profits for a given period.

Performance-based compensation is probably most compatible with expectancy theory. That is, employees should perceive a strong relationship between their performance and the rewards they receive if motivation is to be maximized. If rewards are allocated solely on nonperformance factors—such as seniority, job title, or across-the-board cost-of-living raises—then employees are likely to reduce their efforts.[17]

Pay-for-performance programs are gaining in popularity in organizations. Their growing popularity can be explained in terms of both motivation and cost control. From a motivation perspective, making some or all of a worker's pay conditional on performance measures focuses his or her attention and effort on that measure, then reinforces the continuation of that effort with rewards. However, if the employee, team, or organization's performance declines, so too does the reward.[18] Thus, there's an incentive to keep efforts and motivation strong. For instance, employees at Hallmark Cards, Inc. have up to 10 per cent of their pay at risk. Depending on their productivity on such performance measures as customer satisfaction, retail sales, and profits, employees turn that 10 per cent into rewards as high as 25 per cent.[19] However, failure to reach the performance measures can result in the forfeiture of the 10 per cent of salary placed at risk. Companies such as Saturn, Hewlett-Packard, and DuPont use similar formulas in which employee compensation is composed of base and reward pay.[20] On the cost-savings side, performance-based bonuses and other incentive rewards avoid the fixed expense of permanent—and often annual—salary increases. The bonuses do not accrue to base salary, which means that the amount is not compounded in future years. As a result, they save the company money.

How Can Employee Stock Ownership Plans Affect Motivation?

Many companies are using employee stock ownership plans for improving and motivating employee performance. An employee stock ownership plan (ESOP) is a compensation program in which employees become part owners of the organization by receiving stock as a performance incentive. Millions of employees in such companies as British Petroleum, Avis, and Starbucks participate in ESOPs.[21] Also, many ESOPs allow employees to purchase additional stocks at attractive, below-market prices. Under an ESOP, employees are often motivated to give more effort because they are owners who will share in any gains and losses. The fruits of their labours are no longer just going into the pockets of some unknown owners—the employees are the owners!

Do ESOPs positively affect productivity and employee satisfaction? The answer appears to be yes. The research on ESOPs indicates that they increase employee satisfaction and frequently result in higher performance.[22] However, other studies showed that productivity in organizations with ESOPs does increase, but the impact is greater the longer the ESOP has been in existence.[23] You shouldn't expect immediate increases in employee motivation and productivity if an ESOP is implemented. But over time, employee productivity and satisfaction should increase.

DESIGNING MOTIVATING JOBS

ASSESSING YOURSELF: IS ENRICHMENT FOR YOU?

People differ in what they like and dislike in their jobs. Following are 12 pairs of jobs. For each pair, indicate which job you would prefer. Assume that everything else about the jobs is the same—pay attention only to the characteristics actually listed for each pair of jobs. If you would prefer the job in the left column (Column A), indicate how much you prefer it by putting a check mark in a blank to the left of the Neutral point. If you prefer the job in the right-hand column (Column B), check one of the blanks to the right of Neutral. Check the Neutral blank only if you find the two jobs equally attractive or unattractive. Try to use the Neutral blank rarely.

COLUMN A   **COLUMN B**

Each item below has a rating scale labeled *Strongly Prefer A — Neutral — Strongly Prefer B*.

1. A job that offers little or no challenge | A job that requires you to be completely isolated from coworkers

2. A job that pays very well | A job that allows considerable opportunity to be creative and innovative

3. A job that often requires you to make important decisions | A job in which there are many pleasant people to work with

4. A job with little security in a somewhat unstable organization | A job in which you have little or no opportunity to participate in decisions that affect your work

5. A job in which greater responsibility is given to those who do the best work | A job in which greater responsibility is given to loyal employees who have the most seniority

6. A job with a supervisor who sometimes is highly critical | A job that does not require you to use much of your talent

7. A very routine job | A job in which your coworkers are not very friendly

8. A job with a supervisor who respects you and treats you fairly | A job that provides constant opportunities for you to learn new and interesting things

9. A job that gives you a real chance to develop yourself personally | A job with excellent vacations and fringe benefits

10. A job in which there is a real chance you could be laid off | A job with very little chance to do challenging work

11. A job with little freedom and independence to do your work in the way you think best | A job with poor working conditions

12. A job with very satisfying teamwork | A job that allows you to use your skills and abilities to the fullest extent

Table source: Reprinted by permission from *Work redesign* (1980).

SCORING DIRECTIONS

This 12-item questionnaire taps into the degree to which you have a strong versus weak desire to obtain growth satisfaction from your work.

Each item on the questionnaire yields a score from 1 to 7 (that is, "Strongly prefer A" scores 1; "Neutral" scores 4; and "Strongly prefer B" scores 7). To obtain the score for your individual growth-need, average the twelve items as follows:

> #1, #2, #7, #8, #11, #12 (direct scoring)
> #3, #4, #5, #6, #9, #10 (reverse scoring)

Average scores for typical respondents are close to the midpoint of 4.0. High scores suggest that you will respond to an enriched job because you have a high growth need. Low scores suggest that you wouldn't find enriched jobs satisfying or motivating.

SKILL BASICS

One of the more important factors that influence an employee's motivational level is the structure of his or her work. Is there a lot of variety or is the job repetitive? Is the work closely supervised? Does the job allow the employee discretion? The answers to questions like these will have a major impact on the motivational potential of the job and hence the level of productivity an employee can expect to achieve.

Job design
The way that tasks are combined to form complete jobs.

We use the term **job design** to refer to the way that tasks are combined to form complete jobs. Some jobs are routine because the tasks are standardized and repetitive; others are nonroutine. Some require a large number of varied and diverse skills; others are narrow in scope. Some jobs constrain the employee by requiring him or her to follow very precise procedures; others allow employees substantial freedom in how they do their work. The point is that jobs differ in the way tasks are combined, and these different combinations create a variety of job designs.

What are the key characteristics that define a job? According to Hackman and Oldham's Job Characteristics Model,[23] there are five, and together they comprise the core dimensions of any job:

1. **Skill variety:** The degree to which the job requires a variety of different activities, enabling the worker to use a number of different skills and talents.

2. **Task identity:** The degree to which the job requires completion of a whole and identifiable piece of work.

3. **Task significance:** The degree to which the job has a substantial impact on the lives or work of other people.

4. **Autonomy:** The degree to which the job provides substantial freedom, independence, and discretion to the individual in scheduling the work and in determining the procedures to be used in carrying it out.

5. **Feedback:** The degree to which carrying out the work activities required by the job results in the individual obtaining direct and clear information about the effectiveness of his or her performance.

Figure 9-14 offers examples of job activities that rate high and low for each characteristic.

When these five characteristics are all present in a job, the job becomes enriched and potentially motivating. Notice that we said potentially motivating. Whether that potential is actualized is largely dependent on the employee's growth-need strength (refer back to Assessing Yourself exercise at the beginning of this section). Individuals with a high growth need are more likely to be motivated in enriched jobs than their counterparts with a low growth need.

Job enrichment increases the degree to which a worker controls the planning, execution, and evaluation of his or her work. An enriched job organizes tasks so as to allow the worker to perform a complete activity, increases the employee's freedom and independence, increases responsibility, and provides feedback, so an individual will be able to assess and correct his or her own performance.

PRACTISING THE SKILL

So what can you do, as a supervisor, to enrich your employees' jobs and increase their motivation? We can suggest five specific actions (see Figure 9-15):

1. **Combine tasks.** Supervisors should seek to take existing and fractionalized tasks and put them back together to form a new and larger module of work. This increases skill variety and task identity.

Skill variety
The degree to which the job requires a variety of different activities so the worker can use a number of different skills and talents.

Task identity
The degree to which the job requires completion of a whole and identifiable piece of work.

Task significance
The degree to which the job has a substantial impact on the lives or work of other people.

Autonomy
The degree to which the job provides substantial freedom, independence, and discretion to the individual in scheduling the work and in determining the procedures to be used in carrying it out.

Feedback
The degree to which carrying out the work activities required by the job results in the individual obtaining direct and clear information about the effectiveness of his or her performance.

Job enrichment
Increasing the degree to which a worker controls the planning, execution, and evaluation of his or her work.

FIGURE 9-14

Skill Variety

High variety — An owner-operator of a garage who does electrical repair, rebuilds engines, does body work, and interacts with customers

Low variety — A body shop worker who sprays paint eight hours a day

Task Identity

High identity — A cabinet maker who designs a piece of furniture, selects the wood, builds the object, and finishes it to perfection

Low identity — A worker in a furniture factory who operates a lathe solely to make table legs

Task Significance

High significance — Nursing the sick in a hospital intensive care unit

Low significance — Sweeping hospital floors

Autonomy

High autonomy — A telephone installer who schedules his or her own work for the day, makes visits without supervision, and decides on the most effective techniques for a particular installation

Low autonomy — A telephone operator who must handle calls as they come according to a routine, highly specified procedure

Feedback

High feedback — An electronics factory worker who assembles a radio and then tests it to determine if it operates properly

Low feedback — An electronics factory worker who assembles a radio and then routes it to a quality control inspector who tests its proper operation and makes needed adjustments

FIGURE 9-14

Examples of high and low job characteristics Reprinted from *Organizational Behavior: Understanding Life at Work,* 3rd ed., by Jennifer George and Gareth Jones (1992), Harper Collins Publishers, Inc.

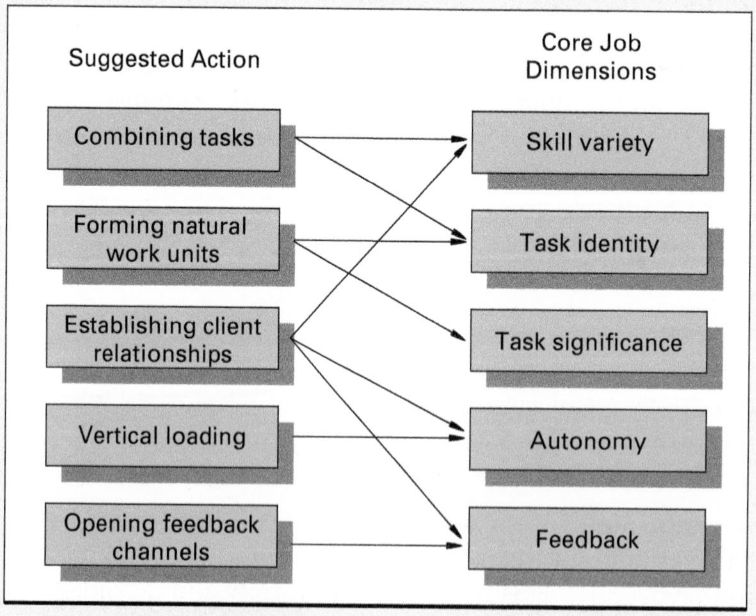

FIGURE 9-15

Guidelines for enriching a job. Reprinted from *Improving Life at Work* (1977), Richard J. Hackman.

2. **Create natural work units.** The creation of natural work units means that the tasks an employee does form an identifiable and meaningful whole. This increases employee ownership of the work and improves the likelihood that employees will view their work as meaningful and important rather than as irrelevant and boring.

3. **Establish client relationships.** The client is the user of the product or service that the employee works on. Wherever possible, supervisors should try to establish direct relationships between workers and their clients. This increases skill variety, autonomy, and feedback for the employee.

4. **Expand jobs vertically.** Vertical expansion refers to giving employees responsibilities and control that were formerly reserved for supervisors and other managers. For example, let employees set work schedules, have a hand in budgeting, select work methods, check quality, and decide how to solve problems.

5. **Open feedback channels.** By increasing feedback, employees not only learn how well they are performing their jobs, but also whether their performance is improving, deteriorating, or remaining at a constant level. Ideally, this feedback about performance should be received directly as the employee does the job, rather than from the supervisor on an occasional basis.

The suggestions we've offered in this section refer to the design of individual jobs. But don't forget that we can also design jobs around work teams: in Chapter 5, we discussed how teams can enrich jobs at the group level, and how they can increase motivation and productivity.

APPLYING YOUR SKILLS

Assume you are the owner of a sports equipment store. Your store specializes in hockey and baseball equipment and makes a good proportion of its money from being the official supplier to local leagues. Several part-time people work for you, all students, and all very athletically inclined. This is ideal as they can speak knowledgeably about the equipment. You're very pleased with the current group of students working for you but are afraid you may lose them. They are all bright young people, attending the local college or university, and they need money. Yet you cannot pay them much, as in all retail positions, because your margins are low. You are contemplating the idea of job design as one way to encourage them to stay through their years at school. Maybe, if they feel they are learning and growing, are interested in the work and challenged by it, they will choose to stay rather than leave for more money elsewhere. Therefore you have written down all the tasks you do and they do. You will then consider how tasks could be reallocated or shared to provide more motivation for your part-time student staff.

Manager's tasks
- Handling banking matters
- Ordering stock
- Visiting manufacturers
- Dealing with team representatives for jersey orders and other special orders
- Preparing displays
- Scheduling of staff
- Training of new staff
- Providing customer service
- Dealing with customers when problems arise
- Dealing with customers with special orders
- Overseeing store maintenance
- Paying bills
- Researching new products

Clerks' tasks
- Providing customer service
- Performing store maintenance
- Pricing
- Taking inventory

Your task is to:
Redesign the clerks' jobs in order to make them more motivational.

1. Explain how your proposed changes will alter the core dimensions of the clerks' jobs.

2. Identify how these changes are likely to affect your job as the owner/manager.

3. Explain how you could determine the probable growth-need strength of these students to see if an enriched job would, in fact, be motivational for them.

You have 30 minutes to complete this task.

SUMMARY

This summary is organized by the Learning Objectives.

1. Motivation is the energizing force creating a willingness to act.
2. Five personality characteristics relevant to understanding the behaviour and motivation of employees are: 1. locus of control—the degree to which people believe they are masters of their own fate; 2. Machiavellianism—the degree to which an individual is manipulative and believes ends can justify means; 3. self-esteem—an individual's degree of liking or disliking for himself or herself; 4. self-monitoring—an individual's ability to adjust his or her behaviour to external, situational factors; and 5. risk propensity—the degree of an individual's willingness to take chances.
3. Maslow focused on the self. His hierarchy of needs proposes that there are five needs (physiological, safety, social, esteem, and self-actualization) and as each need is sequentially satisfied, the next need becomes the dominant motivating force.

   Theory X–Theory Y proposes two views of human nature, then argues that employees are essentially hard working, committed, and responsible. Therefore, to maximize motivation, employees should be allowed to participate in decision making and be given responsible and challenging jobs; and supervisors should strive to achieve good group relations among employees.

   According to the motivation-hygiene theory, if you want to motivate employees, you must emphasize achievement, recognition, the work itself, responsibility, and growth, These are the characteristics that people find intrinsically rewarding.
4. High achievers prefer jobs that give them personal responsibility for finding solutions to problems, where they can receive rapid and unambiguous feedback on their performance, and where they can set moderately challenging goals.
5. Reinforcement theory proposes that people will exert high levels of effort in tasks that are reinforced.
6. People don't only look at absolute rewards they receive from their job. They also look at relative rewards. A focus on equity deals with this fact.
7. The three relationships in expectancy theory that determine an individual's level of effort are effort-performance, performance-rewards, and rewards-personal goals.
8. To maximize employee motivation, supervisors should set clear expectations, recognize individual differences, match people to jobs, set challenging goals, encourage participation, individualize rewards,

give recognition, link rewards to performance, check for equity, and not ignore money.

9. Low-pay service workers suffer both from essentially permanent low pay and limited promotional opportunities. They are most likely to respond to job flexibility and variety, recognition, and social support. In contrast, money is relevant to professionals mostly from an equity perspective. Professionals prefer enriched jobs. Additionally, their loyalty to their profession typically overrides their loyalty to their employer.

KEY TERMS AND CONCEPTS

Autonomy

Distributive justice

Equity theory

Expectancy theory

Feedback

Goal setting

Hierarchy of needs theory

Job enrichment

Locus of control

Machiavellianism

Motivation

Theory X–Theory Y

Motivation-hygiene theory

Need

Need for achievement

Need for affiliation

Need for power

Pay-for-performance programs

Procedural justice

Reinforcement theory

Risk propensity

Self-actualization

Self-esteem

Self-monitoring

Skill variety

Task identity

Task significance

REVIEWING YOUR KNOWLEDGE

1. How does an unsatisfied need create motivation?
2. Contrast behavioural predictions between people with an internal versus an external locus of control.
3. Contrast behavioural predictions between high and low self-monitors.
4. Compare the assumptions of Theory X with Theory Y.
5. What does a supervisor need to do to motivate a high achiever?
6. Describe expectancy theory.
7. What motivational challenges does a diversified workforce create for supervisors?
8. What are the five core dimensions in a job?
9. What is job enrichment?

CASE 9.A

Soccer Coaching Principles Applied to Management

Bonnie Shepherd, National Manager of Business Development for the United Nations Children's Fund (UNICEF) in Canada, sees a close link between her motivational approach as a manager at UNICEF and her approach as a soccer coach. Bonnie previously coached varsity soccer for 6 years, and co-owns a business called Christie Kicks, where she hires varsity athletes to coach community soccer programs. She describes a book that changed her entire philosophy of coaching: *Catch Them Being Good*, by Diccio and Hacker.

"I spent most of my own playing years being coached by an "old school" style of leadership, which focused on what was being done wrong and what should be corrected. When I read this book, it opened me to another way of leadership, where athletes don't need to walk away from each performance thinking about what they did wrong. This book's approach became my strategy for connecting with the players and infiltrated my management style at work as well. The approach is to identify a positive behaviour being demonstrated and call it out in front of the team as a model of behaviour that you want to see in the whole team. Let them know you saw it and it's on the right track. The focus is on identifying strengths and celebrating them. This way, everyone knows what to aim for, what's considered the

FIGURE 9-16

Bonnie Shepherd at UNICEF believes it is important to identify strengths and celebrate them, and to understand the motivations of individuals.

'best practice' expectation for delivery. It's especially important in this method to spread the attention around and recognize "best practice" behaviours from different individuals to avoid favouritism. This model is easily carried over to the workplace—for example during a team meeting, I love to call people out about things worth celebrating—even if it's just taking the time to comment on a great idea supplied by someone."

"It's important to understand what motivates people individually, what their goals are, what do they define as success. For example, for one person, it may be that having their work organized and correct is a "win" whereas someone else wants more opportunity to be out the door at external meetings, driving new business and serving as a front-facing member representing the organization. One individual on my team identified in a one-on-one meeting that she thought she may be interested in developing her presentation and business development skills, so I brought her on calls with me, and then we selected an account that we both felt comfortable she could lead. We did the initial exploratory meeting together and then she was the lead on the relationship from there. I kept connected with her throughout the process, checking in with her to help her determine what she saw as the next steps in the partnership development and why. It created a safe space for learning because she knew she was the lead, but that she had full support to make the right strategic decisions. And it was important that she knew she had sealed the deal in the end. She felt confident enough to try in a safe space, knowing she was supported, and it ended in success, but she also understood where she needs to develop and grow."

RESPONDING TO THIS CASE

1. How would you characterize Bonnie in terms of Machiavellianism and self-monitoring?

2. Does Bonnie appear to abide by Theory X or Theory Y assumptions? Explain.

3. Select the principles of motivation that Bonnie is using

4. Explain how the five job characteristics could explain

    a. Why soccer is highly motivating to many participants

    b. Why working at UNICEF would be highly motivating to some people

CASE 9.B

Tim O'Shea: An Outsider Tackles Motivation

"When I was transferred from Canada to manage an office in the UK for a European pharmaceutical client, one of the first things I noticed, after I had spoken with each staff member privately, was that the office was physically untidy. There was paper and clutter everywhere. In fairness, the staff had been consumed with work, work and more work to the exclusion of regular 'housekeeping'. A key leadership team member was returning from disability leave and two key analysts had departed; so the office was decimated while at the same time hugely busy.

Here I was...parachuted in from Canada and, reportedly, 'here to help'. I was sure that my credentials were well known, but I wasn't personally known. I was sure that there were misgivings as to what value I could bring. I wondered how I was going to get on-side with these folks and make them comfortable so that I

FIGURE 9-17

Parachuted in from Canada, Tim O'Shea turned around a struggling department.

could contribute and manage in a meaningful way quickly without being a distraction. They were war-weary with a huge agenda and with very demanding clients. Several significant projects had to be 'fit for purpose' and delivered to 11,000 employees within a short time frame. There was no 'honeymoon' period available.

After a week of trying to get to know the team individually, I asked for a few extra hours from everyone from 3 to 8 pm to clean and organize the office, shredding paper and putting things in storage. I ordered pizza, served the coffee, hauled garbage, vacuumed the office debris and helped where I could. Through the chat, I found out who was married, other personal things about their background and aspirations, and lots of information about what was going well in the office and what wasn't. It helped me get a grip on the agenda, whom I could count on, and whom I needed to see to free up logjams and other sources of irritation. The next day the place was neat as a pin. And the boss, who came in weekly, said, "Wow! What did you do differently?"

I committed to the team that I would 'run interference' with senior executive for more resources; that I would take the rap when something went wrong; and that team members would take the public credit when things went well. It was a promising start...for a while.

A few days later, when I got resistance from someone about something I was suggesting, I asked the person to tell me more and give me suggestions. Then I followed the advice; the team knew the answers to the problems; I simply encouraged action, dialogue and resolve. That also changed people's attitudes toward me as the new interim manager. I could be trusted to keep my word and treat the team members as adult equals. My focus was on communicating what was happening externally with our clients, prioritizing demands and giving feedback factually and fairly; the fact that there became no basis for mistrust helped immensely and saved time and needless effort.

Whereas the department had been gossiped about by some as a place to avoid from a career perspective, things changed positively over time. When two new positions were posted, lots of people were interested. We were back on the map and perceived as a 'can do and go to' department.

My staff still e-mail me on my birthday and get together when I am on vacation. I was proud to have served with them and learned from them."

RESPONDING TO THIS CASE

1. Tim notes that the department used to have a bad reputation and people didn't want to work there. What seemed to be the demotivating factors before Tim stepped in?
2. Identify how Tim applied motivational concepts effectively.

10 PROVIDING LEADERSHIP

Courtesy of Stockbroker/Alamy

LEARNING OBJECTIVES

After reading this chapter, you should be able to:

1. Define *leadership*.
2. Distinguish between those we call leaders and those who supervise others.
3. Explain the trait approach to leadership.
4. Contrast task-focused and people-focused styles of leadership.
5. Explain how the behavioural approach differs from the situational approach to leadership.
6. Explain the differences in how men and women lead.
7. Describe how emotional intelligence and emotional labour concepts are leadership considerations.

CHAPTER OUTLINE

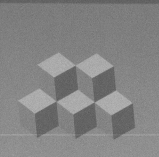

FIGURE 10-1

As a young leader, Ron McLester has successfully dealt with a variety of challenges and found an approach that works for him

Ron McLester manages Aboriginal Education & Student Services at Mohawk College in Hamilton, Ontario. In this position he supervises two counsellors and 5 support staff, and two elders work on contract with the team.

"Before I got here, the department had not developed clear processes. I wanted standards and clear accountability and transparency. Bringing in those processes was resisted by some of the staff because they felt comfortable with the way things had been. It was a rough go when I started 18 months ago. I was 29, the youngest administrator at the college and I must admit I had anxiety for a while. Before, there had been three different office locations within the one campus location and little sense of cohesion. I centralized the services in one large space that is really appealing and meets everyone's needs. I standardized the team meetings and brought in performance plans. I took some Indigenous processes and weaved them into our office procedures. For example, each month each subgroup of the team has a meeting to discuss day-to-day operational issues. But then there's also a monthly meeting of the entire group where we discuss strategic issues, what is affecting all of us, where we are headed. This aligns with the Iroquois governance system where, for example, the three clans of the Oneidas (wolf, bear and turtle) would each have their own meetings but then would also gather together in a grand council meeting to discuss common issues. I attend the operational meetings but don't play a very active role – I'm there for information and support if needed. On the other hand, I play a larger role in the larger team or council meeting, discussing what I have learned about upcoming events and college initiatives and how it may affect our department.

In our language (Iroquois), "chief" means "he speaks for the people". I believe in a consensus style of management and that's what I strive for. Sometimes in meetings, the team will override my views. That's OK. When I started in management, I was too much into consensus and they pushed back, saying they needed someone to make decisions. So I flipped and became much more directive but that didn't work either. I think I now have found a middle ground where we work hard to decide together but I can and do make decisions that are needed at a management level.

In Iroquois culture, leaders are chosen by clan mothers who watch kids grow up and assess their ability to handle leadership positions. Leadership skills are something you have to demonstrate to others, or at least the potential of developing those skills in the right circumstances. They are looking for a combination of honesty, bravery, humility, generosity and charisma. The latter is because you have to be able to speak well. You are a leader within the group itself but you also have to be able to represent the group well to outsiders. Ironically, although a person was never "born" into a leadership position in indigenous culture, the colonial influence has changed this. Hereditary leadership used to mean the position went to someone within the clan but now it means "my son."

Ron has successfully led his group through growth and transformation and has become an influential figure within the college community. His story demonstrates a number of leadership concepts we will discuss in this chapter: leadership as initiating change for the better, the issue of whether leadership skills are born or acquired, and the need to change leadership style to get the best out of a situation.

WHAT IS LEADERSHIP?

Leadership is the ability you demonstrate when you influence others to act in a particular way. Through direction, encouragement, sensitivity, consideration, and support, you inspire your followers to accept challenges and achieve goals that may be viewed as difficult to achieve. As a leader, you're also someone who sees and can get the best out of others - helping them develop a sense of persona and professional accomplishment. Being a leader means building commitment to goal attainment among those being led, as well as a strong desire for them to continue to follow your leadership.

When you think of leaders, you may often view them as those individuals who are in charge of others. These people would include yourself, as an authority over your employees; your boss; and anyone else who holds a position of power over you—like your professor in this class. Obviously, through a variety of actions, you and the other leaders have the ability to influence. Yet, leadership frequently goes beyond formal positions. In fact, sometimes this person of power is not around, yet leadership may still exist (see Dealing with a Difficult Issue). Let's look at this pair of issues.

LEADERS AND SUPERVISORS

Let's begin by clarifying the distinction between those who supervise others and those we call leaders. The two are frequently used as if they mean the same thing, but they do not.

Those who supervise others are appointed by the organization. They have legitimate power that allows them to reward and punish their

Leadership
The ability to influence others to act in a particular way through direction, encouragement, sensitivity, consideration, and support.

Dealing with a Difficult Issue

INFLUENCING WITHOUT POWER

Leadership is about your influence over others—especially in those instances where you don't have formal authority over them—and the "power" you wield. The use or misuse of power can generate ethical questions about right and wrong. For instance, consider the following scenario.

Your boss has been dissatisfied with the way one of your supervisor colleagues is handling a project. She has reassigned the project to you, but your colleague hasn't been told of this action. You've been told to work with this colleague to find out what he's already done, discuss any other necessary information that he might have, and to prepare a project report by the end of next month.

Your colleague is not giving you the information you need to even start, much less complete, the project. He finds your questions unusual. After all, it's his project, and he doesn't have time to stop and talk to you. That would delay him more—and jeopardize the success of his department. However, without this information, you won't be able to meet your deadline either. If that happens, you both may lose.

Do you see any problem in talking to your colleague and telling him the reason you're getting involved? How can you influence him in gaining his cooperation? What would you do in this situation?

employees. Their ability to influence employees is based on the formal authority inherent in their positions. In contrast, *leaders* influence others to perform *beyond* the actions dictated by formal authority. They may emerge from within a group as an informal leader. People must do what a supervisor asks them to do if the request is within the supervisor's authority. On the other hand, people choose to follow a leader. A supervisor who is also a leader gains this influence not from his or her position but through actions and characteristics that earn others' respect.

What else distinguishes leaders? When you consider the supervisors you have worked under, those that seemed more like leaders were likely those that were visionary, unsatisfied with the status quo, looking to improve things and try new approaches. Leaders are leading you in a direction whereas people focused on pure management tend to emphasize making the status quo workable. A leader initiates change, creating a direction for a team and for each individual—employees feel confident that they are part of something important and have the capacity to contribute their part.

LEADERSHIP SKILLS

People promoted into a supervisory position for the first time will take time to settle into the new role, a role that can be intimidating in its expectations. As they gain comfort with the tasks, they will be in a position to consider how they might initiate change, leading the team to do things differently. A variety of skills will support their success as a leader, all of which can be developed. These include technical skills, conceptual skills, networking skills and human relations skills.

TECHNICAL SKILLS

It's a rare occurrence when you can influence others even though you have absolutely no idea of what they are doing. Although people may respect you as a person, when it comes to influencing them, they would like to believe you have the experience to make recommendations. This experience generally comes from your technical skills.

Technical skills are those tools, procedures, and techniques that are unique to your specialized situation. You need to "master" your job in your attempt to be viewed as a source of help—the "expert." Others generally won't come to you unless they need assistance. It's often the exceptions that they can't—or are ill equipped to—handle. That's when they'll look to you for guidance. By having the technical skills, you're able to assist. Because of this emphasis on technical knowledge, it's important that you keep up-to-date. Even if you are no longer doing the job of an operational employee, you should understand what they are dealing with as equipment, methods and challenges change.

What if you are managing employees who have technical skills beyond you so you are not in a position to help? You recognize and defer to their expertise and, when they do need assistance, you make sure they get it. You ensure there are support systems in place to resolve their issues (e.g. specific people to contact over tough problems). This way you are still seen as an integral part of resolving technical challenges.

CONCEPTUAL SKILLS

Conceptual skills are your mental ability to coordinate a variety of interests and activities. Having conceptual skills means having the ability to think in the abstract, analyze lots of information, and make connections between the data. Earlier, we described an effective leader as someone who could create a vision. In order to do this, you must be able to think critically and conceptualize how a situation *could be*, as well as understanding how it presently *is*.

Thinking conceptually is not as easy as you may believe. You must look at the "big picture." Too many times, we get caught up in the daily grind, focusing our attention on the minute details. Not that focusing on the details isn't important—without it, little may be accomplished. But setting long-term directions requires you to think about the future. It requires you to deal with uncertainty and the risk of the unknown. To be a good leader, then, you must be able to make some sense out of this chaos and envision what could be.

NETWORKING SKILLS

Networking skills are your ability to socialize and interact with outsiders—those not associated with your unit. It's understood that as a leader, you cannot do everything by yourself. Therefore, you need to know where to go to get the things your followers need. This may mean "fighting" for more resources or establishing relationships outside your area that will provide some benefit to your followers. Networking, if you're making the connection, means having good political skills. That's a point that shouldn't be overlooked.

Your employees will often look to you to provide them what they need to do an excellent job. If they can depend on you for giving them the tools (or "running the interference" they need), then you'll once again inspire a level of confidence in them. They are also likely to respond better if they know you're willing to fight for them.

Networking also involves those outside of the organization. For example, through professional associations and trade shows, you can keep in touch with new directions for the industry and for particular professions. Through the use of social media (like LinkedIn for professional connections), you can keep in touch with people of potential use to your team. Your connections outside the organization can help you conceptualize your own situation in a way that helps you envision new possibilities.

HUMAN RELATIONS SKILLS

Human relations skills focus on your ability to work with, understand, and motivate those around you. As you've been reading this book, you'll notice that these skills have been highlighted. Good human relations skills require you to be able to effectively communicate—and especially to communicate your vision—with your employees and those outside your unit. They also involve listening to what others have to say. A good leader is not a "know it all," but rather someone who freely accepts and encourages involvement from his or her followers.

Human relations skills are those "people skills" that are frequently mentioned in today's discussion of effective supervision. They lie in the coaching, the facilitating, and supporting of others around you;[1] in understanding yourself, and being confident in your abilities; in your honesty in dealing with others and the values you live by; in your confidence in knowing that by helping others succeed—and letting them get the credit—you're doing the right thing for them, the organization, and yourself.

If you fail as a leader, it most likely won't be because you lack technical skills. Rather, it's more likely that your followers, as well as others, have lost respect for you because of your lack of human relations skills. If that ever happens, your ability to influence others will be seriously impaired.

LEADERSHIP RESEARCH AND THEORIES

Because leadership is believed to have such a strong impact on an organization's success, people have been looking to explain effective leadership for a long time. The thinking on this has evolved through three stages: trait approach, behavioural approach and situational approach.

TRAIT APPROACH

Early theorists believed that leaders were born to be leaders, characterized by features or **traits** that simply made them more effective leaders. The old phrase "blue blood" used to describe people of royal lineage illustrates that people assumed those in leadership positions were basically different from the rest of us. This led to research attempts to isolate those special features. If we could identify those leadership traits, we could seek people who matched the leadership profile. Why waste time training people to be leaders or promoting people who will never have what it takes?

Traits
Inborn qualities

The research examined physical attributes (e.g. height, age, appearance, health), personality characteristics (e.g. introversion-extroversion, dominance), and abilities (e.g. social skills, intelligence). They did find some evidence that leaders tend to be different from the average group member. Leaders tended to be characterized by self-confidence, intelligence, sociability, determination and integrity.[2] But the results were not consistent and were not strong. There are many exceptions. For example, Steve Jobs was seen to be a brilliant leader at Apple but was certainly not known for his social skills.

A more recent re-emergence of the trait approach to leadership is the interest in charismatic leadership.[3] **Charismatic leaders**, like Steve Jobs, have profound and extraordinary effects on their followers. Research suggests these leaders have a compelling and idealized vision and strong convictions about their goal, can communicate that vision well to followers,

Charismatic leader
Has profound and extraordinary effect on followers

and are assertive and unconventional in their behaviour. Many believe that charisma is something a person is born with; others have made attempts to teach people to be more charismatic.

BEHAVIOURAL APPROACH

The failure of the trait approach to reveal a set of characteristics common to all leaders led people to instead look at leadership behaviours.[4] They wondered, is there a particular style of leadership that is much more effective than all others? If behaviours are important rather than traits, could we teach people to use that ideal style? Two basic leadership dimensions emerged from the research examining leadership: task-focused behaviour and people-centered behaviour. **Task-focused behaviour** by a leader emphasizes activities that ensure the job is done properly. This includes creating structures and systems, establishing clear organization and communication patterns, and enforcing rules and regulations. On the other hand, **people-centred behaviour** emphasizes building strong working relationships and a trusting, respectful and motivated team. Some theorists claimed that a combination of the two dimensions would be ideal, with a strong emphasis on both the task and the people. Others claimed that a people-centered style is all that is needed because if you take care of the people, they will take care of the job. Research looked for the "one best style" and did not find it. There is no leadership approach that suits all situations.

Task-focused behaviour
Emphasizes activities that ensure the job is done properly

People-centered behaviour
Emphasizes building strong working relationships and a trusting, respectful and motivated team

SITUATIONAL APPROACH

The behavioural approach was no more successful than the trait approach in painting a picture of the ideal leader. The next research step was a recognition of the complexity of the situation. There is no one best way to lead in all situations. Can we then pin down a better understanding of what leadership approaches are suitable in different circumstances? This is the underlying thinking of the situational approach to leadership—exploring the match between varying situations and leadership behaviours.

Situational approach
Explores the match between varying situations and leadership behaviours

FIEDLER

The first to tackle this was Fiedler, who proposed that effective leadership required a match between the leader's style of interacting with employees and the amount of control and influence the leader has.[5] When a leader has strong formal power, the task is highly structured and the leader has good relations with the employees, Fiedler considered the situation highly favourable for the leader. When he actually tracked different combinations of these factors in work situations to see the leadership performance, he discovered interesting correlations (see Figure 10-2). The task-

	High Favourability			Moderate			Low Favourability	
Situational Factors	I	II	III	IV	V	VI	VII	VIII
Respect for Followers	Good	Good	Good	Good	Poor	Poor	Poor	Poor
Structured Jobs	High	High	Low	Low	High	High	Low	Low
Influence Over Employment Process	Strong	Weak	Strong	Weak	Strong	Weak	Strong	Weak
Preferred Leader Behaviour	Task Centred	Task Centred	Task Centred	People Centred	People Centred	People Centred	Task Centred	Task Centred

FIGURE 10-2

Fiedler's leadership findings

centred approach was correlated with more effective performance in highly unfavourable conditions, where decisive action is respected, and in highly favourable conditions, where the leader is so well established that he or she need not worry about offending employees with a directive approach and can focus on getting the job done. On the other hand, the people-focused approach was more successful in situations of moderate favourability. Interestingly, Fiedler believed that no supervisor is capable of switching from a task-focused approach to a people-centred approach or vice versa. Therefore different situations called for different people in the leadership position. Later theorists disagreed with this conclusion.

HERSEY AND BLANCHARD

Hersey and Blanchard's situational approach[6] asserts that leaders can adjust their style, and should do so in line with the maturity or readiness level of their 'followers'. As seen in Figure 10-3, they have identified four stages of follower readiness and four matching leadership styles that involve different combinations of task- and people-focused behaviour.

R1: At the lowest level of readiness, employees are unable and feeling unwilling or insecure about doing the job. A 'Telling' style is recommended, with a high focus on task and a low focus on the relationship.

R2: The employee is unable but willing or confident. A 'Selling' approach is recommended, combining high task and relationship behaviour.

R3: The employee is able but unwilling or insecure. A 'Participating' approach that focuses on the relationship and not on the task is recommended.

R4: The employee is both able and willing (or confident) to do the job. Delegating is recommended, showing low task and relationship behaviour.

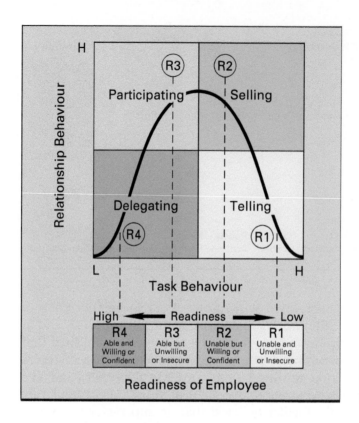

FIGURE 10-3

Situational leadership

Let's see how this model works by going through an example of a new employee in your department and her first day on the job.

When this employee first arrives at work, she is anxious. She's uncertain about what she is getting into and how to handle the job responsibilities. You feel that the employment process worked well in properly matching her to the job and orienting her to the organization. Now it's time for her to start the job she was hired to do. Imagine if at this point you just assigned a list of tasks for her to complete and walked away. She would probably have some difficulty. Why? Because at this time, she's not ready (R1). It's doubtful she even knows the right questions to ask. Communications between you and the employee, at this point, need to be one-way: you need to tell her what to do and give her specific directions on how to do it. According to situational leadership, at this stage you are using a *telling* style of leadership.

But this new employee won't stay at R1 forever. After having been provided with ample directions and becoming more familiar with the job, she's moving to stage R2. At the R2 stage of work development, the employee is becoming more involved in her job, but she still lacks some ability. She's not yet fully trained. She's asking questions about things she may not fully understand. She may question why certain things have to be done as you have asked. Accordingly, you may need to *sell* this employee on some of your ideas to get her to accept them. At this point, high degrees of both one-way and two-way communication are happening simultaneously.

At some later point (R3), this employee has become the expert on her job. She knows her duties better than anyone else, and she's beginning to put her special mark on things. You no longer need to tell her what to do, but the reality is, you still need to be involved in what she's doing. She has not quite reached the point where you can feel comfortable leaving her totally alone. That's not an insult—it's just that you recognize that this employee still has some developing to do. Accordingly, you will best deal with this situation by being supportive of her and not being overly task-centred. Hersey and Blanchard refer to this as a *participating* style of leadership.

Finally, this employee has fully developed. She has your trust and can carry out her duties with little, if any, direction (R4). In this situation, she basically needs to be left alone. At this *delegating* stage of leadership, you simply assign the tasks and let her do her job. You now know—based on your appraisal of her performance—that she can and will get the job done. If she needs help, you're always available to deal with the exceptions.

An important aspect of situational leadership is that an employee can be in all four quadrants at the same time. To lead properly, you must be able to exhibit the correct leadership style given what each employee needs. If a seasoned employee generally at stage R4 gets a new assignment, you cannot assume that he or she will necessarily be at R4 for the new tasks. In fact, the employee may need to be clearly directed in these new tasks—and that implies a telling style of leadership. If that doesn't occur, problems may arise. On the other hand, if an employee who has been at R4 for some time gets additional assignments that require a telling style, problems will arise if that individual is treated like an R1 employee on *all* aspects of his or her job. If, all of a sudden, the employee is being told how to do what he or she has been doing for many months or years, it can have the effect of implying that you perceive the employee as not doing the job properly. The point is, you need to demonstrate a leadership style that's consistent at all times with your employees' abilities and confidence.

PATH-GOAL THEORY

Path-goal theory[7] is a third situational approach to leadership. Based on the expectancy theory of motivation (discussed in Chapter 9), this approach by House and Evans suggests that it is the leader's role to clear the path for employees reaching their goals. Remember that expectancy theory relates motivation to employee perceptions of the linkages between their effort, their performance and the outcomes. To the extent that a leader can strengthen an employee's belief that their effort will be worthwhile in leading them to a valued outcome, the performance will be enhanced. House and Evans suggested the leader use the most appropriate of four different styles to help followers clarify the paths that lead them to their personal and work goals. Both characteristics of the employees and the work environment are important in considering the choice of style. Figure 10-4 shows the four leadership styles and some of those work and employee characteristics.

As an example of an application, a highly trained professional working on a challenging but attainable task may be best led through an achievement-oriented style. This means setting challenging goals for followers and showing strong confidence in their capacity to achieve those goals. In a very different example, when dealing with an inexperienced employee facing an ambiguous, unstructured task, the leader may be most successful using a directive style that gives specific guidance about what is expected and how to approach the task.

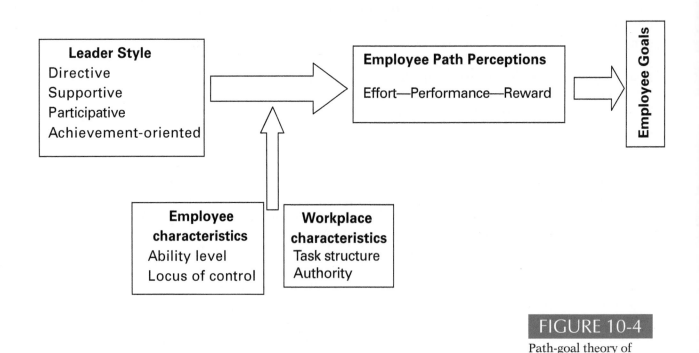

FIGURE 10-4

Path-goal theory of leadership

SITUATIONAL CONCLUSIONS

In the end, we realize that the situational approach has much more to offer us than the trait or behavioural approach. We need to diagnose the needs of the situation to determine the right leadership approach. We can go back to the people versus task dichotomy to consider those needs. Is there something lacking in the task structure that is holding people back? Do they understand what is expected? Have they the right systems and resources? Is it an issue of motivation or comfort level or trust? Is it a combination? Are there different needs for different people or for the same person in different circumstances? This takes us back to the discussions in chapters 8 and 9 around performance management issues and motivation. Talking to employees is important in order to understand their goals, their needs and their perceptions of their own capability and the adequacy of the work environment. It is only by knowing the people and thoroughly investigating particular situations that we can determine the next best approach.

Diagnosis is one step, and adjustment of style is another. Neither is easy. Are you capable of adjusting your style? How far? At what point is it better to bring in someone else with a different style? Do not feel you have to be all things to all people. When challenged with a particular situation, seek advice from your own supervisor or from colleagues who are supervisors, or from the HR department.

CONTEMPORARY LEADERSHIP ROLES

Let's turn our attention to some important issues that every effective supervisor today is, and will continue to be, concerned about. Specifically, how do you build credibility and trust with your employees and what are the issues around empowerment?

CREDIBILITY AND TRUST

Employees want leaders who are credible and whom they can trust. But what do these terms—credibility and trust—really mean?

Credibility is your believability in the role. If you are credible as a leader, employees believe you can fill the role effectively. This is influenced by your competence, your influence and your professionalism. In terms of competence, you do not have to be technically strong in all the employees' tasks but you do need to understand what they do, how and why and ensure the support they need. You need to be willing to problem-solve the issues with employees. In terms of influence, a supervisor who seems to be disconnected to the management structure and out of the loop in communications and decision making will not be seen as a very credible leader. Your professionalism is reflected in your behaviour. A supervisor who uses profanity or has temper tantrums will not be accepted as a professional. Extremely casual language and clothing that was accepted when you were an operational employee may not get the same reaction once you become a supervisor. Frequent lateness for meetings or missing deadlines for work will also detract from your credibility.

Trust is belief in the leader's integrity, and influences a leader's credibility. Employee perceptions of managerial trustworthiness have been linked to the following managerial behaviour:[8]

Credibility
Believability in the role

Trust
Belief in person's integrity

1. **Consistency**: does the supervisor handle similar situations in a consistent way?
2. **Integrity**: do the supervisor's actions match the supervisor's words?
3. **Sharing and delegation of control**: does the supervsior invite the participation of employees in decisions that affect them and respect their opinions?
4. **Communication**: does the supervisor share information in an open, timely way and offer explanations for events?
5. **Demonstration of concern**: does the supervisor behave in a considerate way towards employees, protecting their interests?

David Goncalves, production supervisor at Mother Parkers Tea and Coffee is adamant about the importance of trust in his role. "Always tell the truth. Admit your mistakes. We all make mistakes, and pretending you didn't or redirecting the blame can get you into trouble. Sometimes I will miss extra time someone put in and they will ask about it. When I check and find the error I apologize and make sure the money is in their next paycheque. I have seen supervisors lose a team's trust because they didn't tell the truth. For example, a lead hand took a message, forgot to pass it on and then blamed an innocent person. Once you lose that trust, it takes a long time to build it up again."

Debbie Hinz, production manager at Precision Biologic, agrees. "The group must trust you, knowing that you will look out for their best interests. When they trust you they know they can say anything to you. This trust is built through listening to them and following through on what you say you'll do. I'm a listener. It's funny how eight years ago, if you'd asked me what makes a good manager, I wouldn't have seen myself in that role. I thought you should be forward and outspoken and assertive and I don't see myself that way. I'm a person who builds slow, steady trust in a relationship. I'm not in people's faces. We do things by consensus; we choose a direction that makes sense. Now I feel successful. It has changed my view of what makes a good manager."

How can you build trust? We've listed several suggestions in Building a Supervisory Skill.

PLAYING FAVOURITES

Another aspect of trustworthiness is not playing favourites. Ainslie White: "It's important to be fair in this role. Especially sensitive areas include vacations, pay increases, workload, ensuring people get their say. Don't show any favouritism or preferential treatment. For example, in the allocation of tasks, divide it up, so the team shares between the crappy less visible jobs."

Yet research shows that supervisors unintentionally do show favourites and this has an impact on their perceived trustworthiness and on employee motivation. The Leader-Member Exchange Theory[9] proposed that leaders tend to divide their employees into in-groups (the preferred or more similar employees) and out-groups. In-group members are given greater attention and responsibilities, leading to greater satisfaction and lower turnover. Out-group members are not in the communication loop and are managed by rules and policies rather than a friendly relationship.

You will inevitably form different relationships with your employees and you need to be cautious of this tendency to create favourites. You're human so you'll naturally find some employees you feel closer to and with whom you want to be more open. But you do not want this favouritism to show.

LEADING THROUGH EMPOWERMENT

Several times in different sections of this book, we've stated that supervisors are increasingly leading by empowering their employees. Millions of individual employees and teams of employees are making key operating decisions that directly affect their work. They are developing budgets, scheduling workloads, controlling inventories, solving quality problems, evaluating their own performance, and so on—activities that until very recently were viewed exclusively as part of the supervisor's job.

The increased use of empowerment is being driven by two forces. The first is the need for quick decisions by those people who are most knowledgeable about the issues. If organizations are to successfully compete in a dynamic global village, they have to be able to make decisions and implement changes quickly. That requires, at times, moving decision making to the employee level. The second force is the reality that the downsizing and restructuring of organizations left many supervisors with considerably larger spans of control than they had before. In order to cope with the demands of an increased workload, supervisors have to empower their people. As a result, they are sharing power and responsibility with their employees.[10] This means their role is to show trust, provide vision, remove performance-blocking barriers, offer encouragement, and motivate and coach employees.[11]

Does this wholesale support of shared leadership appear strange given the attention paid earlier to contingency theories of leadership? If it doesn't, it should. Why? Because empowerment proponents are essentially advocating a noncontingent approach to leadership. That means they claim that empowerment will work anywhere. Such being the case, directive, task-oriented leadership is out.

The problem with this kind of thinking is that the current empower-

Culture Could Affect Your Leadership Style

A general conclusion that surfaces from learning about leadership is that no single style suits every situation. One of the situational variables we have not discussed yet is culture. This refers to both national culture and organizational culture.

National culture affects leadership style by way of your employees. You are constrained by the cultural conditions those employees come to expect.[12] For example, an autocratic leadership style is more compatible with cultures where power is unequal, such as those found in Arabic and Latin countries.[13] This cultural "power" ranking should be a good indicator of employees' willingness to accept participative leadership. Participation is most likely effective and expected in cultures where power is more equally distributed, such as those in Norway, Sweden, Finland[14] and Denmark.

Organizational culture also affects an individual's leadership style[15] and here the influence is generally from above rather than below. Chief executive officers with a distinct and strong style are likely to expect a similar approach down the hierarchy. A highly controlling, directive CEO will expect all management to ensure employees stick to the rules and do what they are expected to do, without stepping out of the boundaries. Initiative will not be encouraged.

ment movement ignores the conditions that facilitate successful shared leadership and the extent to which leadership can be shared. Because of factors such as downsizing, which results in the need for higher-level employee skills, commitment of organizations to continuous training, implementation of continuous improvement programs, and introduction of self-managed teams, the need for shared leadership is certainly increasing. But that is not true in all situations, and blanket acceptance of empowerment or any universal approach to leadership is inconsistent with the best and most current evidence we have on the subject.

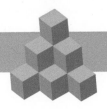

BUILDING TRUST

ABOUT THE SKILL

Given the importance trust plays in the leadership role today, supervisors should actively seek to build trust among their employees. Here are some suggestions for achieving that goal.[16]

PRACTISING THE SKILL

1. **Practise openness.** Mistrust comes as much from what people don't know as from what they do know. Openness leads to confidence and trust. Keep people informed, make the criteria on how decisions are made overt and clear, explain the rationale for your decisions, be candid about problems, and fully disclose relevant information.
2. **Be fair.** Before making decisions or taking actions, consider how others will perceive them in terms of objectivity and fairness. Give credit where it's due, be objective and impartial in performance appraisals, and pay attention to equity perceptions when you distribute rewards.
3. **Speak your feelings.** Supervisors who convey only hard facts come across as cold and distant. If you share your feelings, others will see you as real and human. They'll know who you are and their respect for you will increase.
4. **Tell the truth.** Because honesty is critical to credibility, you must be perceived as someone who tells the truth. Employees are more tolerant of learning something they "don't want to hear" than of finding out that their leader lied to them.
5. **Show consistency.** Employees want predictability. Mistrust comes from not knowing what to expect. Take the time to think about your values and beliefs. Then let them consistently guide your decisions. When you know your central purpose, your actions will follow accordingly, and you'll project a consistency that earns trust.
6. **Fulfill your promises.** Trust requires that employees believe you're dependable. So you need to ensure that you keep your word. Promises made must be promises kept.
7. **Maintain confidences.** You trust those whom you believe to be discreet and whom you can rely on. Employees feel the same way. If they make themselves vulnerable by telling you something in confidence, they need to feel assured that you won't discuss it with others or betray that confidence. If employees perceive you as someone who leaks personal confidences or someone who can't be depended on, you won't be perceived as trustworthy.
8. **Demonstrate confidence.** Develop the admiration and respect of others by demonstrating technical and professional ability. Pay particular attention to developing and displaying your communication, negotiation, and other interpersonal skills.

LEADERSHIP ISSUES TODAY

We'll finish this chapter by looking at two current debates about leadership. These are 1. the issue of differing leadership styles between men and women, and 2. whether emotional intelligence is a key part of effective leadership.

Do Men and Women Lead Differently?

Are there differences in leadership styles based on gender? Are men more effective leaders or does that honour belong to women? Just asking these questions is certain to evoke emotions on both sides of the debate. Before we attempt to respond to them, let's set down one important fact: the bottom line is that the two sexes are more alike than different in terms of the way they lead.[17] Much of this similarity is based on the fact that leaders, irrespective of gender, perform similar activities in influencing others. That's their job, and both sexes do it equally well. This is similar to what can be said of nurses. Although the stereotypical nurse is a woman, men are equally effective—and successful—in this career choice.

However, there is evidence of some notable differences between men and women as leaders. The most common difference lies in leadership style. Women tend to lead more with a democratic style. This implies that they encourage participation of their followers and are willing to share their positional power with others. In addition, women tend to influence others best through their "charisma, expertise, contacts, and interpersonal skills."[18] Men, on the other hand, tend to use a task-centred leadership style more often. Their directing of activities and reliance on their positional power to control the organization's activities tend to dominate the way they influence others. And yet even this difference is blurred, because other things being equal, when a woman leads in a traditionally male-dominated job (like that of a police officer), she too tends to lead in a manner that is more task-centred.[19] We must be careful about jumping to conclusions about gender differences in leadership because most research has been carried out only on men, simply because they were the ones historically in those positions.

Further compounding this issue is the changing role of supervisors in today's organizations. With more emphasis on teams, employee involvement, and interpersonal skills, democratic leadership styles are more in demand. Supervisors need to be more sensitive to their employees' needs, be more open in their communication, and build more trusting relationships. Ironically, many of these are behaviours that women have typically grown up developing.

Go to the library and find two or three recent articles that discuss the issue of gender differences in leadership. Summarize these articles. Then, respond to the following: Do you believe that in today's organizations, both "masculine" and "feminine" approaches to leadership are equally important? Discuss. Also, explain how the specific situation one faces may affect one's leadership style.

EMOTIONAL INTELLIGENCE

Some suggest that emotional intelligence is a characteristic of effective leaders.[20] **Emotional intelligence** is the ability to recognize and manage emotions in yourself and in others. We already touched on the issue of a supervisor's own emotional control in the credibility discussion when we noted that a supervisor who has a temper tantrum is seen as unprofessional. Emotions spread easily, which is why a supervisor's emotional control is critical. Facing a difficult situation, a supervisor's calm handling sets the tone for others. And taking stressful situations in stride is simply an expectation for someone in a position of responsibility.

> **Emotional intelligence**
> The ability to recognize and manage emotions in yourself and in others

You will be in many situations where you feel frustrated or angry or overwhelmed and yet you must hide these feelings and, instead, act patient and positive. This describes **emotional labour**, the effort required to manage emotions in order to perform your job effectively. Your employees will also be in situations where they need to pretend they are feeling something they are not. For example, customer service requires friendly, courteous behaviour, which is difficult to maintain when dealing with a truly rude client. The supervisor can help employees by preparing them to deal with emotionally difficult situations, by stepping in to assist when needed, and by supporting those who are having difficulty.

> **Emotional labour**
> The effort required to manage emotions in order to perform your job effectively

With emotional intelligence being a relatively new concept, research has not yet established clear evidence of its link to effective leadership.[21] But supervisors will tell you that handling people issues is often the toughest part of their job because of the emotional element. They admire leaders who can terminate an employee in a way that protects the employee's dignity, who can spark passion in their employees, and who can coach serious performance issues without getting frustrated or stressed.

NETWORKING: HAVING CONVERSATIONS WITH PEOPLE YOU DO NOT KNOW WELL

ASSESSING YOURSELF: HOW WELL CAN YOU CONNECT WITH NEW PEOPLE?

Indicate the degree to which you think the following statements are true or false by circling the appropriate number; for example, if a statement is always true, you would circle the 5 next to that statement.

5 = Always true
4 = Generally true
3 = Somewhat true, but with exceptions
2 = Somewhat false, but with exceptions
1 = Generally false
0 = Always false

1. In social situations, I approach people I have never met and introduce myself.

   5 4 3 2 1 0

2. In work situations, if I am around new people, I wait for them to introduce themselves or others to introduce us to each other; I wouldn't approach them.

   5 4 3 2 1 0

3. I know how to start a conversation with a person I have never met before.

   5 4 3 2 1 0

4. Once I have started a conversation with a new person, I can effectively keep the conversation going.

   5 4 3 2 1 0

5. I believe that only extraverted people can effectively network, making connections with people they do not know.

   5 4 3 2 1 0

6. The opening line one uses in starting a conversation is critical in determining the effectiveness of the conversation.

   5 4 3 2 1 0

7. One cannot "prepare" for a conversation when meeting a new person.

   5 4 3 2 1 0

8. You can tell when you approach a new person whether the person is willing to be approached.

   5 4 3 2 1 0

9. Starting a conversation with a new
   person means taking a bit of a risk.   5   4   3   2   1   0

10. The trick to making a conversation
    work is focusing on making the other
    person feel comfortable.   5   4   3   2   1   0

SCORING DIRECTIONS

This questionnaire measures your awareness of what it takes to start conversations with new people and your willingness to do so. To obtain your total score, add up the numbers circled, except reverse scores for questions 2, 5, 6, and 7. On those, a circled 5 becomes a 0, 4 becomes 1, and so forth.

The lower your score, the less comfortable you are in starting conversations with new people, probably because you are not familiar with the steps you can take to do so effectively. The higher the score, the more comfortable you are at this important networking skill, probably because you know how to do it.

SKILL BASICS

Being able to connect on a personal level with other people at work will make a big difference to your success. You will appear more trustworthy and you will be more visible. Conversational skills can help you turn business circumstances into an opportunity to establish strong relationships that will help you in the future, whether the relationship is with a customer, a subordinate, or a boss. You will develop business friendships and, all things being equal, people like to do business with their friends.

Approaching a Person. You must take the risk to initiate contact rather than wait for the other person to approach you. You do not have to be an extrovert to do this. Approach someone who is standing or sitting by him or herself. Provide eye contact first—if the person responds, rather than looking away, he or she is approachable. Smile and introduce yourself, for example, "Hi, I'm Cynthia Rall; this is my first time at this conference." The other person will likely pick up on your cue, model your lead, and give you material for continuing the conversation. Note that we decide as someone approaches whether we're willing to be approached so it doesn't matter if you have the perfect opening line.

Starting a Conversation. The focus in starting and sustaining a conversation must be on making the other person comfortable. If you do this, you take the pressure off yourself as the focus and provide a relaxing situation for the other person. You can start with a statement, for example, "It's hot in this room," or, "I didn't expect so many people to show up at this," but people will not always pick up on your cue so you need to follow up with an open-ended question. Some sample open-ended questions are: "How was the traffic for you on the way here?" "What got you into marketing/teaching/whatever?" "How did you get involved in ...?"

Preparing for a Conversation. This is not only possible but advisable if you know you will be meeting new people and are unsure of what to talk about with them. Make yourself think beforehand of several things to discuss, just in case the conversation lags, for example, something going on in the community, something on the news today, or something about the situation you have in common.

During the conversation, learn the other person's name; don't rush through introductions to get to the business at hand. Concentrate on his or her name and repeat it out loud at least once after hearing it. Keep on digging; pick up on what the person has said. For example, "How was your day?" "Busy." "What's a busy day like for you?" Use information available to you; you will get cues from appearance—for example, you see a diploma on the wall and ask "What made you choose U.B.C.?"; behaviour—for example, you notice that the person is left-handed and ask about the challenges of using the right-handed equipment at the company; or the occasion—for example, all the people are connected to the same event so you ask "What brought you here?"

Listening is an essential part of a good conversation and it does not mean not talking. Use eye contact, nodding, and body language to show you're interested and "tuned in." Contribute to the conversation, encouraging the person to continue, by saying, for example, "Oh, I see," "What happened then?" Use paraphrasing to clarify and let the person know you heard him or her. This means recapping what the person just said in your own words. For example, "It sounds like you're really disappointed that the project has been shelved temporarily."

Small talk and starting conversations with new people is not easy for most people but it becomes easier with practice. Consider every conversation to be an opportunity. Conversation is what connects us to others and makes people feel good about being with us.

APPLYING YOUR SKILLS

Have conversations with three new people. These could be three people you've never met before or people you know or have met but have simply never had a conversation with before, such as a boss, customer, teacher, coworker, or another student.

Write up a report covering the following points:

For each conversation, describe
- why you chose this person
- how you prepared
- how you started the conversation
- how you sustained the conversation
- what you felt before/during/after the conversation
- your analysis of why it did or did not go well

After discussing the conversations individually, consider them as a whole and discuss what you learned from doing this, and explain why being able to "do small talk" effectively would be a useful skill for someone in your career, or future career. Give specific circumstances where this skill would be helpful.

SUMMARY

This summary is organized by the Learning Objectives.

1. Leadership is the ability to influence others.
2. Supervisors have the formal power to get people to act in ways within the boundaries of their authority but leaders influence others to perform beyond the limitations of authority. People choose to follow leaders whereas they must comply with a supervisor's direction.
3. The trait approach to leadership looked for qualities that characterize effective leaders. Although research found leaders typically higher on some characteristics (like adaptability and intelligence), the results were not strong.
4. Task-focused leadership emphasizes activities that ensure the job is done properly. People-focused leadership emphasizes building strong relationships and a trusting, respectful and motivated team.
5. The behavioural approach looked for a style of leadership that was effective regardless of the situation. In contrast, the situational approach says there is no one ideal style, and that the 'best' style depends on the situation.
6. While there are some differences, men and women are more alike than different in how they lead. The differences that do exist lie in leadership styles. Women tend to rely on charisma, expertise, and interpersonal skills to influence others. Men, on the other hand, tend to use positional power to direct and control organizational activities.
7. Emotional intelligence is the ability to recognize and manage emotions in yourself and in others. Emotional labour is the effort required to manage emotions in order to perform your job properly. Some believe that high emotional intelligence is characteristics of effective leaders. This includes handling the many situations in which a supervisor must disguise feelings, and supporting employees in work demanding emotional labour.

KEY TERMS AND CONCEPTS

Charismatic leader
Credibility
Emotional intelligence
Emotional labour
Leadership
Path-goal theory

People-centered behaviour
Situational approach
Task-focused behaviour
Traits
Trust

REVIEWING YOUR KNOWLEDGE

1. "All supervisors should be leaders but not all leaders should be supervisors." Do you agree or disagree? Support your position.
2. How is intelligence related to leadership?
3. What is the difference between a task-focused and a people-focused supervisor? Which one do you believe employees would prefer to work for? Why? Which one would you prefer to work for? Explain.
4. Do you believe, like Fiedler, that a leader has one basic style? Or, like Hersey and Blanchard, that a leader can adjust style to the situation?
5. How can supervisors be both flexible and consistent in their leadership styles? Aren't these contradictory? Explain.
6. How could a professor apply situational leadership with students in a classroom setting?
7. If leaders play favourites, is it good or bad for their department's performance? Discuss.
8. "Given the emphasis on caring for employees, women may be more effective supervisors." Do you agree or disagree? Support your position.
9. Generate examples of supervisors illustrating high or low emotional intelligence from your own work experience.
10. Discuss work you have done that required emotional labour. How did the supervisor assist you in dealing with it? What else could have helped?

CASE 10.A

Leading a Film Crew

Kim Derko is a cinematographer who has worked on TV series, feature films, documentaries, music videos and TV movies. As the director of photography (DOP) for a film production, she is the head of the camera and lighting departments. She works with the director to translate what the director and script want in terms of the look of a film. The director, producer and Kim together plan how to shoot the film based on budget, format, and vision, etc. "My role is to translate the vision into the technical stuff. The director has visions. I have a bag of tricks to satisfy their vision."

Kim works on contract and hires on contract. "I hire three crew leaders: the gaffer (head electrician), grip (head rigger for camera movement) and the head of the camera department. Each of these then hires a team of 6 or 7 people. I hire people based on skill, speed and ability to get along. So do the leads. Film production is like a team sport—each person has their position to play. If you don't, you let everyone down."

"I love my job. I love the fact that it's different every minute. Even on the same show, we go to different locations. For example, in the studio we have a controlled environment where we can set up lighting boards with dimmers, keep them set and delegate duties. On location we must go in and out quickly. We have to move in like an army, build the rigging, set up the power. We do everything with extreme precision so I need a team I can trust, for example, to patch a cable correctly. We have to change the lighting and camera movement in every setting and when we're on location there are often things we can't control so we just roll with the demands.

Planning and operational execution are critical but, ironically, I'm not a micromanager. My strategy has always been—I assume everyone knows their job and is good at it. I can tell quickly if someone is not competent at their job.

I give people 100% trust when they're hired and then it's a demerit system from there. It's fine. I can tell within a day if they can't perform and they're gone. Instead of telling people what to do, I kind of put the burden on them and let them use their skills. They do a way better job as a result because they take responsibility for it. I do not go into minute detail unless a person is not working out. The brilliant thing about this strategy is that people have fabulous ideas. I try not to tell people what to do. I tell them what the director wants to achieve, what he wants the film to look like. And here's the budget. So I offer creative parameters rather than giving them demands. It sounds like I'm a lazy boss.

We do end up creating very specific detailed visuals to plan for the execution but there are no standard templates. We are given the plans of a studio and we indicate on this where items go to the gaffer or crew using our own shorthand. We create plan view diagrams. If we are going to shoot on a location we send someone to lay out technical requirements once the location is chosen and we do a survey for technical viewing, usually based on photographs.

We work in a strictly regulated union setting, especially IATSE for the camera people. It's a very competitive union and most people are very good at their job due to the strictness of the union hierarchy (first you're a trainee, then a second camera assistant, then a first camera assistant, then a camera operator, then a DOP; that was my career ladder). It takes years. Coworkers hire you and control your career because those higher than you build their teams for contracts. So camera people have rigid guidelines for quality of work. The union hierarchy helped me as a manager because everyone is conditioned to accept the hierarchy and assumes my credibility, especially since women cinematographers are unusual.

I've worked in a lot of non-union productions (commercials and music videos) and loved the creative freedom especially in music videos. But there was little money so gradually I had to shift away to make a living. The problem with non-union productions is that there are no regulations about the number of hours people work so people are taken advantage of. Producers will hire film students, exploiting them at $50 a day for 14-hour days.

As a woman in this position, I've had little trouble. With a few crew members, I can see it in their eyes—perhaps Kim is doing it because of some affirmative action thing. I've seen women directors who are up-and-coming not get opportunities, I don't know why, the door just doesn't open. I know extremely talented women who work their way up to first camera assistant and then have to fight and fight to become first camera operator. They become disillusioned because they see men get the opportunities after three years when five or eight years later they have not been given a chance. It's blatant discrimination but you can't call people on it because in show business they can always say it was a creative choice. There's no test to pass, there's always the fall back position of creative choice if directors/producers continue to hire their pals. I see it happen all the time.

I can tell there's a reaction from men when I'm being interviewed by a director or producer for the first time. Because there are not many women in a DOP position, they can't always visualize me in the position. A lot of those who hire me are men who first hired me because they thought I was a freak of nature; then it worked out and they hire me repeatedly because they realize my skills after the first collaboration. Grips are used to having a male boss. Until they're in the position of having a woman boss, they can't picture it either. So they're a little uncomfortable with it at first. It's the same with some of the other crew, but I can work through it. I try to hire women camera assistants who I know have strong skills because I know they are not being given breaks by others.

The stressful part of my job is the time limitations we often have on what we must shoot in a day—"x" shots in "y" hours so no messing around (we'll lose an actor or be out of the location or go into triple overtime). I need the team to back me up here—the producer won't rehire me if I go into major overtime or am off schedule.

It's an intense environment and getting along, working as a team is critical. How I talk to them is important. For example, there's a lot of tricky technical stuff to get done. If the first camera assistant alerts me to trouble like a camera down, I thank them for letting me know and I send them off to deal with it. Someone else will step into their role. Even if new, I expect them to have the same skill if not the same experience. That spirit enlivens a presence with all the crew. People love stepping up. When I miss something and a gaffer points it out, I'll say, "Thank god, you saved my butt again." I'm a little selfish, I want everyone to contribute and I learn so much from people by not micromanaging. They feel like they're part of it, not just punching a clock. We have a lot of fun."

RESPONDING TO THIS CASE

1. Does Kim strike you as a supervisor, a leader or both? Why?
2. Describe Kim's effectiveness in terms of the various leadership skills: technical, conceptual, networking, human relations.
3. Apply the various leadership theories to explain Kim's effectiveness in her role.
4. What evidence is there that Kim has credibility and trustworthiness in the eyes of her team? How does Kim illustrate the use of empowerment?
5. Does Kim strike you as using a "female" leadership style?
6. What evidence indicates Kim's emotional intelligence?

FIGURE 10-5
Kim Derko

CASE 10.B

Padma Learns How Not to Lead[1]

Padma had a lot to think about in deciding whether or not to accept a supervisory position with the City of Montreal. She had worked in several companies under both terrible and excellent supervisors. She appreciated how difficult supervision can be, and she knew that a supervisor makes all the difference to the daily life of the employees.

One of her fears was that she would fall into the patterns she had witnessed in her supervisor, Marla, at a manufacturing company. "Everyone lived in fear. We had seen her get rid of people who spoke up. Marla wasn't open to any kind of feedback, and she didn't give us any feedback. There was no formal performance appraisal and no informal feedback. It was sink or swim. Even though she pressured people to come in early and stay late, she was first out the door at 4:30. She was totally reactive and we were stressed because she didn't prepare us for dealing with things she knew were coming. We needed good systems and they weren't there.

Marla had a tough time keeping employees. When people chose to leave, she would say "good riddance". I think it was her defence mechanism. She didn't want to face up to why people kept leaving. She gave people impossible jobs and then blamed them if there was a problem. For example, my position was left vacant for a year before I was hired to deal with the backlog. Then she gave me impossible timelines and little autonomy to actually deal with things the way I needed to. She wasn't available when I needed help. And she wouldn't give direct answers to my questions. In fact she was reluctant to put anything in writing in case she was held to it." Padma started looking for another position. Interestingly, the moment the supervisor found out, she fired Padma.

Padma had a very different experience at another manufacturing company where she felt like she'd hit the jackpot. "My boss was understanding, flexible and open. Lucas wasn't a clock watcher so people weren't afraid to explain the need for time. He understood we all have a job to do but that things happen and people need time off and support. He had regular weekly meetings, shared with everyone on the team the sales and labour issues, the projected overtime and what we had to plan for. We had to bring updates so we were all on the same page. We all knew where we fit into the picture. Lucas ensured everyone was clear on what was expected. Each morning he would say good morning to each of us. He went out on the shop floor every day and stopped to chat at each machine. He saw value in relationships. Employees gave back to him. They wanted to work hard and were willing to work extra. He was a positive person in a tough job because he had to be a leader through the recession. He minimized fears, spoke positively of initiatives, talked about how everyone in the team was part of the greater good, and how it was everyone's joint contributions that were letting them pull through the recession."

Padma loved working in that environment, but she wanted more stability than the manufacturing industry could provide. So she took on a management position at the City of Montreal. "What did I learn from my previous experience about how to be a good supervisor? I need to meet with my employees regularly, ensuring duties are clear, and people see where they fit into the bigger picture. I'm up-to-date on the status of projects. I expose people to as much as I can, depending on their goals and what they are looking for in a job. I get them involved in projects, sometimes pushing them when they're not keen because they don't know what they don't know. Later they understand what they gained from it. I am honest with people, not a sugar coater. For example, with feedback, if something is not being done well, I make the feedback as objective as possible. This is what is happening. This is what needs to happen and why; let's figure out a process. It's important to give factual but supportive feedback, so people know they can come to me for anything and not feel judged, especially if they need help."

---

[1] This case is based on a true story, with names and details changed to protect anonymity.

Padma's earlier bad experience under a poor supervisor taught her a lot and helped prepare her to make the most of her own opportunity in management. "One of my biggest fears was of picking up Marla's bad habits. I don't want to become like her and I remind myself of it regularly."

RESPONDING TO THIS CASE

1. Explain Marla's failure as a supervisor by referring to the leadership skills and leadership theories.

2. Explain Lucas's success as a leader by referring to the leadership skills and theories.

3. Do you believe Padma will be an effective leader, given what she describes having learned? Why or why not?

11

COMMUNICATING EFFECTIVELY

Courtesy Daniel Dempster Photography/Alamy

LEARNING OBJECTIVES

After reading this chapter, you should be able to:

1. Define communication.
2. Contrast formal and informal communication.
3. Explain how electronic communications affect the supervisor's job.
4. List barriers to effective communication.
5. Describe techniques for overcoming communication barriers.
6. List the essential requirements for active listening.
7. Explain what behaviours are necessary for providing effective feedback.

CHAPTER OUTLINE

PERFORMING EFFECTIVELY

WHAT IS COMMUNICATION?

COMMUNICATION SKILLS

METHODS OF COMMUNICATION
Oral Communication
Written Communication
Electronic Communication
Something to Think About
Something to Think About
Nonverbal Communication
The Grapevine

THE SUPERVISOR'S DAY-TO-DAY COMMUNICATION

BARRIERS TO EFFECTIVE COMMUNICATION
Language
Poor Listening Habits
Lack of Feedback
Differences in Perception
Role Requirements
Choice of Information Medium
Lack of Honesty
Dealing with a Difficult Issue: Should You Tell the Whole Truth?
Emotions

IMPROVING YOUR COMMUNICATION EFFECTIVENESS
Think First!
Something to Think About
Constrain Emotions
Learn to Listen
Tailor Language to the Receiver
Match Words and Actions
Supervision in Action: Communication Differences in a Global Village
Utilize Feedback
Participate in Assertiveness Training
Building a Supervisory Skill: Confronting

THE IMPORTANCE OF FEEDBACK SKILLS
What's the Difference Between Positive and Negative Feedback?
How Do You Give Effective Feedback?

FROM CONCEPTS TO SKILLS: ACTIVE LISTENING
Assessing Yourself: Do You Listen Actively?
Skill Basics
Applying Your Skills

UNDERSTANDING THE BASICS
Summary
Key Terms and Concepts
Reviewing Your Knowledge

PERFORMING YOUR JOB
Case 11.A: Communicating Workload
Case 11.B: Long-distance Meetings

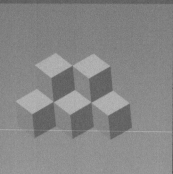

FIGURE 11-1

Rob Watson of Fusion Homes emphasizes the importance of supervisors communicating. This includes communicating positive attitudes that support the company and its values.

Rob Watson is the Vice President of Construction at Fusion Homes in south-western Ontario (London, Guelph, Kitchener and Waterloo). Fusion prides itself on its excellent reputation, having won Ontario Builder of the Year in both medium and large volume categories an unprecedented three times. In the history of the company, Fusion Homes has never missed or even extended a closing date. The company has maintained its prominent position over its short history through fostering open lines of communication with their customers. Each purchaser is given access to a sales professional who stays with them throughout the pre-home buying experience and then a project coordination team member who stays with them throughout the post-home buying experience. Customer feedback is sought both 30 days and one year after purchasers move in, and company goals are set around achieving excellent customer service comments and ratings. Watson comments "I oversee construction and drafting but every department in the company impacts customer service, even accounting and estimating, because subtrades that are happy due to being paid on time and treated with respect go the extra mile to give exemplary service."

Effective communication with customers underlies Fusion decisions and operations, and its success. But it is communication *within* Fusion that allows the coordination and implementation of those operations. All levels of management are the key players in communication.

Communication starts early in a construction company. Rob is in touch with each of his five general managers and drafting staff every morning between 6:45 and 8:30 am. Those general managers in turn meet their site supervisors, service professionals and site personnel. The entire construction team deals directly with their site crew. Each morning, the company president calls Watson to stay up-to-date on all aspects of the construction operation. Rob has a face-to-face meeting with each of his managers every week. In short daily phone calls, people tend to discuss things that need immediate attention so longer face-to-face meetings are good for identifying or dealing with the more substantive issues. In addition, Rob also meets with each construction site supervisor on a random basis in person, getting the supervisor to walk through a house with him, chatting about progress. Twice a year employees at each level meet with their manager for a performance appraisal meeting.

As with many workplaces today, much of the communication is electronic. "With cell phones and 2-way radios, managers are involved in non-stop communication. They can be too available so it's important that people recognize when it is appropriate to call, to email, to cc information. Managers must be available when needed, but they also need to encourage staff to problem-solve on their own. This teaches the team members how to think for themselves, and it allows managers to get their own work done. On the other hand, when managers get inundated with requests and information through email technology, they need to learn how to deal with these emails, organizing them, responding in a timely manner, keeping them down to 10 to 15 actionable items."

Although operational information is at the core of most Fusion communication, Rob is also very attuned to the more subtle attitudinal aspects communicated by management. "If a site supervisor rolls his eyes when he hears about a new policy or I hear him taking the side of the supplier instead of explaining why the company needs things done a certain way, then I'll flag that person and put steps in motion for further investigation or coaching on their behaviour. In everything they do, I need a supervisor to be communicating that they are committed to the company and that they believe in our values. I need them to be leaders and portray what is required of them, and go along with a request from upper management even if they disagree with it. In dealing with their staff, I need them to communicate that they take a personal interest and that they respect this person's time and knowledge." Rob believes that the two key skills for all managers are communication and interpersonal skills; and those skills are essentially inseparable.

All supervisors need strong communication skills. Like Rob, they are involved in frequent communication with employees, managers, peers, and people in other parts of the company in order to get organizational objectives involved. Communications skills alone don't make an effective manager but ineffective communication will lead to a string of problems for the supervisor and the organization.

WHAT IS COMMUNICATION?

Communication is the transference and understanding of meaning. Perfect communication, if such a thing were possible, would exist when a transmitted thought or idea was perceived by the receiver exactly as it was intended by the sender.

Communication is integral to everything a supervisor does. Since the supervisor's focus is on getting work done through other people, effective communication with those people means the difference between strong and weak performance.

What does a supervisor want to consistently communicate?

1. Clear expectations about what is needed from the employee and why

2. Respect for the employee

3. Personal commitment to organizational goals and values; and the importance of alignment between employee actions and organizational goals

All three are critical in order to support both operations and relationships.

Communication
The transference and understanding of meaning.

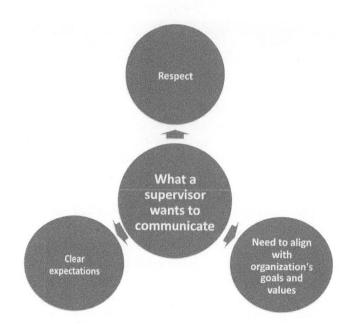

FIGURE 11-2

What a supervisor
wants to consistently
communicate

COMMUNICATION SKILLS

Five communication skills distinguish more effective supervisors, according to a review of research on manager-employee communication[1]. These include being expressive, informative, showing empathy, being a sensitive person, and being persuasive. You need not have all these skills to be effective in your particular role, and some organizations will value particular ones more. But all will potentially contribute to your team's performance and your relationships with your employees.

EXPRESSIVE

Effective communicators have to make the choice to speak up and make their thoughts known. Effective supervisors express their ideas and tend to speak up at meetings. Supervisors who choose not to communicate leave their employees uninformed or confused. Introverted supervisors may have to make a point of pushing themselves to share information and seek interaction with others.

INFORMATIVE

Effective supervisors keep their employees well informed, while selectively sharing information so that employees are not overloaded. They explain the rationale underlying decisions and they give advance notice of changes.

EMPATHY AND SENSITIVITY

These two skills are linked and focus on the supervisor as a listener. Empathy means showing a nonjudgemental understanding of the other person. It requires both hearing the content of their message and picking up on undercurrents, especially emotional undertones. Empathy can be shown nonverbally and through paraphrasing.

Some employees like public praise, others are embarrassed by it. Criticism should always be handled in private. A good supervisor is sensitive to others' feelings and adjusts behaviour accordingly. A combination of empathy and sensitivity will contribute to the supervisor's approachability and trustworthiness in the eyes of employees.

PERSUASIVE

Persuasiveness in writing or in speech means influencing others through the communication. Whether directed at persuading those above or below in the hierarchy, this skill moves objectives forward and by convincing others that the suggestion being pushed is in their interest to support. The persuasiveness can focus on rational or emotional reasons.

METHODS OF COMMUNICATION

Supervisors participate in two types of communication. One is **formal communication**. It addresses task-related issues and tends to follow the organization's authority chain. When supervisors give orders to an employee, provide advice to a team in their department, are offered suggestions by employees, interact with other supervisors on a project, or respond to a request made by their boss, they are engaged in formal communication. It is deliberate. The other type is **informal communication**. This casual type of communication moves in any direction, skips authority levels, and is as likely to satisfy social needs as it is to facilitate task accomplishments.

Supervisors engage in formal communication through speech, written documents, electronic media, and nonverbal behaviour. Informal communication takes place on the **grapevine**.

Formal communication
Addresses task-related issues and tends to follow the organization's authority chain.

Informal communication
Moves in any direction and is as likely to satisfy social needs as to facilitate task accomplishments.

Grapevine
The means by which informal communication takes place.

ORAL COMMUNICATION

Supervisors rely heavily on oral communication. They meet one-on-one with an employee, lead departmental meetings, engage in a problem-solving session with a group of employees, or talk on the phone to a disgruntled customer.

What are the advantages of oral communication? You can transmit information quickly through the spoken word, and oral communications include a nonverbal component that can enhance the message. A phone call, for instance, conveys not only words but also tone and mood. A one-on-one meeting further includes gestures and facial expressions. Additionally, today's supervisors are becoming increasingly aware that not only are oral communications an effective means for quickly conveying information, but they also have positive symbolic value. In contrast to a memo or e-mail message, the spoken word is more personal. It conveys more intimacy and caring. As a result, some of the best supervisors rely extensively on oral communication even when the use of written or electronic channels would seem to be as effective. They have found, through experience, that reliance on oral communication tends to build trust with employees and creates a climate of openness and support. Bonnie Shepherd of UNICEF finds great value in the weekly one-on-one meetings she has with staff. "I see huge positive results of spending time one on one with my team members. Close the door, turn off the computer and the phone and give them my full attention. They are the ones getting the work done and they need to feel supported. They appreciate the check-in with undivided attention. They give me updates on their accounts and we touch base to see if there are highlights to celebrate or challenges to think through. Outside of that hour, when I'm flying around the office, I don't get moments to understand where they are. Through this regular meeting where we communicate openly and honestly, trust is built and it becomes a safe space. Things don't fester."

FIGURE 11-3

Bonnie Shepherd of UNICEF values the weekly meeting she has with each staff member.

WRITTEN COMMUNICATION

When your message is intended to be official, when it has long-term implications, and when it is highly complex, you'll want to convey it in written form. Introducing a new departmental procedure, for instance, should be conveyed in writing so there will be a permanent record to which all employees can refer. Providing a written summary to employees following performance reviews is a good idea because it helps reduce misunderstandings and creates a formal record of what was discussed. Departmental reports that contain lots of detailed numbers and facts are best conveyed in writing because of their complexity.

The fact that written communications provide better documentation than the spoken word is both a plus and a minus. On the plus side, written documents provide a reliable "paper trail" for decisions or actions that are later called into question. They also reduce ambiguity for recipients. But on the negative side, obsessive concern with documenting everything in writing leads to risk avoidance, decision paralysis, and creation of a highly politicized work environment. At the extreme, task accomplishment becomes subordinated to "covering your rear" and ensuring that no one person is held responsible for any questionable decision.

Do men and women communicate in the same way? The answer is "not always." The differences in communication styles between men and women may lead to some interesting insights.[2] When men talk, they tend to do so to emphasize status and independence; whereas women tend to use communications to create connections and intimacy. For instance, men frequently complain that women talk too much about their problems. Women, however, criticize men for not listening. What's happening is that when a man hears a woman talking about a problem, he frequently asserts his desire for independence and control by providing solutions. Many women, in contrast, view conversing about a problem as a means to promote closeness. The woman presents the problem to gain support and connection—not to get the male's advice.

Some research suggests that men are more likely to boast, and less likely to apologize, or to seek help when they need it. Women are more likely to be indirect in their requests, and men more blunt and direct, which can lead to women sometimes being viewed as manipulative and sneaky, and men as insensitive.

Because effective communication between the sexes is important to all supervisors for meeting departmental goals, how can you manage the differences in communication style? Preventing gender differences from becoming persistent barriers to effective communication requires acceptance, understanding, and a commitment to adaptive communication across gender lines. Both men and women need to acknowledge that there are differences in communication styles, that one style isn't better than the other, and that it takes real effort to "talk" with each other successfully.

What do you think? Do men and women really communicate differently? How would the apparent "women's" style of communication potentially affect their success in business?

ELECTRONIC COMMUNICATION

Smartphones, computers and digitalization are dramatically increasing a supervisor's communication options. Today, you can rely on a number of sophisticated electronic media to carry your communications. These include e-mail, the intranet, electronic paging, cellphones, video conferencing, modem-based transmissions, and other forms of network-related communications.

THE PROS AND CONS OF E-MAIL

"Because it's so fast and efficient, we use e-mail a lot," says Tammy Abel, the student placement coordinator who supervises all four Student Employment Centres in Winnipeg. "But it's not necessarily the most effective, and it can easily lead to overload."

"E-mail is an effective business tool that can go very wrong. To pass on an attached report, fine. But to try to discuss an issue—no, it can mess things up. You need to hear the tone, see the expression. Phone is better, face-to-face best," adds Susan Mocsan. "Sometimes people say something in an e-mail that they would never say in person—somehow feeling anonymous."

Tammy and Susan's comments bring up the pros and cons. E-mail allows easy transmission of documents and transfer of straightforward information. It is quick and can contact as many people as you want simultaneously. On the other hand, it has led to a far greater stream of information for most supervisors, not all of it useful or desirable. It has led to discipline issues—to be discussed later in the chapter on discipline. When used inappropriately, it can cause miscommunication and greater problems.

How do you decide when it is appropriate to use e-mail versus another form of communication? What skills are required in using e-mail effectively? How can a supervisor coach a subordinate in the appropriate use of e-mail? How do you feel about your company reading your e-mails—do you feel they are company property or yours?

Supervisors are increasingly using many of these technological advances. E-mail (see Something to Think About) and voice mail allow people to transmit messages 24 hours a day. Even though you're away from your office, others can still leave messages for you to review on your return. And for important and complex communiques, a permanent record of e-mail messages can be obtained by printing out a hard copy. Cell phones are dramatically changing the role of the telephone as a communication device. In the past, telephone numbers were attached to physical locations. Now, the phone number attaches to the individual. As such, supervisors can be in constant contact with department members,

FIGURE 11-4

Words, either written or spoken, don't have to exist for meaning to be transferred. This sign tells you plenty.
Courtesy of Arcady/Shutterstok

other supervisors, and key members of the management team, regardless of where they are physically located. Smartphones are now a primary communication device for supervisors like Rob Watson, described at the beginning of the chapter. Because they allow 24-7 availability by phone and email, they can be seen as both convenient and interfering. Network-related communications allow supervisors to monitor the work of employees whose jobs are done on computers, to participate in electronic meetings, and to communicate with suppliers and customers on interorganizational networks.

NONVERBAL COMMUNICATION

Some of the most meaningful communications aren't spoken, written, or transmitted on a computer. These are **nonverbal communications** (see Figure 11-4). A loud siren or a red light at an intersection tells you something without words. When a supervisor is conducting a training session, he doesn't need words to tell him that people are bored when eyes become glassy. Similarly, he can tell in an instant by his boss's body language and verbal intonations whether she's angry, upbeat, anxious, or distracted.

Body language refers to gestures, facial configurations, and other movements of the body. A snarled face, for example, says something different from a smile. Hand motions, facial expressions, and other gestures can communicate emotions or temperaments such as aggression, fear, shyness, arrogance, joy, and anger.

Nonverbal communications Communication that sends messages without words.

Body language Gestures, facial configurations, and other movements of the body.

Verbal intonations
The emphasis some-
one gives to words or
phrases.

Verbal intonation refers to the emphasis someone gives to words or phrases. To illustrate how intonations can change the meaning of a message, consider the employee who asks a colleague a question. The colleague replies, "What do you mean by that?" The employee's reaction will vary, depending on the tone of the colleague's response. A soft, smooth tone creates a different meaning from one that is abrasive and puts a strong emphasis on the last word. Most of us would view the first intonation as coming from someone who sincerely sought clarification, whereas the second suggests that the person is being aggressive or defensive.

The fact that every oral communication also has a nonverbal message cannot be overemphasized. Why? Because the nonverbal component is likely to carry the greatest impact. One study found that 55 percent of an oral message is derived from facial expression and physical posture, 38 percent from verbal intonations, and only 7 percent from the actual words used.[3] Most of us know that animals respond to the way we say something rather than the content of what we say. Apparently, people aren't much different.

When the verbal and nonverbal parts of a message conflict, we believe the nonverbal message. Why? Because it's a lot easier to lie with words than with your body. For example, imagine someone apologizing but their tone sounds insincere; a colleague congratulating you on your promotion with a very strained look on their face; someone agreeing to do something for you but they avoid looking you in the eye and rush away. The lesson for you as a supervsior is twofold: tune into the nonverbal messages in others to determine what they are really thinking or feeling; and ensure congruence between your own words and actions so you will be seen as sincere.

THE GRAPEVINE

The grapevine is active in almost all organizations. In fact, studies typically find that informal chats are the means by which most operative employees first hear about important changes introduced by management. It rates ahead of supervisors, official memoranda, and other formal sources.

Is the information that flows along the grapevine accurate? The evidence indicates that about 75 percent of what is carried is accurate.[4] But what conditions foster an active grapevine? What gets the rumour mill rolling?

It is frequently assumed that rumours start because they make titillating gossip. Such is rarely the case. Rumours have at least four purposes:

- to structure and reduce anxiety;
- to make sense of limited or fragmented information;
- to serve as a vehicle to organize group members, and possibly outsiders, into coalitions; and

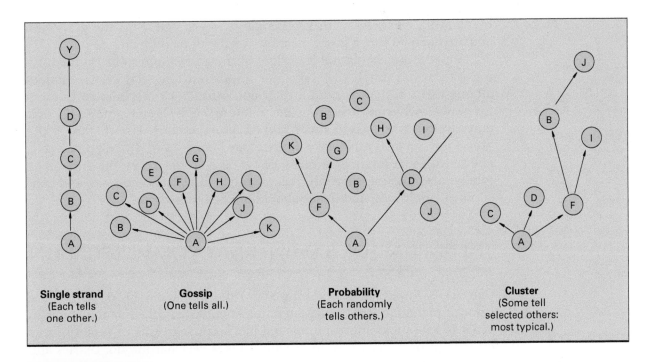

FIGURE 11-5

Grapevine patterns. (*Source:* John W. Newstrom and Keith Davis, *Organizational Behavior: Human Behavior at Work*, 9th ed., New York: McGraw Hill, 1993, p. 445. Reproduced with permission.)

- to signal a sender's status (I'm an insider and you're not) or power (I have the power to make you into an insider).

Studies have found that rumours emerge as a response to situations that are *important* to us, where there is *ambiguity*, and under conditions that arouse *anxiety*. Work situations frequently contain these three elements, which explains why rumours flourish in organizations. The secrecy and competition that typically prevail in large organizations—around such issues as the appointment of new bosses, the relocation of offices, the realignment of work assignments, and layoffs—create conditions that encourage and sustain rumours on the grapevine. A rumour will persist either until the wants and expectations creating the uncertainty underlying the rumour are fulfilled or the anxiety is reduced.

What can we conclude from this discussion? Certainly, the grapevine is an important part of any group or organization's communication system and is well worth understanding. Moreover, it's never going to be eliminated, so supervisors should use it in beneficial ways.

Given that only a small set of employees typically passes information to more than one other person, supervisors can analyze grapevine information and predict its flow. Certain messages are likely to follow predictable patterns (see Figure 11-5). Supervisors might even consider using the grapevine informally to transmit information to specific individuals by planting messages with key people who are active on the grapevine and are likely to find a given message worthy of passing on.

Supervisors should not lose sight of the grapevine's value for identifying issues that employees consider important and that create anxiety among them. It acts as both a filter and a feedback mechanism, picking up issues that employees consider relevant, and planting messages that employees want passed on to upper management. For instance, the grapevine can tap employee concerns (see Figure 11-6). If the grapevine is abuzz with a rumour of a mass layoff, and if you know the rumour is totally false, the message still has meaning. It reflects the fears and concerns of employees, and hence should not be ignored.

THE SUPERVISOR'S DAY-TO-DAY COMMUNICATION

Chapter 2, Supervisory Planning and Time Management, described the value of planning. It was suggested that supervisors schedule their time in order to minimize interruptions and block out segments of time to focus on high-priority activities. In practice, this is very hard to do. Diaries and observations of supervisory activities reveal three interesting findings that relate to communication.[5]

1. **Supervisors are busy.** The typical supervisor's day is made up of hundreds of separate incidents. Instead of planning their days in great detail, supervisors are often forced to react to events and people on the spur of the moment.
2. **Supervisory work is fragmented.** Interruptions are frequent in supervisory work, allowing little time to be devoted to any single activity. Tasks are completed quickly.
3. **Supervisors rely on oral communication.** Supervisors spend most of their time communicating verbally on the telephone, in meetings, or in one-on-one personal contacts.

Taken together, these findings remind us that a supervisor's day-to-day communications are made up of literally dozens of brief encounters

FIGURE 11-6

Information that is shared is often fodder for the workplace grapevine. Courtesy of Richard Lord/The Image Works

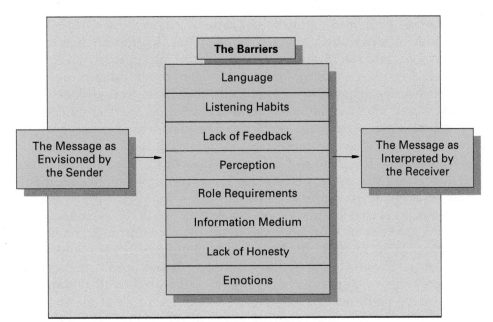

FIGURE 11-7

Barriers to effective
communication

punctuated by constant interruptions. At any given moment, a supervisor might be reading correspondence, involved in a phone conversation, responding to an e-mail message, participating in a formal or informal meeting, taking an observational tour, or cornered in a hallway by his or her immediate manager or by an employee with a question. The effective supervisor learns to differentiate important messages from the unimportant ones and not to let the constant disruptions deter him or her from the pursuit of paramount goals.

BARRIERS TO EFFECTIVE COMMUNICATION

As noted earlier, the goal of perfect communication is to transmit a thought or idea from a sender to a receiver so that it is perceived by the receiver exactly as it was envisioned by the sender. That goal is almost never achieved because of distortions and other barriers (see Figure 11-7). In this section, we will describe some of the more serious barriers that hinder effective communication. In the following section, we'll offer some suggestions for how to overcome these barriers.

LANGUAGE

Words means different things to different people. Age, education, and cultural background are three of the more obvious variables that influence the language people use and the definitions they give to words. In an organization, employees usually come from diverse backgrounds. Furthermore, horizontal differentiation creates specialists who develop their own jargon or technical language. In large organizations, members are often widely dispersed geographically, and those in each locale will use terms and phrases that are unique to their area. Vertical differentiation can also cause language problems. For instance, differences in the meaning of words such as incentives and quotas occur at different levels of management. Top managers often speak about the need for *incentives* and *quotas*, yet these terms have been found to imply manipulation and create resentment among supervisors.

The point is that while you and I may both speak the same language (English), our use of that language is far from uniform. A knowledge of how each of us modifies the language would minimize communication difficulties. The problem is that you don't know how your various employees, peers, superiors, customers, and others with whom you interact have modified the language. Senders tend to assume that the words and terms they use mean the same to the receiver as they to do them. This, of course, is often incorrect, and thus creates communication difficulties.

Language use is altered by the medium. For example, texting on Smartphones encourages the use of very concise language, often with short forms and acronyms. Choice of words often implies emotion or attitude and can be misinterpreted. For example, imagine the potential difference in reaction to a texted "My office ASAP" versus an email or voicemail that explains, "Something has come up that needs immediate attention and I'd appreciate your input. Could you please drop by my office as soon as it's convenient?"

POOR LISTENING HABITS

Most of us hear but we always don't listen! Hearing is merely picking up sound vibrations. Listening is making sense out of what we hear. That is, listening requires that you pay attention, interpret, and remember what is being said.

Most of us are pretty poor listeners. And if you don't have good listening skills, you're not going to get the full message as the sender meant to convey it. There are common flaws that many of us share regarding listening. We get distracted and end up hearing only parts of a message. Instead of listening for meaning, we listen to determine whether we agree or disagree with what's being said—selective perception. We begin thinking about our response to what's being said rather than listening for the complete message. Each of these flaws in our listening habits contributes to messages being received differently from the way the sender intended.

LACK OF FEEDBACK

Effective communication means the transference and *understanding* of meaning. But how do you know if someone has received your message and comprehended it in the way that you meant? The answer is: Use feedback. When a supervisor requests that each member of her staff submit a specific report, receipt of the report is feedback. When your instructor tests you on the material in this book, he gets feedback on your understanding of the text material and his lectures.

When a sender fails to use feedback, he or she never knows if the message has been received as intended. So lack of feedback creates the potential for inaccuracies and distortions.

DIFFERENCES IN PERCEPTION

Our attitudes, interests, past experiences, and expectations determine how we organize and interpret our surroundings. This explains how we can look at the same things and perceive them differently (see Figure 11-8). In the communication process, the receiver selectively sees and hears messages based on his or her background and personal characteristics. The receiver also projects his or her interests and expectations into communications when interpreting them. Since senders and receivers of communications each bring their own set of perceptual biases, the messages they seek to transfer are often subject to distortions.

FIGURE 11-8

What do you see— an old woman or a young girl?

ROLE REQUIREMENTS

People in organizations play **roles**. They engage in behaviour patterns that go with the position they occupy in the organization (see Figure 11-9).

Roles
Behaviour patterns that go with the position one occupies in the organization.

FIGURE 11-9

Union-management negotiations, such as those between Ford and the Canadian Auto Workers, require the parties to play roles.
Courtesy of Jim West/Alamy

Managerial jobs, for instance, come with role identities. Managers know they are supposed to be loyal to, and defend, their boss and the organization. Union leaders' roles typically require loyalty to union goals such as improving employee security. Marketing roles demand efforts to increase sales, while the roles of people working in the credit department emphasize minimizing losses from bad debts.

With the differing role requirements of different members come communication barriers. Each role comes with its own jargon that sets the role apart from others. Additionally, fulfilling role requirements often requires individuals to selectively interpret events. They hear and see the world in a way that is consistent with their role requirements. The result is that people in different roles often have difficulty communicating with each other. Marketing people say they want to "increase sales." So, too, do the people in credit. The difference is that the marketing people want to sell everything to anybody, while credit only wants to sell to those who are creditworthy. Labour and management representatives have difficulty negotiating because their roles encompass very different language and interests. Many of the internal communication breakdowns in organizations are merely individuals enacting behaviours consistent with the roles they are playing.

CHOICE OF INFORMATION MEDIUM

Richness of information
The amount of information a medium is capable of transmitting.

The amount of information transmitted in a face-to-face conversation is considerably greater than that received from a flyer posted on a bulletin board. The former offers multiple information cues (words, posture, facial expressions, gestures, intonation), immediate feedback, and the personal touch of "being there," all of which the flyer lacks. This reminds us that media differ in the **richness of information** they transmit. Figure 11-10

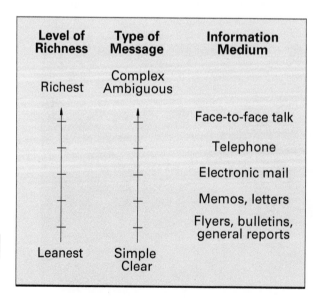

FIGURE 11-10

Hierarchy of information richness

Dealing with a Difficult Issue

SHOULD YOU TELL THE WHOLE TRUTH?

Effective communication in both your personal life and work life is built on the expectation that appropriate and accurate information is being given. In any communications encounter, people should be afforded the respect and dignity of being given complete and factual information. Under what circumstances, then, is it appropriate to withhold information from someone?

One instance that calls for discretion in conveying information is when the issue of confidentiality is involved. The decision to withhold confidential information is sometimes a must—especially at work. Take a situation where one of your employees has just been diagnosed with a treatable form of cancer. He's confided in you about the status of his health. He's also asked you not to say a word to anyone because he considers his health to be a personal matter.

Over the next few months, your employee is absent frequently, especially during his radiation treatments. Because of the circumstances surrounding his illness, you do not feel his absences are a major problem. In part, that's because some of his duties involve direct computer work, which he can do while at home and forward electronically to the appropriate people. You've also discreetly divided the rest of his work among other employees in your work unit. Your employees, though, are wondering what is wrong. Many have come to you to you to find out. You simply, and politely, decline to discuss the issue about this employee with his coworkers. However, a number of them think that you're giving him preferential treatment, and they are ready to go to your boss to complain. You know that if they only knew what was going on, they'd understand, but you can't reveal the reason for his absence. On the other hand, if some individuals begin to make trouble for you or for this employee, it could create more problems for him. That's something he doesn't need right now in his life.

Is it ever appropriate to withhold or filter information in an organization? Should you tell your other employees the whole story? What do you think? Would your views change if this employee had a contagious disease and was working in close contact with his coworkers?

illustrates the hierarchy of information richness. The higher a medium rates in richness, the more information it is capable of transmitting.

Generally speaking, the more ambiguous and complicated the message, the more the sender should rely on a rich communication medium.

For example, as a supervisor, if you want to share with your employees a major new product line that your company will be introducing—and which will affect everyone in your department—your communication is more likely to be effective in a face-to-face departmental meeting than through use of an email. Why? Because this message is likely to initiate apprehension among employees and require clarification. In contrast, a modest change in tomorrow's departmental production schedule can be effectively communicated in an email. Unfortunately, people in organizations don't always match the medium to the message, and thereby create communication problems.

LACK OF HONESTY

A colleague asks you what you think of the ideas he suggested in the recent team meeting in which you both participated. You personally think his suggestions were weak. But you don't tell him that. Rather, you compliment his ideas and say how much they contributed to the final results.

A good deal of what passes as "poor communication" is nothing other than individuals purposely avoiding honesty and openness (see Dealing with a Difficult Issue). To avoid confrontations and hurting others' feelings, some organizational members engage in practices such as conveying ambiguous messages, saying what they think others want to hear, or cutting off communication altogether.

Some people run from confrontation. They want everyone to like them. As such, they avoid communicating any messages they think might be displeasing to the receiver. What they end up doing is increasing tension and further hindering effective communication.

EMOTIONS

How the receiver feels at the time of receipt of a message will influence how he or she interprets it. A message received negatively when you're angry or distraught is likely to be interpreted differently when you're in a neutral disposition. Extreme emotions such as jubilation or depression are most likely to hinder effective communication. In such instances, we are most prone to disregard our rational and objective thinking processes and to substitute emotional judgements. These are also the times we're most likely to use inflammatory language that we later regret.

IMPROVING YOUR COMMUNICATION EFFECTIVENESS

A few of the barriers we've described are part of organizational life and will never be fully eliminated. Perceptual and role differences, for example, should be recognized as barriers but should not be considered easy to correct. However, most barriers to effective communication can be overcome. The following suggestions provide you with some guidance.

THINK FIRST!

"Think before you speak!" That cliché can be expanded to include all forms of communication. Before you speak or write, ask yourself: What message am I trying to convey? Then ask: How can I organize and present my message so that it will achieve the desired outcome?

Most of us follow the "think first" rule when writing a message. The formal and deliberate process of writing encourages thinking through what we want to say and how best to say it. The concept of "working on a draft" implies that the written document will be edited and revised. But few of us give anywhere near the same attention to our verbal communications. That's a mistake. Before you speak, make sure you know what you want to say. Then present your message in a logical and organized fashion so it will be clear and understood by your receiver.

Even our nonverbal messages must be carefully considered. See Something to Think About regarding unintended messages.

SOMETHING TO THINK ABOUT
• AND TO PROMOTE CLASS DISCUSSION •

UNINTENDED MESSAGES
What is the supervisor communicating in the following examples? What is likely to be the consequence?

- The supervisor is looking down and tapping away on a Smartphone while one of his team members is making a presentation to the entire team.
- The supervisor cancels the third meeting in a row with an employee. No explanation is offered.
- The supervisor sighs and rolls her eyes while announcing a new HR policy.
- An employee was badly injured on the shipping dock and has just been taken to hospital. When the supervisor who was absent during the event finally arrives, the first thing he says is, "What happened to the delivery? Did it make it out on time?"

CONSTRAIN EMOTIONS

It would be naive to assume that supervisors always communicate in a fully rational manner. Yet we know that emotions can severely cloud and distort the transference of meaning. If you as a supervisor are emotionally upset over an issue, you are more likely to misconstrue incoming messages and fail to clearly and accurately express outgoing messages. What can you do? The simplest answer is to pause and wait until you have regained composure. Count to 10. Talk to yourself to get you through a situation without losing control. Draft a response and review it a day later before sending to ensure it is a constructive message.

LEARN TO LISTEN

We stated earlier that most of us are poor listeners. But that doesn't mean we can't improve our listening skills. There are specific behaviours that have been found to be related to effective listening. We present those skills in the From Concepts to Skills section at the end of this chapter.

TAILOR LANGUAGE TO THE RECEIVER

Since language can be a barrier, supervisors should choose words and structure their messages in ways that will make them clear and understandable to the receiver. The supervisor needs to simplify his or her language and consider the audience to whom the message is directed, so the language will be tailored to the receivers (see Figure 11-11). Remember that effective communication is achieved when a message is both received and *understood* (see Supervision in Action). Understanding is improved in many cases by simplifying the language used. This means, for example, that a nursing supervisor should always try to communicate in clear and easily understood terms, and that the language used in messages to a patient should be purposely different from that used with the medical staff. Jargon can facilitate understanding when used with those who know what it means, but it can cause innumerable problems when used outside that group.

MATCH WORDS AND ACTIONS

If actions speak louder than words, then it's important to watch your actions to make sure they align with and reinforce the words that go along with them. As a supervisor, you must ensure your verbal and nonverbal communication match. Otherwise, your words will not be trusted. When you must discipline someone, don't smile to soften the blow—you'll seem like a hypocrite. When you give positive feedback, use an enthusiastic voice. If you are aware that you show little expression in your face, consider compensating through animation in your voice. You may be misinterpreted if you don't look like you really mean what you are saying.

As a supervisor, your employees will look at your behaviour as a model. If your verbal comments are backed up by your actions, you will

FIGURE 11-11

Supervising a group of animators at Nelvana in Toronto, Brian Lemay sometimes used cartoon memos to get his message across—a vivid example of tailoring the message to the audience. Courtesy of Brian Lemay/Nelvana (Toronto)

Supervision in Action

Communication Differences in a Global Village

It's important to recognize that communication isn't conducted in the same way around the world.[6] For example, contrast countries that place a high value on individualism (such as Canada) with countries where the emphasis is on collectivism (such as Japan).[7]

Owing to the emphasis on the individual in countries such as Canada, communication patterns are individual-oriented and rather clearly spelled out. For instance, North American supervisors rely heavily on memoranda, announcements, position papers, and other formal types of communication to stake out their positions in the organization. They also often hoard secret information in an attempt to promote their own advancement and as a way of inducing their employees to accept decisions and plans. For their own protection, lower-level employees also engage in this practice.

In collectivist countries such as Japan, there is more interaction for its own sake and a more informal manner of interpersonal contact. The Japanese manager, in contrast to Canadian managers, will engage in extensive verbal consultation over an issue first and will draw up a formal document later, only to outline the agreement that was made. Face-to-face communication is encouraged. Additionally, open communication is an inherent part of the Japanese work setting. Work spaces are open and crowded with individuals at different levels in the work hierarchy. In contrast, Canadian organizations emphasize authority, hierarchy, and formal lines of communication.

gain credibility and build trust. If, on the other hand, you say one thing and do another, your employees will ignore what you say and model themselves on what you do. At the extreme, people stop listening because they no longer believe your words have credibility.

UTILIZE FEEDBACK

Many communication problems can be directly attributed to misunder-standings and inaccuracies. These problems are less likely to occur if the supervisor uses feedback. This feedback can be verbal or nonverbal.

If a supervisor asks a receiver, "Did you understand what I said?" the response represents feedback. But feedback should include more than yes and no answers. And if the person claims to understand, that answer is often not true because the person is too embarrassed to admit not under-standing. The supervisor can ask a set of questions about a message in order to determine whether the message was received as intended. Better yet, the supervisor can ask the receiver to restate the message in his or her own words. If the supervisor then hears what was intended, under-standing and accuracy should be enhanced. Colleen Murphy of the City of Brampton will ask a subordinate, "What do you think I just said?" in order to check understanding. She checks because she often finds misinterpretation.

Feedback does not have to be conveyed in words. The sales super-visor who sends his staff a directive, in which he describes a new monthly sales report that all sales personnel will need to complete, receives feed-back if some of the salespeople fail to turn in the new report. This feed-back suggests that he needs to clarify further the initial directive. Similarly, when you give a speech to a group of people, you watch their eyes and look for other nonverbal clues to tell you whether they are getting your message. This may explain why television performers on comedy shows prefer to tape their programs in front of a live audience. Immediate laughter and applause, or their absence, convey to the per-former whether the message is getting across as intended.

A supervisor must focus not only on ensuring that others understand his or her messages but also that the supervisor him- or herself is also "getting the message" sent by others. Paraphrasing is an effective way to do this. This means that the listener expresses in his or her own words what he or she understood the speaker to have said. This can be even more effective if the listener also includes a reflection of feeling, as this demonstrates how "tuned in" to the total message the listener is. For example, if a subordinate says in a subdued voice, "Look, send someone else on this training. I'm too old to learn this high tech stuff," the super-visor could reply, "You seem apprehensive about this training—as if it's not worth even trying." The subordinate is more likely to open up and discuss his or her concerns than if the supervisor replies, "So you want me to send someone else instead."

PARTICIPATE IN ASSERTIVENESS TRAINING

Many people have no trouble asserting themselves. Being open and hon-est comes naturally to them. Some, in fact, are too assertive. They cross over the line to become aggressive and abrasive. Other individuals suffer from a constant fear of upsetting others and fall back on avoidance or ambiguous communication, when what they need is to be open and assertive. Such people would benefit from participation in assertiveness training. An effective supervisor needn't always be assertive, but should be capable of being so when it's needed.

Assertiveness training is designed to make people more open and self-expressive. Assertive people confront issues in a straightforward manner. They say what they mean, but without being rude or thoughtless.

Individuals who take assertiveness training learn verbal and nonverbal behaviours that enhance their ability to communicate openly and unambiguously. These behaviours include direct and unambiguous language; the use of "I" statements and cooperative "we" statements; a strong, steady, audible voice; good eye contact; facial expressions matched to the message; an appropriately serious tone; and a comfortable but firm posture.

One communication skill that is part of assertiveness and is very useful is confrontation. This skill is explained in Building a Supervisory Skill.

Assertiveness training
Training designed to make people more open and self-expressive.

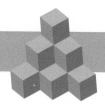

Building a Supervisory Skill

CONFRONTING

About the Skill

Confronting refers to the pointing out of discrepancies in attitudes, thoughts, or behaviours in the other person. It is giving feedback in a factual, non-judgemental way. The purpose is to help the other person look at a situation more realistically and accurately.

For example, you note that, despite promising to show up at an important meeting to contribute to a decision that affected her, the employee did not appear. When you return to the office, the employee says nothing. As supervisor, you could choose to let it pass. This would avoid discomfort but you would still be in the dark. You could be confrontational in an ineffective way, like sarcastically commenting, "Glad you thought we'd handle the meeting so well that you didn't need to be there" or being more aggressive, "How can I count on you when you don't follow through on simple promises like showing up at a meeting?" These would worsen the relationship and still yield no information about their behaviour.

Effective confronting remains nonjudgemental and points out the discrepancy. For example, "I'm puzzled. You said the decision was important to you and you wanted to contribute, but you didn't come to the meeting for

Confronting
Pointing out discrepancies in attitudes, thoughts or behaviours in another person in a non-judgemental way.

the vote. What happened?" The tone used is pivotal. You need to be genuinely concerned about the answer, not critical or flippant. The gentle confrontation is respectful and invites a serious reflection on the discrepancy.

Confrontations can address various types of discrepancies. For example, between two different actions: "On the one hand, you assigned him a low performance rating and, on the other hand, you put him in charge of that new project." Or between words and action: "Your email said you would submit your section by last Friday. However, you have not yet sent it." Or between verbal and nonverbal messages: "I hear you say you're happy to take on that assignment but the way you said it suggests some reluctance or concern about taking it on." The objective of a confrontation is to respectfully point out a discrepancy so the underlying issue can be brought out into the open and explored.

STEPS IN PRACTISING THE SKILL

1. **Notice the discrepancy.** Observe contradiction in words, actions, emotions.

2. **Consider how to word your feedback, pointing out the discrepancy.** A common way to help you get started is to think in terms of "On the one hand... but on the other hand..."

3. **Calmly express the conflicting variables.** Identify the two confronting aspects, describing them in a factual way, with no judgement attached. For example, "You told me that you were having no problems with the report, yet you still have not completed it and it was due two days ago."

4. **Stay silent and let the person respond.** The person may feel somewhat awkward about your feedback, and not respond immediately. Don't try to make it easy for him or her by jumping in with an explanation. Let the person think and respond in his or her own time.

5. **Calmly follow up on the response with pertinent facts and implications.** Continue the conversation in a problem-solving way, remaining constructive and refraining from any accusations. If the person simply denies the truth you have presented, the person may not be prepared to deal with it yet. It may be useful to drop the issue for the moment and follow up later when he or she has thought about it.

TRY IT YOURSELF

Consider the appropriate confronting response in the following situations:

a) "Yeah, I know it's important and needs to get done. Just give me some time. I have other things that need to get done first. I know I promised it to you for this week but there's just no way. I hate to disappoint you; I know how critical this is for you. I'll get it done as soon as possible."

b) "I really want to work on that project. Can you get me on that committee?" The subordinate who says this to you annoyed the team members on his last project by not pulling his weight. You discussed this issue with him in a recent performance review. He has not shown any particular initiative since that discussion.

c) Your manager says to you, "Thanks for doing such a great job. I really appreciate your contribution to this. I don't know what we'd do without you." Meanwhile, you are aware that you received the lowest performance bonus of all the supervisors.

THE IMPORTANCE OF FEEDBACK SKILLS

Ask a supervisor about the feedback he or she gives to employees, and you're likely to get a qualified answer. If the feedback is positive, it's likely to be given promptly and enthusiastically. Negative feedback is often treated very differently. Like most of us, supervisors don't particularly enjoy communicating bad news. They fear offending or having to deal with the receiver's defensiveness. The result is that negative feedback is often avoided, delayed, or substantially distorted.[8] The purposes of this section are to show you the importance of providing both positive and negative feedback and to identify specific techniques to help make your feedback more effective.

WHAT'S THE DIFFERENCE BETWEEN POSITIVE AND NEGATIVE FEEDBACK?

We stated that supervisors treat positive and negative feedback differently. So, too, do receivers. You need to understand this fact and adjust your feedback style accordingly.

Positive feedback is more readily and accurately perceived than negative feedback. Furthermore, while positive feedback is almost always accepted, you can expect negative feedback to meet resistance. Why? The logical answer appears to be that people want to hear good news and block out the rest. Positive feedback fits what most people wish to hear and already believe about themselves.

Does this mean, then, that you should avoid giving negative feedback? No, what it means is that you need to be aware of potential resistance and learn to use negative feedback in situations in which it's most likely to be accepted.[9] That is, negative feedback should be used when it's supported by hard data—numbers, specific examples, and the like.

Both positive and negative feedback contribute to learning, and the shaping of behaviour. Positive feedback is more satisfying to hear, but negative feedback is typically more effective in improving subsequent performance[10]. It is therefore essential not to avoid discussions of performance issues.

How Do You Give Effective Feedback?

There are seven specific suggestions that we can make to help you become more effective in providing feedback, which we will discuss below.

INVOLVE THE EMPLOYEE

Employees are generally quite aware of their performance strengths and weaknesses. Consider inviting the employee to review a performance, what went well and why, and what they would do differently next time. If you start off the discussion with "Tell me about how you think the client meeting went", the employee is quite likely to bring up any issues and you can focus on coaching them and drawing out the positive, rather than delivering bad news.

FOCUS ON SPECIFIC BEHAVIOURS

Feedback should be specific rather than general. Avoid such statements as "You have a bad attitude" or "I'm really impressed with the good job you did." They're vague and, while they provide information, they don't tell the receiver enough to correct the "bad attitude" or on what basis you concluded that a "good job" has been done so the person knows what behaviours to repeat.

KEEP FEEDBACK IMPERSONAL

Feedback, particularly the negative kind, should be descriptive rather than judgemental or evaluative. No matter how upset you are, keep the feedback focused on job-related behaviours and never criticize someone personally because of an inappropriate action. Telling people they're incompetent, lazy, or the like is almost always counterproductive. It provokes such an emotional reaction that the performance deviation itself is apt to be overlooked. When you're criticizing, remember that you're censuring job-related behaviour, not the person. You might be tempted to tell someone he or she is rude and insensitive (which might just be true); however, that's hardly impersonal. It's better to say something more specific like, "You've interrupted me three times with questions that weren't urgent when you knew I was talking long distance to a customer in Brazil."

KEEP FEEDBACK GOAL-ORIENTED

Feedback should not be given primarily to "unload" on another person. If you have to say something negative, make sure it's directed toward the receiver's goals. Ask yourself whom the feedback is supposed to help. If the answer is essentially you—"I've got something I just want to get off my chest"—bite your tongue and hold the comment. Such feedback undermines your credibility and lessens the meaning and influence of future feedback sessions.

MAKE FEEDBACK WELL TIMED

Feedback is most meaningful to a receiver when there is a very short interval between his or her behaviour and the receipt of feedback about that behaviour. For example, a new employee who makes a mistake is more likely to respond to suggestions for improving right after the mistake or at the end of the work day—rather than during a performance review session six months later. If you have to spend time recreating a situation and refreshing someone's memory of it, the feedback you're providing is likely to be ineffective.[11] Moreover, if you're particularly concerned with changing behaviour, delays in providing timely feedback on the undesirable actions lessens the likelihood that the feedback will be effective in bringing about the desired change. Of course, making feedback prompt merely for promptness' sake can backfire if you have insufficient information or if you're emotionally upset. In such instances, "well timed" might be better defined as "somewhat delayed."

ENSURE UNDERSTANDING

Is your feedback concise and complete enough that the receiver clearly and fully understands your communication? Remember, every successful communication requires both transference and understanding of meaning. If feedback is to be effective, you need to ensure that the receiver understands it. Consistent with our discussion of listening techniques, you should have the receiver rephrase the content of your feedback to find out whether it fully captured the meaning you intended.

DIRECT NEGATIVE FEEDBACK

Negative feedback is effective when it is used to correct behaviour, not when it is used to punish. Therefore the feedback should be directed toward behaviour the employee can do something about. There's no value in reminding a person about a shortcoming over which he or she has no control (e.g. the power failure on the subway system that made them an hour late for work). With the feedback on the unsuccessful behaviour, there needs to be a discussion of what alternative behaviours would lead to success in future.

FROM CONCEPTS TO SKILLS

ACTIVE LISTENING

This chapter has repeatedly noted that most of us suffer from poor listening skills. Listening is difficult and often more tiring than talking. It demands intellectual effort and concentration. The average person speaks at a rate of about 150 words per minute, whereas we have the capacity to listen at the rate of over 1000 words per minute. The difference leaves idle time for the brain and opportunities for the mind to wander.

This section is designed to help you correct and improve your listening habits.

ASSESSING YOURSELF: DO YOU LISTEN ACTIVELY?

For each of the following questions, select the answer that best describes your listening habits.

	Usually	Sometimes	Seldom
1. I maintain eye contact with the speaker.	❑	❑	❑
2. I determine whether a speaker's ideas are worthwhile solely by his or her appearance and delivery.	❑	❑	❑
3. I try to align my thoughts and feelings with those of the speaker.	❑	❑	❑
4. I listen for specific facts rather than for "the big picture."	❑	❑	❑
5. I listen for both factual content and the underlying emotion.	❑	❑	❑
6. I ask questions for clarification and understanding.	❑	❑	❑
7. I withhold judgment of what the speaker is saying until he or she is finished.	❑	❑	❑

8. I make a conscious effort to evaluate
the logic and consistency
of what is being said. ❏ ❏ ❏

9. While listening, I think about
what I'm going to say as soon as
I have my chance. ❏ ❏ ❏

10. I try to have the last word. ❏ ❏ ❏

SCORING KEY AND INTERPRETATION

For questions 1, 3, 5, 6, 7, and 8, give yourself three points for Usually, two points for Sometimes, and one point for Seldom. For questions 2, 4, 9, and 10, give yourself three points for Seldom, two points for Sometimes, and one point for Usually.

Total up your points. A score of 27 or higher means that you're a good listener. A score of 22 to 26 suggests you have some listening deficiencies. A score below 22 indicates that you have developed a number of bad listening habits.

SKILL BASICS

Passive listening
Absorbing information as it is literally transmitted.

Active listening
Listening with intensity, empathy, acceptance, and a willingness to take responsibility for completeness.

Effective listening is active rather than passive. In **passive listening**, you are much like a tape recorder. You absorb the information given. If the speaker provides you with a clear message and makes his or her delivery interesting enough to keep your attention, you'll probably get most of what the speaker is trying to communicate. But **active listening** requires you to understand the communication from the speaker's point of view.

There are four essential requirements for active listening. You need to listen with

1. intensity,
2. empathy,
3. acceptance, and
4. a willingness to take responsibility for completeness.

Because listening presents the opportunity for the mind to wander, the active listener concentrates intensely on what the speaker is saying and tunes out thousands of miscellaneous thoughts (work deadlines, money, personal problems) that create distractions. What do active listeners do with their idle brain time? Summarize and integrate what has been said! They put each new bit of information into the context of what has preceded it.

Empathy requires you to put yourself in the speaker's shoes. Try to understand what the speaker wants to communicate rather than what you want to understand. Notice that empathy demands from you both knowledge of the speaker and flexibility. Suspend your own thoughts and feelings and adjust what you see and feel to your speaker's world. In that way, you increase the likelihood that you will interpret the message being spoken in the way the speaker intended.

An active listener demonstrates acceptance. He or she listens objectively without judging content. This is no easy task. It is natural to be distracted by the content of what a speaker says, especially when we disagree with it. When we hear something we disagree with, we begin formulating mental arguments to counter what is being said. Of course, in doing so, we miss the rest of the message. The challenge for the active listener is to absorb what is being said and to withhold judgement on content until the speaker is finished.

The final ingredient of active listening is taking responsibility for completeness. That is, the listener does whatever is necessary to get the full intended meaning from the speaker's communication.

The following guide summarizes 14 specific techniques to use for effective listening.

1. **Be motivated.** If a listener is unwilling to exert the effort to hear and understand, no amount of additional advice is likely to improve listening effectiveness. As we previously noted, active listening is hard work. So your first step toward becoming an effective listener is a willingness to make the effort.

2. **Make eye contact.** How do you feel when somebody doesn't look at you when you're speaking? If you're like most people, you're likely to interpret this as aloofness or lack of interest. It's ironic that while "you listen with your ears, people judge whether you are listening by looking at your eyes." Making eye contact with the speaker focuses your attention, reduces the likelihood that you will become distracted, and encourages the speaker.

3. **Show interest.** The effective listener shows interest in what is being said. How? Through nonverbal signals. Affirmative head nods and appropriate facial expressions, when added to good eye contact, convey to the speaker that you're listening. Verbal signals—comments such as "I see," "Yes," and "I know what you mean"—offer even more direct evidence that you are listening. Leaning slightly forward in your seat suggests interest, whereas leaning back suggests the opposite.

4. **Avoid distracting actions.** The other side of showing interest is avoiding actions that suggest your mind is somewhere else. When

listening, don't look at your watch, shuffle papers, play with your pencil, or engage in similar distractions. They make the speaker feel you're bored or uninterested. Maybe more importantly, they indicate that you aren't fully attentive and may be missing part of the message that they want to convey.

5. **Empathize.** We said the active listener tries to understand what the speaker sees and feels by putting herself in his shoes. Don't project your own needs and intentions onto the speaker. When you do so, you're likely to hear what you want to hear. So ask yourself: Who is this speaker and where is he coming from? What are his attitudes, interests, experiences, needs, and expectations?

6. **Take in the whole picture.** The effective listener interprets feelings and emotions as well as factual content. If you listen to words alone and ignore other vocal cues and nonverbal signals, you will miss a wealth of subtle messages. To test this point, read the script of a play. Then go and see that play live in a theatre. The characters and the message take on a much richer meaning when you see the play acted on stage.

7. **Ask questions.** The critical listener analyzes what he or she hears and asks questions. This behaviour provides clarification, ensures understanding, and assures the speaker that you're listening.

8. **Paraphrase.** Paraphrasing means restating what the speaker has said in your own words. The effective listener uses phrases like: "What I hear you saying is…" or "Do you mean…?" Why rephrase what's already been said? Two reasons! First, it's an excellent control device with which to check whether you're listening carefully. You can't paraphrase accurately if your mind is wandering or if you're thinking about what you're going to say next. Second, it's a control for accuracy. By rephrasing what the speaker has said in your own words and feeding it back to the speaker, you verify the accuracy of your understanding.

9. **Don't interrupt.** Let the speaker complete his or her thought before you try to respond. Don't try to second-guess where the speaker's thoughts are going. When the speaker is finished, you'll know it!

10. **Integrate what's being said.** Use your spare time while listening to better understand the speaker's ideas. Instead of treating each new piece of information as an independent entity, put the pieces together. Treat each part of the message as if it were an additional

piece of a puzzle. By the time the speaker is done, instead of having 10 unrelated bits of information, you'll have 10 integrated pieces of information that form a comprehensive message. If you don't, you should ask the questions that will fill in the blanks.

11. **Don't overtalk.** Most of us would rather speak our own ideas than listen to what someone else says. Too many of us listen only because it's the price we have to pay to get people to let us talk. While talking may be more fun and silence may be uncomfortable, you can't talk and listen at the same time. The good listener recognizes this fact and doesn't overtalk.

12. **Confront your biases.** Evaluate the source of the message. Notice such things as the speaker's credibility, appearance, vocabulary, and speech mannerisms. But don't let them distract you. For instance, all of us have "red flag" words that prick our attention or cause us to draw premature conclusions. Examples might include terms such as *racist, gay, conservative, liberal, feminist,* or *blue collar*. Use information about the speaker to improve your understanding of what he or she has to say, but don't let your biases distort the message.

13. **Make smooth transitions between speaker and listener roles.** In most work situations, you're continually shifting back and forth between the roles of speaker and listener. The effective listener makes transitions smoothly from speaker to listener and back to speaker. From a listening perspective, this means concentrating on what a speaker has to say and practising not thinking about what you're going to say as soon as you get your chance.

14. **Be natural.** An effective listener develops a style that is natural and authentic. Don't try to become a compulsive listener. If you exaggerate eye contact, facial expressions, the asking of questions, showing of interest, and the like, you'll lose credibility.

A good listener is not a manipulator. Use moderation and develop listening techniques that are effective and fit well with your interpersonal style.

APPLYING YOUR SKILLS

This is a role play to practise listening skills. Break into groups of three. One person will be the observer. He or she will evaluate the two other role players and provide feedback on their listening skills using the 14 points listed above.

Choose one of the following role-plays to enact and decide who will play each character.

Why Lose the Good and Keep the Bad An employee has come to speak to his supervisor. This employee is frustrated that a friend who has been a contract worker at the plant is being laid off after 18 months of excellent work. Meanwhile, other full-time employees who are much less competent than this contract employee are keeping their jobs. It does not seem fair that this is how good work is rewarded. It also seems like a stupid decision from the point of view of the company and its productivity. The supervisor needs to work with this person to have him understand that if contract employees remain too long with the company, then they are considered full-time by the government and incur additional expenses for the company (such as benefits). The company does not want to increase its full-time staff. It wants to cover additional work with the flexibility of contract workers.

What Should I Do? One supervisor has approached another supervisor for advice on dealing with a subordinate. He believes that one of his subordinates has been stealing from the company. Several pieces of the new computer equipment have disappeared; the supervisor has heard this employee, named Peter, make cracks about the great new equipment he has at home, and he makes no secret that in his previous position at the company, he was allowed to "borrow" software packages, books, and audiovisual equipment. But the supervisor has no proof of the theft; it is simply a suspicion. He is aware that Peter is a close friend of an executive at the firm and if the supervisor makes a wrong move in handling this, it could mean big trouble.

Can We Work Something Out? An employee is approaching her supervisor to discuss her needs for accommodation at work. One of her parents is critically ill and the other is not in strong health. She needs to spend a lot of time with them helping them cope with daily issues such as shopping, cleaning their house, and accompanying them to medical appointments. Plus, she has her own life to lead. It's a very stressful time in her life. Her employer has been good to her in the past and she is hoping they will continue to be so. She would like them to allow her to work flexible hours and she may need to take a leave of absence. The supervisor has never dealt with a situation like this. The two role players will need to decide what kind of job the employee does.

After each person has read the appropriate roles, begin the exercise. You have up to 15 minutes. When completed, the observer should provide feedback to both of the role players on how well they listened to each other.

SUMMARY

This summary is organized by the Learning Objectives.

1. Communication is the transference and understanding of meaning.
2. Formal communication addresses task-related issues and tends to follow the organization's authority chain. Informal communication moves in any direction, skips authority levels, and is as likely to satisfy social needs as it is to facilitate task accomplishments.
3. Electronic communications allow supervisors to transmit messages 24 hours a day and stay in constant contact with department members, other supervisors, and key members of the management team regardless of where they are physically located. Networks also allow supervisors to participate in electronic meetings and interact with key people outside the organization. Electronic communications mean much greater accessibility which can be a boon, but also create difficulties in separating work and home life.
4. Barriers to effective communication include language differences, poor listening habits, lack of feedback, differences in perception, role requirements, poor choice of information medium, lack of honesty, and emotion.
5. Techniques for overcoming communication barriers include thinking through what you want to say before communicating, constraining emotions, learning to listen, tailoring language to the receiver, matching words and actions, utilizing feedback, and participating in assertiveness training.
6. The essential requirements for active listening are: 1. intensity, 2. empathy, 3. acceptance, and 4. a willingness to take responsibility for completeness.
7. Behaviours that are necessary for providing effective feedback include involving the employee, focusing on specific behaviours; keeping feedback impersonal, goal-oriented, and well-timed; ensuring understanding; and directing negative feedback toward behaviour that the recipient can control.

KEY TERMS AND CONCEPTS

Active listening

Assertiveness training

Body language

Communication

Confronting

Formal communication

Grapevine

Informal communication

Nonverbal communication

Passive listening

Richness of information

Roles

Verbal intonation

REVIEWING YOUR KNOWLEDGE

1. "Everything a supervisor does involves communicating." Build an argument to support this statement.
2. When is a written communication superior to an oral one?
3. "Do what I say, not what I do." Analyze this phrase in terms of supervisors being effective communicators.
4. How can nonverbal messages be powerful communicators?
5. What are the purposes of rumours?
6. Can supervisors control the grapevine? Discuss.
7. Given all the barriers to communication, how is it possible for any two people in an organization to accurately transfer information?
8. "A supervisor should always select the information medium that rates highest in information richness." Do you agree or disagree? Discuss.
9. Why is the ability to effectively use confrontation likely to gain you respect?
10. Why is active listening so difficult for many people to accomplish?

CASE 11.A

Communicating Workload

Wendy Chiu, President and Managing Director of Katalogic Inc., has developed subtle communication techniques that help everyone keep on task and at the same time avoid overloading themselves or others.

"The trick I have found is to write things down and make things visible & public as much as you can. Everyone complains of being overworked all the time, and that there is far too much being asked of them. So you'll see whiteboards and a lot of huge post-it sheets around our offices. I do a lot of measurement, and review of stats, and documentation of productivity to ensure everyone knows what's going on—what they have on their plates and what their colleagues have. And I like to have my staff members record what they're working on. If someone gets to the point where they feel there's too much, I want them to write it on their whiteboard so everyone can see it. Then there can be a negotiation about workload. If I walk by Steven's office and see a whiteboard with ten activities and dates, and I had been ready to give him a task, I'm more likely to pause and check someone else's list. The employee can use it to manage their time and not over commit, especially those who tend to say yes to everything. The board is a reminder to themselves and others. Whiteboards, task logs, to-do lists also let everyone brag silently about what they did that day (not everyone's comfortable communicating successes at team meetings). People used to complain to me that Tim is always surfing the net or Joan is chatting on msn. Everyone needs a mental break now and then. Now the whiteboards make it clear what is being accomplished so people don't question someone doing a coffee run when they see the person has already closed ten tickets."

RESPONDING TO THIS CASE

1. The simple task of recording current projects and posting them so others can see them is actually serving several purposes. List them.
2. Wendy runs a company that creates software and supports customer use of their software. Yet she describes the value of old-fashioned pencil on paper. What advantages does this public documentation of work have over a similar digital record?
3. How does the use of task documentation tackle the communication barriers of: role requirements, differences in perception, lack of honesty and poor listening?
4. Reflecting on the importance of choosing the right information medium, why is the public documentation suitable for communicating task information? What information would it not be suitable for?

FIGURE 11-12

Wendy Chiu

CASE 11.B

Long-Distance Meetings[1]

Alex Lawrence heads up a team of 20 from her Toronto office but those team members are located all around the world. As a result, she has perfected the long-distance meeting. "The chal-

---

[1] Names and details have been changed to protect the identity of "Alex".

lenges are time zones, cultural expectations, levels of knowledge, and multitasking. Simply coordinating to connect at times convenient for everyone can be tough. And people vary in their comfort with speaking up. I find some cultures are much more reticent about offering ideas or asking questions; others are only too happy to blow their own horn. I have to be sensitive to people having different levels of experience and familiarity with issues. And the multitasking issue happens whether the meeting is in person or long-distance. When you're in the same room, you can see people distracted by their Smartphones. When they're at a distance I can still hear them tapping away on their keyboard. My guidelines for an effective meeting are as follows:

- Have an agenda and stick to relevant discussion

- Be clear on the issues and repeat critical points

- Ensure people understand the level of decision making they will have. Are they advising, making a decision or simply implementing something decided elsewhere? Sometimes people get upset when they are asked for their thoughts and then their ideas are not implemented. They need to know their role upfront.

- Make people accountable; record actions to be taken and follow up in subsequent meetings regarding what was done (report on agenda obligations)

- Skip the updates; it becomes more about personality than actual achievements. Some people can blow up one small accomplishment into something impressive sounding whereas the shyer but more effective employee can condense major achievements into an understatement so no one appreciates what they've done.

- Do team building and build trust. Ensure they know what is confidential and cannot go beyond the meeting.

- Encourage disagreement but ensure everyone is on board with the final decision. It means an issue is fully discussed.

- Ensure full participation–it's part of their accountability.

RESPONDING TO THIS CASE

1. Alex's meetings are sometimes purely oral (teleconferencing) and sometimes oral and written (using software that allows them to hear each other but also share documents). What are the benefits and challenges of these techniques for her team in terms of communication effectiveness?

2. Consider which barriers to effective communication may be at play in long-distance meetings with participants around the world. Discuss how Alex's guidelines on how to run an effective meeting will or will not address those barriers.

3. What communications should Alex share with individual employees rather than at these meetings? Why?

PART FIVE

COPING WITH WORKPLACE DYNAMICS

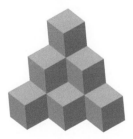

12 MANAGING CONFLICT AND POLITICS

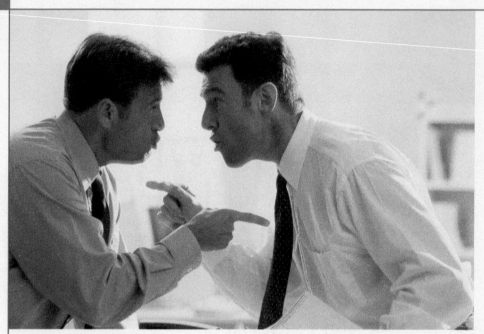

Coutesy of Corbis Bridge/Alamy

LEARNING OBJECTIVES

After reading this chapter, you should be able to:

1. Define conflict.
2. Identify the three general sources of conflict.
3. List the five basic techniques for resolving conflict.
4. Describe how a supervisor could stimulate conflict.
5. Define politicking.
6. Explain the existence of politics in organizations.
7. Describe the situational factors that determine political options.
8. List specific guidelines for developing and improving political skills.
9. Contrast distributive and integrative bargaining.

CHAPTER OUTLINE

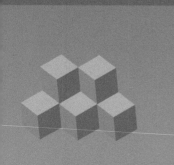

FIGURE 12-1

Diane Hebert describes the conflict created by inconsistent organizational practices. Her solution required sensitivity to company politics.

Diane Hebert describes a challenging situation illustrating the link between conflict and politics. "We had real problems because of inconsistent practices between managers. Some new hires were getting $30,000 to move (to our northern location), others only $10,000. As employees talked to each other, it became a morale issue. My department, Human Resources, should have been involved in writing letters of offer but it was not the standard practice and managers were giving the shop away or causing potential legal problems for the company by not following legislated employment standards. I said, "Let us develop a standard template and then you can customize it. If you don't have a standard, then you must live with the consequences." The president refused to enforce the use of a template – I think there was suspicion that HR was a threat, trying to take power from upper management. They had no experience with a strong and capable HR team so didn't understand HR's value or function. Trying to reason with the executives didn't work. So what did we do? We developed a template anyway. We worked with a few managers who were friendly to the process. Then I asked my staff to offer the template to managers as an optional tool when they were hiring. Now 95% use it, despite it still being "optional". The 5% not using it still causes the other managers grief.

Coaching my staff on how to get things done in an environment where their skills and services are not appreciated, I call it "commando management". We strategize together. I am the youngest of 14 so I've learned to get along in all situations. For example, an interaction with one of my team went like this: Her: We shouldn't have to suck up to x. Me: We do need an approach that will work with him. Her: But he should understand! Me: But he doesn't, that's the issue, so we have to keep going back to him, and stay professional in all our dealings. She had a hard time asking four times for something. I told her she needed to go back and ask again, eventually they will learn. Just last week there was a manager who was a huge holdout. He came and said, "I think my shop people are being paid less and are unhappy; what can we do?" So I offered to do a survey of eight local companies with comparable positions. All of a sudden the switch went on and he realized what a resource HR could be. All of a sudden he's coming to my office willing to go with the letter of offer template.

Handling conflict is an inevitable part of a supervisor's job—whether it is with clients, within the team, or with other parts of the organization, as in Diane's case. Diane exemplifies focusing on resolving the conflict in a functional way and not getting caught up in the emotions or the political power struggles.

In this chapter we'll define conflict, explore what brings it about and examine the various ways supervisors can handle it. Then we'll discuss organizational politics—why understanding politics is important for all supervisors and how you can make politics work for you.

WHAT IS CONFLICT?

Conflict is a process in which one party consciously interferes in the goal-achievement of another party. This interference can be between a supervisor and a member of his or her department, between two employees within a department, between a supervisor and his or her boss, or involve interdepartmental parties, such as two supervisors in separate departments. Conflicts with customers are also often handled by supervisors.

Conflict
A process in which one party consciously interferes in the goal-achievement efforts of another party.

ARE ALL CONFLICTS BAD?

Most of us have grown up with the idea that all conflicts are bad. We were told not to argue with our parents or teachers, to get along with our brothers and sisters, and that countries spent billions of dollars on military outlays to preserve peace. But conflicts aren't *all* bad, especially in organizations.

Conflict is a natural phenomenon of organizational life. It can't be completely eliminated. Why? For the following reasons:

1. Organizational members have different goals.
2. There are scarce resources, such as budget allocations, which various people want and are willing to fight over.
3. People in organizations don't all see things alike, as a result of their diverse backgrounds, education, experiences, and interests.

However, the existence of conflict in organizations has a positive side. It stimulates creativity, innovation, and change. And only through change can an organization adapt and survive (see Figure 12-2). For instance, a positive level of conflict in an organization supports disagreements, the open questioning of others, and challenging the status quo. If organizations were completely devoid of conflict, they would become apathetic, stagnant, and unresponsive to change.

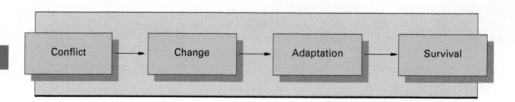

FIGURE 12-2

The positive role of conflict

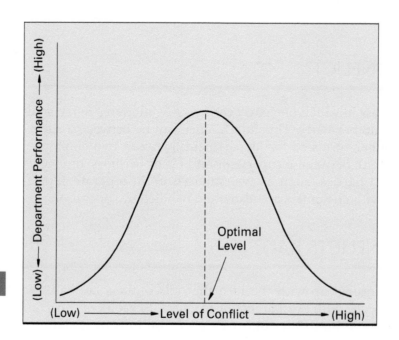

FIGURE 12-3

Conflict and department performance

Supervisors should consider conflict as having an upside as well as a downside. They should encourage enough conflict to keep their departments viable, self-critical, and creative. Of course, too much conflict is bad and should be reduced. The supervisor's goal should be to have enough conflict in the department to keep the unit responsive and innovative, but not so much as to hinder departmental performance (see Figure 12-3).

We are saying that some conflict is functional and some is dysfunctional. Functional conflict is healthy, constructive disagreement. It focuses on effective goal accomplishment and at the same time does not damage relationships. Functional conflict tends to emphasize ideas rather than emotions. On the other hand, dysfunctional conflict is unhealthy, destructive conflict that tends to focus on the conflict rather than the work goal. It often arises from emotional issues and involves inappropriate behaviours like threats.[1]

SOURCES OF CONFLICT

Conflicts don't pop out of thin air. They have causes. These causes can be separated into three general categories: communication differences, structural differences, and personal differences.

COMMUNICATION DIFFERENCES

Communication differences encompass those conflicts arising from misunderstandings and different meanings attached to words, from someone not having needed communication passed on to them, or from an overload of information that makes it difficult to know what is important.

One of the major myths that most of us carry around with us is that poor communication is the only reason for conflicts—"If we could just communicate with each other, we could eliminate our differences." Poor communication is certainly not the source of all conflicts, though there is considerable evidence to suggest that problems in the communication process act to hinder collaboration and stimulate misunderstanding.

STRUCTURAL DIFFERENTIATION

As explained earlier in this book, organizations are horizontally and vertically differentiated. Management divides up tasks, groups common tasks into departments, and establishes rules and regulations to facilitate standardized practices between departments.

This structural differentiation often causes conflicts. Individuals disagree over goals, decision alternatives, performance criteria, and resource allocations. These conflicts, however, are not due to poor communication or personal animosities. Rather, they are rooted in the structure[2] of the organization itself. The "goodies" that people want—budgets, promotions, pay increases, additional staff, office space, influence over decision—are scarce resources that must be divided up. The creation of horizontal units (departments) and vertical levels (the management hierarchy) brings about efficiencies through specialization and coordination, but at the same time produces the potential for structural conflicts. People tend to see their needs as paramount and may be unaware or uncaring of the needs of others in the organization. Some refer to see this as a "**silo mentality**". A structure of separated, unintegrated business units creates a focus on unit success rather than organizational success.

Silo mentality Organizational business units focus on their unit's success rather than organizational success.

Jurisdictional ambiguity is also a source of conflict connected with structural differentiation. If there is something that is not explicitly allocated to a particular person or group, who is to handle it? If it is a highly desirable task or responsibility (e.g. easy and visible), conflict may arise from various people claiming they should be the ones to handle it. If it is undesirable (e.g. risky, difficult and thankless), there will be conflict because no one wants to take it on.

PERSONAL DIFFERENCES

The third source of conflict is personal differences. These include value systems and personality characteristics that account for individual idiosyncrasies and differences.

For example: Your values emphasize acquiring material possessions, while mine focus on developing close family ties. An employee in your department thinks salary increases should be based on seniority. You think the criterion should be job performance. These value differences stimulate conflicts. Similarly, the chemistry between some people makes it hard for them to work together. Factors such as background, education, experience, and training mould each individual into a unique personality. Some personality types are attracted to each other, while some types are like oil and water—they just don't mix. The result is that some people may be perceived by others as abrasive, hard to work with, untrustworthy, or strange. This creates interpersonal conflicts.

TECHNIQUES FOR MANAGING CONFLICT

As a supervisor, you want to have the optimum level of conflict in your department. That means you need to manage it. You'll want to *resolve* conflict when it is too high and disrupts your department's performance. You'll want to *stimulate* conflict when it's too low. So **conflict management** is defined as the application of resolution and stimulation techniques to achieve the optimum level of departmental conflict.

Conflict management
The application of resolution and stimulation techniques to achieve the optimum level of departmental conflict.

RESOLUTION TECHNIQUES

Let's start by discussing the goals in conflict resolution. We tend to assume that the goal of resolving a conflict is achieving what we think is the best solution. Ideally, there are two goals in any conflict:

1. A resolution that effectively meets the organization's needs in the situation.
2. A resolution that protects the relationship.

There are five basic options for eliminating or reducing conflicts: avoidance, accommodation, force, compromise and collaboration. They emphasize these two goals to different degrees.

As shown in Figure 12-4, they differ in terms of the emphasis they place on concern for others versus concern for oneself. Each technique

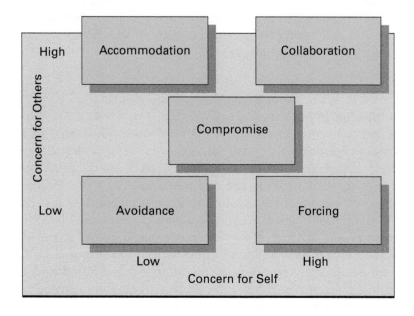

FIGURE 12-4

Basic techniques for resolving conflicts

has particular strengths and weaknesses, and no single technique is ideal for every situation. You should consider each technique as a tool in your conflict management tool chest. While you may be better at using some tools than others, the skilled supervisor knows what each tool can do and when it is likely to be most effective.

AVOIDANCE

Sometimes **avoidance** is the best solution—just withdrawing from the conflict or ignoring its existence. When would that be? When the conflict is trivial, when emotions are running high and time can help cool things down, or when the potential disruption from a more assertive action outweighs the benefits of resolution. The thing to be concerned about with this approach is that some supervisors believe that they can run away from all conflicts. These conflict avoiders are often very poor supervisors. They frustrate their employees and usually lose their respect. For example, such a supervisor may fail to confront an employee who is not doing his work adequately or is breaking rules. The lack of action can anger the other employees. There *are* times when the best action is no action, but that shouldn't be the way you respond to every conflict.

Avoidance
The desire to withdraw from or ignore a conflict.

ACCOMMODATION

The goal of **accommodation** is to maintain harmonious relationships by placing another's needs and concerns above your own. You might, for example, yield to another person's position on an issue or try to defuse a conflict by focusing on points of agreement. This approach is most viable

Accommodation
The willingness of one party in a conflict to place the opponent's interests above his or her own.

when the issue under dispute isn't important to you or when you want to build up "credits" for possible later issues. It is also appropriate when you realize you are wrong, or when the issue is much more significant and consequential to the other person.

FORCING

Forcing
The desire to satisfy your own needs at the expense of the other party.

With **forcing**, you attempt to satisfy your own needs at the expense of the other party. In organizations, this is most often illustrated by supervisors and managers using their formal authority to resolve a dispute. The use of physical threats, intimidation, majority-rule voting, or stubborn refusal to give in on your position are other examples of force. Force works well 1. when you need a quick resolution, 2. on important issues where unpopular actions must be taken, and 3. where commitment by others to your solution is not critical. However, force can damage morale, and cause resistance and a future lack of cooperation. Forcing is a last resort that may be necessary when gentler techniques have failed and the issue is critical—for example, if safety is at risk. If politely reminding someone that they must wear their safety harness is ignored, a supervisor must make it clear that this is an order, not a request.

COMPROMISE

Compromise
A situation in which each party to a conflict is willing to give up something of value.

A **compromise** approach requires each party to give up something of value. This is typically the approach taken by management and unions in negotiating a new labour contract. Supervisors often use compromise to deal with interpersonal conflicts. For instance, a supervisor in a small printing company wanted one of his employees to come in over a weekend to finish an important project. The employee didn't want to spend his whole weekend at work. After considerable discussion, they arrived at a compromise solution: the employee would come in on Saturday only, the supervisor would also come in and help out, and the employee would receive eight hours of overtime pay plus the following Friday off.

Compromise is seen by many as an ideal solution. In fact, it often leads to subpar solutions for the organization. For example, suppose you and I are asked to find someone to fill a key new position. In the hiring process, you prize one particular candidate, I prefer another strong candidate and we both agree on a third person who is "okay" but not great. To avoid either of us losing face we might compromise by selecting the third candidate. This decision likely creates a poorer result for the organization than hiring either lead candidate would have created.

When should a supervisor look to compromise as an option? When conflicting parties are about equal in power, when it is desirable to achieve a temporary solution to a complex issue, or when time pressures demand an expedient solution.

COLLABORATION

The ultimate win-win solution is **collaboration**. All parties to the conflict seek to satisfy their interests. This technique is typically characterized by open and honest discussion among the parties, intensive listening in order to understand differences and identify areas of mutual agreement, and careful deliberation over a full range of alternatives in order to find a solution that is advantageous to all. Effective collaboration yields a solution that both meets the organization's needs in the situation and builds the relationship between the parties involved. When is collaboration the best conflict approach? When time pressures are minimal, when all parties seriously want a solution, and when the issue is too important to be compromised. A discussion of the skills used in collaborating is presented in Building a Supervisory Skill.

Collaboration
A situation where the parties to a conflict each desire to satisfy fully the concerns of all parties.

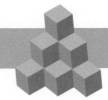

Building a Supervisory Skill

HANDLING CONFLICT THROUGH A ROLE-REVERSAL TECHNIQUE

ABOUT THE SKILL

You approach a conflict from the belief that the best way to solve a conflict is to understand the other person's position. Using this technique, you are much more likely to gain two goals in a conflict—a solution acceptable to both, and a healthy relationship between the two. You may assume, after reading the description below, that the technique would take a long time and therefore not gain the third goal in many conflicts—a timely solution. However, ironically, because it is respectful, future-oriented, and constructive, it often takes less time than an approach that arouses strong emotions.

STEPS IN PRACTISING THE SKILL

1. **Use paraphrasing.** After the other person has spoken, paraphrase the main points before you go on to explain your viewpoint. This means you summarize what they have just said in your own words. By doing this, you force yourself to concentrate on the other person and listen to his or her points, you can clarify any misunderstanding, and you immediately gain greater credibility from the speaker, who knows you really are listening. Note that it is not effective to simply say, "I see" or "I understand how you feel." You may think that is true, but the other

person will not believe you and you have not proven with your words that you really do understand.

2. **Stay calm.** You are a professional. This means you control your emotions. Losing your temper or crying will not win respect. Staying calm despite obvious tension in the situation and perhaps some goading from the other person *will gain you respect.*

3. **Focus on the issue, not the other person.** If you stick to the issue without bringing in anything personal about the other person, emotions are more likely to stay under control, and the conversation is more likely to stay constructive.

4. **Concentrate on what can be done in the future to resolve the problem rather than looking for blame.** Blaming arouses emotions and is usually a waste of time. Focusing on resolving the issue presents an opportunity for both parties to contribute positively to the discussion.

5. **Assume the other person means well.** Few people are intentionally malicious. Usually, a conflict has happened despite the genuinely well-meaning efforts of those involved. It is safer to assume that this has happened in a particular situation—until proven otherwise.

6. **Protect your own interests.** You still want a solution that works for you, but you don't want to sacrifice the relationship in order to get it.

WHICH CONFLICTS SHOULD YOU TACKLE?

Not every conflict justifies your attention. Some might not be worth the effort; others might be unmanageable. While avoidance might appear to be a "cop-out," it can sometimes be the most appropriate response. You can improve your overall management effectiveness, and your conflict management skills in particular, by avoiding trivial conflicts. Choose your battles judiciously, saving your efforts for the ones that count.

Regardless of our desires, reality tells us that some conflicts are unmanageable.[3] When antagonisms are deeply rooted, when one or both parties wish to prolong a conflict, or when emotions run so high that constructive interaction is impossible, your efforts to manage the conflict are unlikely to meet with much success. Don't be lured into the naive belief that a good supervisor can resolve every conflict effectively. Some aren't worth the effort. Some are outside your realm of influence. Still others may be dysfunctional and, as such, are best left alone. Those you choose to handle, you need to know how to handle in the best way possible.

CHOOSING THE APPROPRIATE RESOLUTION TECHNIQUE

Now that you're familiar with your options, how should you proceed if you find you have a conflict that needs resolving?

Start by considering your *preferred conflict-handling style* (see Assessing Yourself: Your Preferred Conflict-Handling Style). Each of us has a basic approach to handling conflict with which we feel most comfortable. Do you try to postpone dealing with conflicts, hoping they'll go away (avoidance)? Do you prefer soothing the other party's feelings so the disagreement doesn't damage your relationship (accommodation)? Are you stubborn and determined to get your way (forcing)? Do you look for middle-ground solutions (compromise)? Or do you prefer to sit down and discuss differences in order to find a solution that will make everybody happy (collaboration)?

Everyone has a basic resolution approach that reflects his or her personality. You should understand what yours is. But most people aren't held prisoner by that approach. They're flexible and can use different approaches if they need to. Unfortunately, some people are extremely rigid and incapable of adjusting their styles. These people are at a severe disadvantage because they can't use all the resolution options. You should know your basic resolution style and try to show flexibility in using others. However, keep in mind that when push comes to shove, most of us fall back on our basic approach because it's the one we know best and feel most comfortable with.

The next thing you should look at is what you want to achieve. The best solution is closely intertwined with your definition of best. Three goals dominate the preceding discussion of resolution approaches: the *importance* of the conflict, concern over maintaining long-term *interpersonal relations*, and

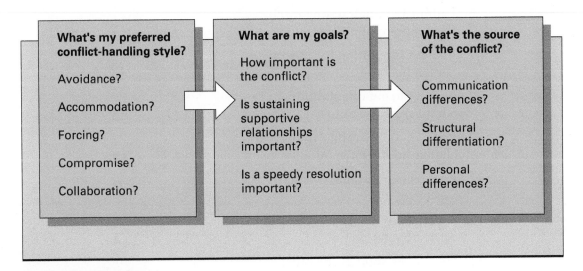

FIGURE 12-5

Choosing the appropriate resolution technique

Assessing Yourself

Your Preferred Conflict-Handling Style

Instructions: Indicate how often you do the following—by checking *seldom, sometimes,* or *usually*—when you differ with someone.

	Seldom	Sometimes	Usually
1. I explore our differences, not backing down, but not imposing my view either.	❑	❑	❑
2. I disagree openly, then invite more discussion about our differences.	❑	❑	❑
3. I look for a mutually satisfactory solution.	❑	❑	❑
4. Rather than let the other person make a decision without my input, I make sure I am heard and also that I hear out the other person.	❑	❑	❑
5. I agree to a middle ground rather than look for a completely satisfying solution.	❑	❑	❑
6. I admit I am half wrong rather than explore our differences.	❑	❑	❑
7. I have a reputation for meeting a person halfway.	❑	❑	❑
8. I expect to get out about half of what I really want to say.	❑	❑	❑
9. I give in totally rather than try to change another's opinion.	❑	❑	❑
10. I put aside any controversial aspects of an issue.	❑	❑	❑
11. I agree early on, rather than argue about a point.	❑	❑	❑
12. I give in as soon as the other party gets emotional about an issue.	❑	❑	❑

	Seldom	Sometimes	Usually
13. I try to win the other person over.	❏	❏	❏
14. I work to come out victorious, no matter what.	❏	❏	❏
15. I never back away from a good argument.	❏	❏	❏
16. I would rather win than end up compromising.	❏	❏	❏

SCORING

Total your choices as follows: give yourself five points for "Usually," three points for "sometimes," and one point for "seldom." Then total them for each set of statements grouped as follows:

Set A:	Items 13–16	Set B:	Items 9–12
Set C:	Items 5–8	Set D:	Items 1–4.

WHAT THE ASSESSMENT MEANS

Treat each set separately. A score of 17 or above on any set is considered high; scores of 12–16 are moderately high; scores of 8–11 are moderately low; and scores of 7 or less are considered low. Sets A, B, C, and D represent different conflict-resolution strategies.

A = Forcing: I win, you lose
B = Accommodation: I lose, you win
C = Compromise: Both you and I win some and lose some
D = Collaboration: Both you and I win

Everyone has a basic underlying conflict-handling style. Your highest scoring set(s) in this exercise indicates the strategy or strategies you rely on most.

*A suggestion: Get someone who knows you well to complete this questionnaire, describing how **you** handle conflicts. That person's evaluation of you may not match yours and the differences may be enlightening.*

the *speed* with which you need to resolve the conflict. All other things held constant, if the issue is critical to your unit's success, collaboration is preferred. If sustaining supportive relationships is important, the best approaches, in order of preference, are accommodation, collaboration, compromise, and avoidance. If it's crucial to resolve the conflict as quickly as possible, then force, accommodation, and compromise—in that order—are preferred.

Lastly, you need to consider the *source of the conflict*. The resolution technique that works best depends, to a large degree, on the cause of the conflict. Communication-based conflicts revolve around misinformation and misunderstandings. Such conflicts lend themselves to collaboration. In contrast, conflicts based on personal differences arise out of disparities between the parties' values and personalities. Such conflicts are most susceptible to avoidance because these differences are often deeply entrenched. When supervisors have to resolve conflicts rooted in personal differences, they frequently rely on force—not so much because it placates the parties, but because it works! The third category, structural conflicts, offers opportunities to use most of the conflict approaches.

This process of blending your personal style, your goals, and the source of the conflict should result in identifying the approach or set of approaches most likely to be effective for you in any specific conflict.

STIMULATION TECHNIQUES

What about the other side of conflict management—situations that require supervisors to stimulate conflict? The notion of stimulating conflict is often difficult to accept. For almost all of us, the term conflict has a negative connotation, and the idea of purposely creating conflict seems to be counter to good supervisory practices. Few of us personally enjoy being in conflict situations. Yet there are situations where an increase in conflict is constructive. Figure 12-6 provides a set of questions that can help you to determine whether a situation might justify conflict stimulation. An affirmative answer to one or more of the questions suggests that an increase in conflict might help your unit's performance.

We know a lot more about resolving conflict than about stimulating it. However, the following are some suggestions you might want to consider if you find your department is in need of an increased level of conflict.

USE COMMUNICATION

Politicians are well known for using communication to stimulate conflict. Senior officials float trial balloons by "planting" possible decisions with the media through the infamous "reliable source" route. For example, a

1. Are you surrounded by "yes people"?

2. Are subordinates afraid to admit ignorance and uncertainties to you?

3. Do you and department members concentrate so hard on reaching a compromise that you lose sight of key values, long-term objectives, or the organization's welfare?

4. Do you believe that it is in your best interest to maintain the impression of peace and cooperation in your unit, regardless of the price?

5. Is there an excessive concern in your department not to hurt the feelings of others?

6. Do people in your department believe that popularity is more important for obtaining rewards than competence and high performance?

7. Is your department unduly focused on obtaining consensus for all decisions?

8. Do employees show unusually high resistance to change?

9. Is there a lack of new ideas?

10. Is there an unusually low level of employee turnover?

FIGURE 12-6

Is conflict stimulation needed? An affirmative answer to any or all of these questions suggests that it may be. (*Source:* Adapted from Stephen P. Robbins, "'Conflict Management' and 'Conflict Resolution' Are Not Synonymous Terms," *California Management Review*, Winter 1978, p. 71.)

policy draft is "leaked" to determine public support. However, if the media or the public do not support the intent of the policy, some high-level official will invariably come forward and make a formal statement such as, "At no time was this policy under consideration."

You can use rumours and ambiguous messages to stimulate conflict in your department. Information that some employees might be transferred, that serious budget cuts are coming, or that a layoff is possible can reduce apathy, stimulate new ideas, and force re-evaluation—all positive outcomes as a result of increased conflict.

Questioning can be a useful technique to create constructive conflict. Ainslie White of Precision Biologic says, "I like to play devil's advocate to spur their thoughts." Rather than simply accepting a suggestion, from an employee, you can push back and ask. "Why? Why not do it a different way?".

BRING IN OUTSIDERS

A widely used method for shaking up a stagnant department is to bring in —either by hiring from outside or by internal transfer—individuals whose backgrounds, values, attitudes, or personalities differ from those of present members. One of the major benefits of the diversity movement (encouraging the hiring and promotion of people who are different) is that it can stimulate constructive conflict and improve an organization's performance.

RESTRUCTURE THE DEPARTMENT

We know that structural variables are a source of conflict. It is therefore only logical that supervisors look to structure as a conflict stimulation device. Centralizing decisions, realigning work groups, and increasing formalization are examples of structural devices that disrupt the status quo and act to increase conflict levels. For example, reallocating some duties or responsibilities is likely to bring new perspectives to bear that will generate healthy discussion.

APPOINT A DEVIL'S ADVOCATE AT MEETINGS

Devil's advocate
A person who purposely presents arguments that run counter to those proposed by the majority or against current practices.

A **devil's advocate** is a person who intentionally presents arguments that run counter to those proposed by the majority or against current practices. He or she plays the role of the critic, even to the point of arguing against positions with which he or she actually agrees.

A devil's advocate acts as a check against groupthink and practices that have no better justification than "that's the way we've always done it around here." When thoughtfully listened to, the advocate can improve the quality of group decision making. On the other hand, others in the group often view devil's advocates as time-wasters; appointment of an advocate is almost certain to delay any decision process. Rotating the role at meetings ensures no one is labelled, and all get the benefit of assuming a questioning perspective.

A WORD OF CAUTION

Even though there are situations in which departmental performance can be enhanced through conflict stimulation, it may not be in your best career interests to use stimulation techniques.

If your organizational culture or your immediate superior view any kind of conflict in your department as a negative reflection on your supervisory performance, think twice before stimulating conflict or even allowing low levels of conflict to exist. Where upper management believes that all conflicts are bad, it's not uncommon for lower-level managers and supervisors to be evaluated on how peaceful and harmonious conditions are in their department. While a conflict-free climate tends to create stagnant and apathetic organizations, and eventually lower performance, it is important for your survival to adopt a conflict-management style that's compatible with your organization. In some cases, that might mean using only resolution techniques.

UNDERSTANDING ORGANIZATIONAL POLITICS

"If your organization's senior management views all conflicts as bad, don't use conflict stimulation techniques, even if they improve your department's performance." This summary of the previous paragraph acknowledges the political nature of organizations. You're not always rewarded for doing the right things. In the real world of organizations, the good guys don't always win. Demonstrating openness, trust, objectivity, support, and similar humane qualities in relationships with others doesn't always lead to improved supervisory performance. There will be times when, to get things done or to protect your interests against the manoeuvering of others, you'll have to engage in politicking. Effective supervisors understand the political nature of organizations and adjust their actions accordingly.

WHAT IS POLITICS?

Politics relates to who gets what, when, and how. **Politicking** is the actions you take to influence, or attempt to influence, the distribution of advantages and disadvantages within your organization. Some examples of political behaviour include creating friendly relationships with others in key organizational positions, withholding key information from decision makers, whistle-blowing, spreading rumours, leaking confidential information about organizational activities to the media, exchanging favours with others in the organization for mutual benefit, and lobbying on behalf of or against a particular individual or decision alternative.

One of the most interesting insights about politics is that what constitutes a political action is almost entirely a judgement call. Like beauty, politics is in the eye of the beholder (see Figure 12-7). A behaviour that one person labels "organizational politics" is very likely to be characterized as an instance of "effective management" by another. This doesn't mean that effective management is necessarily political, though in some

Politicking
The actions you take to influence, or attempt to influence, the distribution of advantages and disadvantages within your organization.

cases it might be. Rather, a person's reference point determines what he or she classifies as organizational politics. Take a look at the contrasting labels in Figure 12-7 that are used to describe the same activities.

POLITICAL LABEL		EFFECTIVE MANAGEMENT LABEL
1. Blaming others	or	Fixing responsibility
2. Kissing up	or	Developing working relationships
3. Apple-polishing	or	Demonstrating loyalty
4. Passing the buck	or	Delegating authority
5. Covering your rear	or	Documenting decisions
6. Creating conflict	or	Encouraging change and innovation
7. Forming coalitions	or	Facilitating teamwork
8. Whistleblowing	or	Improving efficiency
9. Nitpicking	or	Meticulous attention to detail
10. Scheming	or	Planning ahead

FIGURE 12-7

Is it politics or effective management? You make the call!

WHY IS THERE POLITICS IN ORGANIZATIONS?

Can you conceive of an organization that is free of politics? It's possible but unlikely.

Organizations are made up of individuals and groups with different values, goals, and interests. This sets up the potential for conflict over resources. Departmental budgets, space allocations, project responsibilities, and salary adjustments are just a few examples of the resources about whose allocation organizational members will disagree.

Resources in organizations are limited, which often turns potential conflict into real conflict. If resources were abundant, then all the various interests within the organization could satisfy their goals. But, because they're limited, not everyone's interests can be provided for. Further, gains by one individual or group are often perceived, accurately or not, as being at the expense of others within the organization. These forces create competition among members for the organization's limited resources.

Maybe the most important factor leading to politics within organizations is the realization that most of the "facts" that are used to allocate the limited resources are open to interpretation. What, for instance, is "good" performance? What's a "good" job? What's an "adequate" improvement? When there is an obvious difference in skill and experience levels between employees, a promotion decision is straightforward. But what if you have to choose between employees with highly similar skill and experience? Then other factors—less objective ones—come into play: attitude, potential, ability to handle stress, and so on. Most managerial decisions in organizations involve tough decisions like these. It is in this large and ambiguous middle ground of organizational life—where the facts *don't* speak for themselves—that politics takes place.

Finally, because most decisions have to be made in a climate of ambiguity—where facts are rarely fully objective, and thus are open to interpretation—people within the organization will use whatever influence they can to taint the facts to support their goals and interests. That, of course, creates motivation for the activities we call politicking.

POLITICS AND YOU

Are you politically astute? That is, do you think you are aware of the political angles to organizational situations, recognizing the way things get done in your organization? Are you then able to act in a way that protects you and your staff, or to achieve what you want using techniques that work? For some people, the thought of being "political" is offensive because it suggests somehow a lack of ethics or getting ahead by being manipulative rather than earning it. Many people are not comfortable with politics and research shows that perceived organizational politics have been negatively correlated with job satisfaction, organizational commitment and job involvement, and positively associated with job stress and turnover intentions.[4]

Take the questionnaire in Assessing Yourself and see how political your score is. In the case at the start of the chapter, Diane Hebert faced an employee who disliked the necessity of being political, playing nice with people who are not doing their job. Diane is a realist who recognizes there are multiple ways to achieve goals without compromising integrity. If you score as not being "political", one of the implications is that you may find the politics in an organization stressful to deal with.

Assessing Yourself

DO YOU HAVE WHAT IT TAKES TO BE POLITICAL?

Are you an individual who likes to play politics? Is it something that you have the ability to do? Even if you prefer not to, can you "play" to protect yourself?

Undoubtedly, politics exist in every organization. Therefore, one of the first steps is understanding your political temperament. Listed below are several statements. Check True or False based on how you feel about the statement most of the time.

	True	False
1. I stay late just to impress my boss.	☐	☐
2. I do not tell others how I do things, so they don't know what I do.	☐	☐
3. I do not use gossip to my advantage.	☐	☐
4. I rarely express my opinion about my organization if my opinions are negative.	☐	☐
5. I go out of my way to make friends with powerful people.	☐	☐
6. I would not raise concerns about someone's ability to do a job, even if we were competing for a promotion.	☐	☐
7. I won't take credit for the work of someone else.	☐	☐
8. I'd tell my boss if a coworker was actively looking for a new job.	☐	☐
9. I would want my name on a group project, even though my effort was minimal.	☐	☐
10. I see nothing wrong in tooting my own horn.	☐	☐
11. I like having decorations all around my work area.	☐	☐
12. I take action only after I am sure it's ethical to do so.	☐	☐
13. I'd be foolish to publicly correct a mistake my boss made.	☐	☐
14. I'd purchase stock in my company even if it was a financial risk.	☐	☐
15. I would not be willing to play the "heavy" or the "big gun" who is brought in to fire people, even if it meant a promotion for me.	☐	☐
16. I want others to fear me more than like me.	☐	☐
17. I would not join in with coworkers making fun of the boss.	☐	☐
18. Getting ahead means promoting my self-interest.	☐	☐
19. I would not want to help a coworker who makes my performance look bad.	☐	☐
20. I think it's important to be friendly with everyone at work—especially those I don't like.	☐	☐

SCORING

Give yourself one point for each response that matches those given below.

1. True	6. False	11. False	16. True
2. True	7. False	12. False	17. True
3. False	8. True	13. True	18. True
4. True	9. True	14. True	19. True
5. True	10. True	15. False	20. True

MAKING SENSE OF THE ASSESSMENT

Your political score on this assessment indicates how likely you are to use politics to gain an advantage in a situation. Scores greater than 14 indicate you have an above-average willingness to use politics to get what you want. Scores from 10 to 13 indicate you use politics mainly to protect yourself - especially from your boss and those you perceive as having power. Scores from 6 to 9 indicate you have a true belief in others - that they are fair, honest, and not likely to mistreat you. Although noteworthy, this score may indicate you don't understand organizational politics, and you may be somewhat naive in assessing the effect politics may have on you. Finally, scores less than 5 indicate an absence of ability to play politics in an organization. Remember, politics isn't always destructive – there's a constructive component that you must use to your advantage.

Source: *Winning Office Politics* by Andrew Dubrin. Copyright © 1990. Reprinted with permission of Prentice Hall.

THE ETHICS OF "PLAYING POLITICS"

Not all political actions are necessarily unethical. To help guide you in differentiating ethical from unethical politicking, there are some questions you should consider (see Figure 12-8, which illustrates a decision tree to guide ethical actions). The three questions are illustrated by the following examples.

The first question you need to answer addresses self-interest versus organizational goals. Ethical actions are consistent with the organization's goals. Spreading untrue rumours about the safety of a new product introduced by your company, in order to make that product's design

FIGURE 12-8

Is a political action
ethical?

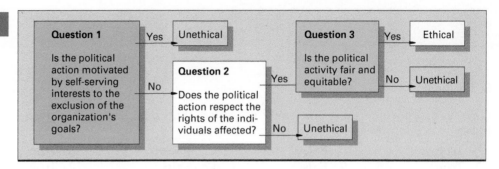

group look bad, is unethical. However, there may be nothing unethical if
you, as a department head, exchange favours with your division's purchasing manager, in order to get a critical contract processed quickly.

The second question is concerned with the rights of other parties. If
you went down to the mail room during your lunch hour and read through
the mail directed to the purchasing manager with the intent of "getting
something on him" so he'd expedite your contract, you'd be acting unethi-
cally. You would have violated the purchasing manager's right to privacy.

The final question you need to address relates to whether the political
activity conforms to standards of equity and justice. If you inflate the performance evaluation of a favoured employee and deflate the evaluation of
a disfavoured employee, and then use these evaluations to justify giving
the former a big raise and nothing to the latter, you have treated the disfavoured employee unfairly.

Here's an example of a situation which a supervisor chose to leave
because he felt that "playing politics" would have been unethical. Haji

FIGURE 12-9

Haji Khurshid stepped
down from a supervi-
sory role because
doing the politically
correct thing compro-
mised his ethics in a
situation.

Khurshid: "I stepped down from my supervisory role because I did not agree with the general manager's way of dealing with things. For example, he did not like one particular employee because he felt he did not show enough respect and he occasionally broke small rules (like a few minutes late). The general manager told me to follow him and find him doing something wrong and fire him. The employee did need improvement but he was a good mechanic and knew the trade. I believe in giving people a chance. The general manager wanted people licking his feet every time he went by and he resented those who didn't, like this mechanic. You cannot always apply your own ethics when you are being dictated to by higher management on how *they* want things to be done." Haji could have protected himself by going along with the general manager. But he chose to quit instead. Which of the ethical questions was being violated in the situation described?

ASSESSING THE POLITICAL LANDSCAPE

Before you consider your political options in any situation, you need to evaluate that situation. The key situational factors are your organization's culture, the power of others, and your own power.

YOUR ORGANIZATION'S CULTURE

The place to begin is an assessment of your organization's culture, to determine which behaviours are desirable and which aren't.

Every organization has a system of shared meaning called its **culture**. This culture is a set of unwritten norms that members of the organization accept and understand, and that guide their actions. For example, some organizations' cultures encourage risk taking, accept conflicts and disagreements, allow employees a great deal of autonomy, and reward members according to performance criteria. But there are cultures that differ by 180 degrees: they punish risk taking, seek harmony and cooperation at any price, minimize opportunities for employees to show initiative, and allocate rewards to people according to such criteria as seniority, effort, or loyalty. The point is that every organization's culture is somewhat different, and if a political strategy is to succeed, it must be compatible with the culture.

> Culture
> A system of shared meaning.

When Diane McArthur was at ServiceOntario, she found her networking strengths particularly important in helping her subordinates when their project moved from the Ministry of Transportation (MTO) to the auspices of the Ministry of Consumer and Commercial Relations (MCCR). Whereas the MTO was filled with engineers and had a methodical, rule-based culture, the MCCR was very small, not dominated by any one profession, and had a more organic culture. In the MCCR, actions succeeded on the basis of relationships as much as rules or structures.

This shift was a challenge for Diane's staff because, although very connected with each other, they did not know people in the new ministry. They needed multiple points of contact to get their jobs done and it was not obvious what they were or how to find out. Diane's skill in getting to know people turned out to be important in the MCCR. She picked up information and got to know people. Consequently, she could link her project people with the appropriate people in the ministry.

THE POWER OF OTHERS

People are either powerful or they're not, right? Wrong! On some issues, a person may be very powerful. Yet that same person may be relatively powerless on other issues. What you need to do, therefore, is determine which individuals or groups will be powerful in a given situation.

Some people will have influence as a result of their formal position in the organization. So that is probably the best place to begin your power assessment. What decision or issue do you want to influence? Who has formal authority to affect that issue? The answer to that question is only the beginning. After determining who has formal authority, consider others—individuals, coalitions, or departments—who may have a vested interest in the decision's outcome. Who might gain or lose as a result of one choice being selected over another? This helps to identify the power players—those motivated to engage in politicking. It also pinpoints your likely adversaries.

Now you need to specifically assess the power of each player or group of players. In addition to each one's formal authority, evaluate the resources each controls and his or her location in the organization. The control of scarce and important resources is a source of power in organizations. Control and access to key information, expert knowledge, and possession of special skills are examples of resources that may be scarce and important to the organization; hence, they become potential means of influencing organizational decisions. In addition, being in the right place in the organization can be a source of power. This explains, for example, the frequent power of secretaries. They are often in the direct flow of key information and control the access of others to their bosses.

Assess your boss's influence in any power analysis. What is his or her position on the issue under concern? For, against, or neutral? If it's for or against, how intense is your boss's stand? What is your boss's power status in the organization—strong or weak? Answers to these questions can help you assess whether the support or opposition of your boss will be relevant.

YOUR POWER

After looking at others' power, assess your own power base. What is your personal power? What power does your supervisory position in the organization provide? Where do you stand relative to others who hold power?

Your power can come from several sources. If you've got a charismatic personality, for instance, you can exert power because others will want to know your position on issues, your arguments will often be persuasive, and your position is likely to carry considerable weight in others' decisions. Another frequent source of power for supervisors is access to important information that others in the organization need.

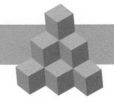

Building a Supervisory Skill

BECOMING POLITICALLY SMART

ABOUT THE SKILL

Although there are few clear-cut ways to avoid getting involved in office politics, here are some suggestions that we offer to help you become more politically smart. These recommendations, however, are not designed to teach you how to take advantage of someone else or of a given situation. Rather, they are intended to help you develop a personal profile, which can assist you if you find yourself in a political situation.

STEPS IN PRACTISING THE SKILL

1. **Frame arguments in terms of organizational goals.** Effective politicking requires covering up self-interest. No matter that your objective is self-serving; all the arguments you marshal in support of it must be framed in terms of the benefits that will accrue to the organization. People whose actions appear to blatantly further their own interests at the expense of the organization's are almost universally denounced, are likely to lose influence, and often suffer the ultimate penalty of being expelled from the organization.

2. **Portray the proper image.** What others think about you is important to your political success. You need to understand the organization's culture and act accordingly. Accept and demonstrate the values, norms, and behaviours that the organization wants. Doing so shows that you know what is important for organizational survival. Portraying the proper image also increases the likelihood that when you do raise an issue, others may give it more legitimacy. An "outcast" who's always complaining rarely gets an audience—even if he or she is right.

3. **Gain control of organizational resources.** The control of organizational resources that are scarce and important is a source of power. Knowledge and expertise are particularly effective resources to control. They make you more valuable to the organization, and therefore

more likely to gain security, advancement, and a receptive audience for your ideas.

4. **Make yourself appear indispensable.** Since we're dealing with appearances rather than objective facts, you can enhance your power by appearing to be indispensable. That is, you don't have to *really* be indispensable, as long as key people in the organization believe that you are. If the prime decision makers believe there is no ready substitute for what you are giving the organization, they are likely to go to great lengths to ensure that your desires are satisfied. How do you make yourself appear indispensable? The most effective means is to develop expertise (through experience, contacts, secret techniques, and natural talents) that is perceived as critical to the organization's operations and that key decision makers believe no one else possesses to the extent that you do. Another way to appear indispensable is to create strong relationships with outsiders to the organization (e.g. key customers, key people linked to government approval).

5. **Be visible.** Because the evaluation of supervisory effectiveness has a substantial subjective component, it is important that your boss and those in power in the organization be made aware of your contribution. If you are fortunate enough to have responsibilities that bring your accomplishments to the attention of others, it may not be necessary to take direct measures to increase your visibility. But your department may handle activities that are low in visibility, or your specific contribution may be indistinguishable because you're part of a team endeavour. In such cases—without creating the image of a braggart—you'll want to call attention to yourself by giving progress reports to your boss and others, being seen at social functions, being active in your professional associations, developing powerful allies who speak positively about your accomplishments, and similar tactics. Of course, the skilled politician actively and successfully lobbies to get those projects that will increase his or her visibility.

6. **Find a mentor.** Nothing helps you avoid land mines better than someone who knows where the land mines are. Getting them to navigate your path makes things so much safer. In organizations, this navigator is called a mentor. A mentor is someone who is usually a more experienced and more senior member of the organization. The mentor is usually already part of the "power" group, and his or her role is to be your support system. Mentors are also people who can vouch for you in the organization. They often are able to get you exposure to the power-brokers in the organization, and provide advice on how to

effectively manoeuvre through the system. From a political point of view, a mentor can act as a sounding-board for you, providing vital suggestions and feedback on how to survive and succeed.

7. **Develop powerful allies.** It helps to have powerful people in your camp. In addition to a mentor, you can cultivate contacts with potentially influential people above you and among other supervisors. They can provide you with important information that may not be available through normal channels. Additionally, there will be times when decisions will be made by those with the greatest support. Sometimes—though not always—there is strength in numbers. Having powerful allies can provide you with a coalition of support if and when you need it.

8. **Avoid tarnished individuals.** In almost every organization, there are fringe members whose status is questionable. Their performance and/or loyalty is under close scrutiny. Such individuals, while they are under the microscope, are "tainted." Carefully keep your distance from them. We all tend to judge others by the company they keep. Given the reality that effectiveness has a large subjective component, your own effectiveness might be called into question if you are perceived as being too closely associated with tainted people.

9. **Support your boss.** Your immediate future is in the hands of your current boss. Since he or she evaluates your performance, you will typically want to do whatever is necessary to have your boss on your side. You should make every effort to help your boss succeed and look good. Provide support if he or she is under siege and spend the time to find out what criteria will be used to assess your effectiveness. Don't undermine your boss. Don't speak negatively of him or her to others. If the individual is competent, visible, and in possession of a power base, she or he is likely to be on the way up in the organization. By being perceived as supportive, you increase the likelihood that you will be pulled along.

Gaining political power and building a power base in an organization is often fostered with the help of a mentor. In the past, however, most of those who were "supported" by an experienced, senior member of the organization often shared something in common. That is, they were usually male and white. But what about women and people of colour? What opportunities lie ahead for them to find and gain this support?

Finding or getting a mentor is rarely easy. In fact, more often than not, you are approached by the other person. What can serve as the "attraction" to bring the two of you together? In the past, it was something a potential mentor saw in you—which was often something they saw in themselves years ago. But how can a male properly relate to a female or vice versa? How can individuals from different races or national origins identify with each other when there's no foundation of commonality between them? Unquestionably, these can be major issues—many of which we've highlighted in previous chapters. Organizations are attempting to bridge this gap. Many recognize that leaving it up to nature just won't work so they establish a formal program that encourages senior members to take junior members under their wing. Even when such programs exist, other problems still may arise. For example, is the male supervisor mentoring a younger female employee exhibiting appropriate mentoring behaviour, or is she getting special treatment because she's a woman? If the two of them develop a close, personal work relationship is there a risk of them crossing the line into sexual harassment?

Despite the potential difficulties diversity offers for mentoring, the fact remains that each of us needs this support. Therefore, if someone doesn't approach you, you can choose to seek a mentor yourself. In either case, being mentored requires work on your part. That effort will only be magnified when your mentor is someone who has personal attributes different from yours.

What do you think about this diversity issue?

FROM CONCEPTS TO SKILLS

NEGOTIATION

As a supervisor, your success in resolving conflict and playing politics will be influenced by your negotiating skills. We know that lawyers and car salespeople spend a lot of time negotiating, but so do supervisors. They have to negotiate salaries for incoming employees, bargain over budgets, work out differences with associates, and resolve conflicts with subordinates. This section will help you to improve your negotiating skills.

ASSESSING YOURSELF: DO YOU UNDERSTAND WHAT IT TAKES TO BE AN EFFECTIVE NEGOTIATOR?

For each of the following statements, indicate your degree of agreement or disagreement by circling one of the five responses.

SA = Strongly agree
A = Agree
U = Undecided
D = Disagree
SD = Strongly disagree

1. I believe everything is negotiable.	SA	A	U	D	SD
2. In every negotiation, someone wins and someone loses.	SA	A	U	D	SD
3. I try to get as much information as possible about the other party prior to negotiation.	SA	A	U	D	SD
4. The other party's initial offer shapes my negotiating strategy.	SA	A	U	D	SD
5. I try to open negotiations with a positive action such as offering a small concession.	SA	A	U	D	SD
6. I build an image of success by focusing on winning as much as possible in every bargaining situation.	SA	A	U	D	SD

SCORING DIRECTIONS AND KEY

For questions 1, 3, and 5, give yourself five points for **SA**, four points for **A**, three points for **U**, two points for **D**, and one point for **SD**. For questions 2, 4, 5 and 6, reverse the scoring; that is, give yourself one point for **SA**, two points for **A**, and so forth.

A score of 25 or above suggests you have a basic understanding of how to be an effective negotiator. Scores of 19 to 24 indicate you have room for improvement. Those who scored 18 or less should find the following discussion and exercise very valuable in improving their overall supervisory effectiveness.

SKILL BASICS

Negotiation
A process in which two or more parties exchange goods or services and attempt to agree upon the exchange rate for them.

What is **negotiation**? It's a process in which two or more parties exchange goods or services and attempt to agree upon the exchange rate for them. For our purposes, we'll also use the term interchangeably with bargaining.

BARGAINING STRATEGIES

There are two general approaches to negotiation: *distributive bargaining* and *integrative bargaining*.

Distributive bargaining
Zero-sum negotiations where any gain by one is at the expense of the other.

You see a used car advertised for sale online. It appears to be just what you're looking for. You go out to see the car. It's great and you want it. The owner tells you the asking price. You don't want to pay that much. The two of you then negotiate over the price. The negotiating process you are engaging in is called **distributive bargaining**. Its most distinctive feature is that it operates under zero-sum conditions. That is, any gain you make is at the other's expense, and vice versa. Every dollar you can get the seller to cut from the car's price is a dollar you save. Conversely, every dollar more he or she can get from you comes at your expense. Thus the essence of distributive bargaining is negotiating over who gets what share of a fixed pie.

Probably the most widely cited example of distributive bargaining is in labour-management negotiations over wages and benefits (see Chapter 15). Typically, labour's representatives come to the bargaining table determined to get as much as they can from management. Because every cent more that labour negotiates increases management's costs, each party bargains aggressively and often treats the other as an opponent who must be defeated.

Figure 12-10 depicts the distributive bargaining strategy. Parties A and B represent the two negotiators. Each has a target point that defines what he or she would like to achieve. Each also has a resistance point, which marks the lowest outcome that is acceptable—the point below which he or she would break off negotiations rather than accept a less favourable settlement. The area between their resistance points is the settlement range. As long as there is some overlap in their aspiration ranges, there exists a settlement area where each one's aspirations can be met.

When engaged in distributive bargaining, your tactics should focus on trying to get your opponent to agree to your specific target point or to get as close to it as possible. Examples of such tactics are persuading your opponent of the impossibility of getting to his or her target point and the advisability of accepting a settlement near yours; arguing that your target is fair, while your opponent's isn't; and attempting to get your opponent to feel emotionally generous toward you and thus to accept an outcome close to your target point.

Now let's look at **integrative bargaining**. Assume a sales representative for a women's sportswear manufacturer has just closed a $15 000 order from a small clothing retailer. The sales rep calls in the order to her firm's credit department. She is told that the firm can't approve credit to this customer because of a past slow-pay record. The next day, the sales rep and the firm's credit supervisor meet to discuss the problem. The sales rep doesn't want to lose the business. Neither does the credit

Integrative bargaining Bargaining under the assumption that there is at least one settlement option that can create a win-win solution.

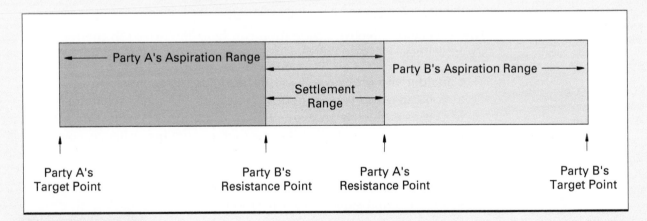

FIGURE 12-10
Staking out the bargaining zone

supervisor, but he also doesn't want to get stuck with an uncollectable debt. The two openly review their options. After considerable discussion, they agree on a solution that meets both their needs: the credit supervisor will approve the sale, but the clothing store's owner will provide a bank guarantee that will assure payment if the bill isn't paid within 60 days.

The sales-credit negotiation is an example of **integrative bargaining**. In contrast to distributive bargaining, integrative problem solving operates under the assumption that there is at least one settlement that can create a win-win solution.

In general, integrative bargaining is preferable to distributive bargaining. Why? Because the former builds long-term relationships and facilitates working together in the future. It bonds negotiators and allows each to leave the bargaining table feeling that he or she has achieved a victory. Distributive bargaining, on the other hand, leaves one party a loser. It tends to build animosities and deepen divisions between people who have to work together on an ongoing basis.

Why, then, don't we see more integrative bargaining in organizations? The answer lies in the conditions necessary for this type of negotiation to succeed. These conditions include openness with information and frankness between parties; sensitivity on the part of each party to the other's needs; the ability to trust one another; and a willingness by both parties to maintain flexibility. Because many organizational cultures and interpersonal relationships are not characterized by openness, trust, and flexibility, it isn't surprising that negotiations often take on a win-at-any-cost dynamic.

BECOMING AN EFFECTIVE NEGOTIATOR

The essence of effective negotiation can be summarized in the following six guidelines.

1. **Consider the other party's situation.** Acquire as much information as you can about your opponent's interests and goals. What are his or her needs and likely strategy? This information will help you understand your opponent's behaviour, predict his or her responses to your offers, and frame solutions in terms of his or her interests. Additionally, when you can anticipate your opponent's position, you are better equipped to counter his or her arguments with the facts and figures that support your position.

2. **Have a concrete strategy.** Treat negotiation like a chess match. Expert chess players have a strategy. They know ahead of time how they will respond to any given situation. How strong is your situation

and how important is the issue? Are you willing to split differences to achieve an early solution? If the issue is very important to you, is your position strong enough to let you play hardball and show little or no willingness to compromise? These are questions you should address before you begin bargaining.

3. **Begin with a positive overture.** Studies on negotiation show that concessions tend to be reciprocated and lead to agreements. As a result, begin bargaining with a positive overture—perhaps a small concession—and then reciprocate your opponent's concessions.

4. **Address problems, not personalities.** Concentrate on the negotiation issues, not on the personal characteristics of your opponent. When negotiations get tough, avoid the tendency to attack your opponent. It's your opponent's ideas or position that you disagree with, not him or her personally. Separate the people from the problem, and don't personalize differences.

5. **Pay little attention to initial offers.** Treat an initial offer as merely a point of departure. Everyone has to have an initial position. These initial offers tend to be extreme and idealistic. Treat them as such.

6. **Emphasize win-win solutions.** Bargainers often assume that their gain must come at the expense of the other party. As noted with integrative bargaining, that needn't be the case. There are often win-win solutions. But assuming a zero-sum game means missed opportunities for trade-offs that could benefit both sides. So if conditions are supportive, look for an integrative solution. Frame options in terms of your opponent's interests and look for solutions that can allow your opponent, as well as yourself, to declare a victory.

APPLYING YOUR SKILLS

Break into groups of three. You will each take on one of the roles described below and attempt to negotiate a solution as to where you will reinvest your company's money. You are three partners in a training firm that specializes in providing experiential events for corporate training, customized "gaming," outdoor challenges for team building—such as high-ropes challenges and Outward Bound-like events. Your four-year-old business has "taken off" recently. Your staff has grown to 10 in the last year (all trainers on contract, however; none are partners like you three). The company has opened offices in Burlington, Vancouver, and Edmonton. Previously the three of you basically worked out of your homes.

You are meeting with your two partners to discuss how you should use the recent profit from the company. You have all agreed to reinvest the money in the growing company but you have not discussed how best to do so.

Person 1 Your feelings are that you need to lure in a really top trainer/marketer to be a partner in the firm. The three of you are spread too thin now that you are offering your services across Canada and even taking on some international contracts. You need another major player who's good at getting and keeping new clients (so can handle the sales end of the business) and can also be an effective facilitator in many of your training activities. This "double duty" is exactly what the three of you have been doing so successfully for four years. But, as the old adage goes: Be careful of what you wish, as your wish may come true. And your business's success has meant no time for any of you other than work. It's now time to share the load.

If you did take on a new partner, his or her deal would be the same as for the rest of you—he or she would be paid based on the work he or she brings in as well as a straight salary for facilitation work. But you'll need money to recruit the right person, to provide training, and to set up the requisite office. Also, you think you need to offer the right person a decent base salary to start with for some security. The candidates you're thinking of will need to be lured away from some pretty good money at their present employer.

Your company's success depends on the people within it. As the company grows, you think it critical to grow the right "talent" along with it.

Person 2 Your feelings are that you need to hire some support staff. You are a company of trainers who are constantly on the move and you have no "secretaries" or support people to staff the offices. You make do with voicemail and email, and the partners are responsible for picking up and distributing messages. This has caused some problems because the partners are often too busy to regularly respond to contacts. Delays have caused some problems with customers. The offices really exist simply for a mailing address and a place to hold meetings when clients prefer to meet at your company's premises rather than their own. There is no live person at any of the offices on a continuous basis.

You think that a live presence is needed in each office to create a professional image, answer the phone, respond to questions when possible, ensure the right partner or contract trainer is informed in a timely manner, and also handle administrative details such as invoices and report production.

Person 3 You believe that the company needs to become much more digitally sophisticated. Money needs to be spent on updating your website. So much could be done to make it into an effective marketing tool rather than simply providing basic information. You also believe there is huge potential for the company to use social media to enhance the online presence of the company and to attract potential employees and potential clients. But none of you are experts in this. You would love to bring in a consulting firm to work with the company on the website and on the potential use of social media. They might also be able to help set up a system for digitally archiving all the project work. This could be used to make case studies for the website, including testimonials from happy clients.

# UNDERSTANDING THE BASICS

SUMMARY

This summary is organized by the Learning Objectives.

1. Conflict is a process in which one party consciously interferes in the goal-achievement efforts of another party.
2. Conflicts generally come from one of three sources: communication differences, structural differences, or personal differences.
3. The five basic techniques for resolving conflict are avoidance, accommodation, force, compromise, and collaboration.
4. A supervisor could stimulate conflict by communicating ambiguous messages, bringing in outsiders with different backgrounds or personalities, restructuring the department, or appointing a devil's advocate.
5. Politicking is the actions you can take to influence, or attempt to influence, the distribution of advantages and disadvantages within your department.
6. Politics exist in organizations because individuals have different values, goals, and interests; because organizational resources are limited; because the criteria for allocating the limited resources are ambiguous; and because individuals seek influence so they can shape the criteria to support their goals and interests.
7. The situational factors that determine political options are 1. your organization's culture, 2. the power of others, and 3. your own power.
8. To develop and improve your political skills, you should frame arguments in terms of organizational goals; develop the right image; gain control of organizational resources; make yourself appear indispensable; be visible; get a mentor; develop powerful allies; avoid "tainted" members; and support your boss.
9. Distributive bargaining creates a win-lose situation because the object of negotiation is treated as fixed in amount. Integrative bargaining treats available resources as variable, and hence creates the potential for win-win solutions.

KEY TERMS AND CONCEPTS

Accommodation

Avoidance

Collaboration

Compromise

Conflict

Conflict management

Culture

Devil's advocate

Distributive bargaining

Forcing

Integrative bargaining

Negotiation

Paraphrasing

Politicking

Silo mentality

REVIEWING YOUR KNOWLEDGE

1. How can conflict benefit an organization?
2. How can an organization's structure create conflict?
3. What is conflict management?
4. When should you avoid conflict? When should you seek compromise?
5. What is a devil's advocate? How does an advocate affect conflict in a department?
6. Can an organization be free of politics? Explain.
7. Is it unethical to "play politics"?
8. How do you assess another person's power in an organization?
9. Why does effective politicking require covering up self-interest?
10. How can increased visibility enhance a person's power?

CASE 12.A

Conflict and Politics in Entrepreneurial Organizations

Vivian[1] has been a manager under several entrepreneurs, starting off in her family's business and now working in a dynamic not-for-profit organization. The experiences have led her to believe that organizations run by entrepreneurial types have a lot in common whether they are for profit or not. The strong personalities drive action and success. But they can also create conflict.

The family business was clearly her parents' baby. Despite growing significantly in size and value, it remained a centralized operation with all decisions made at the top. "My parents were very protective of their position. My father said 'Only you and I will come up with any good ideas, the staff won't.' I fought against this and it was a source of tension. We built a successful company with great people but dad didn't value the staff. Because it's a very proprietary industry, he had to be very protective of his designs and tools. There's no sharing in the industry and he didn't want anything confidential getting outside.

When I worked with another entrepreneur in a different industry, it was a growth experience for me to see how a person operated who did value staff and who constantly sought external advice as well. I've tried to introduce this approach in my current position in the not-for-profit organization but my director has resisted. When I mention putting together a consultation group from the community to get outside input, she says, "good idea", but it never happens. It has to be her idea or pitched to her in just the right way. She might be into it if she experienced it but I don't know that she'd allow it to happen."

Vivian's current boss (the executive director of a not-for-profit community organization) has no related education or training but is a visionary who saw a need, created an organization to meet the need, and has led the organization through 25 years, as it has consistently grown in impact. Vivian notes that entrepreneurs like her father and this executive director have vision and ambition but no management training. "They started from the grass roots but they don't always make the best managers. They don't always follow systems and structures—they've been successful because they've been willing to step outside of the box. Also, they tend to jump from one thing to another. Plans change. You can turn on a dime in a small organization. It's dynamic but doesn't support structures for people management or smart growth strategy. It can be very fly-by-the-seat-of-your-pants. They don't follow best practice. They follow their gut. Instinct drives visibility and growth in both for-profit and not-for-profit but it can make for unstable staff structures.

There's no set structure. Everything's always two steps ahead of the resources to support it. It's great if you're a person who wants to sink their teeth in and run with projects but can mean not a lot of accountability – this can be both good and bad. Then it becomes crucial you hire the right people. Without specific direction or structure, some people are left flailing. It's a sink-or-swim environment. If you're a swimmer, it's great because you get a sense of accomplishment. You can move ahead in projects without a lot of consulting or formal reporting. But there are people in that environment who are not excited to step up to the challenge and see the lack of structure as poor management. They're stressed and demotivated. They sit back and do nothing because they're not being told what to do."

For those whose jobs rely on clear, consistent systems, life can be tough in this environment. "The managing director is the executive director's polar opposite. They butt heads explosively. She realizes she needs his approach but sometimes will discount his input and do what

---

[1] The names and details of this case have been changed to protect confidentiality.

she wants. He wants things to be organized and planned and a budget set at the beginning of the year and not changed. The executive director will play a shell game regarding budgeting and managing money. She focuses on what excites her, and will pull money out of an area for another project that comes along. It's okay to respond to opportunities but this is to an extreme. It can work to your advantage if you want to pitch a project, if it excites her and you can get her buy-in."

RESPONDING TO THIS CASE

1. Identify the sources of conflict described.
2. Identify the conflict resolution techniques observed in the case.
3. Explain the steps the executive director could take to reduce and manage conflict in her organization. How likely is it that she would undertake these steps?
4. Assess the political landscape of the community organization. What does this indicate about options open to employees? Is the political landscape at the family business any different?
5. If you worked for the community organization and had a fabulous idea, outline how you could apply the "politically smart" steps to convincing the executive director of your idea.

CASE 12.B

Joe and Catalino Deal with Angry Clients

Supervisors of front-line service employees are often drawn into dealing with customer/employee interactions that have gone wrong. The supervisor is in the unenviable position of trying to win over an angry customer plus avoid humiliating the employee, who likely did his or her best to handle the situation in the first place. Catalino Misenas, sales manager at Russell Food Equipment in Vancouver, and Joe Puiia, supervisor at the HRDC office in Summerside, PEI, describe their experiences.

"When I deal with an angry client, I find that often all they really need is attention and having someone listen to them. I get them away from the open office into a quiet place. I might say, 'Gee, I don't blame you for being upset. Please tell me what happened.' Then I do some creative fact-finding and allow them to vent. There are a lot of grey areas in policies and regulations, like who is eligible to join a skills development program. So I explain the policies and programs, and I spend a lot of time in definitions, for example, defining strict eligibility," says Joe Puiia.

Catalino's approach is similar. "I thrive on the goal of making an upset customer my best customer. I really listen to what the customer is saying. I repeat what he says and probe what the concern is. Once I've listened and grasped it, I can deal with it. I know I have to deal with a problem right away. For example, I learned that a customer was upset about a whipped-cream dispenser not being delivered—there had been a misunderstanding between the customer and the sales rep. I called her myself and apologized for the error, saying we would rectify the situation immediately. She was happy."

RESPONDING TO THIS CASE

1. What principles and techniques of conflict management are evident in their handling of these customer conflicts?
2. How can a supervisor both satisfy the customer yet treat the employee who dealt with the customer as a competent professional? Consider the supervisors you have seen in this type of situation—how successful were they, and what was the impact?
3. Suppose a supervisor pacifies a customer by incorrectly blaming the employee, saying the employee was out of line and had no right to say what he or she did. Is this unethical? Under what grounds?
4. How can the skills Catalino and Joe illustrate above in dealing with customers also be potentially useful to them in dealing with the internal politics of their organizations?

13

MANAGING CHANGE AND STRESS

Courtesy of Denkou Images/Alamy

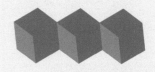

LEARNING OBJECTIVES

After reading this chapter, you should be able to:

1. Contrast Lewin's view with contemporary views of change.
2. Identify the forces for change in today's organizations.
3. Explain why people resist change.
4. Identify ways supervisors can reduce resistance to change.
5. Define stress.
6. Explain what brings about employee stress.
7. Describe two models of stress.

CHAPTER OUTLINE

Jamie Dumas has been incorporating therapeutic programming at the City of Mississauga fitness centre where she is a supervisor, a stressful but exciting change for Jamie and her staff.

As the supervisor of the fitness centre at the City of Mississauga's Huron Park facility, one might think Jamie Dumas's job would be predictable: schedule classes as needed; hire fitness instructors, weight room exercise counsellors, and personal trainers; keep an eye on things to make sure all is going well. However, the role of the community centre is evolving and so is Jamie's job. Specifically, there has been a big push to recognize therapeutic programming as a line of business.

"We do offer traditional programs with fitness classes, and hospitals take care of rehabilitation, but there are gaps for residents who come out of hospital (e.g. relearning how to walk), then come home and have nothing to do; we're trying to fill the gap to continue the process of recovery. It started with the aquatics program and the therapeutic pool we built in our last renovation. Now the fitness side is also playing a part. We've been really successful–developing programs for fall prevention, chronic obstructive pulmonary disease, diabetes, rehab for hips and knees (both pre and post surgery); also dealing with an aging population that needs to stay active."

For Jamie, "the most difficult thing is finding staff qualified and able to deal with both the fitness side and the medical side. Fitness certifications are good but don't touch the recovery area; we get medical support to help train staff, but new certificates are really needed to cover the two areas. To get qualified staff, we talked to the Canadian Centre for Activity in Aging (CCAA) to see if they have anything that will meet our needs in terms of training. They did in fall prevention, but not regarding chronic disease. We dealt with governing bodies in the fitness area, and hospital contacts to get some in-house training. We have to build the skills rather than hire for them. Luckily, staff are interested in learning because it's a marketable skill."

Jamie has also had to engage in training herself to become more familiar with how to deal with the therapeutic area, taking training with the CCAA, becoming an older adult specialist in the fitness area, and getting involved in stroke symposiums and conferences on topics like older adults. Through the local health system, Jamie is now sitting on a board with a group of community specialists focused on chronic disease prevention, representing the recreation side.

This move into therapeutic programming has been stressful for Jamie. "There are no guidelines. We're breaking new ground, and there's no one to hold your hand. At the same time it is exciting because there is a lot of brainstorming. Within the organization there are tensions around it. We know it's the right thing for the community but there's huge indecision between the budget process, business planning and community needs; it's a challenge to support the programming financially and market or communicate it to bring people in. We are on a user pay system so we need to recover our costs. Many people with disabilities are on a fixed income yet the equipment is expensive. And so are the supports needed. For example, we did a Stroke Survivors class in partnership with Trillium hospital. It ran two times a week and needed a staff to student ratio of 1:5 instead of the regular 1:20. The diabetes class we offer requires an extended class time of two hours instead of one because we need to test glucose and blood pressure before and after the class.

Now we're at a crux: how far do we go into the medical side? We're not rehab specialists or physiotherapists but there's a gap and we can be instrumental in keeping people healthy."

Jamie's organization and her department are changing with the needs of the community they serve. This affects her role and all her staff. Jamie is expected to manage the change skilfully, dealing with implementation challenges through effective problem-solving, and ensuring staff are prepared and supportive. Effectively managing change and the accompanying stresses is a component of most supervisory roles. In this chapter, we will address the typical sources of change, the way people react to change, and how supervisors and organizations can ease the experience for all. Then we look at stress - what it is and what can do done about it.

FORCES FOR CHANGE

NEW TECHNOLOGIES

Smartphones, e-mail, and computers are technological changes that have affected many jobs. If you talk to supervisors at Canada Post, they'll tell you how automated readers and sorters have changed the jobs of those responsible for sorting the mail. Take a look at today's automobile assembly lines. Thousands of jobs on these assembly lines have been replaced with automated robots. Few jobs today have not been directly affected by technological change.

The introduction of new equipment, tools, methods, automated machinery, and computerization allows employees and supervisors to do their jobs better and faster. We can expect that technological changes will continue to modify the way work is done. Most importantly, because these technological changes tend to be focused at the operating level, supervisors will have the primary responsibility for introducing and managing these change efforts.

Technological changes have made a huge impact on the work of Garth Dallman, project manager and assistant production manager at Research Casting International (RCI), one of the world's largest providers of museum technical services, including creating dinosaur exhibits:

"There are many aspects of technology that have changed our job. Thirteen years ago when I started, there was no use of digital photos, email, and the internet. We have fantastic research tools at hand now, get more accurate images, can liaise easily with paleontologists, they can Photoshop back with changes. Getting in touch, sending pictures and getting feedback used to take a lot of time. One of the things that has had a big impact on our business is laser scanning and rapid prototype printing. At one point if you had a left femur and wanted a right femur, you would have to sculpt and texture it. Now you can scan the left, mirror and print it and have an exact replica except the opposite side. So the role of sculptors is being reduced but, from a paleontologist's view, it's more accurate. By laser scanning fossils, now we can send data anywhere and anytime. And we can combine information from different locations. For example, we've been asked to produce an alamosaurus for a museum in Dallas, which is interesting because they have some parts, Texas has some and the Smithsonian has others. We will scan data from all three areas, scale it so it's the same size and cut bones to the appropriate size." Asked for advice on handling change, Garth's response is: "It may be a cliché, but stay open to change, embrace new technologies and be a lifelong learner."

FIGURE 13-2

Garth Dallman works with ancient bones using highly sophisticated technology to reconstruct skeletons.

ENVIRONMENTAL DYNAMICS

Changes that occur outside the organization can affect supervisors. These changes include new government regulations, changing social and political trends, new tax laws, changes in labour market conditions, and new strategies taken by competitors. For example, when human rights legislation was passed, many supervisors had to fill out additional reports, modify historical hiring criteria, and participate in the redesign of physical facilities to reduce barriers for people with disabilities. Similarly, the trend toward supervisors having wider spans of control has been largely driven by global competition and the need for organizations to cut costs.

Jamie Dumas's story at the start of the chapter describes changes based on shifts in the needs of the organization's community clientele. Another change faced by many managers is dealing with the implications of the new laws in several provinces regarding psychological harassment or bullying.

INTERNAL FORCES

In addition to technological and environmental factors, internal forces can stimulate the need for change. These internal forces include changes in the organization's overall strategy, reorganizations, changes in the composition of the workforce, introduction of new equipment, and the need to modify employee attitudes. Case 13.B at the end of the chapter describes a supervisor terminating everyone in her department because of an organizational strategy that moved jobs out of North America to eastern Europe.

An organization's workforce is rarely static. Its composition changes in terms of age, education, gender, and ethnicity. The increasing number of women and minorities in the workforce has required many supervisors to become more sensitive to diversity and to change some of their previous practices. The introduction of new equipment represents another internal force for change. Employees may have their jobs redesigned, need to undergo training to operate the new equipment, or be required to establish new interaction patterns within their formal work group. Employee attitudes, such as increased job dissatisfaction, may lead to increased absenteeism, more voluntary resignations, and even strikes. Such events will, in turn, often lead to changes in supervisory practices.

HOW READY ARE YOU FOR COPING WITH WORK-RELATED CHANGE?

Instructions: Listed below are some statements a supervisor made about working in a large, successful corporation. If your job had these characteristics, how would you react to them? After each statement are five letters, A to E. Circle the letter that best describes how you think you would react according to the following scale:

A I would enjoy this very much; it's completely acceptable.
B This would be enjoyable and acceptable most of the time.
C I'd have no reaction to this feature one way or another, or it would be about equal parts enjoyable and unpleasant.
D This feature would be somewhat unpleasant for me.
E This feature would be very unpleasant for me.

1. I regularly spend 30 to 40 per cent of my time in meetings.　　　　A　B　C　D　E

2. Eighteen months ago, my job did not exist, and I have been essentially inventing it as I go along.　　　　A　B　C　D　E

3. The responsibilities I either assume or am assigned consistently exceed the authority I have for discharging them.　　　　A　B　C　D　E

4. At any given moment in my job, I have on the average about a dozen emails to be returned.　　　　A　B　C　D　E

5. There seems to be very little relationship in my job between the quality of my performance and my actual pay and benefits.　　　　A　B　C　D　E

6. About two weeks a year of formal supervisory training is needed in my job just to stay current.　　　　A　B　C　D　E

7. There is no objective way to measure my effectiveness.

    A   B   C   D   E

8. I report to three different bosses for different aspects of my job, and each has an equal say in my performance appraisal.

    A   B   C   D   E

9. On average, about a third of my time is spent dealing with unexpected emergencies that force all scheduled work to be postponed.

    A   B   C   D   E

10. When I have to have a meeting of the people who report to me, it takes my secretary most of a day to find a time when we are all available, and even then, I have yet to have a meeting where everyone is present for the entire meeting.

    A   B   C   D   E

11. The degree I earned in preparation for this type of work is now obsolete, d I probably an should go back for another degree.

    A   B   C   D   E

12. My job requires that I absorb 100–200 pages per week of technical materials.

    A   B   C   D   E

13. I am out of town overnight at least one night per week.

    A   B   C   D   E

14. My department is so interdependent with several other departments in the company that all distinctions about which departments are responsible for which tasks are quite arbitrary.

    A   B   C   D   E

15. I will probably get a promotion in about a year to a job in another department that has most of these same characteristics.

    A   B   C   D   E

16. During the period of my employment here, either the entire company or the department I worked in has been reorganized every year or so.   A   B   C   D   E

17. While there are several possible promotions I can see ahead of me, I have no real career path in an objective sense.   A   B   C   D   E

18. While there are several possible promotions I can see ahead of me, I think I have no realistic chance of getting to the top levels of the company.   A   B   C   D   E

19. While I have many ideas about how to make things work better, I have no direct influence on either the business policies or the personnel policies that govern my department.   A   B   C   D   E

20. My company has recently put in an "assessment centre" where I and all other supervisors will be required to go through an extensive battery of psychological tests to assess our potential.   A   B   C   D   E

21. My company is a defendant in an antitrust suit, and if the case comes to trial, I will probably have to testify about some decisions that were made a few years ago.   A   B   C   D   E

22. Advanced computer and other electronic office technology is continually being introduced into my division, necessitating constant learning on my part.   A   B   C   D   E

23. The computer terminal and screen I have in my office can be monitored in my bosses' offices without my knowledge.   A   B   C   D   E

SCORING

Give yourself four points for each A, three points for each B, two points for each C, one point for each D, and no points for each E. Compute your total, and divide that score by 23. Round your answer to one decimal place.

WHAT THE ASSESSMENT MEANS

While the results of this assessment are not intended to be more than suggestive, the higher your score, the more comfortable you appear to be with change. The test's author suggests analyzing scores as if they were grade point averages. In this way, a 4.0 average is an "A," a 2.0 is a "C," and scores below 1.0 "flunk." Using replies from nearly 500 students and individuals new to supervisory positions, the range of scores was found to be relatively narrow: between 1.0 and 2.2. The average score was between 1.5 and 1.6—a D+/C− sort of grade!

FOR DISCUSSION

Which of the 23 items were particularly distressing to consider? Why?

Source: Peter B. Vail, *Managing as a Performing Art: New Ideas for a World of Chaotic Change*, Exhibit 1, pp. 8–9. © 1989 Jossey-Bass, Inc., Publishers.

CAN YOU SERVE AS A CHANGE AGENT?

Change agents
People who act as catalysts and assume the responsibility for overseeing the change process.

Planned changes within an organization need a catalyst. People who act as catalysts and assume the responsibility for overseeing the change process are called **change agents**.

Any supervisor can be a change agent. The change agent can also be a nonmanager—for example, an internal staff specialist or outside consultant whose expertise is in change implementation. For major systemwide changes, company officials will often hire outside consultants to provide advice and assistance. Because they are from the outside, they often can offer an objective perspective usually lacking in insiders. However, outside consultants may be at a disadvantage because they have an inadequate understanding of the organization's history, culture, operating procedures, and personnel. Outside consultants are also prone to initiate more drastic changes than insiders—which can be either a benefit or a disadvantage—because they do not have to live with the repercussions of the change after it is implemented. In contrast, supervisors who act as change agents may be more thoughtful—and possibly more cautious—because they must live with the consequences of their actions.

CHANGING PERSPECTIVES ON CHANGE

Supervisors historically treated the management of change as a periodic activity with a distinct beginning and end. A problem surfaced that required a change. That change would then be introduced, and the situation would return to a state of equilibrium. This perspective on change is no longer very accurate. Today's supervisor is increasingly finding that change is a constant. It has no distinct beginning or end. Supervisors are having to learn to manage in a world of continuous change.

LEWIN'S VIEW OF CHANGE

Change process
Unfreezing the status quo, changing to a new state, and refreezing the new change to make it permanent.

Lewin's view of change is best illustrated in the classic three-step model of the **change process**[1] (See Figure 13-3).

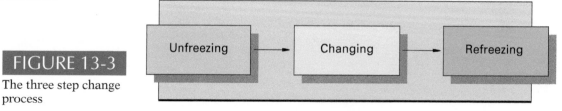

FIGURE 13-3

The three step change process

According to this model, successful change requires unfreezing the status quo, changing to a new state, and refreezing the new change to make it permanent. The status quo can be considered an equilibrium state. To move from this equilibrium, unfreezing is necessary. It can be achieved in one of three ways:

1. The driving forces that direct behaviour away from the status quo can be increased. For example, convince people of the value of the change and its benefits to them.
2. The restraining forces that hinder movement from the existing equilibrium can be decreased. Deal with resistance; address concerns about the change.
3. The two approaches can be combined.

This preparation stage is critical. Without it, the change will likely fail, as Bill Angelopoulos observes: "There was a manager at our organization who got into some difficulties because she introduced change without getting permission in the first place and without getting the buy-in of her staff. She had been recently promoted and had ideas she wanted to implement immediately. She came across as rough and confrontational in her manner so anything she said was resisted. The staff felt her ideas were wrong so productivity suffered. Because she did not check in with the store manager before implementing changes, she had not anticipated the issues involved. The store manager ended up having to do a lot of damage control and dealing with her employees."

Once unfreezing is accomplished and people are prepared for the change, the change itself can be implemented. However, the mere introduction of the change does not ensure that it will take hold. The new situation therefore needs to be *refrozen* so that it can be sustained over time. Glitches with the implementation need to be dealt with so that people don't abandon the change and slide back to the old ways. Enforcement and support of the change must be in place. Policies or procedures may need to be rewritten, training sessions may be required. The objective of the refreezing, then, is to stabilize the new situation by balancing the driving and restraining forces in support of the changed circumstances. An example where the three-step change process was implemented is discussed in Supervision in Action.

Note how this three-step process treats change as a break in the organization's equilibrium state. The status quo has been disturbed and change is necessary to establish a new equilibrium state. This view might have been appropriate to the relatively calm environment that most organizations faced in the late twentieth century. But this model does not describe the world in which current supervisors must manage. However, the model *is* useful in emphasizing the importance of follow-up to ensure that a new change is absorbed appropriately.

The Three-Step Change Process Applied at Precision Biologic

Ainslie White, Manager of Information Systems at Precision Biologic, discusses a major change for which he was the change agent:

"We put in a new and very different computer system. We had done a lot of work to prepare people for it but it was a huge change in the way of doing things. We gave tutorials and informed them what to do, but issues got magnified when we first went live, they couldn't figure out what to do. Luckily, since I figured we would need to focus on integration and resolving issues for the first three months, I had planned no other projects. The first 90 days was a lot of handholding to get people up to speed on the new system. People were definitely frustrated initially and we had to build in time for dealing with that, and understand where they were coming from. It doesn't matter how much you prepare for a change and warn people. It still hits them hard. So it takes a lot of following up. You have to be open. They will rant and rave. You must stay calm and say "OK, let me show you." Discussing things face to face is important. Most people, given time, see things rationally."

How does Ainslie's approach illustrate the three-step change process? Why was it appropriate that Precision Biologic used an insider, Ainslie, as the change agent rather than an outside consultant?

FIGURE 13-4

Ainslie and his IT team

The Contemporary View of Change

The contemporary view of change takes into consideration that environments are both uncertain and dynamic. To get a feeling for what directing change might be like when you have to continually manoeuvre, consider going on a ski trip and facing the following scenario: The ski slopes that are open vary in length and difficulty. Unfortunately, when you start a "run," you don't know what the ski course will be. It might be a simple course, or one that is very challenging. Furthermore, you've planned your ski vacation assuming that the slopes will be open. After all, it's January—and that is prime ski time at the resort. But the course does not always open. As if that were not bad enough, on some days the slopes are closed for no apparent reason at all. Oh yes, and one more thing—lift ticket prices can change dramatically on the hour. And there is no apparent pattern to the price fluctuations.

To succeed under these conditions, you would have to be incredibly flexible and be able to respond quickly to every changing condition. Those who were too slow or too structured would have difficulty—and clearly no fun!

A growing number of supervisors are coming to accept that their job is much like what one might face on such a ski vacation. The stability and predictability of the traditional view of change may not exist. Disruptions in the status quo are not occasional and temporary, and followed by a return to "calm waters." Many of today's supervisors never get out of the rapids. They face constant change. These supervisors are being forced to play a game they've never played before, which is governed by rules that are created as the game progresses.[2]

RESISTANCE TO CHANGE

One of the most well-documented findings in the study of people at work is that individuals resist change. As Mark Smith of KPMG Canada puts it, "No one likes change except a wet baby."[3]

Resistance to change surfaces in many forms. It can be overt, implicit, immediate, or deferred. It is easiest for supervisors to deal with resistance when it is overt and immediate. For instance, a change is proposed and employees quickly respond by voicing complaints, engaging in a work slowdown, threatening to go on strike, or the like. The greater challenge is managing resistance that is implicit or deferred. Implicit resistance efforts are more subtle, for example, loss of loyalty to the organization, loss of motivation to work, increased errors or mistakes, increased absenteeism due to "sickness," and hence more difficult to recognize. Similarly, deferred actions cloud the link between the source of the resistance and the reaction to it. A change may produce what appears

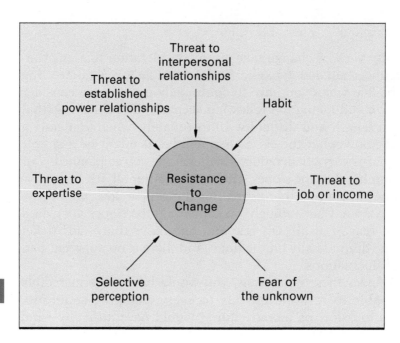

FIGURE 13-5

Why employees resist
change

to be only a minimal reaction at the time it is initiated, but then resistance surfaces weeks, months, or even years later. A single change that in and of itself might have little impact can become the straw that breaks the camel's back. Reactions to change can build up and then explode in some response that seems totally out of proportion to the particular change action it follows. The resistance, of course, has merely been deferred and stockpiled. What surfaces is a response to an accumulation of previous changes.

So why do people resist change? There are a number of reasons (see Figure 13-5).

HABIT

As human beings, we're creatures of habit. Life is complex enough; we don't need to consider the full range of options for the hundreds of decisions we have to make every day. To cope with this complexity, we all rely on habits or programmed responses. But when confronted with change, our programmed responses are no longer appropriate. So when your department is moved to a new office building across town, it means your employees are likely to have to change many habits: waking up 10 minutes earlier, taking a new route to work, finding a new parking place, adjusting to the new office layout, developing a new lunch-time routine, and so on.

THREAT TO JOB OR INCOME

Employees fear any change they think may reduce their job security or income. New labour-saving equipment, for instance, may be interpreted as the forerunner of layoffs. People are also often threatened by changes in job tasks or established work routines if they are fearful that they won't be able to perform them successfully. This is particularly threatening where pay is closely tied to productivity.

FEAR OF THE UNKNOWN

Human beings don't like ambiguity. But changes substitute ambiguity and uncertainty for the known. If the introduction of a new system means that staff will have to learn to do their entire jobs on computers, some of these people may fear that they will be unable to learn the intricacies of the system. They may, therefore, develop a negative attitude toward working with the system or behave dysfunctionally—complaining, purposely working slowly, undermining department morale—if required to use the system.

SELECTIVE PERCEPTION

Individuals shape the world through their perceptions. Once they have created this world, it resists change. So individuals are guilty of selectively processing what they see and hear in order to keep their perceptions intact. They often hear what they want to hear. They ignore information that challenges the world they've created. For example, trainers faced with the requirement to shift their efforts to developing online training instead of face-to face teaching, may have a bias that affects their perception of

FIGURE 13-6

Labour-saving equipment, like assembly-line robots, have replaced thousands of workers in automobile plants. Many auto workers fear changes because they're afraid their jobs might be eliminated. Courtesy of Prisma Bildagentur AG/ Alamy

relevant information. They may only note and remember the issues and challenges and not tune into the important information about potential benefits and opportunities offered by this new focus.

THREAT TO EXPERTISE

Changes in organizational policies and practices may threaten the expertise of specialized groups and departments. The introduction of decentralized personal computers, which allow supervisors and managers access to information directly from a company's mainframe, is an example of a change that was strongly resisted by many information systems departments in the early 1980s. Why? Because decentralized end-user computing was a threat to the specialized skills held by those in the centralized information systems departments.

THREAT TO ESTABLISHED POWER RELATIONSHIPS

Any redistribution of decision-making authority can threaten existing power relationships within an organization. Efforts by top management to empower operating employees or introduce self-managed work teams have frequently been met by resistance from supervisors who are threatened by a loss of power.

THREAT TO INTERPERSONAL RELATIONSHIPS

Work is more than a means to earn a living. The interpersonal relationships that are part of a person's job often play an important role in satisfying the individual's social needs. We look forward to going to work to interact with coworkers and make friends. Change can be a threat to those relationships. Reorganizations, transfers, and restructuring of work layouts change the people that employees work with, report to, and regularly interact with. Since such changes are often seen as threats, they tend to be resisted.

REDUCING RESISTANCE TO CHANGE

The resistance we've described to change can be overcome. We offer five specific techniques:

1. Build trust.
2. Open channels of communication.
3. Involve employees.
4. Provide emphathy and support.
5. Provide incentives.

Resistance is most likely to be eliminated when supervisors implement all four of the techniques. The techniques are discussed below.

BUILD TRUST

If employees trust and have confidence in you, they're less likely to be threatened by changes you propose.

Trust takes a long time to develop. It's also very fragile; it can be destroyed easily. What can you do to build trust? Be fair and impartial. Be consistent and predictable in your decisions and in the way you treat your employees. Develop a reputation for making good on your promises, both explicit and implied. Be supportive. Employees trust supervisors who offer praise, are good listeners, exhibit confidence in their people, and protect their interests. Finally, be candid and honest. Your people should believe that you'll tell them the truth.

OPEN CHANNELS OF COMMUNICATION

Resistance can often be reduced by communicating with employees to help them see the logic of a change.

When employees receive the full facts and any misunderstandings are cleared up, resistance often fades. A longitudinal study of a work reorganization found that employees who felt they were well informed about the change were much more open to the change when it occurred than were those who felt less informed.[4] Opening communication channels, however, will only be effective when there is a climate of trust and where the organization is truly concerned with the welfare of its employees. In a hospital implementing empowerment among nurses, different nurses heard the management message differently depending on how much they trusted management. Those who trusted management were more likely to believe the reasons management gave for the empowerment. Those who did not trust management were more likely to be suspicious of the real reasons behind their decision.[5]

Improved communication is particularly effective in reducing threats created by ambiguity. For instance, when the grapevine is active with rumours of cutbacks and layoffs, honest and open communication of the true facts can be a calming force. Even if the news is bad, a clear message often wins points and opens people to accepting change. When communication is ambiguous and people are threatened, they often contrive scenarios that are considerably worse than the actual "bad news."

INVOLVE EMPLOYEES

Many organizations are asking employees to participate in planning major change programs. Why? It's difficult for individuals to resist a change decision in which they have participated. So solicit employee input early in the change process. When employees have been involved in a change from its beginning, they will usually actively support the change. No one wants to oppose something that he or she helped develop.

PROVIDE EMPATHY AND SUPPORT

A supervisor can play a key role in helping employees deal with a change through expressing understanding and support. By actively listening, the supervisor shows concerned interest and is alerted to concerns that can then be addressed. Emotional support and encouragement significantly reduce the stress employees feel during a change. When employees feel supported by their leader, it actually changes their perceptions of the change itself so they experience less uncertainty and a greater sense that the change is well planned.[6] One aspect of support is a supervisor's patience. People often relapse into old habits several times before they maintain the new behaviour[7]–a supervisor's calm support through these relapses is appreciated.

In order to provide information and support during times of change, a supervisor must be there. Yet, research indicates that managers sometimes withdraw during large-scale change processes in order to get the situation under control for themselves.[8] And managers responsible for downsizing often use avoidance tactics to avoid dealing with needy or upset employees.[9] During those stressful times of change, even when you are tempted to lock yourself away in your office to sort out the challenges, remember that your availability is a key component in an effective change management process.[10]

PROVIDE INCENTIVES

Our last suggestion is to make sure that people see how supporting a change is in their best interests. What's the source of their resistance? What do you control that might overcome that resistance? Are they afraid they won't be able to do a new task? Provide them with new-skills training. Layoffs can become opportunities for those who remain. Jobs can be redesigned to provide new challenges and responsibilities. A pay increase, a new title, flexible work hours, or increased job autonomy are additional examples of incentives that can help reduce resistance.

Graham Van Brunt, director of plant operations and maintenance at Churchill Falls Labrador Corp., a huge hydro facility, knows the value of preparing people for change through training. "When we put in new equipment, like a new relay or a new annunciating system, a substantial part of our expense is in training, to make sure employees understand and can operate the new equipment. We typically do a pilot where consultants train key personnel on site in one localized area. Then we use those employees to train others in the organization." Graham's approach must

FIGURE 13-7

Graham Van Brunt, director of plant operations at Churchill Falls Labrador Corp.
Courtesy of Churchill Falls Labrador Corporation

SAME PLACE, NEW JOB

Churchill Falls Labrador Corp. (CFLC) switched to activity-based budgeting. As a result, management responsibilities were drastically altered to align with activities. Graham Van Brunt describes the changes. "For example, whereas before a superintendent would look after all welders and equipment in an area—tools, labour, generator—now the labour and assets are split. For example, one superintendent looks after the people, and another will manage the generator. The latter, therefore, does not have to worry about training, absenteeism, or employee relations. He must try to get the work done well and inexpensively; this means he could go to the labour manager for staff, but he could also go outside the organization and arrange for the work to be done by someone locally. The decision would rest on factors like cost, professionalism, reaction, the big-picture impact on the company.

"Some employees loved the change. Others hated it—one said 'It feels like someone kicked me in the stomach.' It would be nice if we had a brand-new company to start with instead of going from old to new. It's tough when you tell someone you're no longer looking after this equipment as you have for the past 20 years. Now, you'll be looking after people, and it will be five times as many as before. There's a fear of the unknown.

"Even now, we're still riding the bumps of that change. Some areas were hard to define and we are still dealing with some 'grey' areas."

The changes described seem to make each supervisor's area of responsibility operate like a mini business unit. The mindset to handle this seems very different from the mindset of a supervisor who is part of a hierarchy in a large corporation. Why would CFLC undertake this change? What supervisory skills would be needed to adjust to this change? What preparation could CFLC give the supervisors to be able to cope with the shift?

be successful as "there is little, if any, resistance to the technology. In fact, most embrace it and the new knowledge. We get people demanding to get training they hear others are getting. For example, we got new governor systems to keep the machines running in synch and at the right speed. Theoretical training was given to the technicians but not to the operators. The operators asked to get the theoretical training, too."

Change at the Churchill Falls hydro facility in recent years has included a major reorganization. This required much more adaptation than working with new equipment (see Something to Think About).

WORK STRESS

One-third of Canadians report feeling 'quite a lot' or 'extremely' stressed at work most days.[11] Stress-related absences cost Canadian employers billions of dollars each year.[12] Stress can harm people's lives and it can harm organizations so all supervisors must pay attention to it. There is an increasing realization that stress is something built into many circumstances people must deal with, not simply the reaction of people not strong enough to handle the demands. The World Health Organization has said that "Most of the causes of work stress concern the way work is designed and the way in which organizations are managed."[13] The way in which organizations manage change can be a major contributor to stress, and the increasing pace and extent of change in organizations means the challenges will be ongoing. Supervisors at the front lines of change implementation will be among the first to see stress talking its toll.

WHAT IS STRESS?

Stress
An adaptive response resulting from any environmental action, situation, or event that places excessive psychological and/or physical demands on a person.

The formal definition of **stress** is complex: an adaptive response resulting from any environmental action, situation, or event that places excessive psychological and/or physical demands on a person. Essentially, the adaptive response we typically associate with stress includes things such as tension, anxiety, or a rush of adrenaline. The demands refer to the potential loss of something that a person desires; for instance, respect, his or her job, or a promotion.

Two conditions are necessary for a potentially stressful situation to create actual stress for a person. There must be uncertainty over the outcome and the outcome must be important. Stress is highest for those who don't know whether they will win or lose and lowest for those who think that winning or losing is a certainty. But importance is also critical. If winning or losing is an unimportant outcome, there is no stress. If keeping your job doesn't hold any importance to you, you have no reason to feel stress over having to undergo a performance review. Athletes typically experience greater stress during championship competition because there is increased importance placed on the outcome.

CONSEQUENCES OF STRESS

So far we have referred to stress as only a negative experience. In fact, stress can be functional or dysfunctional.

Have you ever surprised yourself by doing some of your best work or coming up with a great idea when you were really under pressure? Consider situations where athletes have come up with incredible performances at key championships, far surpassing their previous bests. These examples illustrate the motivational power of stress. The immediate fight or flight stage of the stress response sends adrenaline surging through the body, activating the body to deal with events. If the stress is at a level reasonable for the individual, this can actually support strong performance. Some people enjoy that "rush" of pressure and seek it out.

However, when stress is too high or continues over an extended period, the negative consequences kick in. Health risks[14] to the employee include greater vulnerability to heart disease, substance abuse, back pain, depression and anxiety disorders. From the organization's viewpoint, high levels of stress are linked to the greater incidence of injuries on the job, to higher absenteeism and lower job satisfaction.[15] So stress levels need to be monitored and lowered if evidence suggests negative consequences.

SOURCES OF WORK STRESS

Work-related stress is brought about by both organizational and individual factors. As shown in Figure 13-8, these in turn are influenced by individual differences. That is, not all people in similar situations experience similar levels of stress.

ORGANIZATIONAL FACTORS

There is no shortage of factors within the organization that can cause stress. Pressures to avoid errors or complete tasks in a limited time

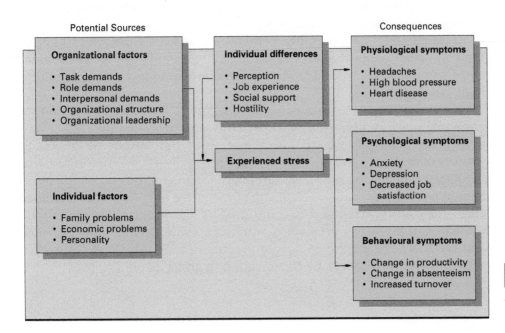

FIGURE 13-8

A closer look at stress

period, a demanding supervisor, and unpleasant coworkers are a few examples. The discussion that follows organizes stress factors into five categories: task, role, and interpersonal demands; organizational structure; and organizational leadership.

Task demands are factors related to an employee's job. They include the job design, dealing with change, time pressures, working conditions and physical demands. The more interdependence between a person's tasks and the tasks of others, the more potential stress there is. Autonomy, on the other hand, tends to lessen stress. Change requires adjustment, and a workplace with ongoing demands to use new methods and equipment can be stressful. Deadlines put pressure on people, especially when the employee must also deal with frequent interruptions. Jobs where employees must deal with extreme temperatures, noise, global travel, strenuous physical demands, hazardous substances or dangers typically put excessive demands on employees.

Role demands relate to pressures placed on an employee as a function of the particular role he or she plays in the organization. **Role conflicts** describe situations in which individuals are confronted by divergent role expectations. For example, conflicting demands within the same role are created when an employee is expected to produce both high quality and high quantity and the combination is impossible. Conflicting demands between two roles are created when a conscientious employee wants to report a major error that needs addressing but as a friend does not want to rat out the colleague who is trying to hide the error. Or, as an employee, you want to meet all expectations but as a parent you feel the need to constrain the hours spent on work. **Role overload** is experienced when the employee is expected to do more than time permits. **Role ambiguity** is created when role expectations are not clearly understood and the employee is unsure of what he or she is to do.

Interpersonal demands are pressures created by other employees. Lack of social support from colleagues and poor interpersonal relationships can cause considerable stress, especially among employees with a high social need.

Organizational structure can increase stress. Excessive rules and an employee's lack of opportunity to participate in decisions that affect him or her are examples of structural variables that might be potential sources of stress.

Organizational leadership represents the managerial style of the organization's senior executives. Some chief executive officers create a culture characterized by tension, fear, and anxiety. They establish unrealistic pressures to perform in the short run, impose excessively tight controls, and routinely fire employees who don't measure up. This style of leadership flows down through the organization to affect all employees.

Role conflicts
Situations in which individuals are confronted by divergent role expectations.

Role overload
Situations where an employee is expected to do more than time permits.

Role ambiguity
Situation where role expectations are not clearly understood and the employee is not sure what he or she is to do.

INDIVIDUAL FACTORS

The typical employee works about 40 hours a week. The experiences and problems that people encounter in the remaining nonwork hours each week can spill over to the job. Our other category, then, encompasses factors in the employee's personal life. Primarily, these factors are *family issues, personal economic problems*, and *inherent personality characteristics*.

Surveys consistently show that people hold family and personal relationships dear. Marital difficulties, the breaking off of a relationship, discipline troubles with children, and relatives with serious illnesses are examples of relationship problems that create stress for employees and that aren't left at the front door when they leave for work.

Economic problems created by individuals overextending their financial resources are another set of personal troubles that can create stress for employees and distract their attention from their work. Regardless of income level (people who earn $80 000 a year seem to have as much trouble handling their finances as those who earn $18 000), some people are poor money managers or have material desires that always seem to exceed their earning capacity.

Personality seems to have the potential to affect stress by influencing both how people perceive situations and how they react to them. High **self-esteem** (feelings of personal worth) and **self-efficacy** (belief in capability to meet demands) seem to buffer people from stress. Stressful circumstances do not seem as threatening and they engage in effective coping strategies. On the other hand, those with 'negative affectivity' seem to be sensitized to experience threat and react strongly to it. Negative affectivity describes a tendency to accentuate the negative aspects of the world around them. Physical measures show these people show greater muscle tension during stress and are slower to recover after the stress is over than those with low negative affectivity.[16] They are also more likely to react to the stress in counterproductive ways because they anger more easily and tend to be impulsive.[17]

Stress factors are additive. A fact that tends to be overlooked when stress factors are reviewed individually is that stress is an additive phenomenon. Stress builds up. Each new and persistent stressor adds to an individual's stress level. A single stressor may seem relatively unimportant in and of itself, but if it is added to an already high level of stress, it can be "the straw that breaks the camel's back." See Assessing Yourself to get a measure of how much stress is currently in your life.

Self-esteem
Feelings of self-worth

Self-efficacy
Belief in one's ability to meet demands

Negative affectivity
A tendency to accentuate the negative aspects of the world around them

Assessing Yourself

HOW MUCH STRESS IN YOUR LIFE?

Below are 20 statements. Use the following scale in responding to each statement:

4 = all the time
3 = often
2 = sometimes
1 = never

1. I'm exhausted by daily demands at work, school, and home.	4	3	2	1
2. My stress is caused by outside forces beyond my control.	4	3	2	1
3. I'm trapped by circumstances that I just have to live with.	4	3	2	1
4. No matter how hard I work to stay on top of my schedule, I can't get caught up.	4	3	2	1
5. I have financial obligations that I can't seem to meet.	4	3	2	1
6. I dislike my work, but I can't take the risk of making a career change (or if not working: I dislike school, but can't take the risk of dropping out).	4	3	2	1
7. I'm dissatisfied with my personal relationships.	4	3	2	1
8. I feel responsible for the happiness of people around me.	4	3	2	1
9. I'm embarrassed to ask for help.	4	3	2	1
10. I don't know what I want out of life.	4	3	2	1
11. I'm disappointed that I have not achieved what I had hoped for.	4	3	2	1
12. No matter how much success I have, I feel empty.	4	3	2	1
13. If the people around me were more competent, I would feel happier.	4	3	2	1
14. People let me down.	4	3	2	1
15. I stew in my anger rather than express it.	4	3	2	1
16. I become enraged and resentful when I am hurt.	4	3	2	1

17. I can't take criticism.	4	3	2	1
18. I'm afraid I'll lose my job (or fail school).	4	3	2	1
19. I don't see the value of expressing sadness or grief.	4	3	2	1
20. I don't trust that things will work out.	4	3	2	1

SCORING

After rating each statement, total your score for the 20 items. Scores of 20-29 indicate a high degree of control, self-esteem, and low stress levels. Scores of 30-49 suggest that your occasional negative self-talk causes you to feel anxious in stressful situations, thus causing moderate levels of stress. Scores of 50-69 indicate a relatively high level of stress. This might indicate you feel trapped. Scores of 70 or more indicate very high stress levels—indicating life has become one crisis and struggle after another for you.

Using this questionnaire as a guide, describe the kinds of things that are causing stress in your life. How are you handling this stress? Do you feel successful? Why or why not? For those who have low stress, what tips could you offer to others for coping with the stress?

Source: Reprinted from *Stress to Strength* (1994), Random House, Inc.

INDIVIDUAL DIFFERENCES

Some people thrive on stressful situations, while others are overwhelmed by them. What is it that differentiates people in terms of their ability to handle stress? Four individual difference factors have been found to be important: perception, experience, social support, and hostility.

One person's fear that he'll lose his job because his company is laying off personnel may be perceived by another as an opportunity to get a large severance allowance and start his own business. Similarly, what one employee perceives as an efficient and challenging work environment may be viewed as threatening and demanding by others. So stress potential doesn't lie in objective conditions. Rather, it lies in an employee's *perception* and interpretation of those conditions. The same situation may be perceived as a challenge by one, but as a burden by another. Those who report challenge-related work stress have higher job satisfaction than those who report hindrance-related work stress.[18]

Experience is said to be a great teacher. It can also be a great stress-reducer. Think back to your first date or your first few days in college. For most of us, the uncertainty and newness of these situations created stress. But as we gained experience, that stress disappeared or at least significantly decreased. The same phenomenon seems to apply to work situations. Why? One explanation is the process of selective withdrawal. Voluntary turnover is more likely among people who experience more stress. Therefore, people who remain with the organization longer are those with more stress-resistant traits, or those who are more resistant to the stress characteristics of their organization. A second explanation is that people eventually develop coping mechanisms to deal with stress. Because this takes time, senior members of the organization are more likely to be fully adapted and experience less stress.

There is increasing evidence that *social support*—collegial relationships with coworkers and supervisors—can buffer the impact of stress. The logic underlying this conclusion is that social support acts as a palliative, lessening the negative effects of even high-stress jobs.

You may have heard of Type A behaviour being used to explain who would be affected by stress. **Type A behaviour** is characterized by feelings of a chronic sense of time urgency and by an excessive competitive drive. Type As try to do more and more in less and less time. The opposite of Type A is **Type B behaviour**. Type Bs never suffer from time urgency or impatience. Until quite recently, it was believed that Type As were more likely to experience stress on and off the job. A closer analysis of the evidence, however, has produced new conclusions. It has been found that only the hostility and anger associated with some Type A behaviour is actually associated with the negative effects of stress. The chronically angry, suspicious, and distrustful person is the one at risk of stressing out.

THE SYMPTOMS OF STRESS

What signs indicate that an employee's stress level might be too high? There are three general ways that stress reveals itself. These include physiological, psychological, and behavioural symptoms.

Most of the early interest over stress focused heavily on health-related or *physiological* concerns. This was attributed to the realization that high stress levels result in changes in metabolism, increased heart and breathing rates, increased blood pressure, headaches, and increased risk of heart attacks. Because detecting many of these symptoms requires the skills of trained medical personnel, their immediate and direct relevance to supervisors is negligible.

Of greater importance to supervisors are psychological and behavioural symptoms of stress. These are things that can be witnessed in the person. The *psychological* symptoms can be seen as increased tension and anxiety, boredom, or procrastination—which can all lead to productivity decreases. So too, can the *behaviourally related* symptoms—changes in

Type A behaviour
Aggressive behaviour in a chronic, incessant struggle to achieve more and more in less and less time.

Type B behaviour
The behaviour of a person who is rarely harried by the desire to obtain a wildly increasing number of things or participate in an endlessly growing series of events in an ever-decreasing amount of time.

eating habits, increased smoking or substance consumption, rapid speech, or sleep disorders. The astute supervisor, upon witnessing such symptoms, does what he or she can to assist the employee in reducing stress levels.

TWO STRESS MODELS

Two comprehensive models examine the basic issues underlying typical sources of stress and use that information to suggest reducing or avoiding stress: the job demand-control-support model and the effort-reward imbalance model.

JOB DEMAND-CONTROL-SUPPORT MODEL

As shown in Figure 13-9, Karacek's **job demand-control-support model**[19] suggests that having high demands accompanied by low control and low support creates strain, and that strain can be modified or prevented by altering these factors. A worker who must accomplish complex and difficult work under deadlines and in poor working conditions, is facing high demands. Lowering those demands somehow would ease the pressure. But, even if the supervisor can do little to alter those demands, the strain can be eased by giving the employee greater decision latitude over what they are doing and by creating supportive working relationships within the team. Low control magnifies the strain in a high demand job but in itself can be highly stressful for some. Similarly, strong support makes a demanding job more bearable but low support on its own can be stressful.

Job demand-control-support model Suggests that having high demands accompanied by low control and low support creates strain

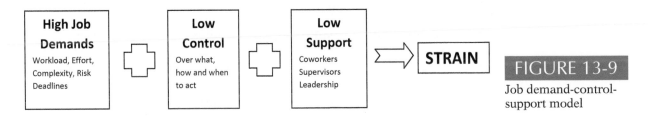

FIGURE 13-9

Job demand-control-support model

EFFORT-REWARD IMBALANCE MODEL

Siegrist's model[20] attributes strain to a combination of high effort and low rewards (see Figure 13-10). As we have seen in previous discussions on the role of fairness (e.g. equity theory in Chapter 9), employees look for a balance between what they contribute and what they receive. In the **effort-reward imbalance model**, an employee feels strained if there is a mismatch between the effort and the consequences. This model suggests that efforts arise not only from external sources (like deadlines, interruptions, workload, emotional labour) but also from internal sources (like

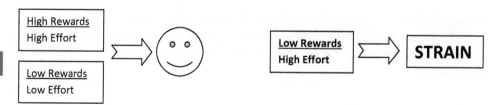

FIGURE 13-10

Effort-reward
imbalance model

need for approval or for achievement). Low rewards could be a matter of low wages, job insecurity or poor benefits but also lack of recognition, lack of career opportunities and disrespectful treatment, as if their efforts are invisible and unappreciated. The strain can lead to adverse health issues.

Both the job demand-control-support model and the effort-reward imbalance model have had strong research support. And they are not mutually exclusive. A Canadian study showed that the two models together were a better predictor of self-reported health status in a group of BC workers than either model alone.[21] Their suggestions on how we can assist employees in avoiding or dealing with stress are included in From Concepts to Skills: Stress Reduction.

COMPANIES TAKE ACTION ON STRESS

With the annual cost of stress in Canadian companies exceeding $12 billion, Canadian companies are implementing a variety of stress-reducing options including flextime, job sharing, telecommuting, and part-time prorated benefits. These companies are responding to the needs of a very different workforce in which:

- 68 per cent of all husband-and-wife families have both spouses working[22]
- 73 per cent of all women with children under 16 work outside the home[23]
- 66 per cent of those caring for elderly family members also have jobs[24]

Much of the stress in the Canadian workforce seems to be centred on the new generation of working parents. This group is vulnerable to work/family stress caused by raising their families and caring for elder family members, with no adult family member at home full-time to take on these tasks as their major responsibility. Companies are beginning to look at options to give greater flexibility in handling both work and personal responsibilities.

For example, consider the health focus of KineMedics, a small (15-person) company that sells sport medicine and surgical rehabilitation products and equipment. Flextime is an official policy that supports stress relief and ongoing physical activity for staff: "We ask our staff to put in a certain amount of hours per week and give them the options to arrange their schedule to suit their needs," explains Simonson. "If a staff member prefers taking a mid-morning run for example, then they can use that as an early lunch hour."[25] There is a customized benefits plan that gives each person a set dollar amount they can use per year to help defray the costs of medical-related expenses such as physiotherapy, prescriptions or sports massage, and a separate recreation allowance of up to $300 a year to reimburse employees for gym membership dues or other fitness and recreation costs like league registration fees. Team involvement in charity events encourages staff to use their athletic prowess for a good cause, while at the same time having fun. For example, as the official medical supplier to the Ottawa Senators Hockey Club, staff of KineMedics support Roger's House, a hospice for terminally ill children, and participate in an annual Walk, Roll & Run for Roger's House and the Roger's House Telethon for which they donate a portion of their sales over a designated week.

STRESS REDUCTION

If employee stress levels are too high in your department, is there anything you can do? The answer is a resounding yes. In this section, we'll review some of your options.

ASSESSING YOURSELF: HOW WELL CAN YOU IDENTIFY STRESSFUL EVENTS?

Which life events typically create the greatest stress? To test your knowledge, rank-order the following 12 events from the most stressful (rank number 1) to least stressful (number 12). Note that positive events can cause stress as well as negative ones.

		Rank
1.	Divorce	_____
2.	Being fired at work	_____
3.	Minor violation of the law such as receiving a traffic ticket	_____
4.	Changing to a different line of work	_____
5.	Death of a spouse	_____
6.	Outstanding personal achievement	_____
7.	Major changes in working hours or conditions	_____
8.	Foreclosure on a mortgage or loan	_____
9.	Gaining a new family member through birth, adoption, or a relative moving in	_____
10.	Major personal injury or illness	_____
11.	Major change in responsibilities at work such as a promotion, demotion, or lateral transfer	_____
12.	Marriage	_____

Source: Based on T.H. Holmes and R.H. Rahe, "The Social Readjustment Scale," *Journal of Psychosomatic Research*, 11 (1967), p. 216.

SCORING DIRECTIONS AND KEY

To find out how you did, transpose your ranking numbers to Column A below. The numbers in Column B represent the correct ranking (from most to least stressful). Now subtract Column B from Column A for each event and put that number in Column C. In Column D, calculate the square of the difference you calculated in Column C e.g., $3^2=9$).

Event	Column A	Column B	Column C	Column D
1	___	5	___	___
2	___	1	___	___
3	___	10	___	___
4	___	12	___	___
5	___	2	___	___
6	___	9	___	___
7	___	4	___	___
8	___	8	___	___
9	___	11	___	___
10	___	6	___	___
11	___	7	___	___
12	___	3	___	___

Total ___ ÷12 = _____

Sum up the total of Column D and divide by 12. The result is a measure of variation. The lower the number, the better you are at identifying the stressfulness of various events. An excellent variation score would be 10 or less.

SKILL BASICS

Low-to-moderate levels of employee stress may not require your attention. The reason, as we noted earlier in the chapter, is that such levels of stress can be functional and can lead to higher employee performance. But high levels of stress, or even low levels sustained over long periods of time, can lead to reduced employee performance and thus require supervisory action.

While a limited amount of stress may benefit an employee's performance, don't expect employees to see it that way. From the individual's standpoint, even low levels of stress are likely to be perceived as undesirable. It's not unlikely, therefore, that you and your employees will differ on what constitutes an acceptable level of stress on the job. What you may consider a positive stimulus that keeps the adrenaline running may be seen as excessive pressure by your employees. Keep this in mind as we discuss techniques for reducing stress.

SELECT EMPLOYEES WITH THE SPECIFIC JOB IN MIND

While certain jobs are more stressful than others, we know that individuals differ in their response to stress situations. Selection and placement decisions should take these facts into consideration. Match personalities to the demands of the job. And remember that, especially in stressful jobs, experienced individuals are likely to adapt better and perform their jobs more effectively.

CLARIFY EXPECTATIONS

Employees are more motivated and less stressed when they clearly understand what is expected of them. This refers to their job description and the work assignments delegated to them but also to clear structure, policies and practices within the company. The use of goals can also reduce stress. Specific goals that employees believe are attainable reduce the stress caused by unrealistic expectations. Additionally, goal feedback reduces uncertainties as to actual job performance. The result is less employee frustration, role ambiguity, and stress.

ENCOURAGE TIME MANAGEMENT

As discussed in Chapter 2, many people manage their time poorly. However, the well-organized employee can often accomplish twice as much as the person who is poorly organized. The understanding and use of basic time-management principles can help individuals better cope with job demands and feel in control of their workday.

REDESIGN JOBS TO ALIGN WITH INDIVIDUAL PREFERENCES

Redesigning jobs to give more autonomy can reduce stress through an increased sense of control. Increasing feedback will reduce ambiguity. Increasing meaningfulness in the job helps the employee feel their efforts are justified in accomplishing something important. Of course, not all employees want enriched jobs. The right job redesign for some employees might then be less responsibility and increased division of labour. If individuals prefer structure and routine, standardizing the job should also reduce uncertainties and stress levels.

LET EMPLOYEES PARTICIPATE IN DECISION MAKING

Role stress is detrimental to a large extent because employees feel uncertain about goals, expectations, how they'll be evaluated, and the like.

By giving employees a voice in those decisions that directly affect their job performance, you can increase employee control and reduce this role stress.

Research has shown that inviting employees to participate in any change process can result in reduced resistance to the change and a greater sense of control over the change, meaning lower stress.[26]

PROVIDE SOCIAL SUPPORT

When colleagues understand the job demands, can joke about them, and lend a hand when needed, an employee's tough job is made easier. When a supervisor shows concern and takes steps to address issues identified by the employee, the employee feels supported. A team atmosphere that focuses on employee well-being as well as team performance means no one will be isolated in dealing with stressful circumstances. This social support is established long before any specific stress arises, through the relationships built up among employees and with the supervisor, through the casual conversations, the humour and the respectful courtesies of everyday interaction.

PROVIDE PRACTICAL SUPPORT

Could physical demands be reduced through job rotation, better ergonomics or better planning to distribute the workload? Could duties be shifted or systems improved? Would increased staffing be feasible to reduce strain on the department? Are flexible work hours a possibility or occasional telecommuting? The supervisor and team members may be able to come up with practical solutions to ease stress in the department.

INCREASE FORMAL COMMUNICATION

Increasing formal communication with employees reduces uncertainty by lessening role ambiguity and role conflict. When employees think they're being kept "in the dark," stress levels rise. When you provide "the light," stress should decline.

GIVE POSITIVE FEEDBACK

We saw earlier that self-efficacy is an individual attribute that influences one's vulnerability to stress. An employee's belief in their ability to meet demands can be enhanced by a solid training base, a consistent support system and also by positive feedback that gives evidence of their success.

An employee whose supervisor openly and frequently acknowledges the employee's skills and performance successes, rather than focusing on weaknesses, is more likely to feel confident in his or her capabilities.

ENCOURAGE EMPLOYEES TO EXERCISE AND RELAX

Noncompetitive physical exercise such as aerobics, race walking, jogging, swimming, and riding a bicycle have long been recommended by physicians as a way to deal with excessive stress levels. These forms of exercise increase heart capacity, lower at-rest heart rate, provide a mental diversion from work pressures, and offer a means to "let off steam."

Employees can also be encouraged to practice relaxation techniques such as meditation, hypnosis, and biofeedback. Fifteen or twenty minutes a day of deep relaxation releases tension and provides a person with a pronounced sense of peacefulness.

Some organizations offer wellness programs that focus on the employees' total physical and mental condition. For example, they provide workshops to help people quit smoking, control alcohol use, lose weight, and eat better. If your organization offers such programs, encourage your employees to participate.

SET AN EXAMPLE—LOOK AT STRESSFUL SITUATIONS AS CHALLENGES

If you curse when unexpected changes happen or appear frustrated with overload or new demands, employees will take their cue from you. If, on the other hand, you treat stressful events with a sense of humour, as one more interesting challenge to face in an interesting job, that interpretation will rub off on others.

APPLYING YOUR SKILLS

Complete the following questionnaire by circling one number in each line across. To what extent does each of the following sentences fit as a description of you?

	Very true	Quite true	Some-what true	Not very true	Not at all true
1. I "roll with the punches" when problems come up.	1	2	3	4	5
2. I spend almost all of my time thinking about my work.	5	4	3	2	1

		Very true	Quite true	Some-what true	Not very true	Not at all true
3.	I treat other people as individuals and care about their feelings and opinions.	1	2	3	4	5
4.	I recognize and accept my own limitations and assets.	1	2	3	4	5
5.	There are quite a few people I could describe as "good friends."	1	2	3	4	5
6.	I enjoy using my skills and abilities both on and off the job.	1	2	3	4	5
7.	I get bored easily.	5	4	3	2	1
8.	I enjoy meeting and talking with people who have different ways of thinking about the world.	1	2	3	4	5
9.	Often in my job I "bite off more than I can chew."	5	4	3	2	1
10.	I'm usually very active on weekends with projects or recreation.	1	2	3	4	5
11.	I prefer working with people who are very much like myself.	5	4	3	2	1
12.	I work primarily because I have to survive, not necessarily because I enjoy what I do.	5	4	3	2	1
13.	I believe I have a realistic picture of my personal strengths and weakness.	1	2	3	4	5
14.	Often I get into arguments with people who don't think my way.	5	4	3	2	1
15.	Often I have trouble getting much done on my job.	5	4	3	2	1
16.	I'm interested in a lot of different topics.	1	2	3	4	5
17.	I get upset when things don't go my way.	5	4	3	2	1
18.	Often I'm not sure how I stand on a controversial topic.	5	4	3	2	1
19.	I'm usually able to find a way around anything that blocks me from an important goal.	1	2	3	4	5
20.	I often disagree with my boss or others at work.	5	4	3	2	1

SCORING AND INTERPRETATION

The author of this questionnaire believes that people who cope with stress effectively have five characteristics.

1. They know themselves well and accept their own strengths and weaknesses.
2. They have a variety of interests off the job, and they are not total "workaholics."
3. They exhibit a variety of reactions to stress, rather than always getting a headache or always becoming depressed.
4. They are accepting of others who have values or styles different from their own.
5. They are active and productive both on and off the job.

Add together the numbers you circled for the four questions contained in each of the five coping scales.

Coping scale	Add together your responses to these questions	Your score (write in)
Knows self	4, 9, 13, 18	_____
Many interests	2, 5, 7, 16	_____
Variety of reactions	1, 11, 17, 19	_____
Accepts other's values	3, 8, 14, 20	_____
Active and productive	6, 10, 12, 15	_____

Then, add the five scores together for your overall total score: _____

Scores on each of the five areas can vary between 5 and 20. Scores of 12 or above suggest that it might perhaps be useful to direct more attention to the area.

The overall total score can range between 20 and 100. Scores of 60 or more may suggest some general difficulty in coping on the dimensions covered.

Source: Reprinted from *Work Stress* (1979), Management Decision Systems, Inc.

GROUP INTERACTION

Break into groups of three or four. Compare your scale and total scores. Discuss what you might be able to do if your score is high.

Have the two people in each group with the highest score and lowest score enact a role-play. The person with the lowest score is the supervisor; the person with the highest is the employee. Assume that the supervisor has concluded that the employee seems to be acting strangely recently on his or her job. You think high stress may be part of the problem. Conduct a counselling session with the employee to discuss what you (the supervisor) might do to help the employee reduce his or her stress level.

SUMMARY

This summary is organized by the Learning Objectives.

1. Lewin's view of change treats change as a break in the organization's equilibrium state. Change is initiated and then stabilized at a new equilibrium. The contemporary view of change is that it is constant. Disequilibria is the natural state.

2. The forces for change in today's organization include new technologies (e.g., automation, computerization, smartphones); environmental dynamics (e.g., new government regulations, changing labour market, increased competition); and internal forces (e.g., reorganizations, change in strategy, new equipment introduced).

3. People resist change out of habit, fear of the unknown, selective perception, or if they perceive the change as a threat to their job, income, expertise, established power relationships, or interpersonal relationships.

4. Supervisors can reduce resistance by building trust, opening channels of communication, involving employees in the change decisions, providing empathy and support, and by providing incentives to employees for accepting change.

5. Stress is an adaptive response resulting from any environmental action, situation, or event that places excessive psychological and/or physical demands on a person.

6. Stress comes from organizational factors such as task and role demands, interpersonal demands, and structural variables; it can also be caused by individual factors such as family problems, economic problems, and personality variables.

7. The job demands-control-support model suggests that strain is created by any one of three factors existing (high demands, low control, low support) and magnified when these are combined. The effort-reward imbalance model attributes strain to the rewards (e.g. recognition, pay) not matching the efforts dedicated by the employee.

KEY TERMS AND CONCEPTS

Change agents
Change process
Effort-reward imbalance
    model
Job demand-control-
    support model
Negative affectivity
Role ambiguity

Role conflict
Role overload
Self-efficacy
Self-esteam
Stress
Type A behaviour
Type B behaviour

REVIEWING YOUR KNOWLEDGE

1. Give several examples of environmental forces that might affect supervisors and require changes in a department.
2. Describe the three-step model of the change process.
3. What signals or cues might tell you that an employee is resistant to a change you're planning to implement?
4. What is selective perception and how is it related to change resistance?
5. How does building trust lessen change resistance?
6. Why should supervisors be concerned with an employee's work-related stress?
7. Does stress increase or decrease when a person becomes a supervisor? Explain.
8. Is all stress bad? Discuss.
9. How can supervisors reduce employee stress?
10. Do supervisors have the right to inquire about, or try to help employees deal with, stresses that result from factors outside the job? Discuss.

CASE 13.A

Change Management at UNICEF

When Bonnie Shepherd became the National Manager of Business Development for the United Nations Children's Fund (UNICEF) in Canada after fundraising at the University of Toronto for years, she did not expect change management to be a key demand in the new job, but it quickly emerged as a fact of life. Bonnie had only been in the position for a short time when her manager, Dee, had to go on a leave for four months and Bonnie was asked to step in as acting Director of Corporate Partnerships. "We have a great working relationship and Dee was already mentoring me to prepare for a potential transition into a Director level role in the future. I was expecting this would be in several years but the situation changed to, 'how about in 6 weeks?"

Although the situation was a bit overwhelming, it was also an opportunity. "When I was approached by UNICEF's senior leadership team to step up and take on the Director position, I didn't hesitate; I saw it as an opportunity to escalate my own learning. Although I was new to the team, I had developed good working relationships with my colleagues and I felt I had the full support of management and my team. I felt we were unified and I was supported which gave the confidence I needed to take on this exciting challenge."

The new role was a huge adjustment not only for Bonnie but also for the rest of the corporate team who now reported directly to Bonnie. When Dee and Bonnie first discussed the possibility of Bonnie becoming acting director to cover her leave, Dee suggested discussing the idea with the staff one on one before the change was made. Bonnie agreed, and they met with each person to see if they were comfortable with the idea and whether they had any concerns that could be addressed ahead of time.

"I never felt isolated leading the team. Dee was an incredible support during the transition phase, as were my colleagues. As I was balancing both the Director position and my regular Business Development role, my days were consumed with internal and external meetings. My team was incredible and helped any way they could; updating my calendar via Blackberry on the fly, providing briefings prior to meetings, prepping my documents, even grabbing me lunch on the busiest days. They were so incredibly helpful. It was truly a team effort."

What Bonnie learned from her immediate immersion into change management has stood her in good stead in dealing with other organizational change. For example, UNICEF Canada phased out some fundraising streams in the corporate portfolio that had existed for years, affecting several people's jobs. "Working with strong leadership during this difficult period of change, I've learned that it is important to communicate major changes as soon as possible to provide opportunity to adjust. Start with general information when the change becomes a possibility–in this case we learned almost a year in advance that there was a chance certain programs would be phased out. The corporate team immediately started discussing how we would address this. The business decision behind the potential change was shared openly and we discussed what opportunities there may be in the new situation. From this experience I learned as change happens, it's important to be honest and give as much lead time as possible. I think this really helped the individuals most impacted feel they had some control over the situation."

Bonnie credits the weekly one on one meetings she has with team members as key to managing change in the workplace. Each meeting is about an hour long and the agenda is set by the team member, not Bonnie. "Meeting one on one with my team members has had tremendous positive impacts. We close the door, turn off the computer and the phone and we give each other our full attention. We do the same when I meet with my own manager as well. One on one meetings provide support and help prioritize our work. We provide updates on our accounts and we touch base to see if there are accomplishments to celebrate or challenges to work through strategically. Outside of that hour the days are busy and we don't always have moments to check in. These regular meetings result in open and honest communication. They build trust and provide a safe space to discuss work. Issues don't fester into larger unaddressed problems. These meetings also provide me with an opportunity to give my team updates, communicating information and updates from the senior level. If there is any change in strategy, very little comes as a surprise to my team. Everything has been communicated as early as possible, so we all feel well prepared to handle it as a team."

RESPONDING TO THIS CASE

1. What were the forces underlying the staff change and the dropping of certain fundraising streams?
2. Explain how the handling of Bonnie's temporary promotion reflects concepts from Lewin's three-step change process.
3. Identify the techniques for reducing resistance to change that are evident in this case.
4. Identify the stress reduction techniques evident in the case.

FIGURE 13-11
Bonnie Shepherd

CASE 13.B

Changes Leave Some Behind

As manager of client satisfaction for a multinational company for almost 20 years, Alex participated in ongoing changes as the company has evolved.

The company's restructuring described in another case (see Trickle Down Restructuring in Chapter 5) meant shifting client relationships for all of Alex's team members, and the need to establish trust and credibility each time. Two further changes made a major impact on her team: reengineering the reporting process across the company, and a decision to move the work of Alex's unit offshore.

Organizations generate many internal reports, summarizing and sharing information on activities and achievements. Alex's company decided that a lot of energy was being wasted creating reports needlessly and they embarked on an initiative to eliminate reports where unnecessary, and simplify and standardize the remaining ones. Applying the Pareto principle to this situation, they reckoned that 80% of the results were driven by 20% of the reports so they wanted to strip down to only those reports that were clearly useful. In Alex's area, some reports were eliminated, some were automated and a standard 25-page report was cut down to 5 pages. What did this mean for her staff? "Some staff wanted to change parts of the report, thinking to improve it, wanting to customize it as they were used to. I had to impress upon them that standardized means just that–no changes. Innovation is not in redesigning the report but in better using the information in the report to move the business forward. They needed to focus their energies on how to use the data well. This was not comfortable for everyone. For example, due to the simplification process, there was less reporting required. So someone who used to spend 75% of their time generating reports (which is a pretty basic task) is now spending only 50% of their time on this and expected to spend the rest of the time coaching, advising and using the data, which is much tougher."

Like many companies where a huge percentage of their costs lies in paying for labour, Alex's organization looked for savings by moving jobs to sources of cheaper labour. Starting with twenty positions in her unit serving all of North America when she stepped into management, there is now one. And it is not Alex. All other positions have been sent offshore to eastern Europe where there is a labour force that is highly educated, motivated, and inexpensive. Alex managed the transition, laying off individuals in North America gradually, and then training the new staff in eastern Europe. "Firing people is the worst part of a management job. Each year managers were asked to provide scenarios with particular budgets (e.g. if you were to cut the budget by 10% or 20%, how could it be done in your department). We would go through the names of staff and say this person would be downsized, this person could be redeployed in this other kind of position; we would provide input, but executives would decide which scenario to go with and when." The company had been clear about their strategy to move jobs to international hubs, and the need to work to specific targets, including reducing labour costs. So no one should have been surprised when it was their turn to be laid off. But some were. "Some felt tainted by being let go - why are others being kept? The whole perception depends on the individual. For example, one young employee took the summer off to be with his kids and appreciated being given the money to do that; he was planning to seek a job in the fall. The most challenging is someone 25 years in the business thinking they would always work with the company. This was a wakeup call, 45 years old and competing with the young for a new job. Many were eligible to retire so it was easier; for the younger who didn`t expect it, it was tougher. I knew what was likely and tried to get staff to investigate opportunities; I did every-

thing I could to get them out of the department, encouraging everyone in the department to do interest interviews to explore other openings in the company, I found mentors, I pushed them to go for job opportunities even if I was personally stuck missing needed support, but I knew what was coming. The relocation to eastern Europe happened over five years. If someone missed the company messages, there was trouble. Every year I explained to all of them that each year we lost one or two, and there was no reason why this year would be different."

In the end, Alex herself walked into one of those termination interviews. "It was strange to be on the other side of the table and see the process take place, having been through HR's training several times about what to say and do in a termination." Alex is taking her time to look for a new direction in her career. She has no bitterness. The company has survived and flourished because they made tough but necessary decisions. She saw the costs and the budget sheets and their actions made sense, even if it meant the end of her career there and that of many friends and colleagues.

RESPONDING TO THIS CASE

1. Describe the forces for change noted in the case.
2. Is Alex a change agent? Why or why not?
3. Describe the evidence of resistance to change illustrated in the case. What are the reasons?
4. Identify the techniques that Alex used to try to deal with the resistance to change.
5. Explain the individual differences that seem to be related to stress experienced.
6. Use the two models of stress to explain the stress experienced by employees in this case.

14

DISCIPLINING EMPLOYEES

Courtesy of VisionsofAmerica/Joe Sohm/Getty Images

LEARNING OBJECTIVES

After reading this chapter, you should be able to:

1. Define *discipline*.
2. Identify the four most common types of discipline problems.
3. List the typical steps in progressive discipline.
4. Explain the "hot stove" rule.
5. Describe the role of extenuating circumstances in applying discipline.
6. Explain the three legal dismissal situations.
7. Describe how a collective bargaining agreement affects the disciplining of unionized employees.

CHAPTER OUTLINE

PERFORMING EFFECTIVELY

WHAT IS DISCIPLINE?

TYPES OF DISCIPLINE PROBLEMS
    Attendance
    On-the-Job Behaviours
    Dishonesty
    Something to Think About
    Outside Activities

DISCIPLINE ISN'T ALWAYS THE SOLUTION

RELUCTANCE TO DISCIPLINE
    Something to Think About

BASIC TENETS OF DISCIPLINE
    Lay the Groundwork
    Make Discipline Progressive
    Follow the "Hot Stove" Rule
    What the Hot Stove Rule
        Doesn't Cover

FACTORS TO CONSIDER IN DISCIPLINING

DISCIPLINE AND THE LAW
    Unionization

FROM CONCEPTS TO SKILLS: DISCIPLINING
    Assessing Yourself: Are You
        Effective at Disciplining?
    Skill Basics
    Applying Your Skills

UNDERSTANDING THE BASICS
    Summary
    Key Terms and Concepts
    Reviewing Your Knowledge

PERFORMING YOUR JOB
    Case 14.A: Supporting an
        Effective Discipline
        Process
    Case 14.B: Terminating the
        Poor Employee Leads to
        More Trouble

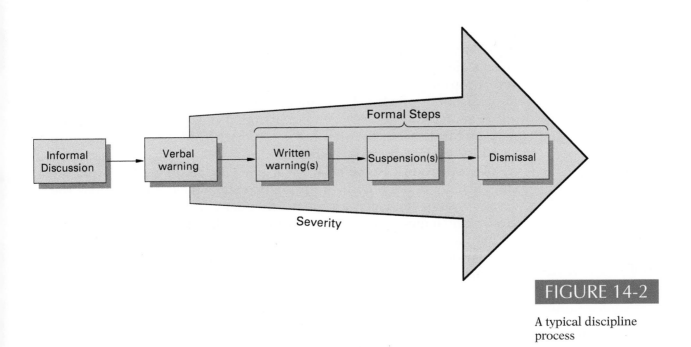

PERFORMING EFFECTIVELY

FIGURE 14-1

Shelby D'Ambrogio sometimes has to discipline employees at AMC Theatres

You read about Shelby D'Ambrogio's experience at the start of Chapter 1. At AMC Theatres, Shelby works hard to prepare and support staff in doing their job well and enjoying their work experience. But sometimes she has to deal with discipline issues, where an employee is capable of performing and is choosing not to.

"At AMC we would start with a discipline warning. It may end up in a termination for severe misconduct. Misconducts range from things like not redeeming a coupon to theft. For lesser infractions, I would record the date and what the employee did and I would sit with the employee and explain why I was writing them up. There would be a discussion as to whether they need coaching or training. I would have them show me the correct action. For serious infractions, I would call home office and ask them what steps they'd like us to follow. I have witnessed a termination by the general manager based on my recommendation. Sometimes employees are given time to fix something and put on a three-month contract for this purpose."

As Shelby describes, discipline is a corrective action, not a punishment. In this chapter we will discuss typical discipline issues, and an effective discipline process.

WHAT IS DISCIPLINE?

Discipline Actions taken by supervisors to enforce an organization's standards and regulations.

What specifically do we mean when we use the term **discipline** in the workplace? It refers to actions taken by a supervisor to enforce the organization's standards and regulations. It generally follows a typical sequence of four steps: verbal warning, written warning, suspension, and dismissal (see Figure 14-2) and is frequently preceded by an informal discussion when the unacceptable behaviour is first noticed.

Formal Steps

Informal Discussion → Verbal warning → Written warning(s) → Suspension(s) → Dismissal

Severity

A typical discipline process

An informal discussion is a check to ensure the employee knows what is expected and is capable of meeting those expectations. For example, Debbie Hinz, production supervisor of a lab at Precision Biologic, describes an informal but critical discussion she had with a young contract worker who was texting at work: "She was shocked that it was an issue. When I spoke with her I explained why it was inappropriate. One, we have lab areas in the building with strict biosafety rules so texting is a safety issue—people remove their gloves to handle the phone and then do not wash their hands so they are contaminating. Two, if you are texting, your focus is not on your work and this opens the door to mistakes—in her case there had been instances of errors. There are specific processes we follow in the production lab and there is no room for interruption of these processes." The employee corrected her behaviour immediately so there was no need for any formal discipline.

The mildest form of discipline is the **verbal warning**. A verbal warning is a temporary record of a reprimand, which is placed in the supervisor's file. This verbal warning typically states the purpose, date, and outcome of the feedback session with you. If the verbal warning is effective, no further disciplinary action is needed. However, if an employee fails to improve his or her performance, he or she will encounter more severe action—the written warning. The **written warning** is the first formal stage of the disciplinary procedure. This is because the written warning becomes part of an employee's official personnel file. In all

Verbal warning
A temporary record of a reprimand, which is placed in the supervisor's file.

Written warning
The first formal stage of the disciplinary procedure; the warning becomes part of an employee's official personnel file.

other ways, however, the written warning is similar to the verbal warning. That is, the employee is advised in private of the violation, its effects, and potential consequences of future violations. All written and verbal warnings also contain suggestions on how to improve behaviour or descriptions of what the desired behaviour is, often quoting relevant policy and procedures. Also, after a period of time if no further disciplinary problems arise, the warning is removed from the file. See Figure 14-3 for a sample discipline letter.

Suspension
Time off without pay; this step is usually taken only if neither verbal nor written warnings have achieved desired results.

A **suspension** or time off without pay may be the next disciplinary step, usually taken only if the prior two steps have not achieved the desired results—although exceptions do exist where suspension may be given without any prior verbal or written warning if the infraction is of a serious nature. Why would you suspend an employee? One reason is that a short lay-off, without pay, is potentially a rude awakening. It may convince the employee that you are serious, and may help him or her to fully understand and accept responsibility for following the organization's rules.

Suspensions may be paid or unpaid. Most are unpaid as "time-outs" for the employee to reflect on the seriousness of their behaviour. Suspensions are paid if there is an internal investigation into the employee's actions because the investigation may clear the employee of responsibility.

Dismissal
Termination of employment.

Your ultimate disciplinary punishment is terminating employment. While **dismissal** is often used for the most serious offences, it may be the only feasible alternative if your employee's behaviour seriously interferes with a department or the organization's operation. A lot of employers are now putting termination clauses in offer letters, dictating the behaviours and infractions that would lead to dismissal, to ensure clear communication.

While many organizations may follow the stepwise process described above, recognize that it may be bypassed if an employee's behaviour is extreme. For example, stealing, or attacking another employee with intent to inflict serious harm, may result in immediate suspension or dismissal. Regardless of any action taken, however, discipline should be fair and consistent. That is, the punishment an employee receives should be appropriate to what he or she did, and others doing the same thing should be disciplined in a like manner.

Re: Summary of Punctuality Issue[1]

Dear EMPLOYEE NAME

This letter is in regards to our meeting on DATE. In attendance were you, myself, and OTHER ATTENDEES (e.g. union representative, human resources consultant). The purpose of the meeting was to discuss your incidents of lateness and to explore options to enable consistent punctuality at work. We discussed your punctuality between DATE to DATE. Below is a summary of the days on which you were late.

LIST DATES ON WHICH EMPLOYEE WAS LATE

At the meeting, we inquired if there was anything contributing to your high rate of lateness. You indicated CONTRIBUTING FACTORS (e.g. family issue, medical reason). We suggested several options for your consideration on how to resolve and cope with the issues at hand. The options we discussed are:

1. OPTION #1 (e.g. variable hours, job share, employee assistance program)
2. OPTION #2 (e.g. variable hours, job share, employee assistance program)
3. OPTION #3 (e.g. variable hours, job share, employee assistance program)

As we discussed, your punctuality is a necessary component in the effective and efficient delivery of services to our clients. Lateness leads to increased workloads for the remaining staff performing the work and disrupts the coordination of your work with theirs. You indicated you understood the importance of punctuality.

It is important that you realize that excessive lateness with no likelihood of change can lead to termination of employment through frustration of the employment contract.

We also agreed to review your progress on DATE. My expectation is that your punctuality will improve and there will be no need for a second written warning.

Sincerely

NAME
TITLE

Copy to Personnel File

---

[1]Adapted from Formal Meeting Phase #1 Form Letter, Attendance Support Policy: Application Guidelines. Public Service Commission, Government of Saskatchewan http://www.psc.gov.sk.ca/attendance

FIGURE 14-3

Sample discipline
letter

TYPES OF DISCIPLINE PROBLEMS

With very little difficulty, we could list several dozen or more infractions that supervisors might believe require disciplinary action. For simplicity's sake, we have classified the more frequent violations into four categories: attendance, on-the-job behaviours, dishonesty, and outside activities.

ATTENDANCE

The most common disciplinary problems facing supervisors undoubtedly involve attendance. For instance, in a study of 200 organizations, 60 per-cent of which employed over 1000 workers, absenteeism, tardiness, abuse of sick leave, and other aspects of attendance were rated as the foremost problems by 79 per cent of the respondents.[1] Importantly, attendance problems appear to be even more widespread than those related to pro-ductivity (carelessness in doing work, neglect of duty, and not following established procedures).

ON-THE-JOB BEHAVIOURS

This blanket label includes insubordination, bullying, harassment, horse-play, fighting, gambling, failure to use safety devices, carelessness, alcohol and drug abuse, and inappropriate use of e-mail and the internet. (see Something to Think About).

DISHONESTY

Although it is not one of the more widespread employee problems con-fronting a supervisor, dishonesty has traditionally resulted in the most severe disciplinary actions. One study found that 90 per cent of surveyed organizations would discharge an employee for theft, even if it was only a first offence. Similarly, 88 per cent would discharge employees who were found to have falsified information on their employment applications.[2] These findings reflect the strong cultural norm against dishonesty in North America. More common dishonesty examples include falsifying time or expense records.

OUTSIDE ACTIVITIES

Our final problem category covers activities that employees engage in outside of work, but which either affect their on-the-job performance or generally reflect negatively on the organization's image. Included here are unauthorized strike activity, outside criminal activities, and working for a competing organization.

EMAIL, SOCIAL MEDIA, AND INTERNET USE CAN LEAD TO DISCIPLINE

Fourteen Vancouver police officers ranging in rank from constable to inspector were disciplined for viewing and e-mailing pornography and other inappropriate and offensive images while at work. "They know better," Chief Chu told reporters. "Our policies are clear, and when this happens, we will hold them accountable."[3] Parks Canada disciplined a group of employees for distributing an email that contained a racist joke portraying aboriginal people and African-Canadians in a negative light. The email was pulled from Parks Canada systems as soon as it came to light.[4]

Two employees of a BC automobile dealing and accessory shop were terminated for posting offensive statements on Facebook. The angry posts were threatening and homophobic and named the employers, calling them crooks and warning people not to spend their money at the shop. The BC Labour Relations Board upheld the dismissals saying there could be no expectation of privacy (especially given they shared the comments with hundreds of Facebook "friends," including other employees), and the comments amounted to insubordination and "egregious" misconduct.[5] A Canada Post employee was also fired for comments on Facebook, some of which targeted and threatened specific managers. The Arbitrator in the hearing found that the comments were "universally nasty in tone and content," "offensive and frightening" and were "publicly disseminated and destructive of workplace relationships." Despite the employee's long service and lack of prior disciplinary issues, the arbitrator agreed with her termination from her position.[6]

A respiratory therapist at an Alberta hospital was dismissed for looking at pornography on a hospital computer. Though he was remorseful, had six years of discipline-free service and had not neglected his duties, the hospital fired him for violating its computer-use policy. An arbitrator upheld the termination because of the trust issue: if word ever got out to the therapist's female patients about his excessive online porn surfing, there would be discomfort. Interestingly, the dismissal of an employee of Citizenship and Immigration Canada for spending more than one-half of his time surfing the Internet, including looking at pornography, was not upheld by an arbitrator because of the employee's 27 years of discipline-free service. However, he did receive a 20-month unpaid suspension.[7]

Disciplining for improper use of email, social media or the internet obviously can be done. But it is not easy. Dismissals have been overturned on the basis that there was no related policy or no proof that the policy was known to the employee. In order to avoid issues with the use of technology, and to support the supervisor if disciplining is required, it is important to:

- Establish policy regarding the use of technology.
- Communicate the policy and the reasons for the policy. Communicate regularly. Ensure employees know the consequences of choosing to violate the policy.
- Educate employees regarding expectations of privacy.[8]

DISCIPLINE ISN'T ALWAYS THE SOLUTION

Just because you have a problem with an employee, don't assume that discipline is the automatic answer. Before you consider disciplining an employee, be sure that the employee has both the ability and the influence to correct his or her behaviour.

If an employee doesn't have the ability—that is, he or she *can't* perform—disciplinary action is not the answer. Similarly, if there are external factors beyond the employee's control that block goal attainment—for example, inadequate equipment, disruptive colleagues, or excessive noise —discipline doesn't make much sense. If an employee *can* perform but won't, then disciplinary action is called for. However, ability problems should be responded to with solutions such as skill training, on-the-job coaching, job redesign, or a job transfer. Serious personal problems that interfere with work performance are typically best met with professional counselling or a medical referral. And, of course, if there are external obstacles in the employee's way, you should act to remove them. The point is that if the cause of an employee's problem is outside his or her control, then discipline is not the answer.

RELUCTANCE TO DISCIPLINE

Supervisors are responsible for taking disciplinary action when necessary. Many do not. They are uncomfortable with the task so they avoid it, feeling unprepared to handle it, hesitant in their own skills to do it effectively, and concerned about harming their relationship with the employee.

Diane Hebert: "Some managers won't deal with poor performance. This causes departmental performance to drop because other staff watch, expecting it to be dealt with. When it's not, morale and productivity are affected. It can also disrupt other departments. For example, there was a young woman from the finance department who would disappear and bother the men in another department. The Manager of that department asked her supervisor three times to deal with her. Finally, the vice president asked me (the HR manager) to sit with her supervisor and show her how to talk to the employee so she would change her behaviour."

It is important the organization train supervisors and provide them with the tools to discipline effectively. Again, Diane explains: "It's not enough to say 'We need to look at absenteeism issues.' You need to develop a program, a way of tracking absenteeism and dealing with it. For example, create a three-month probation tool so managers know what to look for and how to evaluate it. You can't leave it up to managers to simply 'know'".

Consistent discipline is critical within a department but also across departments. Supervisors need to know specific expectations (e.g. at what point does lateness become a discipline issue?) and precedents so they can present a united support for policies and procedures at the organization. Diane Hebert explains: "One manager only allows one smoke break in the morning and one in the afternoon, whereas another manager allows smokers to take hourly breaks. People want rules and regulations. They make comparisons and see inconsistencies and unfairness. It affects morale and productivity. Yes, they also want flexibility, but reasonable exceptions can be made to a situation that others will understand."

See Dealing With a Difficult Issue to consider the interesting situation of a supervisor being disciplined for not effectively disciplining staff members.

SOMETHING TO THINK ABOUT
• AND TO PROMOTE CLASS DISCUSSION •

BEING DISCIPLINED FOR NOT DISCIPLINING

Below is a discipline letter sent to a supervisor. Amongst infractions noted, the letter describes the supervisor as not being consistent and effective in disciplining employees. After reading the letter, consider what the underlying issues may be for this supervisor's performance. What actions could the company take to support improvement in the supervisor's performance?

"Dear _____

This letter will confirm our meeting on April 12, 20XX where we discussed various performance issues pertaining to your position as Production Supervisor.
During our discussion I expressed to you my concern with your overall performance in the position of Production Supervisor, and

the inability to meet the expectations of your role. I expressed my concern to you regarding your leadership, being unapproachable to operators, and consistency and effectiveness of discipline. Being in a leadership role, it is imperative that you lead by example, and meet the Company expectations for acceptable performance.

On April 6, I met with you to discuss the overall expectations and objectives of a Production Supervisor. It was discussed that as a Production Supervisor it is your responsibility to create a positive environment and motivate employees to be efficient and effective in their roles. There have been occasions where operators and co-workers have found you to be unapproachable and feel uncomfortable coming to you with concerns or problems. As a Supervisor it is important to always display a positive attitude and to promote a team environment.

We also discussed the importance of effective and consistence performance management. At times you have neglected to discipline employees to avoid confrontation. Supervisors are responsible for consistent, fair and effective discipline. By avoiding disciplinary action employees will lose respect for supervisors, policies and procedures.

During our discussion I asked you if you would like to continue in your role as Production Supervisor or pursue other opportunities. You have decided to remain in your current role. During our discussion, you agreed that your performance needed to improve and you reassured me that I would see an improvement with the areas of concern outlined above.

I will be reviewing with you the performance concerns as outlined in this letter, in (8) eight weeks (date), to determine if improvements have been made. This is sufficient time for you to make improvements in your performance as a Production Supervisor. Should your performance not improve, and you do not meet our expectations by the week of June 12, further disciplinary action will be taken which may result in your discharge from the Company. I am confident that further discussions regarding your performance will not be necessary. If improvement is not made with respect to your job performance, further disciplinary action may be taken."

BASIC TENETS OF DISCIPLINE

Based on decades of experience, supervisors have learned what works best when administering discipline. In this section, we'll review some of the lessons learned. We'll present the basic groundwork that needs to be laid prior to any punitive action, the importance of making discipline progressive, and how the "hot stove" rule can guide your actions.

LAY THE GROUNDWORK

Any disciplinary action you take should be perceived as fair and reasonable. This increases the likelihood that the employee will change his or her behaviour to align with the organization's standards, and also prevents unnecessary legal entanglements. The foundation of a fair and reasonable disciplinary climate is created by ensuring that employees are given adequate advance notice of disciplining rules and that a proper investigation precedes any action.

Evidence must be documented and substantiated. The organization should have thorough and well communicated policies and procedures which are up-to-date and available to all employees. Some companies require all employees to sign off that they have read, understood and will comply with the policy manual. Any changes to policy or procedures need to be clearly communicated.

ADVANCE NOTICE

Employees have a right to know what is expected of them and the probable consequences should they fail to meet those expectations. They should also understand just how serious different types of offences are. This information can be communicated in employee handbooks, company newsletters, posted rules, or labour contracts. The fact that CP Rail had a message informing users about unauthorized use of the company's e-mail whenever users logged on was instrumental in upholding a dismissal for improper e-mail use.[9] It is always preferable to have these expectations in writing. This provides protection for you, the organization, and your employees.

PROPER INVESTIGATION

Fair treatment of employees demands that a proper investigation precede any decision. Employees should be treated as innocent until proven guilty. And importantly, no judgement should occur before all the relevant facts have been gathered.

As the employee's supervisor, you will typically be responsible for conducting the investigation. However, if the problem includes an interpersonal conflict between you and the employee, a neutral third party should be chosen to conduct the investigation.

The investigation should focus not only on the event that might lead to discipline but also on any related matters. This is important because these related concerns may reveal mitigating factors that will need to be considered. And, of course, the employee must be notified of the offence with which he or she is being charged so that a defence can be prepared. Remember, you have an obligation to listen objectively to the employee's interpretation and explanation of the offence. A fair and objective investigation will include identification and interviewing of any witnesses and documentation of all evidence that is uncovered.

Failure to conduct a full and impartial investigation can carry high costs. A good employee may be unjustly punished, the trust of other employees may be severely jeopardized, and you may place your organization under possible risk for financial damages should the employee file a suit.

Make Discipline Progressive

Progressive discipline Penalties are made progressively stronger if, or when, an offence is repeated.

Punishment should be applied in steps. That is, penalties should get progressively stronger if or when an offence is repeated. As outlined at the start of this chapter, progressive disciplinary action typically begins with a verbal warning, and then proceeds through written reprimands, suspension, and finally, in the most serious cases, dismissal (see Figure 14-2).

The logic underlying **progressive discipline** is twofold. First, stronger penalties for repeated offences discourage repetition. Second, progressive discipline is consistent with court and arbitration rulings that mitigating factors (such as length of service, past performance record, or ambiguous organizational policies) be considered when taking disciplinary action.

Follow the "Hot Stove" Rule

"Hot stove" rule Principles that can guide disciplining; the action should be immediate, offer advance warning, be consistent, and impartial, and guide future behaviour.

The **"hot stove" rule** is a frequently cited set of principles that can guide you in effectively disciplining an employee.[10] The name comes from the similarities between touching a hot stove and administering discipline.

When you touch a hot stove, you get an immediate response: the burn you receive is instantaneous, leaving no doubt in your mind about the cause and the effect. You have ample warning: you know in advance what happens if you touch a red-hot stove. Further, the result is consistent: every time you touch a hot stove, you get the same response—you get burned. The result is impartial. Regardless of who you are, if you touch a hot stove, you will be burned. Finally, there is a clear guide to future behaviour: avoid being burned by refraining from touching the hot stove. The analogy with discipline should be apparent, but let's briefly expand on each of these points because they are central tenets in developing your disciplining skills.

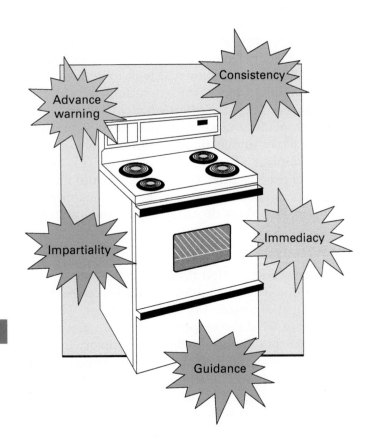

FIGURE 14-4
The "hot stove" rule

IMMEDIACY

The impact of a disciplinary action will be reduced as the time between the infraction and the penalty's implementation lengthens. The more quickly the discipline follows the offence, the more likely it is that the employee will associate the discipline with the offence rather than with you as the imposer of the discipline. Of course, the immediacy requirement should not result in undue haste. Fair and objective treatment should not be compromised for expediency.

ADVANCE WARNING

As we noted earlier, you have an obligation to give advance warning before initiating formal disciplinary action. This means the employee must be aware of the organization's rules and accept its standards of behaviour. Disciplinary action is more likely to be interpreted as fair by employees when they have received clear warning that a given violation will lead to discipline and when they know what that discipline will be.

CONSISTENCY

Fair treatment of employees demands that disciplinary action be consistent. If you enforce rule violations in an inconsistent manner, the rules will lose their impact. Morale will decline and employees will question your competence. Productivity will suffer as a result of employee insecurity and anxiety. Your employees will want to know the limits of permissible behaviour and they will look to your actions for guidance. If Hans is reprimanded today for an action he took last week, at which time nothing was said, these limits become blurry. Similarly, if Pooja and Nitu are both goofing around at their desks and only Pooja is reprimanded, Nitu is likely to question the fairness of the action. The point, then, is that discipline should be consistent. This need not result in treating everyone exactly alike, because that would mean ignoring mitigating circumstances. But it does put the responsibility on you to clearly justify disciplinary actions that may appear inconsistent to employees.

IMPARTIALITY

The next guideline that flows from the "hot stove" rule is to keep the discipline impartial. Penalties should be connected with a given violation, not with the personality of the violator. That is, discipline should be directed at what the employee has done, not at the employee. As a supervisor, you should make it clear that you are avoiding personal judgements about the employee's character. You are penalizing the rule violation, not the individual. And all employees committing the violation can be expected to be penalized. Further, once the penalty has been imposed, you must make every effort to forget the incident. You should attempt to treat the employee in the same manner you did prior to the infraction.

Discipline is meant to correct, not to humiliate or degrade the employee. Treating the employee in a demeaning, disrespectful way will likely lead to consequences not bargained for. The resentful employee may comply but will be generally demotivated and will work only to the minimum standard. Meanwhile, colleagues who learn of the poor treatment will lose respect for the supervisor and question the fairness of other decisions made by the supervisor. Employees may become less than cooperative with the supervisor. One discipline situation with an individual can lead to a morale issue in the whole team.

GUIDANCE

The last guideline refers to informing the employee about what will happen in future if they repeat the infraction and clarifying what behaviour is expected to avoid future disciplinary action. "Once burned, twice shy" describes the quick lesson we learn from touching a hot stove. Similarly, an employee in a disciplinary situation should leave with a crystal clear understanding of what will happen if they repeat the offence and what behaviour is expected of them.

FACTORS TO CONSIDER IN DISCIPLINING

Defining what is "reasonable in relation to the offence" is one of the most challenging aspects of the discipline process. Why? Because infractions vary greatly in terms of severity. Suspending an employee is considerably more stringent than issuing a verbal warning. Similarly, the decision to fire someone—the organizational equivalent of the death penalty—is dramatically more punitive than a two-week suspension without pay. If you fail to recognize relevant extenuating factors and make the proper adjustments in the severity of penalties, you risk having your action perceived as being unfair. The following factors (summarized in Figure 14-5) should be taken into consideration when applying discipline:

1. **Seriousness of the problem.** How severe is the problem? Dishonesty, for example, is usually considered a more serious infraction than reporting to work 20 minutes late.
2. **Duration of the problem.** Have there been other discipline problems with this employee, and if so, over how long a time span? A first occurrence is usually viewed differently from a third or fourth offence.
3. **Frequency and nature of the problem.** Is the current problem part of an emerging or continuing pattern of discipline infractions? Continual infractions may require a different type of discipline from that applied to isolated instances of misconduct.
4. **Employee's work history.** How long has the employee worked for the organization, and what has been the quality of his or her performance? For many violations, the punishment will be less severe for those who have developed a strong track record.

- Seriousness of the problem

- Duration of the problem

- Frequency and nature of the problem

- Employee's work history

- Extenuating circumstances

- Degree of warning

- History of the organization's discipline practices

- Implications for other employees

- Upper-management support

FIGURE 14-5

Relevant factors determining the severity of penalties

5. **Extenuating circumstances.** Are there extenuating factors, such as influences outside the employee's control, that lessen the severity of the infraction? The employee who missed the plane for an important meeting because his wife went into labour with their first child is likely to have his violation assessed more leniently than would his peer who missed the same plane because he overslept.

6. **Degree of warning.** To what extent has the employee been previously warned about the offence? Did he or she know and understand the rule that was broken? As we have noted several times previously, discipline severity should reflect the degree of knowledge the violator holds of the organization's standards of acceptable behaviour. In addition, an organization that has formalized written rules governing employee conduct is more justified in aggressively enforcing violations than is an organization whose rules are informal or vague.

7. **History of the organization's discipline practices.** How have similar infractions been dealt with in the past within your department? Within the entire organization? Equitable treatment of employees must take into consideration precedents within the unit where the infraction occurs, as well as previous disciplinary actions taken in other units within the organization.

8. **Implications for other employees.** What impact will the discipline selected have on other workers in the unit? There is little point in taking a certain action against an employee if it will have a major dysfunctional effect on others within the unit. The result may be to convert a narrow and single disciplinary problem into a severe supervisory headache. Conversely, failure to impose discipline where it's justified can reduce departmental morale, undermine your credibility, and lessen employee concern for obeying the rules. For instance, more than 40 per cent of respondents to a survey felt their managers were too lenient with poor performers, which generated resentment among hard-working employees.[11]

9. **Upper-management support.** If a disciplined employee decides to appeal the case to a higher level of management, will you have reasonable evidence to justify your decision? If you have the data to support your action, can you count on your superiors backing you up? Your disciplinary actions aren't likely to carry much weight if violators believe that they can get your decision overridden.

DISCIPLINE AND THE LAW

Making a mistake when disciplining an employee can have very serious repercussions for an organization. As a result, most large organizations have specific procedures that supervisors are required to follow.

Supervisors typically are provided training in how to handle the discipline process. Moreover, they are encouraged to work closely with staff specialists in the human resources department.

Most large corporations have specific rules to follow, including documentation and progressive steps, in cases that might lead to eventual dismissal. As a supervisor, it is your responsibility to defend your disciplinary actions. Proper documentation is the best protection against employees who claim, "I never knew there was any problem," or, "I was treated unfairly." In addition, you will want to obey **due process** when taking any disciplinary action. This includes:

1. a presumption of innocence until reasonable proof of an employee's role in an offence is substantiated;
2. the right of the employee to be heard, and in some cases to be represented by another person; and
3. discipline that is reasonable in relation to the offence involved.

Does the threat of legal action then prevent companies from letting employees go? Certainly not. In Canada, there are three basic ways to dismiss employees.

DISMISSAL WITH JUST CAUSE

These cases involve employees with documented offences such as disobedience of a lawful and reasonable order, gross negligence, or criminal activities. The supervisor must have documented proof of such offences.

Impeccable documentation is essential in all cases of just cause. When a just cause dismissal is challenged in court, the burden of proof that the action was justified will lie with the organization.

DISMISSAL WITH REASONABLE NOTICE

An employee can be discharged, even if performance is entirely satisfactory, as long as reasonable notice is given. Provincial Employment Standards Acts and the federal Labour Code define the minimum notice periods. Since these regulations change frequently, supervisors need to take care to keep abreast of the legislative updates.

DISMISSAL WITH REASONABLE COMPENSATION

Again, a satisfactory employee might be let go immediately, with reasonable compensation in lieu of notice. Provincial and federal acts again outline the conditions of minimum compensation.

UNIONIZATION

What if your employees are unionized and are protected by a collective bargaining agreement? How does this affect the disciplinary process?

Where employees belong to a union, there will be a *collective bargaining agreement*. This agreement, among other things, will outline rules governing the behaviour of union members. It will also identify disciplinary procedures and clarify the steps members are to follow if they believe that they are receiving arbitrary or unfair treatment.

The collective bargaining agreement will typically define what represents a rule violation and what penalties are applicable. Keep in mind that the more serious actions - suspension or dismissal of an employee—usually can be expected to be vigorously opposed by both the employee and the union.

Most collective bargaining agreements

1. stipulate that employees can only be disciplined for "just cause";
2. provide a grievance procedure; and
3. afford opportunities for third-party review if employees believe they have been wronged.

Disciplining unionized employees, therefore, tends to be a more quasi-legal undertaking than disciplining nonunion employees. The bargaining contract, the existence of a grievance procedure, the right to have differences evaluated and resolved by a third party, and the whole quasi-legal labour-management relationship all act to reduce your authority as a supervisor in taking disciplinary action.

Union leaders tend to argue in favour of resolution of problems rather than discipline, except in the case of criminal actions by employees. Depending on the maturity of the workplace relationship, the union can play a role in helping to solve the problem. Many unions view discipline as a draconian system that represses the workers, and if coupled with a lean operating philosophy, discipline measures often come down hard on absenteeism. A real problem can develop if legitimate time off is challenged. Increased pressure is felt by all workers because those at work are expected to produce despite a workforce depleted by absent employees. Union members would prefer to look at resolving the bigger issue of what causes absenteeism than face discipline for days away from work.

Specific examples and challenges of disciplining within a unionized environment are discussed in Chapter 15.

DISCIPLINING

Let's translate what you've learned about disciplining into specific skills you can apply on the job. As we've done throughout this book, we'll begin by testing your current basic skill level.

ASSESSING YOURSELF: ARE YOU EFFECTIVE AT DISCIPLINING?

For each of the following statements, select the answer that best describes you. Remember to respond as you have behaved or would behave, not as you think you should behave. If you have no supervisory experience, answer the statements assuming you were a supervisor.

WHEN DISCIPLINING AN EMPLOYEE:	Usually	Sometimes	Seldom
1. I provide ample warning before taking formal action.	❑	❑	❑
2. I wait for a pattern of infractions before calling it to the employee's attention.	❑	❑	❑
3. Even after repeated offences, I prefer informal discussion about correcting the problem rather than formal disciplinary action.	❑	❑	❑
4. I delay confronting the employee about an infraction until his or her next performance-appraisal review.	❑	❑	❑
5. In discussing an infraction with the employee, my style and tone are serious.	❑	❑	❑
6. I explicitly seek to allow the employee to explain his or her position.	❑	❑	❑
7. I remain impartial in allocating punishment.	❑	❑	❑
8. I allocate stronger penalties for repeated offences.	❑	❑	❑

SCORING KEY AND INTERPRETATION

For questions 1, 5, 6, 7, and 8, give yourself three points for Usually, two points for Sometimes, and one point for Seldom.

For questions 2, 3, and 4, give yourself three points for Seldom, two points for Sometimes, and one point for Usually.

Total up your points. A score of 22 points or higher indicates excellent skills at disciplining. Scores in the 19 to 21 range suggest some deficiencies. Scores below nineteen indicate considerable room for improvement.

SKILL BASICS

The following dozen principles should guide you when you have to discipline an employee.

1. **Before you accuse anyone, do your homework.** What happened? If you didn't personally see the infraction, investigate and verify any accusations made by others. Was it completely the employee's fault? If not, who or what else was involved? Did the employee know and understand the rule or regulation that was broken? Document the facts: date, time, place, individuals involved, mitigating circumstances, and the like.

2. **Provide ample warning.** Before you take formal action, be sure you've provided the employee with reasonable previous warnings and that those warnings have been documented. Ask yourself: if challenged, will my action be defensible? Did I provide ample warning to the employee before taking formal action? It's very likely that applying stiffer punitive actions later on will be judged as unjust by the employee, an arbitrator, and the courts if it is determined that these punitive actions could not be readily anticipated by the employee. New supervisors, whose predecessors were lax on discipline, often move quickly to tighten discipline practices. Their frequent mistake is failing to provide adequate notice to employees of this change. In these cases, employees have a good basis for claiming arbitrary and discriminatory practices.

   The preliminary warning should typically be informal and of the verbal variety. That is, you point out the rule violation, the problem that this infraction has caused, what the correct behaviour should be, and the specific consequences if the infraction is repeated.

   It's a good idea to make a temporary record of this oral reprimand and place it in the employee's file. Once the employee has corrected the problem, the record of the reprimand can be removed.

Of course, if this warning is ineffective, you have documentation of your warning.

3. **Act in a timely fashion.** When you become aware of an infraction and it has been supported by your investigation, do something and do it quickly. Delay weakens the link between actions and consequences, sends the wrong message to others, undermines your credibility with your subordinates, creates doubt that any action will be taken, and invites repetition of the problem.

4. **Conduct the discipline session in private.** Praise employees in public but keep punishment private. Your objective is not to humiliate the violator. Public reprimands embarrass an employee and are unlikely to produce the change in behaviour you desire.

5. **Adopt a calm and serious tone.** Many interpersonal situations are facilitated by a loose, informal, and relaxed manner on the part of a supervisor. The idea in such situations is to put the employee at ease. Administering discipline is not one of those situations. Avoid anger or other emotional responses, and convey your comments in a calm and serious tone. But do not try to lessen the tension by cracking jokes or making small talk. Such actions are only likely to confuse the employee because they send out conflicting signals. At the same time, your communication must be respectful, whether it is the words you choose or your body language. An employee who has made a major error still wants to maintain their dignity.

6. **Be specific about the problem.** When you sit down with the employee, indicate that you have documentation and be specific about the problem. Define the violation in exact terms instead of just citing company regulations or the union contract. Explain why the behaviour can't be continued by showing how it specifically affects the employee's job performance, the unit's effectiveness, and the employee's coworkers.

7. **Keep it impersonal.** Criticism should be focused on the employee's behaviour rather than on the individual personally. For instance, if an employee has been late for work several times, point out how this behaviour has increased the workload of others or has lowered departmental morale. Don't criticize the person for being thoughtless or irresponsible.

8. **Get the employee's side of the story.** Regardless of what your investigation has revealed, due process demands that you give the employee the opportunity to explain his or her position. From the employee's perspective, what happened? Why did it happen? What was his or her perception of the rules, regulations, and circumstances? If there are significant discrepancies between your version of the violation and the employee's, you may need to do more investigating. Of course, you'll want to document your employee's response for the record.

   Keep an open mind and use your active listening skills. It is possible that your initial information on the violation was biased or in error. Additionally, there might be extenuating circumstances of which you were unaware. The point is that you should not merely go through the motions to meet "due process" requirements; rather, you should solicit the employee's explanation to ensure that you have all the relevant facts.

9. **Keep control of the discussion.** In most interpersonal exchanges with employees, you want to encourage open dialogue. You want to give up control and create a climate of communication between equals. This won't work in administering discipline. Why? Violators are prone to use any leverage to put you on the defensive. In other words, if you don't take control, they will. Disciplining, by definition, is an authority-based act. You are enforcing the organization's standards and regulations. So take control. Ask the employee for his or her side of the story. Get the facts. But don't let the employee interrupt you or divert you from your objective.

10. **Agree on how mistakes can be prevented next time.**
    Disciplining should include guidance and direction for correcting the problem. Let the employee state what he or she plans to do in the future to ensure that the violation isn't repeated. For serious violations, have the employee draft a step-by-step plan to change the problem behaviour. Then set a timetable, with follow-up meetings in which progress can be evaluated. If the employee is genuinely unable to develop a satisfactory solution to the problem, you may be called upon to become a counsellor. You might need to help the employee understand the problem, identify courses of corrective action, assess the advantages and disadvantages of each, and plan a specific strategy for improving the situation. When the root of the problem is personal (relationships, children, financial, or the like) or has considerable emotional content, you may need to direct the employee to a professional counsellor.

11. **Select progressive disciplinary action and consider mitigating circumstances.** Choose a punishment that is appropriate to the crime. For the typical minor infraction, begin with a verbal warning, and then progress up the disciplinary chain. For more serious violations (for example, stealing, falsification of records, sabotage, gross insubordination, selling drugs at the work site, or attacking another employee with the intent to do serious harm) stronger punishments are justified from the outset. The punishment you select should be viewed as fair and consistent. But once you've arrived at your decision, tell the employee what the action will be, your reasons for taking it, and when it will be carried out.

12. **Fully document the disciplinary session.** To complete your disciplinary action, make sure that your ongoing documentation (what occurred, the results of your investigation, your initial warnings, the employee's explanation and responses, the discipline decision, and the consequences of further misconduct) is complete and accurate. This full documentation should be made part of the employee's permanent file. In addition, it's a good idea to give the employee a formal letter that highlights what was resolved during your discussion, specifics about the punishment, future expectations, and what actions you are prepared to take if the behaviour isn't corrected or the violation is repeated.

Applying Your Skills

Divide into groups of three or four and take turns being the observer and the two role players in the following four role-plays. Only read your role-play when it is your turn. The "supervisor" in each role-play is expected to handle the disciplinary situation using the guidelines described in the chapter.

1. What a Mess!

BRIEFING FOR THE SUPERVISOR

You feel you must speak to one of your subordinates about her untidy work area. It is important that tools be put back where they belong, that only current projects be in the work area, and that nothing be misplaced such that it could cause a hazard (e.g., someone tripping over it). This

one employee is excellent at her job and you have no complaint with the quantity and quality of her work. But you are not pleased with how she keeps her work area. It is so messy that you suspect it slows her down looking for things and you are concerned about hazards. You have tried to make her aware of it with jokes but it obviously has not worked so you've decided you must have a meeting with her and make it official.

BRIEFING FOR THE SUBORDINATE

Your boss has asked to speak with you. It sounds serious. Usually the supervisor is a friendly person who jokes around but there was no joking this time. You don't know what it is about. You are a strong member of the supervisor's team, producing very good work, both in terms of speed and accuracy. You don't think there can be any complaint about your work. Occasionally you are a few minutes late getting back from break, and you're not the most organized person around. Your work area is not in good shape but you know where everything is. And it's just the way you work. Even your supervisor has made cracks about it. No, maybe it's about you not going out of your way to help the new guy. He's a pain, asking too many questions and not listening to the answers. Who knows what the supervisor wants? You'll just have to wait and see.

2. TIME IS MONEY

BRIEFING FOR THE SUPERVISOR

You have decided to speak to one of your subordinates about her very loose interpretation of the work schedule. This person has been arriving a few minutes late all week and leaving a few minutes early each shift. Normally, you don't even watch out for the exact moment your staff start and stop. After all, they're all reliable, good workers. And there hasn't been a problem recently with any of them. But one of the other workers made a comment about how this particular subordinate must be getting promoted to management because she seems to set her own clock. So you watched more closely and indeed this subordinate is taking advantage and working close to half an hour less than she should be. It is setting a bad example and needs to stop.

This person is normally one of your best workers. You don't know this person well because she is a very quiet, private person.

BRIEFING FOR THE SUBORDINATE

Your supervisor has asked to speak with you. You hope it is not a problem because you have enough to deal with these days. One of your children is very sick and, although your mother is staying at your home to help out, you are very concerned about your child and you know it's really too much for your mother. Plus, you have to take your child to various specialists' appointments and your mother can't drive. So you have been cutting time at work, coming in a little late and leaving a little early. You don't feel guilty because you have been taking a short lunch to make up some of the time. Plus, you've always been a very reliable worker. This is only a temporary problem, you hope.

You are not keen on discussing this matter with your supervisor as you consider it a private affair. It is up to you how much you will reveal.

3. Face It, It's Over

BRIEFING FOR THE SUPERVISOR

One of your subordinates, a young woman, has just complained to you about another worker who also reports to you. She reported that he had grabbed her behind some packing boxes and tried to kiss her. She and he had previously dated but had parted over a year ago and, since then, she has become engaged to someone else. She has made it absolutely clear that she wants no personal relationship beyond work. She says he won't face that and she expects you to make sure he treats her with respect.

You are aware of their former relationship and you are also aware that he was very unhappy when they broke up. He hasn't dated since. You have asked him to come speak with you.

BRIEFING FOR THE SUBORDINATE

Your supervisor has just asked to speak with you. You aren't sure but you think it's about your former girlfriend since you just saw her leave the supervisor's office (you both work in the same company under the same supervisor). You did a stupid thing this morning. You ran into her accidentally in a packing area and decided on the spur of the moment to take advantage of the privacy. You grabbed her and tried to kiss her. She pulled away and left, telling you in no uncertain terms what she thought of you. The two of you split up over a year ago and she is now engaged to someone else. But you know her new relationship is a mistake and you really want her to give you another chance. It was not the best approach to take, you realize. Well, you hope your supervisor stays out of the situation because it is none of his business.

4. No, It's Not Private

BRIEFING FOR THE SUPERVISOR

You have just received some interesting information from a computer consultant who was hired by the company to set up some new policies and practices linked to the new programs. As part of his job, he does occasional audits of computer use by company personnel. He came to you to show you how one of your subordinates has been using his e-mail. This subordinate has been receiving and sending pornographic material, as well as receiving and sending a variety of jokes, some fairly mild, many seriously inappropriate. At the moment there is no policy regarding using e-mail for personal use. But, regardless, this is certainly using company property and time in an unacceptable way. You are shocked at this and must deal with the situation immediately. You have called the employee to your office.

BRIEFING FOR THE (male) SUBORDINATE

Your supervisor has just asked to speak with you. You don't know what it's about but you have a sick feeling in your stomach. You just saw the company's computer consultant leave the supervisor's office and you know that the consultant has been doing occasional audits of how company personnel are using the computer. You were praying he wouldn't check up on you. You do quite a bit of work on the computer but you also use it for a bit of fun. You have a group of friends who pass around material by e-mail. Some dirty jokes, a few pictures. Nothing too obscene. But the company may not be too happy about it.

UNDERSTANDING THE BASICS

SUMMARY

This summary is organized by the chapter Learning Objectives.

1. Discipline refers to actions taken to enforce the organization's rules and standards.

2. The most common disciplinary problems facing supervisors relate to attendance issues such as absenteeism, tardiness, and abuse of sick leaves. The other major types of discipline problems are on-the-job behaviours (including insubordination and substance abuse), dishonesty, and outside activities that affect on-the-job performance or reflect poorly on the organization.

3. The typical steps in progressive discipline are: 1. a verbal warning, 2. written reprimands, 3. suspension, 4. dismissal. There is often an informal discussion before the verbal warning.

4. The "hot stove" rule states that discipline should be administered in the same way that people are burned by a hot stove. The response should be immediate; there should be a warning; the result should be consistent; the result should be impartial, and there should be clear guidance about next steps.

5. Fairness demands that extenuating circumstances be considered before applying negative discipline. Factors such as the duration of the problem, the employee's work history, and past discipline practices in the organization are all legitimate factors that can influence the degree of disciplinary action.

6. The three methods of dismissal permitted by law are dismissal with just cause, dismissal with reasonable notice, and dismissal with reasonable compensation.

7. In disciplining unionized employees, the bargaining contract, the existence of a grievance procedure, the right to have differences evaluated and resolved by a third party, and the entire quasi-legal labour-management relationship all act to reduce a supervisor's range of discretion.

UNDERSTANDING THE BASICS

KEY TERMS AND CONCEPTS

Discipline   Progressive discipline
Dismissal   Suspension
Due process   Verbal warning
"Hot stove" rule   Written warning

REVIEWING YOUR KNOWLEDGE

1. "A good supervisor will never have to use discipline." Do you agree or disagree with this statement? Discuss.
2. Why is an informal discussion often the unofficial first step of a discipline procedure?
3. Why is it common for an organization to immediately dismiss a high-performing employee who lied about his educational qualifications on his application but take less harsh action against an average employee who misses a day of work to go fishing? Is this fair?
4. Why isn't discipline always the solution?
5. If you see a violation of an organizational rule by one of your employees with your own eyes, do you still need to investigate? Discuss.
6. Why is it so important to document, in writing, any disciplinary action you take against an employee?
7. What authority, if any, do you think human resource departments should have over a supervisor's disciplinary practices?
8. What should you do to follow due process when taking disciplinary action?

CASE 14.A

Supporting an Effective Discipline Process

Diane Hebert worked with a group of managers regarding how to deal with a disruptive employee. This engineer had angered a client so much that the client had threatened to pull a $10 million contract. The employee also refused to stamp drawings after his own people had worked on them for months because he didn't "like" them. The engineer was a strong personality and the managers had procrastinated in dealing with him.

As the HR manager, Diane organized a half day strategizing session with several managers to decide next steps. It was not her decision to make but she could see that some planning was needed to support the managers determining what to do. She helped them identify the issues and laid them out in a chart with three columns: 1) factual description of behaviours of concern; 2) description of impact of behaviour (on clients, colleagues...); 3) strategy to improve. "It was important to clarify these aspects for the managers. They needed to see the facts in black and white. It helped them to prepare for the meeting with the engineer and recognize what needed to be communicated to him. By the end of the strategizing, they were also prepared for the engineer's likely reaction. They knew he would get defensive and sabotage the whole meeting by trying to defend himself against every point. Diane taught them how to prevent this from happening. So, when the meeting with four managers started and he interrupted, they told him he would get a chance to speak at the end but first needed to hear what they had to say. They laid out the facts of his behaviour and the effects of those behaviours, and required improvement within two months or he would be terminated. In the end, after he went away and thought about it, the engineer chose to resign. Although the outcome was not what they pre-ferred happen, his leaving caused morale and productivity to improve in his department. The managers found the exercise so efficient that they used it from that point on when dealing with performance issues. Diane considered that a successful outcome.

RESPONDING TO THIS CASE

1. Explain why you believe the managers procrastinated in dealing with the disruptive engineer.

2. Rather than using all steps of a typical discipline process, the managers chose to give a two-month improvement period with termination as endpoint if performance was unsatisfactory. Use the "factors to consider in disciplining" (Figure 14-5) to explain why they chose this approach.

3. Identify the elements of effective discipline that were instituted with Diane's assistance.

4. Describe what it was in Diane's "exercise" that led managers to adopt it for dealing with future performance issues.

FIGURE 14-6

Diane Hebert

Terminating the Poor Employee Leads to More Trouble*

Liz hired Kosta with high expectations, bringing him in to a team of strong performers that were all strongly supportive of each other and loyal to the department. However, within the first few weeks of Kosta's hire, she started getting poor feedback about his performance, particularly his way of dealing with clients. He was unprepared for meetings and offhand in his manner. He had come with strong references so this surprised her. Liz decided that she had been premature in allowing him to work fully independently with clients. So she started meeting with him regularly, coaching him and attending occasional client meetings with him where she was able. It was a strain because Kosta resented the oversight and the implication that he could not do his job well. His performance when Liz observed him directly was satisfactory although not exceptional but she continued to hear less than positive feedback about situations where she was not in attendance. Although client interactions were an issue, Kosta had no problem fitting in with Liz's team and became fast friends with the sociable group.

Increasingly concerned about Kosta's lack of improvement and his unwillingness to even admit there was a problem, Liz documented the issues over the ensuing months. These included issues like lack of follow-through on commitments to clients, missed appointments, and inaccurate or missing reports. In meetings and in letters, she made clear to Kosta both the performance expectations and the fact that if he did not improve, he would not make it through probation. As in all good management practice, Liz dealt with the performance issues in a confidential manner. This meant that the rest of the team were unaware of both the performance issues with clients and the fact that he may not make it through probation. Only Liz, her own manager, Kosta and the Human Resources department were aware of Kosta's tenuous position at the company.

When another round of client feedback yielded continuing problems, Liz made the decision (supported by the company) to let Kosta go before his probation period had ended. She was relieved to have him gone from the team. However, the rest of the team did not feel the same way. They liked Kosta and felt she had betrayed the team by terminating his employment. Because Liz herself was a new manager, only recently promoted from the team ranks, there were rumblings that she was letting the position go to her head. So at a meeting with the team the day after he left, Liz announced the decision and answered questions. When challenged about why Kosta was terminated, Liz explained:

> *Like all new hires, Kosta went through regular performance reviews as part of the probation process and the organization decided that the fit was not there. I am not in a position to give details about specific situations. As you all would expect if you were the subject of performance discussions, the confidentiality of the performance management process must be respected.*

When pushed with comments like, "Come on, he was a great guy. What could he possibly have done that was so unacceptable?" Liz responded:

> *"I cannot give that information and you will simply have to trust me that this decision was necessary and that all efforts were made to make the situation workable and to avoid this unfortunate decision."*

The tension was palpable. Liz was frustrated that her long-time colleagues were questioning her ethics and her intentions. She concentrated on remaining calm and choosing not to

---

* Based on a true story, with names and details altered.

take the situation personally, knowing that the decision had been the correct one. She was tempted to give the details to at least a few of the team, those that she considered personal friends. They would get the word out and everyone would likely understand the situation better. But she knew that was wrong and could get her into more trouble, so she chose not to share any specifics with anyone on the team. After the meeting, most seemed to accept the decision and move on but tension remained as an undercurrent with a couple of the team members. One strong performer who was a team lead on several projects brought up the issue at her performance review months later, saying "I'm not sure I can continue taking on the project leads under your direction given your questionable treatment of Kosta." Liz's response was:

> *I understand your disappointment at losing someone you considered a member of the team. Since that time, you and I have in fact worked together effectively in our professional roles and I would hope that this could continue. I value both your work and your support of the team. Given our history together I would hope you see that I, too, am focused on what is best for the team. And consider that the decision about Kosta was made in that light.*

The employee chose to continue accepting project lead roles under Liz's leadership.

Six months after Kosta's termination, Liz feels that the termination decision continues to take a toll on her. Dealing with a poor hire was bad enough, but dealing with the fallout from an unpopular termination was an unexpected and lingering stress on her.

RESPONDING TO THIS CASE

1. Liz was essentially disciplining Kosta, even though it was not called that because he was on probation.

    a. Explain how the discipline was progressive.
    b. Identify how Liz followed the basic tenets of discipline, and the discipline "skill basics".

2. Discuss why Kosta's colleagues thought the termination inappropriate.

3. Discuss how Liz handled the reaction of Kosta's colleagues – was it appropriate? Is there anything else you felt she could have done?

15 THE SUPERVISOR'S ROLE IN EMPLOYEE RELATIONS

Courtesy of Andrey Popov/Shutterstock

LEARNING OBJECTIVES

After reading this chapter, you should be able to:

1. Describe the current status of labour unions in Canada.
2. Explain the appeal of unions to employees.
3. Identify the legislation pertinent to employee relations.
4. Identify the primary purpose of collective bargaining.
5. Describe the supervisor's role in labour matters.
6. Discuss who a union steward is and what a supervisor's relations with this person should be.
7. Describe where supervisors most often get into trouble in contract administration.
8. Describe the steps for handling a grievance.

CHAPTER OUTLINE

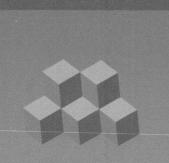

From his experience working in a grocery store chain, Liam (an alias) has some interesting observations about the challenges of supervising in a unionized workplace:

"Employees know the collective agreement like the back of their hands, particularly those in a steward role. They go by the book and this can create a lack of flexibility in dealing with a situation. Scheduling is a big issue. Certain employees are entitled to certain hours because of seniority. At times a supervisor drafts the schedule incorrectly and it becomes a grievance issue. A manager needs to know the collective agreement thoroughly, how many hours an employee is entitled to and how to do the schedule so everyone gets suitable hours.

We had a steward who was not an ideal employee who was given disciplinary action and it became almost a game for the steward and manager to find each other at fault. The steward would hassle the manager over not doing something right and then the manager would catch the steward breaking a rule. It became like kids in a playground, not a professional environment where people are focused on clarifying expectations and working together to achieve something.

I've seen a few situations where an employee claimed harassment against a manager. It is always taken seriously so we investigated but never once in my experience was it found to be a case of harassment. The manager simply didn't have the skills required. They were attempting to deal with a performance issue and not doing it well. Harassment claims seem to come up when an employee feels disrespected and not given equal treatment to others in the department. For example, when a manager has daily conversations with employees about their roles and duties, they cannot treat everyone the same way because the circumstances are different, but it is tricky to be seen as fair at the same time. A strong employee does not need to be spoken to or trained as much. Some employees take the "different" treatment the wrong way.

If going to speak to an employee about a discipline issue, we have to have a union steward present. This can create a problem, having to rearrange schedules so the steward and employee and store manager can all be available at the same time when handling a performance issue. So the discussion is not always timely."

As you see from Liam's description, when a supervisor is working in a unionized workplace, the presence of the union and the collective agreement mean there are more "rules" to be aware of in dealing with employees, and there is another layer of scrutiny watching whatever the supervisor does. In this chapter we'll discuss why employees join unions, review the key labour laws you need to know about, and then consider the role that supervisors play in labour matters.

WHAT IS EMPLOYEE RELATIONS?

Employee relations includes all the activities within a company that involve dealing with a union and its members. But what's a **union**? It's an organization that represents workers and seeks to protect their interests through collective bargaining.

In Canada, about one in three workers is a member of a union or covered by a collective bargaining unit.[1] Membership varies greatly by region, by industry, by occupation and by sector, with higher membership in the public sector than the private sector. As shown in Figure 15-1, you are more likely to be supervising unionized employees in Quebec or Newfoundland and Labrador, which have the highest rates, than in Alberta, which has the lowest rate. Figure 15-2 illustrates that unionization is highest in education, public administration and utilities industries but very low in finance, agriculture and insurance industries, amongst others.

Employee relations
All activities within a company that involve dealing with a union and its members.

Union
An organization that represents workers and seeks to protect their interests through collective bargaining.

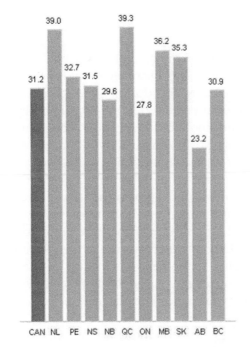

Source: HRSDC calculations based on Statistics Canada, http://www4.hrsdc.gc.ca/.3ndic.1t.4r@eng.jsp?iid=17#M.4

FIGURE 15-1

Unionization rate, by region, 2011 (percent of employees)[2]

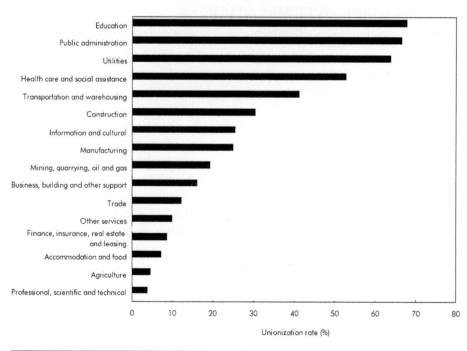

FIGURE 15-2

Unionization rate, by industry, 2011

Source: Statistics Canada, http://www.statcan.gc.ca/pub/75-001-x/2011004/article/11579-eng.htm

Spillover effect
Successes made by unions at the negotiating table influence the wages, working conditions, and terms of employment for workers who are not unionized.

Union membership in the major industrialized countries, as a percentage of the civilian workforce, has been declining for many years. A number of factors have contributed to this decline. The economic sectors where union strength has traditionally been greatest—particularly blue-collar manufacturing jobs in the automobile, steel, rubber, and chemical industries—have significantly cut their North American workforces. Many of these jobs have been eliminated through automation or exported to countries with lower labour costs. The growth in the labour force since the late 1960s has been among women, professionals, government employees, and service workers—groups that have sometimes been more resistant to labour's effort to organize them. And, of course, unions have suffered directly as a result of their own success. Labour union growth in the 1930s and 1940s was largely a result of responding to the depressed status of the working class. But as unions succeeded in raising wages and improving working conditions, the reasons for their very existence became less obvious.

However, in many key industries, for instance, mining, construction, railways, and trucking, most workers are unionized. Most importantly, we can't overlook the **spillover effect**. Successes made by unions at the negotiating table spill over to influence the wages, working conditions, and terms of employment for workers who are not unionized (particularly in the same industry).

A BASIC QUESTION: WHY WOULD
EMPLOYEES JOIN A UNION?

What do employees seek to gain when they join a union? The answer to this question varies with the individual and the union context, but the following captures the most common reasons.

HIGHER WAGES AND BENEFITS

There's power in numbers. As a result, unions are often able to obtain higher wages and benefit packages for their members than these employees would be able to negotiate individually. Canadian unionized workers do generally receive higher wages[2] and are also more likely to enjoy non-wage benefits such as coverage in employer-sponsored pension, dental or medical plans.[3] One or two employees walking off the job over a wage dispute is unlikely to significantly affect most businesses, but hundreds of workers going out on strike can temporarily disrupt or even close down a company. Additionally, professional bargainers employed by the union may be able to negotiate more skilfully than any individual could do on his or her own behalf.

GREATER JOB SECURITY

Unions provide members with a sense of independence from management's power to arbitrarily hire, promote, or fire. The collective bargaining contract will stipulate rules that apply to all members, thus providing fairer and more uniform treatment. Greater accessibility to a grievance system is thought to provide greater protection against exploitation, abuse or unfair treatment by their employer.[4]

INCREASED OPPORTUNITIES TO INFLUENCE WORK RULES

Where a union exists, workers are provided with an opportunity to participate in determining the conditions under which they work, and an effective channel through which they can protest conditions they believe are unfair. Therefore, a union not only represents the worker but also provides rules that define channels through which complaints and concerns of workers can be registered. Grievance procedures and rights to third-party arbitration of disputes are examples of practices that are frequently defined and regulated as a result of union efforts.

COMPULSORY MEMBERSHIP

Many labour agreements require that individuals must join the union (such a workplace is referred to as a **union shop**) or at least pay dues (an

Union shop
A workplace where employees must join the union.

Agency shop
A workplace where employees do not have to join the union but must pay union dues if they want to keep their jobs.

agency shop) if they want to keep their jobs. These requirements are typically imposed by the unions themselves on free riders (employees who gain the benefits of union membership without paying fees and dues).

UNHAPPINESS WITH A SUPERVISOR

Setting aside the other reasons why employees join a union, there appears to be one common factor—you, the supervisor. If employees are upset with the way you handle problems or the way you disciplined one of their co-workers, they are likely to seek help from a union. In fact, research has shown that when employees vote to unionize, it's often a vote against their immediate supervisor rather than a vote in support of a particular union.

LABOUR LEGISLATION YOU NEED TO KNOW ABOUT

Supervisors don't need to be labour lawyers to deal with legal issues surrounding union-management relations. But there are some basic laws with which you need to be familiar.

In Canada, there are three legislative areas that deal with the relationships among employees, unions and employers: the federal Labour Relations Act, provincial Labour Relations Acts, and the federal Charter of Rights and Freedoms. Again, as with other legislation, the jurisdiction will be largely determined by the nature of the company.

FEDERAL AND PROVINCIAL LABOUR RELATIONS ACTS

The labour relations acts set out the responsibilities and rights of employees and their unions, generally outlining the following issues:

- rules for starting a union
- rules for joining a union
- supporting or not supporting a union
- collective bargaining procedures
- administration of collective agreements
- unfair labour practices

These acts specifically prohibit employers from:

1. interfering with, restraining, or coercing employees in the exercise of the rights to join unions and bargain collectively
2. dominating or interfering with the formation or administration of any labour organization
3. discriminating against anyone because of union activity

4. discharging or otherwise discriminating against any employee because he or she filed charges or gave testimony under the act
5. refusing to bargain collectively with the representatives chosen by the employees

These acts also prohibit union actions that may not be in the best interests of the employees. Specifically, a union may not:

1. force an employee to bargain through it if the union is not the bargaining agent
2. participate or interfere with the administration of the company
3. attempt, at the workplace or during working hours, to persuade an employee to become a union member, except with the employer's consent
4. expel or suspend an employee from the union by applying union membership rules in a discriminatory manner
5. penalize a member for filing a complaint or testifying pursuant to the code

Each jurisdiction has a labour relations board that regulates the actions of both unions and companies, playing a role in settling disputes in contract administration and collective bargaining.

THE CHARTER OF RIGHTS AND FREEDOMS

The Charter of Rights and Freedoms, passed by the federal government in 1982, also influences the relationship between employees and their union representative. Any action that contravenes an individual's fundamental freedom can be challenged. For example, fundamental freedoms include freedom of religion; freedom of expression; freedom of association; freedom of peaceful assembly; and freedom of thought, belief and opinion. By joining a union, an employee does not surrender these fundamental freedoms guaranteed by the charter.

FROM CONFLICT TO COOPERATION

Historically, the relationship between labour and management was built on conflict. The interests of management and labour were seen as basically at odds; each treated the other as the enemy.

But times have changed. Management has become increasingly aware that successful efforts to increase productivity, improve quality, and lower costs require employee involvement and commitment. And labour unions have come to recognize that they can help their members more by cooperating with management than by fighting them.

Ironically, current labour laws, passed in an era of mistrust and antagonism between management and labour, have become barriers to these parties putting their differences aside and becoming cooperative partners.

Graham Van Brunt agrees with the cooperative approach. As director of plant operations and maintenance at Churchill Falls Labrador Corporation, a huge hydro facility, he has seen both conflict and cooperation in relationships with the union. "We went through a labour strike and you never want to do that in a small town. It is important to keep the union happy. You do that by working with them as closely as possible. Some management don't like the union at their elbows watching them but that's the old way of thinking. I've seen things work much better if we keep the union involved. For example, now we have joint programs, like the safety program, to which both the union and management are committed. In day-to-day operations, there's nothing wrong with sitting down with the union and listening to what they have to say about the business. Keep them close. Keep the lines of communication open. Explain why you're making the decisions you're making. In most cases, it doesn't hurt to tell them what you're thinking. It saves a lot of grief in the long run."

AN OVERVIEW OF THE COLLECTIVE BARGAINING PROCESS

As a supervisor, you won't typically be directly involved in the collective bargaining process. You will, however, be affected by the process and outcome. The next section will describe things you can and cannot legally do during the period when a union is attempting to organize employees in your company; it will also show how you play a major part in the administration of the final union contract. So you need a basic understanding of collective bargaining.

Collective bargaining is a process for negotiating a union contract and for administrating the contract after it has been negotiated (see Figure 15-3). The following discussion briefly summarizes how the process typically flows in the private sector.

ORGANIZATION AND CERTIFICATION

Efforts to organize a group of employees may begin when employee representatives ask union officials to visit the employees' organization and solicit members or when the union itself initiates a membership drive. Either way, the law requires that a union must secure signed authorization cards from a specified percentage of the employees it desires to represent. If the percentage goal is achieved, either the union or management will file a petition with the Labour Relations Board

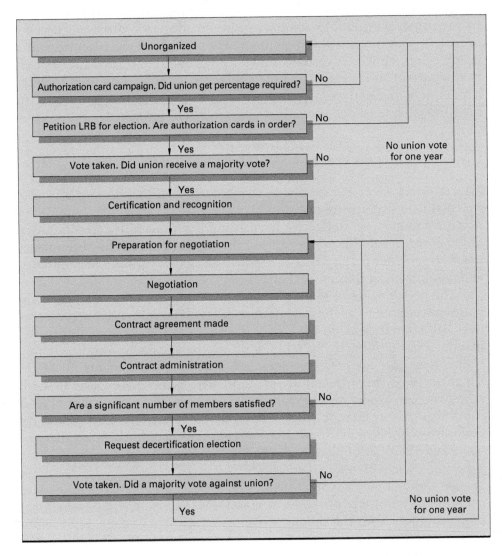

FIGURE 15-3

The collective bargaining process

(LRB), requesting a representation election. The percentage of employees needed to hold an election varies from a low of 35 per cent in Quebec to a high of 45 per cent in British Columbia.[5]

When the LRB receives the required number of authorization cards, it evaluates them, verifies that legal requirements have been satisfied, and then clarifies the appropriate **bargaining unit**; that is, it identifies which employees the union will represent if it wins the election.

Bargaining unit
Identifies which employees the union will represent if it wins an election.

A secret-ballot election is usually called within 25 days after the LRB receives the authorization cards. If the union gets a majority in this election, the LRB certifies the union and recognizes it as the exclusive bargaining representative for all employees within the specified bargaining unit. Should the union fail to get a majority, another election cannot be held for one year.

Occasionally, employees become dissatisfied with a certified union. In such instances, employees may request a decertification election by the LRB. If a majority of the members vote for decertification, the union is out. However, recognize two things about decertification. First, most contracts forbid it during the contract's term. Second, union members cannot decertify today and bring in another union tomorrow. In most cases, at least one year must transpire between votes.

OK, THE UNION WON—WHAT NOW?

After a union has been certified—meaning it won the election and was successful in organizing a group of workers—the collective bargaining process commences. **Collective bargaining** is a process for negotiating a union contract and for administering the contract after it has been negotiated. It includes preparing to negotiate, the actual contract negotiations, and administering the contract after it has been ratified.

The people who do the negotiating for both the union and the company are referred to as the negotiations teams. The company's representatives will often depend on the size of the organization. In a small firm, for instance, bargaining is probably done by the president—and probably some other staff the president feels are necessary participants. In larger organizations, there is usually an industrial relations expert. In such cases, you can expect the company to be represented by the senior official for industrial relations, other company executives, and company lawyers—with support provided by legal and economic specialists in wage and salary administration, labour law, benefits, and so forth. As a supervisor, you will not be involved.

On the union side, you typically can expect to see a bargaining team made up of an officer of the local union, local shop stewards, and some representation from the union. Again, as with the company, representation is modified to reflect the size of the bargaining unit. If negotiations involve a contract that will cover many employees at company locations throughout Canada, the team will be dominated by several union officers, with a strong supporting cast of economic and legal experts employed by the union. In a small firm or for local negotiations covering special issues at the plant level for a nationwide organization, bargaining representatives for the union might be the local officers and a few specially elected committee members.

PREPARATION FOR NEGOTIATION

Once a union has been certified, management will begin preparing for negotiations. It will gather information on the economy, copies of recently negotiated contracts between other unions and employers, cost-of-living data, labour market statistics, and similar external factors. It will

Collective bargaining
A process for negotiating a union contract and for administrating the contract after it has been negotiated. It includes preparing to negotiate, the actual contract negotiations, and administering the contract after it has been ratified.

also gather internal information on complaints and accident records, employee performance reports, and overtime figures.

This information will tell management their organization's current labour-performance status, what similar organizations are doing, and what it can anticipate from the economy in the near term. Management then uses these data to determine what it can expect to achieve in the negotiation. What can it expect the union to ask for? What is management prepared to give?

NEGOTIATION

Negotiation customarily begins when the union delivers a list of demands to management. These are typically ambitious in order to create room for trading in the later stages of negotiation. Not surprisingly, management's initial response may be to counter by offering little more than the terms of the previous contract or, in an increasing number of cases, to even propose reductions in current wages, benefits, and previously agreed-to conditions.

These introductory proposals usually initiate a period of long and intense bargaining. Compromises are made, and after an oral agreement is achieved, it is converted into a written contract. Finally, negotiation concludes with the union's representatives submitting the contract to its members for ratification.

CONTRACT ADMINISTRATION

Once a contract is agreed upon and ratified, it must be administered. The way in which it will be administered is specified in the contract itself.

Probably the most important element of contract administration— particularly in terms of the supervisor's job—has to do with the spelling out of a procedure for handling contractual disputes. Almost all collective bargaining agreements contain formal procedures for resolving grievances over the interpretation and application of the contract.

THE SUPERVISOR'S ROLE IN LABOUR MATTERS

Now let's turn our attention to the various demands placed on supervisors as a result of labour-management relations.

ORGANIZING DRIVES

If your employees aren't currently unionized, you may experience a union organizing drive. If that happens, be very careful about what you say and do. For example, the law is clear in stating that you can't threaten or intimidate employees in order to get them to vote against the union.

Because supervisors are the closest level of management to the workers, you represent the best source of information about intentions and actions. So pay attention. If you see that union-organizing activities are taking place among employees, report your observations to your boss or to the human resources department. Early detection can allow your company to plan a proper response.

Figure 15-4 provides a list of guidelines to lessen the likelihood that you'll break the law or hinder your company's response to the union's organizing effort. You are free to express your views and opinions about unions to your employees. But the law forbids you from interfering in your employee's right to choose a union to represent them. And because the line is often vague about where your free speech becomes interference, you must be cautious.

- If your employees ask for your opinion on unionization, respond in a neutral manner. For example, "I really have no position on the issue. Do what you think is best."

- You can prohibit union organizing activities in your workplace during work hours only if they interfere with work operations.

- You can prohibit outside union organizers from distributing union information in the workplace.

- Employees have the right to distribute union information to other employees during break and lunch periods.

- Don't question employees publicly or privately about union-organizing activities. For example, "Are you planning to go to that union rally this weekend?" But if an employee freely tells you about the activities, you may listen.

- Don't spy on employees' union activities, for example, by standing in the lunchroom to see who is distributing pro-union literature.

- Don't make any threats or promises that are related to the possibility of unionization. For example, "If this union effort succeeds, upper management is seriously thinking about closing down this plant. But if it's defeated, they plan to push through an immediate wage increase."

- Don't discriminate against any employee who is involved in the unionization effort.

- Be on the lookout for efforts by the union to coerce employees to join its ranks. This is illegal. If you see this occurring, report it to your boss or the human resources department. Your company may want to file a complaint against the union with the LRB.

FIGURE 15-4

Supervisory guidelines during a union organizing drive

Negotiation

Supervisors typically play a minor part in the actual negotiation of the contract. Basic responsibility for this activity lies with specialists in the human resource department and top management.

The supervisor's role during the negotiation period tends to be limited to that of a resource person. You may be called upon to provide your organization's negotiators with departmental information on past problems with work-shift schedules, seniority rights, transfers, discipline, or ambiguous terminology in the current contract. This suggests that it's important for you to keep careful records of labour problems you experience during the current contract period so that these problems can be addressed during the next contract negotiation.

Contract Administration

Once a formal agreement is in place, you must manage your department within the framework established by that contract. This means that you must fully understand all the "fine print" in the contract—and you need to make sure departmental members have the contract information, too.

Large and small organizations alike will hold supervisory training sessions and meetings to help you understand the contract and to clarify new provisions. You'll be given a copy of the agreement to study, an opportunity to get questions answered, and procedures to follow when problems arise.

Why do organizations place so much emphasis on ensuring that supervisors know and understand the contract? Because supervisors are the primary link between management and the employees. For the typical unionized employee, the supervisor is his or her sole contact with management. What supervisors say and do, then, largely determines the labour-management climate in the organization. If you misinterpret a contract provision, treat an employee unfairly, or engage in a contract violation, the consequences for you and the company might be immediate, or they might be postponed until the next negotiation. The union's representatives will keep track of these incidents and they'll use them to help win concessions in the next contract.

Keep in mind that working under a labour contract and supervising unionized employees does not take away your rights to make decisions or manage your people. What it does is spell out limitations to your authority and establish procedures for employees to challenge any action you take that they see as a violation of the labour agreement. So, for instance, you can still assign work schedules, make job transfers, and discipline problem employees—but you must do so within the framework defined in the labour contract.

Remember, too, that the labour contract is a bilateral agreement. It also specifies responsibilities for employees, and procedures you can take when employees fail to comply with provisions in the contract. So the labour agreement constrains employees as well as management.

Depending on the relationship that has been built between the supervisor and workers, a looser interpretation of the contract can lead to agreement in solving day-to-day problems.

A labour specialist describes the two extremes with which new supervisors sometimes approach administering a collective agreement: "Some read the collective agreement in detail and manage strictly by what is stipulated in the agreement; if an issue is not addressed by the collective agreement, they assume there is no pathway to address the issue; this can create a problem of perceived rigidity and can also interfere with operational effectiveness. By contrast, some managers coming from a nonunionized environment to a unionized environment don't realize that managing in a unionized environment is different. They often struggle with adjustment and face resistance from their staff. In some environments a grievance is launched as soon as a new manager fails to comply with the collective agreement. In environments with more positive labour relations, the Human Resources department might get a courtesy call early on from the union asking that the new manager be educated about the collective agreement provisions. Often new managers manage their departments in a way that they feel is reasonable or based on the practices they've experienced in other organizations, not realizing the collective agreement is very prescriptive in some matters. For example, the first time someone asks for professional development leave, or to schedule a vacation, or for overtime, they apply a "reasonable person" standard, not considering seniority or what the collective agreement requires. The result of this is that employees raise the issue with the union, feeling the request should have been handled differently, or that their rights under the collective agreement have been violated. It is good practice for the employer to give managers training early on, especially providing coaching and support for those who have not worked in a unionized environment before. Where there are shades of gray, it doesn't mean the manager's hands are tied. They need to learn how to navigate the shades of gray."

RELATIONS WITH THE UNION STEWARD

Union steward
An employee who is the elected representative of the employees in a work unit, and is there to protect the rights of the union members.

The **union steward** in your department is essentially to the union what you are to the company. Just as you're there to protect the rights of management, he or she is an employee who is the elected representative of the employees in your work unit, and is there to protect the rights of the union members.

What authority does a union steward have in running your department? Very little to none! The steward cannot tell you or any employee what to do. The only authority stewards have is to give advice. They can offer advice to you and employees as to their understanding of how the contract limits your actions.

Just because union stewards have limited formal authority doesn't mean they can't be troublesome. Poor relations with your steward are likely to result in increased challenges to your actions and increased grievance filings. So getting along with your union steward tends to make your life at work a lot more pleasant.

The role of steward comes with certain expectations from employees. The steward is their representative. He or she is elected to protect their rights. You have to expect the steward's loyalties to lie with the union members. That doesn't mean, however, that you can't attempt to minimize hostilities with your steward. The best means for developing a cooperative relationship is to show respect for the steward and to keep him or her informed of problems you're having and of any changes that will affect the people in your department. A good supervisor-steward relationship can allow problems to be resolved quickly in the department and avoid the stress and cost associated with a lengthy dispute.

CHALLENGES IN CONTRACT ADMINISTRATION

Some of the issues that new managers have to address early in their new roles are those that are often clearly prescribed in the collective agreement, including scheduling (shifts, overtime, lieu time) and vacation. Supervisors are well advised to become familiar with the collective agreement and to administer the collective agreement appropriately. Often a manager new to a unionized environment will assess the operations of their department and decide that it would make more sense if work arrangements were altered. They announce shift changes and don't realize the requirements in the collective agreement to, for instance, consult with the union, give notice of shift change, give preference based on seniority, etc. New managers are advised to consult with the Human Resources department who can assist them to meet their collective agreement obligations and avoid complaints or even grievances from employees. It's important to be familiar with the provisions of the collective agreement that are governed by seniority and to manage those provisions accordingly.

Supervisors need to recognize the importance of responding promptly to grievances. A **grievance** is a work-related dispute arising out of the interpretation, application, administration or alleged violation of the specific terms of the collective agreement. Employees in a unionized environment have this resource available to them if they feel their rights under the collective agreement have been violated. Sometimes new managers simply don't realize that this recourse is possible and are not familiar with the very prescriptive requirements outlined in most collective agreements with regard to meetings, formal responses and timelines that

Grievance
A work-related dispute arising out of the interpretation, application, administration or alleged violation of the specific terms of the collective agreement.

must occur in response to the grievance. Often new managers are surprised when a grievance lands on their desk in response to a decision they have made or an action they have taken, and they may make the mistake of not taking any action in response to the grievance. They don't realize that time is ticking and the employer needs to adhere to the required timelines for formal responses. Even if there is no basis for the grievance, the employer is expected to respond to the grievance within the prescribed timeline, and the employer's ability to successfully defend against the grievance can be negatively affected by undue delays in the process.

A new area that employers need to pay attention to is the language around workplace harassment and workplace violence in the Occupational Health and Safety Act in several provinces. Each employer is obligated to provide a work environment free from violence and harassment. Accusations of bullying or harassment can be very difficult to deal with for employers as well as for unions. Such allegations are sometimes against coworkers, even coworkers within the same bargaining unit or different bargaining units. The latter is particularly challenging because the two people are represented by two different unions or union locals seeing things with their own perspective, each with a duty to represent their own members. In the event of an allegation of harassment, employers are obligated to investigate. This process can be very difficult for people to endure and can be disruptive to the workplace in general. A supervisor or manager needs to keep their eyes open for potential issues and be responsive if an employee brings an incident or concern of this nature to their attention.

Does Unionization Tie a Supervisor's Hands?

The contract creates a framework in which a supervisor must work but it does not prevent management from managing effectively. "One manager made the transition from a nonunion environment to a unionized environment and was not prepared for the difference it would make to how he managed his staff. The nonunionized environment had been a demanding, high-volume production environment with tight deadlines, a lack of process for assigning overtime, and no additional compensation for staff who worked overtime. The new environment was similarly demanding with high volumes and tight deadlines; however, because it was a unionized environment, his attempts to manage in the fashion he was accustomed to in the previous organization met with resistance. That manager did not last long in his new role as he found the new environment interfered with his ability to manage his staff and meet his operational targets. Managers need to understand that there are differences between managing in non-union environments versus union environments, and they need to familiarize themselves with those differences to successfully meet their operational priorities. It is often all about using a reasonable approach and being fair. Most people will respond positively to a supervisor who treats them with respect and handles situations consistently in a fair way. If a manager is rigid or oblivious (to the union framework), this leads to trouble. When a manager understands the collective agreement so they are not committing any violations and not getting people's backs up, and they approach situations from a fair, reasonable perspective, there is no reason why they can't motivate and build a strong team atmosphere, even if it is a unionized environment" explains a labour relations specialist in the public sector.

WHEN AN IMPASSE IS REACHED IN NEGOTIATIONS

Sometimes representatives of management and labour cannot reach an agreement on a new contract. When this happens, the union may choose to call a **strike**. In a strike, employees leave their jobs and refuse to come to work until a contract has been signed. Realize, too, that there's a company equivalent to a strike. It's called a **lockout**. That is when management denies unionized employees access to their jobs.

Historically, the strike was a potent weapon. By withholding labour, the union could impose financial hardships on an employer. However, beginning in the early 1980s, strikes began to lose much of their potency. For one thing, public sentiment supporting their use by unions has declined. As well, employers in some provinces are allowed to hire replacement workers during a strike, which tends to nullify the impact. Permanent replacement workers are banned in most jurisdictions (except New Brunswick, Nova Scotia, and Prince Edward Island). Quebec, Ontario and British Columbia also ban the use of temporary replacement workers.[6]

When labour and management cannot reach a satisfactory agreement themselves, they may need the assistance of an objective third-party individual. This assistance comes in the form of conciliation and mediation, fact-finding, or interest arbitration.

Conciliation and **mediation** are two very closely related impasse resolution techniques. Both are techniques whereby a neutral third party attempts to get labour and management to resolve their differences. Under conciliation, the role of the third party is to keep the negotiations ongoing. In other words, this individual is a go-between—advocating a voluntary means through which both sides can continue negotiating. Mediation goes one step further. The mediator attempts to pull together the common ground that exists and make settlement recommendations for overcoming the barriers that exist between the two sides. A mediator's suggestions, however, are only advisory. That means that the suggestions are not binding on either party.

Strike
A situation in which employees leave their jobs and refuse to come to work until a contract has been signed.

Lockout
A company action equivalent to a strike; occurs when management denies unionized employees access to their jobs.

Conciliation
An impasse-resolution technique in which a third party acts as a go-between with the aim of keeping negotiations ongoing.

Mediation
An impasse-resolution technique in which a mediator attempts to pull together the common ground that exists and make settlement recommendations for overcoming the barriers that exist between the two sides in a conflict.

Fact-finding
A technique whereby a neutral third-party individual conducts a hearing to gather evidence from both labour and management.

Interest arbitration
Arbitration in which a panel of three individuals hears testimony from both sides and renders a decision on how to settle the current contract negotiation dispute.

Wildcat strike
An illegal strike where employees refuse to work during the term of a binding contract, often due to ambiguities in the current contract.

Fact-finding is a technique whereby a neutral third-party individual conducts a hearing to gather evidence from both labour and management. The fact-finder then renders a decision as to how he or she views an appropriate settlement. Similar to mediation, the fact-finder's recommendations are only suggestions—they, too, are not binding on either party.

The final impasse resolution technique is called **interest arbitration**. Under interest arbitration, generally a panel of three individuals—one neutral and one each from the union and management—hears testimony from both sides. After the hearing, the panel renders a decision on how to settle the current contract negotiation dispute. If all three members of the panel are unanimous in their decision, that decision may be binding on both parties. Interest arbitration is found more frequently in public-sector collective bargaining; its use in private-sector labour disputes is rare.

There is little you can do to directly resolve a strike. However, if your employees go out on strike, you may be called upon to assume an increased number of nonsupervisory tasks in order to keep the business going. Or if management decides to replace striking workers, you will have to train and orient the new employees.

A more troublesome situation for supervisors is the **wildcat strike**. This is an illegal strike where employees refuse to work during the term of a binding contract. Such strikes can be brought about by a number of factors, but they usually involve ambiguities in the current contract. For instance, employee concerns over management's right to contract out some assembly work has resulted in wildcat strikes at several electronic-component manufacturers. The key point to remember is that wildcat strikes are illegal. Grievance procedures exist precisely to settle such differences. Should you find yourself in the middle of a wildcat strike, Figure 15-5 provides you with some guidelines to follow.

- Stay on the job.
- Notify higher management.
- Carefully record the events as they happen.
- Pay strict attention to who the leaders are and record their behaviour.
- Record any lack of action by union officials.
- Report all information as fully and as soon as possible to higher management.
- Encourage employees to go back to work.
- Ask union officials to instruct employees to go back to work.
- Don't discuss the cause of the strike.
- Don't make any agreements or say anything that might imply permission to leave work.
- Make it clear that management will discuss the issue when all of the employees are back at work.

FIGURE 15-5

Supervisory guidelines for handling wildcat strikes. Reprinted by permission from *Supervision: Key Link to Productivity*, 4th ed., (1993).

HANDLING GRIEVANCES

We've used the term grievance at several points in this chapter to refer to a dispute. But how does a supervisor go about handling a grievance? Of all the activities that supervisors of unionized employees get involved in, none are more important than the handling of grievances. In this section, we'll help you develop your grievance-handling skills.

ASSESSING YOURSELF: ARE YOU AN EFFECTIVE GRIEVANCE-HANDLER?

Answer each of the following questions as you have or would behave, not as you think you *should* behave.

	Strongly Agree	Agree	Undecided	Disagree	Strongly Disagree
1. If an employee has a grievance, the *first* thing I do is review the relevant clause in the union contract.	❑	❑	❑	❑	❑
2. As soon as an employee informs me of a grievance, to avoid escalation I specifically provide him or her with management's side of the story.	❑	❑	❑	❑	❑
3. If I'm unsure about wording or an interpretation in the contract, I contact a labour specialist in the organization for counsel.	❑	❑	❑	❑	❑
4. I research all the facts pertinent to the dispute, regardless of how much time it may take.	❑	❑	❑	❑	❑
5. I avoid letting personalities or personal preferences influence my decision on a grievance.	❑	❑	❑	❑	❑
6. If a grievance has merit, I assume I have the authority to take immediate corrective action.	❑	❑	❑	❑	❑
7. I keep comprehensive records on every grievance in expectation that my decision will be appealed.	❑	❑	❑	❑	❑

SCORING DIRECTIONS AND KEY

For questions 3, 5, and 7, give yourself five points for Strongly Agree, four points for Agree, three points for Undecided, two points for Disagree, and one point for Strongly Disagree. For questions 1, 2, 4, and 6, reverse the scoring (for example, one point for Strongly Agree). Add up your total score. The range will be between 7 and 35. Scores of 30 and above indicate good grievance-handling skills. Scores of 25 to 29 indicate room for improvement. Scores of less than 25 suggest a strong need to work on these skills.

SKILL BASICS

Almost all collective bargaining agreements contain formal procedures to be used in resolving disputes surrounding the interpretation and application of the contract. These procedures are typically designed to resolve disputes as quickly as possible and at the lowest level in the organization. Whenever possible, then, the supervisor is encouraged to resolve employee grievances without involving upper levels of management and senior union officials.

Consistent with this belief that grievances should be handled at the lowest level possible in the organization, the typical grievance procedure looks like Figure 15-6. An employee's first efforts should be directed at attempting to resolve the complaint with his or her immediate supervisor.

If dissatisfied with the supervisor's response, the grievance typically escalates through the following stages: the supervisor and union steward discuss the complaint; the supervisor and a labour specialist from the human resources department discuss the complaint with the chief union steward or union grievance committee; the facilities manager and the labour specialist meet with the union grievance committee; the organization's top management meet with the union grievance committee and a representative of the national union to try to work out a solution. If the grievance still cannot be resolved, the dispute will be referred to an impartial third-party **arbitrator** who will hear the case and make a ruling. In practice, 98 percent of all collective bargaining agreements provide for arbitration as the final step in an impasse. Grievance arbitration usually focuses on one of two issues—contract interpretation and discipline and discharge. The party claiming that the contract language has been improperly interpreted has the burden of going forward in presenting its case. In discipline and discharge cases, because the action was initiated by the company, the company officials have the burden of showing that they had

Arbitrator
An impartial third party who hears grievances and makes rulings on them.

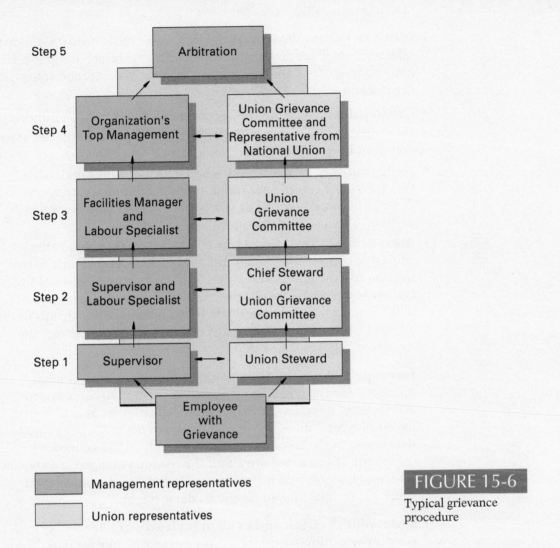

Step 5   Arbitration

Step 4   Organization's Top Management   ↔   Union Grievance Committee and Representative from National Union

Step 3   Facilities Manager and Labour Specialist   ↔   Union Grievance Committee

Step 2   Supervisor and Labour Specialist   ↔   Chief Steward or Union Grievance Committee

Step 1   Supervisor   ↔   Union Steward

Employee with Grievance

◾ Management representatives

◻ Union representatives

FIGURE 15-6

Typical grievance procedure

just cause. As for who pays the arbitrator, it's often dependent on who's raising the issue. More often, though, the labour agreement will stipulate who pays, or how the costs of arbitration will be divided.

The previous steps describe the overall grievance procedure. But our concern is in building supervisory skills. So we need to address a more specific question: how should you, as a supervisor, respond if an employee or union steward presents a formal grievance? We suggest you do the following:

1. **Listen to the employee's complaint.** Don't be defensive and don't take the complaint personally. Employees regularly have grievances and you're the first contact point in the process that represents the organization.

   - Calmly listen to the employee's complaint. Keep an open mind.
   - Very importantly at this stage, don't argue with the employee. What you want to do is gain understanding.
   - Using your active listening skills will help you better understand the employee's complaint. Additionally, hostilities and tensions are likely to become subdued as you honestly demonstrate your willingness to understand the grievance.
   - Ask questions to make sure you get to the real problem. Is the employee complaining about unfair allocation of overtime when the real issue is that the employee is having serious personal financial problems and was counting on lots of overtime to help pay bills? You want to make sure you fully understand the details of the grievance and what specific provision of the labour contract the employee believes is involved.

2. **Investigate to get the facts.** You want to separate facts from opinions. Are the facts, as presented by the employee, complete and factual? Interview any key people who may be able to verify the employee's claims. Review all pertinent documents. Go over the clauses in the labour contract that apply to the employee's complaint. If you're unsure about the contract's language or how a relevant clause should be interpreted, get counsel from a labour specialist in your human resources department.

3. **Make your decision and explain it clearly.** You need to complete your investigation promptly so you can reach your decision in a relatively short period of time. Why? Because most labour agreements specify a definite time period within which a grievance must be answered.

   - If you determine that the grievance is unfounded, verbally give the employee and union steward your interpretation. Be sure to back up your decision with specific reasons for denying the grievance, citing evidence from your investigation and/or language from the contract. You should then follow up the verbal answer with a written response.
   - If the grievance has merit, provide a written response to the employee and union steward stating this fact. Additionally, you

should describe the corrective action you plan to take. But before you write this response, be sure that your remedy is consistent with established practices, doesn't set any new precedents, and is within your authority. When in doubt, get approval from your boss or a manager in human resources. You should be very careful about making individual exceptions to past practices. This might seem like an easy way to make the grievance disappear, but you could end up setting a precedent that might seriously hurt the organization in future contract negotiations or in future arbitration decisions.

4. **Keep records and documents.** It's important to document everything you do relating to a grievance. Remember that the labour agreement is a binding, legal contract. As such, formality is important. You have to follow the language of the contract. To protect yourself and the organization against charges that you have not followed the contract as intended, you must keep all the records that you've accumulated on every grievance.

5. **Be prepared for appeals.** If you rule against the employee, you should expect the employee or the union steward to appeal your decision to a higher level. Be prepared to be questioned by union officials and various labour specialists from your organization's human resource group. Don't let this shake you. And don't let an employee or union representative's threat of appeal influence your decision.

The grievance procedure is essentially a formal appeals system. It is designed to protect an employee's rights. Your judgement may be overruled at a higher level. But that's OK. If you've followed the contract's procedures, made your decision in good faith, and carefully documented your actions, you've correctly fulfilled your obligations in the grievance procedure.

PREVENTING GRIEVANCES

"Keep your nose clean. If you are going to be at an employee's machine, make sure you have a valid reason for doing it. You have to watch how you deal with reprimands. You must follow the book. For example, you must go by the progressive discipline procedure and not play favourites with anyone," says Tina Payton, prepress supervisor at Robinson-Blackmore, a printing company in St. John's, Newfoundland.

"Treat employees fairly. Make the limits clear. And recognize that you'll never make everyone happy," comments Larry Bowzeylo, Operations Integration Manager for Suncor in Fort McMurray, Alberta.

"If you follow the appropriate steps in disciplining someone, the union can't do anything. And if you treat people with respect and integrity, so they know you're fair and won't backstab anybody, you'll be fine," adds Paula Aylward, a shift manager at Cavendish Farms in PEI.

"Be very honest and forthright with the shop steward. Let them know if there's a concern. For example, if there's an incident where I have to speak to the cook about yelling and swearing, I will invite the shop steward to be there, even though it is not necessary. Be fair and make sure everyone understands what's on the table. Show respect regardless of what's happening. Be diplomatic; people can get heated and emotional," says Tricia Mah, director of support services at a large Vancouver nursing home.

Applying Your Skills

Break the class into groups of three. This role-play requires one person to play the role of the supervisor, another the role of the employee (Naveen), and the third will play the union steward.

All players should read the following scenario and the excerpt from the union's contract and a letter of understanding. Then you are to role-play a meeting in the supervisor's office. This role play should take no more than 15 minutes.

SCENARIO

Naveen is a plant worker who works day shifts from Monday to Friday and enjoys the opportunity to occasionally make overtime money when the plant is busy and requires weekend work. He is unhappy that he was not allowed to sign up for overtime on the weekend.

Naveen was absent from Monday to Thursday due to illness and returned to work on Friday, feeling fine. He discovered that there had been a request for substantial overtime on the weekend so he submitted an offer on Friday to work on both Saturday and Sunday. The offer was refused by his supervisor. Naveen is now entering a meeting with his supervisor and union steward. As a senior worker at the plant, Naveen feels that he should have had the first opportunity to work the extra hours. The supervisor feels that proper procedure was followed in allocating overtime to those who signed up for it by the deadline.

RELEVANT CONTRACT LANGUAGE

5.6 *Overtime Distribution.* All overtime must be authorized in advance by the Company and shall be distributed between competent employees in an equitable manner on a rotational basis. An agreed system shall be implemented to effectively monitor the distribution of overtime.

In order to accomplish such equitable distribution of overtime the Company shall:

(a) post all scheduled overtime in the plant on a weekly basis, and

(b) post an overtime request form (Tuesday at 9:00 am, prior to the weekend in which overtime is required) listing each regular employee's name.

Employees who wish to work overtime that weekend shall sign the Overtime Request Form by 9:00am on the Wednesday prior to the weekend. The confirmed scheduled overtime shall be posted by 5:00pm on the Thursday prior to the weekend; it is understood that should the Company's circumstances change subsequent to its posting, the schedule may be revised.

Daily overtime, (Monday to Friday) of an expected duration of one (1) hour or less in conjunction with an employee's regular shift, will normally be assigned to the employee performing the job on the shift where overtime is required. Overtime in excess of an expected duration of one (1) hour shall first be offered to the senior employee on shift.

The company shall maintain up-to-date records of overtime worked which shall be reviewed with the Plant Committee Chairperson on a monthly basis. Where discrepancies occur in the assignment of overtime every reasonable effort shall be made to adjust such discrepancies in the subsequent month.

SUMMARY

This summary is organized by the Learning Objectives.

1. Union membership has been gradually declining but still remains high in the public sector. But this decline should not be interpreted as implying that labour union influence is low. Labour unions still represent the majority of workers in many key industries. Additionally, wages and benefits won by labour unions typically spill over to influence the wages and benefits of nonunionized employees.

2. Unions are appealing to employees because their power offers the promise of higher wages and benefits, greater job security, and increased opportunities to influence work rules.

3. The federal Canada Labour Code and provincial labour relations acts provide guidelines for both companies and unions. The Charter of Rights and Freedoms further protects all individual rights of every Canadian.

4. The primary purpose of collective bargaining is to negotiate a union contract and spell out the terms for administering that contract.

5. The supervisor plays a very important role in contract administration. He or she needs to know the details of the contract in order to interpret it and carry out its procedures. What supervisors say and do largely determines the labour-management climate in the organization.

6. A union steward is the elected representative of the employees in a work unit and is there to protect the rights of union members. Ideally, the relationship between the union steward and supervisor should be a cooperative one. The supervisor should share information regarding changes coming in the unit and keep the steward informed regarding any problems, for example, having given verbal warnings to an employee repeatedly regarding lateness.

7. The most common trouble areas in contract administration are scheduling and vacation. Lack of promptness in handling grievances can also be an issue. Increasingly, dealing with claims of bullying or workplace harassment is a challenge.

8. The steps involved in handling a grievance are: 1. listen to the employee's complaint; 2. investigate to get the facts; 3. make your decision and explain it clearly; 4. keep records and documents; and 5. be prepared for appeals.

KEY TERMS AND CONCEPTS

Agency shop
Arbitrator
Bargaining unit
Collective bargaining
Conciliation
Employee relations
Fact-finding
Grievance
Interest arbitration

Lockout
Mediation
Spillover effect
Strike
Union
Union shop
Union steward
Wildcat strike

REVIEWING YOUR KNOWLEDGE

1. What might explain the decline in union membership over the past 50 years?
2. Contrast agency and union shops.
3. How are labour issues influenced by legislation?
4. Describe the supervisor's role in the collective bargaining process.
5. "An employer might not want to stifle a union organizing effort. In fact, an employer might want to encourage his employees to join a union." Do you agree or disagree with this statement? Discuss.
6. What is collective bargaining?
7. What is the purpose of a grievance procedure? Describe the typical steps in the grievance process.
8. "You can predict strikes. Union administrators have to call a strike every now and then just to demonstrate to their membership that they're fighting hard for them." Do you agree or disagree with this statement? Explain.
9. How would the existence of a union and a collective bargaining contract affect a) employee recruitment and selection, b) compensation, and c) discipline?

PERFORMING YOUR JOB

CASE 15.A

Making a Union Unnecessary

You are a supervisor at a chicken processing plant. It started out small but the owners are ambitious and energetic and the company is rapidly growing. You and the others on the management team are concerned about preventing unionization at the plant. There has been some talk among the employees about organizing, and the increase in the size of the workforce at the plant makes it a likely target for a union drive. There are many unionized companies in the area.

Employees are paid competitive wages but the jobs are not exciting. The place is kept very clean and the newly hired HR manager is ensuring that all appropriate health and safety precautions and procedures are followed. The benefit package is meagre, as the company has been reinvesting heavily in its growth. The jobs are unskilled yet it is a challenge to recruit all the staff needed because the unemployment rate is low in the region.

RESPONDING TO THIS CASE

1. Why do you and the other managers fear unionization? What specific consequences do you fear?
2. What would attract the employees to a union? What benefits would they anticipate?
3. How could you and/or the other managers find out what issues employees have, both immediately and on an ongoing basis, in order to resolve these issues and create a more positive relationship?
4. The plant workers have relatively low education whereas the supervisors and managers, including you, have a college or university education. How can this create a division? How can this division be bridged? What can the company do to integrate these two quite different "types" of employees? What can the individual supervisors and managers do to create a relationship that feels to the employees like a partnership, rather than a hierarchical and authoritarian relationship?

CASE 15.B

Dealing with Harassment Charges[1]

At the government agency where she manages a large group of staff, Nina has been dealing with Cole's performance issues for a year now. Despite carefully following procedures in handling it, Nina has had a grievance filed against her by Cole, claiming the management of his performance has been unfair, followed by a charge of workplace harassment that was formally investigated by the province. In the end, she was entirely vindicated of any wrongdoing. But the entire process took its toll and leaves Nina wondering whether she has the strength to provide much needed supervision of Cole in the future.

In a tumultuous work environment, Nina was the third manager to supervise Cole within his probationary period. It was quickly clear to her that he was not meeting the expectations of the job. She worked closely with Cole to support his development so that he would be successful in the performance of his job functions. Unfortunately, the previous two managers had taken a hands off approach to management of all staff, and had not documented any concerns specific to Cole's performance. Cole made it through probation. As with all her staff, Nina expected accountability from Cole. But he did not take kindly to her approach, perhaps because of the lax supervision he had previously received leading him to believe he could do what he wanted. Cole submitted expenses and could not produce receipts. He was absent from work for several days without reporting in and could not be reached, despite Nina needing critical information from him. Given straightforward parameters that he and all staff in his position must follow in dealing with clients, and in meeting ministry established headlines, he changed procedures to suit his own preferences.

Cole also had difficulties working with his colleagues. He did not show up for meetings and then became angry when they stopped inviting him. He claimed some of the work they did was second rate and insisted that he replace certain elements with his own work, even though he had not been present to discuss issues and concerns with colleagues. Then he did not follow through with the work he had promised. In one instance, colleagues chose to submit a major report without his name because of his lack of contribution.

Nina therefore had documented issues regarding expenses, not following procedures, and absenteeism, plus complaints from both staff and clients about Cole's behaviour. Early on, she asked to sit in on some client meetings as part of the probationary process, standard procedure that Cole nevertheless resented. He asked for a union representative to also come and she readily agreed. She praised the good work she observed, both formally in the appraisal and informally in emails and conversation. As issues mounted, however, Nina spoke to him, privately and in a constructive way, about what was happening. She tried to understand the reasons behind his choices, and guide him towards acceptable behaviour. His behaviour did not change. The union representative was invited to meetings to discuss the lack of progress. Ultimately, with issues continuing, Nina moved on to a formal written discipline letter. At this point, Cole got angry and insisted that the discipline letter be removed from his file. He lodged a grievance with the union against Nina, claiming her action was unfair. At the same time he approached the Human Resources department and lodged a formal complaint of workplace harassment against Nina, noting 16 specific incidents. This led to a formal investigation of the harassment charge by an external investigator, involving interviews with Cole, Nina and witnesses. It was an intimidating process for all involved. Nina spent about 60 hours dealing with the harassment charges, through meeting with the investigator for the formal interview and then answering follow-up questions, pulling together documentation to support her case and creating a 24-page formal response to the charges, including all her documentation of their interactions. It was a stressful time, both in taking her away from ongoing demands of her job, and in leading others to question her actual handling of Cole, believing perhaps "where there's smoke, there's fire."

---

[1] Names and details have been changed to protect identities.

"I'm tough and I'm process-driven but I found this difficult. I've seen others in my position ruined by this kind of situation. Part of the issue is that as a manager, you're alone. The employee has the full weight of the union behind them. And HR doesn't want to take sides; they want to be seen as neutral so they did not help me. I was lucky to have the full support of my own manager. I get why the workplace harassment legislation was brought in. I know there are managers who take advantage of their position and treat employees badly. But that was not the case here, yet I was the one under scrutiny.

In this situation I learned a few things. One was how important it is for me to not confide in my staff. Despite them complaining to me about Cole, I had not discussed how I was handling it, or agreed with them or criticized him in any way. When they were randomly called as witnesses by the external investigator, it would have been an issue if they had heard me divulge confidential information about his performance. I also learned that, when you are considering dealing with a performance issue, you have to take a long-term view. Nothing is a short term fix. And there are consequences in dealing with performance issues, so I need to wonder whether something is worth the effort or just needs to be suffered through."

Nina's troubles with Cole are not over. During the investigation he went on stress leave. He is returning to work shortly. An HR department representative suggested to Nina's boss that Nina be reassigned to a different employee group to avoid her having to deal with Cole. This stunned them, since Cole was the problem, not Nina. She had been cleared of any suspicion of harassment and, in fact, the investigator had praised her handling of the situations under review. No, Nina is staying where she is. HR has agreed to warn Cole that, if he brings up any of the harassment complaints again, after months of effort proved them groundless, he will be terminated.

RESPONDING TO THIS CASE

1. Describe how Nina's situation may have been different if the workplace was not unionized. Consider both the positives and the negatives of the union having been involved in the performance issues.
2. Discuss how the new workplace harassment legislation in several provinces can complicate normal contract administration and management for a supervisor.

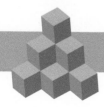

COMPREHENSIVE CASES

Benoit

Benoit works for a management systems outsourcing and consulting company. As manager of support services, he has two very different roles to play: one focused externally on the client; the other focused internally on the team that provides the service to the client.

As the prime contact with a client whose project his team is handling, Benoit represents his company and must provide a professional face that assures the client that their needs will be fully met in a timely way (even when he is not so confident himself, given various operational challenges). He must have a firm grasp on the client's needs so he can translate that into a series of tasks for his team. He must also have a firm grasp on how challenging it will be to achieve what the client wants so that he can communicate reasonable expectations to the client and not put his team in a position of having to achieve the impossible.

As the lead for his team, Benoit has to ensure they have the capacity to complete those tasks. This means expectations regarding tasks, deadlines and quality must be clear and the team must have the physical, human and time resources needed. Benoit won't be doing any of the work himself but will play a key role when it comes to troubleshooting.

Reporting to Benoit are five people, split into two very different roles. The 3 business analysts work with their clients on an ongoing basis to ensure business requirements are met (acting as a bridge between business and the technical team that develops customized IT solutions; also testing solutions, doing training for clients, writing procedures to support business requirements, troubleshooting issues with the current system). The two coordinators process daily runs, set up code in the system, and carry out standardized items, spending most of their time on computers.

The coordinator position is often a step towards becoming a business analyst. Benoit's team often require the assistance of technical consultants (IT specialists) who actually report to Benoit's colleague, the director of consulting services.

Above Benoit in the organizational structure is the president and managing director of the company. Beside him in the structure is the director of consulting services, who previously held Benoit's position. Benoit was hired to replace her.

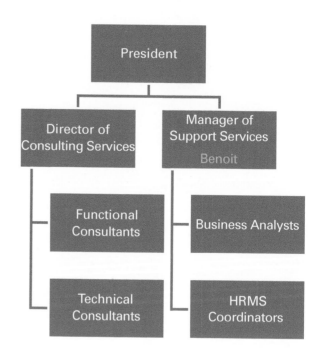

RESPONDING TO THIS CASE

1. Benoit came from a large organization where he was a specialist serving the company. He had limited experience as an acting manager supervising one employee. Now he has five staff in two different roles and external clients to deal

with. Describe the challenges this transition would involve and the skills needed to handle it well.

2. Describe how Benoit fulfills the four management functions in his role.

3. Explain how emotional labour seems to be a part of Benoit's job.

4. Benoit's predecessor remained at the company, simply moving into another role. What are the potential advantages and challenges of this?

5. Before joining this outsourcing/consulting company, Benoit worked for a huge national company. He was far removed from the executive level and felt like he was a very small cog in a large industrial complex. Now he reports directly to the president, an innovative entrepreneur who started the company and continues to head up the organization as it grows. It means Benoit gets a chance to be involved in decisions that affect everyone and has the opportunity to be involved in anything he wants. Contrast these two different positions, outlining the pros and cons of each for someone in Benoit's position.

6. In order to meet clients' needs, Benoit's team sometimes needs the input of technical consultants at the company. These technical consultants actually report to the consulting side despite being responsible for contributions to both consulting and outsourcing projects. What are the political aspects of this for Benoit and his team?

7. Identify the potential sources of conflict that Benoit must deal with.

Dominic

Dominic has just walked into a challenging situation as a new supervsior. At 25, he is younger than all the staff, and he does not have the IT background that they have. But in the selection process, the team itself got the chance to interview all candidates and they agreed with management's recommendation to hire Dominic. Now, at the two-month point of his having started, his apprehensions about fitting in with the older, more ex-

perienced group have disappeared. More challenging than his youth, perhaps, is the fact that this is a new position no one has ever filled and Dominic is crafting it with the help of his management colleagues and his team.

Dominic's Background

Dominic had never held a supervisory position and neither had anyone in his family. So what prepared him for this leadership role? One was a volunteer position at university during his undergraduate degree. As one of three student directors working with the Student Life office and 30 volunteers, he helped organize alternative night life events for students under drinking age. This involved strategizing on what events to hold (e.g. amazing race, movie night, yoga), organizing and running them, doing budgeting, and organizing facilities for events. "It was like running a small business: recruiting, retaining, recognizing, planning events, running events, being accountable to the university (because of liability issues)." The second leadership experience was as a youth leader at his church, running a few events a year, usually sports or picnics, just for fun to get more youth engaged with the church community. It involved fundraising and organizing events. "We started small with a baseball tournament; then families kept coming to events. We started with 12 to 20 year olds, now we have 5 year olds and 150 kids; it gave me experience in crowd control and organizing events."

Dominic's Education and Experience

After doing a graduate degree in economics, Dominic took on a corporate research position that required him to assess the viability of current organizational projects and proposed projects. He had to work with several databases and occasionally seek out information from external organizations. The work required analytical, statistical, research and writing skills. It also helped that he was comfortable with a variety of software programs to manipulate the data. Dominic became the go-to person in the department regarding coding issues and pulling data out of the management information system. Known for his calm, positive presence and his ability to come up with an answer to any question, Dominic fit in easily with the older, all-female team. Dominic was not unhappy in the position but realized he was looking for more, so he was open to a friend's suggestion he apply to supervise a research department at another organization, a department that was reinventing itself. This is how he described the appeal of the job before actually taking it on:

"I like the idea of helping the department move to becoming a service centre and working with the executives to sort out how to make it happen effectively. It sounds like 50% of the job is project management, working with stakeholders. The team is doing work a lot like what I have been doing in my current role but I can take it further, helping the team organize how to do it well. I will be doing less of the nitty-gritty data crunching; reporting and presenting will be my responsibility, which is the really interesting part of research. And because I have direct contact with the programmers that handle the data manipulation, I will have more control over the process and can get done what is needed."

A New Organization and A New Role

The organization had made a decision to entirely reorganize their institutional research department. Previously, there had been ten analysts who worked under a director and associate director and took on whatever research requests came to them from the organization. This led to duplication of effort (e.g. someone would make the request to three analysts to ensure someone got them the information needed in a timely way) and no use of specialized talents (no match between the researcher and the kind of research they were skilled and interested in). It also meant a lack of communication amongst the analysts so that, even when working on a common project, there was little interaction. The department wanted to be able to handle large projects and ad hoc requests from the corporate community in a more

efficient way. So the decision was made to add three managers and to cluster the analysts into four groups, each focusing on different aspects of research: data analytics (Dominic's team of four analysts); evaluation and accounting (under another new manager); budget and resource planning (under a new manager) and policy (reporting directly to the associate director).

Interestingly, the analysts themselves had a major role in deciding the new structure. The associate director had presented the new structural plan and said, "This is the operational plan; go in teams to say where you think your boundaries begin and end, negotiate with the other teams, and create a first draft." Not only did they draft team boundaries, outlining what they thought each should handle, they also drafted what the role of the manager would be in supporting each group. When Dominic began his position, he was handed a list of responsibilities that had been created by his team. He and the other two managers are following the guidelines set by the staff, and tweaking them as events dictate adjustment is needed.

Did Empowerment Work?

Empowerment is supposed to motivate workers. Did it do the trick here? "Workers were certainly empowered but there are little things they don't like, and the negativity clouds everything; for example, the whole data analytics team was moved to another office when we needed to reorganize space to cluster teams. The director simply decided who was going, with no consultation. All this wonderful work (empowerment) and one decision throws it out. Another issue is that we have groups empowered to make decisions but when an executive decision is needed, it does not come. There was an issue of a boundary between the data group and the evaluation group and there was no resolution reached through internal discussion; they needed the associate director's expertise and power, but she just deferred to the evaluation team. Why did she defer? The team thinks it's a personality issue (she doesn't want to take ownership) but I feel it could be that she is trying to get them to resolve their own issues. I feel caught in the middle. There have been a number of situations where people have gone looking for her assistance in making a decision, especially about boundaries and roles and responsibilities, and it just bounces back on us, so now we don't go to her. We're just muddying through. But only 5% is an issue, the rest is OK. She is using this same approach with the management team. She will always say "What do you think?" Sometimes this is frustrating but it has always worked out."

DOMINIC'S TEAM

"The group is pulling together as a team. As much as they didn't like the move, having five desks in a small area where they're facing each other does encourage communication and shared problem-solving; but it's not good for privacy. Because they're the data team, people often stop in and disturb all of us when they have a data request for one person or just pause for a casual chat. Interestingly the data area has also become the technical support for the whole department because of their special skills, so lots drop in for help. But they do see the benefit of being in the same space together; it got rid of duplicate requests.

I've been surprised at how well I fit in with this IT team. I was apprehensive of their acceptance; but we have had to make a lot of decisions and we've learned how to work together. They generate ideas, then discuss them and ask, what do you think, Dominic? There's lots of joint problem-solving; they take the time to explain, I ask questions. Then, based on what they've outlined to me, I say, "Do this – it sounds good". They like that. In a way, my lack of familiarity with their work can help. My questions and the short briefings they give help me sort out what sounds best, and I choose on the basis of what will meet needs. I think it is the bigger picture, operational perspective I bring that helps."

None of the team members had applied for Dominic's position. Dominic understands one is near retirement and probably didn't want the hassle. He doesn't understand two of them holding back. The fourth is a brilliant technical expert but wouldn't enjoy the role. "He knows everything, and has built databases but is rigid and tends to be critical. He is a great resource for the team but not

a decision maker. He doesn't take into account operational needs, understanding the role of others and meeting their needs. The others respect him and often go to him first for his thoughts in a situation, but don't rely on him to make a decision. They like having me there to say, Jim's right, or Sorry, Jim."

CONTINUING CHALLENGES: STRUCTURE, STRATEGY AND CREDIBILITY

The new structure is certainly engaging the staff and funnelling projects more efficiently. But all the kinks have not been worked out. "There's an interesting path of communication. An analyst in evaluation is expected to go to his manager if he thinks my team should be involved in something he's working on. Then that manager goes to me and I work with my team over the specific request. It seems to slow things down on the surface but allows me to manage workload, so we still need to work out boundaries here. The grey areas where it is not clear who does what remain frustrating. And the perceived lack of support from above could be an issue. I think it is a matter of empowerment but many of the staff feel it is a lack of leadership."

Not only is the department reorganizing itself, but the organization is rethinking how the databases are set up for the company, who has access and what the role of institutional research should be. Because various departments have had access to a central database, and then copy and manipulate the data in the ways they prefer, they come up with different answers to the same question. Plus there are issues of security and confidentiality of data. It's a huge institution so solving all data needs while maintaining security and saving resources is an issue. So Dominic is involved in strategic discussions with executives about how to move forward. A frustrating aspect is that other parts of the organization are hiring people to program and deal with data when centrally (through Dominic's area) it could be done more quickly and securely. It seems that Dominic's department has a credibility issue dating back to the old management information system, now being replaced, that would drop records or generate different answers to the same question. He wants people from across the organization to use the services of his team, so he will need to work with the other managers in institutional research on both communicating their value and availability, and rebuilding the trust that had somehow been lost.

RESPONDING TO THIS CASE

1. Discuss Dominic in terms of the four categories of management competence.
2. Describe the kinds of plans Dominic will have to deal with in this position.
3. Explain why setting goals with his analysts may be a challenge and how this could be addressed.
4. Give Dominic advice on managing his time.
5. Explain what the focus of control efforts will be in the institutional research department where Dominic works.
6. Discuss the kind of group decision making that Dominic appears to use, whether it is appropriate and why.
7. Use organizing concepts to describe how the department has changed.
8. Discuss whether the small clusters now referred to as "teams" truly are teams, according to the characteristics of real teams.
9. Describe the challenges of performance management in a work environment that is dependent on work requests from other parts of the organization.
10. Describe the indications that Dominic is a leader as well as a supervisor.
11. Explain what factors seem to have supported his team members learning to trust him.
12. Identify the potential sources of conflict in Dominic's situation.
13. Apply Lewin's three step change process to assess how well the restructuring has been implemented.
14. Describe why some of the employees may have been resistant to the restructuring change, and what techniques appear to have been used to reduce or avoid this resistance.

Karen

Karen is the manager of operations at a third party audit company that audits and processes payments of freight bills for large companies. Almost 30 people report to Karen in two departments: the audit group that handles customer account administration and has a lot of communication with the customer, and the data entry team that inputs information into the computer system. "We do not book or carry shipments; we process the payments, issue the cheques to carriers in some cases or in other cases upload to their financial system so they can pay carriers directly. It is a deadline-driven business. We must get things done right and on time."

Karen has been with the company for years, having originally done data entry on a part-time basis. This means she has a good understanding of the system. If there is a programming issue or a data error, she can often be a trouble shooter.

Her supervisory duties include:

- Delegating workload
- Approving and tracking vacations
- Arranging coverage for sick days and vacations
- Hiring
- Orienting new hires
- Training of new hires (all training of data entry people; whereas, for audit staff, Karen spends the first half day with them and then the supervisor of quality control steps into the training)
- Arranging cross-training to ensure back-up
- Troubleshooting problems
- Performance feedback
- Administering bonus program

Karen also takes on what she refers to as a "non" supervisory role, setting up processes for new customers, for example, and helping with ongoing projects.

Karen and the HR person do all the hiring together, interviewing and deciding by consensus. "We have a common understanding of the skills required. We always look for someone with a transportation background. It's too difficult to train on a new system as well as a new industry.

When we bring in someone new, after the 20 minute orientation that HR gives them, I take them around and introduce them to everyone. Sometimes I set up a "buddy" so they have someone to take them for lunch. When I'm training someone, they sit side by side with me. Our company and software are unique. They will have many questions so instead of having them trained by someone with a full workload, I have more flexibility to work with them. I want the new person to have a fair chance since everyone is busy.

Performance appraisals are done annually but not for the last two years because the company decided not to do increases due to the economy. We do have a quarterly performance-based bonus system for the auditors and data entry staff. People are given targets and they vary with accounts because some are more complex or more detail-oriented. They are given hours against the account so they must accomplish the targets within certain time limits. Other aspects that contribute to the bonus include customer service (e.g. praise, complaints) and meeting deadlines. The bonus has to be earned and is not given to all. You are paid to do a job. If you go above and beyond, you are given a bonus.

But even if there is no formal performance appraisal, I still keep track of what is happening. If there is a problem, I speak with the person immediately. My door is always open and I connect with people in the kitchen or passing by. I don't formally walk up and say "What's going on?" But I'm usually aware of anything early on. They realize I can help them resolve issues or indicate next steps. For example, if there is a rude carrier on the phone looking for payment, my staff will forward it to me. The person may be threatening but we can't process payment or request funds prematurely. Another reason for them to come to me would be if something is not going right in the weekly schedule. For example, reports are due Friday noon but will be late and they are wondering if they should contact the customer. Sometimes they may simply be informing me and not actually looking for direction. I do get involved with a lot of customers, jumping in where needed. Some customers will ask me questions. If there's been a problem with an account, they like to know someone senior is working on it. Often if auditors go to meet customers, I go with them to build rapport.

An example of a challenge I had to deal with was with a senior auditor who was not happy with his bonus being reduced significantly. He was used to getting a substantial payout. But this time one quarter of his targets were out. He had much higher hours against the account in the period than planned and it was not clear why—if I know something has happened to affect an account, I can always adjust expectations. We had a meeting and he was very upset that his bonus was not the usual. He raised his voice and walked out of my office. But we don't want the bonus to be perceived as a negative. So the next day I sent him an email saying I would like to discuss this further—the bonus is a fair process that is earned. Please come by. He did come by and he left smiling. I explained how the bonus works, how we use the time sheets and the documents in the system for records; we don't just pull them from the sky. I explained that, if he was having a problem, he needed to let me know (and now he does). It's a complex bonus program and most don't understand how it works; they just look at the results."

Karen works long hours. "My staff work eight hours and get flex hours so a lot come in at 7 am and at 2:59, they're gone. I come in at 7:30 and leave at 4:30 but there are many days I'm here until 5 or 6 to make a deadline. My staff know I work hard and it can be an issue at times because they may see asking a question as an interruption.

What advice would I give to a new manager? Moving from data entry into a supervisory position after a couple of years meant I knew the company and people well but it was an adjustment going from being a friend to a supervisor. For some that's a problem. But I knew I wanted to be a supervisor who treated everyone the same.

I had a supervisor working under me a few years back who took her position as '*I'm* the supervisor'. But you can be a leader without pushing it. She was pushing her weight around, which caused conflict because staff would skip her to come to me and I said you must deal with her, which caused more conflict. Working with her, I explained how I preferred her to deal with things —if this comes up again, this is how I suggest you deal with it. But she chose to leave. I tried to guide her according to what worked well for me. I don't push my weight around but I know what's right for the company. I can help people understand that. If I'm questioning how to deal with a situation myself, I'll go to the VP or HR for suggestions.

We've had situations where employees don't get along and they end up in my office. I feel like "mother". If one comes in and says "she did this", I suggest they work it out themselves so I don't make it into a bigger issue.

The hardest thing in supervising is learning how to deal with the personalities. Some are easier to give instructions or information to. Others will challenge you so you need to learn how to approach them. It's the end product that's important. We're a service provider. Some individuals can be difficult to deal with because they always have an excuse at hand for why an error was made and don't take accountability. I explain the situation; go through the steps of what happened and what should have happened. I let them walk through the situation and I ask them why they took certain steps (because I understand their job and we all make mistakes). I point out issues not to criticize them but to ensure it won't happen again. If they don't know, they will repeat an error so they must be made aware. When you point out an error to some they will say "Oh, I can't believe it" and are quick to address the issue, but others are full of excuses.

RESPONDING TO THIS CASE

1. Describe examples of Karen fulfilling each of the management functions.
2. Discuss the value of the company promoting from within, as in Karen's case, versus hiring from outside.
3. Describe:
   a. the pros and cons of the training approach used by Karen.
   b. how the effectiveness of the training could be evaluated.
4. Discuss the wisdom of Karen's company suspending performance appraisals when there are no increases.
5. Use the motivation guidelines to discuss the likely value of the bonus system as a motivator.
6. Identify two different conflict management styles used by Karen and their appropriateness.
7. Describe your reaction to Karen's story:
   a. Does it encourage you to consider taking on a supervisory role?
   b. Does she appeal to you as a supervisor you might work under? What specific aspects of her explanations of handling things did you like/not like? Discuss this with colleagues.

ENDNOTES

Chapter 1

[1] Allen I. Kraut et al, "The Role of the Manager: What's Really Important in Different Management Jobs," *Academy of Management Executive*, November 1989, pp. 286–293.

[2] This section is based on Linda A. Hill, *Becoming a Manager: Master of a New Identity* (Boston, Harvard Business School Press, 1992)

[3] Robert L. Katz, "Skills of an Effective Administrator," *Harvard Business Review* (September/October 1974), pp. 90–102.

[4] Daniel Goleman, *Working with Emotional Intelligence* (NY: Bantam Books, 1998), p.318 .

[5] D. Farrell and J.C. Petersen, "Patterns of Political Behaviour in Organizations," *Academy of Management Review* (July 1982), p. 405.

[6] R.E. Boyatzis, *The Competent Manager: A Model for Effective Performance* (NY: John Wiley and Sons, 1982), p. 33.

[7] Based on John Newstrom and Keith Davis, *Organizational Behavior at Work*, 9th ed. (NY: McGraw-Hill, 1993), p. 239.

[8] See Richard E. Crandall, "First-Line Supervisors: Tomorrow's Professionals", Personnel (November 1988), pp. 24–31.

[9] B. Moses, Role Call: It's tougher to be a manager now, The Globe and Mail, March 17, 2010 (accessed at www.theglobeandmail.com/report-on-business/managing/barbara-moses on October 26, 2010)

[10] T. Roberts, "Who are the high-tech home workers?" *Inc. Technology*, 1994, p. 31.

[11] T. Krywulak and M. Roberts. *Winning the "Generation Wars" Making the Most of Generational Differences and Similarities in the Workplace*, Conference Board of Canada, November 2009, http://www.conferenceboard.ca/temp/ef62 db65-6be7-4941-9bcf-014b573c4089/10-070-CanCompete_GenerationWars.pdf

[12] Geert Hofstede, *Culture's Consequences: International Differences in Workplace Values* (Gage Publications, 1997)

[13] Hofstede called this last dimension masculinity/femininity.

[14] http://geert-hofstede.com/canada.html

[15] S. Hebert and R. Ravary. *Employers' Lessons from Quebec's Experience with Psychological Harassment*, June, 2008, http://blogs.hrhero.com/northernexposure /2008/06/24/lessons-from-quebecs-experi-ence-with-psychological-harassment/

Chapter 2

[1] H. Mintzberg, *The Rise and Fall of Strategic Planning* (New York: Free Press, 1994).

[2] Ibid.

[3] K. Rebello and P. Burrows, The Fall of an American Icon, *Business Week*, February 5, 1996, pp. 34–42.

[4] D. Miller, "The Architecture of Simplicity," *Academy of Management Review*, January 1993, pp. 116–138.

[5] Cited in Harold E. Fearon and others, *Fundamentals of Production/ Operations Management*, 3rd ed. (St. Paul, MN: West Publishing, 1986), p. 97.

Chapter 3

[1] IBM Business Conduct Guidelines, http://www.ibm.com/investor/pdf/BCG20 12.pdf

[2] This list is based on James J. Semrodek Jr., "Nine Steps to Cost Control," *Supervisory Management*, April 1976, pp. 29–32

[3] "Supervisor Liability for Safety Violations", OHS Insider, October 29, 2010, http://ohsinsider.com/do-dili-gence/supervisor-liability-for-safety-violations

[4] Material adapted from Canadian Centre for Occupational Health and Safety (www.ccohs.ca)

[5] http://www.ccohs.ca/youngworkers/ resources/realWorld.html

[6] Material adapted from Worker's Compensation Board of B.C. video discussion guide,

http://www2.worksafebc.com/PDFs/Young Worker/LostYouthGuide.pdf

[7] S. Lam, C. Hui and K.S. Law, "Organizational Citizenship Behavior: Comparing Perspectives of Supervisors and Subordinates Across Four International Samples," *Journal of Applied Psychology*, 1999, Vol 84 (4), pp. 594–601.

[8] Cited in G. Bylinsky, "How Companies Spy on Employees," *Fortune*, November 4, 1991, pp. 131–140

[9] Cited in Archie B. Carroll, "In Search of the Moral Manager," *Business Horizons*, March/April 1087, p. 7.

Chapter 4

[1] Alan J. Rowe, James D. Boulgarides, and Michael R. McGrath, *Managerial Decision Making, Modules in Management Series* (Chicago, IL: SRA, 1984), pp. 18–22.

[2] Saul W. Gellerman, Why "Good" Managers Make Bad Ethical Choices, *Harvard Business Review*, July/August 1986, p. 89.

[3] Adapted from Laura L. Nash, Ethics Without the Sermon, *Harvard Business Review*, November/December 1981, p. 81.

[4] SConference Board of Canada, April 12, 2010, http://www.newswire.ca/en/story/683185/l eaders-can-learn-the-skills-needed-to-nav-igate-the-future-world-of-work; M. Bloom, The office of 2020: We need it yesterday, The Globe and Mail, April 9, 2010, http://www.theglobeandmail.com/comme ntary/the-office-of-2020-we-need-it-yes-terday/article1366766/

[5] R. Richards et al., "Assessing Everyday Creativity: Characteristics of the Lifetime Creativity Scales and Validation with Three Large Samples," *Journal of Personality and Social Psychology*, March 1988, pp. 476–85.

[6] Adapted from J. Calano and J Salzman, "Ten Ways to Fire up Your Creativity," *Working Woman* (July 1989), pp. 94–95.

Chapter 5

[1] www.hamiltonsteel.ca/hamilstonsteel/operations.asp(Sept 30, 2012).

[2] Henry Mintzberg, *Structure in Fives: Designing Effective Organizations* (Englewood Cliffs, NJ: Prentice-Hall, Inc., 1983), p. 157.

[3] A Master Class of Radical Change, *Fortune* (December 13, 1993), p. 83.

[4] Ibid, p. 88.

[5] Jon R. Katzenbach and Douglas K. Smith, *The Wisdom of Teams* (Boston, MA: Harvard Business School Press, 1993), pp. 43–64.

[6] J. Mathieu, T. Heffner, G. Goodwin, E. Salas, J. Cannon Bowers, The Influence of Shared Mental Models on Team Process and Performance, *Journal of Applied Psychology*, April 2000, pp. 273-283.

[7] See James A. Shepperd, "Productivity Loss in Performance Groups: A Motivation Analysis," *Psychological Bulletin*, January 1993, pp. 67–81.

[8] Fernando Bartolome, "Nobody Trusts the Boss Completely—Now What?" *Harvard Business Review*, March/April 1989, pp. 135–42.

[9] K. Dirks, "The Effects of Interpersonal Trust on Work Group Performance," *Journal of Applied Psychology*, June 1999, pp. 445–455.

[10] P. Tesluk and J. Mathieu, "Overcoming Roadblocks to Effectiveness: Incorporating Management of Performance Barriers into Models of Work Group Effectiveness," *Journal of Applied Psychology*, 1999, Vol. 84, No. 2, pp. 200–217.

[11] This questionnaire is adapted from L. Steinmetz and R. Todd, *First Line Management*, 4th ed. (Homewood, IL: Irwin, 1986), pp. 64–67. With permission.

Chapter 6

[1] http://www.ag.gov.bc.ca/human-rights-protection/pdfs/EmployerInfo.pdf

[2] Lyle Spencer and Signe Spencer, *Competence at Work: Models for Superior Performance*, (John Wiley, 1993).

[3] G. A. Neuman and J. Wright, "Team Effectiveness: Beyond Skills and Cognitive Ability," *Journal of Applied Psychology*, 1999, Vol. 84, No. 3, pp. 376–389.

[4] Allan Halcrow, "Employees Are Your Best Recruiters," *Personnel Journal*, November 1988, pp. 42–49.

[5] Wayne F. Cascio, *Applied Psychology in Personnel Management*, 4th ed. (Englewood Cliffs, NJ: Prentice Hall, 1991), p. 265.

[6] John B. Miner, *Industrial and Organizational Psychology* (New York: McGraw-Hill, 1991), pp. 504–11.

[7] Walter C. Borman and Glenn L. Hallman, "Observation Accuracy for Assessors of Work Sample Performance: Consistency Across Task and Individual Differences Correlates," *Journal of Applied Psychology*, February 1991, pp. 11–18.

[8] See Robert L. Dipboye, *Selection Interviews: Process Perspectives* (Cincinnati: South-Western, 1992), Chapter 2.

[9] Irwin L. Goldstein, "The Application Blank: How Honest Are the Responses?" *Journal of Applied Psychology*, October 1971, pp. 491–92.

[10] Cited in "If You Can't Say Something Nice," *Wall Street Journal*, March 4, 1988, p. 25.

[11] T. Janz, L. Hellervik and D. Gilmore, *Behavior Description Interviewing* (Allyn & Bacon, 1986).

[12] See, for example, S. L. Premack and J. P. Wanous, "A Meta-Analysis of Realistic Job Preview Experiments", *Journal of Applied Psychology*, November 1985, pp. 706–20.

Chapter 7

[1] Much of this is based on Albert Bandura, *Social Learning Theory* (Englewood Cliffs, N.J.: Prentice Hall, Inc, 1977)

[2] Information on the St. Michaels Hospital simulation centre from http://www.stmichaelshospital.com/media/detail.php?source=hospital_news/2011/20111028_hn and http://www.stmichaelshospital.com/education/simulation/simulation-equipment.php

[3] Dr. Grantcharov at St. Michael's was quoted from http://www.stmichaelsfoundation.com/inspiringstories/michaelstories/index.aspx?c=GFs1dXVE&a=1

[4] Jermyn, D. Reverse mentorship opens minds at work, *Globe and Mail*, February 1, 2011.

[5] Ibid

[6] Auto Parts Certificate, Automotive Parts Sectoral Training council, Jeffry Piker, Educational Consultant.

[7] http://www.rogers.com/web/Careers.portal?_nfpb=true&_pageLabel=C_TR&_page=3

[8] http://www.ocadu.ca/about_ocad/accessibility/online_training_module.htm

[9] http://www.uwo.ca/humanresources/facultystaff/learn_car_dev/training.htm

[10] http://www.jobquality.ca/interviews/interview_rbc.shtml

[11] http://www.imperialoil.ca/Canada-English/community_ccr2011_development_diversity.aspx

[12] Johnson, G. Bombardier: Giving women wings, *The Globe and Mail*, February 20, 2011. http://www.theglobeandmail.com/report-on-business/careers/top-employers/bombardier-giving-women-wings/article567311/

[13] http://www.mcss.gov.on.ca/en/mcss/about/stories/banking.aspx

[14] http://jobs.fourseasons.com/workingatfourseasons/learninganddevelopment/Pages/LearningandDevelopment.aspx

[15] Lessons in management: What would Walt Disney do?, *The Globe and Mail*, July 16, 2012. http://m.theglobeandmail.com/report-on-business/careers/management/lessons-in-management-what-would-walt-disney-do/article4418115/?service=mobile

[16] C.D. Orth, H.E. Wilkinson and R.C. Benfari, "The Manager's Role as Coach and Mentor," *Organizational Dynamics*, Spring 1987, p.67.

Chapter 8

[1] Gary P. Latham and Kenneth N. Wexley, *Increasing Productivity Through Performance Appraisal* (Reading, MA: Addison-Wesley, 1981), p. 80.

[2] Peter M. Blau, *The Dynamics of Bureaucracy*, rev. ed. (Chicago, IL: University of Chicago Press, 1963).

[3] See, for example, Michael J. Kavanagh, "Evaluating Performance," in K. M. Rowland and G. R. Ferris, eds., *Personnel Management* (Boston: Allyn & Bacon, 1982), pp. 187–126.

[4] K. R. Murphy and V. A Pardaffy, "Bias in Behaviorally Anchored Rating Scales: Global or Scale Specific," *Journal of Applied Psychology*, April 1989, pp. 343–46; and M. J. Piotrowski, J. L. Barnes-Farrell, and F. H. Esris, "Behaviorally Anchored Bias: A Replication and Extension of Murphy

and Constans," *Journal of Applied Psychology*, October 1988, pp. 827–28.

[5]R. Mayer and J. Davis, "The Effect of the Performance Appraisal System on Trust for Management: A Field Quasi-Experiment," *Journal of Applied Psychology*, February 1999, pp. 123–136.

[6]J. Conway, Distinguishing Contextual Performance from Ask Performance for Managerial Jobs, *Journal of Applied Psychology*, February 1999, pp. 3–13.

[7]H. John Bernardin, "The Effects of Rater Training on Leniency and Halo Errors in Student Rating of Instructors," *Journal of Applied Psychology*, October 1975, pp. 550-55.

[8]L. O'Brien, "Improving Performance Appraisal Interviews," *Supply Management*, May 4, 2000, pp. 36–37.

[9]W. Bridges, "The End of the Job," Fortune, September 19, 1984, p. 64.

[10]This discussion is based on Scott A. Snell and Kenneth N. Wexley, "How to Make Your Performance Appraisals More Effective," *Personnel Administrator*, April 1985, pp. 117–118.

[11]J. Wisinski, "A Logical Approach to a Difficult Employee," *HR Focus*, January 1992, p. 9.

[12]G. D. Cook, Employee Counseling Session, *Supervision*, August 1989, p. 3.

[13]Norman R. F. Maier, *The Appraisal Interview: Three Basic Approaches* (La Jolla, CA: University Associates, 1976).

[14]"How Do I Love Me? Let Me Count the Ways," *Psychology Today*, May 1980, p. 16.

[15]Ronald J. Burke, R. J. Weitzel, and T. Weir, "Characteristics of Effective Employee Performance Review and Development Interviews: Replication and Extension," *Personnel Psychology*, Winter 1978, pp. 903–19.

[16]Latham and Wexley, *Increasing Productivity through Performance Appraisal*, (Reading, MA: Addison-Wesley, 1981), p. 151.

Chapter 9

[1]A. Maslow, *Motivation and Personality* (NY: Harper and Row, 1954)

[2]D. McGregor, *The Human Side of Enterprise* (NY: McGraw-Hill, 1960)

[3]F. Herzberg, B. Mausner and B. Snyderman, *The Motivation to Work* (NY: John Wiley and Sons, 1959)

[4]D.C. McClelland, *The Achieving Society* (NY: Van Nostrand Reinhold, 1961)

[5]J.S. Adams, "Inequity in Social Exchanges," in L. Berkowitz (ed.), *Advances in Experimental Social Psychology*, Vol. 2 (NY: Academic Press, 1965), pp. 267–3.00

[6]J.A. Colquitt, D. E. Conlon, M.J. Wesson, C.O.L.H. Porter, and K.Y.Ng, "Justice at the millennium: A meta-analytic review of 25 years of organizational justice research. *Journal of Applied Psychology*, Vol. 86(3), (2001) pp. 425–445.

[7]Y. Cohen-Charash and P. E. Spector, "The Role of Justice in Organizations: A Meta-Analysis," *Organizational Behavior and Human Decision Processes*, Vol. 86 (2), 2001, pp. 278–321

[8]J.R. Hackman and G.R. Oldham, "Motivation through the design of work: test of a theory, Organizational Behavior and Human Performance, Vol. 16 (2), 1976, pp. 250–279.

[9]Ibid

[10]A.M. Grant, "The significance of task significance: Job performance effects, relational mechanisms, and boundary conditions. *Journal of Applied Psychology*, Vol 93(1), 2008, pp.108–124.

[11]V.H. Vroom, *Work and Motivation* (NY: John Wiley, 1964)

[12]A. M. Grant, "Employees Without a Cause: The Motivational Effects of Prosocial Impact in Public Service," *International Public Management Journal*, 11 (2008), pp. 48–66

[13]M. Erb, ".How to Stop Micromanaging Your Team", Entrepreneur, January 31, 2011.

[14]E.A. Locke et al, "The Relative Effectiveness of Four Methods of Motivating Employee Performance," in K. D. Duncan, M.M. Gruneberg and D. Wallis, eds., *Changes in Working Life* (London: John Wiley, 1980), pp. 363–383.

[15]A.M. Dickinson and K.L.Gillette, "A Comparison of the Effects on Productivity: Piece-Rate Pay versus Base Pay Plus Incentives," *Journal of Organizational Behavior Management*, spring 1994, pp. 3–82

[16]See, for example, D. Fenn, "Compensation: Bonuses that Make Sense," *Inc.*, March 1996, p. 95.

[17]G. Grib and S. O'Donnell, "Pay Plans that Reward Employee Achievement," *HRMagazine*, July 1995, pp.49–50.

[18]"Compensation: Sales Managers as Team Players," *Inc.*, August 1994, p. 102.

[19]D. Fenn, "Compensation: Goal-Driven Incentives," *Inc.*, August 1996, p. 91; M.A. Verespej, "More Value for Compensation," *Industry Week*, June 17, 1996, p. 20.

[20]S. Overman, "Saturn Teams Working and Profiting," *HRMagazine*, March 1995, p. 72.

[21]K. Capell, "Options for Everyone," *Business Week*, July 22, 1996, pp. 80–88.

[22]See, for example, T.R. Stenhouse, "The Long and the Short of Gainsharing," *Academy of Management Executive*, Vol.9 (1), 1995, pp. 77–78.

[23]S.A. Lee, "ESOP is a Powerful Tool to Align Employees with Corporate Goals," *Pension World*, April 1994, pp. 40–42.

[24]J.R. Hackman and G.R. Oldham, "Motivation through the design of work: test of a theory, Organizational Behavior and Human Performance, Vol. 16 (2), 1976, pp. 250–279.

Chapter 10

[1]See, for example, S. Cammaniti, "What Team Leaders need to Know," *Fortune*, February 20, 1995, pp. 93–100.

[2]P.G. Northouse, *Leadership: Theory and Practice*, 6th edition (Thousand Oaks, California: Sage Publications, 2013).

[3]B.M. Bass, The *Bass Handbook of Leadership: Theory, Research, and Managerial Applications*, 4th edition (NY: Free Press, 2008).

[4]ibid

[5]F.E. Fiedler, *A Theory of Leadership Effectiveness* (NY: McGraw-Hill, 1967)

[6]P. Hersey and K.H. Blanchard, *Management of Organizational Behavior: Utilizing Human Resources*, 5th ed. (Englewood Cliffs, NJ:Prentice Hall Inc, 1988)

[7]R.J. House and T.R. Mitchell, "Path-Goal Theory of Leadership," *Journal of Contemporary Business*, Autumn 1974, pp. 81–97.

[8]E. M. Whitener, S.E. Brodt, M. A. Korsgaard & J. M. Werner. "Managers as initiators of trust: An exchange relationship framework for understanding managerial trustworthy behavior", Academy of Management Review, 23 (1998), pp. 513–530.

[9]B.M. Bass, *The Bass Handbook of Leadership: Theory, Research, and*

Managerial Applications, 4th edition (NY: Free Press, 2008).

[10]G. Hofstede, "Motivation, Leadership and Organization: Do American Theories Apply Abroad?" Organizational Dynamics (Summer 1980), p. 57.; and A. Ede, "Leadership and Decision Making: Management Styles and Culture," *Journal of Managerial Psychology* (July 1992), pp. 28–31.

[11]For example, see T. Morris and C.M. Pavett, "Management style and productivity in two cultures," *Journal of International Business Studies*, Vol. 23 (1), 1992 , pp. 169–179.

[12]For example, see R. Mehta, A.J. Dubinsky and R. E. Anderson, "Leadership style, motivation and performance in international marketing channels: An empirical investigation of the U.S.A., Finland and Poland," *European Journal of Marketing*, Vol. 37, 2003, pg. 50–85

[13]P. Lok, J. Crawford, "The effect of organisational culture and leadership style on job satisfaction and organisational commitment: A cross-national comparison", *Journal of Management Development*, Vol. 23 (4), 2004, pp. 321–338.

[14]This skills box is based on F. Bartolome, "Nobody Trusts the Boss Completely – Now What?" Harvard Business Review, March/April 1989, pp. 35-142; and J.K. Butler Jr., "Toward Understanding and Measuring Conditions of Trust: Evolution of a Condition of Trust Inventory," *Journal of Management*, September 1991, pp. 643–663.

[15]L. Holpp, "Applied Empowerment," *Training*, February 1994, pp. 39–44.

[16]See, for example, R. Wellins and J. Worklan, "The Philadelphia Story,", *Training*, March 1994, pp. 93–100

[17]E. Chavez, M.T. Green and D. Garza-Ortiz, "Leadership style differences between men and women: A review of the scholarly literature," in R.A. Oglesby, H.P. LeBlanc III, and M.G. Adams (eds.), *Business Research Handbook*, Vol. 17, 2010, pp. 474–478

[18]S.P. Robbins, *Organizational Behaviour: Concepts, Controversies and Applications*, 7th ed. (Englewood Cliffs, NJ: Prentice-Hall Inc, 1996), p. 441.

[19]ibid.

[20]R.E. Boyatzis, C. Soler, "Vision, leadership and emotional intelligence transforming family business", *Journal of Family Business Management*, Vol. 2 (1), 2012, pp.23–30

[21]J. Antonakis, N.M. Ashkenasy and M.T. Dasborough, "Does leadership need emotional intelligence?" The Leadership Quarterly 20, 2009, pp. 247–261.

Chapter 11

[1]F. M. Jabin, "Superior-Subordinate Communication: The State of the Art," Psychological Bulletin 86, 1979, pp.1201-1222; W. C. Reddin, Communication Within the Organization: An Interpretive Review of Theory and Research (New York: Industrial, Communication Council, 1972)

[2]D. Tannen, *Gender and Discourse* (NY: Oxford University Press, 1994)

[3]A. Mehrabian, "Communication Without Words," *Psychology Today*, September 1968, pp. 53–55

[4]K. Davis, cited in R. Rowan, "Where Did That Rumor Come From?" *Fortune*, August 13, 1979, p. 134.

[5]See, for example, M.W. McCall Jr., A.M. Morrison and R.L. Hannan, "Studies of Managerial Work: Results and Methods," *Technical Report No. 9* (Greensboro, NC: Center for Creative Leadership, 1978), pp. 7-9; F. Luthans and J.K. Larsen, "How Managers Really communicate," *Human Relations*, February 1986, pp. 161–178.

[6]See, for example, L.K. Larket, "Toward a Theory of Communicative Interactions in Culturally Diverse Workgroups," *Academy of Management Review*, June 1996, pp. 463–491; R.V. Lindahl, "Automation Breaks the Language Barrier," *HRMagazine*, March 1996, pp. 79–82; D. Lindorff, "In Beijing the Long March is Just Starting," *Business Week*, February 12 1996, p. 68; L. Miller, "Two Aspects of Japanese and American Coworker Interaction: Giving Instructions and Creating Rapport," *Journal of Applied Behavioral Science*, June 1995, pp. 141–161.

[7]Based on S.D. Saleh, "Relational Orientation and Organizational Functioning: A Cross-Cultural Perspective," *Canadian Journal of Administrative Sciences*, September 1987, pp. 276–293.

[8]C. Fisher, "Transmission of Positive and Negative Feedback to Subordinates," *Journal of Applied Psychology*, October 1979, pp. 433–540.

[9]SF. Bartolome, "Teaching About Whether to Give Negative Feedback," *The Organizational Behaviour Teaching Review*, Vol. 9 (2), 1986-7, pp. 95–104.

[10]S. L. Ryne, B. Gerhart and L. Parks, "Personnel Psychology: Performance Evaluation and Pay for Performance," *Annual Review of Psychology* 56, 2005, pp. 571–600.

[11]K.S. Verderber and R.F. Verderber, *Inter-Act: Using Interpersonal Communication Skills*, 4th ed. (Belmont, CA: Wadsworth, 1986).

Chapter 12

[1]A. Armstrong, J. Condie, D.L. Nelson, J.C. Quick, *ORGB* (Toronto: Nelson, 2011)

[2]J.A. Wall Jr. and R.R. Callister, "Conflict and Its Management," *Journal of Management*, Vol 21 (3), 1995, pp. 515–558.

[3]L. Greenhalgh, "Managing Conflict," *Sloan Management Review, Summer* 1986, pp. 45–51.

[4]M.A. Bodla and R.Q. Danish, "Politics and Workplace: An Empirical Examination of the Relationship between Perceived Organizational Politics and Work Performance," South Asian Journal of Management, Vol. 16 (1), 2009, pp. 44-59.

Chapter 13

[1]K. Lewin, *Field Theory in Social Science* (NY: Harper and Row, 1951).

[2]See, for instance, T. Peters, *Thriving on Chaos* (NY: Alfred and Knopf, 1987).

[3]G. Pitts, "The Fine Art of Managing Change," The Globe and Mail, January 4, 2010

[4]C. Wanberg and J. Banas, "Predictors and Outcomes of Openness to Changes in a Reorganizing Workplace," *Journal of Applied Psychology*, February 2000, pp. 132–142.

[5]D. N. Rousseau and S. A. Tijoriwala, "What's a Good Reason to Change? Motivated Reasoning and Social Accounts in Promoting Organizational Change," *Journal of Applied Psychology*, 1999, Vol. 84, No. 4, pp. 514–528.

[6]A. E. Rafferty and M. A. Griffin, "Perceptions of Organizational Change: A Stress and Coping Perspective," *Journal of Applied Psychology* 91, 2006, pp. 1154–1162.

[7]K. E. Weick and R. E. Quinn, "Organizational Change and development," *Annual Review of Psychology* 59, 1999, pp. 361–386

[8]M. F. R. Kets de Vries and K. Balazs, "The Downside of Downsizing," *Human Relations* 50, 1997, pp. 11–50

[10]P. O. Saksvik, S. D. Tvedt, K. Nytro, G. R. Andersen, T. K. Andersen, M. P. Buvik, and H. Torvatn, "Developing Criteria for Healthy Organizational Change, " Work and Stress 21, 2007, pp. 243–263.

[11]J. Park, "Work Stress and Job Performance," *Perspectives on Labour and Income*, Statistics Canada, December 2007, catague no. 75-001-XIE, http://www.statcan.gc.ca/pub/75-001-x/75-001-x2007112-eng.htm

[12]Cited in C. W, "Sources of Workplace Stress," Perspectives on Labour and Income, Statistics Canada, June 2003, http://www.statcan.gc.ca/pub/75-001-x/00603/6533-eng.htm

[13]S. Leka, A. Griffiths and T. Cox, *Work Organisation and Stress: Systematic Problem Approaches for Employers, Managers and Trade Union Representatives*, World Health Organization, 2003.

[14]A.E. Nixon, J.J. Mazzola, J. Bauer, J.R. Krueger and P.E. Spector, "Can work make you sick? A meta-analysis of the relationships between job stressors and physical symptoms," *Work and Stress*, Vol 25 (1), 2011, pp. 1-22.

[15]N.G. Boyd, J.E. Lewin and J.K. Sager, "A model of stress and coping and their influence on individual and organizational outcomes," Journal of Vocational Behaviour, Vol. 75 (2), 2009, pp. 197–211.

[16]K. L. Zellars, J. A. Meurs, P. L. Perrewe, C. J. Kacmar and A. M. Rossi, "Reacting to and Recovering from Stressful Situation: The Negative Affectivity-physiological Arousal Relationship," *Journal of Occupational Health Psychology* 14, 2009, pp.11-22

[17]N. A. Bowling and K. J. Eschleman, "Employee Personality as a Moderator of the Relationships Between Work Stressors and Counterproductive Work Behavior, *Journal of Occupational Health Psychology* 15, 2010, pp. 91-103

[18]M. Cavanaugh, W. Boswell, M. Roehling and J. Boudreau, "An Empirical Examination of Self-Reported Work Stress among U.S. Managers," *Journal of Applied Psychology*, February 2000, pp. 65-74.

[19]R. A . Karacek, "Job Demands, Job Decision Latitude, and Mental Strain: Implications for Job Redesign," Administrative Science Quarterly 24, 1979, pp. 285-310; Karasek, R., & Theorell, T. *Healthy work: Stress, productivity, and the reconstruction of working life*. (New York: Basic Books, 1990).

[20]J. Siegrist, "Adverse Health Effects of High effort/Low Reward Conditions," *Journal of Occupational Health Psychology* 1, 1996, pp. 27-41

[21]A. S. Ostry, S. Kelly, P. A. Demers, C. Mustard and C. Hertzman, "A Comparison between the Effort-reward Imbalance and Demand Control Models," BMC Public Health 3, 2003, p.10

[22]http://www.statcan.gc.ca/pub/75-001-x/2009104/pdf/10837-eng.pdf

[23]http://www.statcan.gc.ca/pub/89-503-x/2010001/article/11387/tbl/tbl005-eng.htm

[24]http://www.statcan.gc.ca/pub/75-001-x/11106/9520-eng.pdf

[25]http://www.phac-aspc.gc.ca/alw-vat/studies-etudes/kinemedics-eng.php

[26]C. Wanberg and J. Banas, "Predictors and Outcomes of Openness to Changes in a Reorganizing Workplace," Journal of Applied Psychology, February 2000, pp. 132-142.

Chapter 14

[1]Employee Conduct and Discipline, personnel Policies Forum, urvey No. 102 (Washington, D.C.: Bureau of National Affairs, August 1973)

[2]ibid

[3]R. Matas, "Vancouver police face discipline for surfing porn," The Globe and Mail, February 16, 2012, http://m.theglobeandmail.com/news/british-columbia/vancouver-police-face-discipline-for-surfing-porn/article2340916/?service=mobile

[4]"Parks Canada employees disciplined over email," Brandon Sun, September 10, 2010. http://www.brandonsun.com/regional/parks-canada-employees-disciplined-over-email-102614814.html?thx=y

[5]P. Nikfarjam, "Facing Discipline For Facebook Postings in Canada," http://grossmancga.com/site/2012/05/10/facing-discipline-for-facebook-postings-canada/

[6]K. Orth, "The Employers' Edge Blog – Social Networking Trips Up Another Employee: Discharge Upheld for Gross Insubordination and Threats Made by Postal Employee in Facebook Posts," April 19, 2012, Crawford, Chondon and Partners, http://www.ccpartners.ca/2012/april-19-2012-the-employers-edge-blog-social-networking-trips-up-another-employee-discharge-upheld-for-gross-insubordination-and-threats-made-by-postal-employee-in-facebook-posts

[7]J.R. Smith, "Employees on the Internet," Canadian HR Reporter, January 4, 2012, http://www.hrreporter.com/blog/employment-law/archive/2012/01/04/employees-on-the-internet

[8]J. Graham and L. Rafuse, "Legal Update: 10 Tips to deal with employee discipline for social media use," McInnes Cooper, March 1, 2012, http://www.mcinnescooper.com/publications/legal-update-10-tips-to-deal-with-employee-discipline-for-social-media-use/

[9]C.Deehy, "Franchising and the use of cyberspace in the workplace," http://www.lapointerosenstein.com/fichier/listelibrary/30/Cde-cyberspace.pdf

[10]Based on D. McGregor, "Hot Stove rules of Discipline," In G. Strauss and L. Sayles (eds.) *Personnel: The Human Problems of Management* (Englewood cliffs, NJ: Prentice-Hall, Inc., 1967).

[11]A study by Wyatt Company, reported in S. Gaines, Salary Levels Taking Back Seat To Concern Over Job Security, *The Chicago Tribune*, November 19, 1987, http://articles.chicagotribune.com/1987-11-19/business/8703270848_1_pay-scores-survey

Chapter 15

[1]HRSDC calculations based on Statistics Canada, http://www4.hrsdc.gc.ca/.3ndic.1t.4r@-eng.jsp?iid=17#M_4

[2]Fang, Tony and Anil Verma. 2002. "Union wage premium." Perspectives on Labour and Income (Statistics Canada, Catalogue 75-001-XPE) 14, no. 4 (Winter): 17-23.

[3]Akyeampong, Ernest B. 2002. "Unionization and fringe benefits." Perspectives on Labour and Income (Statistics Canada, Catalogue 75-001-XPE) 14, no. 3 (Autumn): 42-46.

[4]Akyeampong, Ernest B. 2003. "Unionization and the grievance system." Perspectives on Labour and Income (Statistics Canada, Catalogue 75-001-

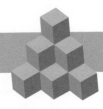

Absenteeism Failure to report to work.

Absolute standards Employees are evaluated within the context of expected behaviour and not compared with others.

Accept errors Accepting those candidates who subsequently perform poorly on the job.

Accommodation The willingness of one party in a conflict to place the opponent's interests above his or her own.

Accountability Holding a person to performing an assignment in a satisfactory manner.

Active listening Listening with intensity, empathy, acceptance, and a willingness to take responsibility for completeness.

Activities Time or resources required to progress from one event to another on a PERT chart.

Agency shop Work setting in which employees do not have to join the union but they must pay union dues if they want to keep their jobs.

Agenda A written statement of a meeting's purpose, who will be in attendance, and the issues that will be discussed.

Apprenticeships A program covering a period of time—typically from one to five years—when an individual is considered to be training to learn a skill.

Arbitrator An impartial third party who hears grievances and makes rulings on them.

Assertiveness training Training designed to make people more open and self-expressive.

Attitudes Evaluative statements or judgments concerning objects, people, or events.

Authority The managerial right to give orders and expect the orders to be obeyed.

Authority after discussion Decision making by a group leader after weighing group members' decisions.

Autonomy The degree to which the job provides substantial freedom, independence, and discretion to the individual in scheduling the work and in determining the procedures to be used in carrying it out.

Avoidance The desire to withdraw from or ignore a conflict.

Baby-boomers Those born 1946-1964.

Bargaining unit Identifies which employees the union will represent if it wins an election.

Behaviour-based interviewing Probing the applicant for specific narrative details of actual events in their past in order to predict their probable behaviour on the job for which they are applying.

Behaviourally anchored rating scales (BARS) A performance appraisal technique in which an evaluator rates employees on specific job behaviours derived from performance dimensions.

Benchmarking The continuous process of measuring products and practices against the toughest competition and those companies recognized as world-class leaders.

Bill C-45 2004 addition to Criminal Code that holds employers and supervisors accountable for employee safety.

Blended departmentalization Mixing different types of departmentalization within the same structure.

Body language Gestures, facial configurations, and other movements of the body.

Bona fide occupational requirements Skills or qualifications essential for performance in the role.

Bottom-up budgeting Budgeting in which budget requests are prepared by those who implement them and are then sent to higher levels of management for approval.

Brainstorming An idea-generation process that specifically encourages any and all alternatives while withholding any criticism of those alternatives.

Budgets Numerical plans.

Business process Visual representation of the sequence of events for a particular process.

Cause and effect diagrams Diagrams used to speculate on potential effects of taking an action, grouping the effects according to common categories.

Central tendency error A reluctance by an evaluator to use the extremes of the appraising scale.

Centralized authority Decision making carried out by senior management.

Chance causes Variations caused by randomness in the process.

Change agents People who act as catalysts and assume the responsibility for overseeing the change process.

Change process Unfreezing the status quo, changing to a new state, and refreezing the new change to make it permanent.

Charismatic leader Has a profound and extraordinary efffect on followers.

Checklist A performance appraisal technique where an evaluator uses a list of behavioural descriptions and checks off those behaviours that apply to the employee.

Coaching Day-to-day, hands-on process of helping employees recognize opportunities to improve their work performance.

Code of ethics A formal document that states an organization's primary values and the ethical rules it expects employees to follow.

Cognitive learning Occurs via mental processes such as reading, watching, and thinking.

Cohesiveness The degree to which members are attracted to each other and are motivated to stay in the group.

Collaboration A situation where the parties to a conflict each desire to satisfy fully the concerns of all parties.

Collective bargaining A process for negotiating a union contract and for administrating the contract after it has been negotiated.

Collectivism A cultural framework emphasizing tight social ties and allegiance to the group.

Communication The transference and understanding of meaning.

Compromise A situation in which each party to a conflict is willing to give up something of value.

Conceptual competence The mental ability to analyze and diagnose complex situations.

Conciliation An impasse-resolution technique that states that the role of the third party is to keep the negotiations ongoing and to act as a go-between.

Concurrent controls Controls that are enacted while an activity is in progress.

Conflict A process in which one party consciously interferes in the goal-achievement efforts of another party.

Conflict management The application of resolution and stimulation techniques to achieve the optimum level of departmental conflict.

Confronting Pointing out discrepancies in attitudes, thoughts or behaviours in another person in a non-judgmental way.

Consensus Agreement to support a decision by all members of a group.

Control by exception Strategic control devices should call attention only to exceptions from standard.

Control charts Charts that show plotting of results over a period of time, with statistically determined upper and lower limits.

Controlling Monitoring activities to ensure that objectives are being met as planned and correcting any significant deviations.

Corrective control Provides feedback, after an activity is finished, to prevent any future deviations.

Creativity The ability to combine ideas in a unique way to make unusual associations between them.

Credibility Believability in the role.

Critical incidents A performance appraisal technique in which an evaluator lists key behaviours that separate effective from ineffective job performance.

Critical path The longest sequence of events and activities in a PERT chart.

Cross-functional teams Managers and employees from different levels and different parts of the organization form teams to solve problems.

Culture A system of shared meaning.

Customer Everyone internally or externally who interacts with the organization's product or service.

Customer departmentalization Grouping activities on the basis of common customers.

Data Raw, unanalyzed facts.

Decentralized authority Top management pushes decision making down to lower levels.

Decision trees A diagrammatic technique for analyzing decisions by assigning probabilities to various outcomes and calculating payoffs for each.

Decision by authority under discussion The decision is made by the group leader after weighing group members' opinions.

Decision by expert The decision is delegated by the group to a person with special skill or knowledge.

Decision by minority vote The decision is made by a subgroup (e.g. a committee).

Decision-making process The eight steps to making rational decisions.

Delegation A four-step process of allocating duties, delegating authority, assigning responsibility, and creating accountability.

Delphi technique A group decision technique where members independently and anonymously contribute to a group discussion through systematic compilation of their thoughts.

Departmentalization Grouping employees based on work functions, product or service, target customer or client, geographic territory, or the process used to turn inputs into outputs.

Devils advocate A person who purposely presents arguments that run counter to those proposed by the majority or against current practices.

Discipline Actions taken by a supervisor to enforce the organization's rules and standards.

Discretionary time The portion of a supervisor's time that is under his or her control.

Dismissal Termination of one's employment.

Distributive bargaining Zero-sum negotiations, where any gain by one is at the expense of the other.

Distributive justice Fairness in who gets what.

Diversity training Training aimed at creating a greater awareness of the issues that arise in a staff of varied background and characteristics, encouraging acceptance and appreciation of that variety, and helping employees learn how to accommodate and work with people of diverse background.

Division of labour The breakdown of jobs into narrow, specialized tasks.

Downsizing A reduction in the workforce and reshaping of operations to create "lean and mean" organizations. The goals of organizational downsizing are greater efficiency and reduced costs.

Due diligence Taking all reasonable care to prevent the occurence of an incident or event.

Due process Assuming an employee is innocent until proved otherwise; giving the employee the right to be heard; and invoking disciplinary action that is reasonable in relation to the offence involved.

E-learning Employees use network technology to gain access to training materials, to "experts", and to other learners.

Effectiveness Doing the right task; goal attainment.

Efficiency Doing a task right; with the least waste of resources.

Effort-reward imbalance model Strain results from a mismatch between effort and consequences.

Emotional intelligence A set of skills including self-awareness, self-regulation, motivation, empathy, and social skills that correlate highly with effectiveness at work; or the ability to recognize and manage emotions in yourself and in others.

Emotional labour The effort required to manage emotions in order to perform our job effectively.

Employee Assistance Programs (EAPs) Programs designed to act as a first stop for individuals seeking psychiatric or substance-abuse help, with the goal of getting productive employees back on the job as swiftly as possible.

Employee development Preparation of employees for future positions that require higher-level skills, knowledge, or abilities.

Employee relations All activities within a company that involve dealing with a union and its members.

Employee stock ownership plan (ESOP) A compensation program that allows employees to become part owners of an organization by receiving stock as a performance incentive.

Employee training Changing skills, knowledge, attitudes, or behaviour of employees. Determination of training needs is made by supervisors.

Employment standards Legislated rules about conditions of employment such as minimum wage, hours of work and overtime, vacation, termination of employment.

Empowered work teams The primary working units in a TQM program who have hands-on involvement in process improvement.

Empowerment Increasing an employee's involvement in making decisions and taking responsibility for work outcomes.

End-users Individuals who take responsibility for accessing and analyzing information they need on their personal computers.

Equity theory Employees perceive what they get from a job situation (outcomes) in relation to what they put into it (inputs), and then compare their input-outcome ratio with the input-outcome ratio of others; then respond so as to eliminate any inequities.

Ethical dilemmas Situations requiring one to define right and wrong conduct.

Ethics Rules or principles that define right and wrong conduct.

Events End points on a PERT chart that represent the completion of major activities.

Expectancy theory The strength of a tendency to act depends on the strength of an expectation that the act will be followed by a given outcome and on the attractiveness of that outcome to the individual.

Expected value analysis Calculating the expected value of a particular alternative by weighting its possible outcomes by the probability of achieving the alternative, then summing up the totals derived from the weighting process.

Experiential learning Relies on practising, experiencing, or doing something.

Expert A person with special skill or knowledge in a particular field.

Fact-finding A technique whereby a neutral third-party individual conducts a hearing to gather evidence from both labour and management.

Feedback The degree to which carrying out the work activities required by the job results in the individual obtaining direct and clear information about the effectiveness of his or her performance.

Fiedler's contingency theory A leadership theory; proposes that effectiveness depends upon a proper match between a leader's style of interacting with subordinates and the degree to which the situation gives control and influence to the leader.

First-level managers Supervisors.

Forcing The desire to satisfy your own needs at the expense of the other party.

Formal communication Addresses task-related issues and tends to follow the organization's authority chain.

Formal group A work group where objectives and work assignments are defined by management.

Functional authority Rights over individuals outside one's own direct areas of responsibility.

Functional departmentalization Grouping activities by functions performed.

Fundamental attribution error The tendency to make attributions to internal causes when focusing on someone else's behaviour.

Gantt chart A bar graph, with time on the horizontal axis and activities to be scheduled on the vertical axis, that shows planned and actual activities.

Gap analysis Involves defining the difference between what is actually happening and what you would like to have happening.

Gen X those born 1964-1980.

Gen Y those born after 1980.

Geographic departmentalization Grouping activities on the basis of territory.

Goal setting Setting specific and measurable targets is motivating.

Grapevine The means by which informal communication takes place; rumour mill.

Graphic rating scale A performance-appraisal technique in which an evaluator rates a set of performance factors on an incremental scale.

Grievance A work-related dispute arising out of the interpretation, application, administation or alleged violation of the specific terms of the collective agreement.

Group Two or more people who come together to achieve a particular objective.

Group order ranking A performance appraisal approach that groups employees into ordered classifications.

Groupthink Group members withhold different views in order to appear to be in agreement.

Halo error A tendency to rate an individual high or low on all factors due to the impression of a high or low rating on some specific factor.

Harassment Inappropriate words or actions that adversely affect the worker's psychological or physical well-being, and may cause a worker to be humiliated or intimidated.

Harshness error The tendency to appraise a set of employees too low.

Hierarchy of needs theory Theory that there is a hierarchy of five needs—physiological, safety, social, esteem, and self-actualization. As each need is sequentially satisfied, the next need becomes dominant.

Horizontal structures Very flat structures used in small businesses as well as giant companies in which job-related activities cut across all parts of the organization.

"Hot stove" rule Principles that can guide disciplining; the action should be immediate, offer advance warning, and be consistent and impartial and inform regarding future action.

Human resource planning Ensuring that a department has the right personnel, who are capable of completing those tasks that help the department reach its objectives.

Incident rate A measure of the number of injuries, illnesses, or lost workdays as it relates to a common base rate of 100 full-time employees.

Incremental budget A budget that develops out of the previous budget.

Individual ranking A performance appraisal approach that ranks employees in order from highest to lowest.

Individualism A cultural framework with loose social ties and emphasis on self-interest.

Informal communication Moves in any direction and is as likely to satisfy social needs as to facilitate task accomplishments.

Informal group Natural formations in the work place that are neither formally structured nor defined by management.

Information Analyzed and processed data.

Integrative bargaining Assumes there is at least one settlement option that can create a win-win solution.

Interactional justice Fairness in how people are treated.

Interest arbitration Arbitration in which a panel of three individuals hears testimony from both sides and renders a decision on how to settle the current contract negotiation dispute.

Intermediate-term plans Plans that cover from one to five years.

Interpersonal competence The ability to work with, understand, and motivate other people, both individually and in groups.

Job analysis The process of collecting information to define a job in terms of its component tasks or duties and the knowledge or skills required to perform them.

Job description A written statement of what a jobholder does, how the job is done, and why it is done.

Job design The way tasks are combined to form complete jobs.

Job enrichment Increasing the degree to which a worker controls the planning, execution, and evaluation of his or her work.

Job evaluation An assessment of the worth of a job.

Job rotation Moving employees horizontally to broaden their skills, knowledge, or abilities; turning specialists into generalists.

Job safety analysis A process of identifying potential hazard on a job and recommending the safest way to do the job.

Job specification The minimum acceptable qualifications an applicant must possess to perform a given job successfully.

Justice view of ethics Decisions that seek fair and impartial distribution of benefits and costs.

Just-in-time (JIT) inventory system A system in which inventory items arrive when they are needed in the production process instead of being stored in stock. See also Kanban.

Leadership The ability to influence a group toward the achievement of goals.

Leading Directing and coordinating people.

Learning curve Learning begins with a steep rise, then increases at a decreasing rate until a plateau is reached.

Leniency error The tendency to appraise a set of employees too high.

Line authority The authority that entitles a supervisor to direct the work of his or her direct reports and to make certain decisions without consulting others.

Lockout A company action equivalent to a strike; when management denies unionized employees access to their jobs.

Locus of control The degree to which people believe they are masters of their own fate.

Long-term plans Plans covering more than five years.

Machiavellianism Degree to which an individual is manipulative and believes ends can justify means.

Majority vote Agreement to a decision by at least 51 percent of a group's members.

Management The process of getting things done, effectively and efficiently, through and with others.

Management by objectives (MBO) A system in which subordinates jointly determine specific performance objectives with their superiors, progress toward objectives is periodically reviewed, and on the basis of which rewards are allocated.

Management competencies General categories of skills necessary to successfully perform a managerial job.

Management functions Planning, organizing, leading, and controlling.

Management information system (MIS) A mechanism to provide managers with needed and accurate information on a regular and timely basis.

Management process The four managerial functions of planning, organizing, leading, and controlling.

Marginal analysis Analyzing decisions in terms of their incremental costs.

Matrix A structural design that assigns specialists from functional departments to work on one or more projects that are led by a project manager.

Matrix assessment Sets up a comparison between alternatives based on weighted criteria.

Mediation An impasse-resolution technique where a mediator attempts to pull together the common ground that exists, and makes settlement recommendations for overcoming the barriers that exist between two sides in a conflict.

Mentoring A formal or informal process for more experienced workers to share their knowledge and guide less experienced workers.

Middle managers All employees below the top-management level who manage other managers.

Motivation The energizing force creating a willingness to act.

Motivation-hygiene theory Intrinsic factors are related to job satisfaction, while extrinsic factors are associated with dissatisfaction.

Need A physiological or psychological deficiency that makes certain outcomes seem attractive.

Need for achievement The need to do things better or more efficiently.

Need for affiation The need for social interaction and strong relationships with others.

Need for power The need to exert influence.

Negative affectivity The tendency to accentuate the negative aspects of the world around them.

Negotiation A process in which two or more parties exchange goods or services and attempt to agree upon the exchange rate for them.

Networking Developing contacts (could be in organization, industry, community) for potential use in future.

Nominal group technique A group decision technique in which all members are present but operate independently.

Noonprogrammed decision A complex and nonroutine decision requiring a creative solution.

Nonverbal communications Communication that sends messages without words.

Normal distribution Variations are assumed to follow a bell-shaped distribution curve.

Norms Acceptable standards of behaviour within a group that are shared by the group's members.

Off-the-job training Training that takes place outside the direct work area.

On-the-job training Training that places employees in actual work situations.

Operative employees Rank-and-file workers who physically produce an organization's goods and services.

Organization A systematic grouping of people brought together to accomplish some specific purpose.

Organizational culture A shared perception of the organization's values.

Organizing Arranging and grouping jobs, allocating resources, and assigning work in a department so that activities can be accomplished as planned.

Orientation An attempt to familiarize new employees with the job, the work unit, and the organization as a whole.

Paraphrasing Summarizing in your own words.

Pareto charts Simple bar charts that rank causes of a problem by their quantity over a certain time.

Pareto principle You achieve 80% of your results from your 20% of your efforts.

Passive listening Absorbing information as it is literally transmitted.

Path-goal theory The leader's job is to assist followers in overcoming obstacles in the way of attaining their goals by providing the proper leadership style.

Pay-for-performance programs Compensation plans that pay employees on the basis of some performance measure.

People-centred leaders Emphasize good interpersonal relations and a trusting, respectful and a motivated team.

Performance appraisal An evaluation and development tool. Involves reviewing past performance to identify accomplishments and deficiencies, and creating detailed plans to improve future performance.

Performance management Steps taken to ensure employee performance aligns with the organization's goals.

PERT chart A technique for scheduling complex projects.

Planning Defining objectives and the means for attaining them.

Policies Broad guidelines for managerial action.

Political competence A supervisor's ability to enhance his or her power, build a power base, and establish the "right" connections in the organization.

Politicking The actions you can take to influence, or attempt to influence, the distribution of advantages and disadvantages within your organization.

Polychronicity The degree to which a person prefers doing two or more things simultaneously.

Power distance The measure of the extent to which a society accepts unequal distribution of power.

Preventive control Controls that anticipate and prevent undesirable outcomes.

Problem A discrepancy between an existing and a desired state of affairs.

Procedural justice Fairness in how things are done.

Procedure A series of steps for responding to a recurring problem.

Process departmentalization Grouping activities on the basis of product or customer flow.

Product or service departmentalization Grouping activities by product line or service.

Program A single-use set of plans for a specific major undertaking.

Programmed decision A simple routine matter for which the supervisor has an established decision rule.

Progressive discipline Penalties are made progressively stronger if, or when, an offense is repeated.

Quality control Identification of mistakes that may have occurred; monitoring quality to ensure that it meets some preestablished standard.

Range of variation The degree of acceptable variation between actual performance and the standard.

Realistic Job Preview Information given to job applicant during hiring process which includes both positive and negative information about the job and company; it creates realistic expectations.

Recency error The tendency for evaluators to recall and give greater importance to employee job behaviours that have occurred near the end of the performance-measuring period.

Reinforcement theory People will exert higher levels of effort in tasks that are reinforced.

Reject errors Rejecting candidates who would later perform successfully on the job.

Relative standards Employee performance is evaluated through comparison with others.

Reliability The ability of a selection device to measure the same thing consistently.

Response time Responding to requests, demands, and problems initiated by others.

Responsibility An obligation to perform assigned activities.

Reverse mentoring Less experienced workers mentor more experienced employees.

Richness of information A measure of the amount of information that is transmitted based on multiple information cues (words, posture, facial expressions, gestures, intonations), immediate feedback, and the personal touch.

Rights view of ethics Decisions emphasize respecting and protecting the basic rights of individuals.

Risk analysis Analyzing decisions in terms of their relative risk.

Risk propensity The degree to which people are willing to take chances.

Role ambiguity A situation where role expectations are not clearly understood and the employee is not sure what he or she is to do.

Role conflicts Situations in which individuals are confronted by divergent role expectations.

Role overload Situations where an employee is expected to do more than time permits.

Roles Behaviour patterns that go with the position one occupies in the organization.

Rule An explicit statement that tells a manager what he or she ought or ought not to do.

Scatter diagrams Illustrate the relationship between two variables.

Scheduling Determining what activities have to be done, the order they are to be done in, who is to do each, and when they are to be completed.

Self-actualization The drive to become what one is capable of becoming.

Self-efficacy Belief in one's ability to tackle events successfully.

Self-esteem The degree to which individuals like or dislike themselves.

Self-monitoring A personality trait that measures an individual's ability to adjust his or her behaviour to external, situational factors. High self-monitors are adaptable in adjusting their behaviour to external situational factors, and are capable of presenting striking contradictions between public personas and private selves. Low self-monitors tend to display their true feelings and beliefs in every situation.

Senior management The highest level of management. Those people responsible for establishing the organization's overall objectives and developing the policies to achieve those objectives.

Sexual harassment Sexually suggestive remarks, unwanted touching and sexual advances, requests for sexual favours, and other verbal and physical conduct of a sexual nature.

Short-term plans Plans that are less than one year in length.

Silo mentality Organizational.

Similarity error Giving special consideration when rating others to those qualities that the evaluator perceives in himself or herself.

Simple structure A non-elaborate structure low in complexity, with little formalization, and with authority centralized in a single person; a "flat" organization.

Single-use plans Detailed courses of action used once or only occasionally.

Situational approach Explores the match between varying situations and leadership behaviours.

Six Sigma A structured quality approach that seeks to improve quality by identifying and removing the causes of defects and minimizing variability in process.

Skill The ability to demonstrate a system and sequence of behaviour that is functionally related to attainment of a performance goal.

Skill variety The degree to which the job requires a variety of different activities so the worker can use a number of different skills and talents.

SMART goals Objectives that are specific, measurable, accepted, reasonable and time-bound.

Social loafing The tendency of group members to do less than they are capable of individually when their individual contribution is not measured.

Span of control The number of subordinates a supervisor can direct efficiently and effectively.

Spillover effect Successes made by unions at the negotiating table influence the wages, working conditions, and terms of employment for workers who are not unionized.

Staff authority A limited authority that supports line authority by advising, servicing, and assisting.

Standard deviation A measure of variability in a group of numerical values.

Standing plans Plans used over and over again for recurring activities.

Status A social rank or the importance one has in a group.

Strategic planning Covering the entire organization, it establishes overall goals and positions the organization's products or services against the competition.

Stress An adaptive response resulting from any environmental action, situation, or event that places excessive psychological and/or physical demands on a person.

Strike Employees leave their jobs and refuse to come to work until a contract has been signed.

Supervisors First-level managers who oversee the work of operatives or nonmanagement employees.

Supervisory competencies Conceptual, interpersonal, technical, and political capabilities.

Suspension Time off without pay; this disciplinary step is usually taken only if neither verbal nor written warnings have achieved desired results.

Tactical planning Specific plans on how overall goals are to be achieved.

Task identity The degree to which the job requires completion of a whole and identifiable piece of work.

Task significance The degree to which the job has a substantial impact on the lives or work of other people.

Task-centred leaders Leaders who emphasize the technical or task aspects of the employee's job.

Team A workgroup whose members are committed to a common purpose, have a set of specific performance goals, and hold themselves mutually accountable for the team's results.

Team discipline Discipline is imposed by group control rather than supervisory control.

Technical competence The ability to apply specialized knowledge or expertise.

Telecommuting The linking by computer and modem of workers at home with coworkers and management at an office.

Theory X–Theory Y Two diametrically-opposed views on human nature. Theory X assumes people are essentially lazy, irresponsible, and lacking ambition; Theory Y assumes people are hard-working, committed, and responsible.

360-degree feedback The use of multiple sources of evaluation of an employee's performance in order to increase accuracy.

Time management A personal form of scheduling; maximizing the allocation of the use of time.

Top-down budgeting Budgets that are initiated, controlled, and directed by top management.

Total quality management (TQM) A philosophy of management that is driven by the constant attainment of customer satisfaction through the continuous improvement of all organizational processes.

Traditional career path A sequence of management positions with increasing responsibilities; characterized by relative predictability, upward vertical movement, and the organization taking responsibility for employee career development.

Traditionalist Those born before 1944.

Training Learning experience that results in a relatively permanent change in an individual that improves his or her ability to perform on the job.

Traits Specific characteristics held by individuals that allow them to effectively lead others.

Trust Belief in the person's integrity.

Type A behaviour Aggressive involvement in a chronic, incessant struggle to achieve more and more in less and less time.

Type B behaviour Rarely harried by the desire to obtain a wildly increasing number of things or participate in an endlessly growing series of events in an ever-decreasing amount of time.

Uncertainty avoidance The extent to which a society is characterized by anxiety over uncertainty, and therefore seeks to avoid it, reducing risk.

Union An organization that represents workers and seeks to protect their interests through collective bargaining.

Union shop Requires that employees must join the union.

Union steward An employee who is the elected representative of the employees in a work unit, and is there to protect the rights of the union members.

Unity of command The principle that a subordinate should have one and only one superior to whom he or she is directly responsible.

Utilitarian view of ethics Decisions are based solely on the basis of their outcomes; the goal is to provide the greatest good for the greatest number.

Validity The proven relationship that exists between a selection device and some relevant criterion.

Variable charts Measure a characteristic on a continuous scale.

Verbal intonation The emphasis someone gives to words or phrases.

Verbal warning A temporary record of a reprimand, which is placed in the supervisor's file.

Vestibule training Employees learn their jobs on the equipment they will be using, but away from the actual work floor.

Wellness programs Any type of program that is designed to keep employees healthy, focusing on such things as smoking cessation, weight control, stress management, physical fitness, nutrition education, high blood-pressure control, and so on.

Wildcat strike An illegal strike where employees refuse to work during the term of a binding contract.

Work sampling A selection device in which job applicants are presented with a miniature replica of a job and are asked to perform tasks central to that job.

Workforce diversity The increasing heterogeneity of organizations with the inclusion of different groups.

Work specialization Also known as division of labour. The process of breaking down a job into a number of steps, with each step being completed by a separate individual.

Written essay A performance appraisal technique in which an evaluator writes out a description of an employee's strengths, weaknesses, past performance, and potential and then makes suggestions for improvement.

Written warning The first formal stage of the disciplinary procedure; the warning becomes part of an employee's official personnel file.

Wrongful discharge Improper or unjust termination of an employee.

Zero-base budget A budget that makes no reference to previous appropriations; all items must be justified.

INDEX

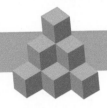